France

Angleterre

MER DU NORD

Pays-Bas

Allemagne

Dunkerque
Calais
Belgique

LA MANCHE

NORD-PAS-
DE-CALAIS
Lille
Valenciennes

Luxembourg

Cherbourg
Le Havre
Caen

HAUTE-
NORMANDIE

Rouen

Amiens

PICARDIE

Reims

Metz
LORRAINE
Nancy

Meuse

Rhin

ALSACE

Strasbourg

VOSGES

Saint-Malo

BASSE-
NORMANDIE

Seine

Versailles

✪ **Paris**

ÎLE-DE-
FRANCE

CHAMPAGNE-
ARDENNE

Troyes

Moselle

Brest

Fougères

Rennes

BRETAGNE

Le Mans

Orléans

Blois   Chambord

BOURGOGNE

Seine

Dijon

Mulhouse

Saône

Besançon

JURA

Suisse

PAYS DE LA LOIRE

Angers

St-Nazaire

Nantes
Chinon

Loire

Tours

Chenonceaux

Azay-le-
Rideau

Bourges

CENTRE

Chalon-sur-
Saône

Nevers

FRANCHE-
COMTÉ

Poitiers

Loire

La Rochelle

LIMOUSIN

Vichy

Clermont-
Ferrand

Rhône

Lyon

Annecy

POITOU-
CHARENTES

Limoges

Saint-Étienne

RHÔNE-ALPES

Italie

OCÉAN

ATLANTIQUE

Périgueux

AUVERGNE

Grenoble

ALPES

Bordeaux

MASSIF CENTRAL

Rodez

Rhône

PROVENCE-
ALPES-
CÔTE-
D'AZUR

AQUITAINE

Garonne

MIDI-PYRÉNÉES

Avignon

Monte-
Carlo

Monaco

Biarritz
Bayonne
Pau

Toulouse

Nîmes
Montpellier

Tarascon

Grasse

Aix-en-
Provence

Nice

PYRÉNÉES

Carcassonne

Béziers
Narbonne

Toulon

Cannes

Marseille

Espagne

LANGUEDOC-
ROUSSILLON

Perpignan

Andorre

MER MÉDITERRANÉE

0   75 km

CORSE

Ajaccio

Canada

Québec

Nouveau-Brunswick

Québec
Montréal

St-Pierre-et-Miquelon

Amérique du Nord

États-Unis

Maine

Nouvelle-Angleterre

Nouvelle-Écosse

Océan Atlantique

Louisiane

La Nouvelle-Orléans

Haïti

Les Antilles

Port-au-Prince

Guadeloupe

Martinique

Océan Pacifique

Guyane française

Cayenne

Amérique du Sud

Wallis et Futuna

Polynésie française

Vanuatu

Tahiti

Australie

Nouvelle-Calédonie

Le monde francophone

Europe

Asie

Bruxelles

Belgique
Luxembourg
Paris
Genève
France
Suisse

Andorre
Monaco
Corse

Tunis
Rabat
Alger
Tunisie
Liban

Maroc

Algérie

Viêt-Nam
Hanoi
Laos
Vientiane

Mauritanie
Mali
Niger
Tchad

Cambodge

Sénégal

Guinée

République
centrafricaine

République
de Djibouti

Pondichéry

Phnom
Penn

Burkina-
Faso
Côte
d'Ivoire

Rép.
démo-
cratique
du Congo

Ruanda

Seychelles

Togo
Gabon

Bénin
Congo
Burundi

Cameroun

Comores
Mayotte

Océan
Indien

Afrique

Maurice
Réunion

Australie

Antananarivo

Madagascar

Océan
Atlantique

Océan
Indien

Antarctique

Océan
Pacifique

Terres australes
et antarctiques
françaises

Pays et régions où le
français est langue officielle

Pays et régions où le
français est langue co-officielle

Pays et régions où le
français est langue administrative

Pays et régions où l'influence
culturelle française reste importante
et où le français est encore une
langue courante

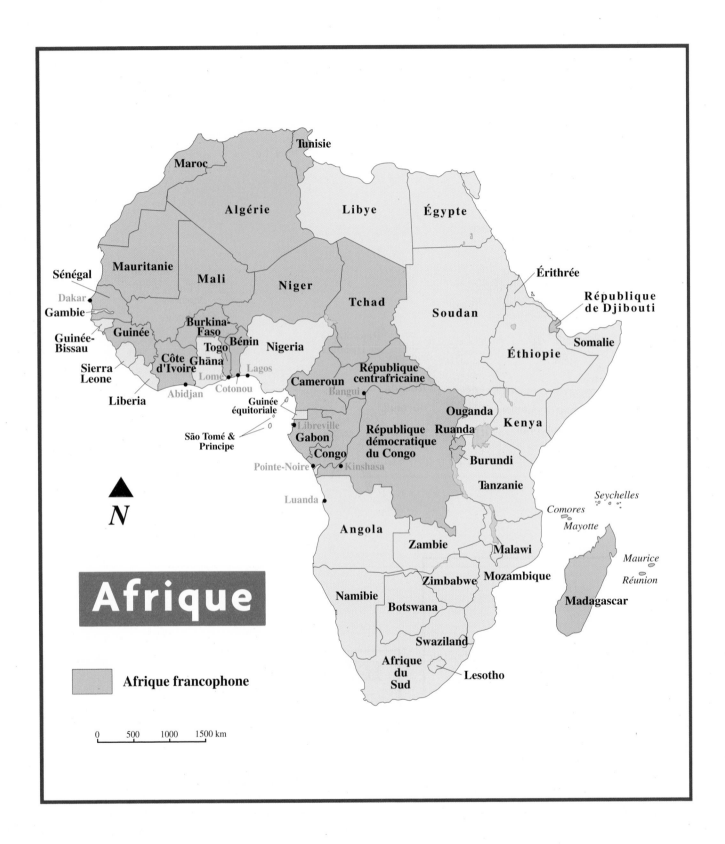

Afrique

N

Maroc
Tunisie
Algérie
Libye
Égypte
Mauritanie
Sénégal
Dakar
Mali
Niger
Tchad
Érithrée
République de Djibouti
Gambie
Soudan
Guinée-Bissau
Guinée
Burkina-Faso
Bénin
Nigeria
Somalie
Togo
Sierra Leone
Côte d'Ivoire
Ghāna
Lagos
Éthiopie
Lomé
Cotonou
Cameroun
République centrafricaine
Liberia
Abidjan
Bangui
Guinée équitoriale
Ouganda
Kenya
São Tomé & Principe
Libreville
Gabon
République démocratique du Congo
Ruanda
Congo
Burundi
Pointe-Noire
Kinshasa
Tanzanie
Luanda
Seychelles
Comores
Mayotte
Angola
Zambie
Malawi
Maurice
Réunion
Mozambique
Zimbabwe
Madagascar
Namibie
Botswana
Swaziland
Afrique du Sud
Lesotho

0   500   1000   1500 km

Afrique francophone

LIAISONS

AN **INTRODUCTION** TO **FRENCH**

WYNNE WONG
THE OHIO STATE UNIVERSITY

STACEY WEBER-FÈVE
IOWA STATE UNIVERSITY

EDWARD OUSSELIN
WESTERN WASHINGTON UNIVERSITY

BILL VANPATTEN
MICHIGAN STATE UNIVERSITY

HEINLE
CENGAGE Learning™

Australia • Brazil • Japan • Korea • Mexico • Singapore • Spain • United Kingdom • United States

CRL 448 WON

HEINLE
CENGAGE Learning™

Liaisons, First Edition

Wong | Weber-Fève | Ousselin | VanPatten

Vice President, Editorial Director:
P. J. Boardman

Publisher: Beth Kramer

Senior Acquisitions Editor: Nicole Morinon

Development Editor: Denise St. Jean

Senior Content Project Manager:
Esther Marshall

Assistant Editor: Kimberly Meurillon

Senior Editorial Assistant: Timothy Deer

Senior Media Editor: Morgen Murphy

Marketing Manager: Daphne Allanore

Marketing Coordinator: Claire Fleming

Marketing Communications Manager:
Glenn McGibbon

Signing Reps: Ellen Schraim, Nick Agnew

Manufacturing Planner: Betsy Donaghey

Senior Art Director: Linda Jurras

Permissions Editor: Julie Low

Production Service: PreMediaGlobal

Text Designer: Polo Barrera

Illustrator: Marie Lafrance

Cover Designer: Polo Barrera

Cover Image: istockphoto.com/ Anton-Marlot

International Edition:

ISBN-13: 978-0-840-02888-4

ISBN-10: 0-840-02888-1

Cengage Learning International Offices

Asia
www.cengageasia.com
tel: (65) 6410 1200

Australia/New Zealand
www.cengage.com.au
tel: (61) 3 9685 4111

Brazil
www.cengage.com.br
tel: (55) 11 3665 9900

India
www.cengage.co.in
tel: (91) 11 4364 1111

Latin America
www.cengage.com.mx
tel: (52) 55 1500 6000

UK/Europe/Middle East/Africa
www.cengage.co.uk
tel: (44) 0 1264 332 424

**Represented in Canada by
Nelson Education, Ltd.**
www.nelson.com
tel: (416) 752 9100 / (800) 668 0671

Cengage Learning is a leading provider of customized learning solutions with office locations around the globe, including Singapore, the United Kingdom, Australia, Mexico, Brazil, and Japan. Locate your local office at: **www.cengage.com/global**

For product information and free companion resources:
www.cengage.com/international
Visit your local office: **www.cengage.com/global**

Printed in the United States of America
1 2 3 4 5 6 7 15 14 13 12 11

Esther Marshall

SCOPE and SEQUENCE

SCOPE and SEQUENCE

SCOPE and SEQUENCE

SCOPE and SEQUENCE

Welcome to **Liaisons!** **Liaisons** is an innovative introductory French program that uses an engaging film of the same title to help you explore the richness of the French language and the fascinating cultures of France and the French-speaking world. Filmed on location in Quebec and in France, the film **Liaisons** is a first-rate production with a stellar cast including the notable talent of Mylène Savoie (from the Canadian film *Exode*), Guillaume Dolmans (from the French television series *Cœur océan*), and Johanne Marie Tremblay (from the Oscar-winning film *Les invasions barbares*). We hope you will enjoy watching this exciting film as much as we all enjoyed making it!

The textbook **Liaisons** will help you acquire a solid foundation of the vocabulary and grammar that beginning level students need in order to express themselves well at this level. The activities have been carefully designed so that you first develop confidence with the new vocabulary and grammar before being required to produce it. Besides learning about the French language and France and other French-speaking cultures, you will also have the opportunity to get to know your classmates and your instructor better as well as learn interesting information from them as you engage in the language practice activities in your book.

As suggested by the title of this book and film, this program contains many **liaisons,** or *connections* and *links*. Great care has been taken to ensure that the film and the different features of the book are linked together. As you learn French with the **Liaisons** program, we hope you will also become aware of how language and culture are intricately linked together as well as see the connections that can be made with different cultures, people in your class, your community, the French-speaking world, and the global world at large.

Liaisons: The Film

Claire Gagner, a graduate student in psychology at McGill University in Montreal, has spent most of her adult life on her own ever since her mother committed herself to a psychiatric hospital. Working as a receptionist at *l'Hôtel Delta* to put herself through school, Claire's life has been defined by work, her studies, and visits with her mother at the hospital. One day Claire receives an envelope with an anonymous prepaid trip to Quebec City. As she embarks on this journey, she encounters mysterious characters and eventually travels to France where the past and the present blend in some startling revelations.

Cast of Characters

CLAIRE
A graduate student in psychology at McGill University and hotel receptionist at *l'Hôtel Delta*

ABIA
Claire's best friend and co-worker at *l'Hôtel Delta*

SIMONE
Claire's mother and psychiatric patient at the *Clinique psychiatrique Laurier*

ALEXIS
A Parisian who is in Canada to deal with family business

ROBERT
Hotel manager of *l'Hôtel Delta* and Claire and Abia's supervisor

MADAME PAPILLON
Friend and neighbor of Claire's uncle in Paris

RÉMY
A mysterious man with an interest in Claire

Student Textbook

The Student Textbook contains the information and activities that you need for in-class use and self-study. The textbook is divided into 12 core chapters, a preliminary chapter, and a final chapter. Each core chapter contains three parts (**parties**), and each part contains a vocabulary and grammar section with presentations, explanations, activities for listening, speaking, and writing practice and cultural information. In each chapter, one page is always dedicated to French pronunciation and two pages help you understand and work with the film *Liaisons*. Special end-of-chapter sections give you the opportunity to develop your reading and writing skills in French and your cultural knowledge of the French-speaking world. Each chapter ends with a French-English vocabulary list of all of the chapter's active vocabulary to help you study for quizzes and exams. At the end of the textbook, you will find a comprehensive reference section including French-English and English-French glossaries and verb charts.

Student Activities Manual

The purpose of the Student Activities Manual (SAM) is to give you extra practice of what you learned in class outside of class. The SAM is both the workbook (comprehension and written practice of the vocabulary and grammar presented in class) and the lab manual (listening and pronunciation practice). In odd-numbered chapters, you will continue to develop your writing skills in French through a blog-style writing activity in which you react to the film *Liaisons*. Even-numbered chapters contain an e-mail-style writing activity related to the chapter's theme.

Acknowledgments

Liaisons is the culmination of many years of research, idea sharing, and hard work. Like all first editions, it is the outcome of endless hours of writing, rewriting, and fine tuning; and years of intensive reviews and piloting. Woven into this project are the voices and dedicated efforts of many and we want to acknowledge and thank them properly.

First and foremost, we want to thank the team at Cengage Heinle for believing in this project and for supporting our vision. In particular, we want to thank P.J. Boardman, Nicole Morinon, Beth Kramer, and Lara Semones. You knew from the beginning that Heinle was the home for *Liaisons* and we thank you for your persistence. Thank you also Nick Agnew for the phone call you made one night which put *Liaisons* on a different course with a bigger vision. We also want to extend a special thanks to acquisitions editor Nicole Morinon who patiently worked with the author team on a day-to-day basis. Thank you, Nicole, for your guidance and for making this project the best it can be! We are also indebted to freelance developmental editor Denise St. Jean for her meticulous editing, her insightful comments, and her amazing attention to the smallest details. Thank you, Denise, for your patience as we tried to master how to count lines. I think we finally got it now! Thank you Esther Marshall, and your team: Marie Lafrance, Cécile Hoene, Sev Champeny, Julie Low, and Melissa Sacco for your excellent production work. We are thrilled to have in our book the art of award-winning freelance artist Marie Lafrance. Thank you, Marie, for your stunning illustrations! Thank you Lindsey Richardson, Glenn McGibbon, Daphne Allanore and Claire Fleming for your marketing vision. Thank you, Linda Jurras, for an outstanding interior design. In addition, we would like to thank Timothy Deer, Kimberly Meurillon, Catharine Thomson, and Liz Kendall. Thank you, Peter Schott, Carolyn Nichols, John Farrell and Dave Waldman for your great contribution on the Video and audio. We are also grateful to Adrienne Barbo, Elizabeth Bishop, Kelly Campbell, Carole Edwards, Jean-Louis Hippolyte, Kelly Kidder, Maël Loubard, Lara Mangiafico, Heather McCoy, Vanessa Reynaud, Florian Vauléon, and Anaïs Wise for their work on the ancillary program. We also want to thank all our sales reps at Heinle for their hard work. You play a significant role in making our books a success and we thank you for your dedication to our projects.

We would also like to thank all the people who made the film *Liaisons* the first-rate production it is! We first want to thank our director Andrei Campeanu of A/T Media. Thank you, Andrei, for making our story come to life so quickly and in such an amazing way. We're sorry you had so much trouble convincing the **Union des artistes** that this was not a feature film, but we take that as a testament to the high quality of this production. We also want to thank Sabrina Aviles, our producer, for her superb organization skills and meticulous call sheets. Special thanks also to Ana Stojanovic, our assistant director, for working so patiently with the language team; and to actor and second assistant director, Pierre-Xavier Martel for his talent and for his role in helping us secure such a stellar cast! We must also recognize the dedication of our production manager in Canada, Lysanne Thibodeau, for putting together such an amazing crew for us and for her willingness to wear so many different hats which included waitressing at the *Cochon dingue*! A very special thanks also to Laurence Deray, our production manager in France, for her hard work, expertise, and professionalism. We are touched that the daughter of a famous French film director liked our script. We're sorry we brought along a snowstorm to Paris, but it made for a beautiful opening scene! To all our actors and to our crew in Canada and in France, we cannot thank you enough for your role in making *Liaisons* come to life. This has truly been a magical experience!

We are also very grateful to our many colleagues across the country who carefully reviewed our script and textbook chapters in their different phases. Your thoughtful comments and constructive criticism were instrumental in making *Liaisons* the project that we are proud of today.

Student Reviewers

Erin Adams	*Southern Illinois University – Carbondale*
Tim Anderson	*Old Dominion University*
David Brennan	*University of Nebraska – Omaha*
Esther Chen	*New York University*
Charles DeVita	*Virginia Commonwealth University*
Holly Doe	*Southern Illinois University – Carbondale*
Jennifer Haggard	*Camden County College*
Valerie Lamour	*New York University*
Kate Lewanowicz	*Virginia Commonwealth University*
Nicole Mattia	*Virginia Commonwealth University*
Ryan McDonnell	*University of Nebraska – Omaha*
Morgen Powell	*Virginia Commonwealth University*
Jessie Price	*Camden County College*
Lauren Shapiro	*New York University*
John Shick	*Old Dominion University*
Sarah Stevenson	*Southern Illinois University – Carbondale*
Carter Tuttle	*Virginia Commonwealth University*
Eliza Warwick	*New York University*

Advisory Board Members

Heather Willis Allen	*University of Wisconsin – Madison*
Martine Howard	*Camden County College*
Stacey Katz Bourns	*Harvard University*
Angèle Kingué	*Bucknell University*
Kathryn Lorenz	*University of Cincinnati*
Heather McCoy	*Pennsylvania State University*
John Moran	*New York University*
Kelly Sax	*Indiana University – Bloomington*

Focus Group Participants

Michele Cao Danh	*Northeastern University*
Eddy Cuisinier	*Western Kentucky University*
Cheryl Hansen	*Weber State University*
Christine Lac	*Carleton College*
Kathryn Lorenz	*University of Cincinnati*
Martine Howard	*Camden County College*
John Moran	*New York University*
José Ortiz-Batista	*County College of Morris*
Marina Peters-Newell	*University of New Mexico*

Deb Reisinger	*Duke University*
Susan Skoglund	*Kirkwood Community College*

Reviewers

Ellen Abrams	*Northern Essex Community College*
Antoinette Alitto-Heigl	*Harrisburg Area Community College*
Heather Willis Allen	*University of Wisconsin – Madison*
Debra Anderson	*East Carolina University*
Eileen Angelini	*Canisius College*
Renée Arnold	*Kapiolani Community College*
Genette Ashby-Beach	*Georgia Perimeter College*
Mariana Bahtchevanova	*Arizona State University*
Julie Baker	*University of Richmond*
Jody Ballah	*University of Cincinnati – Raymond Walters College*
Elizabeth Barrow	*Kent State University – Tuscarawas*
Barbara Bateman	*Georgia Perimeter College*
Dikka Berven	*Oakland University*
Carolyn Bilby	*Bellevue College*
Thomas Blair	*City College of San Francisco*
Lisa Blair	*Shaw University*
Geraldine Blattner	*Florida Atlantic University*
Sylvie Blum-Reid	*University of Florida*
John Boitano	*Chapman University*
Tammie Bolling	*Tennessee Technology Center – Jacksboro*
Amelia Bowen	*Old Dominion University*
Marie Lorraine Bruno	*Immaculata University*
Elizabeth Bull	*Northern Virginia Community College*
Thomas Buresi	*Southern Polytech State University*
Joanne Burnett	*University of Southern Mississippi*
Ruth Caldwell	*Luther College*
Anne Carlson	*Southern Illinois University – Carbondale*
Culley Carson-Grefe	*Austin Peay State University*
Krista Chambless	*University of Alabama – Birmingham*
Matthieu Chan Tsin	*Coastal Carolina University*
Rosalie Cheatham	*University of Arkansas*
Rebecca Chism	*Kent State University*
Stephanie Coker	*University of Kentucky*
Hervé Corbé	*Youngstown State University*

(Continued)

Reviewers (*Continued*)

Nathalie Cornelius	*Bloomsburg University*
Donna Coulet du Gard	*University of Delaware*
Tamara Cox	*Gardner – Webb University*
Eddy Cuisinier	*Western Kentucky University*
Laurel Cummins	*Bronx Community College – City University of New York*
Margaret Dempster	*Northwestern University*
Nicole Denner	*Stetson University*
Jean-Luc Desalvo	*San José State University*
Georges Detiveaux	*Lone Star College – Cyfair*
Constance Dickey	*Syracuse University*
Sébastien Dubreil	*University of Texas – Knoxville*
John Duffy, Jr.	*University of South Carolina*
Stephanie Duisberg	*Pima Community College – NorthWest*
Catherine Dunand	*Northeastern University*
Lucile Duperron	*Dickinson College*
Brenda Dyer	*Drexel University*
Vicki Earnest	*Calhoun College*
Mary Ellen Eckhert	*East Los Angeles College*
Wade Edwards	*Longwood University*
Shirin Edwin	*Sam Houston State University*
Claudia Esposito	*University of Massachusetts – Boston*
Betty Rose Facer	*Old Dominion University*
Timothy Farley	*Truman State University*
Jennifer Forrest	*Texas State University – San Marcos*
Claude Fouillade	*New Mexico State University*
Laura Franklin	*Northern Virginia Community College*
Jonathan Fulk	*University of Minnesota*
Jeanette Funaro	*Johnson County Community College*
Claire Gallou	*Phillips Academy*
Katherine Gantz	*St. Mary's College of Maryland*
Carolyn Gascoigne	*University of Nebraska – Omaha*
Christine Gaudry-Hudson	*Millersville University*
Abdou Gaye	*Ulster County Community College*
Anne George	*Whatcom Community College*
Claudine Giacchetti	*University of Houston*
Sage Goellner	*University of Wisconsin – Madison*
Katie Golsan	*University of the Pacific*
Christelle Gonthier	*Duke University*
Eve Goodhue	*Simpson College*
Marvin Gordon	*University of Illinois – Chicago*
David Graham	*Clinton Community College*
Frederique Grim	*Colorado State University*
Luc Guglielmi	*Kennesaw State University*
Sharon Hahnlen	*Liberty University*
Mark Hall	*Ithaca College*
Lana Hamon	*Trinity School*
Brigitte Hamon-Porter	*Hope College*
Cheryl Hansen	*Weber State University*
Patricia Harrigan	*Community College of Baltimore County – Essex*
Elaine Harris	*Northeastern Illinois University*
Steve Haslam	*Westminster College*
Alexander Hertich	*Bradley University*
Mary Jane Highfield	*St. John's University*
Jean-Louis Hippolyte	*Rutgers University – Camden*
Dominique Hitchcock	*Riverside Community College*
Lethuy Hoang	*Springfield College*
Martine Howard	*Camden County College*
Amy Hubbell	*Kansas State University*
Anna Hudson	*Dickinson College*
Andrew Irving	*University of Wisconsin – Madison*
Charlotte Jackson	*Long Beach City College*
Andrea Javel	*Boston College*
Judith Jeon-Chapman	*Worcester State College*
Warren Johnson	*Arkansas State University*
Caroline Jumel	*Oakland University*
Mary Helen Kashuba	*Chestnut Hill College*
Stacey Katz Bourns	*Harvard University*
Matt Kemp	*Kent State University*
Kelly Kidder	*Lipscomb University*
Angèle Kingué	*Bucknell University*
Elizabeth Knutson	*United States Naval Academy*
Nedialka Koleva	*Mesa Community College*
Christine Lac	*Carleton College*
Elizabeth Lang	*American University*
Bérénice Le Marchand	*San Francisco State University*
Mikle Ledgerwood	*Samford University*
Kathy Leis	*College of DuPage*
Jacek Lerych	*Grays Harbor College*
Marie Level	*Baylor University*
Tamara Lindner	*University of Louisiana – Lafayette*
Jane Lippmann	*University of Texas – Austin*
Gary Ljungquist	*Salem College*
Jean-Francois Llorens	*High Point University*
Lara Lomicka	*University of South Carolina*
Joanne Lonay	*Seattle Central Community College*
José Lopez-Marron	*Bronx Community College – City University of New York*
Kathryn Lorenz	*University of Cincinnati*
Amy Lorenz	*Loras College*
Jin Lu	*Purdue University – Calumet*
Paula Luteran	*Hutchinson Community College*
Mary Katherine Luton	*Charleston Southern University*
Elizabeth Martin	*California State University – San Bernardino*
Sharla Martin	*University of Texas – Arlington*
Alix Mazuet	*University of Central Oklahoma*
Stuart McClintock	*Midwestern State University*
Heather McCoy	*Pennsylvania State University*
Anne McGovern	*Mary Baldwin College*
Betty McLane-Iles	*Truman State University*
Catherine Mennear	*Wake Technical Community College*
Christiane Métral	*Smith College*
Jessica Miller	*University of Wisconsin – Eau Claire*
Isabelle Miller	*Everett Community College*
Anne-Hélène Miller	*East Carolina University*
Nicole Mills	*Harvard University*
Blandine Mitaut	*Shippensburg University*
Julie Molnar	*Columbus State Community College*
Aileen Mootoo	*Southeastern Louisiana University*
John Moran	*New York University*
Brigitte Moretti-Coski	*Ohio University*
Christine Moritz	*University of Northern Colorado*
Kristina Mormino	*Georgia Gwinnett College*
Shawn Morrison	*College of Charleston*
Martine Motard-Noar	*McDaniel College*
Markus Muller	*California State University – Long Beach*
Kathryn Murphy-Judy	*Virginia Commonwealth University*
Stéphane Natan	*Rider University*
Patricia Newman	*Trident Technical College*
Karen Nichols	*Xavier University of Louisiana*
Barbara Nissman-Cohen	*Lebanon Valley College*
Eva Norling	*Bellevue College*
Sylvette Norré	*George Fox University*

Reviewers (*Continued*)

Frances Novack	*Ursinus College*
Philip Ojo	*Agnes Scott University*
Marie-Noelle Olivier	*University of Nevada – Las Vegas*
Kory Olson	*Richard Stockton College*
Geraldine O'Neill	*Pace University*
Jennifer Orlikoff	*West Virginia University*
Brahim Oulbeid	*Westfield State University*
Kate Paesani	*Wayne State University*
Keith Palka	*Central Michigan University*
Juliette Parnell-Smith	*University of Nebraska – Omaha*
Gloria Pastorino	*Fairleigh Dickinson University*
Kelly Peebles	*Clemson University*
Marina Peters-Newell	*University of New Mexico*
Janel Pettes-Guikema	*Grand Valley State University*
Brigitte Philippe	*University of South Florida*
Lewis Porter	*Walsh University*
Joseph Price	*Texas Tech University*
Bonnie Pytlinski	*St. Leo University*
Alain Ranwez	*Metropolitan State College of Denver*
Esther Ratner	*Brandeis University*
Deb Reisinger	*Duke University*
Gail Riley	*American University*
Daniel Rivas	*Irvine Valley College*
Radonna Roark	*Oklahoma Baptist University*
Molly Robinson Kelly	*Lewis & Clark College*
Peggy Rocha	*San Joaquin Delta College*
Susan Rosenstreich	*Dowling College*
Nicole Rudolph	*Adelphi University*
Love Sanchez-Suarez	*York Technical College*
Anna Sandstrom	*University of New Hampshire*
Prosper Sanou	*State University of New York – Stony Brook*
Rosemarie Sarkis	*Riverside Community College*
Bonnie Sarnoff	*Limestone College*
Alan Savage	*Wheaton College*
Kelly Sax	*Indiana University – Bloomington*
Patricia Scarampi	*Lake Forest College*
Cheryl Schaile	*Texas A&M University*
Timothy Scheie	*University of Rochester – Eastman School of Music*
Leslie Sconduto	*Bradley University*
Sandhya Shanker	*Michigan State University*
Thomas Shealy	*Winthrop University*
Jennifer Shotwell	*Randolph – Macon College*
Patricia Siegel	*State University of New York – The College at Brockport*
Gregg Siewert	*Truman State University*
Louis Silvers	*Monroe Community College*
Lee Slater	*Old Dominion University*
Elizabeth Smith	*Southwest Virginia Community College*
Janet Solberg	*Kalamazoo College*
Emese Soos	*Tufts University*
Karen Sorenson	*Austin Peay State University*
Janet Starmer	*Guilford College*
Victoria Steinberg	*University of Tennessee – Chattanooga*
Edith Stetser	*Arcadia University*
Kathryn Stewart-Hoffmann	*Oakland Community College*
Jessica Sturm	*Purdue University*
Amye Sukapdjo	*Gainesville State College*
Kimberly Swanson	*University of Kansas*
Bernadette Takano	*University of Oklahoma*
Kendall Tarte	*Wake Forest University*
Valerie Thiers-Thiam	*Borough of Manhattan Community College – City University of New York*
Ellen Thorington	*Ball State University*
James Tomek	*Delta State University*
Fred Toner	*Ohio University*
Rick Treece	*University of Minnesota*
Madeline Turan	*Stony Brook University*
Sandra Valnes Quammen	*Duke University*
Carmen Vergès	*Virginia Highlands Community College*
Nancy Virtue	*Indiana University – Purdue University Fort Wayne*
Irene Wallaert	*Indiana University of Pennsylvania*
Andrew Wallis	*Whittier College*
Sadik Wardeh	*Valencia Community College*
Anna Weaver	*Mercer University*
Catherine Webster	*University of Central Oklahoma*
Arlene White	*Salisbury University*
William White	*Buffalo State College*
Georgeanna Wielkoszewski	*Chandler Gilbert Community College*
Leanne Wierenga	*Wittenberg University*
Donna Wilkerson-Barker	*State University of New York – The College at Brockport*
Sharon Wilkinson	*Simpson College*
Larry Wineland	*Messiah College*
Dierdre Wolownick	*American River College*
Valerie Wust	*North Carolina State University*
Bonnie Youngs	*Carnegie Mellon University*

Wynne's acknowledgments

This project has been a longtime aspiration of mine and I am thrilled to see it finally come to fruition. I want to thank my family, friends, and colleagues for their unwavering support and encouragement through the bumps along the way, and for sharing in the excitement as we witnessed this project come together. A special thanks to my brother William who gave us inspiration for the film's ending. It goes without saying that I am deeply indebted to my co-authors for their dedication and hard work. Thank you, Edward, for your culture expertise. Thank you, Bill, for all your *input* (pun intended), for being such an ingenious **scénariste**, for giving our profession structured input, and for making everything we do so much fun! Thank you, Stacey, for your devotion to this project from the beginning and for being such a great and reliable co-author. Our idea sharing sessions together during the early stages were instrumental in making *Liaisons* what it is today.

I also want to personally thank Heinle, Cengage Learning for making this project even better than I had envisioned and for the reminder that a closed door can indeed sometimes lead to greater things.

Stacey's acknowledgments

I would first and foremost like to thank Wynne Wong for having invited me to join her on this project. This experience has made me not only a better scholar and researcher but a better educator. This project taught me to look at all my teaching from a new perspective and with an eye to language-acquisition needs across all levels of the French language curriculum and in every target-language course I teach from beginning to advanced. I am also indebted to Bill VanPatten for his expertise, guidance, and wicked sense of humor! You helped Wynne and me maintain our sanity. Thank you, Edward Ousselin, for your native-speaker language and culture expertise, and Nicole Morinon and Denise St. Jean for your never-ending patience. I would also like to thank the Iowa State University French 101 class of Fall 2010 for trying out many of these activities in class while we wrote and revised the early chapters. You all were such good sports! Finally, I would like to thank my family and colleagues for their love and support; and last but not least, I send a special thanks and gratitude to my husband Sébastien Fève for patiently answering my countless questions on how to accurately phrase this or that in French for this level of textbook. There are no words to express how much I love you and how much I appreciate all that you do.

Bill's acknowledgments

I am grateful to my wonderful co-authors who are dedicated, disciplined, and just plain fun to work with. Extra kudos to Wynne Wong, who has skillfully led this team and worked harder than anyone I've ever seen to get this project completed. Thanks are also due to Heinle, Cengage Learning for accepting this project and for shaping and guiding it. I'd like to thank Murphy—the best Havanese in the world. He reminds me everyday of the simple things.

Bienvenue

En bref   In this preliminary chapter, you will:

- learn greetings and introductions
- learn subject pronouns
- learn the verb **être** and some of its basic uses
- learn vocabulary for common objects in the classroom
- learn the numbers 0–60
- talk about courses and majors

- learn some adjectives and learn about their formation, agreement, and position
- learn about articles and the gender and number of nouns
- learn about the French alphabet and accent marks
- read about French as a world language and read about some famous French speakers

 You will also watch the **PROLOGUE** of the film *Liaisons*.

Ressources

 audio   🌐 http://www.cengagebrain.com

🔊 Comment ça va?
CD1-2

How is it going?

- The most common way to greet people in French is to say **bonjour** *(hello)*. However, in informal situations between friends and people who know each other well, **salut** *(hi)* and the **tu** form of verbs are often used.

LYDIE	**Salut, Annie! Comment vas-tu?**	*Hi, Annie. How are you?*
ANNIE	**Salut, Lydie! Je vais très bien. Et toi?**	*Hi, Lydie. I'm fine. And you?*
LYDIE	**Très bien, merci!**	*Very well, thanks!*

ALEX	**Salut, Marc! Quoi de neuf?**	*Hi, Marc. What's new?*
MARC	**Pas grand-chose. Et toi?**	*Not much. And you?*
ALEX	**Rien de nouveau. Au revoir.**	*Nothing new. Bye.*
MARC	**À bientôt, Alex.**	*See you soon, Alex.*
ALEX	**À plus!**	*See ya!*

- When greeting people in formal situations and in situations where you need to show respect to someone, **bonjour** and the **vous** form of verbs must be used.

PROFESSEUR	**Bonjour, Marie. Comment allez-vous?**	*Hello, Marie. How are you?*
MARIE	**Très bien, merci. Et vous, monsieur?**	*Very well, thank you. And you, sir?*
PROFESSEUR	**Très bien aussi. Merci.**	*Very well also. Thank you.*

MADAME GILLES	**Bonjour, Jean. Comment vas-tu?**	*Hello, Jean. How are you?*
JEAN	**Très bien, madame. Et vous?**	*Very well, Ma'am. And you?*
MADAME GILLES	**Très bien aussi. Merci.**	*Very well, too. Thank you.*
JEAN	**Au revoir, Madame Gilles.**	*Goodbye, Madame Gilles.*
MADAME GILLES	**Au revoir, Jean.**	*Goodbye, Jean.*

- French speakers usually shake hands when introduced to each other. Note that **enchanté** is used when the speaker is male and **enchantée** when the speaker is female.

PIERRE	**Salut, Paul. Salut, Alex. Je vous présente mon amie Marie.**	*Hi, Paul. Hi, Alex. I introduce to you my friend Marie.*
PAUL	**Bonjour, Marie. Enchanté.**	*Hello, Marie. Pleased to meet you.*
ALEX	**Enchanté, Marie.**	*Pleased to meet you, Marie.*
MARIE	**Enchantée.**	*Pleased to meet you.*

Vocabulaire complémentaire

un (meilleur) ami *(m.)* / une (meilleure) amie *(f.)* *a best friend*

un(e) camarade de chambre *a roommate*

un copain *(m.)* / une copine *(f.)* *a friend*

un garçon / une fille *a boy / a girl*

un homme / une femme *a man / a woman*

un petit ami / une petite amie *a boyfriend / a girlfriend*

Comment t'appelles-tu? *What's your name?*

Je m'appelle Victor. *My name is Victor.*

Mon prénom est Annick. *My first name is Annick.*

Quel est ton nom (de famille)? *What is your (last) name?*

Mon nom (de famille) est Dubois. *My (last) name is Dubois.*

Comment s'appelle-t-il? *What is his name?*

Il s'appelle Henri. *His name is Henry.*

Comment s'appelle-t-elle? *What is her name?*

Elle s'appelle Isabelle. *Her name is Isabelle.*

Son nom (de famille) est... *His/Her last name is . . .*

Son prénom est... *His/Her first name is . . .*

Ravi(e) de faire ta *(informal)* connaissance. *Pleased to meet you.*

Ravi(e) de faire votre *(formal)* connaissance. *Pleased to meet you.*

Comment ça va? / Ça va (bien)? *How are you?*

Ça va (bien). Et toi? *Fine. And you?*

Moi aussi. *Me too.*

Pas mal. *Not bad.*

Bonsoir. *Good evening.*

Bonne nuit. *Good night.*

Bonne journée. *(Have a) Good day.*

Au revoir. *Goodbye.*

À demain. *See you tomorrow.*

À bientôt. *See you soon.*

À plus (tard). *See you (later).*

Il n'y a pas de quoi. / De rien. *You're welcome.*

Voici... *Here is . . . / Here are . . .*

Voilà... *There is . . . / There are . . .*

Note de vocabulaire

Copain / copine may be used in more informal situations. Depending on context, it may mean boyfriend or girlfriend.

Liaisons musicales

© Ghnassia Anthony/SIPA/Newscom

Born in Corsica in 1984, the French singer Alizée was discovered after winning a talent show in France called *Graines de star* in 1999. One of her hits is *Mademoiselle Juliette*, a song inspired by Juliet Capulet from *Roméo & Juliette.* Find and listen to a performance of *Mademoiselle Juliette* on the Internet. How would you characterize its musical style?

Un mot sur la langue

Monsieur, madame et mademoiselle

Monsieur *(Mister)* is used to refer to adult males. It can also mean *sir* when used alone, not followed by someone's last name. The final **r** in **monsieur** is never pronounced.

Madame *(Mrs.)* is typically used for married women while **mademoiselle** *(Miss* or *Ms.)* is reserved for girls or unmarried women. In Quebec, however, all adult women are usually called **madame** regardless of marital status. In France, it is common to use **madame** for women who are over 30, regardless of marital status.

In writing, when used before a family name, **Monsieur, Madame,** and **Mademoiselle** are capitalized and often abbreviated as: **M. (M. Durand), Mme (Mme Martin),** and **Mlle (Mlle Leroux).** There is no period after the feminine forms.

• Would you use **madame** or **mademoiselle** for the following people?

1. a professor   2. your five-year-old niece   3. your boss

ACTIVITÉ Ⓐ **Mettez-les dans l'ordre!** Put these phrases in the order in which the speakers would most likely say them.

A. _____ Très bien aussi. Merci.

_____ Ça va très bien.

_____ Salut, François! Comment ça va?

_____ Et toi, Manuel?

B. _____ Au revoir, madame.

_____ Bonjour, madame.

_____ Comment allez-vous?

_____ Pas mal. Merci.

C. _____ À plus tard.

_____ Bonjour, Paul. Enchanté.

_____ Bonjour, Marc. Je vous présente Paul.

_____ Enchanté, Marc.

D. _____ Rien de nouveau. À demain.

_____ Pas grand-chose. Et toi?

_____ Bonsoir, David. Quoi de neuf?

_____ Au revoir.

ACTIVITÉ Ⓑ **Questions** You will hear some questions. Select the answer to each one.

CD1-3

1. a. Ça va bien.   b. Je m'appelle Carla.   c. Salut!

2. a. Ça va très bien, merci.   b. Mon nom est Auger.   c. Bonsoir.

3. a. Au revoir.   b. Moi aussi. Merci.   c. Je m'appelle Thomas.

4. a. À demain.   b. De rien.   c. Rien de nouveau.

ACTIVITÉ Ⓒ **Les personnes célèbres**

CD1-4

Étape 1. You will hear introductions to some famous people. Select the correct first or last name to complete each introduction.

1. a. Catherine   b. Deneuve   **4.** a. Gérard   b. Depardieu

2. a. Nicolas   b. Sarkozy   **5.** a. Harry   b. Potter

3. a. Sasha   b. Obama   **6.** a. Marion   b. Cotillard

Étape 2. Indicate if each person is **un garçon, une fille, un homme** or **une femme.**

Modèle: Catherine Deneuve est une femme.

ACTIVITÉ Ⓓ **Meilleur(e)s ami(e)s et petit(e)s ami(e)s** Complete each sentence with the appropriate name.

1. Mon/Ma *(My)* meilleur(e) ami(e) s'appelle _____.

2. Mon/Ma camarade de chambre s'appelle _____.

3. La petite amie de *(of)* Mickey Mouse s'appelle _____.

4. Le petit ami de Daisy Duck s'appelle _____.

5. Le copain de Charlie Brown s'appelle _____.

ACTIVITÉ **E** **Répondez** You will hear a series of questions and statements. What would you say in response?

CD1-5

1.   **2.**   **3.**   **4.**   **5.**   **6.**   **7.**   **8.**   **9.**   **10.**

ACTIVITÉ **F** **À vous: Faisons connaissance!**

Étape 1. Move around the room, greeting and introducing yourself to at least four people. Write down their first and last names.

Étape 2. Be prepared to introduce at least two of the people you just met.

Modèle: **Je vous présente Carrie Smith et Tom Baker.**

ACTIVITÉ **G** **Petits sketchs** Prepare a small skit with your classmates. Write out the dialogue and be prepared to act it out. Choose one or two of the following situations.

1. Good friends run into each other on campus on the way to class.

2. A student/Students run(s) into a professor on campus.

3. Your roommate introduces a friend to you at a party.

4. You run into your professor and introduce your friend to the professor.

Si vous y allez

Fondation Alliance française

The mission of the **Alliance française** is to promote the appreciation of French and Francophone cultures among French, Francophone, and American people through various educational and cultural activities. Most major cities have an **Alliance française.** To meet other francophiles, go to the website of your local **Alliance française** to see what activities are offered in your city.

Un mot sur la culture

© Stockbyte/Getty Images

Les salutations (Greetings)

In the French-speaking world, when people first meet each other, it is customary for them to shake hands regardless of their age or gender. When friends or family greet each other, men generally shake hands with each other while women kiss each other on the cheek. Men will kiss female family members and female friends on the cheek. The number of kisses **(les bises)** varies depending on the region and other factors and is difficult to anticipate. Two kisses, one on each cheek, is the most common combination throughout most of France. Three kisses are often exchanged in Paris and Provence or between close friends. Four kisses are reportedly exchanged in Nantes or as a sign of affection between the closest of friends or family members. However, no matter how many the number of kisses exchanged, the French always start with the right cheek.

• Do you think it is customary for the following cultures to greet with a kiss or kisses?

	Oui	Non			Oui	Non
1. les Américains	☐	☐	**3.** les Japonais		☐	☐
2. les Mexicains	☐	☐	**4.** les Africains		☐	☐

Pour parler de nos origines

Le verbe **être** / Les pronoms sujets / Les questions

DU FILM *LIAISONS*

Un coup d'œil sur la grammaire

In the **Prologue** of the film *Liaisons*, a woman is reading a document that she has written.

© Heinle/Cengage Learning

Je **suis** Madeleine Prévost de Paris...

Now answer these questions about the woman's message.

1. What part of speech is the word **suis**?
    a. noun   b. verb   c. adverb

2. What do you think **je suis** means?
    a. *I am*   b. *I have*   c. *very well*

Les verbes-clés

Note de grammaire
Être is the infinitive form of the verb. The infinitive is the basic form of the verb that you will find in a dictionary.

•••➤ In French, the verb **être** means *to be*. One very common use of **être** is to express one's place of origin. In this case, it is used with the preposition **de** + a city, which means *from* in this particular expression.

Céline Dion **est de** Charlemagne, au Québec.
Céline Dion is from Charlemagne, Quebec.

Catherine Deneuve **est de** Paris, en France.
Catherine Deneuve is from Paris, France.

•••➤ Another common use of **être** is to express one's occupation.

Voici Monsieur Leroux. Il **est professeur**.
Here is Mr. Leroux. He is a professor.

Nathan **est étudiant**.
Nathan is a student.

Catherine **est étudiante**.
Catherine is a student.

•••➤ The following are the present tense forms of the verb **être** and the subject pronouns (*I, you, he, she, it, we,* and *they*).

Note de prononciation
The **s** of **nous, vous, ils,** and **elles** is not pronounced. However, if the word that follows these pronouns begins with a vowel, the **s** is pronounced as **z** in **vous êtes**.

être *(to be)*	
je suis *I am*	**nous sommes** *we are*
tu es *you are*	**vous êtes** *you are*
il est *he/it* (m.) *is*	**ils sont** *they* (m. pl.) *are*
elle est *she/it* (f.) *is*	**elles sont** *they* (f. pl.) *are*
on est *one is*	

There are formal and informal ways to address people in French. When talking to someone whom you do not know well, who is older, or who is in a position of respect, use **vous** *(formal)*. When talking to a friend, family member, or a child, use **tu** *(informal)*. When talking to more than one person, use **vous** *(plural, formal, and informal)*.

When talking about several persons or a group of people, use **elles** if everyone is female. Use **ils** if at least one person is male.

Carole et Sarah, **elles** sont de Paris.   *Carole and Sarah, **they** are from Paris.*

Ahmed et Nourdine, **ils** sont de Nice.   *Ahmed and Nourdine, **they** are from Nice.*

Antoine et Marie, **ils** sont de Montréal.   *Antoine and Marie, **they** are from Montreal.*

To ask a yes/no question in French, you can make a statement and raise the pitch of your voice at the end. This is called rising intonation. Such questions are considered informal.

—**Pauline est étudiante?**   *—Is Pauline a student?*

—**Oui, elle est étudiante.**   *—Yes, she's a student.*

You can also place **est-ce que** (**est-ce qu'** before a vowel sound) in front of a statement. Your voice also rises at the end of these questions.

—**Est-ce qu'elle est de Chicago?**   *—Is she from Chicago?*

—**Non, elle est de Cleveland.**   *—No, she is from Cleveland.*

ACTIVITÉ **H** **Quelle ville?**

Étape 1. Complete each sentence with the correct information about yourself. Then share your information with the class. How many of your classmates are from the same city as you? How many of you are from the same city as your parents? If you have children and/or a spouse, are they from the same city as you are?

1. Je suis de *(city)*…
2. Mes *(My)* parents sont de…
3. Mes enfants *(children)* sont de…
4. Mon mari *(husband)* / Ma *(My)* femme *(wife)* est de…
5. Mes grands-parents sont de…
6. Mon/Ma camarade de chambre est de…

Étape 2. Now ask two people next to you where they are from. Are they from the same city as you? To ask someone which city he/she is from, you can say **Tu es de quelle ville?** To ask about a classmate's parents, grandparents, or children, say **Tes parents / Tes grands-parents / Tes enfants, ils sont de quelle ville?** To ask about a spouse or roommate, say **Ton mari / Ta femme / Ton (Ta) camarade de chambre est de quelle ville?**

🔊 Liaisons avec les mots et les sons

CD1-6

L'alphabet et les accents

The letters in the French alphabet look the same as those in the English alphabet, but they do not sound the same.

a (a)	**h** (ache)	**o** (o)	**v** (vé)
b (bé)	**i** (i)	**p** (pé)	**w** (double vé)
c (cé)	**j** (ji)	**q** (ku)	**x** (iks)
d (dé)	**k** (ka)	**r** (erre)	**y** (i grec)
e (eu)	**l** (elle)	**s** (esse)	**z** (zède)
f (effe)	**m** (emme)	**t** (té)	
g (gé)	**n** (enne)	**u** (u)	

Some French words have written accents. These are part of their spelling and cannot be omitted. In later lessons, you will learn how these accents may change the way a word is pronounced. For now, you need to recognize these accent marks and, when you spell a word aloud, include the name of the accent after the letter.

Accent	Name	Example	Spelling
´	accent aigu	pr**é**nom	P-R-E-**accent aigu**-N-O-M
`	accent grave	tr**è**s bien	T-R-E-**accent grave**-S B-I-E-N
^	accent circonflexe	h**ô**pital	H-O-**accent circonflexe**-P-I-T-A-L
¨	tréma	Rapha**ë**l	R-A-P-H-A-E-**tréma**-L
,	cédille	**Ç**a va	C-**cédille**-A V-A

Pratique A. Listen to and practice spelling these French names. Don't forget the accents.

1. Noël	**3.** Stéphane	**5.** Benoît	**7.** Eugène
2. Anaïs	**4.** Béatrice	**6.** François	**8.** Zoé

Pratique B. The **h** in French is usually silent and treated as a vowel as in these names. Listen to, repeat, and practice spelling these names. Notice the silent **h** as you say the names.

Hélène   Héloïse   Henri   Hermès   Honoré   Hugh

Pratique C. Listen to and practice spelling the names of these characters from the film *Liaisons*.

Claire Gagner

Abia Ndono

Alexis Prévost

ACTIVITÉ ① **Enchanté(e)** Greet and introduce yourself to four people in your class to find out their names and the city (**ville**) they are from. You may have to spell your name or the city. Be prepared to present your findings to the rest of the class.

Nom	Ville
1. _____	_____
2. _____	_____
3. _____	_____
4. _____	_____

ACTIVITÉ J **Francophone ou francophile?** Indicate where the following people are from and whether each person is **francophone** or **francophile**.

Modèle: Catherine Deneuve / Paris
Catherine Deneuve est de Paris. Elle est francophone.

1. Julia Child / Pasadena
2. Céline Dion / Charlemagne (Québec)
3. Zinedine Zidane / Marseille
4. Jodie Foster / Los Angeles
5. Gérard Depardieu / Châteauroux (France)
6. Marion Cotillard / Paris
7. Tennessee Bob Peckham / Martin (Tennessee)
8. Le professeur de français / [ville]

Un mot sur la langue

Francophones et francophiles

The term **francophone** is typically used as an adjective meaning *French-speaking* (as a primary language) and may be used to refer to individuals, groups of people, or places.

Montréal est une ville **francophone**.
Amadou est **francophone**.

The term **francophone** may also be used as a noun to refer to a native speaker of French, regardless of ethnicity or geographical location. When used in English, the "F" is capitalized.

Il y a des **francophones** à mon université.   *There are **Francophones** at my university.*

The word **francophiles** refers to people who identify themselves with speakers of French and admire the French language and its cultures. The opposite of **francophile** is **francophobe**.

• Est-ce que vous êtes francophone, francophile ou francophobe?

En **classe**

In class

une carte

une fenêtre

un écran

un tableau

une horloge

une brosse (à tableau)

une craie

un professeur

une porte

un ordinateur

une chaise

un bureau

un livre

une poubelle

une calculatrice

un stylo

une table

une étudiante

un étudiant

un sac

un cahier

un sac à dos

un crayon

une feuille de papier

Une salle de classe

Note de **vocabulaire**

The **h** in **horloge** and in **huit** is not pronounced because the **h** in French is usually silent.

Vocabulaire complémentaire

Les nombres de 0 à 20

0 **zéro**

1 **un**	6 **six**	11 **onze**	16 **seize**
2 **deux**	7 **sept**	12 **douze**	17 **dix-sept**
3 **trois**	8 **huit**	13 **treize**	18 **dix-huit**
4 **quatre**	9 **neuf**	14 **quatorze**	19 **dix-neuf**
5 **cinq**	10 **dix**	15 **quinze**	20 **vingt**

En classe

Dans la classe, il y a... *In the classroom, there is . . . , there are . . .*
une affiche *a poster*
une agrafeuse *a stapler*
un baladeur MP3 *an MP3 player*
un CD *a compact disc, a CD*
un classeur *a folder, a binder*
un examen *an exam*
une gomme *an eraser*
un iPod® *an iPod®*
un marqueur *a marker*
un ordinateur (portable) *a (laptop) computer*
un (téléphone) portable *a cell phone*
un projecteur *a(n) (overhead) projector*

un(e) camarade de classe *a classmate*
une classe *a class*

ACTIVITÉ A Dans notre *(In our)* salle de classe Read these sentences and indicate whether the objects are in your classroom.

	Oui	Non
1. Il y a une porte.	☐	☐
2. Il y a une fenêtre.	☐	☐
3. Il y a une calculatrice.	☐	☐
4. Il y a un projecteur et un écran.	☐	☐
5. Il y a un ordinateur.	☐	☐
6. Il y a des livres.	☐	☐
7. Il y a des cahiers.	☐	☐
8. Il y a une poubelle.	☐	☐
9. Il y a une horloge.	☐	☐
10. Il y a un tableau.	☐	☐

Conclusion Notre salle de classe est bien équipée *(well equipped).* Oui / Non

© Ferenc Szelepcsenyi/Shutterstock.com

Si vous y allez

© Ludovic/REA/Redux

If you go to France, visit the store Fnac, one of the largest retail chains specializing in cultural and electronic products such as books, DVDs, CDs, and computers. If you can't make it to France, check out their website at: www.fnac.com

ACTIVITÉ B Dans mon (In my) sac (à dos)

Étape 1. Indicate if these objects are in your bag.

Dans mon sac (à dos)…

	Oui	Non		Oui	Non
1. il y a une calculatrice.	☐	☐	7. il y a un (téléphone) portable.	☐	☐
2. il y a une affiche.	☐	☐	8. il y a des marqueurs.	☐	☐
3. il y a un examen.	☐	☐	9. il y a une agrafeuse.	☐	☐
4. il y a un crayon.	☐	☐	10. il y a une gomme.	☐	☐
5. il y a un iPod®.	☐	☐			
6. il y a un baladeur MP3.	☐	☐			

Étape 2. Ask a classmate if the items in **Étape 1** are in his/her bag.

Modèle: Étudiant(e) 1: **Est-ce qu'il y a une calculatrice dans ton (in your) sac (à dos)?**
Étudiant(e) 2: **Oui. / Non.**

Étape 3. Based on your findings, which statement best describes your classmate? Might he/she be a good person to borrow something from?

a. Mon/Ma (My) camarade de classe est bien équipé(e).

b. Ma/Mon camarade de classe n'est pas bien équipé(e) (is not well equipped).

ACTIVITÉ C Les salles de classe en 1970 et aujourd'hui

Étape 1. How have classrooms changed since 1970? Make a list of typical things one would find in a classroom in the 1970s and another list of things that one would find in a typical classroom today.

1970	Aujourd'hui (Today)
un tableau _____	_____
_____	_____
_____	_____
_____	_____

Étape 2. Now look at your classroom and review your two lists. How would you describe your French classroom?

a. Ma (My) salle de classe est comme (like) une salle de classe de 1970.

b. Ma salle de classe est une salle moderne.

ACTIVITÉ D Quel numéro le suit? (Which number follows it?)

CD1-7 You will hear a number. Select the number that follows it.

1. a. 6	b. 8	c. 10	**4.** a. 4	b. 11	c. 3
2. a. 12	b. 15	c. 18	**5.** a. 6	b. 13	c. 18
3. a. 20	b. 17	c. 9	**6.** a. 19	b. 17	c. 18

ACTIVITÉ **E** **Combien?** *(How many?)* How many of these people or things are in your classroom?

Dans la salle de classe, il y a…

1. _____ chaise(s).
2. _____ sac(s) à dos.
3. _____ iPod(s)®.
4. _____ affiche(s).
5. _____ professeur(s).
6. _____ ordinateur(s).
7. _____ étudiant(e)(s).
8. _____ camarade(s) de classe.
9. _____ horloge(s).
10. _____ poubelle(s).

ACTIVITÉ **F** **Les courriels** *(e-mails)*

Étape 1. Write down your instructor's e-mail address. Here is some useful vocabulary to help you.

at or @ = **arobase** *dash* = **tiret** *dot* = **point** *underscore* = **tiret bas**	

- Le courriel de mon professeur: _____

Étape 2. Ask three students in your class to spell aloud their e-mail addresses. Write what you hear.

Modèle: Étudiant(e) 1: **Quelle est ton adresse électronique?**
Étudiant(e) 2: **Mon adresse électronique est s-m-i-t-h arobase a-b-c point e-d-u.**
Étudiant(e) 1 *writes:* **smith@abc.edu**

Un mot sur la culture

© Yu Yang/Xinhua/Landov

La francophonie

The term **francophonie** was created in 1880 by the French geographer Onésime Reclus (1837–1916) to refer to a community of people and countries whose culture, regardless of ethnicity and geographical location, is primarily associated with the French language. The concept of **francophonie** was popularized by Léopold Sédar Senghor in the 1960s, and gradually became institutionalized, leading to the first **Sommet de la Francophonie** in Paris in 1986. Today, **la francophonie** with a small "**f**" refers to a community of people who use French as a language of communication and in their daily life; **la Francophonie** with a capital "**F**" refers to a group of governments or countries which forms the **Organisation Internationale de la Francophonie** (OIF).

- What countries make up the **Organisation Internationale de la Francophonie**?

Pour être précis(e)

Les articles indéfinis / Le genre et le nombre

DU FILM LIAISONS

Un coup d'œil sur la grammaire

Here is a description of an image you will see when you watch the **Prologue** of the film *Liaisons* later in this chapter.

© Heinle/Cengage Learning

Il y a **une** femme avec **un** stylo qui écrit sur *(on)* **une** feuille de papier dans *(in)* **une** chambre *(room)* à Paris.

The words **une** and **un** both mean *a* or *an* in English. Why is **une** used with **femme** and **feuille de papier,** but **un** with **stylo**?

1. The article **une** is used with nouns that have _____ grammatical gender.

    a. masculine   b. feminine

2. The article **un** is used with nouns that have _____ grammatical gender.

    a. masculine   b. feminine

As in English, French nouns have number (**le nombre**): singular or plural. Unlike English, French nouns also have grammatical gender (**le genre**). Every noun (a person, an animal, a place, a thing, or an idea) is classified as being either masculine or feminine. Sometimes nouns that refer to females are feminine (**une femme** *a woman*, **une fille** *a girl*) and nouns that refer to males are masculine (**un homme** *a man*, **un garçon** *a boy*). However, in most cases, especially with inanimate nouns, gender is unpredictable. Therefore, you must learn the gender along with the noun. Gender is often expressed not only in the noun, but also in the article that introduces it.

Indefinite articles: gender and number				
	singular		**plural**	
masculine	**un** livre	*a book*	**des** livres	*(some) books*
	un ordinateur	*a computer*	**des** ordinateurs	*(some) computers*
feminine	**une** table	*a table*	**des** tables	*(some) tables*
	une horloge	*a clock*	**des** horloges	*(some) clocks*

The indefinite articles (**les articles indéfinis**) mean *a, an,* or *some.* **Un** is used before masculine singular nouns; **une** is used before feminine singular nouns; and **des** is used before plural nouns. While *some* is often omitted in English, **des** cannot be omitted in French.

In most cases, an **s,** which is not pronounced, is added to a singular noun to make it plural. Nouns that end in **-eau** like **un tableau** and **un bureau** add an **x: des tableaux, des bureaux.**

Nouns that have been borrowed from the English language are usually masculine: **un CD, un iPod®, un DVD.**

Some nouns that refer to people can be changed from masculine to feminine by adding an **e.**

un étudiant *(m.)*	*a student*	une étudiante *(f.)*	*a student*
un ami *(m.)*	*a friend*	une amie *(f.)*	*a friend*
un Français	*a French man*	une Française	*a French woman*

Pour aller plus loin
C'est vs. *Ce sont*

To identify objects or people, use **c'est** *(this is)* followed by a singular article and noun and **ce sont** *(these are)* followed by a plural article and noun.

Qu'est-ce que c'est?	*What is this?*
C'est un stylo Montblanc.	*This is a Montblanc pen.*
Ce sont des classeurs.	*These are folders.*

ACTIVITÉ Ⓖ **La garderie** Select the item that goes with each article. Then indicate if that item is typically found in the playroom of **une garderie** *(a daycare center).*

					Oui	Non
1.	une…	a. table	b. écran	c. stylos	☐	☐
2.	des…	a. calculatrice	b. chaises	c. livre	☐	☐
3.	un…	a. porte	b. examen	c. crayons	☐	☐
4.	une…	a. affiche	b. livres	c. tableau	☐	☐
5.	des…	a. crayon	b. livres	c. porte	☐	☐
6.	une…	a. horloge	b. écrans	c. ordinateur	☐	☐
7.	des…	a. marqueurs	b. tableau	c. cahier	☐	☐
8.	un…	a. feuille de papier	b. calculatrice	c. crayon	☐	☐
9.	une…	a. poubelle	b. étudiants	c. professeur	☐	☐
10.	des…	a. agrafeuse	b. amis	c. classeur	☐	☐

🔊 **ACTIVITÉ H** **Je vais acheter...** You will hear parts of statements about what
CD1-8 someone needs to buy for school. Pay attention to the article to determine what that
object is.

Modèle: *You hear:* Je vais acheter *(I am going to buy)* une…
You see: a. agrafeuse   b. livre   c. stylos
You select: **a**

1. a. calculatrice   b. cahier   c. écrans
2. a. affiche   b. chaise   c. stylos
3. a. ordinateur   b. calculatrice   c. tables
4. a. brosse   b. affiches   c. crayon
5. a. iPod®   b. cahiers   c. chaise
6. a. cahiers   b. tableau   c. projecteur
7. a. horloge   b. téléphone portable   c. agrafeuses
8. a. gomme   b. sac   c. CD

ACTIVITÉ I **Qu'est-ce que c'est?** Listen and watch as your instructor
points to various objects in the room. Answer his/her questions with **C'est…** or
Ce sont…

Modèle: Professeur: **C'est un tableau ou une table?** *(points to blackboard)*
Étudiant(e)s: **C'est un tableau.**

ACTIVITÉ J **Fais-moi un dessin!** *(Draw me a picture!)*
The class will be divided into two teams to play a picture-drawing game. One person
from each team will take turns drawing. The drawers **(dessinateurs / dessinatrices)**
for each team will go to the instructor who will show them a card with a word on
it. Each drawer must then go back to his/her team and draw the picture on the card
while the rest of the team tries to guess what the object is. The first person from a
team that says the correct object and article (for example, **C'est un crayon!**) gets
a point!

ACTIVITÉ K **Trois objets**

Étape 1. If you could only take three objects with you to class everyday, what
would they be? Complete this sentence with three objects from **Vocabulaire 2.**

• Mes trois objets sont:

_____

_____

_____.

Étape 2. Compare what you wrote with a classmate. How would you describe your partner based on his/her response? Complete the following sentence with your partner's name and select the appropriate adjective.

Conclusion _____ est pratique / original(e) / extravagant(e) parce que *(because)* ses trois objets sont _____, _____ et _____.

ACTIVITÉ (L) **Une salle de classe idéale**

Étape 1. Make a list of what should be in an ideal classroom, using vocabulary you know. Include the ideal quantity of each object. Write out the numbers in French.

• Dans une salle de classe idéale, il y a…

Étape 2. Share what you wrote with a classmate. Did you write similar things? Decide with your classmate whether the following statement is true or false for your classroom.

Conclusion Notre *(Our)* salle de classe est une salle de classe idéale.   V / F

ACTIVITÉ (M) **À acheter**

Étape 1. According to the National Retail Federation, the average college student in the U.S. spends approximately $956.93 on back-to-school items every year. What do you still need to buy this semester / term for **la rentrée**? Make a list in French of what you are going to buy at the bookstore.

À acheter… *(To buy…)*

un stylo _____

_____

_____

_____

_____

_____

_____

_____

_____

Étape 2. Based on your list, how much do you think you will need to spend? Check the best answer.

Lexique

< : **moins de** *(less than)*   > : **plus de** *(more than)*

☐ < $5,00   ☐ >$5,00   ☐ > $10,00

☐ > $15,00   ☐ >$20,00

Liaisons musicales

Patrick Bruel (1959–) is a French singer of Algerian descent. One of his popular songs, *La place des grands hommes*, is a song about school friends wondering what their lives will be like if they meet again in 10 years. Look for the music video of this song on the Internet. Did you and your friends ever wonder about the same thing in high school?

Les **études**
Studies

**le commerce
(international)**

l'art *(m.)*

l'astronomie *(f.)*

la biologie

le journalisme

la littérature

les mathématiques
(f. pl.)

la musique

la psychologie

Les cours à l'université

Vocabulaire complémentaire

Quelle est ta spécialisation? *What's your major?*

Qu'est-ce que tu étudies? *(sing.)* *What are you studying?*

Qu'est-ce que vous étudiez? *(pl.)* *What are you studying?*

J'étudie... *I am studying . . .*

Je ne sais pas encore. *I don't know yet.*

Combien de cours *(m.)* **as-tu ce semestre / trimestre?** *How many courses / classes
do you have this term?*

les devoirs *(m. pl.)* *homework*

l'école *(f.)* *school*

les études *(f.)* *studies*

l'université *(f.)* *university*

Les lettres *(f.)*, **les langues** *(f.)* **et les arts** *(m.)*

les langues
    l'allemand *(m.)* *German*
    l'anglais *(m.)*
    le chinois *Chinese*
    l'espagnol *(m.)*
    le français
    le russe *Russian*
la philosophie

Les sciences *(f.)* **humaines / sociales**

l'anthropologie *(f.)*
l'histoire *(f.)*
la psychologie
la sociologie

Les sciences naturelles

la chimie *chemistry*
la physique *physics*

L'administration *(f.)*, **l'économie**

la comptabilité *accounting*
le droit *law*
l'économie *(f.)* *economics*
la gestion *business administration*

D'autres cours / spécialisations

le génie (civil, mécanique, électrique) *engineering*
l'informatique *(f.)* *computer science*
les sciences politiques *(f. pl.)*
les TIC (technologies de l'information et de la communication)

Les nombres de 20 à 60

20 **vingt**	25 **vingt-cinq**	30 **trente**
21 **vingt et un**	26 **vingt-six**	31 **trente et un**
22 **vingt-deux**	27 **vingt-sept**	40 **quarante**
23 **vingt-trois**	28 **vingt-huit**	50 **cinquante**
24 **vingt-quatre**	29 **vingt-neuf**	60 **soixante**

Pour aller plus loin
Les articles définis

In French, definite articles (**les articles définis**) are used with majors and courses because one function of definite articles is to designate nouns that are used in a general sense. In this case in English, no article is used. The French definite articles are **le** *(m., sing.)*, **la** *(f., sing.)*, **l'** (*sing.* before a vowel sound), and **les** (*m. pl.* and *f. pl.*).

Tran étudie **la** psychologie.   *Tran studies psychology.*

Le français est intéressant.   *French is interesting.*

ACTIVITÉ A Associations

CD1-9

Étape 1. Indicate the item you associate with the subject matter you hear.

1. a. un microscope   b. les guerres mondiales *(world wars)*
2. a. Picasso   b. B. F. Skinner
3. a. Beethoven   b. *Les Misérables*
4. a. la Bourse *(stock market)*   b. le musée *(museum)*
5. a. la géométrie   b. les ordinateurs
6. a. Friedrich Nietzsche   b. une calculatrice

Étape 2. Go back to the items you didn't choose. Can you give a subject matter association from **Vocabulaire 3** for each one?

ACTIVITÉ B On étudie…

Using the following columns, make logical sentences.

Modèle: Dans un cours **d'économie**, on étudie *(one studies)* **la Bourse.**

Dans un cours…	…on étudie
1. _____ d'histoire	a. la gestion
2. _____ d'astronomie	b. l'actualité *(current events)*
3. _____ d'économie	c. les éléments chimiques
4. _____ de physique	d. la rotation des planètes
5. _____ de journalisme	e. les événements historiques
6. _____ de chimie	f. les réactions nucléaires

> **Note de grammaire**
> In French, **de** *(of)* is used in front of words that begin with consonants and **d'** is used in front of words that begin with a vowel or silent *h:* **un cours de chimie, un cours d'astronomie, un cours d'histoire.**

ACTIVITÉ C Quelle est sa spécialisation?

Read these statements by several people. Can you guess what each person's major is?

1. Je m'appelle Sophie. Mes cours ce semestre sont la géométrie, le calcul et l'algèbre. Ma spécialisation est…

2. Je m'appelle Mustapha. Mes cours ce trimestre sont la comptabilité, l'économie et la gestion des affaires. Ma spécialisation est…

3. Je m'appelle Anouk. Mes cours ce semestre sont la littérature française du Moyen Âge *(Middle Ages)*, la grammaire avancée et le cinéma français. Ma spécialisation est…

4. Je m'appelle Jean-Marc. Mes cours ce trimestre sont Freud et la psychanalyse, l'interprétation des rêves *(dreams)* et les théories de Jean Piaget. Ma spécialisation est…

Liaisons musicales

French composer Bruno Coulais (1954–) composed the music for *Les Choristes,* a film about how a music teacher changed the lives of his students at a boys' boarding school in France. This soundtrack was nominated for an Oscar in 2005 in the Best Achievement in Music Written for Motion Pictures. Listen to excerpts of the soundtrack on the Internet.

ACTIVITÉ D Et vous? Quelle est votre spécialisation?

Ask three people what their classes are and then try to guess their major. If someone has not yet chosen his/her major, he/she can say **Je ne sais pas encore.**

Modèle: Étudiant(e) 1: **Ce semestre / trimestre, quels sont tes *(your)* cours?**
Étudiant(e) 2: **Ce semestre / trimestre, mes cours sont le français, la comptabilité et l'économie.**
Étudiant(e) 1: **Est-ce que ta spécialisation est le commerce international?**
Étudiant(e) 2: **Oui.**

ACTIVITÉ E Les nombres (numbers) You will hear a number. What is the most logical thing it could be referring to?

1. a. le prix *(price)* d'un livre
   b. le prix d'un iPod®

2. a. le prix d'un crayon
   b. le prix d'une calculatrice

3. a. le prix d'une agrafeuse
   b. le prix d'un projecteur

4. a. le prix d'un ordinateur
   b. le prix d'une chaise

5. a. le prix d'un classeur
   b. le prix d'une horloge

6. a. le nombre d'états *(states)* aux États-Unis
   b. le nombre de crédits du cours de français

ACTIVITÉ F Combien?

Étape 1. Answer these questions with the number that answers each question correctly for you. If you do not know, you can say **Je ne sais pas.**

1. Combien de cours as-tu *(do you have)* ce semestre?
2. Combien de crédits as-tu ce semestre?
3. Combien de crédits de français sont nécessaires pour *(for)* le diplôme de français?
4. Combien de crédits au total *(total)* sont nécessaires pour ta spécialisation?
5. Combien de devoirs as-tu ce soir?

Étape 2. Who in the class has the greatest number of credit hours this semester?

Conclusion _____ a le plus grand nombre de crédits ce semestre.

Un mot sur la culture

La dictée

The French **dictée** *(dictation)* is more than a spelling exercise; it is a cultural phenomenon. The French are so attached to this practice that it has been made into a popular TV show, *Les dictées de Bernard Pivot.* Host Bernard Pivot reads texts with tricky grammar and complex spelling (French does not always sound like the way it is written) to challenge participants and viewers. Besides the game show, this passion has sparked the establishment of **dictée** competitions all over the world, including the U.S., and the creation of two best-selling **dictée** books by Pivot.

- Do you think a dictation game could be popular in the U.S.?
- Would you like to participate in a **dictée** competition?

© Olga Besnard/Shutterstock.com

Pour décrire

Les articles définis / Les adjectifs qualificatifs

DU FILM *LIAISONS*

Un coup d'œil sur la grammaire

The film *Liaisons* that you will be watching in this course has a scene that takes place at McGill University. Here is what a student has to say about his courses there.

© Heinle/Cengage Learning

J'ai deux cours ce semestre: la sociologie et l'anglais. Pour moi, la sociologie est **fascinante**. Mon cours d'anglais est **intéressant** et il est **important** parce qu'il y a beaucoup d'anglophones à McGill.

1. The words **fascinante, intéressant,** and **important** are adjectives. Why is there an **e** at the end of **fascinante,** but not at the end of **intéressant** and **important**?

2. What two definite articles do you recognize in the student's statements?

Les articles définis

Si vous y allez

© Arpad Benedek/
iStockphoto.com

If you go to Paris, check out **la Sorbonne.** Founded by Robert de Sorbon in 1253, **la Sorbonne** is one of France's oldest universities. You can take a virtual tour at www.sorbonne.fr

···❖ As you saw in **Vocabulaire 3,** French has four definite articles: **le** *(m., sing.),* **la** *(f., sing.),* **l'** *(sing.* before a vowel sound), and **les** *(m. pl.* and *f. pl.).* They are often used to refer to nouns that were previously mentioned or to talk about specific nouns. In this usage, the definite article is equivalent to *the* in English.

—C'est qui?	—*Who is that?*
—C'est **le** professeur.	—*That's the professor.*
Voici **l'**agrafeuse.	*Here's the stapler.*
J'aime **le** stylo rouge.	*I like the red pen (as opposed to the blue pen).*

···❖ Another use of definite articles is to designate nouns in a general sense. In this case, no article is used in English.

J'étudie **les** langues.	*I study languages.*
Ma spécialisation est **le** chinois.	*My major is Chinese.*

···❖ Definite articles are also used to indicate possession with the preposition **de** and the name of a person. When the person's name begins with a vowel sound, **de** becomes **d'.**

C'est **le** professeur **de** Paul.	*This is Paul's professor.*
Ce sont **les** stylos **de** Paul et **de** Guy.	*These are Paul and Guy's pens.*
Voici la table **d'**Anne.	*Here is Anne's table.*

Les adjectifs qualificatifs

Adjectives are words used to describe people, places, things, and ideas: *serious student, intelligent young woman*. In French, adjectives must agree with the noun or pronoun they modify. This means that they must agree in gender and number, just as articles (**le, la, les, un, une, des**) do. Descriptive adjectives (**les adjectifs qualificatifs**) normally follow the nouns they modify.

For most adjectives, an **e** is added to the masculine form to create the feminine form. Add an **s** to the masculine and feminine forms to make them plural.

amusant(e) *funny*	**embêtant(e)** *annoying*	**intelligent(e)**
brillant(e)	**fascinant(e)**	**intéressant(e)**
charmant(e)	**impatient(e)**	**méchant(e)** *mean*
content(e)	**important(e)**	**patient(e)**
doué(e) *gifted*	**indépendant(e)**	**récent(e)**

Tom est intelligent.   Sylvie est intelligent**e**.

Ils sont charmant**s**.   Elles sont charmant**es**.

- When an adjective of this type describes a group of males and females or objects that are both masculine and feminine in grammatical gender, use the masculine plural form.

  Tom et Sylvie sont intelligent**s**.   L'art *(m.)* et la musique sont important**s**.

- In the masculine singular form of adjectives of this type, the final consonant is silent. In the feminine singular form, the final consonant is pronounced. The final **s** of the plural forms is silent.

  Pierre est intelligen**t**.   Claire est intelligent**e**.

  Ils sont intelligent**s**.   Elles sont intelligent**es**.

Some adjectives have the same feminine and masculine forms. Most adjectives of this type end in **e**.

célèbre *famous*	**moderne**	**pratique**
dynamique	**modeste**	**sociable**
énergique	**nécessaire**	**timide**
facile *easy*	**optimiste**	**utile** *useful*
inutile *not useful*	**pessimiste**	

Le journalisme est **utile**. La biologie est **difficile**.
Mon professeur est **dynamique**.
Norah Jones est **célèbre**.

Note de **grammaire**
Adjectives like these that end in **e** and have the same masculine and feminine forms are often cognates, meaning they have the same or similar spellings and meanings in French and English. An exception is **chic,** which does not end in **e**: Il/Elle est **chic**. Ils/Elles sont **chics**.

Note de **grammaire**
Some adjectives are irregular and have different masculine and feminine forms. You will learn these adjectives in **Chapitre 2**.

ACTIVITÉ G Les possessions Your instructor will point to different objects that belong to you or your classmates. Indicate who that object belongs to.

Modèle: Professeur: **C'est le livre de qui?**

Étudiants: **C'est le livre de Mark.**

🔊 **ACTIVITÉ H Les cours** You will hear adjectives that describe various courses.

CD1-11 Select the course you feel fits the adjective used. You may select more than one course.

1. a. le chinois   b. le français   c. le journalisme
2. a. la biologie   b. la chimie   c. la littérature
3. a. l'astronomie   b. l'astrologie   c. la danse folklorique
4. a. la comptabilité   b. la musique   c. la sociologie
5. a. l'allemand   b. l'anglais   c. le français
6. a. la comptabilité   b. l'économie   c. l'histoire

🔊 **ACTIVITÉ I Quel cours? (Which class?)** A French exchange student is

CD1-12 describing courses she is taking. Listen carefully to the form of the adjectives in order to determine to which class she is referring.

1. a. la biologie   b. le français
2. a. le chinois   b. la littérature
3. a. l'art *(m.)*   b. la musique
4. a. le génie   b. la chimie
5. a. l'anglais *(m.)*   b. l'informatique *(f.)*
6. a. le journalisme   b. la gestion des affaires

ACTIVITÉ J Les Clinton

World leaders, past or present, always make the news. A journalist in Senegal recently wrote an article on the Clintons. Pay attention to the form of the adjectives to determine if they refer to Bill or to Hillary. Write either Bill or Hillary in each blank. Then, indicate whether you agree or disagree with what the journalist wrote.

© Daniel Barry/epa/Corbis

	Je suis d'accord.	Je ne suis pas d'accord.
1. _____ est dou**é**e.	☐	☐
2. _____ est passionnant**e**.	☐	☐
3. _____ est intelligent.	☐	☐
4. _____ est patient.	☐	☐
5. _____ est amusant**e**.	☐	☐
6. _____ est content.	☐	☐

ACTIVITÉ **K** **Nicolas Sarkozy et Carla Bruni-Sarkozy**

Étape 1. Does Nicolas Sarkozy have a lot in common with his wife Carla Bruni-Sarkozy? Decide which traits you think each one has. Select both names if you think they both have that trait. You may also decide some traits do not apply to either one.

© Ian Langsdon/epa/Corbis

	Nicolas Sarkozy	Carla Bruni-Sarkozy
1. dynamique	☐	☐
2. timide	☐	☐
3. pratique	☐	☐
4. moderne	☐	☐
5. sociable	☐	☐
6. pessimiste	☐	☐
7. modeste	☐	☐
8. chic	☐	☐

Étape 2. Write sentences to describe Carla Bruni-Sarkozy and Nicolas Sarkozy based on how you responded in **Étape 1.** Share your sentences with a classmate. Were your sentences similar or different?

ACTIVITÉ **L** **Les cours et les professions** What course or courses do you think are **nécessaires** and **utiles** to prepare for these professions? Is there a course that is **inutile**? Share responses with a partner to see if you have similar views.

Modèle: un comptable *(accountant)*

> **La comptabilité est nécessaire. Les mathématiques sont utiles.**
> **La musique est inutile.**

1. un professeur de littérature
2. un journaliste
3. un économiste *(economist)*
4. un artiste

ACTIVITÉ **M** **Je suis comme...** *(I am like . . .)*

Étape 1. From the adjectives you've learned so far, select three that you think describe you well. Write three sentences.

Modèle: Je suis très dynamique. Je suis intelligent(e). Je suis sociable.

Étape 2. Get together with a classmate and read him/her your sentences. Based on your description of yourself, your classmate will decide which famous person you are most like. Tell your classmate whether you agree or not.

Modèle: Étudiant(e) 1: **Tu es comme** *(like)* **Jennifer Lopez.**
> Étudiant(e) 2: **Oui, je suis d'accord. / Non, je ne suis pas d'accord.**

Avant de visionner

You are about to watch the **Prologue** of the film *Liaisons.* Don't worry if you do not understand all of the language you hear. As a beginning student of French, you aren't expected to! However, you should be able to grasp the central ideas of each film segment you watch. The activities in this book are designed to help you understand as much as possible.

As you may know, cinematographic elements of a film such as sound and camera techniques play a role in helping you understand what is going on in any given scene. These cinematographic elements are part of what the French call **la mise en scène** which includes: **le décor, les costumes et les objets; les couleurs; l'éclairage** (*lighting*)**; le son** (*sound*)**; and les mouvements de la caméra.** You may rely on context and elements of **la mise en scène** to help you understand. As your proficiency in French increases, so will your comprehension of the language.

ACTIVITÉ A Un coup d'œil sur une scène

Here is a scene from the **Prologue** of *Liaisons.*

CLAIRE Bonjour, Maman.

MME GAGNER C'est toi, Claire? Ce n'est pas une de mes hallucinations…?

CLAIRE Non, Maman. C'est moi.

With a classmate, try to answer the following questions based on the scene. You will check your answers later when you watch the **Prologue.**

© Heinle/Cengage Learning

1. What is the relationship between these two characters?
2. What does Madame Gagner ask Claire?
3. Where do you think this scene takes place?

Regarder le Prologue
You will now watch the **Prologue** of the film *Liaisons.* Use the context and **la mise en scène** to help you understand. Also, verify your answers to **Activité A.**

Après le visionnage

Le contexte One skill you will want to develop as you study French is to guess the meaning of language from context. Here are lines between the man and the woman from the opening **Prologue.**

HOMME Maman, maman, ça va?

FEMME Oui, oui, mon fils. Ça va.

ALEXIS Tiens.

FEMME Attends! *(coughs)* Je suis Madeleine Prévost de Paris, *(coughs)* née Tremblay, femme de Henri Prévost et mère de... *(coughs)*

1. In the first line, the woman identifies herself as she dictates to the man what to write down. What is her name? Where is she from?

2. The woman also says she is **femme d'Henri Prévost.** What do you think **femme** means in this context: *wife* or *woman*?

3. The woman also says née **Tremblay.** What does this indicate?

4. Is the woman reading a will, a confession, or something else? What are your clues?

5. The man calls the woman **maman.** Can you deduce what the word **fils** means?

ACTIVITÉ **C** **Vérifiez votre compréhension** Answer each question based on what you remember from watching the second part of the **Prologue** in which you meet Claire Gagner.

1. C'est _____. a. le passé b. le temps présent

2. Claire Gagner est étudiante à _____. a. Montréal b. Paris

3. Claire étudie _____. a. l'anglais b. la psychologie

ACTIVITÉ **D** **Premières impressions: Claire Gagner**

Étape 1. What are your first impressions of the main character Claire Gagner? Use the verb **être** and three adjectives to describe her.

Étape 2. Now share your impressions with a classmate. Do you have similar or different impressions of Claire?

© Heinle/Cengage Learning

Dans les coulisses

Some believe that the opening shots and prologue of a film sometimes contain all the information needed to understand it. What are your initial impressions of the film after viewing the prologue? What kind of film do you think it is? Can you guess what some of its themes might be?

Le monde parle français... et maintenant vous aussi!

LE FRANÇAIS: LANGUE DU MONDE

By choosing to study French, you will not only learn how the French language works, you will be exposed to cultures and information that will enrich your understanding and appreciation of different perspectives of the world and its peoples.

What do you already know about French in the world? Take this quiz to find out.

1. French is spoken on how many continents in the world?
   a. two   b. three
   c. four   d. five

2. French is an official language in how many countries in the world?
   a. 6   b. 17
   c. 29   d. 38

3. French is a language of diplomacy in the world (and one of the official languages of the United Nations).
   a. True   b. False

4. French is considered a critical language by the CIA.
   a. True   b. False

5. Approximately how many people in the world speak French as a first language?
   a. 50 million   b. 100 million   c. 150 million   d. more than 200 million

6. French is an official language in the United States.
   a. True   b. False

7. Approximately how many people in the United States speak French?
   a. less than 1 million   b. more than 1 million   c. more than 2 million

8. One of the most translated books in the world is a French book. What is this book's title?
   a. *Candide*   b. *Les Trois Mousquetaires*   c. *Le Petit Prince*

What is your current knowledge of French in the world?
15–18 points: **Bravo!** Your knowledge is quite impressive!
10–14 points: **Très bien.** You know quite a bit.
6–8 points: **Pas mal.** Not too bad. You probably learned some new facts today.
5 or less: **Courage.** You will have many more opportunities to learn.

8. c, written by Antoine de Saint-Exupéry (5 points)
6. a, official in Louisiana along with English since 1968 (1 point) 7. b (3 points);
1. d (3 points); 2. c (3 points); 3. a (1 point); 4. a (1 point); 5. b (3 points);

Answers to the quiz:

Parlez-vous the language of 200 million people?

Learning French opens the doors to dozens of countries and cultures and millions of French-speakers. Across the globe there are 55 French-speaking countries, each offering a unique travel, study abroad or pen pal experience. On the Internet French is the third most common language, providing a wealth of information, networking and learning opportunities. Visit TheWorldSpeaksFrench.org to learn more about the benefits of French language education.

TheWorldSpeaksFrench.org   The French Language Initiative

Visuals and pictures help you interpret the message of written texts. You are going to read about some prominent personalities and a company in the francophone world. Use the visuals to help you match the following French words to their English equivalents.

1. chanteur
2. entreprise
3. joueuse
4. réalisateur

a. business, company
b. player
c. film director
d. singer

Luc Besson: réalisateur français

Né° à Paris, le réalisateur Luc Besson (1959–) est célèbre en France et aux États-Unis pour° ses films *Le Grand Bleu* (1988), *Nikita* (1990), *The Fifth Element* (1998) et *The Messenger* (1999). Besson a aussi écrit° le scénario pour *Taken* (2008), un film mettant en vedette° Liam Neeson et Maggie Grace.

Né *Born* **pour** *for* **a écrit** *wrote* **mettant en vedette** *starring*

© ITAR-TASS /Landov

© Paul Vreeker/Reuters /Landov

Justine Henin: joueuse de tennis belge

Originaire de Liège (Belgique), Justine Henin (1982–) est l'une des joueuses de tennis les plus importantes des années 2003 à 2008 avec un palmarès° de 41 titres. Elle a remporté° la médaille d'or° aux Jeux olympiques en 2004.

avec un palmarès *with a list of titles* **a remporté** *won* **médaille d'or** *gold medal*

Faudel: chanteur français d'origine algérienne

Né dans une banlieue° de Paris, Faudel Belloua (1978–), «le petit prince» du raï, rend hommage° à ses deux cultures: la culture française et la culture algérienne. Sa musique est caractérisée par les rythmes orientaux et africains, le reggae et le rock.

banlieue *suburb* **rend hommage** *pay tribute*

Le Cirque du Soleil: entreprise québécoise

Entreprise québécoise de divertissement° artistique, la compagnie a été fondée en 1984 par deux artistes de rue°, Guy Laliberté et Daniel Gauthier. Le Cirque du Soleil est un cirque contemporain avec des acrobates, des costumes et de la musique spectaculaires.

divertissement *entertainment* **rue** *street*

Compréhension

1. Qui est chanteur?
2. Qui est joueuse de tennis?
3. Qui est réalisateur?
4. Quelle entreprise est connue pour le cirque contemporain?

Activités Internet

- Many celebrities in the United States speak French as a foreign language. Find at least ten famous Americans who speak French. Be prepared to share your list with the rest of your class. Let's see who in your class can come up with the longest list!

- Find three famous people from different French-speaking countries. Say where they are from and what they do for a living.

- **L'entreprise Bic** is a company based in France. Find three interesting pieces of information about this company. What are other significant companies in the French-speaking world?

You may access all end-of-chapter vocabulary audio at **iLrn** and on the *Liaisons* Premium Website.

PARTIE 1

LES SALUTATIONS

À bientôt.	*See you soon.*
À demain.	*See you tomorrow.*
À plus (tard).	*See you (later).*
Au revoir.	*Goodbye.*
Bonjour.	*Hello.*
Bonne journée.	*Good day.*
Bonne nuit.	*Good night.*
Bonsoir.	*Good evening.*
Comment allez-vous?	*How are you?*
(pl./sing., formal)	
Comment vas-tu?	*How are you?*
(sing, informal)	
Comment ça va?	*How is it going?*
(sing., informal)	
Ça va bien.	*Fine.*
Ça va très bien. Et toi?	*Very well. And you?*
Ça va mal. / Ça ne va pas très bien.	*Not well.*
Je vais très bien.	*I'm doing very well.*
Très bien aussi.	*Very well, too (also).*
Comment s'appelle-t-il?	*What is his name?*
Il s'appelle Henri.	*His name is Henry.*
Comment s'appelle-t-elle?	*What is her name?*
Elle s'appelle Isabelle.	*Her name is Isabelle.*
Son nom (de famille) est…	*His/Her last name is…*
Son prénom est…	*His/Her first name is…*
Comment t'appelles-tu?	*What's your name?*
Je m'appelle…	*My name is…*
Mon prénom est…	*My first name is…*
Quel est ton nom (de famille)?	*What is your (last) name?*
Mon nom (de famille) est…	*My (last) name is…*
De rien. / Il n'y a pas de quoi.	*You're welcome.*
Et toi? (sing., informal)	*And you?*
Et vous? (pl./sing., formal)	*And you?*
Je vous présente…	*I introduce to you…*
Enchanté(e).	*Pleased to meet you.*
Ravi(e) de faire ta connaissance. (sing., informal)	*Pleased to meet you.*
Ravi(e) de faire votre connaissance. (pl. / sing., formal)	*Pleased to meet you.*
Merci.	*Thank you.*
Moi aussi.	*Me, too.*
Madame (Mme)	*Ma'am, Mrs.*
Mademoiselle (Mlle)	*Miss*
Monsieur (M.)	*Sir, Mr.*
Quoi de neuf?	*What's new?*
Pas grand-chose.	*Not much.*
Rien de nouveau.	*Nothing new.*
Salut.	*Hello, hi.*

Voici…	*Here is…*
Voilà…	*There is…*
un(e) meilleur(e) ami(e)	*a best friend*
un(e) camarade de chambre	*a roommate*
un copain (m.) / une copine (f.)	*a friend*
une fille	*a girl*
un garçon	*a boy*
une femme	*a woman*
un homme	*a man*
un(e) petit(e) ami(e)	*a boyfriend / girlfriend*

VERBE

être	*to be*

DIVERS

de	*from*

PARTIE 2

UNE SALLE DE CLASSE

un(e) camarade de classe	*a classmate*
une classe	*a class (of students)*
un(e) étudiant(e)	*a student*
un professeur	*a professor, a teacher*
une affiche	*a poster*
une agrafeuse	*a stapler*
un baladeur MP3	*an MP3 player*
une brosse (à tableau)	*a board eraser*
un bureau	*a desk*
un cahier	*a notebook*
une calculatrice	*a calculator*
un CD	*a compact disc, a CD*
une chaise	*a chair*
une classe	*a class*
un classeur	*a folder, a binder*
une craie	*(a piece of) chalk*
un crayon	*a pencil*
un écran	*a screen*
une fenêtre	*a window*
une feuille de papier	*a sheet of paper*
une gomme	*an eraser*
une horloge	*a clock*
un iPod®	*an iPod®*
un livre	*a book*
un marqueur	*a marker*
un ordinateur (portable)	*a (laptop) computer*
une porte	*a door*
une poubelle	*a waste basket*
un projecteur	*a(n) (overhead) projector*
un sac	*a bag, a purse*
un sac à dos	*a backpack*
un stylo	*a pen*
une table	*a table*
un tableau	*a chalkboard*
un (téléphone) portable	*a cell phone*

LES NOMBRES DE 0 À 20

0 zéro	7 sept	14 quatorze
1 un	8 huit	15 quinze
2 deux	9 neuf	16 seize
3 trois	10 dix	17 dix-sept
4 quatre	11 onze	18 dix-huit
5 cinq	12 douze	19 dix-neuf
6 six	13 treize	20 vingt

DIVERS

Dans la classe, il y a...	*In the classroom, there is . . . , there are . . .*
Qu'est-ce que c'est?	*What's that?*
C'est...	*This is . . .*
Ce sont...	*These are . . .*

PARTIE 3

LES LETTRES, LES LANGUES ET LES ARTS

l'art *(m.)*	*art*
les langues *(f. pl.)*	*languages*
l'allemand *(m.)*	*German*
l'anglais *(m.)*	*English*
le chinois	*Chinese*
l'espagnol *(m.)*	*Spanish*
le français	*French*
le russe	*Russian*
la littérature	*literature*
la musique	*music*
la philosophie	*philosophy*

LES SCIENCES HUMAINES / SOCIALES

l'anthropologie *(f.)*	*anthropology*
l'histoire *(f.)*	*history*
la psychologie	*psychology*
la sociologie	*sociology*

LES SCIENCES NATURELLES

l'astronomie *(f.)*	*astronomy*
la biologie	*biology*
la chimie	*chemistry*
la physique	*physics*

LE DROIT, L'ADMINISTRATION ET L'ÉCONOMIE

le commerce (international)	*business*
la comptabilité	*accounting*
l'économie *(f.)*	*economy*
la gestion	*business administration*

D'AUTRES COURS / SPÉCIALISATIONS

le génie (civil, mécanique, électrique)	*engineering (civil, mechanical, electrical)*
l'informatique *(f.)*	*computer science*
le journalisme	*journalism*
les mathématiques *(f. pl.)*	*mathematics*
les sciences politiques *(f. pl.)*	*political science*
les TIC (technologies de l'information et de la communication) *(f. pl.)*	*information technology*

DIVERS

Quelle est ta spécialisation?	*What's your major?*
Qu'est-ce que tu étudies? *(sing.)*	*What are you studying?*
Qu'est-ce que vous étudiez? *(pl.)*	*What are you studying?*
J'étudie...	*I am studying . . .*
Je ne sais pas encore.	*I don't know yet.*
Combien de cours as-tu ce semestre / trimestre?	*How many courses / classes do you have this term?*
le cours	*course*
les devoirs *(m. pl.)*	*homework*
l'école *(f.)*	*school*
les études *(f. pl.)*	*studies*
l'université *(f.)*	*university*

LES NOMBRES DE 20 À 60

20 vingt	28 vingt-huit
21 vingt et un	29 vingt-neuf
22 vingt-deux	30 trente
23 vingt-trois	31 trente et un
24 vingt-quatre	40 quarante
25 vingt-cinq	50 cinquante
26 vingt-six	60 soixante
27 vingt-sept	

ADJECTIFS

amusant(e)	*funny*
brillant(e)	*brilliant*
célèbre	*famous*
charmant(e)	*charming*
content(e)	*happy, content*
difficile	*difficult*
doué(e)	*gifted*
dynamique	*dynamic*
embêtant(e)	*annoying*
énergique	*energetic*
facile	*easy*
fascinant(e)	*fascinating*
impatient(e)	*impatient*
important(e)	*important*
indépendant(e)	*independent*
intelligent(e)	*intelligent*
intéressant(e)	*interesting*
inutile	*not useful, useless*
méchant(e)	*mean*
moderne	*modern*
modeste	*modest*
nécessaire	*necessary*
optimiste	*optimistic*
patient(e)	*patient*
pessimiste	*pessimistic*
pratique	*practical*
récent(e)	*recent*
sociable	*sociable*
timide	*shy*
utile	*useful*

Une **vie** équilibrée

En bref   In this chapter, you will:

- learn numbers 60–100

- learn some regular **-er** verbs

- learn the pronoun **on**

- learn how to make statements negative

- learn about stressed pronouns

- learn the days of the week

- learn adverbs of intensity and frequency

- learn some irregular adjectives

- learn how to express time

- learn the verb **avoir** and some expressions with **avoir**

- read about how people spend time in some French-speaking countries

 You will also watch **SÉQUENCE 1: L'étranger** of the movie *Liaisons*.

Ressources

 audio   http://www.cengagebrain.com

© eddie linssen / Alamy

VOCABULAIRE 1

🔊 Nos **activités**
CD1-13

Our activities

cuisiner et manger

déjeuner au café

dîner au restaurant

travailler au bureau

étudier à la bibliothèque

jouer *(to play)*

marcher au parc

pratiquer le sport

inviter des amis

écouter des CD

regarder la télé

voyager / aimer

Les activités de Kim-Lee pendant la semaine

Les nombres de 60 à 100

60 soixante
61 soixante et un
62 soixante-deux
63 soixante-trois
64 soixante-quatre
65 soixante-cinq
66 soixante-six
67 soixante-sept
68 soixante-huit
69 soixante-neuf
70 soixante-dix
71 soixante et onze
72 soixante-douze
73 soixante-treize

74 soixante-quatorze
75 soixante-quinze
76 soixante-seize
77 soixante-dix-sept
78 soixante-dix-huit
79 soixante-dix-neuf
80 quatre-vingts
81 quatre-vingt-un
82 quatre-vingt-deux
83 quatre-vingt-trois
84 quatre-vingt-quatre
85 quatre-vingt-cinq
86 quatre-vingt-six
87 quatre-vingt-sept

88 quatre-vingt-huit
89 quatre-vingt-neuf
90 quatre-vingt-dix
91 quatre-vingt-onze
92 quatre-vingt-douze
93 quatre-vingt-treize
94 quatre-vingt-quatorze
95 quatre-vingt-quinze
96 quatre-vingt-seize
97 quatre-vingt-dix-sept
98 quatre-vingt-dix-huit
99 quatre-vingt-dix-neuf
100 cent
100% cent pour cent

Vocabulaire complémentaire

pendant *during*
la semaine *the week*
le week-end *the weekend*

Note de vocabulaire

The number 80, **quatre-vingts**, = 4 × 20. When **quatre-vingts** is followed by another number, there is no **s** after **vingt**: **quatre-vingt-deux**.

ACTIVITÉ A Est-ce que c'est essentiel? You will hear a series of activities. Indicate whether or not you feel they are essential for a balanced life.

CD1-14

1. oui / non
2. oui / non
3. oui / non
4. oui / non

5. oui / non
6. oui / non
7. oui / non

8. oui / non
9. oui / non
10. oui / non

ACTIVITÉ B Une vie équilibrée?

CD1-15

Étape 1. Listen and follow along as you hear statements about students' daily activities at Claire Gagner's university, McGill University. Select the number that you hear.

1. _____ des étudiants déjeunent tous les jours.
   a. 61%   b. 75%   c. 87%   d. 95%

2. _____ des étudiants étudient pendant le week-end.
   a. 54%   b. 68%   c. 84%   d. 96%

3. _____ des étudiants travaillent pendant le week-end.
   a. 24%   b. 68%   c. 79%   d. 88%

4. _____ des étudiants dînent avant *(before)* 8h le soir.
   a. 41%   b. 63%   c. 76%   d. 80%

5. _____ des étudiants pratiquent un sport.
   a. 69%   b. 77%   c. 83%   d. 91%

6. _____ des étudiants regardent la télévision pendant le week-end.
   a. 32%   b. 52%   c. 64%   d. 73%

Étape 2. Based on the answers to **Étape 1,** would you say that students at McGill University have **une vie équilibrée?**   oui / non

🔊 **ACTIVITÉ C Quel âge?** *(What age?)*

CD1-16

Étape 1. You will hear how old each of these people were when they died. Write the number you hear. You do not need to spell it out.

1.

Jacques Brel _____

5.

Léopold Sédar Senghor _____

2.

Édith Piaf _____

6.

Mahatma Gandhi _____

3.

François Mitterrand _____

7.

Mère Teresa _____

4.

Félix Leclerc _____

8.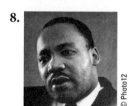

Martin Luther King _____

Étape 2. These people all had special talents when it came to relating to the public. Brel, Piaf, and Leclerc were singers. Mitterrand, Senghor, and Gandhi were politicians. Mère Teresa and M.L. King were humanitarians and civil rights activists. Match these people with their special talents.

1. Brel, Piaf, Leclerc   a. travailler pour *(for)* le public
2. Mitterrand, Senghor, Gandhi   b. chanter *(sing)* pour le public
3. Mère Teresa et M.L. King   c. parler *(speak)* au public

• Which of these people had **une vie équilibrée**? If you don't know some of the people, learn about them through an Internet search or print resources in the library.

ACTIVITÉ D Les activités

Étape 1. Indicate what percentage of time on average each week day you do the following activities. Provide the word for each number.

Pendant une journée de la semaine *(a week day)*:

1. _____ %: étudier le français
2. _____ %: être à l'université
3. _____ %: travailler
4. _____ %: cuisiner

5. _____ %: pratiquer un sport
6. _____ %: regarder la télé
7. _____ %: marcher au parc
8. _____ %: manger

Étape 2. Do **Étape 1** again, but this time, for a day on the weekend. Do any of your answers change? Now select the statement that best describes you.

a. Ma vie pendant la semaine est plus *(more)* équilibrée.

b. Ma vie pendant le week-end est plus équilibrée.

ACTIVITÉ E Notre classe

Étape 1. Poll your classmates to see if they like to do the following activities. If they answer **oui,** put their names next to that item. If they answer **non,** move on and ask other classmates.

Modèle: Est-ce que tu aimes cuisiner?

_____ cuisiner

_____ déjeuner à l'université

_____ étudier pendant le week-end

_____ regarder des émissions de télé-réalité *(reality shows)*

_____ inviter des amis

_____ dîner dans un restaurant élégant

_____ pratiquer un sport

_____ jouer aux jeux vidéo

_____ voyager

_____ écouter des CD

Étape 2. Your instructor will now poll the entire class to see how many people like these activities.

✈ ·····
Si vous y allez

© Olivier Rieu

If you go to Paris, visit the restaurant **Des Gars dans la Cuisine** for a bite to eat. This off-beat, contemporary restaurant was started by two friends, Gil and Jean-Jacques, also known as **les gars** *(the guys).* Find the restaurant's website to take a virtual tour and read reviews.

Note de **vocabulaire**
The French word **gars** comes from **garçon** which means *boy.* **Gars** is a colloquial expression for *guy.*

Un mot sur la culture

Téléphoner en France

© Jack Sullivan / Alamy

French phone numbers appear in pairs and are said in pairs. For example, the phone number 06 14 36 76 89 is said like this: **zéro six, quatorze, trente-six, soixante-seize, quatre-vingt-neuf.**

• Practice saying these phone numbers for restaurants in France.

1. Restaurant Le Marrakech: 04 93 85 81 55
2. Des Gars dans la Cuisine: 01 42 74 88 26
3. Couleur Café: 03 80 70 10 47
4. Restaurant Chez Mireille: 04 93 85 27 23

Pour parler de nos activités

Les verbes du premier groupe en **-er** / Le pronom sujet **on** / La négation / Les pronoms disjoints

DU FILM *LIAISONS*

Un coup d'œil sur la grammaire

In **Séquence 1** of the film *Liaisons,* Claire makes these statements about her mother to her friend.

© Heinle/Cengage Learning

Elle **mange,** elle **joue** aux cartes, elle lit et elle dort. Elle **mange,** elle **joue** aux cartes, elle lit et elle dort. Elle **existe,** c'est tout. C'est trop triste...

1. You have already encountered the verb forms **mange** and **joue** in **Vocabulaire 1.** Do you remember what they mean?

2. The infinitive forms of the verbs **mange** and **joue** are **manger** and **jouer.** These verbs end in **-er.** The verb **existe** follows the same pattern. What is the infinitive form of the verb **existe?**

Les verbes du premier groupe en *-er*

⋯ Verbs in French are grouped according to the ending of their infinitive. In **Vocabulaire 1** of this chapter, you learned the meaning of several **-er** verbs. Now you will learn the different forms of the verbs in this group.

⋯ To form the present tense of **-er** verbs, you drop the **-er** from the infinitive form and add these endings: **-e, -es, -e, -ons, -ez, -ent.**

travailler *(to work)*			
je	travaill**e**	nous	travaill**ons**
tu	travaill**es**	vous	travaill**ez**
il/elle/on	travaill**e**	ils/elles	travaill**ent**

⋯ While **-er** verbs have five different written forms (the forms for **je** and **il/elle/on** are identical), there are only three distinguishable spoken forms: 1) **travaille / travailles / travaillent** (same pronunciation), 2) **travaillons,** and 3) **travaillez.**

⋯ In English, the present tense can be expressed in three ways. In French, these meanings are expressed with a single verb.

Je travaille. ⎰ *I work.*
⎱ *I am working.*
⎰ *I do work.*

Ils jouent. ⎰ *They play.*
⎱ *They are playing.*
⎰ *They do play.*

Le pronom sujet *on*

⟫ The indefinite pronoun **on** can mean either *one* or *they*. It may also be used to refer to *you* or *people* in general. In conversational French, **on** is frequently used instead of **nous.** **On** always takes the same form of the verb as **il** and **elle.** When the word after **on** begins with a vowel sound, there is a liaison. (See pronunciation section **Liaisons avec les mots et les sons** on p. 59).

On voyage à Paris souvent.   *People travel to Paris often.*

On étudie ce soir?   *Shall we study tonight?*

On arrive bientôt.   *We are arriving soon.*

⟫ Here are some regular **-er** verbs in addition to the ones you learned in **Vocabulaire 1.** They are conjugated the same way as **travailler.**

Les verbes-clés

adorer	*to adore*	danser (avec)	*to dance (with)*	passer un examen	*to take an exam*
aimer bien	*to like*	détester	*to hate*	penser	*to think*
aimer mieux	*to prefer*	habiter	*to live (in a place), to reside*	rater un examen	*to fail an exam*
chanter	*to sing*	naviguer sur Internet	*to surf the Internet*	téléphoner	*to telephone*
chercher	*to look for*	parler	*to speak, to talk*	trouver	*to find*

⟫ Verbs that end in **-ger** like **manger** and **voyager** that you learned in **Vocabulaire 1** have a spelling change in the **nous** form. They are conjugated as **nous mangeons** and **nous voyageons** (**-eons** instead of the normal **-ons** ending).

⟫ The following questions are useful when asking about activities.

—**Qu'est-ce que tu fais?**   —*What are you doing?*

—**Je travaille.**   —*I'm working.*

—**Qu'est-ce qu'il/elle fait?**   —*What is he/she doing?*

—**Il/Elle déjeune.**   —*He/She is having lunch.*

⟫ Sometimes two verbs can be used together to express an idea. In these cases, the first verb is conjugated and the second verb is in the infinitive form. Some common verbs that can be followed by an infinitive are **adorer, aimer, aimer mieux,** and **détester.**

J'**aime étudier** le français.   *I like to study French.*

Nous **détestons danser.**   *We hate to dance.*

La négation

⟫ To make a sentence negative, place **ne** (**n'** before a vowel sound) before the conjugated verb and **pas** after it.

Je **ne** regarde **pas** la télé.   *I don't watch television.*

Vous **n'**étudiez **pas** le week-end? *You don't study on weekends?*

⟫ In the case of two verbs used together, **ne** (**n'**)... **pas** goes around the first conjugated verb.

Je **n'**aime **pas** danser.   *I don't like to dance.*

Note de vocabulaire
Note that **passer un examen** means *to take an exam* and not *to pass an exam.* In French, *to pass an exam* is **réussir à un examen.** You will learn this verb in **Chapitre 4.**

Note de prononciation
For verbs that begin with a vowel sound, **je** becomes **j':** J'aime le français!

Les pronoms disjoints

❖ You have already learned subject pronouns in French (**je, tu, il, nous,** etc). Another category of pronouns is called **les pronoms disjoints** (*stressed pronouns*).

je → **moi**	il → **lui**	nous → **nous**	ils → **eux**
tu → **toi**	elle → **elle**	vous → **vous**	elles → **elles**

❖ **Les pronoms disjoints** are used after prepositions and conjunctions such as **et, mais** (*but*), **à** or **de.**

Alex et **toi,** vous étudiez ce soir?	*Alex and you, you're studying tonight?*
Coralie est française mais pas **moi.**	*Coralie is French but not me.*
Moi, je suis américaine.	*Me, I'm American.*
Je pense beaucoup à **elles.**	*I think about them (fem. pl.) a lot.*

❖ Stressed pronouns are also used after **c'est** and **ce sont.**

| —C'est Marc? | —Ce sont M. et Mme Tremblay? |
| —Oui, c'est **lui.** | —Oui, ce sont **eux.** |

ACTIVITÉ **F** Select the correct **pronom disjoint.**

1. C'est Richard? Oui, c'est _____. a. lui b. elle

2. Ce sont Marc et Alain? Oui, ce sont _____. a. vous b. eux

3. C'est Fatima? Oui, c'est _____. a. elle b. nous

4. C'est toi, Dien? Oui, c'est _____. a. moi b. vous

5. Tu penses beaucoup à moi? Oui, je pense beaucoup à _____. a. lui b. toi

6. Tu penses souvent à Nicole et Anne? Oui, je pense souvent à _____. a. eux b. elles

🔊 **ACTIVITÉ** **G** **C'est qui?** Because there are only three discernible verb forms
CD1-17 in spoken French, context is very important in determining who the speaker may be referring to. Another hint is the /z/ sound of the plural form. With verbs that begin with a vowel sound, the **s** of the plural form of **ils** or **elles** is pronounced like the sound /z/. The presence of the /z/ sound tells you that the subject is plural (**ils écoutent**) while the absence of the /z/ sound tells you the subject is singular (**il écoute**). This /z/ sound is also known as a **liaison** sound which you will learn about on p. 59 of this chapter. A reporter is interviewing a French family about their activities. Listen and determine who the reporter is referring to.

1. a. Grégoire	b. Grégoire et Pierre	6. a. Marie	b. Marie et sa maman
2. a. Marie	b. Marie et sa maman	7. a. Marie	b. Marie et sa maman
3. a. Pierre	b. Pierre et Grégoire	8. a. Grégoire	b. Grégoire et Pierre
4. a. Grégoire	b. Grégoire et Pierre	9. a. Grégoire	b. Grégoire et Pierre
5. a. Marie	b. Marie et Pierre	10. a. Marie	b. Marie et sa maman

ACTIVITÉ H *FLASH* **sur les actrices du film** *Liaisons*

Étape 1. Pierre Brassard, host of the talk show *FLASH* in Quebec, is interviewing the actresses of the film *Liaisons*, Mylène Savoie (Claire Gagner) and Johanne Marie Tremblay (Simone Gagner). Pay attention to the verbs to determine whom he is referring to.

1. _____ voyag**ent** toujours *(always)* pour le travail.
   a. Mylène   b. Mylène et Johanne

2. _____ travaill**ent** 65 heures par semaine.
   a. Mylène   b. Mylène et Johanne

3. _____ ne déjeun**ent** pas.
   a. Mylène   b. Mylène et Johanne

4. _____ détes**te** le sport.
   a. Mylène   b. Mylène et Johanne

5. _____ ne mang**ent** pas bien.
   a. Mylène   b. Mylène et Johanne

6. _____ regar**de** des films d'horreur.
   a. Mylène   b. Mylène et Johanne

Conclusion Which sentence do you think best describes the actresses of the film *Liaisons*?

   a. Leur *(Their)* vie est équilibrée.   **b.** Leur vie **n'**est **pas** équilibrée.

Étape 2. Brassard interviews actress Michèle Labonté (Mme LeGrand) who travels with her dog Demoiselle. Michèle is describing some of her activities. Do the activities refer to Michèle or to Michèle and Demoiselle?

1. _____ chant**e** souvent devant *(in front of)* le miroir.   a. Je   b. Nous

2. _____ déjeun**ons** à 11h30.   a. Je   b. Nous

3. _____ cherch**ons** des papillons *(butterflies)* au parc.   a. Je   b. Nous

4. _____ jou**e** au Frisbee®.   a. Je   b. Nous

5. _____ mang**eons** une glace *(ice cream cone)* le soir.   a. Je   b. Nous

Étape 3. *FLASH* interviews skaters Isabelle Brasseur and Lloyd Eisler. Determine if the questions are only for Isabelle or for both Isabelle and Lloyd.

1. _____ aim**ez** les émissions *(programs)* culturelles?   a. Tu   b. Vous

2. _____ aim**es** le rap?   a. Tu   b. Vous

3. _____ habit**ez** dans un grand appartement?   a. Tu   b. Vous

4. _____ pens**ez** que le français est une langue importante?   a. Tu   b. Vous

5. _____ ador**es** danser?   a. Tu   b. Vous

Et vous? How would you answer these questions if Pierre Brassard interviewed you?

ACTIVITÉ I **Un jour avec Regis et Kelly**

Étape 1. A viewer gets to spend a day with the show hosts of *Live with Regis and Kelly*. Using the following cues, create sentences to describe how she spends this day with them.

> **Activités possibles**
>
> chanter dans le studio
>
> cuisiner un repas (*meal*) français
>
> danser le tango
>
> dîner dans un restaurant marocain
>
> écouter des chansons d'Elvis
>
> jouer au Frisbee®
>
> naviguer sur Internet pour trouver des potins (*gossip*)
>
> regarder le tournage de *Live with Regis and Kelly*
>
> trouver une boîte de nuit (*night club*)

Liaisons musicales

© Patrick Hertzog/AFP/ Getty Images

Dur dur d'être bébé (It's Tough to be a Baby), was recorded by the French singer Jordy Lemoine in 1992 at the age of 4. The worldwide success of this dance single earned Jordy a listing in the *Guinness Book of World Records* as the youngest singer to have a #1 hit song on the singles charts. Search the Internet to find the lyrics of this song. If you had to write a song called *Dur dur d'être étudiant,* what would you say?

1. Je/J' _____

2. Kelly et moi _____

3. Regis _____

4. Kelly _____

5. Regis et Kelly _____

6. Regis, Kelly et moi _____

Étape 2. Which of the activities do you adore doing, like doing, prefer doing, and hate doing?

1. J'adore…   **2.** J'aime bien…   **3.** J'aime mieux…   **4.** Je déteste…

ACTIVITÉ J **Les activités**

Étape 1. Create sentences indicating whether you do or do not do the following activities.

1. regarder la télé-réalité

2. parler deux langues ou plus (*or more*)

3. passer des examens pendant le week-end

4. manger trois repas par jour

5. écouter la musique de Céline Dion

6. habiter à la résidence universitaire

7. rater des examens

8. inviter des amis

 Étape 2. Now ask a classmate if he/she does these activities. Jot down your partner's answers so you are prepared to share information with the rest of the class.

Modèle: É1: **Est-ce que tu regardes la télé-réalité?**

É2: **Oui, je regarde la télé-réalité. / Non, je ne regarde pas la télé-réalité.**

Étape 3. What are some things that you and your partner have in common? Refer to your notes from **Étape 2** and prepare a few sentences summarizing how you and your partner are the same or different.

Modèle: **Jack et moi, nous étudions pendant le week-end.**

ACTIVITÉ K Le détecteur de mensonges

Do you know the show *Lie Detector*? The contestants give three statements about themselves. Two statements are true and one is a lie. Opponents try to guess which statement is a lie. If the opponents correctly guess which statement is false, they win! If the opponents guess wrong, the contestant wins!

Étape 1. Create three statements about yourself. At least one statement must be a negative statement, and one must be a lie.

1. _____

2. _____

3. _____

Étape 2. In groups of 3 or 4 take turns being the contestant. The contestants read their sentences. Their opponents try to guess and say which statement is the lie. For example: **Numéro 1 est faux.** Opponents may ask the contestants questions about the statements if they wish to help them guess. Switch roles.

La parole est à vous!

Une vie équilibrée: Est-ce que c'est possible pour les étudiants d'aujourd'hui?

On dit que° les étudiants sont trop occupés° aujourd'hui. Ils travaillent, ils étudient et parfois° ils ont des enfants°. Une vie équilibrée: Est-ce que c'est possible pour les étudiants?

• Émilie de Montréal: «Non, ce n'est pas possible pour moi. Je vais à° l'université pendant la semaine, je travaille le soir et j'étudie le week-end. Trouver le temps pour bien manger et pour me reposer°, c'est difficile.»

• Romain de Rennes (France): «Ce n'est pas facile mais c'est possible. Je suis très occupé avec mes cours pendant la semaine mais le week-end, je me repose même si° j'ai beaucoup de devoirs. La vie est trop courte°.»

On dit que *They say that* **occupés** *busy* **parfois** *sometime* **enfants** *children* **Je vais à** *I go to* **me reposer** *to rest* **même si** *even if* **courte** *short*

Et vous? Qu'en pensez-vous?

Une vie équilibrée: Est-ce que c'est possible pour les étudiants d'aujourd'hui?

🔊 Les **jours** de la **semaine**

Days of the week

Mon agenda

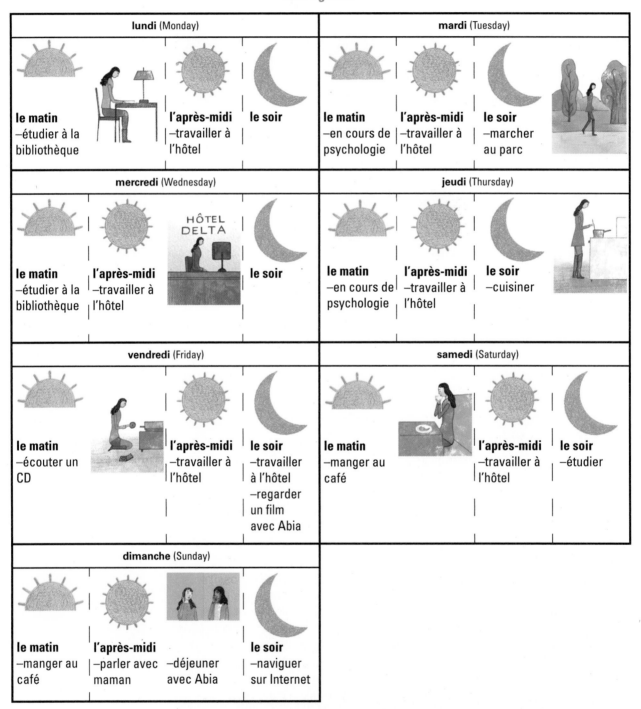

lundi (Monday)		
le matin –étudier à la bibliothèque	**l'après-midi** –travailler à l'hôtel	**le soir**

mardi (Tuesday)		
le matin –en cours de psychologie	**l'après-midi** –travailler à l'hôtel	**le soir** –marcher au parc

mercredi (Wednesday)		
le matin –étudier à la bibliothèque	**l'après-midi** –travailler à l'hôtel	**le soir**

jeudi (Thursday)		
le matin –en cours de psychologie	**l'après-midi** –travailler à l'hôtel	**le soir** –cuisiner

HÔTEL DELTA

vendredi (Friday)		
le matin –écouter un CD	**l'après-midi** –travailler à l'hôtel	**le soir** –travailler à l'hôtel –regarder un film avec Abia

samedi (Saturday)		
le matin –manger au café	**l'après-midi** –travailler à l'hôtel	**le soir** –étudier

dimanche (Sunday)			
le matin –manger au café	**l'après-midi** –parler avec maman	–déjeuner avec Abia	**le soir** –naviguer sur Internet

Une semaine typique pour Claire Gagner

Vocabulaire complémentaire

après *after*	**le lendemain** *the next / following day*
aujourd'hui *today*	**la nuit** *night*
avant *before*	**la semaine** *week*
demain *tomorrow*	**tous les jours** *everyday*
hier *yesterday*	**tous les soirs** *every evening*
	Quel jour sommes-nous? *What day is it?*
l'emploi du temps *(m.) schedule*	**Nous sommes mardi.** *It's Tuesday.*
l'horaire *(m.) schedule*	**Qu'est-ce que tu fais / vous faites?** *What are you doing?, What do you do?*

- In French, days of the week are masculine and are not capitalized. To say that something occurs during a particular part of the day or regularly on a particular day, use the definite article **le** + the day of the week or part of the day.

  Je regarde un film **le vendredi**.   **Le soir,** j'étudie.
  *I watch a movie **every Friday (on Fridays)**.*   *In the evening, I study.*

- When an event occurs once or on a specific day, do not use **le**.

  Vendredi, je cherche un appartement.   Nous sommes **mercredi**.
  *I am looking for an apartment **on Friday**.*   *It's **Wednesday**.*

🔊 **ACTIVITÉ A** **À la Clinique Laurier** Listen to the passage about Nurse
CD1-18 Nicole's activities at the **Clinique Laurier** (where Claire's mother is a patient) and determine if she does each activity weekly or just once this week.

1. a. chaque *(each)* mercredi   b. ce *(this)* mercredi
2. a. chaque jeudi   b. ce jeudi
3. a. chaque samedi   b. ce samedi
4. a. chaque mardi   b. ce mardi
5. a. chaque dimanche   b. ce dimanche

🔊 **ACTIVITÉ B** **Le lendemain** You will hear days of the week. Select the day
CD1-19 that comes *after* the day you hear.

1. a. lundi   b. dimanche   c. jeudi
2. a. mardi   b. samedi   c. mercredi
3. a. jeudi   b. mardi   c. samedi
4. a. lundi   b. mercredi   c. dimanche
5. a. dimanche   b. samedi   c. vendredi
6. a. vendredi   b. lundi   c. mercredi

ACTIVITÉ C Avant et après Complete these sentences with the day *before* or *after* the day that is mentioned.

1. Le jour avant dimanche, c'est…
2. Le jour après mardi, c'est…
3. Le jour avant samedi, c'est…
4. Le jour avant mercredi, c'est…
5. Le jour après jeudi, c'est…
6. Le jour avant lundi, c'est…
7. Le jour après mercredi, c'est…
8. Le jour après dimanche, c'est…

ACTIVITÉ D Les activités de Claire Gagner You will hear a series of
CD1-20 questions about Claire's activities. Look at her **agenda** on page 44 and answer the questions.

Modèle: *You hear:* Qu'est-ce que Claire fait samedi après-midi?
You say: **Elle travaille à l'hôtel.**

Conclusion Quelles activités est-ce que Claire fait *(does)* beaucoup?

ACTIVITÉ E Quelle(s) journée(s) de la semaine? Quel(s) jour(s) de la semaine est…

1. Pâques *(Easter)*?
2. Thanksgiving (ou l'Action de grâce)?
3. la fête du Travail?
4. le cours de français?
5. le week-end?
6. ta journée préférée *(your favorite day)*?

ACTIVITÉ F Le meilleur soir What day of the week is the best evening to do these activities?

Modèle: le meilleur *(best)* soir pour jouer au bingo
C'est mercredi soir!

1. le meilleur soir pour regarder un film au cinéma
2. le meilleur soir pour manger au restaurant
3. le meilleur soir pour regarder la télévision
4. le meilleur soir pour passer un examen
5. le meilleur soir pour jouer au football américain
6. le meilleur soir pour inviter des amis
7. le meilleur soir pour téléphoner aux parents
8. le meilleur soir pour étudier

ACTIVITÉ G **L'emploi du temps / L'horaire**

👫 **Étape 1.** Using the table as a guide, interview a classmate to find out what days of the week he/she has classes and what those classes are. Indicate whether the classes occur **le matin, l'après-midi,** or **le soir.**

Modèle: É1: **Quels cours est-ce que tu as** *(have)* **le lundi matin?**
É2: **français et sociologie**

	lundi	mardi	mercredi	jeudi	vendredi
le matin					
l'après-midi					
le soir					

Étape 2. Share your classmate's responses with the rest of the class.

Modèle: **Le lundi matin, Paul a** *(has)* **français et sociologie. Le mardi après-midi, il a philosophie et biologie.**

Conclusion Who has a busier schedule this quarter/semester? You or your partner?

Liaisons musicales

© Jean Pierre Amet/
Bel Ombra/Corbis

Inspired by the music and texts of Bob Dylan, French singer-songwriter-guitarist, Francis Cabrel (1953–) released his first album in 1977 and remains a much appreciated and favorite artist of the francophone world. Visit his official website and search the Internet to find videos of some of his songs. 🌐

Un mot sur la culture

lundi	mardi	mercredi	jeudi	vendredi	samedi	dimanche
		1	2	3	4	5
6	7	8	9	10	11	12
13	14	15	16	17	18	19
20	21	22	23	24	25	26
27	28	29	30	31		

Le calendrier français

In the U.S. and in English-speaking Canada, calendars list Sunday as the first day of the week. Because the Bible makes the Sabbath (Saturday) the last day of the week, it is common in Jewish and Christian practice to designate Sunday as the first day of the week. However, if you look at a French calendar, you will see that Monday is the first day of the week and not Sunday. Since, in Catholic tradition, the day of the Lord **(le jour du Seigneur)** is Sunday, the first day of the week is Monday. Another reason for this could be that modern culture views Monday as the beginning of the work week and the school week.

• Which day of the week is the first day for you?

Pour donner des descriptions

Les adverbes / Les adjectifs irréguliers

DU FILM *LIAISONS*
....

Un coup d'œil sur la grammaire

© Heinle/Cengage Learning

Elle mange, elle joue aux cartes, elle lit et elle dort. Elle existe, c'est tout. C'est **trop triste...**

In **Séquence 1** of the film *Liaisons,* Claire says this statement about her mother to her friend. You saw this statement in **Grammaire 1.** Do you remember what it means?

What do you think **trop triste** means?

a. a little sad   b. too sad

Les adverbes

You have already encountered some adverbs in **Chapitre préliminaire.** You will see them again in this chapter plus additional adverbs that will help you be more precise when giving descriptions and talking about activities.

Adverbs of intensity		
trop	Je mange **trop.**	*I eat too much.*
beaucoup	Il mange **beaucoup.**	*He eats a lot.*
assez	Nous mangeons **assez.**	*We eat enough.*
un peu	Elle mange **un peu.**	*She eats a little.*

Note de **grammaire**

Ne... jamais functions like **ne... pas.** The **ne** goes before the conjugated verb and **jamais** goes after it. You will learn more about this and other negative expressions in subsequent lessons.

Adverbs of frequency		
toujours	Anne travaille **toujours.**	*Anne always works.*
souvent	Marc travaille **souvent** le lundi.	*Marc often works on Mondays.*
parfois, quelquefois	Je travaille **parfois** le week-end.	*I sometimes work on weekends.*
rarement	Il travaille **rarement.**	*He rarely works.*
ne... jamais	Elle **ne** travaille **jamais.**	*She never works.*

Les adjectifs irréguliers

Descriptive adjectives (**les adjectifs qualificatifs**) allow you to be more precise when talking about activities and giving descriptions. You already encountered several descriptive adjectives in the **Chapitre préliminaire** and know that they must agree with the noun or pronoun they modify by adding an **e** (when they modify feminine nouns), an **s** (when they modify plural nouns) or **es** (when they modify plural feminine nouns). In French, adjectives normally follow the nouns they modify. Adjectives can also modify the subject of a sentence when they follow the verb **être**.

Je préfère **les gens** *(m. pl.)* **intéressants**.	*I prefer interesting people.*
Nadine est **une personne intelligente**.	*Nadine is an intelligent person.*
Les femmes indépendantes travaillent beaucoup.	*Independent women work a lot.*

Some Irregular Adjectives				
masculine singular	**feminine singular**	**masculine plural**	**feminine plural**	
fier	fière	fiers	fières	*proud*
naïf	naïve	naïfs	naïves	*naive*
sportif	sportive	sportifs	sportives	*athletic*
gentil	gentille	gentils	gentilles	*nice*
intellectuel	intellectuelle	intellectuels	intellectuelles	*intellectual*
travailleur	travailleuse	travailleurs	travailleuses	*hardworking*
ambitieux	ambitieuse	ambitieux	ambitieuses	*ambitious*
courageux	courageuse	courageux	courageuses	*courageous*
ennuyeux	ennuyeuse	ennuyeux	ennuyeuses	*boring*
heureux	heureuse	heureux	heureuses	*happy*
malheureux	malheureuse	malheureux	malheureuses	*unhappy*
paresseux	paresseuse	paresseux	paresseuses	*lazy*
sérieux	sérieuse	sérieux	sérieuses	*serious*
talentueux	talentueuse	talentueux	talentueuses	*talented*

Pour aller plus loin
N'est-ce pas?

In French, **n'est-ce pas** can be added to yes/no questions when one expects an affirmative answer as an expression of affirmation.

Tu aimes la philosophie, **n'est-ce pas**?	*You like philosophy, don't you?*
Le livre est intéressant, **n'est-ce pas**?	*The book is interesting, isn't it?*

ACTIVITÉ **H** **Un bon étudiant** Do these statements describe a good student? Answer **oui** or **non**. Then, select the statements that are true for you.

Un bon étudiant…

1. … rate **rarement** les examens.
   oui / non

2. … **n'écoute jamais** le professeur.
   oui / non

3. … étudie **beaucoup** le soir.
   oui / non

4. … parle **souvent** avec le professeur.
   oui / non

5. … mange **parfois** en cours.
   oui / non

6. … étudie **assez** le week-end.
   oui / non

7. … **ne** regarde **jamais** la télé.
   oui / non

8. … navigue **souvent** sur Internet
   en classe.   oui / non

ACTIVITÉ **I** **Quand est-ce que vous… ?** Which days of the week do you study or do other activities a lot or less frequently? Pay attention to the adverb and indicate which days of the week you do these activities with the level of frequency indicated.

Modèle: J'étudie souvent **le lundi et le jeudi soir.**

1. J'étudie **beaucoup** _____.
2. J'étudie **un peu** _____.
3. J'étudie **rarement** _____.
4. Je mange **parfois** avec des amis _____.
5. Je regarde **souvent** la télévision _____.
6. Je **ne** cuisine **jamais** _____.

© Supri Suharjoto/Shutterstock.com

ACTIVITÉ **J** **Une vie équilibrée?**

Étape 1. Indicate how often you actually do the following activities.

	rarement	parfois	souvent	toujours
1. Je pratique un sport…				
2. Je regarde la télé…				
3. J'étudie…				
4. Je voyage…				
5. Je passe des examens…				
6. Je mange…				

Étape 2. Exchange responses with a classmate. Look at how your classmate responded and decide if he/she has a balanced life.

Conclusion Est-ce que votre camarade de classe a *(have)* une vie équilibrée?

Étape 3. Provide a complete sentence to explain why you think your classmate has a balanced life or why his/her life is not balanced.

Modèles: Ma camarade de classe a *(has)* une vie équilibrée parce qu'elle étudie souvent et elle voyage parfois. / Mon camarade n'a pas *(does not have)* une vie équilibrée parce qu'il étudie toujours et il mange rarement.

ACTIVITÉ K Les différents types de personnes Different types of people perform activities with different degrees of frequency or intensity. Complete each sentence with a logical adverb to describe these people's activities.

1. Les hommes sportifs pratiquent _____ un sport.
2. Les femmes ambitieuses travaillent _____.
3. Les enfants *(children)* naïfs écoutent _____ leurs parents.
4. Les étudiants paresseux étudient _____ le week-end.
5. Les parents fiers parlent _____ de leurs enfants.
6. Les gens *(people)* malheureux voyagent _____.

Note de **grammaire**
You will learn more about the position of adverbs in **Chapitre 2.**

ACTIVITÉ L Barack ou Michelle Obama? A talk show host in France recently made some comments about Barack and Michelle Obama. Pay attention to the forms of the adjectives in order to determine if the comment refers to **Monsieur Obama** or **Madame Obama.** Complete each statement with **Monsieur (M.)** or **Madame (Mme)** based on the form of the adjectives. Then indicate if you agree or disagree with the statements.

	Je suis d'accord.	Je ne suis pas d'accord.
1. _____ est gentille.	☐	☐
2. _____ est courageuse.	☐	☐
3. _____ est intellectuel.	☐	☐
4. _____ est talentueux.	☐	☐
5. _____ est travailleur.	☐	☐
6. _____ est fière.	☐	☐
7. _____ est ambitieuse.	☐	☐
8. _____ est sérieux.	☐	☐

ACTIVITÉ M Les frères ou les sœurs? A reporter is talking about Mary-Kate and Ashley Olsen and Stephen and Alec Baldwin. Pay attention to the forms of the adjectives in order to determine if the comment refers to **les frères Baldwin** ou **les sœurs Olsen.** Complete each statement with **les frères Baldwin (a)** or **les sœurs Olsen (b)** based on the forms of these adjectives. Then indicate if you feel each statement is negative or positive.

	commentaire positif	commentaire négatif
1. _____ sont heureux.	☐	☐
2. _____ sont souvent naïves.	☐	☐
3. _____ sont courageuses.	☐	☐
4. _____ sont un peu paresseux.	☐	☐
5. _____ sont toujours fiers.	☐	☐
6. _____ sont rarement talentueuses.	☐	☐
7. _____ sont ennuyeux.	☐	☐

✎ **ACTIVITÉ** Ⓝ **Les célébrités**

Étape 1. Decide whether each adjective describes the celebrities indicated. Use the negative form if you do not think the adjective describes the people. Use the appropriate form of the adjective.

Modèle: (sérieux) Jeb et George W. Bush **sont sérieux.**
Margaret Cho et Ellen DeGeneres **ne sont pas sérieuses.**

1. (ambitieux)

Nicolas Sarkozy et Carla Bruni-Sarkozy _____ .

Jessica et Ashlee Simpson _____ .

2. (courageux)

Paris Hilton et Britney Spears _____ .

Les soldats *(soldiers)* américains _____ .

3. (naïf)

Courtney Cox et David Arquette _____ .

Hillary et Chelsea Clinton _____ .

4. (travailleur)

Emilio Estevez et Charlie Sheen _____ .

LaToya et Janet Jackson _____ .

5. (sportif)

Le prince William et le prince Harry _____ .

Serena et Venus Williams _____ .

6. (fier)

Barack et Michelle Obama _____ .

Malia et Sasha Obama _____ .

👥 **Étape 2.** Share your answers with a classmate. Did you come up with similar statements?

✎ **ACTIVITÉ** Ⓞ **Nous sommes observateurs?**

Étape 1. How well do your classmates know you? Let's see how observant **(observateurs/observatrices)** they've been. From the adjectives you've learned so far, select six that you think describe you or don't describe you and prepare six sentences.

Modèle: Je suis ambitieux. Je suis un peu sociable. Je ne suis pas optimiste…

👥 **Étape 2.** Share your six adjectives—not your sentences—with a classmate. Your classmate will guess what sentences you wrote with those adjectives. Was your classmate able to guess correctly? Rate how observant your classmate is with the following scale.

• Mon/Ma camarade de classe est _____ observateur/observatrice.

   a. très   b. assez   c. un peu

✈ ·····
Si vous y allez

© Megapress / Alamy

If you go to Montreal and want to people watch, stop in the **Café Cherrier** for a drink or a bite to eat. Located on **rue St. Denis** just north of the Latin Quarter, this European style bistro is a popular gathering for intellectuals, artists, and TV personalities in Montreal.

ACTIVITÉ **P** **Les dessins animés** Prepare sentences about these cartoon characters using the verb **être** and the cues provided. You may use the adverbs more than once but each adjective can only be used once. Can you guess which cartoons (**dessins animés**) are of French or Francophone origin?

© Photo 12/Alamy

Adjectifs possibles		
ambitieux	gentil	naïf
amusant	heureux	paresseux
courageux	intellectuel	sérieux
ennuyeux	malheureux	sportif
fier	méchant	talentueux

Adverbes possibles		
parfois	rarement	toujours
quelquefois	souvent	trop

Modèle: Bart Simpson est **souvent paresseux.**

1. Lisa Simpson _____
2. Blanche Neige *(Snow White)* _____
3. Batgirl et Wonderwoman _____
4. Tintin et Milou _____
5. Astérix et Obélix _____
6. Jessica Rabbit _____
7. Rémy (de *Ratatouille* de Disney) _____
8. Shrek et la princesse Fiona _____

La parole est à vous!

Est-ce que le week-end est trop court et la semaine de travail trop longue?

- Paul de Dijon (France): «Oui, absolument! Le week-end est trop court°. Trois jours, ce n'est pas assez. Pour avoir une vie équilibrée, on devrait avoir° quatre jours!»
- Todd, étudiant américain à Dijon: «Je préfère un long week-end aussi mais une semaine de travail de cinq jours est aussi nécessaire. Une semaine de travail de quatre jours n'est pas pratique.»

court *short* **devrait avoir** *should have*

Et vous? Qu'en pensez-vous?

Est-ce que le week-end est trop court et la semaine de travail trop longue?

🔊 Quelle **heure** est-il?

What time is it?

Il est une heure.

Il est deux heures.

Il est trois heures douze.

Il est quatre heures et quart.

Il est cinq heures et demie.

Il est sept heures moins vingt.

Il est neuf heures moins le quart.

Il est onze heures moins cinq.

Il est midi *(noon)*.
Il est minuit *(midnight)*.

Vocabulaire complémentaire

être en avance *to be early*
être à l'heure *to be on time*
être en retard *to be late*

À quelle heure est-ce qu'on mange? *(At) What time are we eating?*
Vers 8h30. *Around 8:30.*
Entre 10h et 11h. *Between 10:00 and 11:00.*
De 10h à 11h. *From 10:00 until 11:00.*

J'ai un cours de français à 9h. *I have a French class at 9:00.*

- To add minutes to the hour, add them after **heure(s)**.

    Il est quatre heures **seize**. *It's 4:16.*

- Note that special words are used to mean quarter of the hour or half-hour.

    Il est trois heures **et quart**. *It's 3:15.*
    Il est onze heures **et demie**. *It's 11:30.*
    Il est midi **et demi**. *It's 12:30.*

- To express a time that is approaching an hour, use the expression **moins** *(less)*.

    Il est neuf heures **moins le quart**. *It's 8:45. (It's a quarter to nine.)*
    Il est dix heures **moins vingt**. *It's 9:40. (It's twenty to ten.)*

- To distinguish between A.M. and P.M., add **du matin, de l'après-midi,** or **du soir**.

    Il est dix heures **du matin**. *It's 10 o'clock in the morning.*
    Il est trois heures **de l'après-midi**. *It's 3 o'clock in the afternoon.*
    Il est huit heures et demie **du soir**. *It's 8:30 in the evening.*

Note de **vocabulaire**
Note that you use **moins *le* quart** but *et* **quart**: Il est deux heures **et quart**. Il est cinq heures **moins le quart**.

🔊 **ACTIVITÉ** Ⓐ **Quelle heure est-il?** Write the times you hear. Be sure to
CD1-21 specify A.M. or P.M.

Modèle: *You hear:* Il est une heure de l'après-midi.
You write: **1:00 P.M.**

1. _____   5. _____
2. _____   6. _____
3. _____   7. _____
4. _____   8. _____

Un mot sur la langue

Heure ou heures?

Use **heure** (singular) for one o'clock and **heures** (plural) for hours after one o'clock. Add an **e** to **demi** if it follows **heure(s)** because **heure** is feminine (**Il est cinq heures et demie**). Do not add an **e** to **demi** if it follows **midi** or **minuit** because they are masculine: **Il est midi et demi**.

- Write out these times in French.

    1. 1:30 P.M. _____
    2. 4:30 P.M. _____
    3. 12:30 A.M. _____
    4. 8:30 A.M. _____
    5. 12:30 P.M. _____
    6. 9:30 P.M. _____

16:30

🔊 **ACTIVITÉ** Ⓑ **L'emploi du temps de Simon** You will hear statements
CD1-22 about Simon's (a classmate of Claire's) activities for Friday. Look at his schedule to determine if the statements are true (**vrai**) or false (**faux**).

vendredi	
7h30	cours d'anglais
9h00	cours de chimie
11h00	cours d'informatique
12h30	déjeuner
2h30	étudier à la bibliothèque (library)
4h15	jouer au football
6h45	dîner avec Claire

1. vrai / faux   **3.** vrai / faux   **5.** vrai / faux
2. vrai / faux   **4.** vrai / faux   **6.** vrai / faux

ACTIVITÉ Ⓒ **Il est l'heure.** Look at each clock and say what time it is.

Liaisons musicales

© Serge Thomann/Wire Image/Getty Images

The youngest of fourteen children, Céline Dion (1968–) first started singing in shopping malls in her hometown in Charlemagne, Quebec. Today she is an international mega pop star singing in both French and English. One of her earlier songs, *Trois heures vingt* is a love song from her 1984 album *Mélanie*. Find a video clip of this song on the Internet, and visit the singer's official website.
🌐

✏️ **ACTIVITÉ** Ⓓ **Une vie saine (healthy) et équilibrée**

Étape 1. Indicate at what time one should do the following activities in order to live a healthy, balanced life. Write out the time in French.

Modèles: On prend le petit déjeuner (have breakfast) **à huit heures du matin.**
On va au (goes to) gymnase **entre neuf heures et dix heures.**

1. On déjeune _____ .

2. On joue au basket-ball _____ .

3. On travaille _____ .

4. On dîne _____ .

5. On prend un goûter (snack) _____ .

6. On dort (sleep) _____ .

Étape 2. Now revisit **Étape 1** and provide the time you usually do these activities.

Conclusion Est-ce que vous avez (have) une vie saine et équilibrée?

Étape 3. Tell a classmate at what time you do these activities. Your classmate will share his/her responses with you. Based on the responses, decide if your classmate is living a healthy, balanced life.

Conclusion Mon/Ma camarade a *(has)* une vie saine et équilibrée.   oui / non

ACTIVITÉ Ⓔ **À l'heure, en avance ou en retard?** Indicate whether you are on time, early, or late in these situations.

Modèle: Le cours de musique est à midi. Tu arrives à midi et quart.
   Donc *(So / In that case),* je suis en retard.

1. Le cours de biologie est à 11h. Tu arrives à 10h40.
2. Le cours de chimie est à 8h30. Tu arrives à 8h30.
3. Le cours de gestion est à 9h15. Tu arrives à 9h30.
4. Le cours de comptabilité est à 10h. Tu arrives à 9h45.
5. Le cours de génie mécanique est à midi. Tu arrives à 12h30.
6. Le cours de psychologie est à 2h. Tu arrives à 2h.
7. Le cours de journalisme est à 3h. Tu arrives à 2h30.
8. Le cours de musique est à 4h. Tu arrives à 4h20.

• En général, est-ce que tu es à l'heure, en avance ou en retard pour les cours?

ACTIVITÉ Ⓕ **À quelle heure?** Ask a classmate at what time he/she usually does these activities.

Modèle: É1: **À quelle heure est-ce que tu écoutes la radio?**
      É2: **J'écoute la radio vers 9h du matin. / J'écoute la radio de 8h à 9h du matin. / J'écoute la radio entre 8h et 9h du matin.**

1. déjeuner pendant la semaine
2. étudier le soir
3. aimer mieux pratiquer le sport
4. cuisiner pendant la semaine
5. arriver à l'université
6. regarder la télévision
7. travailler le week-end
8. aimer mieux dîner le week-end

ACTIVITÉ Ⓖ **Nos emplois du temps**

Étape 1. Provide 1–2 things you do in the morning, in the afternoon, and in the evening for each day of the work week. Include the time when you do these activities.

	lundi	mardi	mercredi	jeudi	vendredi
le matin	10h cours de français	11h cours de musique	10h cours de français	11h cours de musique	10h cours de français
l'après-midi					travailler de 4h à 6h
le soir					

Étape 2. Ask a classmate what he/she does during the times and days that you have activities on your schedule.

Modèle: É1: **Qu'est-ce que tu fais le lundi à 10h du matin?**
É2: **J'ai un cours à 10h.**
É1: **Qu'est-ce que tu fais le vendredi à 7h du soir?**
É2: **Je travaille.**

Étape 3. Using the information you obtained in **Étape 2,** complete this statement with the appropriate adjective. Try to give two pieces of information to support your choice.

Conclusion Nos *(Our)* emplois du temps sont similaires / différents.

ACTIVITÉ **H** **Expressions utiles** Which of these expressions would you use to respond to these questions?

Expressions		
Bien sûr! *(Of course!)*	**Pas du tout!** *(Not at all!)*	**Peut-être.** *(Perhaps.)*

1. Aimez-vous passer un examen à 7h du matin?
2. Aimez-vous dîner après 9h du soir?
3. Aimez-vous dormir jusqu'à midi?
4. Aimez-vous étudier le dimanche?
5. Aimez-vous regarder les films français?
6. Aimez-vous parler français?

Un mot sur la culture

Le système des 24 heures

In most French-speaking countries, the 24-hour clock is used in formal conversations, in the news, and in publications like course schedules, train and plane schedules, movie times, and TV programs. With the 24-hour clock, you use 13 to 24 to express the hours of 1:00 P.M. through midnight. For example, 3:00 P.M. is **15h00 (quinze heures)** and 5:45 P.M. is **17h45 (dix-sept heures quarante-cinq).** The expressions **et demi(e), et quart, moins le quart, midi,** and **minuit** are not used. Thus, if your favorite TV show is on at 8:30 P.M., you will see it listed as **20h30** in the TV guide.

• Can you convert the following times to the 24-hour clock?
   1. 11:45 P.M.   2. 10:05 A.M.   3. 4:30 P.M.   4. 8:20 P.M.

© Khafizov Ivan Harisovich/Shutterstock.com

Liaisons avec les mots et les sons

CD1-23

La liaison et l'enchaînement

Note de prononciation
In a liaison, **s** and **x** are pronounced **z**, and in an **enchaînement**, **f** is pronounced **v**.

Liaison and **enchaînement** refer to the linking of the final consonant sound of one word with the vowel sound of the following word. A **liaison** occurs when a word that normally ends in a silent consonant (**s, t, x** or **n**) is followed by a word that begins with a vowel sound. When **liaison** and **enchaînement** occur, the first word needs to modify or qualify the second word in some way as in the following examples.

Subject pronouns

Il est professeur.   Elle est professeur.   On aime le français.
Nous adorons la chimie.   Vous étudiez beaucoup.   Elles habitent à Paris.

Articles

un écran   une étudiante   les affaires   les heures

Adverbs or adjectives

C'est ambitieux.   C'est important.   C'est très intéressant.   C'est assez sérieux.

Numbers

Il est cinq heures.   Il est six heures.   Il est huit heures.
Il est neuf heures.   Il y a deux hommes.   Il y a trois étudiants.

Pratique A. Listen carefully and mark (‿) the two sounds that have a **liaison**.

1. Les étudiants mangent à neuf heures.
2. C'est une femme très intelligente.
3. Elle est très ambitieuse.
4. On est des étudiants travailleurs.
5. Il a cinq affiches dans son sac.
6. Il y a deux horloges dans la salle de classe.

Pratique B. Listen to these lines from the film *Liaisons* and indicate with (‿) where the **liaisons** should be.

CLAIRE Elle existe, c'est tout.

ABIA Et les hallucinations?

CLAIRE Elle a des moments de lucidité...

ABIA Il est presque quinze heures. Il faut travailler.

🔊 **À vos stylos! C'est l'heure de la dictée!**

CD1-24 You will hear three sentences. Listen closely to them. You will then hear the sentences a second time. Write the three sentences you hear.

Sujet Claire et Abia

Pour parler de nos horaires et de nos possessions

Le verbe **avoir**

DU FILM *LIAISONS*

Un coup d'œil sur la grammaire

In **Séquence 1** of the film *Liaisons,* Claire makes the following statement to a friend after she returns from visiting her mother.

Elle **a** des moments de lucidité mais...

The word **a** comes from the verb **avoir**. What does this verb mean?

a. to be   b. to do   c. to have

Les verbes-clés

Note de **prononciation**
Note that **as** and **a** have the same pronunciation. Make sure you pronounce the **liaison** /z/ for all the plural forms (**nous avons, vous avez, ils ont, elles ont**) and the **liaison** /n/ for **on a.**

◇ **Avoir** is an irregular verb that is used to express possession. You have already seen some of the forms of this verb in the **Chapitre préliminaire** and this chapter. Here are all the forms of the present tense of **avoir**.

avoir *(to have)*	
j'**ai**	nous **avons**
tu **as**	vous **avez**
il/elle/on **a**	ils/elles **ont**

Nous **avons** un cours de français à 10 heures.	*We have a French class at 10 o'clock.*
Est-ce que tu **as** un stylo?	*Do you have a pen?*
J'**ai** un cours le mardi et le jeudi.	*I have a class Tuesdays and Thursdays.*

◇ The indefinite articles **un, une,** and **des** becomes **de** (**d'** before a vowel sound) in negative sentences with **avoir** as well as with many other verbs.

Tu as **une** calculatrice?	*Do you have a calculator?*
Je n'ai pas **de** calculatrice.	*I don't have a calculator.*
Anne a **un** ordinateur.	*Anne has a computer.*
Marc n'a pas **d'**ordinateur.	*Marc does not have a computer.*
Rachid cherche **des** stylos.	*Rachid is looking for some pens.*
Il ne cherche pas **de** crayons.	*He is not looking for pencils.*

◇ The definite article (**le, la, l', les**) does not change in negative sentences.

—Vous avez **le** livre de biologie?	*Do you have the biology book?*
—Non, je n'ai pas **le** livre.	*Non, I don't have the book.*

◇ **Avoir** is also used to express age.

J'**ai** 18 ans.   *I am 18 years old.*   Ils **ont** 21 ans.   *They are 21 years old.*

Many common expressions in French also use the verb **avoir**.

avoir besoin de	*to need*	**avoir peur de**	*to be afraid of*
avoir de la chance	*to be lucky*	**avoir raison**	*to be right*
avoir envie de	*to feel like doing or having something*	**avoir sommeil**	*to be sleepy*
		avoir tort	*to be wrong*

J'**ai besoin** d'une agrafeuse.	*I need a stapler.*
Nous **avons besoin** d'étudier.	*We need to study.*
Tu **as de la chance**!	*You are lucky!*
Il n'**a** pas **envie de** travailler.	*He does not feel like working.*
Elle **a peur de** dépenser de l'argent.	*She is afraid to spend money.*
Ils **ont** très **sommeil.**	*They are very sleepy.*
Tu **as raison** mais moi, j'**ai tort.**	*You are right, but, me, I'm wrong.*
Elle **a peur de** parler français.	*She is afraid to speak French.*

The expression **avoir peur de** may be followed by a noun. Note that **de** must combine with definite articles (**le, la, l', les**) in the following ways.

de + le = du	J'**ai peur du** professeur.	*I am afraid of the professor.*
de + la = de la	Elles **ont peur de la** fille méchante.	*They are afraid of the mean girl.*
de + l' = de l'	Luc a **peur de l'**étudiant italien.	*Luc is afraid of the Italian student.*
de + les = des	Il a peur **des** cours difficiles.	*He is afraid of (the) difficult classes.*

Note de grammaire

The expression **il y a** *(there is / there are)* that you learned in **Chapitre préliminaire** also uses the verb **avoir**.

Si vous y allez

© Richard Cummins / SuperStock

Do you like haunted houses? Located in Sainte-Claire in the province of Quebec, **Québec Halloween** is a haunted house that promises to scare! Attractions include haunted mazes, and ghosts and goblins of all kinds. You can even have your photo taken with your favorite horror character. **Est-ce que vous avez peur?!** Look for the website by doing a search with the words **Québec, maison hantée,** and **Sainte-Claire.**

🔊 **ACTIVITÉ I** **Qui est-ce? / C'est qui?** *(Who is it?)* You will hear
CD1-25 statements about classes Marc and Arthur have. Listen to the verb to determine if Marc has the course or if both Marc and Arthur have the course.

1. a. Marc   b. Marc et Arthur   4. a. Marc   b. Marc et Arthur
2. a. Marc   b. Marc et Arthur   5. a. Marc   b. Marc et Arthur
3. a. Marc   b. Marc et Arthur   6. a. Marc   b. Marc et Arthur

ACTIVITÉ J **Les camarades de chambre**

Étape 1. Two sets of roommates are talking about their courses and things they need. Pay attention to the verbs to determine the subject of the sentence.

1. _____ **avons** un cours de musique à 8h30.   a. Nous   b. Vous
2. _____ **avez** un cours de psychologie à midi.   a. Nous   b. Vous
3. _____ **avez** un cours d'anglais à 11h00.   a. Nous   b. Vous
4. _____ **ai** besoin d'un sac à dos.   a. J'   b. Tu
5. _____ **as** besoin d'un cahier.   a. J'   b. Tu
6. _____ **ai** besoin d'une calculatrice.   a. J'   b. Tu

ACTIVITÉ K **Avoir raison ou avoir tort?** React to the following statements made by a sixth-grader with **(a) Oui, tu as raison** or **(b) Non, tu as tort.**

1. Deux plus deux font douze.
2. Onze plus cinq font seize.
3. La capitale de la France est Québec.
4. La capitale du Canada est Ottawa.
5. Les devoirs sont importants.
6. Les examens sont embêtants.
7. Je n'ai pas besoin d'étudier.
8. J'ai besoin de manger des légumes (*vegetables*).

ACTIVITÉ L **Qu'est-ce que nous avons?** *(What do we have?)*

Étape 1. Florian and Hisham will be housemates. They are making a list of things they have and don't have. Pay attention to the articles to determine whether they have or do not have the things mentioned. Remember that when **avoir** is used in the negative, the indefinite articles **un, une,** and **des** becomes **de (d'** before a vowel sound). Complete each sentence with **(a) Nous avons** or **(b) Nous n'avons pas.**

1. _____ **de** chaises (*f.*).
2. _____ **une** télévision.
3. _____ **des** lampes (*f.*).
4. _____ **de** table (*f.*).
5. _____ **un** réfrigérateur.
6. _____ **d'**affiches (*f.*).
7. _____ **un** ordinateur.
8. _____ **d'**horloge (*f.*).
9. _____ **des** bureaux.
10. _____ **une** poubelle.

Étape 2. Look at the items that Florian and Hisham do not have. Write complete sentences indicating what they need. Hint: They need four items from the list. Use the expression **avoir besoin de.**

Modèle: Ils n'ont pas d'horloge.
Ils ont besoin d'une horloge.

1. _____
2. _____
3. _____
4. _____

ACTIVITÉ M **Quel âge est-ce qu'ils ont?** *(How old are they?)* At what age are people more likely to do the following activities? Provide complete sentences using the verb **avoir** to express the persons' ages.

Modèle: Elle vote. 11 ans / 21 ans **Elle a 21 ans.**

1. Elle cuisine un hamburger.
   5 ans / 15 ans
2. Il a une carte de crédit.
   10 ans / 30 ans
3. Elle joue à la marelle (*hopscotch*).
   8 ans / 96 ans
4. Elles adorent *Sesame Street*.
   6 ans / 56 ans
5. Ils jouent au hockey.
   22 ans / 98 ans
6. Ils dansent la polka.
   18 ans / 67 ans
7. Elles naviguent sur Internet.
   21 ans / 95 ans
8. Ils cherchent un emploi (*job*).
   34 ans / 81 ans

Étape 1. Do you know how old these famous people are? Look at the year they were born and say how old they are.

1. 1955

2. 1971

3. 1976

4. 1975

5. 1982

6. 1948

7. 1981

8. 1986

Étape 2. Answer these questions.

1. Quel âge avez-vous?
2. Quel âge a votre camarade de classe?
3. Quel âge a votre meilleur(e) *(best)* ami(e)?
4. Quel âge a le président de votre université?

5. Quel âge a le président des États-Unis?
6. Quel âge a le vice-président des États-Unis?
7. Quel âge a le maire *(mayor)* de votre ville?
8. Quel âge a votre camarade de chambre?

Étape 3. Answer these questions.

1. Qui est le/la plus jeune *(youngest)* dans l'Étape 2?
2. Qui est le/la plus âgé(e) *(oldest)* dans l'Étape 2?

ACTIVITÉ O **Les étudiants typiques de mon université** What are typical students at your college or university like? Read the statements and determine whether the statements are true or false.

Les étudiants typiques de mon université…	Vrai	Faux
1. ont envie de passer des examens.	☐	☐
2. ont envie de parler avec leurs parents.	☐	☐
3. ont souvent sommeil en cours.	☐	☐
4. ont de la chance d'avoir de bons professeurs.	☐	☐
5. ont de la chance d'avoir une bonne bibliothèque.	☐	☐
6. n'ont pas envie de manger à la résidence universitaire.	☐	☐
7. n'ont pas envie d'étudier.	☐	☐
8. n'ont pas sommeil le matin.	☐	☐

Et vous? Est-ce que vous êtes un(e) étudiant(e) typique de votre université? Pourquoi ou pourquoi pas?

ACTIVITÉ P **Nos envies et nos besoins**

Étape 1. Make a list of at least three activities that you feel like doing this weekend. Make another list of things that you need to do this weekend.

Modèle: **J'ai envie de regarder un film avec mes amis.**
J'ai besoin de travailler à la bibliothèque.

Étape 2. Share what you wrote with a classmate. Look at what you both want to do and what you both need to do and decide who is more likely to have a good weekend.

Conclusion Qui va passer *(Who is going to spend)* un bon week-end?

ACTIVITÉ Q **Les préférences** Poll your classmates to see if they have the following favorite things. If you find someone who does, jot down his/her name and his/her favorite thing.

Modèle: É1: **Est-ce que tu as un professeur préféré?**
É2: **Oui, j'ai un professeur préféré: le professeur de français.**

1. un cours préféré
2. un film préféré
3. un CD préféré
4. un sport préféré
5. un livre préféré
6. un magasin *(store)* préféré
7. un auteur *(author)* préféré
8. un jour de semaine préféré

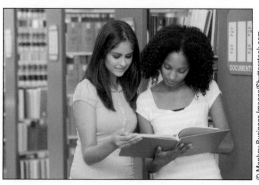

© Monkey Business Images/Shutterstock.com

ACTIVITÉ R Est-ce que vous avez peur?

Étape 1. Indicate if you are afraid of these things.

	Oui	Non
1. des professeurs	☐	☐
2. des monstres	☐	☐
3. des clowns	☐	☐
4. de voyager à l'étranger *(abroad)*	☐	☐
5. de marcher seul(e) *(alone)* sur le campus le soir	☐	☐
6. de cuisiner	☐	☐
7. de chanter	☐	☐
8. de danser	☐	☐
9. de manger des insectes	☐	☐
10. de regarder des films d'horreur	☐	☐

Étape 2. Ask a classmate whether he/she is afraid of these things.

Modèle: É1: **Est-ce que tu as peur des professeurs?**
É2: **Non, je n'ai pas peur des professeurs.**

Étape 3. Based on the information from **Étape 1** and **Étape 2**, what things are both you and your classmate afraid of?

Modèle: **Nous avons peur des clowns et de cuisiner.**

© 37719031?/Shutterstock.com

La parole est à vous!

Est-ce qu'il est important d'être à l'heure?

En général dans le monde francophone, quand on a un rendez-vous, on arrive à l'heure. Mais entre amis, le concept de l'heure est parfois flexible. Est-ce qu'il est important d'être à l'heure?

- Diane de Columbus, Ohio (États-Unis): «Oui, il est important d'être toujours à l'heure. On est tous° très occupés. Être en retard pour les rendez-vous et chez des amis, c'est très impoli!»
- Lupenga du Congo: «Non, dans ma culture, le concept de l'heure est flexible. Quand on a une invitation pour le déjeuner à midi, il n'est pas impoli d'arriver à 14h30. J'ai l'impression que les Américains sont toujours pressés°.»

tous *all* **pressés** *in a hurry*

Et vous? Qu'en pensez-vous?

Est-ce qu'il est important d'être à l'heure?

Avant de visionner

ACTIVITÉ A **Vous rappelez-vous? (*Do you remember?*)** Indicate if each sentence is **vrai** or **faux** based on what you remember from the **Prologue** of *Liaisons*.

	Vrai	Faux
1. Claire étudie à l'Université McGill.	☐	☐
2. Claire est étudiante en littérature française.	☐	☐
3. Claire va à l'hôpital après son cours.	☐	☐
4. Mme Gagner souffre de psychose.	☐	☐

ACTIVITÉ B **Un coup d'œil sur une scène** In this scene from **Séquence 1**, Claire talks with her co-worker Abia after visiting her mother. With a classmate, try to figure out which words—those in option a or in option b—go in the blanks. You will check your answers later when you watch this scene.

ABIA Ah, Claire. (1) _____ es déjà arrivée.

CLAIRE Oui. Quelle (2) _____ est-il?

ABIA 14h45 à peu près.

CLAIRE (3) _____?

ABIA Oui. Très (4) _____. *[noticing her expression].* Qu'est-ce (5) _____?

CLAIRE Ma mère.

1. a. Je b. Tu	4. a. bien b. mal
2. a. heure b. semaine	5. a. que tu cherches b. qu'il y a
3. a. Pas mal b. Ça va, toi	

- What do you think the questions **Qu'est-ce que tu cherches?** and **Qu'est-ce qu'il y a?** mean?

Regarder la séquence

You will now watch **Séquence 1** of the film *Liaisons*. Don't worry if there are words or expressions you do not understand. Use the context and images to help you understand what you hear.

Après le visionnage

ACTIVITÉ **C** **Vérifiez votre compréhension!**

1. Claire travaille dans un hôpital.   V / F

2. Claire et Abia sont collègues et amies.   V / F

3. Mme Gagner mange, lit *(reads)*, joue aux cartes et dort *(sleeps)* toute la journée.   V / F

4. Un homme donne *(gives)* une enveloppe à Claire.   V / F

5. Claire rencontre Alexis Prévost qui a besoin d'une brosse à dents *(toothbrush)*.   V / F

6. Claire trouve le nom de M. Prévost dans le registre de l'hôtel *(hotel registry)*.   V / F

ACTIVITÉ **D** **Avez-vous compris?** Review your answers to **Activité B** of **Avant de visionner.** How did you do?

ACTIVITÉ **E** **Premières impressions: Abia**

Étape 1. What are your first impressions of Abia? Write 1–2 sentences to describe her, using adjectives you have learned so far.

© Heinle/Cengage Learning

Étape 2. Compare what you wrote with a classmate. Do you have similar impressions?

Liaisons avec la culture

Montréal—Ville internationale et cosmopolite

Montreal is the second largest city in Canada next to Toronto and the second largest French-speaking city in the world next to Paris. The official language in Montreal is French but, if you take a stroll in downtown Montreal, you are likely to hear English and many other languages because Montreal is home to many different ethnic communities including **le quartier chinois** and **le quartier italien**. Montreal is also a center for film and television production, as well as the home of many internationally-known festivals like **le festival Juste pour rire** *(Just for Laughs Festival)* and **le Festival international de jazz de Montréal**.

© Sebastian Rich / Corbis

Les études, le travail et les vacances

OUTILS DE LECTURE
Using cognates

Cognates are words that are similar in spelling and meaning in French and in English. While you may not know every word in a French text, your ability to recognize cognates will help you understand most of the meaning in a text.

1. Look at this sentence from the text **Étudier en France et au Sénégal: En général, les étudiants universitaires obtiennent une licence, qui est comparable au B.A. américain, en trois ans.** What are the cognates in this sentence?

2. Using the cognates and any other words in the sentence that you already know, what do you think this sentence means?

Étudier en France et au Sénégal

Le système universitaire du Sénégal est semblable° au système français. Pour être admis à s'inscrire° à l'université, il faut réussir° au baccalauréat, une série d'examens qu'on passe à la fin de la dernière année au lycée°. En général, les étudiants universitaires obtiennent une licence°, qui est comparable au B.A. américain, en trois ans. Il y a des différences avec° le système universitaire américain. En France et au Sénégal, les études universitaires sont presque gratuites°. Le sport est moins important qu'aux États-Unis: il n'y a pas de grandes équipes° universitaires.

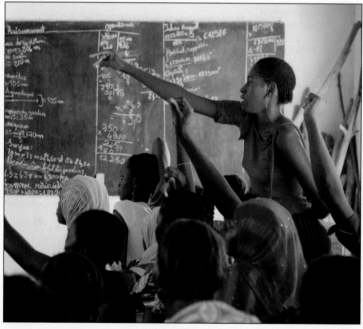

© Olivier Asselin / Alamy

semblable *similar* **s'inscrire** *register* **réussir** *pass* **lycée** *high school* **obtiennent une licence** *earn a degree* **avec** *with* **gratuites** *free of charge* **équipes** *teams*

Vrai ou faux?

1. Aux États-Unis, les études universitaires sont gratuites.   V / F

2. En France et au Sénégal, le baccalauréat est très important.   V / F

3. On obtient une licence en 3 ans.   V / F

4. Il y a beaucoup d'équipes de sport universitaires en France et au Sénégal.   V / F

© Moodboard Premium/Glow

Au travail en France et en Suisse

La France et la Suisse sont des pays voisins°, mais leurs attitudes envers° le travail sont très différentes. En général, les Suisses travaillent entre 40 et 45 heures par semaine avec quatre semaines de vacances par an. En France, par contre°, les Français travaillent 35 heures par semaine et ils ont cinq semaines de vacances par an. Pour les Français, les vacances sont très importantes pour avoir une vie équilibrée. En effet°, pour certains Français, les vacances sont plus° importantes que l'argent°. Selon CBS news, l'argent n'est pas la priorité la plus importante parce que la France a un excellent système de soins médicaux et d'éducation qui est presque° gratuit°.

pays voisins *neighboring countries* **envers** *toward* **par contre** *on the other hand* **En effet** *In fact* **plus** *more* **l'argent** *money* **presque** *almost* **gratuit** *free*

Vrai ou faux?

1. Les Suisses ne travaillent pas beaucoup. V / F

2. Les vacances sont très importantes pour les Français. V / F

3. Les Suisses travaillent moins que *(less than)* les Français. V / F

4. La France a un excellent système de soins médicaux. V / F

En vacances au Québec

Parce que l'hiver est une réalité importante dans la vie des Québécois, il y a beaucoup d'activités pour passer le temps durant cette longue saison. Le Carnaval de Québec est un festival pour fêter° l'hiver au mois de février. Pendant le carnaval, il y a de nombreuses activités sportives et artistiques: des courses de traîneaux à chiens°, un concours° international de sculptures de glace°, la tire sur neige°, la danse folklorique, le bain de neige°, la visite au château de glace, etc. La mascotte du carnaval est le Bonhomme Carnaval. Les Québécois attendent° avec impatience son arrivée en février au grand défilé° du bonhomme. Que la fête commence!°

© Images Distribution / Newscom

fêter *celebrate* **traîneaux à chiens** *dogsled races* **un concours** *contest* **sculptures de glace** *ice sculpture* **la tire sur neige** *taffy making on snow* **le bain de neige** *snow bath* **attendent** *wait* **défilé** *parade* **Que la fête commence!** *Let the partying begin!*

Vrai ou faux?

1. L'hiver est court *(short)* au Québec. V / F

2. Il y a des activités sportives et artistiques au Carnaval. V / F

3. Le Carnaval de Québec est au mois de juin. V / F

4. La mascotte du Carnaval de Québec est le Bonhomme Carnaval. V / F

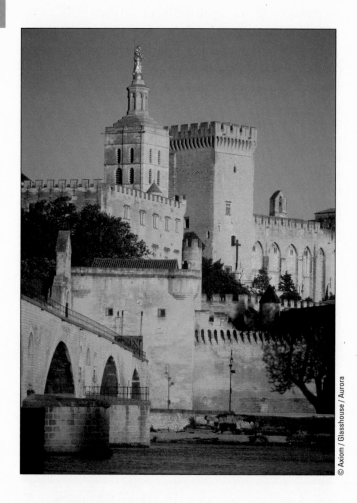

© Axiom / Glasshouse / Aurora

Le festival de théâtre d'Avignon

Le festival d'Avignon existe depuis° 1947. C'est un grand événement artistique et touristique. Ce festival de théâtre dure° de trois à quatre semaines chaque été°. La ville est remplie° d'artistes et de spectateurs. On peut voir° des pièces de théâtre classique ou expérimental. Avignon, une ville du sud de la France, a une histoire unique. Au quatorzième siècle°, les papes° de l'Église catholique vivaient° à Avignon. La ville a été contrôlée par l'Église jusqu'à° la Révolution française (1789). Actuellement°, le palais des Papes d'Avignon est utilisé comme décor de théâtre pendant le festival.

depuis *since* **dure** *lasts* **chaque été** *each summer* **remplie** *filled* **peut voir** *can see* **Au quatorzième siècle** *In the fourteenth century* **les papes** *popes* **vivaient** *lived* **jusqu'à** *until* **Actuellement** *Currently, Today*

Vrai ou faux?

1. Le festival d'Avignon est un festival de théâtre.　　V / F

2. Le festival est en octobre.　　V / F

3. Avignon est dans le nord de la France.　　V / F

4. Les papes de l'Église catholique vivaient au palais à Avignon avant la Révolution française.　　V / F

🌐 Activités Internet

- Do an Internet search to find the university you would most like to attend in France or Senegal if you were to study abroad for one academic year.

- Do an Internet search on a francophone country in North or West Africa to find out how many hours a week people in that country typically work and how many weeks of vacation they typically have.

- Go to the official website of **le Carnaval de Québec** to see a program of activities and to watch videos of the festival. Make note of the dates of the next winter **carnaval** and of three interesting activities to share with the class.

- Type **festival été** into your search engine to find at least three summer festivals in France and the cities in which they are held. Be prepared to share this information with the class.

PARTIE 1

VERBES

adorer	*to adore*
aimer bien	*to like*
aimer mieux	*to prefer*
chanter	*to sing*
chercher	*to look for*
cuisiner	*to cook*
danser	*to dance*
déjeuner (au café)	*to have lunch (at a café)*
détester	*to hate*
dîner (au restaurant)	*to have dinner (at a restaurant)*
écouter (des CD)	*to listen to (CDs)*
étudier (à la bibliothèque)	*to study (at the library)*
habiter	*to live (in a place), to reside*
inviter (des amis)	*to invite (friends)*
jouer	*to play*
manger	*to eat*
marcher (au parc)	*to walk (in the park)*
naviguer sur Internet	*to surf the Internet*
parler	*to speak, to talk*
passer un examen	*to take an exam*
penser	*to think*
pratiquer le sport	*to play sport*
rater un examen	*to fail an exam*
regarder (la télé)	*to watch (television)*
téléphoner	*to telephone*
travailler (au bureau)	*to work (at the office)*
trouver	*to find*
voyager	*to travel*

LES NOMBRES DE 60 À 100

60 soixante
61 soixante et un
62 soixante-deux
63 soixante-trois
64 soixante-quatre
65 soixante-cinq
66 soixante-six
67 soixante-sept
68 soixante-huit
69 soixante-neuf
70 soixante-dix
71 soixante et onze
72 soixante-douze
73 soixante-treize
74 soixante-quatorze
75 soixante-quinze
76 soixante-seize
77 soixante-dix-sept
78 soixante-dix-huit
79 soixante-dix-neuf
80 quatre-vingts
81 quatre-vingt-un
82 quatre-vingt-deux
83 quatre-vingt-trois
84 quatre-vingt-quatre
85 quatre-vingt-cinq
86 quatre-vingt-six
87 quatre-vingt-sept
88 quatre-vingt-huit
89 quatre-vingt-neuf
90 quatre-vingt-dix
91 quatre-vingt-onze
92 quatre-vingt-douze
93 quatre-vingt-treize
94 quatre-vingt-quatorze
95 quatre-vingt-quinze
96 quatre-vingt-seize
97 quatre-vingt-dix-sept
98 quatre-vingt-dix-huit
99 quatre-vingt-dix-neuf
100 cent
100% cent pour cent

DIVERS

avec	*with*
mais	*but*
pendant	*during, throughout*
la semaine	*the week*
le week-end	*the weekend*
Qu'est-ce que tu fais?	*What are you doing?*
Qu'est-ce qu'il/elle fait?	*What is he/she doing?*

You may access all end-of-chapter vocabulary audio at **GLrn** and on the *Liaisons* Premium Website.

PARTIE 2

LES JOURNÉES ET L'EMPLOI DU TEMPS

lundi	*Monday*
mardi	*Tuesday*
mercredi	*Wednesday*
jeudi	*Thursday*
vendredi	*Friday*
samedi	*Saturday*
dimanche	*Sunday*
après	*after*
aujourd'hui	*today*
avant	*before*
demain	*tomorrow*
hier	*yesterday*
l'emploi du temps (*m.*)	*schedule*
l'horaire (*m.*)	*schedule*
le lendemain	*the next / following day*
la nuit	*night*
tous les jours	*everyday*
tous les soirs	*every evening*
Quel jour sommes-nous?	*What day is it?*
Nous sommes mardi.	*It's Tuesday.*

Qu'est-ce que tu fais / vous faites?	*What are you doing?, What do you do?*

ADVERBES

assez	*enough*
beaucoup	*a lot*
ne… jamais	*never*
un peu	*a little*
parfois	*sometimes*
quelquefois	*sometimes*
rarement	*rarely*
souvent	*often*
toujours	*always*
trop	*too, too much*

LES ADJECTIFS IRRÉGULIERS

fier / fière	*proud*
naïf / naïve	*naive*
sportif / sportive	*athletic*
gentil / gentille	*nice*
intellectuel / intellectuelle	*intellectual*
travailleur / travailleuse	*hard-working*
ambitieux / ambitieuse	*ambitious*
courageux / courageuse	*courageous*
ennuyeux / ennuyeuse	*boring*
heureux / heureuse	*happy*
malheureux / malheureuse	*unhappy*
paresseux / paresseuse	*lazy*
sérieux / sérieuse	*serious*
talentueux / talentueuse	*talented*

DIVERS

les gens *(m. pl.)*	*people*
l'hôtel *(m.)*	*hotel*
une personne	*person*

PARTIE 3

QUELLE HEURE EST-IL?

Quelle heure est-il?	*What time is it?*
Il est une heure. / Il est deux heures.	*It's one o'clock. / It's two o'clock.*
Il est midi / minuit.	*It's noon / midnight.*
et quart	*a quarter past*
et demi(e)	*half past*
moins le quart	*a quarter to*
du matin	*in the morning*
de l'après-midi	*in the afternoon*
du soir	*in the evening*
À quelle heure… ?	*At what time . . . ?*
vers 8h30	*around 8:30*
entre 10h et 11h	*between 10:00 and 11:00*
de 10h à 11h	*from 10:00 until 11:00*
J'ai un cours de français à 9h.	*I have a French class at 9:00.*
être en avance	*to be early*
être à l'heure	*to be on time*
être en retard	*to be late*

VERBES

avoir	*to have*
avoir… ans	*to be . . . years old*
avoir besoin de	*to need*
avoir de la chance	*to be lucky*
avoir envie de	*to feel like*
avoir peur de	*to be afraid*
avoir raison	*to be right*
avoir sommeil	*to be sleepy*
avoir tort	*to be wrong*

DIVERS

donc	*so, therefore*
bien sûr	*of course*
pas du tout	*not at all*
peut-être	*perhaps*

Les **plaisirs** de la **vie**

En bref   In this chapter, you will:

- talk about the months, seasons, and weather

- learn the verb **aller** and the preposition **à**

- talk about sports and leisure-time activities

- learn the verbs **faire, lire, écrire,** and **dire**

- learn about contractions with the preposition **de**

- learn more about adverbs

- learn about silent consonants

- read about rugby in Toulouse, France

- write a brief portrait

 You will also re-watch **SÉQUENCE 1: L'étranger** of the film *Liaisons*.

Ressources

 audio   http://www.cengagebrain.com

🔊 Le **climat**

Climate

Il fait gris.

Il pleut.

le printemps (mars, avril, mai)

Il fait du soleil.

Il fait chaud.

l'été (juin, juillet, août)

Il fait du vent.

Il fait frais.

l'automne (septembre, octobre, novembre)

Il neige.

Il fait froid.

l'hiver (décembre, janvier, février)

Les mois de l'année et le temps

Vocabulaire complémentaire

un an / une année *year*
un mois *month*
une saison *season*

l'averse (f.) *shower*
le brouillard *fog*
le ciel *sky*
l'étoile (f.) *star*
la lune *moon*
la météo *weather forecast*
la neige *snow*
des nuages (m.) *(some) clouds*
l'orage (m.) *storm*
l'ouragan (m.) *hurricane*

la pluie *rain*
la tornade *tornado*
le verglas *(black) ice*

annoncer *to forecast*

Quel temps fait-il? *What's the weather like?*
Le ciel est couvert. *It's cloudy / overcast.*
Il fait beau. *The weather is nice.*
Il fait bon. *The weather is good / warm.*
Il fait lourd. *It's humid / muggy.*
Il fait mauvais. *The weather is bad.*

- In most of the French-speaking world, temperature is given in Celsius, not Fahrenheit. The conversion formulas are $F = (C \times 1.8) + 32$ and $C = (F - 32) \times 0.56$.

  —**Quelle température fait-il?**   —*What's the temperature?*
  —**Il fait 14 degrés.**   —*It's 14 degrees Celsius. / It's 57° Fahrenheit.*

- In French, dates are expressed with **le** + the numbers 2–31 + the month. To say it's the first of the month, use **le premier**. In writing, dates are abbreviated by placing the day before the month, for example, **5/10 = le 5 octobre**.

  —**Quelle est la date aujourd'hui?**   —*What is today's date?*
  —**On est le 23 novembre.**   —*It's November 23.*
  —**Nous sommes le 23 novembre.**   —*It's November 23.*
  —**C'est quand ton / votre anniversaire?**   —*When is your birthday?*
  —**C'est le 10 janvier.**   —*It's the 10th of January.*
  —**C'est quand l'anniversaire de Samir?**   —*When is Samir's birthday?*
  —**C'est le premier mai.**   —*It's the first of May.*

- **Le temps** means both *weather* and *time* in French.

  Le temps est agréable aujourd'hui.   *The weather is nice today.*
  Olivier regarde la télé quand il a le temps.   *Olivier watches TV when he has time.*

© Heinle/Cengage Learning

🔊 **ACTIVITÉ A Quel mois?** Montreal,
CD1-26 where Claire from the film *Liaisons* lives, has
a four-season climate. You will hear weather
expressions for Montreal. In which month of
the year are these weather conditions likely
to occur?

1. a. en décembre	b. en avril	c. en juillet
2. a. en avril	b. en août	c. en janvier
3. a. en octobre	b. en juin	c. en février
4. a. en septembre	b. en janvier	c. en mai
5. a. en juillet	b. en mars	c. en décembre
6. a. en février	b. en novembre	c. en septembre

🔊 **ACTIVITÉ B Quelle saison?** Listen to these weather conditions and decide if
CD1-27 they are **vrai** or **faux.**

1. V / F	**5.** V / F
2. V / F	**6.** V / F
3. V / F	**7.** V / F
4. V / F	**8.** V / F

ACTIVITÉ C Quelle ville? With which cities or states do you associate these
weather conditions?

1. les tornades	**5.** le brouillard
2. les ouragans	**6.** les orages
3. la neige	**7.** le soleil
4. la pluie	**8.** le vent

ACTIVITÉ D Étoiles, lune ou soleil? Complete each sentence with
les étoiles, la lune, or **(le) soleil.**

1. On voit *(sees)* _____ le matin.

2. On voit _____ le soir.

3. Les vampires aiment _____.

4. Louis XIV est le roi *(king)* _____.

5. Les astronomes étudient _____.

6. Les loups-garous *(werewolves)* aiment _____.

ACTIVITÉ **E** **Quelle saison et quel temps?** Complete these sentences with the appropriate seasons or weather conditions.

Modèle: À New York, il pleut souvent _____.

À New York, il pleut souvent **au printemps et en été.**

1. À Chicago, il fait du vent _____.

2. À Paris, il neige _____.

3. À Miami, il fait lourd _____.

4. À Los Angeles, _____ en hiver.

5. À Montréal, _____ en automne.

6. À Boston, _____ en été.

Note de vocabulaire

En is used with the months of the year (**en janvier, en décembre**) and with **automne, été,** and **hiver,** but **au** is used with **printemps.**

ACTIVITÉ **F** **La météo** Prepare sentences predicting the weather forecast for your area for the entire week starting with **lundi.**

Modèle: **Lundi, il fait beau. Mardi, il pleut.**

ACTIVITÉ **G** **Quelle est la date?** Provide the dates for these events or holidays.

Modèle: la rentrée scolaire   **C'est le 6 septembre.**

1. Halloween
2. la fête nationale américaine
3. Noël
4. la Saint-Patrick
5. la fête nationale en France
6. la Saint-Valentin

ACTIVITÉ **H** **C'est quand votre anniversaire?** Ask at least five classmates when their birthday is. Jot down the names of your classmates and their birthdays. Try to find out who has a birthday coming up. Circle the birthday that is coming up soon.

Liaisons musicales

© Franck Seguin/Corbis

Quebecois singer Robert Charlebois (1944–) is often known as the Elvis of the French-speaking world. His songs deal with different realities of Quebec, sometimes political and often humorous, such as *Demain l'hiver* which starts with **Demain l'hiver / je m'en fous** *(I don't care)* / **je m'en vais** *(I'm going away)* **dans le sud** *(south)* **au soleil…** Look for this song as well as more information on Charlebois on his official website. 🌐

Un mot sur la culture

L'hiver au Québec

Winter is such a significant part of Quebec's reality that poet Gilles Vigneault wrote in a much cherished song: *Mon pays ce n'est pas un pays c'est l'hiver!* In fact, the Quebecois have even created winter-related terms that are unique in the French language.

- Can you guess the meaning of these expressions?

1. banc de neige
2. Il fait frette.
3. la poudrerie

a. *blowing fine powdery snow*
b. *snow drift*
c. *It's very (dang) cold.*

© Ron Erwin/All Canada Photos/Photolibrary

Pour parler des destinations

Le verbe **aller** / La préposition **à**

DU FILM *LIAISONS*

....

Un coup d'œil sur la grammaire

Look at these photos from the film *Liaisons* and their captions, paying special attention to the verbs and prepositions used.

Claire **va au** cours de psychologie
à l'université McGill.

Claire **va à la** chambre de
Madame Gagner.

1. What do you think the verb **va** means?
2. Both **à** and **au** mean *to*. Why is **au** used with **cours** and **à la** used with **chambre**?

🔑 **Les verbes-clés**

⋯ The verb **aller** *(to go)* is an irregular verb.

The present tense of **aller** *(to go)*	
je **vais**	nous **allons**
tu **vas**	vous **allez**
il/elle/on **va**	ils/elles **vont**

⋯ **Aller** is often used with prepositions to indicate locations or destinations, especially the preposition **à** *(to, at)*. This preposition may appear by itself or it may contract with the definite article, depending on the gender and number of the object it is modifying.

à + le	**au** (masculine, singular)
à + les	**aux** (plural, masculine or feminine)
à + la	**à la** (feminine, singular)
à + l'	**à l'** (singular, before a vowel sound)

Les étudiants **vont** tous les jours à l'école.	*Students **go to** school everyday.*
Le professeur ne **va** pas **au** bureau.	*The professor **is not going to** the office.*
Mon professeur **va à** Paris en été.	*My professor **goes to** Paris in the summer.*

The verb **aller** may also be used to express events that will happen in the near future. Called **le futur proche** *(the near future)*, this construction consists of a form of the present tense of **aller** followed by an infinitive.

Je **vais aller** à Paris cet été.	*I **am going to go** to Paris this summer.*
Nous **allons aller** à l'université demain.	*We **are going to go** to the university tomorrow.*
Abia **ne va pas aller** au café ce soir.	*Abia **is not going to go** to the café tonight.*

ACTIVITÉ I Les activités

Étape 1. Indicate whether these activities refer to **le professeur** or **les étudiants.**

1. _____ **vont** au cours de français tous les jours. a. Le professeur b. Les étudiants

2. _____ **va** travailler à la bibliothèque. a. Le professeur b. Les étudiants

3. _____ **va** à Paris cet été. a. Le professeur b. Les étudiants

Étape 2. Select the subjects of these sentences.

4. _____ **vais** au cours de sciences politiques à 8h. a. Je b. Tu

5. _____ **vas** au cours de mathématiques à 10h30. a. Je b. Tu

6. _____ **vais** au cours de philosophie à 11h. a. Je b. Tu

Étape 3. Select the subjects of these sentences.

7. _____ **allez** au campus le lundi, le mercredi et le vendredi. a. Nous b. Vous

8. _____ **allons** au restaurant le vendredi soir. a. Nous b. Vous

9. _____ **allez** au cinéma le samedi après-midi. a. Nous b. Vous

Et vous? Est-ce que vous allez faire *(do)* ces activités aujourd'hui? Lesquelles *(Which ones)?*

Si vous y allez

© Alan Schein Photography/Corbis

Si vous allez à Montréal, allez au Biodôme. It allows visitors to experience replicas of five ecosystems in the Americas: 1) Tropical Rainforest, 2) the Laurentian Wilderness, 3) St. Lawrence Marine, 4) the Arctic, and 5) Antarctic. Search for **biodôme Montréal** on the Internet and take a virtual tour.

ACTIVITÉ J Où je vais? Pay close attention to the prepositions in order to figure out where this person is going. Once finished, reread the sentences and decide which sentences are true for you.

1. Le lundi, je vais **à l'…**
   a. hôtel.   b. cours de français.

2. Le samedi, je vais **au…**
   a. campus.   b. université.

3. Le week-end prochain, je vais **à l'…**
   a. café.   b. université.

4. Le mercredi, je vais **aux…**
   a. jardins publics. b. école.

5. Mardi prochain, je vais **à l'…**
   a. cours de biologie,
   b. appartement de mon ami(e).

6. Après le cours aujourd'hui, je vais **à la…**
   a. salle de gymnastique.
   b. café.

7. Le jeudi, je vais **au…**
   a. cours de musique.
   b. université.

8. Cet après-midi, je vais **à la…**
   a. école.
   b. bibliothèque.

ACTIVITÉ K **Qu'est-ce qu'on va faire** *(to do)?* Finish the sentences with an activity that you think the people are going to do today.

Modèle: Aujourd'hui, mon professeur **va travailler au bureau.**

1. Aujourd'hui, mes amis…
2. Aujourd'hui, mon voisin/ma voisine *(my neighbor)*…
3. Aujourd'hui, les étudiants du cours de français et moi …
4. Aujourd'hui, ma/mon camarade de chambre…
5. Aujourd'hui, je…
6. Aujourd'hui, mon professeur...

ACTIVITÉ L **Quel jour de la semaine?** What day of the week do you think you will do these activities?

Modèle: danser   **Je vais danser samedi soir.**

1. cuisiner
2. dîner dans un bon restaurant
3. étudier
4. regarder la télévision
5. déjeuner à l'université
6. travailler
7. aller au cours de français
8. parler avec la famille

ACTIVITÉ M **Boule de cristal** *(Crystal ball)* With a partner, make real or imaginary predictions for these people. Think about what they're going to be like, what they're going to need or desire, and what they're going to do in the future. Use your knowledge of popular culture and your creativity!

Modèle: Brendan Fraser

> **Il va rester sexy. Il va jouer dans un autre film comme** *The Mummy.* **Et il va avoir envie d'étudier le français mais il ne va pas avoir besoin d'aller à l'université.**

1. Bill Gates
2. Brad Pitt et Angelina Jolie
3. Oprah Winfrey
4. Rachael Ray et Martha Stewart
5. Prince William et Prince Harry
6. Natalie Portman
7. Moi, je…
8. Claire du film *Liaisons*

Si

In French, **si** means *if*. **Si** becomes **s'** in front of a vowel sound.

Si Tom aime le sushi, on va manger au restaurant japonais.	*If Tom likes sushi, we are going to eat at the Japanese restaurant.*
S'il neige, je ne vais pas aller à l'école.	*If it snows, I am not going to go to school.*

Si, not **oui,** is also used to say *yes* in response to a negative question.

—Ils ne parlent pas français?	— *They don't speak French?*
—**Si,** ils parlent français.	— *Yes, they speak French.*
—Tu ne vas pas étudier ce soir?	— *You are not going to study tonight?*
—**Si,** je vais bientôt étudier.	— *Yes, I am going to study soon.*

Essayez! Answer these questions affirmatively.

1. Tu ne vas pas manger?
2. Tu n'as pas de cours aujourd'hui?
3. Tu n'aimes pas le français?

La parole est à vous!

Est-ce que le climat change aujourd'hui?

Aujourd'hui, on parle beaucoup du «réchauffement de la planète»°. Qu'en pensez-vous? Est-ce que le climat est en train de changer aujourd'hui et va-t-il continuer à changer à l'avenir°?

- Marc-André d'Ottawa (Canada), âge 33 ans: «Oui, le climat change chaque année. Les températures sont plus° extrêmes et il y a plus d'ouragans, de tornades et de cyclones chaque saison.»

- Fabien de Lille (France), âge 17 ans: «Non, je ne crois° pas. Le réchauffement de la planète n'est pas vraiment une réalité. C'est une idée inventée par les scientifiques° qui passent toutes leurs journées dans un laboratoire.»

réchauffement de la planète *global warming* **avenir** *future* **plus** *more* **crois** *believe* **scientifiques** *scientists*

Et vous? Qu'en pensez-vous?

1. Est-ce que le climat est en train de changer aujourd'hui?
2. Le climat va-t-il continuer à changer à l'avenir?

Les **sports**

Sports

le baseball

le basket-ball / le basket

le football / le foot

le football américain

le golf

le hockey

le rugby

le tennis

le tennis de table

le volley-ball

Les activités sportives

Vocabulaire complémentaire

faire de l'aérobic *to do aerobics*

faire du bowling *to go bowling*

faire du cheval *to go horseback riding*

faire de la gym / du sport *to work out, to exercise*

faire du patinage *to iceskate, to go iceskating*

faire de la planche à voile *to go wind-surfing*

faire de la plongée sous-marine *to scuba dive*

faire du ski (alpin) *to go (downhill) skiing*

faire du ski de fond *to go cross-country skiing*

faire du surf *to surf*

faire du yoga *to do yoga*

pratiquer *to play, to do a sport*

une équipe *a team*

un joueur / une joueuse *a player*

un match (de + sport) *a match, a game (of + sport)*

faire du jogging

faire de la marche

faire de la natation

faire du vélo

faire du ski nautique

Les expressions avec *faire*

- To talk about the sports you play, use an expression with the verb **faire** *(to do, to make)* or use the verb **jouer à** *(to play)* plus the name of the sport.

J'aime faire du jogging tous les jours.	*I like to go jogging everyday.*
Mes amis jouent souvent au foot.	*My friends play soccer often.*

Un mot sur la langue

Expressions intéressantes

Games and sports are important activities and conversation topics to many cultures. France is no exception. There are many everyday expressions in French that use games and sports-related vocabulary to express different ideas.

- Can you guess the meaning of these expressions?

  1. C'est un jeu *(game)* d'enfant *(child)*.
  2. marquer un point
  3. À vous de jouer!

  a. *It's your turn/move (now).*
  b. *It's very easy.*
  c. *to get one up, to have an advantage*

🔊 **ACTIVITÉ Ⓐ Quel sport?** Select the famous athlete that plays the sport
CD1-28 mentioned in each sentence you hear.

1. a. Richard Simmons	b. Andy Roddick	c. LeBron James
2. a. Mia Hamm	b. Serena Williams	c. Danica Patrick
3. a. David Beckham	b. Tony Parker	c. Sidney Crosby
4. a. Roger Federer	b. Phil Mickelson	c. Martin Brodeur
5. a. Michael Jordan	b. Michael Phelps	c. Apolo Anton Ohno
6. a. Kobe Bryant	b. Thierry Henri	c. Lance Armstrong
7. a. Jane Fonda	b. Justine Henin	c. Venus Williams
8. a. Shawn Johnson	b. Laila Ali	c. Kim Yu-Na

🔊 **ACTIVITÉ Ⓑ Les championnats** Which one of the championships
CD1-29 corresponds to the sport you will hear?

1. a. le Super Bowl	b. le Stanley Cup	c. la Coupe du Monde *(World Cup)*
2. a. la Coupe du Monde	b. le Super Bowl	c. le Gran Premio Santander d'Italia
3. a. le Stanley Cup	b. le Super Bowl	c. le tournoi de Roland-Garros
4. a. le Presidents Cup	b. le Tour de France	c. le Grand Prix de Monaco
5. a. le World Series	b. la Coupe du Monde	c. l'U.S. Open
6. a. l'Open d'Australie	b. l'Indianapolis 500	c. le Larry O'Brien Championship

ACTIVITÉ Ⓒ Des athlètes ou des téléspectateurs? Is your class a group
of athletes, TV sports watchers, a mix of both, or none of the above? Select your
personal sports-related habit (a, b, c, or d) for these sports.

a. Je pratique ce *(this)* sport.   **c.** Je pratique ce sport et je regarde ce sport à la télé.
b. Je regarde ce sport à la télé.   **d.** Aucune de ces réponses. *(None of these answers.)*

1. le ski alpin	**3.** le golf	**5.** le bowling	**7.** le patinage
2. la natation	**4.** le volley-ball	**6.** le tennis de table	**8.** le football américain

ACTIVITÉ Ⓓ Faire ou jouer?

Étape 1. Complete these sentences with either **jouer** or **faire.**

Les étudiants aiment _____

1. de la natation.	**3.** du cheval.	**5.** au football.	**7.** de la marche.
2. au tennis.	**4.** du jogging.	**6.** du yoga.	**8.** du vélo.

Étape 2. Finish each sentence with sports or physical activities that you like to do
or play.

1. J'aime **faire** _____.   **2.** J'aime **jouer** _____.

Étape 3. Which activity do you think Claire from the film *Liaisons* enjoys?

Claire Gagner aime _____.

ACTIVITÉ **E** **Vos préférences**

Étape 1. Pay attention to the articles to determine which sport is being referred to. Then, indicate whether each statement is **vrai** or **faux** for you.

1. J'aime faire du	a. ski nautique	b. planche à voile	V/F
2. J'aime faire de la	a. jogging	b. marche	V/F
3. J'aime faire de l'	a. aérobic	b. gym	V/F
4. J'aime faire de la	a. marche	b. yoga	V/F
5. J'aime faire du	a. plongée sous-marine	b. surf	V/F
6. J'aime faire du	a. bowling	b. natation	V/F

Et vous? Complete the sentences with activities from this lesson.

1. Mes amis et moi, nous aimons faire _____.

2. Mon/Ma camarade de chambre aime faire _____.

ACTIVITÉ **F** **Quel match en quelle saison?** Which professional sport games do people typically go see in each season of the year?

Modèle: en automne **On regarde un match de football américain en automne.**

1. en automne **2.** en hiver **3.** au printemps **4.** en été

ACTIVITÉ **G** **Les joueurs (joueuses) et les équipes** Which sports are associated with these players or teams?

Modèles: Michael Jordan **Michael Jordan est un joueur de basket-ball.**
Les Chicago White Sox **Les Chicago White Sox sont une équipe de baseball.**

1. Serena Williams **3.** John McEnroe **5.** Les Black Hawks
2. Les Dallas Cowboys **4.** Zinedine Zidane **6.** Les Los Angeles Lakers

ACTIVITÉ **H** **Qu'est-ce que vos amis aiment faire?**

Étape 1. What kinds of sports do your friends like to play or what kinds of physical activities do they like to do in these weather conditions? You can also answer with what they do *not* like to do.

Modèle: **Quand il fait beau, mes amis aiment faire du jogging.**
Quand il fait froid, mes amis n'aiment pas jouer au golf.

1. quand il fait frais **4.** quand il neige
2. quand il fait bon **5.** quand il pleut
3. quand il fait du vent **6.** quand il faut chaud

Étape 2. Share your preferences from **Étape 1** with two or three other classmates. Do you think any of your friends would get along with your classmates' friends?

Si vous y allez

Si vous allez à Toulouse, allez au Stade Toulousain. Founded in 1907, the **Stade Toulousain** is one of the finest rugby clubs in Europe. They won the Heineken Cup in 1996, 2003, and 2005. Take a virtual tour at the **stade**'s official website.

ACTIVITÉ I Préférences

Étape 1. Do you and your classmates like or dislike the same sports or physical activities? Prepare three questions to ask your classmates based on your likes and dislikes.

Modèles: Est-ce que tu aimes faire du yoga? / Est-ce que tu joues au golf?

Étape 2. Now ask your three questions to three different students. Fill in the grid with the appropriate information. Which likes and dislikes do you have in common? Be ready to share your information in French with your instructor and classmates.

	Prénom	**Réponse 1**	**Réponse 2**	**Réponse 3**
É1				
É2				
É3				

ACTIVITÉ J Est-ce que vous êtes sportif/sportive?

Étape 1. Interview a classmate to find out if he/she is athletic or not. Note his/her answers. If your partner answers **non** to a question, go on to the next one. If your partner answers **oui,** indicate the frequency with which he/she does this activity: **tous les jours, régulièrement, de temps en temps** (occasionally).

Modèle: É1: **Est-ce que tu aimes faire du jogging?**
É2: **Oui.**
É1: **Tous les jours? Régulièrement? De temps en temps?**
É2: **Régulièrement.**

			Oui	Non
1. Est-ce que tu aimes faire du jogging?				
☐ Tous les jours	☐ Régulièrement	☐ De temps en temps	☐	☐
2. Est-ce que tu aimes faire de l'aérobic?				
☐ Tous les jours	☐ Régulièrement	☐ De temps en temps	☐	☐
3. Est-ce que tu aimes faire de la marche?				
☐ Tous les jours	☐ Régulièrement	☐ De temps en temps	☐	☐
4. Est-ce que tu aimes faire de la gym?				
☐ Tous les jours	☐ Régulièrement	☐ De temps en temps	☐	☐
5. Est-ce que tu aimes faire du vélo?				
☐ Tous les jours	☐ Régulièrement	☐ De temps en temps	☐	☐
6. Est-ce que tu aimes faire de la natation?				
☐ Tous les jours	☐ Régulièrement	☐ De temps en temps	☐	☐

Étape 2. Now look back at your partner's answers to **Étape 1** and count them up. Write your partner's score and share it with him/her.

Non = 0 points	**Régulièrement = 2 points**
De temps en temps = 1 point	**Tous les jours = 3 points**

Étape 3. Write down your personal score and see what conclusion your score earns. If you finish early, share your results with another classmate or another pair of classmates.

0–3 = Pas du tout sportif/sportive. Attention! Un peu de sport est important pour une vie équilibrée.

4–8 = Pas très sportif/sportive. Vous n'êtes pas très sportif/sportive mais vous aimez faire des efforts quand même *(nevertheless)*. Essayez de faire un peu plus *(more)* d'efforts!

9–14 = Bravo! Vous êtes sportif/sportive. C'est très bien et très important pour la prévention des problèmes de santé et pour rester en forme *(stay in shape)*. Continuez.

15–18 = Très sportif/sportive. Vous êtes très sportif/sportive. En général, c'est bien d'être sportif. Mais attention! Vous risquez de vous blesser *(hurt yourself)*.

Un mot sur la culture

Jeu de paume

Royal Tennis, frontispiece from 'Jeu Royal de la Paume', 1632 (engraving, French); Bibliothèque des Arts Decoratifs, Paris/ Archives Charmet/The Bridgeman Art Library

Tennis is a popular spectator sport in France where it is also widely practiced. It is a British adaptation of an old French sport called **jeu de paume** that dates back to the 14th century. Following the Battle of Azincourt (1415), the French Duke of Orleans was imprisoned in England. During this period, he introduced the game to his English captors. Originally players used the palm of their hand. Gloves were soon worn and then bats were added. Early in the 16th century, wooden rackets were introduced. In England, the game evolved into tennis and then spread to France in the 19th century. **Jeu de paume** is still played in France, but it is nowhere near as popular as tennis.

• Do you know any other modern-day sports that have historical origins?

Pour parler des activités et poser des questions

Le verbe **faire** / L'inversion

DU FILM *LIAISONS*

Un coup d'œil sur la grammaire

© Heinle/Cengage Learning

Look at this photo from the film *Liaisons* and its caption.

MME SIMONE GAGNER Qu'est-ce que tu **fais** là-bas? Viens jouer avec moi.

You have seen the verb **fais** from the infinitive **faire** many times. Do you remember what this verb means?

Le verbe *faire*

Les verbes-clés

✤ **Faire** *(to do, to make)* is another irregular verb in French.

The present tense of **faire** *(to do, to make)*	
je **fais**	nous **faisons**
tu **fais**	vous **faites**
il/elle/on **fait**	ils/elles **font**

✤ **Faire** may be used with or without an object and may be used in questions as well as in general statements.

—Qu'est-ce que **tu fais**?　　　　—*What **are you doing**?*

—**Je fais** mes devoirs.　　　　　—***I am doing** my homework.*

—Qu'est-ce qu'**il fait** à manger?　—*What **is he making** to eat?*

—**Il fait** des pâtes.　　　　　　　—***He's making** pasta.*

✤ The questions **Qu'est-ce que tu fais?**, **Qu'est-ce qu'ils font?**, etc. may be answered with verbs other than **faire.**

—Qu'est-ce qu'ils **font**?　　　　　　　　—*What are they doing?*

—Ils **cherchent** un appartement.　　　　—*They are looking for an apartment.*

—Qu'est-ce que tu vas **faire** ce soir?　　—*What are you going to do this evening?*

—Je **vais jouer** au tennis avec un ami.　—*I am going to play tennis with a friend.*

✤ As you learned in **Chapitre 1**, indefinite articles (**un, une, des**) are replaced by **de/d'** in negative sentences. The partitive articles that make up some expressions used with **faire** (**du, de la, de l', des**) also become **de/d'** in negative sentences.

—Je fais **de la** gym tous les jours.　　　—*I work out everyday.*

—Je **ne** fais **pas de** gym tous les jours.　—*I don't work out everyday.*

Note de grammaire

Recall that definite articles (**le, la, l', les**) do not change in negative sentences.

Samira **ne** fait **pas les** devoirs de français. *Samira is not doing French homework.*

Elle fait **les** devoirs de biologie. *She is doing biology homework.*

L'inversion

••• You have already learned two ways to ask questions in French: **est-ce que (Est-ce que tu as un stylo?)** and intonation **(Ça va?)**. Another way to ask questions is to use inversion which means inverting the subject pronoun and the conjugated verb. Generally speaking, inversion is considered more formal and is more often used in writing or more formal and polite conversation.

| **Parlez-vous** français? | *Do you speak French?* |
| Claire et Abia **sont-elles** amies? | *Are Claire and Abia friends?* |

••• If the verb ends in a vowel and the subject pronoun is **il, elle,** or **on**, a **-t-** is added to facilitate pronunciation.

| Comment **va-t-elle**? | *How's she doing?* |
| **Y a-t-il** un examen aujourd'hui? | *Is there an exam today?* |

••• In a negative question with inversion, **ne… pas** goes around the inversion.

| **Ne mangent-ils pas** avec nous? | *Are they not eating with us?* |

ACTIVITÉ K Activités populaires Finish these sentences by choosing the correct subject. Then, indicate if people typically practice these activities or watch them, or both.

		On pratique cette activité.	On regarde cette activité.
1. _____ **faisons** du cheval.	a. Nous b. Vous	☐	☐
2. _____ **faites** du vélo.	a. Nous b. Vous	☐	☐
3. _____ **faisons** de la natation.	a. Nous b. Vous	☐	☐
4. _____ **faisons** de l'aérobic.	a. Nous b. Vous	☐	☐
5. _____ **faites** du patinage.	a. Nous b. Vous	☐	☐
6. _____ **faites** de la marche.	a. Nous b. Vous	☐	☐

••• **Et vous?** Which of the above activities do you like? **Moi, j'aime…**

ACTIVITÉ L En été ou en hiver? Finish these sentences by choosing the correct subject. Then, indicate if each activity is typically done during the summer or the winter, or during both seasons.

			en été	en hiver
1. _____ **fait** de la marche.	a. Je	b. Pierre	☐	☐
2. _____ **fait** du ski nautique.	a. Tu	b. Elle	☐	☐
3. _____ **fais** du ski alpin.	a. Tu	b. Hélène	☐	☐
4. _____ **fait** de la plongée sous-marine.	a. Je	b. Marc	☐	☐
5. _____ **fais** du ski de fond.	a. Je	b. Monique	☐	☐
6. _____ **fais** de la gym.	a. Tu	b. Il	☐	☐

ACTIVITÉ M Qui fait... ? Which classmates are most likely to do the following activities? Do you remember how they responded earlier in activities in **Vocabulaire 2**? Use the name of your classmates (and even your instructor) to complete these sentences. Finish the last item with an activity of your choosing.

1. _____ **fait** du vélo.

2. _____ **font** de la marche.

3. _____ ne **font** pas de yoga.

4. _____ **fait** souvent de la gym.

5. _____ ne **fait** pas de jogging.

6. _____ **font** _____.

ACTIVITÉ N Qu'est-ce qu'ils font? What activities are the following people most likely to do? Complete each statement with a form of the verb **faire** and the most logical activity.

1. Lance Armstrong

2. Bruce Irons

3. Jacques Cousteau

4. Forrest Gump

5. Moi

6. Mon/Ma camarade de chambre et moi, nous

Lance Armstrong, cycliste américain

ACTIVITÉ O Oui ou non? With a partner, answer these trivia questions.

	Oui	Non
1. Barack Obama **parle-t-il** français?	☐	☐
2. Justine Henin **joue-t-elle** au tennis?	☐	☐
3. Les Français **mangent-ils** du fromage?	☐	☐
4. Les Américains **sont-ils** fans de rugby?	☐	☐
5. Martha Stewart **aime-t-elle** la cuisine française?	☐	☐
6. Mikhail Baryshnikov **fait-il** du ballet?	☐	☐
7. Luc Besson et Steven Spielberg **sont-ils** réalisateurs?	☐	☐
8. Joël Robuchon et Emeril Lagasse **cuisinent-ils** bien?	☐	☐
9. Faudel **chante-t-il** en français?	☐	☐
10. Le Cirque du Soleil **est-il** américain?	☐	☐

ACTIVITÉ **P** **Les activités pour un Cercle français**

Étape 1. Ask your classmates if they do these activities. If someone answers yes, note his/her name. Remember that **du, de la, de l'** and **des** become **de** in negative sentences.

Modèles: faire du ski   **Faites-vous du ski?**

1. cuisiner des repas *(meals)* français
2. chanter des chansons françaises
3. regarder des films français
4. écouter de la musique francophone

5. faire du cheval
6. jouer au tennis de table
7. jouer au bowling
8. danser des danses folkloriques françaises

Étape 2. What three activities are most popular? Who does these activities? Who doesn't do these activities?

Modèle: **Darla, Kim et David cuisinent des repas français. Ils ne jouent pas au tennis de table et ils ne regardent pas de films français.**

Pour aller plus loin

Les mots utiles: *avec, mais* et *pour*

Avec *(with),* **mais** *(but)* and **pour** *(for)* are useful **mots utiles** in communication.

Essayez! Complete these sentences with the correct **mots utiles.**

1. J'ai un livre _____ toi.
2. Nous mangeons _____ le professeur.
3. Je parle français _____ je ne parle pas italien.
4. Je joue au tennis _____ Marc.

Liaisons musicales

© Francis Apesteguy/ Sardine Photos/Newscom

A French icon, Serge Gainsbourg (1928–1991) was a singer, songwriter, actor, and director. His music mixed a variety of styles including jazz, ballads, pop, Afro-Caribbean, and **chanson française.** Find three of Gainsbourg's songs on the Internet. List their titles and their musical styles.

La parole est à vous!

Est-ce que les athlètes professionnels sont trop adorés?

Beaucoup d'athlètes professionnels gagnent bien leur vie° aujourd'hui et il y a beaucoup de gens partout° dans le monde° qui adorent les athlètes professionnels. Qu'en pensez-vous? Les athlètes professionnels sont-ils trop adorés et trop payés?

- Asmaou de Dakar (Sénégal), âge 45 ans: «Oui, je dirais° que oui. Les athlètes professionnels ont du talent, c'est sûr. Mais pourquoi gagnent-ils tant° d'argent? Je ne comprends pas.»

- Henri de Charleroi (Belgique), âge 22 ans: «Certainement que non! Les athlètes professionnels sont spéciaux. Ils sacrifient beaucoup pour jouer à un niveau° supérieur. Ne méritent°-ils pas tout dans la vie?»

gagnent bien leur vie *earn a good living* **partout** *everywhere* **dans le monde** *in the world* **dirais** *would say* **tant** *so much* **niveau** *level* **méritent** *deserve*

Et vous? Qu'en pensez-vous?

Les athlètes professionnels sont-ils trop adorés et trop payés?

Les loisirs

Pastimes

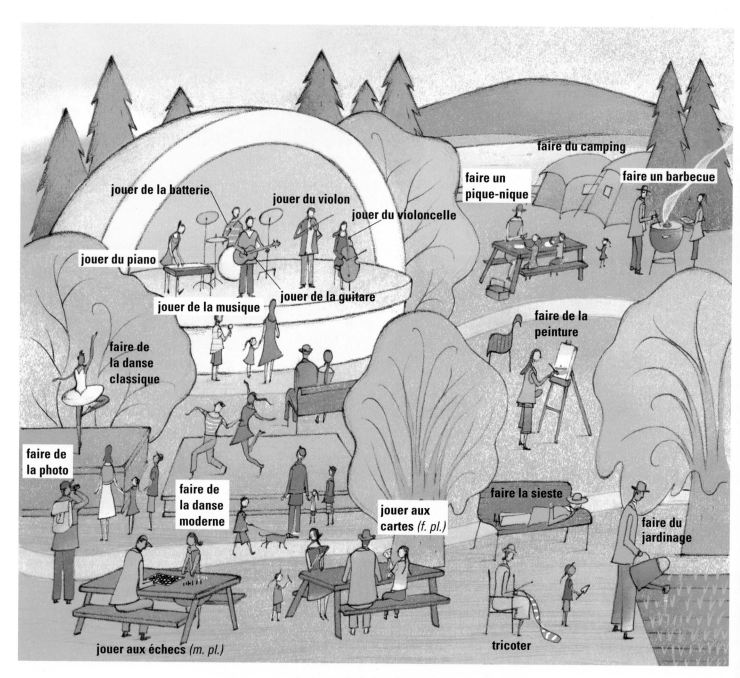

- jouer de la batterie
- jouer du violon
- jouer du violoncelle
- jouer du piano
- jouer de la guitare
- jouer de la musique
- faire du camping
- faire un pique-nique
- faire un barbecue
- faire de la peinture
- faire de la danse classique
- faire de la photo
- faire de la danse moderne
- jouer aux cartes (f. pl.)
- faire la sieste
- faire du jardinage
- jouer aux échecs (m. pl.)
- tricoter

Les activités de loisir

Vocabulaire complémentaire

aller au spa *to go to the spa*
commander une pizza *to order a pizza*
dessiner *to draw, to sketch*
écrire des lettres *to write letters*
écrire des poèmes *to write poems*
écrire des textos *to write text messages*

faire du bricolage *to do home improvement*
faire des courses *to run errands*
faire la cuisine / cuisiner *to cook*
faire la fête *to party*
faire la grasse matinée *to sleep in*
faire du karaoké *to do karaoke*
faire du lèche-vitrine *to window-shop*

faire une promenade *to take a walk*
faire du shopping *to shop*
faire un voyage *to take a trip*

jouer au poker *to play poker*
jouer aux jeux de société *(m. pl.)* *to play board games*

lire les courriels *to read e-mails*
lire le journal *to read the newspaper*
lire de la poésie *to read poetry*
lire un roman *to read a novel*

un loisir *a leisure activity*
un passe-temps *a pastime, a hobby*

Note de vocabulaire
You will learn the conjugations of **écrire** and **lire** in **Grammaire 3.**

ACTIVITÉ A Où fait-on ces activités? You will hear a series of activities. Where are they typically conducted: **a) à l'intérieur** *(inside)*, **b) à l'extérieur** *(outside)*, or **c) les deux** *(both)*?

1. _____
2. _____
3. _____
4. _____
5. _____

6. _____
7. _____
8. _____
9. _____
10. _____

ACTIVITÉ B Qui fait l'activité? You will hear another series of activities. Which of these people are famous for them?

1. a. Carlos Santana   b. Mick Jagger   c. Mickey Hart
2. a. Kenny G   b. Michelle Obama   c. Maya Angelou
3. a. Yo Yo Ma   b. Bill Gates   c. Jay Leno
4. a. Claude Monet   b. Sarah Bernhardt   c. Frédéric Chopin
5. a. Andrew Lloyd Webber   b. Louis Armstrong   c. John Mayer
6. a. Anne Geddes   b. Jim Carrey   c. Lance Armstrong

ACTIVITÉ C Plaisirs ou obligations?

Étape 1. Decide if each activity is **un plaisir** or **une obligation.**

	un plaisir	une obligation		un plaisir	une obligation
1. faire la cuisine	☐	☐	**5.** faire des courses	☐	☐
2. faire du jardinage	☐	☐	**6.** faire la sieste	☐	☐
3. lire les courriels	☐	☐	**7.** lire un roman	☐	☐
4. faire de la peinture	☐	☐	**8.** lire le journal	☐	☐

Étape 2. Share your answers with a partner to see if you have similar ideas, and be ready to report back to the class.

Modèle: **Faire la cuisine est un plaisir pour moi mais une obligation pour mon partenaire.**

ACTIVITÉ D Vos préférences

Étape 1. Use the preposition and articles to finish these sentences.

1. On aime **jouer au**	a. piano	b. poker	c. cartes
2. On aime **jouer du**	a. violoncelle	b. poker	c. échecs
3. On aime **faire du**	a. lèche-vitrine	b. fête	c. cuisine
4. On aime **jouer aux**	a. musique	b. violoncelle	c. jeux de société
5. On aime **commander une**	a. pizza	b. danse classique	c. loisir
6. On aime **faire un**	a. fête	b. pique-nique	c. promenade
7. On aime **faire la**	a. poker	b. grasse matinée	c. batterie
8. On va **au**	a. spa	b. piano	c. lèche-vitrine

Étape 2. Finish each sentence with a recreational activity that you like to do.

1. J'aime **faire** _____. **2.** J'aime **jouer** _____. **3.** J'aime _____.

Étape 3. Do you remember which activity Claire's mother likes to do at the hospital?

Madame Gagner aime **jouer** _____.

ACTIVITÉ E Qu'est-ce qu'on fait ici? What kinds of activities do you generally do in these locations?

Modèle: dans une salle de répétition *(rehearsal room)*
On joue du piano.

1. dans un bar
2. au conservatoire de musique
3. dans une boîte de nuit *(nightclub)*
4. dans une pizzeria
5. au conservatoire de danse
6. à l'université
7. dans un parc
8. à la maison *(at home)*

Liaisons musicales

© Fabien Klotchkoff/Visual Press Agency/Photoshot

Quebecoise cellist Jorane (1975–) is known in Quebec and in Europe for her alternative musical style and for her haunting voice as she sings and plays cello at the same time. Jorane's musical style and cello playing is sometimes compared to Tori Amos and her piano. Go to Jorane's official website to listen for yourself. 🌐

ACTIVITÉ F **Qui a un talent secret?** Ask the following questions to different classmates to see if they have hidden talents. When you find someone who says yes, note his/her name next to the activity. Don't forget that **un, une, du, de la, de l'** and **des** become **de/d'** in negative sentences.

Modèle: jouer de la guitare   **Est-ce que tu joues de la guitare?**

Qui a un talent pour...

1. dessiner?
2. faire du bricolage?
3. bien faire la cuisine?
4. bien jouer au poker?
5. tricoter?
6. faire la fête?
7. bien faire du karaoké?
8. jouer de la guitare?

© Diego Cervo/Shutterstock.com

ACTIVITÉ G **Les professeurs ou les étudiants?**

Étape 1. Make a list of four activities that you typically associate with students and four that you associate with professors at your university.

Modèle: **Généralement, les étudiants jouent de la batterie.**
Généralement, les professeurs font du jardinage.

Étape 2. Read your list to a partner and tell him/her whether you agree (**Je suis d'accord.**) or do not agree (**Je ne suis pas d'accord.**) with his/her statements.

Modèle: É1: **Typiquement les professeurs font du jardinage.**
É2: **Oui, je suis d'accord. / Je ne suis pas d'accord. Les professeurs et les étudiants jouent de la batterie.**

ACTIVITÉ H **Itinéraire** Plan an intinerary for an exchange student with at least two activities you will do together **le matin, l'après-midi** and **le soir.** Be prepared to share your itinerary with the class so it can decide whose activities are the most interesting.

Modèle: **Le matin, nous allons faire une promenade.**

ACTIVITÉ I **Le plus grand plaisir dans la vie** What do students in your class think is the biggest pleasure in life? Select your top three activities from those presented in **Vocabulaire 3** in order of preference. Your instructor will take a poll to see which activity is the greatest pleasure for your class.

Modèle: **Mes plus grands plaisirs sont 1) aller au spa, 2) commander une pizza et 3) faire de la photo(graphie).**

Pour aller plus loin

Depuis combien de temps

If you would like to ask someone in French how long he/she has been doing something or going somewhere, use the construction **depuis combien de temps** plus the present tense of the verb. To answer the question, recycle **depuis** and give the length of time.

—**Depuis combien de temps joue-t-il de la guitare?**

—*How long has he been playing guitar?*

—**Depuis quatre semaines.**

—*For four weeks.*

—**Depuis combien de temps fais-tu de la danse classique?**

—*How long have you been doing classical dance?*

—**Depuis cinq ans.**

—*For five years.*

Essayez! Answer the following questions with **depuis**.

Modèle: Depuis combien de temps est-ce que tu fais la sieste?

Depuis vingt minutes.

1. Depuis combien de temps est-ce que tu étudies le français?
2. Depuis combien de temps est-ce que tu es étudiant(e) à l'université?
3. Depuis combien de temps est-ce que tu habites dans cette *(this)* ville?
4. Depuis combien de temps est-ce que tu écoutes ton professeur aujourd'hui?

Un mot sur la culture

© Peter Frank Edwards/Redux

Regarder passer les gens: passe-temps populaire

According to France's Ministry of Culture report in 2007, French households spend approximately €1,385 (1,385 euros) a year on culture, leisure activities, sports, and games. One of the most popular past-times, however, is free. This activity is **regarder passer les gens** *(people-watching)*. It is so popular that cafés are designed to promote people-watching by having all their café chairs face the street. The wait staff also helps promote this activity by not rushing to bring you your check right away so you can enjoy a leisurely coffee or meal while watching the world go by.

- Aimez-vous regarder passer les gens?
- Où sont les meilleurs endroits *(best places)* pour regarder passer les gens?

🔊 **Liaisons avec les mots et les sons**

CD1-32 # Les consonnes finales muettes

In general, final consonants in French are silent.

> salu~~t~~   nou~~s~~   stylo~~s~~   alleman~~d~~   concer~~t~~   chocola~~t~~

However, there are some final consonant letters that are generally pronounced: **q, k, b, c, r, f,** and **l.** To help you remember these consonants, think of the consonants in the phrase **QuiCK—Be CaReFuL!**

> cin**q**   publi**c**   anora**k**   clu**b**   chi**c**   classeu**r**   neu**f**   journa**l**

An exception is **r** in words ending in **-ier** and **-er.**

> cahie~~r~~   papie~~r~~   regarde~~r~~   travaille~~r~~   parle~~r~~

If a word ends in an unaccented **e** or in **es,** the preceding consonant is always pronounced, but the **e** / **es** remains silent.

> por**te**   alleman~~d~~ / alleman**de**   peti~~t~~ / peti**te**   gran~~d~~ / gran**de**

You learned a major exception in **Chapitre 1:** Some final consonants that are normally silent will be pronounced if there is **une liaison** (for example, between an article and a noun).

> les‿étudiants   les‿hallucinations   les‿averses   les‿orages

Pratique A. Listen and select the word you hear.

1. chez / chef
2. français / française
3. c'est / cinq
4. intéressant / intéressante
5. publie / public
6. étudiant / étudiante

Pratique B. Listen to and repeat these statements about **les loisirs.** Which words have pronounced final consonants? Don't forget the **liaison.**

Quand il fait beau, on fait du cheval et on joue au golf. Mais quand il fait mauvais, on fait de l'aérobic ou on joue aux cartes.

🔊 **À vos stylos! C'est l'heure de la dictée!**

CD1-33 You will hear three sentences from the film *Liaisons*. Listen closely to them. You will then hear the sentences a second time. Write the three sentences you hear.

Sujet Claire parle de sa mère.

Pour parler de la communication

Les verbes **lire, écrire, dire** / Les adverbes

DU FILM *LIAISONS*

Un coup d'œil sur la grammaire

© Heinle/Cengage Learning

Do you remember this opening scene from the prologue of the film *Liaisons*? Read the description under the photo.

Une femme **écrit lentement** sur une feuille de papier.

1. What does the verb **écrit** mean?
2. **Lentement** is an adverb. Which adjective does it come from?

Les verbes-clés

Les verbes *lire, écrire, dire*

Lire, écrire, and **dire** are three useful verbs of communication. They share a similar conjugation pattern. Here are their present tense forms.

lire *(to read)*	
je **lis**	nous **lisons**
tu **lis**	vous **lisez**
il/elle/on **lit**	ils/elles **lisent**

dire *(to say)*	
je **dis**	nous **disons**
tu **dis**	vous **dites**
il/elle/on **dit**	ils/elles **disent**

écrire *(to write)*	
j'**écris**	nous **écrivons**
tu **écris**	vous **écrivez**
il/elle/on **écrit**	ils/elles **écrivent**

© Tracey Whitefoot/Alamy

Si vous y allez

Si vous allez à Québec, allez à la Bibliothèque Saint Jean-Baptiste. In the **Quartier Saint Jean-Baptiste** of Quebec City on **rue Saint Jean,** this library is inside the old Anglican Church of St. Matthew, a historical landmark in Quebec. On the grounds of this church / library is a cemetery that houses the remains of British soldiers from the battle of 1759 when New France was lost to the British.

Nous **lisons** le journal.

Qu'est-ce que vous **dites**?

Je **lis** le texte rapidement.

Elle **écrit** un courriel à son amie.

*We **are reading** the newspaper.*

*What **are you saying**?*

*I **am reading** the text rapidly.*

*She **is writing** an e-mail to her friend.*

Les adverbes

Adverbs allow you to be more precise in your descriptions. They modify verbs, adjectives, and other adverbs. You already saw some adverbs like **beaucoup, souvent, trop,** and **très** in **Chapitre 1.**

- Most adverbs are formed by adding **-ment** to the feminine form of an adjective.

Feminine Adjective	Adverb
active	activement *actively*
sérieuse	sérieusement *seriously*

- If the masculine form of the adjective ends in a vowel, add **-ment** to it.

Masculine Adjective	Adverb
absolu	absolument *absolutely*
poli	poliment *politely*
vrai	vraiment *really, truly*

- If the masculine form of the adjective ends in **-ent** or **-ant,** replace the ending with **-emment** and **-amment,** respectively. Both endings have the same pronunciation.

Masculine Adjective	Adverb
évident	évidemment *evidently*
patient	patiemment *patiently*
constant	constamment *constantly*
courant	couramment *fluently*

- Some adverbs are irregular.

Adjective	Adverb
bon/bonne	bien *well*
mauvais/mauvaise	mal *badly*
gentil/gentille	gentiment *nicely*

- **Vite** means *quickly* or *fast* and can also be used as an exclamation to mean *hurry.*

Il mange trop **vite.**	He eats too **fast.**
Vite! Vite!	**Hurry! Hurry!**

- When adverbs modify adjectives or other adverbs, they usually precede them.

Anne est **très** intelligente.	Anne is **very** intelligent.
Tom regarde **trop souvent** la télé.	Tom watches TV **too often.**

- When an adverb modifies a verb, it usually goes after the verb.

Je mange **rapidement.**	I eat **quickly.**
On travaille **bien** ensemble.	We work **well** together.

- In a negative construction, the adverb comes after **pas.**

Je ne parle pas **bien** le français.	I don't speak French **well.**
Je ne fais pas **rapidement** les courses.	I don't run errands **quickly.**

© Elena Elisseeva/Shutterstock.com

ACTIVITÉ J Activités d'aujourd'hui ou d'autrefois? How have forms of communication changed? Finish the sentences below by choosing the correct subject. Afterwards, indicate if this is an activity of today (**aujourd'hui**), an activity of the past (**autrefois**), or both (**les deux**).

	Aujourd'hui	Autrefois	Les deux
1. … **écrivons** des lettres à la main *(hand)*. a. Je b. Elle c. Nous	☐	☐	☐
2. … **écrivent** des courriels. a. Tu b. Ils c. Vous	☐	☐	☐
3. … **lis** les infos *(news)* sur Internet. a. Il b. Je c. Elles	☐	☐	☐
4. … **lisez** des romans. a. Vous b. On c. Nous	☐	☐	☐
5. … **écrit** des textos. a. Je b. Ils c. Il	☐	☐	☐
6. … **lisons** des poèmes. a. Tu b. Nous c. On	☐	☐	☐
7. … **dis** «bonjour» à Maman au téléphone. a. Je b. Nous c. Vous	☐	☐	☐
8. … **dites** «salut» par message instantané. a. Tu b. Elles c. Vous	☐	☐	☐

Conclusion Est-ce que la communication d'aujourd'hui est très différente de la communication d'autrefois?   oui / non

ACTIVITÉ K Est-ce que vous dites la vérité?

Étape 1. Read each situation with a partner and tell each other whether or not you would tell the truth: **Oui, je dis la vérité. / Non, je ne dis pas la vérité.**

Est-ce que vous dites la vérité si…

1. un(e) ami(e) a une coupe de cheveux *(haircut)* horrible. Il/Elle vous demande: «Est-ce que tu aimes ma coupe de cheveux?»
2. le café de votre ami(e) est très mauvais. Il/Elle vous demande: «Est-ce que tu aimes mon café?»
3. la robe *(dress)* de votre amie est très belle. Elle vous demande: «Est-ce que tu aimes ma robe?»
4. un(e) ami(e) impoli(e). Il/Elle vous demande: «Est-ce que je suis impoli(e)?»
5. un(e) camarade de chambre a un(e) petit(e) ami(e) méchant(e). Il/Elle vous demande: «Est-ce que tu aimes mon/ma petit(e) ami(e)?»

Étape 2. Est-ce que votre camarade de classe et vous êtes similaires ou différent(e)s? Est-ce que vous êtes honnêtes?

ACTIVITÉ **L** Les activités de communication

Étape 1. How often do you do the following activities? Answer with **rarement, constamment,** or **trop souvent.**

Modèle: écrire des lettres à la main   **J'écris rarement des lettres à la main.**

1. écrire des lettres à la main
2. écrire des courriels
3. écrire des textos
4. écrire des lettres d'amour
5. lire les courriels
6. lire les infos sur Internet
7. lire le journal papier
8. lire l'horoscope
9. dire «bonjour» à ton professeur
10. dire la vérité *(truth)*

ACTIVITÉ **M** Un(e) bon(ne) ou mauvais(e) étudiant(e)?

Étape 1. Read the following descriptions about student activities and decide if each statement describes **un(e) bon(ne) étudiant(e)** or **un(e) mauvais(e) étudiant(e).**

	bon(ne) étudiant(e)	mauvais(e) étudiant(e)
1. Il/Elle fait **patiemment** les devoirs.	☐	☐
2. Il/Elle n'écrit pas **intelligemment**.	☐	☐
3. Il/Elle réussit *(succeeds)* **brillamment** aux examens.	☐	☐
4. Il/Elle répond *(answers)* **intelligemment** aux questions.	☐	☐
5. Il/Elle ne va pas **fréquemment** aux cours.	☐	☐
6. Il/Elle étudie **sérieusement**.	☐	☐
7. Il/Elle parle **méchamment** aux professeurs.	☐	☐
8. Il/Elle est **rarement** en retard pour les cours.	☐	☐

© ARENA Creative/Shutterstock.com

Étape 2. Now ask a classmate if he/she does these activities to determine if he/she is **un(e) bon(ne) étudiant(e)** or **un(e) mauvais(e) étudiant(e).**

Modèle: É1: **Est-ce que tu fais patiemment les devoirs?**
  É2: **Non, je ne fais pas patiemment les devoirs. Je fais rapidement les devoirs.**
  É1: **Est-ce que tu écris intelligemment?**
  É2: **Oui, j'écris intelligemment.**

Étape 3. Based on you and your partner's responses in **Étape 2,** indicate whether the two of you are **bon(ne)s** or **mauvais(e)s étudiant(e)s.**

ACTIVITÉ N **Comment font-ils?** With a classmate, decide how or how frequently you think the following celebrities do these activities.

Modèles: John Meyer / écrire de la musique rock acoustique
John Meyer écrit brillamment de la musique rock acoustique.

Paris Hilton / faire les courses
Paris Hilton fait rarement les courses.

1. Bette Midler et Céline Dion / donner des concerts
2. Ben Affleck / jouer au poker
3. Beyoncé / faire de la danse classique
4. Wolfgang Puck / faire la cuisine
5. Jim Carrey et Will Ferrell / jouer des rôles sérieux au cinéma
6. Jackie Chan / jouer au football américain
7. Kanye West / écrire des poèmes
8. Madonna et Lance Armstrong / parler français

ACTIVITÉ O **Vos tendances**

Étape 1. Answer these questions using an adverb.

LEXIQUE

attentivement	élégamment	mal	sérieusement
bien	fréquemment	prudemment	souvent
brillamment	(im)patiemment	rapidement	toujours
constamment	horriblement	rarement	vite

Modèles: Comment écrivez-vous les courriels?
J'écris impatiemment les courriels.

À quelle fréquence *(With what frequency)* écrivez-vous des textos?
J'écris presque *(almost)* constamment des textos.**

Comment...

1. faites-vous vos devoirs?
2. écrivez-vous les compositions?
3. mangez-vous le dîner?
4. faites-vous les courses?
5. faites-vous la cuisine?

À quelle fréquence…

6. lisez-vous vos courriels?
7. dites-vous la vérité?
8. faites-vous de la gym?
9. faites-vous du sport?
10. allez-vous au spa?

Étape 2. Ask a partner the questions and note his/her answers. Based on your partner's answers, which adjective would you use to describe him/her?

LEXIQUE

équilibré(e)	paresseux/paresseuse	stressé(e) *(stressed)*
farfelu(e) *(scatter-brained)*	sérieux/sérieuse	travailleur/travailleuse

ACTIVITÉ P Sondage

Étape 1. Ask questions to different classmates to try to find someone who engages in these activities at the frequency or in the manner indicated. When you find someone, make note of his/her name, and be ready to share your answers with the class.

Modèle: Trouvez quelqu'un qui fait constamment la fête.

Est-ce que tu fais constamment la fête?

Trouvez quelqu'un qui...

1. écrit tous les jours sur Facebook.
2. compose élégamment de la poésie *(poetry)*.
3. dit rarement des mensonges *(lies)*.
4. fait constamment la fête.
5. joue sérieusement aux jeux de société.
6. écoute attentivement du jazz.
7. lit un roman en ce moment.
8. commande fréquemment des pizzas.

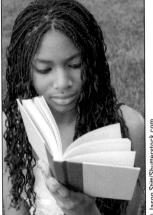

© Jason Stitt/Shutterstock.com

Étape 2. Based on what you found out in this activity, how do you think your class appears in the eyes of the instructor? **Bizarre? Excessive? Normale? Chanceuse** *(Lucky)*? **Malchanceuse? Gâtée** *(Spoiled)*?

La parole est à vous!
Les petits plaisirs vont-ils disparaître?

Les petits plaisirs de la vie sont en train de disparaître°. Beaucoup de gens sont inquiets° parce que nous sommes aujourd'hui trop collés° à la télé et à Internet et que nous oublions° comment faire d'autres activités. Qu'en pensez-vous? Est-ce qu'on passe trop de temps devant la télé ou l'ordinateur?

- Karim de Beyrouth (Liban), âge 17 ans: «Mais non! Je corresponds constamment avec mes amis. On écrit des textos, des courriels et des messages sur Facebook. On joue même° aux jeux ensemble par Internet.»

- Yvonne de Mulhouse (France), âge 76 ans: «Oui. Aujourd'hui les moyens° de communication électronique servent de médiateur° entre les gens. Les lettres écrites à la main... cet art, ce plaisir est fini, malheureusement.»

disparaître *die out* **inquiets** *worried* **collés** *glued* **nous oublions** *we forget* **même** *even*
les moyens *means* **médiateur** *mediator*

Et vous? Qu'en pensez-vous?

1. Est-ce qu'on passe trop de notre vie aujourd'hui devant la télé ou sur Internet?
2. Est-ce que les autres petits plaisirs de la vie sont en train de disparaître aujourd'hui?

GRAMMAIRE 3 *cent trois* **103**

DEUXIÈME
PROJECTION

Avant de visionner

ACTIVITÉ A **Qui l'a dit?** Do you remember who said these lines in **Séquence 1**?

	Claire	Abia	Alexis
1. «Elle mange, elle joue aux cartes, elle lit et elle dort.»	☐	☐	☐
2. «Qu'est-ce qu'il y a?»	☐	☐	☐
3. «Elle a des moments de lucidité mais…»	☐	☐	☐
4. «Et les hallucinations?»	☐	☐	☐
5. «Vous êtes Claire… ?»	☐	☐	☐
6. «J'ai oublié ma brosse à dents chez moi.»	☐	☐	☐

ACTIVITÉ B **Vous rappelez-vous?** In **Séquence 1,** Claire met a man named Alexis Prévost at the hotel. With a classmate, fill in the missing words from part of their encounter. You will check your answers later.

ALEXIS Claire. C'est votre (1) _____, n'est-ce pas?

CLAIRE Oui. Je (2) _____ Claire. Claire Gagner.

ALEXIS (3) _____, Claire Gagner.

CLAIRE Enchantée.

ALEXIS C'est joli.

CLAIRE Pardon?

ALEXIS Votre prénom. C'est un (4) _____ prénom, Claire.

CLAIRE Merci. Euh, vous (5) _____ client de (6) _____, monsieur?

ALEXIS Oui. Excusez-moi, Mademoiselle. Je m'appelle (7) _____.

Regarder la séquence

You will now watch **Séquence 1.** Verify your answers to **Activité B.**

Après le visionnage

ACTIVITÉ C **Les deux hommes**

In **Séquence 1,** Claire meets two men at the hotel: a man who hands her an envelope and a man who needs a toothbrush. Decide if the following adjectives describe **l'homme avec l'enveloppe, Alexis, les deux** *(both)* or **ni l'un ni l'autre** *(neither).*

1. Il est sérieux.   **2.** Il est sociable.   **3.** Il est beau.   **4.** Il est mystérieux.

ACTIVITÉ D **Résumé de la Séquence 1** Complete the summary of **Séquence 1** by supplying the missing words. Not all the words listed will be used, so be careful!

avec   depuis   enveloppe   mère   nous   parle   psychiatrique   vous

Claire travaille à l'hôtel (1) _____ son amie Abia. Claire (2) _____
avec Abia de sa (3) _____ qui est à l'hôpital (4) _____. Simone
Gagner est à l'hôpital (5) _____ plus de *(more than)* six ans. À l'hôpital, un
homme mystérieux donne à Claire une (6) _____ et il disparaît *(disappears).*

a   l'hôtel   il   ont   Prévost   sympathique

Claire rencontre un homme qui (7) _____ besoin d'une brosse à dents.
(8) _____ est client de (9) _____ et il s'appelle Alexis
(10) _____. Claire trouve cet homme (11) _____ et très beau.

Dans les coulisses

In **Séquence 1,** Claire meets two somewhat mysterious men. One gives her an envelope. The other asks for a toothbrush, claiming he is a guest of the hotel. What makes these men mysterious? Which of the two might have an important role in the film? What are your reasons for thinking this? As you ponder these questions, consider time on screen, information exchanged during conversations, and Claire's actions. All of these are tools that writers and directors use to indicate relationships among people and to suggest what might appear later in the story.

LIAISONS AVEC LA LECTURE

À DÉCOUVRIR: La France et le rugby à Toulouse

À DÉCOUVRIR: La France

Pays: La France
Géographie: En Europe de l'Ouest, entre la Belgique et l'Espagne (France métropolitaine)
Climat: Hivers frais et étés doux mais hivers doux et étés chauds dans le sud (France métropolitaine)
Population: 63,2 millions (France métropolitaine)
Capitale: Paris

Activité Internet
Type **je découvre la France** into your search engine and find something interesting to see or do in France.

À DÉCOUVRIR: La ville de Toulouse

Région: Midi-Pyrénées
Département: Haute-Garonne
Population: Plus de 400 000
Réputation: Une technopole européenne pour les industries aéronautique, de l'espace (aérospatiale) et de l'information
Climat: Tempéré océanique à influences méditerranéenne et continentale

Avant de lire

France is a relatively diverse country with different climates, cuisines, regional identities, traditions, and favorite pastimes. In the upcoming reading, you will discover a popular pastime in the city of Toulouse.

Que savez-vous déjà?

1. Est-ce que vous connaissez quelque chose de *(something)* célèbre à Toulouse?
2. Quelles industries ou entreprises se trouvent *(are found)* à Toulouse?

OUTILS DE LECTURE
Using glosses

Glosses are translations of words whose meanings may be more challenging to guess from context. To develop good reading skills, it is best to try to guess the meanings of unfamiliar words from context first and then use the glosses to confirm your guesses. As you read **Découvrir le rugby à Toulouse,** try to guess the meaning of unfamiliar words and then use the glosses to check your predictions.

Découvrir le rugby à Toulouse

Alors que° le football est de loin° le sport le plus populaire en France et à travers le monde°, le rugby est particulièrement populaire dans le sud-ouest de la France. Le Championnat de France est régulièrement dominé par les clubs des villes du sud-ouest: Bordeaux, Montpellier, Narbonne, Pau, Perpignan, Tarbes... et Toulouse, qui a remporté° dix-sept titres de Champion de France. Au niveau° international, la France participe au Tournoi annuel° des Six Nations (avec l'Angleterre°, l'Écosse°, l'Irlande, l'Italie, le Pays de Galles°) et à la Coupe du Monde, une compétition qui a lieu° tous les quatre ans.

Toulouse, qui est un des grands centres technologiques en France (le siège° du constructeur aéronautique Airbus), est aussi célèbre pour son club de rugby, le Stade Toulousain, qui est un grand club professionnel. Au niveau sportif, les supporters du Stade Toulousain sont passionnés par leur équipe, dont° les joueurs portent des maillots° rouge et noir.

Clément Poitrenaud est un des joueurs les plus célèbres de l'équipe de rugby de Toulouse. Il joue généralement en poste d'arrière°. Il est connu° pour son jeu spectaculaire, pour son goût du° risque, mais aussi pour ses blessures°.

Alors que *While* **de loin** *by far* **à travers le monde** *throughout the world* **a remporté** *won* **niveau** *level* **Tournoi annuel** *yearly tournament* **l'Angleterre** *England* **l'Écosse** *Scotland* **le Pays de Galles** *Wales* **qui a lieu** *which is held* **le siège** *corporate headquarters* **dont** *whose (of which)* **maillots** *jerseys* **en poste d'arrière** *in the position of fullback* **est connu** *is known* **goût du** *taste for* **blessures** *injuries*

Après avoir lu

Compréhension

1. Est-ce que le rugby est le sport le plus *(most)* populaire en France?   Oui / Non
2. Est-ce que le club de Toulouse a eu *(has had)* beaucoup de succès en France?   Oui / Non
3. Est-ce que Toulouse est seulement une ville de rugby?   Oui / Non
4. Est-ce que Clément Poitrenaud est connu pour son jeu médiocre?   Oui / Non

Et vous?

1. Est-ce que tu joues au rugby?
2. Est-ce que tu portes parfois le maillot de ton équipe de sport préférée?
3. Est-ce qu'il y a un(e) athlète professionnel(le) que tu aimes regarder?

Activité Internet
The reading mentions several cities in southwestern France. Type **franceguide** into your search engine and look for other cities in the south of France. Choose one and write 2–3 sentences about it.

LIAISONS AVEC LA LECTURE ET L'ÉCRITURE Le portrait

Here is a **portrait** for rugby player Clément Poitrenaud.

Clément Poitrenaud (1m88, 91 kilos [*approx. 6ft 2in, 200 lbs.*]) est un joueur très célèbre de l'équipe de rugby de Toulouse. Né le 20 mai 1982 à Castres dans le sud-ouest de la France, Poitrenaud joue aussi en équipe nationale de France. Il joue généralement en poste d'arrière mais quelquefois il joue au centre aussi. Il est connu pour son jeu spectaculaire, pour son goût du risque, mais aussi pour ses blessures. Les autres joueurs du club de Toulouse pensent que Poitrenaud est très fidèle au sport et à l'équipe. Ils aiment beaucoup jouer avec lui au Stade Toulousain.

© Jean-Paul Pelissier/Reuters/Landov

Avant d'écrire

1. List the kinds of information that appear in Poitrenaud's **portrait**.

2. Answer the following questions to help you write your own **portrait**.

   a. Qui es-tu? Tu es étudiant(e)? Parent? Athlète?

   b. Tu es de quelle ville? De New York? De Columbus?

   c. Quelles sont tes caractéristiques personnelles? Tu es sociable? Travailleur (travailleuse)?

   d. As-tu des talents particuliers? Tu joues de la guitare?

   e. Qu'est-ce que tu vas faire après tes études *(studies)*? Tu vas être professeur?

Écrire

Using information from **Avant d'écrire**, write your own portrait of 6–8 sentences in French.

Après avoir écrit

Exchange your **portrait** with a partner. 1) Circle all the descriptors and verify that all the adjectives agree in number and gender. 2) Underline all the adverbs and verify that your partner correctly conjugated all of the verbs. 3) Put a * next to the sentence that best communicates your partner's personal information. 4) How would you characterize your partner's portrait: **unique, banal, stéréotypé, original, intéressant, amusant, drôle, sarcastique, vantard** *(boastful)*, **modeste,** etc.? Discuss your reactions together and then write a second version of your **portrait,** taking into account your partner's comments and corrections.

PARTIE 1

LES MOIS DE L'ANNÉE

janvier	*January*
février	*February*
mars	*March*
avril	*April*
mai	*May*
juin	*June*
juillet	*July*
août	*August*
septembre	*September*
octobre	*October*
novembre	*November*
décembre	*December*
un an / une année	*year*
un mois	*month*
une saison	*season*

LES SAISONS

l'automne *(m.)*	*fall*
l'été *(m.)*	*summer*
l'hiver *(m.)*	*winter*
le printemps	*spring*

LE TEMPS / LA MÉTÉO

Quelle température fait-il?	*What's the temperature?*
Il fait 20 degrés.	*It's 20 degrees Celsius. / It's 68° Fahrenheit.*
Quel temps fait-il?	*What's the weather like?*
Il fait beau.	*The weather is nice.*
Il fait bon.	*The weather is good / warm.*
Il fait chaud.	*It's hot.*
Il fait frais.	*It's cool.*
Il fait froid.	*It's cold.*
Il fait gris.	*It's dreary.*
Il fait lourd.	*It's hot and muggy.*
Il fait mauvais.	*The weather is bad.*
Il fait (du) soleil.	*It's sunny.*
Il fait du vent.	*It's windy.*
Il neige.	*It's snowing.*
Il pleut.	*It's raining.*
Le ciel est couvert.	*It's cloudy / overcast.*
l'averse *(f.)*	*shower*
le brouillard	*fog*
l'étoile *(f.)*	*star*
la lune	*moon*
la météo	*weather forecast*
la neige	*snow*
des nuages *(m.)*	*(some) clouds*
l'orage *(m.)*	*storm*
l'ouragan *(m.)*	*hurricane*
la pluie	*rain*
le soleil	*sun*

la tornade	*tornado*
le verglas	*(black) ice*

LA DATE

Quelle est la date (aujourd'hui)?	*What's the date (today)?*
C'est le premier (1er) mai.	*It's May first.*
C'est / On est / Nous sommes le 10 novembre.	*It's the 10th of November.*
C'est quand ton / votre anniversaire?	*When is your birthday?*
C'est quand l'anniversaire de Samir?	*When is Samir's birthday?*

VERBES

aller	*to go*
annoncer	*to forecast*

DIVERS

depuis combien de temps	*for how long*
pour	*for*

PARTIE 2

LES SPORTS ET LES ACTIVITÉS SPORTIVES

le baseball	*baseball*
le basket-ball / le basket	*basketball*
le football / le foot	*soccer*
le football américain	*football*
le golf	*golf*
le hockey	*hockey*
le rugby	*rugby*
le tennis	*tennis*
le tennis de table	*ping-pong, table tennis*
le volley-ball	*volleyball*
faire	*to do, to make*
faire de l'aérobic	*to do aerobics*
faire du bowling	*to go bowling*
faire du cheval	*to go horseback riding*
faire de la gym	*to work out, to exercise*
faire du jogging	*to go jogging*
faire de la marche	*to walk (for exercise)*
faire de la natation	*to swim (for exercise)*
faire du patinage	*to ice skate, to go iceskating*
faire de la planche à voile	*to go wind-surfing*
faire de la plongée sous-marine	*to scuba dive*
faire du ski (alpin)	*to go (downhill) skiing*
faire du ski de fond	*to go cross-country skiing*
faire du ski nautique	*to water-ski*
faire du sport	*to work out, to exercise*
faire du surf	*to surf*
faire du vélo	*to go bike riding*
faire du yoga	*to do yoga*

jouer (à + sport)	to play (a sport)	jouer au poker	to play poker
pratiquer	to play / to do (a sport)	jouer de la batterie	to play the drums
		jouer de la guitare	to play the guitar
une équipe	a team	jouer de la musique	to play, to listen to music
un joueur / une joueuse	a player		
un match (de + sport)	a match, a game (of a sport)	jouer du piano	to play the piano
		jouer du violon	to play violin
		jouer du violoncelle	to play cello

PARTIE 3

LES ACTIVITÉS DE LOISIR		lire les courriels	to read e-mail
		lire le journal	to read the newspaper
aller au spa	to go to the spa	lire de la poésie	to read poetry
commander une pizza	to order a pizza	lire un roman	to read a novel
cuisiner	to cook		
dessiner	to draw, to sketch	tricoter	to knit
écrire des lettres	to write letters		
écrire des poèmes	to write poems	un loisir	a leisure activity
écrire des textos	to write text messages	un passe-temps	a pastime, a hobby
faire un barbecue	to have a BBQ	un plaisir	a pleasure
faire du bricolage	to tinker, to do odd jobs, to act the handyman/woman	**VERBES**	
		dire	to say
faire du camping	to go camping	écrire	to write
faire les courses	to run some errands	lire	to read
faire la cuisine	to cook		
faire de la danse classique	to do classical dance	**DIVERS**	
faire de la danse moderne	to do modern dance	la vie	life
faire la fête	to party		
faire la grasse matinée	to sleep in	**ADVERBES**	
faire du jardinage	to garden	absolument	absolutely
faire du karaoké	to do karaoke	activement	actively
faire du lèche-vitrine	to window-shop	constamment	constantly
faire de la peinture	to paint	couramment	fluently
faire de la photo(graphie)	to practice photography	évidemment	evidently
faire un pique-nique	to (have/go on a) picnic	gentiment	nicely
faire une promenade (en ville)	to take a walk (in town)	lentement	slowly
		patiemment	patiently
faire du shopping	to shop, to go shopping	poliment	politely
faire la sieste	to take a nap	sérieusement	seriously
faire un voyage	to take a trip	vraiment	really, truly
jouer aux cartes (f. pl.)	to play cards	bien	well
jouer aux échecs (m. pl.)	to play chess	mal	badly
jouer aux jeux de société (m. pl.)	to play board games	vite, rapidement	fast, quickly, hurry!

Nos origines

En bref   In this chapter, you will:

- learn nationalities and countries

- learn prepositions to express geographical locations

- learn the verbs **venir** and **devenir**

- learn possessive and demonstrative adjectives

- learn adjective placement to talk about physical traits and colors

- learn **-ir** verbs like **sortir, partir, dormir, and sentir**

- learn about oral vowels

- read about the origins of family names, of linguistic and cultural differences, and of people in France and the Francophone world

 You will also watch **SÉQUENCE 2: La décision** of the movie *Liaisons.*

Ressources

 audio   🌐 http://www.cengagebrain.com

L'origine **culturelle**

Cultural origins

Les nationalités

les Allemand(e)s
les Anglais(es)
les Américain(e)s
les Belges
les Brésiliens / Brésiliennes
les Canadiens / Canadiennes
les Chinois(es)
les Espagnol(e)s
les Français(es)
les Irlandais(es)
les Italiens / Italiennes
les Ivoiriens / Ivoiriennes
les Japonais(es)
les Marocain(e)s
les Mexicain(e)s
les Québécois(es)
les Roumain(e)s
les Russes
les Sénégalais(es)
les Suisses
les Tunisiens / Tunisiennes
les Vietnamiens /
   Vietnamiennes

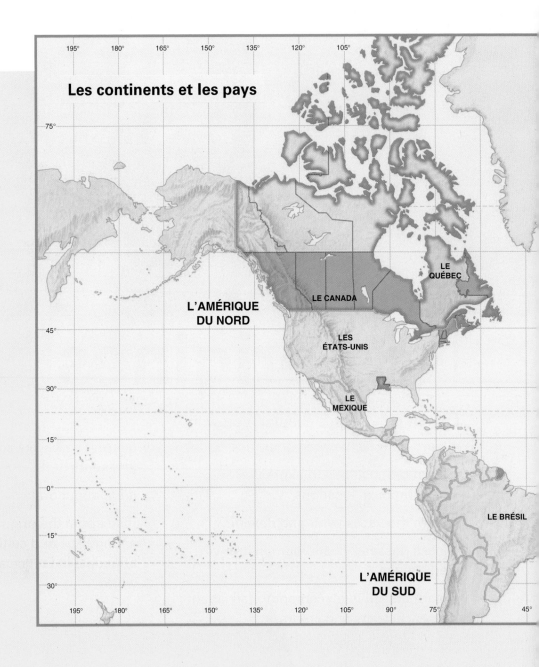

Les continents et les pays

C'est vs. Il/Elle est

C'est is followed by the name of a person or place or by an article and a noun. It is primarily used to identify. **Il/Elle est** is usually followed by an adjective and is used to describe.

C'est Gérard Depardieu.
That's Gérard Depardieu.

Il est français.
He is French.

C'est une Italienne.
That's an Italian (woman).

Elle est italienne.
She's Italian.

Essayez! Complétez chaque phrase avec **C'est** ou **Il/Elle est** et identifiez une personne de cette nationalité.

Modèle: **Elle est** espagnole.
C'est Penelope Cruz.

1. _____ américain.
2. _____ une Québécoise.
3. _____ anglaise.
4. _____ un Italien.

ACTIVITÉ A **Quel continent?** Vous allez entendre *(hear)* le nom d'un pays.
CD1-34 Le pays se trouve *(is found)* dans quel(s) continent(s)?

1. a. l'Amérique du Sud   b. l'Afrique du Nord   c. l'Asie

2. a. l'Afrique de l'Est   b. l'Asie   c. l'Europe de l'Est

3. a. l'Afrique du Nord   b. l'Europe de l'Ouest   c. l'Amérique du Nord

4. a. l'Amérique du Sud   b. l'Asie   c. l'Amérique du Nord

5. a. l'Asie   b. l'Amérique du Sud   c. l'Afrique du Nord

6. a. l'Afrique de l'Ouest   b. l'Europe de l'Ouest   c. l'Amérique du Nord

7. a. l'Amérique du Sud   b. l'Afrique de l'Ouest   c. l'Europe de l'Ouest

8. a. l'Afrique du Nord   b. l'Asie   c. l'Europe de l'Est

ACTIVITÉ B **Les pays et leurs produits ou activités** Vous allez entendre
CD1-35 *(hear)* une série de pays. Associez le pays que vous entendez à un produit ou à une activité.

1. a. le baseball   b. le football

2. a. le Coca-cola   b. le sushi

3. a. le saké   b. la tequila

4. a. *Les Misérables*   b. *Don Quichotte*

5. a. Toyota   b. Volkswagen

6. a. le chocolat   b. la pizza

ACTIVITÉ C **La Francophonie** Quels pays sont dans l'Organisation Internationale de la Francophonie? Cherchez les pays sur Internet si nécessaire.

ORGANISATION
INTERNATIONALE DE
la francophonie

ACTIVITÉ D **Les nationalités et les pays** Vous allez entendre *(hear)* une
CD1-36 série de nationalités. Associez la nationalité que vous entendez à un pays.

1.   **2.**   **3.**   **4.**   **5.**   **6.**   **7.**   **8.**   **9.**   **10.**

Si vous y allez

Courtesy Le Colonial
San Francisco

Si vous allez à Chicago ou
à San Francisco, allez au
restaurant Le Colonial pour
goûter la cuisine franco-
vietnamienne.

ACTIVITÉ E **Associations** Quelles nationalités associez-vous aux choses suivantes?

1. le Château Frontenac   **5.** la Grande Muraille de Chine

2. Mercedes-Benz   **6.** le TGV

3. la Maison Blanche *(White House)*   **7.** la Tour de Pise

4. Astérix   **8.** le chocolat Nestlé

ACTIVITÉ F **L'origine nationale / La nationalité** Identifiez leur origine nationale.

Modèles: George Washington / américain **Il est américain.**
Hillary Clinton / américain **Elle est américaine.**

1. Saint Patrick
2. Heidi Klum
3. Léopold Sédar Senghor
4. Marie-Antoinette
5. Ludwig van Beethoven
6. Frida Kahlo

ACTIVITÉ G **L'origine / La nationalité / La culture** Abia, le personnage du film *Liaisons,* est de culture québécoise et de nationalité canadienne. Mais les ancêtres d'Abia sont d'origine ivoirienne. Et vous?

© Heinle/Cengage Learning

Étape 1. Quelle est votre nationalité? Quelle est votre origine culturelle?

1. Je suis de nationalité _____.
2. Je suis d'origine culturelle _____.

Étape 2. Trouvez la nationalité et l'origine culturelle de trois personnes dans la classe et complétez la grille *(fill in the grid)*. Posez les questions suivantes:

1. Quelle est ta nationalité?
2. Quelle est ton origine culturelle?

Nom	La nationalité	L'origine culturelle
_____	_____	_____
_____	_____	_____
_____	_____	_____

Étape 3. Faites une liste de toutes les nationalités et origines culturelles de la classe. Soyez prêt(e)s à partager *(Be ready to share)* vos réponses. Ensuite, regardez vos listes et répondez aux questions suivantes:

1. Est-ce qu'il y a plusieurs *(several)* nationalités dans votre classe?
2. Est-ce qu'il y a plusieurs origines culturelles dans votre classe?

Un mot sur la culture

Ying Chen

© Ulf Andersen/Getty Images

Ying Chen (1961–) est une écrivaine québécoise qui habite à Montréal. Elle est née° à Shanghai en Chine, elle est donc d'origine chinoise. Son livre *L'Ingratitude* (1995) a obtenu le Prix Paris-Québec. Ce livre est publié aux États-Unis en anglais sous le titre *Ingratitude.* Ying Chen écrit en français mais elle parle aussi le chinois, le russe, l'italien et l'anglais.

née *born*

• Connaissez-vous l'origine culturelle de ces personnes?
1. Carla Bruni-Sarkozy
2. Zinédine Zidane
3. Édith Piaf
4. Julia Child

Pour parler des pays, des villes et de nos origines

Les prépositions et les lieux géographiques / Les verbes **venir** et **devenir**

DU FILM *LIAISONS*

Un coup d'œil sur la grammaire

Look at these photos from the film *Liaisons* and their captions. Note the different prepositions used in French to express that one is *in* a geographical location.

Claire habite **au** Canada, **à** Montréal.

L'oncle Michel habite **en** France, **à** Paris.

Abia habite **au** Canada, **à** Montréal.

La famille d'Abia habite **en** Côte d'Ivoire.

Unlike English, the use of prepositions with geographical locations in French depends on if the place is a country or city and if a country is masculine or feminine. Answer these questions based on the photo captions.

1. Is the preposition **à** used with cities or countries?   a. cities   b. countries
2. Is the preposition **en** used with cities or countries?   a. cities   b. countries
3. Is the preposition **au** used with cities or countries?   a. cities   b. countries

Countries and Continents

••❖ To say that you are *in* or going *to* a country, use the preposition **au** with masculine countries and **en** with feminine countries.

J'étudie **au** Canada.	*I am studying **in** Canada.*
Nous allons **au** Maroc.	*We are going **to** Morocco.*
Pierre habite **en** France.	*Pierre lives **in** France.*
Anne va **en** Espagne.	*Anne is going **to** Spain.*

••❖ Use the preposition **aux** to express *in* or *to* with countries that have plural grammatical gender like **les États-Unis.**

Les Tremblay habitent **aux** États-Unis.	*The Tremblays live **in** the United States.*
Nous retournons **aux** États-Unis.	*We are returning **to** the United States.*

•••• Use the preposition **en** to express *in* or *to* with continents because they are feminine.

Le Canada est **en** Amérique du Nord.　　*Canada is **in** North America.*

Nous allons **en** Europe.　　*We are going **to** Europe.*

•••• To express *from* a country or continent, use the prepositions **du** *(m.)*, **de** *(f.)*, **d'** *(before vowel)* or **des** *(pl.)*, depending on the location's grammatical gender.

Maria est **du** Brésil.　　*Maria is **from** Brazil.*

Abia est **de** Côte d'Ivoire.　　*Abia is **from** the Ivory Coast.*

Je suis **d'**Asie.　　*I am **from** Asia.*

Nous rentrons **des** États-Unis.　　*We are returning **from** the United States.*

States and Provinces

•••• States and provinces follow the same rules as countries and continents.

Sarah habite **en** Californie *(f.)*.　　*Sarah lives **in** California.*

Nous allons **au** Mexique *(m.)*.　　*We are going **to** Mexico.*

Elle étudie **au** Québec *(m.)*.　　*She is studying **in** Quebec [province].*

Jean va **en** Provence *(f.)*.　　*Jean is going **to** Provence.*

Tom est **du** Colorado *(m.)*.　　*Tom is **from** Colorado.*

Marie est **de** Lorraine *(f.)*.　　*Marie is **from** Lorraine.*

Je suis **de** l'Ohio.　　*I am **from** Ohio.*

Cities

•••• To express *in* or *to* a city, use the preposition **à.** To express *from* a city, use the preposition **de.**

Nous allons **à** Paris.　　*We are going **to** Paris.*

Claire est **à** Québec.　　*Claire is **in** Quebec City.*

Luciano est **de** Rome.　　*Luciano is **from** Rome.*

Note de vocabulaire

See the vocabulary list at the end of this chapter for a list of U.S. states in French.

Liaisons musicales

© Heinz Ruckemann/UPI/Landov

Daniel Lavoie est un chanteur du Manitoba (au Canada) qui a obtenu de nombreux prix et distinctions. Sa chanson *Je voudrais voir* (I would like to see) *New York* (1986) parle des villes et des pays qu'il aimerait voir. Cherchez les paroles *(lyrics)* de cette chanson. Nommez les villes et les pays mentionnés. 🌐

Les verbes-clés

Les verbes *venir* et *devenir*

❖ The verbs **venir** *(to come)* and **devenir** *(to become)* are another class of **-ir** verbs and take the following conjugations.

venir *(to come)*		devenir *(to become)*	
je **viens**	nous **venons**	je **deviens**	nous **devenons**
tu **viens**	vous **venez**	tu **deviens**	vous **devenez**
il/elle/on **vient**	ils/elles **viennent**	il/elle/on **devient**	ils/elles **deviennent**

Elsa **vient** du Maroc.　　　　　　*Elsa **comes** from Morocco.*

Vous **venez** dîner ce soir?　　　　*Are you **coming** to dinner this evening?*

Lise **devient** citoyenne américaine.　*Lise **is becoming** an American citizen.*

Venir de + infinitive

❖ When **venir de** is followed by a verb in the infinitive, the meaning changes from *to come from* to *to have just done something a few moments ago*.

Nous **venons de terminer** nos devoirs.　　　　*We **just finished** our homework.*

Il **vient de rentrer** du Maroc.　　*He **just returned** from Morocco.*

ACTIVITÉ Ⓗ **Où vont-ils?** Des étudiants parlent de leurs projets de vacances. Utilisez les prépositions pour déterminer où va chaque étudiant(e).

1. Je vais **au…**	a. Maroc	b. Paris	c. Espagne
2. Je prends des cours **en…**	a. Marseille	b. Italie	c. Canada
3. Nous allons **à…**	a. Sénégal	b. New York	c. Brésil
4. Je prends mes vacances **en…**	a. Rome	b. Mexique	c. Tunisie
5. Nous allons **à…**	a. Montréal	b. France	c. Belgique
6. Je vais **au…**	a. Tokyo	b. Colorado	c. Los Angeles
7. Mon ami va **en…**	a. Suisse	b. Maroc	c. Québec
8. Nous allons **au…**	a. Irlande	b. Viêt Nam	c. Berlin

❖ **Et vous?** Où est-ce que vous aimeriez aller en vacances?

ACTIVITÉ I **D'où viennent-ils?**

Étape 1. Le directeur d'une auberge de jeunesse *(youth hostel)* vous présente ses clients. Utilisez les prépositions pour déterminer d'où vient chaque personne.

1. Je vous présente Coralie. Elle vient **de**…
   a. Mexique   b. Montréal   c. Irlande

2. Voici Kim. Elle vient **du**…
   a. Japon   b. Tokyo   c. Chine

3. Nicoleta vient **de**…
   a. Viêt Nam   b. Roumanie   c. Allemagne

4. Laura vient **des**…
   a. Brésil   b. Italie   c. États-Unis

5. Bernard vient **d'**…
   a. Allemagne   b. Russie   c. France

6. Gabrielle et Caroline viennent **de**…
   a. Ohio   b. Californie   c. Canada

Étape 2. Répondez à ces *(these)* questions.

1. D'où venez-vous? _____

2. D'où vient un(e) de vos camarades de classe? _____

ACTIVITÉ J **Dans quelle ville?** Dans quelle ville peut-on *(can one)* trouver les choses suivantes?

Modèle: On trouve le meilleur *(best)* café **à Seattle.**

1. On trouve la meilleure pizza _____.

2. On trouve la meilleure équipe de baseball _____.

3. On trouve les meilleurs restaurants _____.

4. On trouve les meilleurs parcs _____.

5. On trouve le meilleur shopping _____.

6. On trouve les meilleurs musées _____.

ACTIVITÉ K **Dans quels pays?**

Étape 1. Lisez ces descriptions. Complétez chaque phrase avec une préposition et un pays.

Modèle: Les femmes sont très élégantes **en France.**

1. Il y a beaucoup d'écologistes _____.

2. Les femmes ont beaucoup de liberté _____.

3. Les habitants ont beaucoup d'enfants _____.

4. On trouve le meilleur *(best)* système de soins médicaux *(healthcare)* _____.

5. On trouve le meilleur système de transport public _____.

6. On trouve la meilleure qualité de vie _____.

✈ ...... **Si vous y allez**

Si vous allez à Québec, allez au restaurant Chez Victor pour les meilleurs hamburgers et les meilleures frites en Amérique du Nord. Visitez le site officiel du restaurant sur Internet.

© Wynne Wong

Étape 2. Partagez *(Share)* vos réponses de l'Étape 1 avec un(e) camarade de classe. Avez-vous écrit les mêmes choses? Voulez-vous changer vos réponses?

Modèle: É1: **Je pense qu'il y a beaucoup d'écologistes aux États-Unis. Et toi?**
É2: **Moi, je pense qu'il y a beaucoup d'écologistes au Canada.**
É1: **Ah oui! Je suis d'accord *(I agree)* avec toi. Il y a beaucoup d'écologistes au Canada. / Non, je ne suis pas d'accord.**

Étape 3. Partagez vos réponses et celles *(those)* de votre partenaire avec la classe. Ensuite, faites un résumé des opinions de votre classe.

La classe pense…

1. qu'il y a beaucoup d'écologistes **au Canada, en France et aux États-Unis.**
2. que les femmes ont beaucoup de liberté _____.
3. que les habitants ont beaucoup d'enfants _____.
4. qu'on trouve le meilleur système de soins médicaux _____.
5. qu'on trouve le meilleur système de transport public _____.
6. qu'on trouve la meilleure qualité de vie _____.

ACTIVITÉ L D'où viennent…?

Répondez à chaque question avec un pays et une phrase complète.

Modèle: D'où viennent les meilleurs hot-dogs?
Les meilleurs hot-dogs viennent des États-Unis.

1. les meilleurs films?
2. les meilleurs athlètes?
3. les meilleurs artistes?
4. les meilleures voitures *(cars)*?

ACTIVITÉ M «Sur Twitter» Une personne célèbre est un client à l'hôtel Frontenac. Un journaliste décrit toutes ses activités sur twitter. Indiquez si chaque activité se passe **maintenant** *(now)* ou vient de se passer **à l'instant** *(a few moments ago)*.

	maintenant	à l'instant
1. Il vient de manger un hot-dog.	☐	☐
2. Il parle avec le serveur.	☐	☐
3. Il lit le journal *La Gazette*.	☐	☐
4. Il vient de lire un texto intéressant.	☐	☐

© Bruno Morandi/Robert Harding World Imagery/ Corbis

ACTIVITÉ N **Qu'est-ce qu'ils viennent de faire?** Regardez ces images du film *Liaisons*. Qu'est-ce que les personnages viennent de faire? Complétez les phrases en utilisant les verbes entre parenthèses.

1. (rencontrer) _____   **2.** (lire) _____

ACTIVITÉ O **Dans un monde idéal** Dans un monde *(world)* idéal, tout le monde a des qualités. Qu'est-ce que les gens peuvent *(can)* devenir?

Modèles: Les gens stupides **deviennent intelligents.**
Une femme méchante **devient gentille.**

1. Un étudiant paresseux _____.   **6.** Les professeurs pauvres _____.

2. Une étudiante timide _____.   **7.** Les gens pessimistes _____.

3. Un enfant *(child)* triste _____.   **8.** Les gens embêtants _____.

4. Les professeurs ennuyeux _____.   **9.** Les gens difficiles _____.

5. Les étudiants impatients _____.   **10.** La classe de français et moi, nous _____.

La parole est à vous!

Est-ce qu'il est important d'apprendre des langues?

On dit que le multilinguisme et l'enseignement° des langues sont au cœur° du projet européen, surtout pour l'Union européenne. Qu'en pensez-vous? Est-ce que vous pensez qu'il est important d'apprendre des langues?

- Jean-Paul de Nantes (France): «Non, pas du tout! Je ne quitte° jamais la France. Je reste° toujours chez moi. Je ne fais pas de voyage. Je n'ai pas besoin de parler une autre langue que le français!»

- Élise de Bruxelles (Belgique): «Je pense que oui, absolument! Les langues que nous parlons sont le reflet de notre culture et de notre identité. Elles permettent la compréhension des autres cultures et des autres peuples.»

l'enseignement *the teaching* **au cœur** *at the heart* **quitte** *leave* **reste** *stay*

Et vous? Qu'en pensez-vous?

Est-ce qu'il est important d'apprendre des langues?

L'origine **familiale**
Family heritage

La famille d'Abia Ndono

La famille proche *(Immediate family)*

Adelai est **le père** d'Abia.

Bisa est **la mère** d'Abia.

Adelai et Bisa sont **les parents** d'Abia.

Abia est **la fille** d'Adelai et de Bisa.

Xavier est **le fils** d'Adelai et de Bisa.

La femme de Xavier, Fatima, est **décédée**.

Abia, Nadia et Xavier sont **les enfants** d'Adelai et de Bisa.

Adelai est **le mari** de Bisa.

Bisa est **la femme** d'Adelai.

Xavier est **le frère** d'Abia.

Nadia est **la sœur** d'Abia.

Patrick est **le neveu** d'Abia et **le petit-fils** d'Adelai et de Bisa.

Aude est **la nièce** d'Abia et **la petite-fille** d'Adelai et de Bisa.

Fifi est **le chat** de Patrick et Aude.

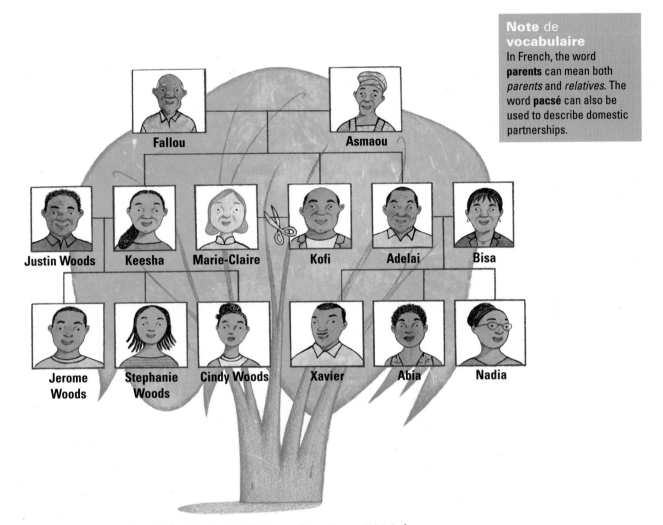

La famille d'Adelai Ndono (le père d'Abia)

Vocabulaire complémentaire

le/la conjoint(e) / partenaire *significant other / domestic partner*
la famille proche *immediate family*
la famille élargie *extended family*
le beau-fils *stepson, son-in-law*
la belle-fille *stepdaughter, daughter-in-law*
l'animal *(m.)* **domestique** *pet*
le chien *dog*
le chat *cat*

célibataire *single*
marié(e) *married*
divorcé(e) *divorced*
décédé(e) *deceased*
veuf / veuve *widower / widow*

La famille élargie *(Extended family)*

Fallou est **le grand-père** d'Abia.

Asmaou est **la grand-mère** d'Abia.

Fallou et Asmaou sont **les grands-parents** d'Abia.

Keesha est **la tante** d'Abia.

Kofi est **l'oncle** d'Abia.

Justin Woods est **le beau-frère** d'Adelai.

Bisa est **la belle-sœur** de Keesha.

Jerome est **le cousin** d'Abia.

Stephanie et Cindy sont **les cousines** d'Abia.

Fallou est **le beau-père** de Justin Woods.

Asmaou est **la belle-mère** de Justin Woods.

ACTIVITÉ A La famille d'Abia—la famille proche Regardez le dessin
CD1-37 *(drawing)* de la famille d'Abia. Vous allez entendre des descriptions. Pour chaque
description, indiquez si c'est vrai ou faux et corrigez les phrases fausses.

1. 2. 3. 4. 5. 6. 7. 8.

ACTIVITÉ B La famille d'Adelai Ndono—la famille élargie d'Abia
Complétez les phrases suivantes à propos de la famille élargie d'Abia.

1. Xavier est _____ d'Adelai.

2. Bisa est _____ de Keesha.

3. Justin est _____ d'Adelai.

4. Jerome, Stephanie et Cindy sont _____ de Justin et Keesha.

5. Abia et Nadia sont _____ d'Adelai et de Bisa.

6. Kofi et Adelai sont _____ de Jerome, Stephanie et Cindy.

7. Bisa est _____ de Jerome, Stephanie et Cindy.

8. Jerome est _____ d'Abia.

9. Asmaou est _____ d'Abia.

10. Fallou est _____ de Bisa.

ACTIVITÉ C Qui dans la famille d'Abia…? Répondez à chaque *(each)*
question avec une phrase complète.

Qui dans la famille d'Abia est / sont...

1. divorcé(s)?

2. célibataire(s)?

3. décédé(s)?

4. veuf(s)?

5. marié(s)?

6. un animal domestique?

ACTIVITÉ D La famille d'Abia

Préparez un paragraphe de 5–6 phrases pour
décrire la famille d'Abia. **SUGGESTIONS:** D'où
vient sa famille? Combien d'enfants est-ce qu'il
y a dans sa famille? Combien de frères et sœurs
est-ce qu'Abia a? Et combien de cousin(e)s?
Quels membres de la famille sont mariés?
divorcés?

© Heinle/Cengage Learning

ACTIVITÉ E Votre famille

Étape 1. Parlez de votre famille avec un(e) camarade de classe. Vous pouvez
utiliser l'Activité D comme modèle.

Étape 2. Posez des questions à votre camarade pour en savoir plus *(to find out more)* sur sa famille.

Questions possibles

Comment s'appelle X?   X est marié(e)?   X est célibataire?

X a des enfants?   Il/Elle a des animaux domestiques?

ACTIVITÉ F Familles célèbres

Étape 1. Connaissez-vous *(Do you know)* des familles célèbres? Créez des phrases pour décrire la famille des personnes suivantes.

Modèle: Carla Bruni-Sarkozy

> **Carla Bruni-Sarkozy est la femme de Nicolas Sarkozy. C'est la fille d'Alberto Bruni. C'est la sœur de Valeria Bruni.**

1. le Prince Charles
2. Jeb Bush
3. Jenna et Barbara Bush
4. Arnold Schwarzenegger

5. Sasha Obama
6. Hillary Clinton
7. Janet et LaToya Jackson
8. Bart et Lisa Simpson

Étape 2. Choisissez *(Choose)* une personne célèbre et écrivez un portrait de cette *(this)* personne. **SUGGESTIONS:** Cette personne est de quel pays? Où habite cette personne? Qui sont ses parents et ses frères et sœurs? Il/Elle est marié(e), célibataire ou divorcé(e)? Il/Elle a des enfants?

David & Valérie DOUILLET
NOTRE GRANDE FAMILLE
Histoire d'une tribu recomposée

© Michel Lafon Publishing, 2007

Un mot sur la culture

La famille recomposée

Les familles recomposées sont devenues ordinaires et acceptées en France. Le terme désigne une famille dans laquelle° des enfants viennent d'une union précédente des parents. Une autre expression pour «famille recomposée» est «famille patchwork». Dans une famille patchwork, il est normal d'avoir un demi-frère ou une demi-sœur et un beau-père ou une belle-mère. David Douillet, un judoka français qui a obtenu la médaille d'or aux Jeux Olympiques (en 1996 et 2000), est un exemple. Il a écrit un livre avec sa femme Valérie à propos de leur famille.

dans laquelle *in which*

À noter | Ces termes ont deux sens: beau-père *(stepfather* or *father-in-law)* et belle-mère *(stepmother* or *mother-in-law)*.

- Est-ce que les familles recomposées sont acceptées dans votre culture?
- Vous connaissez des familles recomposées célèbres?

Pour parler des familles

Les adjectifs possessifs / Les adjectifs démonstratifs

DU FILM *LIAISONS*

Un coup d'œil sur la grammaire

Look at these photos from the film *Liaisons* and their captions. Note the words used to express ownership.

© Heinle/Cengage Learning

CLAIRE Et elle? Comment va-t-elle?

INFIRMIÈRE (NURSE) Elle va mieux ces jours-ci. Elle est dans **sa** chambre. Allez la voir.

© Heinle/Cengage Learning

SIMONE C'est toi, Claire? Ce n'est pas une de **mes** hallucinations?

What do you think the following expressions mean?

1. **sa** chambre
   a. my room
   b. your room
   c. her room
2. **mes** hallucinations
   a. my hallucinations
   b. your hallucinations
   c. her hallucinations

Les adjectifs possessifs

In French, possessive adjectives must agree both in gender and number with the nouns they modify, *not* with the person(s) who own(s) the nouns.

Voici **mon** père et **ma** mère.		*Here are **my** father and **my** mother.*
Mes parents vivent en France.		***My** parents live in France.*

masculine singular	feminine singular	plural	
mon	ma	mes	*my*
ton	ta	tes	*your (fam. & sing.)*
son	sa	ses	*his/her/its*
notre	notre	nos	*our*
votre	votre	vos	*your (form. or pl.)*
leur	leur	leurs	*their*

⋯ The masculine singular forms **mon, ton,** and **son** are also used with feminine singular nouns if those nouns begin with a vowel sound.

Mon amie va à Québec.	***My*** *friend is going to Quebec.*
Ton étudiante est ici.	***Your*** *student is here.*
Son école est fermée.	***His/Her*** *school is closed.*

⋯ **Notre, votre,** and **leur** are used for both masculine and feminine singular nouns.

Notre mère s'appelle Aline.	***Our*** *mother's name is Aline.*
Votre père est beau.	***Your*** *father is handsome.*
Leur voiture est belle.	***Their*** *car is beautiful.*

⋯ Note that **sa, son,** and **ses** can mean either *his, her,* or *its.* The context usually makes the meaning clear.

Tom adore **son** frère.	*Tom loves **his** brother.*
Anne adore **son** frère aussi.	*Anne loves **her** brother too.*
Sarah vient avec **sa** sœur.	*Sarah is coming with **her** sister.*
Pierre vient avec **sa** cousine.	*Pierre is coming with **his** cousin.*
Salima adore **ses** amis.	*Salima loves **her** friends.*
Marc adore **ses** amis.	*Marc loves **his** friends.*

Les adjectifs démonstratifs

⋯ Demonstrative adjectives *(this, that, those, these)* allow you to be more specific when you identify or describe things. Like possessive adjectives, demonstrative adjectives in French must agree in gender and number with the nouns they modify.

masc. sing.	masc. sing. before a vowel sound	fem. sing.	masc./fem. plural
ce livre	**cet** étudiant	**cette** fille	**ces** enfants
		cette étudiante	

Ce garçon est mon neveu.	***This*** *boy is my nephew.*
Cet homme est mon oncle.	***This*** *man is my uncle.*
Cette étudiante est ma nièce.	***This*** *student is my niece.*
Ces filles sont mes cousines.	***These/Those*** *girls are my cousins.*

⋯ To be more precise, **-ci** and **-là** may be added to the noun to indicate *here* (close by) and *there* (farther away), respectively.

Cette fille**-ci** est ma nièce.	***This*** *girl **(over here)** is my niece.*
Ce garçon**-là** est mon neveu.	***That*** *boy **(over there)** is my nephew.*
J'aime **cette** photo**-ci**.	*I like **this** photo **(here)**.*
Il préfère **ces** stylos**-là**.	*He prefers **those** pens **(over there)**.*

Liaisons musicales

© Vittorio Zunino Celotto/ Getty Images

Carla Bruni-Sarkozy, la femme de Nicolas Sarkozy, est une chanteuse française. Sa chanson, *L'amoureuse* (2008) est dédiée *(dedicated)* à son mari. Trouvez une vidéo de la chanson sur Internet. 🌐

🔊 **ACTIVITÉ G Vrai ou faux? Les possessions de notre classe de**
CD1-38 **français** Vous allez entendre *(hear)* des phrases. Pour chaque *(each)* phrase,
indiquez si c'est vrai ou faux.

1.　　　2.　　　3.　　　4.　　　5.

ACTIVITÉ H Les photos de famille Un étudiant à l'Université McGill vous
montre *(shows)* ses photos de famille. Complétez ses descriptions.

1. Voici **ma**…	a. mère	b. père	c. parents
2. Et voici **mon**…	a. mère	b. père	c. parents
3. Ici, ce sont **mes**…	a. tante	b. sœur	c. frères
4. Ils aiment bien **leurs**…	a. sœur	b. oncle	c. parents
5. Je n'aime pas **cette**…	a. enfant	b. fille	c. garçon
6. C'est **notre**…	a. cousins	b. cousine	c. oncles
7. J'aime bien **ces**…	a. enfants	b. garçon	c. fille
8. Ce sont **nos**...	a. neveux	b. nièce	c. cousin

ACTIVITÉ I Qui le dit? Un professeur ou un(e) étudiant(e)? Qui dit
ces phrases? Un professeur? Un(e) étudiant(e)? Les deux *(Both)*? Personne *(Nobody)*?

1. J'aime bien **cette** université.　　3. J'aime bien **ce** cours de français.

2. J'aime bien **cette** salle de classe-**ci**.　　4. J'aime bien **ces** étudiant(e)s-**là**.

ACTIVITÉ J Claire ou Alexis?

Étape 1. Décidez si ces descriptions des
personnages du film *Liaisons* décrivent
(describe) Claire, Alexis ou les deux.

© Heinle/Cengage Learning

	Claire	Alexis	Les deux
1. **Ses** cheveux sont courts.	☐	☐	☐
2. **Sa** langue maternelle, c'est le français.	☐	☐	☐
3. **Sa** meilleure amie est Abia.	☐	☐	☐
4. **Son** accent est français.	☐	☐	☐
5. **Son** nom de famille est Gagner.	☐	☐	☐
6. **Ses** cours sont à l'Université McGill.	☐	☐	☐

Étape 2. Et toi? Répondez aux questions.

1. **Tes** cheveux sont courts ou longs?

2. Quelle est **ta** langue maternelle?

3. Qui est **ton/ta** meilleur(e) ami(e)?

4. Quel est **ton** nom de famille?

ACTIVITÉ K Connaissez-vous bien l'Université McGill?

Étape 1. Voici des phrases sur les étudiants ou les professeurs de l'Université McGill. Est-ce que chaque phrase est vraie ou fausse? Corrigez les phrases fausses.

	Vrai	Faux
1. **Leur** université est grande. McGill a environ 31 000 étudiants.	☐	☐
2. **Leur** campus est dans le centre-ville de Québec.	☐	☐
3. **Leurs** étudiants parlent anglais et français.	☐	☐
4. 20% de **leurs** étudiants sont francophones.	☐	☐

Étape 2. Avec un(e) camarade, préparez des phrases pour décrire **votre** université.

Modèle: Notre université est grande aussi...

ACTIVITÉ L Vos préférences

Étape 1. Répondez aux questions et écrivez vos réponses dans la colonne **Moi**. Ensuite, trouvez un(e) partenaire. Posez ces questions à votre partenaire. Écrivez ses réponses.

	Moi	Mon/Ma partenaire
1. Quel est **ton** cours préféré?	_____	_____
2. Quel est **ton** film préféré?	_____	_____
3. Quelle est **ta** voiture préférée?	_____	_____
4. Quelle est **ta** boisson *(drink)* préférée?	_____	_____
5. Quels sont **tes** restaurants préférés?	_____	_____
6. Quelles sont **tes** villes préférées?	_____	_____

Étape 2. Préparez 3 à 4 phrases pour décrire les préférences de votre camarade et partagez-les *(share them)* avec la classe.

La parole est à vous!

Est-ce que la famille moderne est en évolution?

On dit que la famille moderne est en train de changer de définition et de structure. La famille est donc différente aujourd'hui. Qu'en pensez-vous? Quelle est la conception de la famille aujourd'hui?

- Marie-Ange de Québec (Canada): «La famille, c'est toujours les parents, les enfants, les grands-parents, les tantes, les oncles et les cousins. Mais on se voit° de moins en moins°. Peut-être juste une fois° par an.»

- François expatrié à New York (USA): «Je ne sais pas. J'aurais dit° que la famille, c'est les parents et les enfants. Mais maintenant que je suis aux États-Unis et que mes parents sont en France, je dirais° que la famille, c'est les amis.»

se voit *sees each other* **de moins en moins** *less and less* **une fois** *once* **aurais dit** *would have said* **dirais** *would say*

Et vous? Qu'en pensez-vous?

1. Quelle est votre conception de la famille aujourd'hui?

2. Est-ce que la famille moderne est en évolution?

Liaisons musicales

© Robert Wagenhoffer/CP Images

Dans les années soixante-dix, le chanteur québécois Richard Séguin a formé avec sa sœur jumelle *(twin)* Marie-Claire le duo Les Séguin. Leur premier album *Séguin* (1973) est un mélange *(mix)* de folk-rock et d'influences amérindiennes. Aujourd'hui, Richard et Marie-Claire sont deux artistes solos très populaires au Québec. Visitez le site officiel de Richard Séguin sur Internet. 🌐

Les traits **physiques**

Physical traits

La famille Dubois

 Vocabulaire complémentaire

les cheveux noirs *black hair*	**chauve** *bald*
les cheveux ondulés *wavy hair*	**laid(e)** *ugly*
les cheveux roux *red hair*	**maigre** *scrawny, skinny*
un(e) blond(e) *a blond*	**mince** *thin, slender, slim*
un roux / une rousse *a redhead*	**musclé(e)** *muscular*

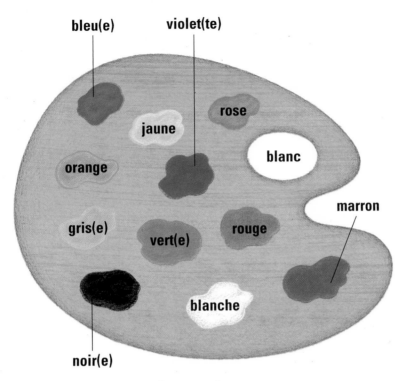

bleu(e) violet(te)

rose

jaune

blanc

orange

marron

gris(e)

vert(e) rouge

blanche

noir(e)

Les couleurs

🔊
CD1-39
ACTIVITÉ A C'est qui? Regardez bien la photo de la famille Dubois et répondez aux questions que vous entendez *(hear)*.

1.　　2.　　3.　　4.　　5.　　6.　　7.　　8.

🔊
CD1-40
ACTIVITÉ B Claire ou Abia? Indiquez si chaque phrase que vous entendez décrit **a) Claire** du film *Liaisons* ou **b) Abia.**

1.　　2.　　3.　　4.

© Heinle/Cengage Learning

ACTIVITÉ C Les traits physiques et les nationalités À quelles nationalités associez-vous ces traits physiques?

1. Ils sont très **grands**.	a. les Japonais	b. les Allemands
2. Ils ont des **taches de rousseur**.	a. les Irlandais	b. les Chinois
3. Elles sont très **minces**.	a. les Françaises	b. les Américaines
4. Elles ont les **cheveux blonds**.	a. les Suisses	b. les Sénégalaises
5. Ils ont **les yeux bleus**.	a. les Américains	b. les Vietnamiens

◄)) **ACTIVITÉ D** **Connaissez-vous bien les drapeaux du monde?** Vous
CD1-41 allez entendre *(hear)* une série de couleurs. Avec quel drapeau *(flag)* associez-vous
ces couleurs?

1. a. le drapeau québécois
   b. le drapeau français
2. a. le drapeau chinois
   b. le drapeau ivoirien
3. a. le drapeau italien
   b. le drapeau canadien
4. a. le drapeau américain
   b. le drapeau belge

© Terra Images/Photolibrary

✎ **ACTIVITÉ E** **Dans la classe: C'est qui?** Vous allez écrire une description
d'un(e) de vos camarades de classe. Ensuite *(Then)*, vos camarades vont deviner
(guess) qui c'est. Si vos camarades ne peuvent pas *(cannot)* deviner qui c'est, ils vont
vous poser *(ask you)* des questions.

Modèle: É1: **Il a les yeux verts. Il a les cheveux courts et bruns. C'est qui?**
　　　　　É2: **Je ne sais pas. Il est petit ou grand?**
　　　　　É1: **Il est grand.**
　　　　　É3: **C'est Mark?**
　　　　　É1: **Oui, c'est Mark.**

ACTIVITÉ F **À qui ressemblez-vous dans votre famille?**

Étape 1. Regardez votre partenaire et faites une liste de ses traits physiques.
Écrivez ces traits dans la première colonne.

Modèle: les yeux bleus

Les traits physiques de mon/ma partenaire	mère	père	les deux	autre parent	personne
1. _____	☐	☐	☐	☐	☐
2. _____	☐	☐	☐	☐	☐
3. _____	☐	☐	☐	☐	☐
4. _____	☐	☐	☐	☐	☐

Étape 2. Interviewez votre partenaire pour déterminer si les traits physiques sur
votre liste semblent *(seem)* venir de sa mère, de son père, des deux, d'un autre parent
ou de personne *(nobody)* dans sa famille. Cochez (✓) ses réponses.

Étape 3. D'après les réponses à l'Étape 2, comment décririez-vous *(would you
describe)* votre partenaire?
Mon/Ma partenaire…

- ressemble plus à sa mère.
- ressemble plus à son père.
- ressemble à sa mère et à son père.
- ressemble à un autre parent.
- ne ressemble à personne dans sa famille.

Un mot sur la culture

Cyrano de Bergerac

© Douglas Pearson/Corbis

Voici un célèbre trait physique dans la culture française: le grand et long nez de Cyrano, le personnage principal dans *Cyrano de Bergerac* (pièce de théâtre d'Edmond Rostand, 1897). Cyrano a peur de déclarer son amour à Roxane parce qu'il est laid. Cyrano aime beaucoup jouer avec la langue française comme dans cette citation: «Tous les mots° sont fins° quand la moustache est fine°». Il y a beaucoup d'expressions en français qui mentionnent des traits physiques.

mots *words* **fins** *witty* **fine** *thin*

- Que veulent dire ces expressions?

1. «mon œil»	a. *under someone's very nose*
2. «au nez et à la barbe de quelqu'un»	b. *by word of mouth*
3. «de bouche à oreille»	c. *no way*

 Liaisons avec les mots et les sons

CD1-42

Les voyelles orales et les voyelles nasales

French vowel sounds mainly fall into two categories: oral and nasal vowels. When forming oral vowels, air escapes through the mouth. When forming nasal vowels, air is concentrated in the nose and the **n** and **m** sounds are not pronounced. Put your hand under your nose and notice the sensations when you pronounce these words.

Oral Vowels	Nasal Vowels	Oral Vowels	Nasal Vowels
beau	bon	mot	mon
leur	lent	ta	temps
vie	vin	fait	fin
vous	vont	nos	nom

An oral vowel sound that does not exist in English is the French **u** sound. To make this sound, place the tip of your tongue behind your lower teeth, round your lips like you are going to whistle and say *ee*.

d**u**	ét**u**des	m**u**sclé	ond**u**lé	t**u**	**u**ne

Pratique A. Écoutez bien et encerclez le mot *(word)* que vous entendez *(hear)*.

1. les / lent   **2.** mot / mon   **3.** vos / vont   **4.** allez / allons   **5.** tes / temps   **6.** une / un

Pratique B. Écoutez et répétez ces répliques du film *Liaisons* à haute voix *(aloud)*. Encerclez toutes les voyelles nasales et soulignez *(underline)* toutes les voyelles orales.

CLAIRE Ça va, mon chat? Tu as faim?

CLAIRE On a payé une réservation pour deux nuits à mon nom à Québec.

À vos stylos! C'est l'heure de la dictée!

CD1-43   Vous allez entendre quatre phrases. Écoutez bien. Vous allez entendre les phrases une deuxième fois. Écrivez les phrases.

Sujet Une scène de la Séquence 2 du film *Liaisons*

Pour parler de nos familles et de nos traits physiques

La position des adjectifs / Les verbes **sortir, partir, dormir** et **sentir**

DU FILM *LIAISONS*

Un coup d'œil sur la grammaire

© Heinle/Cengage Learning

À l'Hôtel Delta, Claire rencontre un client **intéressant**: un **bel** homme **charmant** aux cheveux **blonds**. Il s'appelle Alexis Prévost.

Look at this photo from the film *Liaisons* and its caption, paying special attention to the adjectives.

Now answer these questions about the position of the adjectives.

1. Which adjectives follow the nouns they modify?
2. Which adjective precedes the noun it modifies?

Les adjectifs prénominaux

•‥‥» In **Chapitre préliminaire** and **Chapitre 1,** you learned that adjectives in French agree in gender and number with the nouns they modify and that they are usually placed after the noun.

Claire est une femme **intelligente.**   Abia a les cheveux **noirs.**

•‥‥» There are several adjectives used to describe people or things that are usually placed *before* the noun. Because they go before the noun, these adjectives are called prenominal adjectives or **adjectifs prénominaux** in French.

Les adjectifs prénominaux		
Masculine	**Feminine**	
C'est un **petit** quartier *(neighborhood)*.	C'est une **petite** ville.	*small*
C'est un **grand** quartier.	C'est une **grande** ville.	*big, tall, great*
C'est un **joli** quartier.	C'est une **jolie** ville.	*pretty*
C'est un **bon** quartier.	C'est une **bonne** ville.	*good*
C'est un **mauvais** quartier.	C'est une **mauvaise** ville.	*bad*
C'est un **jeune** homme.	C'est une **jeune** femme.	*young*

Note de grammaire

Note that **jeune** is used with both masculine and feminine nouns.

•‥‥» **Grand** can mean *big, tall,* or *honorable* depending on its placement.

C'est un homme **grand.**   *That's a **tall** man.*

C'est un **grand** homme.   *That's a **great** man.*

♦ Three prenominal adjectives have different masculine singular forms when they precede consonants and vowels or a mute *h* (**h muet**).

Masculine before a consonant	Masculine before a vowel or *h* muet	Feminine	
un **beau** quartier	un **bel** appartement	une **belle** ville	*beautiful*
	un **bel** homme		*handsome*
un **nouveau** quartier	un **nouvel** appartement	une **nouvelle** ville	*new*
un **vieux** quartier	un **vieil** appartement	une **vieille** ville	*old*
	un **vieil** homme		

♦ When prenominal adjectives precede a plural noun, the plural indefinite article **des** usually becomes **de**. Note that some prenominal adjectives have irregular plural forms.

Masculine plural before a consonant	Masculine plural before a vowel or *h* muet	Feminine plural
de **beaux** quartiers	de **beaux** appartements	de **belles** villes
	de **beaux** hommes	
de **nouveaux** quartiers	de **nouveaux** appartements	de **nouvelles** villes
de **vieux** quartiers	de **vieux** hommes	de **vieilles** villes

Il y a **des** quartiers **intéressants** à Montréal.   *but*

Il y a **de beaux quartiers** à Montréal.

Il y a **de vieux appartements** dans mon quartier.

J'ai **de nouvelles lampes** dans mon nouvel appartement.

La bibliothèque a **de nouveaux livres.**

♦ Adjectives may also immediately follow the verb **être.**

Les quartiers à Montréal **sont beaux.**

Les appartements **sont vieux.**

L'homme aux yeux bleus **est beau,** n'est-ce pas?

Les verbes *dormir, partir, sentir* et *sortir*

♦ You have already studied several classes of verbs in French. There is a subset of verbs ending in **-ir**. These **-ir** verbs follow the same pattern.

dormir *(to sleep)*	
je **dors**	nous **dormons**
tu **dors**	vous **dormez**
il/elle/on **dort**	ils/elles **dorment**

partir *(to leave)*	
je **pars**	nous **partons**
tu **pars**	vous **partez**
il/elle/on **part**	ils/elles **partent**

Si vous y allez

© Brigitte MERLE/ Photolibrary

Si vous allez à Paris, visitez le quartier asiatique pour ses bons restaurants chinois, surtout pendant le nouvel an chinois.

Les verbes-clés

sentir *(to smell)*	
je **sens**	nous **sentons**
tu **sens**	vous **sentez**
il/elle/on **sent**	ils/elles **sentent**

sortir *(to go out)*	
je **sors**	nous **sortons**
tu **sors**	vous **sortez**
il/elle/on **sort**	ils/elles **sortent**

Mon frère **dort** beaucoup.

Papa, tu **pars** déjà?

Les cheveux de maman **sentent** bon.

Nous **sortons** souvent le samedi.

*My brother **sleeps** a lot.*

*Dad, you're **leaving** already?*

*Mom's hair **smells** good.*

*We **go out** often on Saturdays.*

🔊 **ACTIVITÉ** Ⓖ **Quel dessin?**

CD1-44

Étape 1. Vous allez entendre une description d'un dessin. Écoutez bien la description et choisissez le bon dessin.

1. a.   b.   2. a.   b.

3. a.   b.   4. a.   b.

5. a.   b.   6. a.   b.

Étape 2. Voici encore des descriptions de dessins. Regardez bien les adjectifs pour déterminer le bon objet dans le dessin.

1. Il y a **une vieille…**
   a. appartement   b. maison *(house)*   c. quartier

2. Ce sont **de nouvelles…**
   a. fenêtres   b. quartiers   c. instruments de musique

3. C'est **un nouvel**
   a. professeur   b. appartement   c. maison

4. Ce sont **de beaux…**
   a. femmes   b. hommes   c. homme

5. C'est **un vieux…**
   a. tableau   b. ordinateur   c. homme

6. C'est **un vieil…**
   a. stylo   b. table   c. ordinateur

7. Ce sont **de vieux…**
   a. amis   b. amies   c. dames

8. Ce sont **de nouveaux…**
   a. étudiantes   b. chaises   c. amis

ACTIVITÉ 🅗 Dans la maison de ma famille

Étape 1. Dans la maison de votre famille, les objets sont-ils pour la plupart *(mostly)* vieux ou nouveaux? Complétez les phrases suivantes avec la forme appropriée de l'adjectif **nouveau** ou **vieux**.

© Peter Horree / Alamy

Dans la maison de _____ [membre de la famille], il y a…

1. un _____ téléviseur.   **5.** de _____ lampes *(f.)*.

2. de _____ chaises.   **6.** un _____ réfrigérateur.

3. un _____ ordinateur.   **7.** de _____ assiettes *(f.) (plates)*.

4. un _____ bureau.   **8.** une _____ table.

Étape 2. Qu'avez-vous dans votre maison ou appartement? Complétez les phrases suivantes avec la forme appropriée de l'adjectif **nouveau** ou **vieux**.

1. J'ai un _____ téléviseur.   **5.** J'ai de _____ lampes.

2. J'ai de _____ chaises.   **6.** J'ai un _____ réfrigérateur.

3. J'ai un _____ ordinateur.   **7.** J'ai de _____ assiettes.

4. J'ai un _____ bureau.   **8.** J'ai une _____ table.

Conclusion En général, préférez-vous les objets dans votre maison ou appartement ou les objets dans la maison de votre famille?

ACTIVITÉ **I** **Portrait d'un membre de votre famille**

Étape 1. Vous allez faire une description d'un membre de votre famille pour un artiste qui va faire son portrait. Choisissez la personne et faites une liste d'adjectifs pour décrire son âge et ses traits physiques.

Membre de ma famille: _____   Son âge: _____

Les traits	**Les adjectifs**
les yeux	_____
le nez	_____
les oreilles *(f.) (ears)*	_____
les cheveux	_____
la bouche *(mouth)*	_____
le corps *(body)*	_____

Étape 2. Écrivez un paragraphe pour décrire ce membre de votre famille. Puis, lisez le paragraphe à un(e) camarade. Votre camarade est l'artiste qui va faire le portrait!

Modèle: **C'est mon grand-père. Il est vieux. Il a les yeux noirs et un petit nez,** etc.

Étape 3. Est-ce que le portrait ressemble au membre de la famille que vous avez décrit?

ACTIVITÉ **J** **Les odeurs**

Étape 1. Un article dans la revue *Châtelaine* dit que les odeurs peuvent évoquer des sentiments *(feelings)* différents pour des personnes différentes. Décrivez l'odeur des choses *(things)* suivantes. Complétez les phrases avec l'adverbe **bon** ou **mauvais.**

Modèle: Les fleurs sentent **bon.**

© Laurent / Yakou / Photo Researchers, Inc

1. Les roses **sentent** _____.
2. La campagne **sent** _____.
3. Le café **sent** _____.
4. La bière **sent** _____.
5. Les hôpitaux *(m.)* **sentent** _____.
6. Les bébés **sentent** _____.

Étape 2. Comparez vos réponses avec celles *(those)* d'un(e) camarade. Avez-vous écrit les mêmes choses ou avez-vous des réponses différentes? Est-ce que l'article avait raison?

Modèle: É1: **Comment sentent les roses?**
           É2: **D'après moi, les roses sentent mauvais. Et toi?**
           É1: **D'après moi, les roses sentent bon.**

Étape 1. Les familles et les adolescents des séries télévisées *(TV shows)* sont souvent stéréotypés. Lisez chaque description et cochez (✓) la période à laquelle elle correspond.

	Les années 1950	Le 21e siècle *(century)*
1. Les enfants **partent** pour l'école ensemble.	☐	☐
2. Les enfants **dorment** jusqu'à midi le week-end.	☐	☐
3. Les enfants **sortent** dans les bars le week-end.	☐	☐
4. La famille **sort** ensemble le vendredi soir.	☐	☐
5. Les garçons préfèrent les **jolies** filles **minces** aux **cheveux longs**.	☐	☐
6. Les filles préfèrent les **beaux** garçons **musclés**.	☐	☐

Étape 2. Posez ces questions à un(e) camarade pour savoir s'il/si elle est plutôt comme un(e) enfant des années 1950 ou un(e) enfant du 21e siècle.

1. Tu pars à l'université avec ton frère ou ta sœur?
2. Combien d'heures dors-tu chaque nuit?
3. Tu sors dans les bars le week-end?
4. Tu sors avec ta famille le week-end?
5. Penses-tu que les garçons préfèrent les jolies filles minces aux cheveux longs?
6. Penses-tu que les filles préfèrent les beaux garçons musclés?

Conclusion Mon/Ma camarade est plus comme un(e) enfant des années 1950 / du 21e siècle.

Quelle famille! (What a Family!) est une série télévisée québécoise des années 1950.

La parole est à vous!

Est-ce que la chirurgie esthétique est bonne ou mauvaise?

On dit que la chirurgie esthétique° est une vraie alternative pour la plupart des gens aujourd'hui. C'est une industrie en pleine expansion°. Qu'en pensez-vous? Est-ce que la chirurgie esthétique est bonne ou mauvaise?

- Christine de Basse-Terre (Guadeloupe): «La chirurgie esthétique facultative° est terrible! Pourquoi changer un trait physique? C'est votre héritage.»
- Marc expatrié à Los Angeles (USA): «C'est très bien! Si je peux rester plus beau et plus sexy quand je suis plus âgé, pourquoi pas? Il faut profiter de la vie!»

la chirurgie esthétique *cosmetic surgery* **en pleine expansion** *growing* **facultative** *elective*

Et vous? Qu'en pensez-vous?

1. Est-ce que la chirurgie esthétique est bonne ou mauvaise?
2. Est-elle un sujet à controverse?

Avant de visionner

ACTIVITÉ Ⓐ **Vous rappelez-vous?**

Vous rappelez-vous *(Do you remember)* ce qui s'est passé *(what happened)* à la Séquence 1 du film *Liaisons*? Pour chaque phrase, indiquez si c'est vrai ou faux.

	Vrai	Faux
1. Claire a reçu une enveloppe d'un homme mystérieux.	☐	☐
2. L'amie de Claire s'appelle Simone.	☐	☐
3. Claire trouve Alexis Prévost très beau.	☐	☐
4. Alexis Prévost avait besoin d'une brosse à dents *(toothbrush)*.	☐	☐

ACTIVITÉ Ⓑ **Un coup d'œil sur une scène** Voici une scène de la Séquence 2 du film *Liaisons* que vous allez regarder. Claire reçoit un appel *(phone call)* de son oncle. Choisissez *(Choose)* la lettre du mot qui correspond à chaque blanc *(blank)* dans le dialogue. Vous allez vérifier vos réponses plus tard.

> **Note** de vocabulaire
> OFF veut dire *(means)* **voix off** *(voice off screen)*.

MICHEL *(OFF)* C'est (1) _____ oncle Michel.

CLAIRE Michel! (2) _____ Je dormais. Je n'ai pas reconnu ta voix *(voice)*...

MICHEL *(OFF)* Claire, (3) _____. Tu dois aller à Québec.

CLAIRE Comment?

© Heinle/Cengage Learning

1. a. ta	b. ton	**3.** a. écoute	b. s'il te plaît
2. a. Ça va?	b. Pardon.		

Regarder la séquence

Vous allez regarder la Séquence 2 du film *Liaisons*. Utilisez le contexte pour comprendre les dialogues.

Après le visionnage

ACTIVITÉ Ⓒ **Vérifiez votre compréhension**

1. Qui a payé la réservation à l'hôtel Frontenac pour Claire?

2. L'oncle Michel a téléphoné à quelle heure?

3. Est-ce qu'Abia est contente que Claire veuille *(wants)* aller à Québec?

4. Qui est-ce que Claire voit *(sees)* à la fin de la Séquence 2?

ACTIVITÉ **D** **Avez-vous compris?** Relisez vos réponses dans l'Activité B. Avez-vous choisi *(choose)* les bons mots? Si nécessaire, regardez la scène encore une fois *(again)* pour vérifier vos réponses.

ACTIVITÉ **E** **Utilisez le contexte** Claire dit à Abia qu'elle va aller à Québec. Regardez bien les mots **en gras** *(bold)* et répondez aux questions.

ABIA Claire, cet homme qui te fait la réservation… c'est peut-être **(1) un meurtrier,** un psychopathe!

CLAIRE **(2) Ne dramatise pas,** Abi. […]

ABIA Et tu ne vas pas changer d'avis?

CLAIRE Non. Tu veux bien **(3) garder** Émile pour moi cette **(4) fin de semaine**?

© Heinle/Cengage Learning

1. Que veut dire le mot **meurtrier**?

2. **Dramatiser** veut dire *to dramatize.* Que veut dire l'expression **Ne dramatise pas**?

3. Le verbe **garder** normalement veut dire *to keep* en anglais. Mais dans le contexte de ce dialogue, **garder** a un sens différent. Dans ce contexte, que veut dire **garder**?

4. **Fin de semaine** est une expression québécoise. Que veut dire **fin de semaine**?

ACTIVITÉ **F** **Vos impressions** On voit encore une fois le personnage d'Alexis Prévost. Quelles sont vos impressions de Monsieur Prévost? Comment est-il physiquement? D'où vient-il? Quels adjectifs utiliseriez-vous *(would you use)* pour décrire sa personnalité? Écrivez 3 à 5 phrases pour décrire vos impressions. Partagez votre description avec un(e) camarade. Avez-vous les mêmes *(same)* impressions?

Liaisons avec la culture

La ville de Québec

La ville de Québec est la capitale nationale de la province du Québec, située sur les rives du fleuve Saint-Laurent. On dit **à Québec** et **de Québec** pour parler de la ville et **au Québec** et **du Québec** pour parler de la province. La ville est fondée en 1608 par l'explorateur français Samuel de Champlain et reste l'un des plus anciens territoires européens en Amérique du Nord. Elle est également la seule ville fortifiée en Amérique du Nord. Depuis 1985, elle figure sur la liste du patrimoine mondial établie par l'UNESCO. 95% de la population de Québec parle français comme langue maternelle. Chaque année, les touristes viennent à Québec pour profiter de son caractère européen et de son patrimoine français.

© Richard T. Nowitz/Corbis

LIAISONS CULTURELLES

Le monde francophone et ses origines

L'origine des noms de famille québécois

Saviez-vous que certains noms de famille sont particulièrement fréquents au Québec: Tremblay, Gagnon, Roy, Côté, Bouchard? Il y a des raisons historiques: ce sont les descendants des premiers Français qui ont émigré en Nouvelle-France. En 1540, l'explorateur Jacques Cartier a essayé° de fonder une colonie française en Amérique du Nord. Ces premières familles d'origine française ont eu beaucoup d'enfants. Avant 1960, la religion catholique a été très importante dans la société québécoise. Sous l'influence de l'Église catholique, les femmes avaient 8 à 12 enfants. Leurs patronymes ou noms de famille sont aujourd'hui les plus répandus° au Québec.

© Bettmann/Corbis

essayer *to try* **répandus** *widespread*

Vrai ou faux?

1. Tremblay, Gagnon, Roy, Côté et Bouchard sont les noms des familles riches au Québec.   V / F
2. Ces noms sont les noms des premiers Français qui sont arrivés en Nouvelle-France.   V / F
3. Avant 1960, la religion protestante était très importante.   V / F
4. Avant 1960, les femmes avaient beaucoup d'enfants.   V / F

Bienvenue chez les CH'TIS

KAD MERAD — DANY BOON

L'origine des différences linguistiques et culturelles en France

Bienvenue chez les Ch'tis (2008), réalisé par Dany Boon, est un grand succès commercial en France. Philippe Abrams, un habitant du sud de la France déménage dans le nord et habite avec les *Ch'tis*, les habitants de la région Nord-Pas-de-Calais qui parlent un dialecte francais qui s'appelle le «ch'ti». Philippe trouve les Ch'tis froids, incultes° et arriérés° mais, petit à petit, il apprécie ses nouveaux amis du nord. Ces différences linguistiques et culturelles trouvent leurs origines dans les différentes régions de la France. La France est divisée en vingt-six régions différentes (dont vingt-deux en France métropolitaine), chacune° avec sa cuisine, son histoire, son climat, son dialecte et parfois sa langue distincte.

incultes *uneducated* **arriérés** *backwards* **chacune** *each*

Vrai ou faux?

1. Les Ch'tis sont les habitants du sud de la France.   V / F
2. Le ch'ti est un dialecte français.   V / F
3. La France a beaucoup de régions, chacune avec sa culture distincte.   V / F

Les origines littéraires aux Antilles

La littérature francophone aux Antilles a connu un grand développement après la Seconde Guerre mondiale°. Elle trouve ses origines dans les traditions littéraires françaises, dans les cultures locales et dans la langue française et les langues créoles. Deux thèmes principaux de cette littérature sont l'héritage culturel et la recherche° de l'identité. Une écrivaine de littérature antillaise très importante—que l'on appelle parfois «la Grande Dame de la littérature antillaise»—s'appelle Maryse Condé. Elle vient de Pointe-à-Pitre en Guadeloupe. Dans ses écrits, elle explore la question du panafricanisme ou de l'unification des Africains et de leurs descendants en dehors de l'Afrique.

la Seconde Guerre mondiale *WWII* **la recherche** *the search*

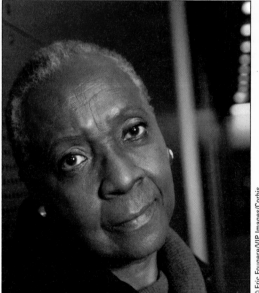

Vrai ou faux?

1. La littérature antillaise a ses origines dans la littérature française.   V / F
2. Maryse Condé vient de Martinique.   V / F
3. Un thème important pour Condé est l'unification des Africains en Afrique.   V / F

© Sandro Campardo/epa/Corbis

Un humoriste d'origine franco-maghrébine

Il y a beaucoup de Français aujourd'hui qui ont un héritage franco-maghrébin. Ils ont des racines dans la culture française et dans la culture d'un pays du Maghreb, c'est-à-dire le Maroc, l'Algérie ou la Tunisie. Ils ont des parents ou des grands-parents qui sont immigrés ou ils sont eux-mêmes° immigrés. Un homme très fier de ses origines franco-maghrébines est l'humoriste Jamel Debbouze. Il est né à Paris en 1975 de parents d'origine marocaine. Debbouze est humoriste, acteur et producteur. Dans ses sketches, il aime se moquer des° différences culturelles entre les Français, les Nord-Africains et les Français nés de parents immigrés du Maghreb. Par exemple, il plaisante° souvent sur le sujet des différences culinaires, musicales, linguistiques et religieuses entre la France et le Maroc.

eux-mêmes *themselves* **se moquer des** *to make fun of*
plaisante *jokes*

Compréhension

1. Nommez un pays du Maghreb.

2. Les parents de Jamel Debbouze sont originaires de quel pays?

3. Qu'est-ce que Debbouze fait comme métier *(job)*?

4. De quels sujets est-ce que Debbouze aime se moquer dans ses sketches?

🌐 Activités Internet

- Faites une recherche sur Internet avec les mots-clés *(key words)* «nom de famille Tremblay» pour savoir *(to know)* combien de personnes en France ont le nom Tremblay et pour connaître l'origine du nom et sa signification.

- Faites une recherche sur Internet avec les mots-clés «26 régions françaises» pour trouver les 26 régions de la France. Préparez un petit reportage sur une région.

- Faites une recherche sur Internet avec les mots-clés «littérature antillaise» pour trouver les noms d'autres écrivains de la littérature antillaise francophone. Choisissez un(e) écrivain(e) et cherchez des informations sur lui/elle.

- Cherchez le nom d'une autre célébrité franco-maghrébine sur Internet. Préparez une petite biographie sur cette célébrité.

PARTIE 1

LES CONTINENTS ET LES PAYS

le continent	*continent*
le pays	*country*
l'Afrique *(f.)* du Nord	*North Africa*
l'Afrique de l'Ouest	*West Africa*
l'Allemagne *(f.)*	*Germany*
l'Amérique *(f.)* du Nord	*North America*
l'Amérique du Sud	*South America*
l'Angleterre *(f.)*	*England*
l'Asie *(f.)*	*Asia*
la Belgique	*Belgium*
le Brésil	*Brazil*
le Canada	*Canada*
la Chine	*China*
la Côte d'Ivoire	*Ivory Coast*
l'Espagne *(f.)*	*Spain*
les États-Unis *(m. pl.)*	*United States*
l'Europe *(f.)* de l'Est	*Eastern Europe*
l'Europe de l'Ouest	*Western Europe*
la France	*France*
l'Irlande *(f.)*	*Ireland*
l'Italie *(f.)*	*Italy*
le Japon	*Japan*
le Maroc	*Morocco*
le Mexique	*Mexico*
le Québec	*Quebec*
la Roumanie	*Romania*
la Russie	*Russia*
le Sénégal	*Senegal*
la Suisse	*Switzerland*
la Tunisie	*Tunisia*
le Viêt Nam	*Vietnam*

LES ÉTATS DES ÉTATS-UNIS

l'Alabama *(m.)*	l'Iowa *(m.)*
l'Alaska *(m.)*	le Kansas
l'Arizona *(m.)*	le Kentucky
l'Arkansas *(m.)*	la Louisiane
la Californie	le Maine
la Caroline du Nord	le Maryland
la Caroline du Sud	le Massachusetts
le Colorado	le Michigan
le Connecticut	le Minnesota
le Dakota du Nord	le Mississippi
le Dakota du Sud	le Missouri
le Delaware	le Montana
l'état *(m.)* de New York	le Nebraska
l'état *(m.)* de Washington	le Nevada
la Floride	le New Hampshire
la Géorgie	le New Jersey
Hawaii (Hawaï)	le Nouveau-Mexique
l'Idaho *(m.)*	l'Ohio *(m.)*
l'Illinois *(m.)*	l'Oklahoma *(m.)*
l'Indiana *(m.)*	l'Oregon *(m.)*

la Pennsylvanie	
le Rhode Island	
le Tennessee	
le Texas	
l'Utah *(m.)*	
le Vermont	
la Virginie	
la Virginie Occidentale	
le Wisconsin	
le Wyoming	

LES NATIONALITÉS

les Allemand(e)s	*Germans*
les Américain(e)s	*Americans*
les Anglais(es)	*British*
les Belges	*Belgians*
les Brésiliens / Brésiliennes	*Brazilians*
les Canadiens / Canadiennes	*Canadians*
les Chinois(es)	*Chinese*
les Espagnol(e)s	*Spaniards*
les Français(es)	*French*
les Irlandais(es)	*Irish*
les Italiens / Italiennes	*Italians*
les Ivoiriens / Ivoiriennes	*of the Ivory Coast*
les Japonais(es)	*Japanese*
les Marocain(e)s	*Moroccans*
les Mexicain(e)s	*Mexicans*
les Québécois(es)	*Quebeckers*
les Roumain(e)s	*Romanians*
les Russes	*Russians*
les Sénégalais(es)	*Senegalese*
les Suisses	*Swiss*
les Tunisiens / Tunisiennes	*Tunisians*
les Vietnamiens / Vietnamiennes	*Vietnamese*

VERBES

devenir	*to become*
venir / venir de	*to come / to have just done something*

LES PRÉPOSITIONS

à	*to, in*
au(x)	*to, in*
de / du	*from*
en	*to, in*

PARTIE 2

LA FAMILLE

le beau-fils	*stepson, son-in-law*
le beau-frère	*brother-in-law, stepbrother*
le beau-père	*father-in-law, stepfather*
la belle-fille	*stepdaughter, daughter-in-law*

la belle-mère	mother-in-law, stepmother
la belle-sœur	sister-in-law, stepsister
le / la conjoint(e), partenaire	significant other, (domestic) partner
le / la cousin(e)	cousin
les enfants (m.)	children
la famille élargie	extended family
la famille proche	immediate family
la femme	wife, woman
la fille	daughter, girl
le fils	son
le frère	brother
la grand-mère	grandmother
les grands-parents (m.)	grandparents
le grand-père	grandfather
le mari	husband
la mère	mother
le neveu	nephew
la nièce	niece
l'oncle (m.)	uncle
les parents (m.)	parents, relatives
le père	father
la petite-fille	granddaughter
le petit-fils	grandson
la sœur	sister
la tante	aunt
l'animal (m.) domestique	pet
le chat	cat
le chien	dog
célibataire	single
décédé(e)	deceased
divorcé(e)	divorced
marié(e)	married
veuf / veuve	widower / widow

LES ADJECTIFS POSSESSIFS

ma/mon/mes	my
ta/ton/tes (fam. & sing.)	your
sa/son/ses	his/her/its
notre/nos	our
votre/vos (formal sing. or pl.)	your
leur/leurs	their

LES ADJECTIFS DÉMONSTRATIFS

ce (m. sing.)	this
cet (m. sing. before vowel)	this
cette (f. sing.)	this
ces	these, those

PARTIE 3

LES TRAITS PHYSIQUES

une barbe	beard
un(e) blond(e)	a blond
les cheveux (m.) blonds	blond hair
les cheveux bouclés / frisés	curly hair
les cheveux bruns	brown hair
les cheveux courts	short hair
les cheveux longs et raides	long straight hair
les cheveux noirs	black hair
les cheveux ondulés	wavy hair
les cheveux roux	red hair
un grand nez	a big nose
un roux / une rousse	a redhead
les taches (f.) de rousseur	freckles
les yeux (m.) bleus	blue eyes
les yeux marron	brown eyes
les yeux verts	green eyes
chauve	bald
gros / grosse	fat
laid(e)	ugly
maigre	skinny, scrawny
mince	slim, lean, slender
musclé(e)	muscular

LES COULEURS

blanc / blanche	white
bleu(e)	blue
gris(e)	grey
jaune	yellow
marron	brown
noir(e)	black
orange	orange
rose	pink
rouge	red
vert(e)	green
violet(te)	violet, purple

VERBES

dormir	to sleep
partir	to leave
sentir	to smell
sortir	to go out

LES ADJECTIFS

beau / bel / belle	handsome, beautiful
bon / bonne	good
grand(e)	big, tall
jeune	young
joli(e)	pretty
mauvais(e)	bad
nouveau / nouvel / nouvelle	new
petit(e)	small, short
vieux / vieil / vieille	old

La littérature dans la francophonie

Victor Hugo

Né à Besançon, Victor Hugo (1802–1885) est un poète,
écrivain, dramaturge°, homme politique, académicien
et intellectuel engagé français. Hugo occupe une place
importante dans l'histoire des lettres françaises et est
considéré comme l'un des plus° importants écrivains
romantiques de la langue française. Cet écrivain est aussi
un romancier° du peuple. Ses succès mondiaux° *Notre-
Dame de Paris* (1831) et *Les Misérables* (1862) restent encore
populaires aujourd'hui.

dramaturge *playwright* **l'un des plus** *one of the most* **romancier** *novelist* **mondiaux**
worldwide

© Danny Martindale/WireImage/Getty Images

© Ginet - Drin/SoFood Collection/Photolibrary

La «madeleine de Proust»

Une madeleine est un petit
gâteau° traditionnel lorrain
en forme de coquillage°. Ces
gâteaux sont très populaires en France en partie° parce que
dans son œuvre° de sept volumes *À la recherche du temps
perdu* (1913–1927), Marcel Proust utilise une madeleine
comme déclencheur° de souvenirs°. Dans ce roman, quand
le narrateur mange une madeleine, il revit° une scène de
son enfance°. À partir de° cette simple madeleine, Proust
écrit des pages et des pages… La «madeleine de Proust»
est aujourd'hui une métaphore pour parler des souvenirs
du passé.

petit gâteau *cookie* **coquillage** *seashell* **en partie** *in part* **œuvre** *work* **déclencheur** *trigger*
souvenirs *memories* **revit** *relives* **enfance** *childhood* **À partir de** *From*

Un mouvement littéraire et culturel: la créolité

En 1989, trois écrivains martiniquais—Jean Bernabé,
Raphaël Confiant et Patrick Chamoiseau—ont publié
l'*Éloge de la créolité*. Le but° de ce mouvement littéraire
est de reconnaître° l'hybridité ou le métissage culturel° des
Antilles, dont la population est d'origine africaine, asiatique
et européenne. La créolité a eu une influence considérable
dans le monde francophone. Ce mouvement constitue un
reflet de la diversité ethnique, culturelle et linguistique de la
Martinique et de la Guadeloupe, deux départements français
d'outre-mer°.

but *purpose* **reconnaître** *recognize* **métissage culturel** *cultural cross-fertilization*
d'outre-mer *overseas*

JEAN
BERNABÉ

PATRICK
CHAMOISEAU

RAPHAËL
CONFIANT

ÉLOGE
DE LA
CRÉOLITÉ

IN PRAISE OF
CREOLENESS

ÉDITION BILINGUE
TRADUCTION ANGLAISE DE M B TALEB KHYAR

GALLIMARD

© Traduction anglaise de M.B. Taleb-Khyar, Gallimard Press.

© RA/Lebrecht Music & Arts

Marguerite Yourcenar

D'origine belge, Marguerite Yourcenar (1903–1987) a vécu° pendant longtemps aux États-Unis. Cette écrivaine française a été poète, traductrice° et critique. Célèbre pour ses romans historiques et ses mémoires autobiographiques, Yourcenar est une des meilleures° romancières du vingtième siècle. Son roman *Mémoires d'Hadrien* a connu un succès mondial°. En 1980, elle est devenue° la première femme élue° à l'Académie française.

a vécu *lived* **traductrice** *translator* **meilleures** *best* **mondial** *worldwide* **est devenue** *became* **élue** *elected*

Ken Bugul

Née° Mariétou Biléoma Mbaye, cette romancière sénégalaise écrit sous son nom de plume°, Ken Bugul. Ironiquement, Ken Bugul signifie en wolof «personne n'en veut°». Dans *Rue Félix-Faure* (2005) et *La pièce d'or* (2006), elle critique son pays natal, le Sénégal. Elle vit° à Porto-Novo au Bénin où elle dirige° Collection d'Afrique, un centre de promotion des œuvres° culturelles et des objets d'art. Elle a obtenu le Grand Prix Littéraire d'Afrique Noire en 1999.

© Elise Fitte-Duval/Maxppp/Landov

Née *Born* **le nom de plume** *pen name* **personne n'en veut** *no one wants any* **vit** *lives* **dirige** *directs* **œuvres** *works*

Révision

1. Quels écrivains sont associés au mouvement de la créolité?

2. Qui écrit sous le nom Ken Bugul?

3. Qui est associé aux madeleines?

4. Qui a écrit *Notre-Dame de Paris*?

5. Qui a été *(was)* la première femme élue à l'Académie française?

🌐 Activités Internet

• Cherchez le site officiel de l'Académie française sur Internet. Nommez trois membres de l'Académie élus au vingt-et-unième siècle.

• Cherchez une recette pour les madeleines sur Internet. Nommez trois ingrédients de cette recette.

• Trouvez une œuvre de Ken Bugul ou de Raphaël Confiant sur Internet. Quel est le titre et le thème de cette œuvre?

Les **espaces**

En bref   In this chapter, you will:

- talk about your house, furniture, and household chores

- learn the present tense of **-ir** verbs like **choisir**, **obéir**, and **finir**

- learn places in the city, on campus, and in the great outdoors

- learn commands to give orders and directions

- learn vocabulary for expressing the sequence of events

- learn prepositions of location and the numbers 100 and above

- learn more about question words and nasal vowels

- read about **Côte d'Ivoire** and the city of Abidjan

- write a brief description of a city

 You will also re-watch **SÉQUENCE 2: La décision** of the film *Liaisons*.

Ressources

 audio   iLrn   🌐 http://www.cengagebrain.com

VOCABULAIRE 1

Les **espaces personnels**

Personal spaces

la salle de bains

un miroir

un lavabo

une douche

les W.-C. *(m. pl.)*

le couloir

la chambre

les étagères *(f.)*

une commode

un lit

une baignoire

un balcon

le premier étage

les rideaux *(m.)*

un (four à) micro-ondes

une cuisinière

un réfrigérateur / un frigo

la salle de séjour

un fauteuil

un téléviseur

une lampe

un canapé

l'escalier *(m.)*

un four

la cuisine

une console de jeux vidéo

un tapis

un lecteur DVD

le rez-de-chaussée

Les pièces et les objets de la maison

Vocabulaire complémentaire

les affaires *(f.)* *things, stuff*

un appareil audiovisuel *piece of audiovisual equipment*

un appareil électroménager *household appliance*

un appartement *apartment*

un bail *lease*

les choses *(f.) things, stuff*

un(e) colocataire *roommate, housemate*

le garage *garage*

un loyer *rent*

un meuble *piece of furniture*

une pièce *room*

un placard *closet*

le règlement de location *rental agreements / renter rules*

la salle à manger *dining room*

le salon *formal living / sitting room*

le sous-sol *basement*

les tâches *(f.)* **ménagères** *chores, housekeeping tasks*

un(e) voisin(e) *neighbor*

---

louer *to rent*

partager *to share*

passer l'aspirateur *(m.) to vacuum*

ranger (la maison) *to pick up (the house), to put things away*

sortir la poubelle *to take out the garbage, trash*

---

faire la lessive *to do the laundry*

faire le ménage *to do the housework*

faire la poussière *to dust*

faire la vaisselle *to do the dishes*

équipé(e) *equipped*

propre *clean*

sale *dirty*

Note de **grammaire**

Remember that verbs ending in **-ger** like **manger**, **ranger**, and **partager** have a spelling change in the **nous** form (**nous rangeons**, **nous partageons**).

Si vous y allez

© Peter Horree/Alamy

Si vous allez à Paris, allez au marché aux puces *(flea market)* de Saint-Ouen pour voir de vieux objets pour la maison et de vieux meubles.

Un mot sur la langue

© Elizabeth Whiting & Associates/Alamy

Les toilettes ou les W.-C.?

En France, on a des expressions différentes pour parler de l'endroit° où on trouve la cuvette des W.-C.° On appelle cette petite pièce **les toilettes** ou **les W.-C.** *(water closet).* Il y a aussi des expressions imagées. On dit aussi **les cabinets, le nécessaire** et **le petit coin°.** Dans tous les cas°, dans les résidences, les toilettes sont généralement séparées de la salle de bains; on n'y trouve donc pas de baignoire et pas de douche!

l'endroit *place* **la cuvette des W.-C.** *toilet bowl* **coin** *corner* **cas** *cases*

● Est-ce que cette séparation des toilettes et de la salle de bains est pratique ou problématique, à votre avis *(in your opinion)*?

🔊
CD2-2 **ACTIVITÉ A** **Où se trouve-t-il?** Dans quelle(s) pièce(s) se trouve chaque objet mentionné?

1. a. le garage   b. le salon
2. a. la chambre   b. le balcon
3. a. la salle de bains b. le couloir
4. a. l'escalier   b. la chambre

5. a. la salle de séjour   b. les W.-C.
6. a. la chambre   b. la salle de bains
7. a. la cuisine   b. la salle à manger
8. a. le balcon   b. le couloir

ACTIVITÉ B **Quel objet?** Trouvez l'intrus *(the one that doesn't belong)*.

1. a. un lavabo   b. une cuisinière   c. un micro-ondes   d. un four
2. a. un canapé   b. une douche   c. les rideaux   d. un lecteur DVD
3. a. des étagères   b. un lit   c. une baignoire   d. des appareils audiovisuels
4. a. une douche   b. une baignoire   c. un miroir   d. un fauteuil
5. a. un fauteuil   b. un tapis   c. une cuisinière   d. une console de jeux vidéo
6. a. un colocataire   b. un voisin   c. un escalier   d. un camarade de chambre
7. a. un loyer   b. un bail   c. un salon   d. le règlement de location
8. a. un appartement   b. une maison   c. une chambre   d. les tâches ménagères

ACTIVITÉ C **Dans quelle pièce?** Où est-ce que vous aimez faire ces activités?

Modèle: parler au téléphone **J'aime parler au téléphone dans ma chambre.**

1. manger
2. étudier
3. lire

4. regarder la télé
5. faire une sieste
6. jouer aux jeux vidéo

7. parler au téléphone
8. écouter de la musique
9. naviguer sur Internet

ACTIVITÉ D **Un appartement typique d'étudiant**

Étape 1. Est-ce qu'un appartement typique d'étudiant a ces objets ou ces pièces?

Modèle: un téléviseur   **Oui, il y a un téléviseur. / Non, il n'y a pas de téléviseur.**

1. un balcon
2. un micro-ondes
3. une salle à manger
4. un frigo

5. une baignoire
6. un canapé
7. un téléviseur
8. une commode

9. des étagères
10. un miroir
11. un salon
12. un lavabo

Étape 2. Quels objets ou quelles pièces sont dans l'appartement de Claire Gagner?

© Heinle/Cengage Learning

Étape 3. Demandez à un(e) camarade de classe s'il/si elle a les pièces ou les objets présentés dans l'Étape 1.

Modèle: É1: **Est-ce que tu as un garage?**
É2: **Oui, j'ai un garage. / Non, je n'ai pas de garage.**

Conclusion Est-ce que l'appartement de votre camarade de classe est bien équipé?

ACTIVITÉ E Qui suis-je? Quel appareil ou objet est décrit *(described)* par chaque phrase suivante?

1. Je suis un appareil électroménager que tu passes pour rendre propre le tapis.
2. Je suis quelque chose que tu signes, un contrat pour habiter en location.
3. Je suis un appareil audiovisuel qui lit les films.
4. Je suis quelque chose que tu paies *(pay)* chaque mois pour louer un logement.
5. Je suis quelque chose à respecter pour éviter *(avoid)* des problèmes avec les voisins.

ACTIVITÉ F Dans quelle pièce ou partie de la maison? Dans quelle pièce ou partie de la maison fait-on chaque activité que vous allez entendre?

CD2-3

1.   2.   3.   4.   5.   6.

ACTIVITÉ G Le ménage

Étape 1. Indiquez la fréquence avec laquelle *(how often)* vous faites ces activités ménagères: **tous les jours, une fois** *(one time)* **par semaine, une fois toutes les deux semaines** *(every other week),* **une fois par mois** ou **jamais.**

1. Je **fais la vaisselle**…
2. Je **passe l'aspirateur**…
3. Je **fais la lessive**…
4. Je **fais le ménage**…

5. Je **sors la poubelle**…
6. Je **fais la poussière**…
7. Je **range la vaisselle**…
8. Je **range la lessive**…

Étape 2. Montrez vos réponses à un(e) partenaire. Est-ce qu'il/elle a une maison plutôt **sale** ou bien **propre?**

ACTIVITÉ H Qui fait quoi? Indiquez qui fait normalement ces tâches ménagères chez vous.

Modèle: Ma sœur et moi faisons la vaisselle.

1. faire la vaisselle
2. faire la lessive
3. passer l'aspirateur

4. sortir la poubelle
5. ranger la salle de séjour
6. ranger la lessive

ACTIVITÉ I **Un(e) colocataire potentiel(le)?** Posez ces questions à un(e) camarade de classe. Décidez s'il/si elle est un(e) colocataire potentiel(le) pour vous.

1. Quel est le loyer que tu peux *(can)* payer?
2. Tu as des meubles?
3. Partager la salle de bains est facile pour toi?
4. Tu aimes mieux un appartement ou une maison?
5. Tu es poli(e) avec tes voisins?
6. Tu as des appareils audiovisuels?
7. Tu fais le ménage?
8. Tu ranges tes affaires?

ACTIVITÉ J **Appartements et maisons à louer et à ne pas louer** Quels critères sont nécessaires pour chaque logement? Pensez aux **pièces**, aux **appareils** et au **règlement de location**. Quel est **le loyer** pour chaque logement? Avec un(e) partenaire, préparez trois à quatre phrases pour chaque description.

Modèle: une maison idéale à louer

Dans une maison idéale à louer, il y a deux chambres et deux salles de bains. La cuisine est propre et équipée avec une cuisinière, un four et un frigo. Les meubles de la salle de séjour sont confortables. Le loyer est de 600 dollars par mois.

1. un appartement à louer
2. la maison de vos rêves *(dreams)*

ACTIVITÉ K **L'Hôtel Château Frontenac**

Étape 1. Dans le film *Liaisons,* Claire va visiter le Château Frontenac, un hôtel quatre étoiles *(stars)* au Québec. Faites la description **des pièces, des objets, des meubles** et **de l'état de propreté** *(cleanliness)* que vous imaginez pour chaque type de chambre.

© Chris Cheadle/All Canada Photos/Corbis

1. une chambre normale
2. une suite exécutive

Étape 2. Cherchez le site officiel de l'Hôtel Château Frontenac sur Internet et trouvez des photos et descriptions des chambres. Comparez vos descriptions aux informations que vous trouvez sur le site. Avez-vous besoin de modifier vos réponses?

ACTIVITÉ L Petite description Préparez une petite description dans laquelle vous décrivez votre appartement ou maison, votre personnalité, vos activités et le genre *(kind)* de colocataire que vous recherchez.

Modèle: Je suis une étudiante de 20 ans et je recherche une colocataire. J'ai un appartement de quatre pièces: deux chambres, un W.C., une salle de bains, une cuisine équipée, une salle de séjour et une salle à manger avec meubles. Je suis calme et polie. Je suis une étudiante sérieuse. Je recherche une jeune femme célibataire. Elle a besoin de partager le ménage. Le loyer est $560 par mois avec $100 de charges.

ACTIVITÉ M Sondage: Le logement idéal Faites un sondage pour déterminer les préférences de vos camarades de classe en matière de logement. Posez chaque question à au moins trois étudiants différents et notez leurs réponses.

Questions	É1	É2	É3
1. Quelles pièces sont essentielles?	_____	_____	_____
2. Quel est le bon nombre de colocataires?	_____	_____	_____
3. Quels appareils électroménagers sont nécessaires?	_____	_____	_____
4. Quelles règles de location sont importantes?	_____	_____	_____
5. Quels meubles sont indispensables?	_____	_____	_____

Un mot sur la culture

Où faire la lessive?

Si vous avez besoin de faire la lessive dans une maison française, vous allez sans doute trouver la machine à laver° et le sèche-linge° dans un endroit différent de celui où vous les trouvez dans votre maison. Aux États-Unis et au Québec, les maisons ont tendance à avoir une lingerie° au sous-sol, à côté de° la cuisine ou près des° chambres. Mais en France, les buanderies° sont assez rares dans les résidences privées. On trouve le plus souvent les appareils ménagers pour le linge° dans la salle de bains ou dans la cuisine parce que c'est dans ces deux endroits qu'on trouve la plomberie° nécessaire à leur installation. C'est aussi assez commun en France pour une famille de ne pas avoir de séchoir°. En général, les Français préfèrent faire sécher° leurs vêtements à l'extérieur (dans le jardin° ou sur le balcon) ou bien à l'intérieur dans la salle de bains.

© Imagehit Inc./Alamy

une machine à laver *washing machine* **un sèche-linge** *clothes dryer* **une lingerie** *laundry room* **à côté de** *next to* **près de** *near*
les buanderies *laundry rooms* **le linge** *laundry* **la plomberie** *plumbing* **séchoir** *dryer* **faire sécher** *to allow to dry* **le jardin** *yard*

- Comment préférez-vous faire sécher vos vêtements: naturellement (dans le jardin, sur un balcon ou dans la salle de bains) ou bien dans un séchoir?

Pour parler de nos maisons et de notre vie

Les verbes **choisir, finir** et **obéir**

DU FILM *LIAISONS*

Un coup d'œil sur la grammaire

Look at these photos from the film **Liaisons** and their captions. Note the verbs used to communicate the actions that are taking place.

© Heinle/Cengage Learning

Claire vient de **finir** son cours de psychologie.

© Heinle/Cengage Learning

Émile, le chat de Claire, n'**obéit** pas toujours.

What do you think these verbs mean?

1. **finir**   a. to begin   b. to obey   c. to finish
2. **obéir**   a. to finish   b. to obey   c. to choose

Les verbes-clés

⋯ **Choisir, finir,** and **obéir** are another class of regular -**ir** verbs that follow a set pattern of endings in the present tense.

finir *(to finish)*	choisir *(to choose)*	obéir (à) *(to obey)*
je fin**is**	je chois**is**	j'obé**is**
tu fin**is**	tu chois**is**	tu obé**is**
il/elle/on fin**it**	il/elle/on chois**it**	il/elle obé**it**
nous fin**issons**	nous chois**issons**	nous obé**issons**
vous fin**issez**	vous chois**issez**	vous obé**issez**
ils/elles fin**issent**	ils/elles chois**issent**	ils/elles obé**issent**

Je **finis** toujours mes devoirs avant 20h.   *I always **finish** my homework before 8 pm.*

Elle **choisit** ses cours aujourd'hui.   *She **is choosing** her classes today.*

⋯ Common expressions used with the verb **obéir (à)** are: **obéir aux règles** *(to obey the rules),* **obéir à la loi** *(to obey the law),* and **obéir aux parents.**

Nous **obéissons** toujours à la loi.   *We always **obey** the law.*

⋯▸ Here are other regular -**ir** verbs that follow the same pattern: **grossir** *(to gain weight)*, **maigrir** *(to lose weight)*, **grandir** *(to grow up)*, **réussir (à)** *(to succeed at/in)*, **réfléchir (à)** *(to reflect upon, to consider)*, and **salir** *(to dirty)*.

Les êtres humains **grossissent** s'ils mangent tout le temps.
*Humans **gain weight** if they eat all the time.*

Nous **maigrissons** si nous faisons du sport.
*We **lose weight** if we exercise.*

De nos jours, les enfants **grandissent** dans une société matérialiste.
*These days, children **grow up** in a materialistic society.*

Est-ce que tu **réussis** toujours **à** tes examens?
*Do you always **pass** your exams?*

Je **réfléchis au** sujet que le professeur propose pour cette rédaction.
*I **am thinking about** the topic that the professor is proposing for this essay.*

Pour aller plus loin
La préposition *chez*

Chez is a preposition that means *to be at one's place* or *at the home of someone*.

Je finis mes devoirs **chez** Claire.	*I am finishing my homework at Claire's (house).*
Les enfants vont grandir **chez** nous.	*The children will grow up at our (house / place).*
Je travaille **chez** moi.	*I'm working at home (my place).*

Essayez! Chez qui aimez-vous faire ces activités?

1. étudier   2. manger   3. regarder un film   4. faire la fête

---

ACTIVITÉ Ⓝ Choisir des meubles et des décorations Choisissez les sujets appropriés.

1. _____ chois**is** des meubles pour l'appartement.	a. Je	b. Il	c. Nous
2. _____ chois**issons** un miroir pour la salle de bains.	a. Nous	b. Vous	c. Elle
3. _____ chois**is** une table pour la salle à manger.	a. Tu	b. On	c. Ils
4. _____ chois**issent** les rideaux pour les chambres.	a. Vous	b. Je	c. Elles
5. _____ chois**issez** un fauteuil pour la salle de séjour.	a. Tu	b. Vous	c. Nous
6. _____ chois**it** un tapis pour le salon.	a. On	b. Elles	c. Tu

⋯▸ **Et vous?** Aimez-vous choisir des meubles et des décorations?

🔊 **ACTIVITÉ Ⓞ La vie aujourd'hui** Choisissez le sujet approprié pour chaque
CD2-4 phrase que vous allez entendre.

1. a. L'enfant b. Les enfants	**4.** a. La fille b. Les filles
2. a. Le garçon b. Les garçons	**5.** a. L'étudiant b. Les étudiants
3. a. La femme b. Les femmes	**6.** a. Le professeur b. Les professeurs

ACTIVITÉ P La vie des personnages de *Liaisons*

Étape 1. Complétez les phrases avec un verbe qui convient: **maigrir, finir, grossir, réfléchir, salir, obéir, grandir** ou **choisir.**

1. Claire _____ au message dans l'enveloppe mystérieuse.
2. Abia et Claire _____ leur journée de travail à l'hôtel à 18h.
3. Le chat de Claire _____ parce qu'il mange beaucoup.
4. Mme Gagner _____ parce qu'elle n'aime pas la cuisine de l'hôpital.
5. La femme de ménage de l'hôtel n'aime pas les clients qui _____ leur chambre.
6. Robert _____ toujours avant de parler aux clients de l'hôtel.

Étape 2. Et vous? Répondez à ces questions.

1. À quelle heure est-ce que vous finissez vos cours?
2. Est-ce que vous grossissez quand vous mangez beaucoup?
3. Est-ce que vos colocataires salissent votre appartement?
4. Est-ce que vous réfléchissez avant de parler avec vos profs?

ACTIVITÉ Q Est-ce que vous êtes un(e) bon(ne) colocataire? Posez ces questions à un(e) partenaire.

Modèle: réfléchir longtemps avant de choisir un appartement
   É1: **Tu réfléchis longtemps avant de choisir un appartement?**
   É2: **Oui / Non, je (ne) réfléchis (pas) longtemps avant de choisir un appartement.**

1. réfléchir avant de signer le bail
2. réussir à payer le loyer chaque mois
3. obéir au règlement de location
4. finir les tâches ménagères
5. choisir des décorations de bon goût *(taste)*
6. salir les meubles et les tapis

ACTIVITÉ R Trouvez quelqu'un qui... Posez chaque question à un(e) étudiant(e) différent(e). Quand vous trouvez quelqu'un qui correspond à chaque action, notez son prénom.

Trouvez quelqu'un qui...   **Prénom de l'étudiant(e)**

1. **finit** toujours ses devoirs avant le cours.   _____
2. n'**obéit** pas toujours à la loi.   _____
3. **choisit** de prendre l'autobus.   _____
4. **réussit à** tous ses cours.   _____
5. **maigrit** à cause du stress.   _____
6. **grossit** pendant les vacances.   _____
7. **réfléchit** souvent **à** son avenir *(future)*.   _____
8. ne **réussit** pas toujours **aux** examens.   _____

Il faut...

When you want to express something that you or someone else must do, use **Il faut** + *infinitive*. Context will determine the precise meaning.

Il faut ranger la chambre.

You have to pick up the bedroom. / I must pick up the bedroom. / We have got to pick up the bedroom. / It is necessary to pick up the bedroom.

Essayez! Avec quelles phrases êtes-vous d'accord? Préparez deux phrases de votre invention pour les numéros 9 et 10.

1. Il faut étudier tous les jours pour réussir à l'école.
2. Il faut toujours obéir aux règles de l'université.
3. Il faut réfléchir avant de parler en classe.
4. Il faut louer un logement près de *(near)* l'université.
5. Il faut souvent faire le ménage.
6. Il faut choisir de bons/bonnes colocataires.
7. Il ne faut pas salir les salles de cours.
8. Il ne faut pas payer son loyer en retard.
9. Il faut…
10. Il ne faut pas…

La parole est à vous!

Est-ce que nous sommes (trop) matérialistes aujourd'hui?

On dit souvent que les étudiants possèdent beaucoup de choses aujourd'hui. Qu'en pensez-vous? Est-ce que les étudiants emportent° trop de choses avec eux à l'université ou dans leur logement?

- Jean-René de Mirecourt (France): «Très certainement. Les étudiants ont trop de choses aujourd'hui. Moi, j'avais° seulement deux valises quand j'ai emménagé dans ma chambre de résidence universitaire: quelques vêtements°, des affaires pour le lit et la toilette, des fournitures scolaires et une radio.»

- Guillaume d'Aix-en-Provence (France): «Mais non! Nous désirons nous sentir comme à la maison. Il faut beaucoup de choses pour se sentir chez soi. C'est le confort qui compte!»

emportent *take* **avais** *had* **vêtements** *clothing*

Et vous? Qu'en pensez-vous?

Est-ce que les étudiants ont trop de choses et est-ce qu'ils sont matérialistes aujourd'hui?

🔊 Les **espaces urbains**

Urban spaces

une banque

une boutique / un magasin

le bureau de poste

le cinéma

une église

un hôpital

un institut de beauté

un magazine

un kiosque à journaux

une librairie

un musée

une laverie automatique

une piscine municipale

Les endroits en ville

Vocabulaire complémentaire

un amphithéâtre *lecture hall*
une banlieue *suburbs*
un bâtiment *building*
un bistro *café-restaurant*
un centre commercial *shopping center / district*
un centre sportif *recreation center*
le centre-ville *downtown*
un endroit *location, place*
un laboratoire *laboratory*
un lycée *high school*
une maison de la presse *newsstand*
un parking *parking lot*

un plan *map (of a city)*
un quartier (résidentiel) *(residential) neighborhood*
une résidence universitaire *residence hall*
un restaurant universitaire *campus cafeteria*
une rue *street*
un stade *stadium*
les toilettes *(f. pl.)* **(publiques) / les W.-C.** *(m. pl.)* **(publics)** *public restrooms*
une ville *a city, a town*

Les prépositions

à côté (de) *next (to)*
au coin (de) *on the corner (of)*
à droite (de) *to/on the right (of)*
à gauche (de) *to/on the left (of)*
derrière *behind*
devant *in front (of)*

en face (de) *across (from)*
entre *between*
loin (de) *far (from)*
près (de) *near*
tout droit *straight ahead*

- Recall that **de** contracts with **le** and **les: de + le = du; de + les = des.** There is no contraction with **la** and **l': de la, de l'.**

La librairie est **en face du** stade.	The bookstore is **across from the** stadium.
Le stade est **loin des** toilettes publiques.	The stadium is **far from the** public toilets.
Le musée est **près de la** piscine.	The museum is **near the** pool.
Le lycée est **à côté de l'**église.	The high school is **next to the** church.

Un mot sur la langue

Une laverie automatique ou un Lavomatique?

Du fait° de leur popularité ou de la publicité°, on a l'habitude en France d'appeler certains objets par le nom de la marque° qui les fabrique° au lieu d'°utiliser le mot de vocabulaire approprié. C'est ce qu'on appelle des noms de marque générique°. Par exemple, on appelle parfois une laverie automatique **un Lavomatique.** C'est le nom d'une société° de laveries automatiques en France. Les noms de marque générique commencent toujours par une majuscule°. On fait la même chose en anglais, par exemple, on dit *un Coke* pour *un soda.*

Du fait *Because of* **publicité** *advertising* **marque** *brand* **fabrique** *makes, manufactures* **au lieu d'** *instead of* **générique** *generic* **une société** *company* **majuscule** *capital letter*

- Connaissez-vous ces exemples: **un Kleenex, du Vicks, du Nutella, une Barbie, un Bic, un Frigidaire, un Jacuzzi, une Jeep, un Stetson, un Tupperware, une Vespa** et **un Zippo**?

ACTIVITÉ A Notre campus

CD2-5

Étape 1. Comment s'appellent ces bâtiments sur votre campus?

Modèle: un laboratoire   **McQuigg Hall**

1.   2.   3.   4.   5.   6.   7.   8.   9.   10.   11.   12.

Étape 2. Les cours de psychologie de Claire Gagner sont dans le Pavillon Stewart sur le campus de McGill University. Dans quels bâtiments sont vos cours?

ACTIVITÉ B La ville et le campus

Étape 1. Quel nom associez-vous à chaque lieu?

Modèle: un musée   **le Louvre**

1. un musée   4. un lycée   7. un hôpital
2. une église   5. une pharmacie   8. un cinéma
3. un bistro   6. un centre commercial 9. un institut de beauté

Étape 2. Demandez à un(e) partenaire si on trouve ces endroits dans son quartier. Décidez s'il/si elle habite dans un quartier intéressant.

Modèle: É1: **Est-ce qu'il y a un musée dans ton quartier?**
É2: **Oui, il y a un musée dans mon quartier: le Columbus Art Museum. /**
Non, il n'y a pas de musée dans mon quartier.

ACTIVITÉ C Où faut-il aller? Vous allez entendre des débuts de phrase. Où est-ce qu'on fait chaque activité?

CD2-6

1.   2.   3.   4.   5.   6.   7.   8.   9.   10.

ACTIVITÉ D Quel bâtiment? Choisissez cinq bâtiments sur votre campus et complétez les phrases. Ensuite, échangez vos phrases avec un(e) partenaire et devinez (*guess*) de quels bâtiments votre partenaire parle.

Modèle: É1: **Ce bâtiment se trouve derrière le stade.**
É2: **C'est le *French Field House*.**

1. Ce bâtiment se trouve **en face de** _____ et **à côté de** _____.
2. Ce bâtiment se trouve **devant** _____ et **entre** _____ et _____.
3. Ce bâtiment se trouve **près de** _____ et **à gauche de** _____.
4. Ce bâtiment se trouve **derrière** _____ et **à droite de** _____.
5. Ce bâtiment est **au coin de** _____. Il est **loin de** _____.

Si vous y allez

© Erwan Le Prunnec/Glow Images

Si vous allez à Plombières-les-Bains en Lorraine (France), allez aux Thermes Napoléon—un institut de beauté et des bains publics romains.

ACTIVITÉ **E** **Énigmes** Identifiez ces mots de vocabulaire.

1. C'est un établissement d'enseignement du second degré.
2. C'est un endroit où on achète (buys) des médicaments (medications).
3. C'est un commerce où on vend (sells) des marchandises.
4. C'est un établissement où on trouve des lettres et des paquets.
5. C'est une partie d'une ville avec certaines caractéristiques ou une certaine unité.
6. C'est la représentation graphique d'une ville, d'une banlieue, d'une région.
7. C'est un café ou un restaurant modeste.
8. C'est un endroit où les spectateurs regardent du sport.

ACTIVITÉ **F** **Quel endroit?** Où aimez-vous faire ces activités? Notez vos réponses. Puis, demandez à votre partenaire où il/elle aime faire ces activités. Qu'est-ce que vous allez peut-être faire ensemble?

Modèle: prendre le déjeuner

   É1: **Où est-ce que tu aimes prendre le déjeuner?**
   É2: **J'aime prendre le déjeuner au restaurant universitaire.**

	Moi	Mon/Ma partenaire
1. étudier?	_____	_____
2. faire la lessive?	_____	_____
3. voir (see) un film?	_____	_____
4. dîner?	_____	_____
5. faire du sport?	_____	_____
6. aller le week-end?	_____	_____

Un mot sur la culture

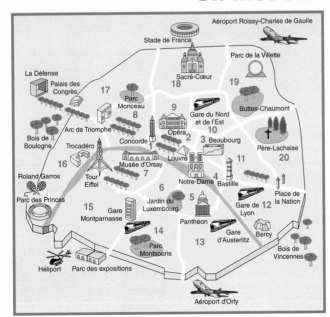

Les arrondissements de Paris

Paris est la capitale de la France mais c'est aussi une métropole°. C'est-à-dire que c'est une grande ville qui inclut° de nombreux quartiers et des banlieues. La ville de Paris est divisée en vingt arrondissements° et compte au moins quinze quartiers distincts et différents. Certains quartiers couvrent deux ou trois arrondissements. On dit souvent que chaque quartier parisien a son propre° caractère ou sa propre personnalité.

métropole *metropolis* **inclut** *includes* **arrondissements** *districts, sections* **propre** *own*

- Y a-t-il des arrondissements ou quartiers différents dans votre ville?

Pour donner des ordres et des indications
L'impératif

DU FILM *LIAISONS*

Un coup d'œil sur la grammaire

Look at these photos from the film *Liaisons* and their captions, paying special attention to the words used to express orders.

MICHEL **Va** à Québec.

CLAIRE Et n'**oublie** pas que mon oncle a téléphoné ce matin...

What do you think these expressions mean?

1. Va à Québec. **2. N'oublie** pas.

❖ The imperative (**l'impératif**) is used to make suggestions and to give commands. For regular verbs and most irregular verbs, the imperative forms are identical to the present tense forms. To form the **tu** form of **-er** verbs and **aller,** however, you drop the final **-s** from the present tense form. You do not use subject pronouns with the imperative.

❖ The verbs **avoir** and **être** have irregular command forms.

	-er *verbs*	-ir *verbs*	aller	avoir	être
(tu)	mang**e**	fin**is**	**va**	aie	sois
(nous)	mang**eons**	fin**issons**	allons	ayons	soyons
(vous)	mang**ez**	fin**issez**	allez	ayez	soyez
	faire	**partir**	**sortir**	**lire**	**dire**
(tu)	**fais**	pars	sors	lis	dis
(nous)	**faisons**	part**ons**	sort**ons**	lis**ons**	dis**ons**
(vous)	**faites**	part**ez**	sort**ez**	lisez	dites

Note de **grammaire**

In spoken French, the **nous** form of commands is less common than **tu** and **vous** commands. The pronoun **on** + the present tense is often used in a question instead of the **nous** command: **On va au restaurant ce soir?** *Let's go to the restaurant tonight.*

Parlez français!
Écoutons le professeur.
Allez à la bibliothèque pour étudier.
Fais le ménage, s'il te plaît.

Speak French!
Let's listen to the professor.
Go to the library to study.
Do the housework, please.

In negative commands, put **ne... pas** around the verb.

N'aie pas peur.	***Don't be*** afraid.
Ne parlons pas de politique, s'il vous plaît.	***Let's not talk*** about politics, please.

Use the imperative to give directions (**des indications**) in French. Here are some common expressions that you will hear and can use.

tourner à droite / à gauche	*to turn right / left*
traverser la rue / la place	*to cross the street / town square*
aller / continuer tout droit	*to go / to continue straight ahead*
aller / continuer jusqu'à	*to go / to continue until*
aller jusqu'au bout	*to go to the end*
aller vers	*to go towards*
Tourne à droite après le stade.	***Turn right*** after the stadium.
Traversons la rue ensemble.	***Let's cross the street*** together.

Liaisons musicales

© RA/Lebrecht Music & Arts

Ne me quitte pas (1959) est une chanson très connue en France et dans tout le monde francophone. Jacques Brel, un chanteur belge, est l'auteur et l'interprète de cette chanson. Les chansons de Brel ont souvent un message socio-politique. Cherchez les paroles de cette chanson sur Internet.

Pour aller plus loin
L'ordre des événements

The following expressions are useful in sequencing series of events or activities.

d'abord	*first*	**plus tard**	*later*
puis / ensuite	*then, next*	**enfin**	*finally*

Essayez! Voici une recette *(recipe)* pour un plat *(dish)* québécois très populaire, la poutine. Mettez *(Put)* les instructions dans le bon ordre.

_____ **Ensuite,** mettez le fromage et la sauce sur les frites.

_____ **Enfin,** dévorez le plat!

_____ **Puis,** faites cuire *(cook)* les frites et réchauffer *(heat up)* la sauce.

_____ **D'abord,** achetez des frites, du fromage en grains et de la sauce.

🔊 **ACTIVITÉ** **G** **À Québec** D'abord, trouvez ces endroits sur le

CD2-7 plan de la ville de Québec. Ensuite, vous allez entendre une série de phrases sur ces endroits. Est-ce que les phrases sont vraies ou fausses?

1. _____ le Château Frontenac

2. _____ le Parc des Gouverneurs

3. _____ la Place de l'Hôtel-de-Ville

🔊 **ACTIVITÉ H** **Dans le cours de français** Vous allez entendre une série
CD2-8 d'ordres. À qui chaque ordre est-il destiné *(intended)*: a) un étudiant ou b) tous les
étudiants?

1.　　　2.　　　3.　　　4.　　　5.　　　6.

ACTIVITÉ I **À qui parle-t-on?** Qu'est-ce que vous diriez *(would say)* à
chaque personne? Quelle suggestion est la meilleure *(best)* à votre avis?

1. au professeur de français
   a. Ne **donne** pas de devoirs.
   b. Ne **donnons** pas de devoirs.
   c. Ne **donnez** pas de devoirs.

2. à votre meilleur(e) ami(e)
   a. **Réfléchis** avant de parler.
   b. **Réfléchissons** avant de parler.
   c. **Réfléchissez** avant de parler.

3. à votre camarade de chambre /
   colocataire
   a. **Sois** sérieux. On a besoin d'étudier.
   b. **Soyons** sérieux. On a besoin
      d'étudier.
   c. **Soyez** sérieux. On a besoin d'étudier.

4. à vous et vos amis
   a. Ne **sors** pas après minuit.
   b. Ne **sortons** pas après minuit.
   c. Ne **sortez** pas après minuit.

5. à vos camarades de classe
   a. **Étudie** tous les jours.
   b. **Étudions** tous les jours.
   c. **Étudiez** tous les jours.

6. à vous et vos camarades de classe
   a. **Fais** les devoirs ensemble au café.
   b. **Faisons** les devoirs ensemble
      au café.
   c. **Faites** les devoirs ensemble
      au café.

ACTIVITÉ J **Des ordres ou des conseils à suivre** Quels ordres ou
conseils est-ce qu'il faut suivre *(follow)* dans ces différents endroits? Suivez-vous
normalement chaque ordre ou conseil?

Modèle: **À la bibliothèque, ne parle pas avec ton voisin.**
À la bibliothèque, fais attention aux livres.

Possibilités					
aller	recopier *(to copy)*	demander	être	manger	oublier
avoir	critiquer	écrire	lire	obéir	parler

1. Dans la salle informatique, _____ près des ordinateurs.

2. Dans le parking, _____ tes clés *(keys)* de voiture.

3. Dans la salle de cours, _____ les devoirs de tes camarades de classe.

4. Dans un restaurant, _____ attentivement la carte *(menu)*.

5. À l'église, _____ respectueux.

6. Dans un cinéma, _____ avec tes voisins pendant le film.

7. Dans le bureau d'un professeur, _____ les autres étudiants de la classe.

8. Dans la queue *(check-out line)* de la librairie universitaire, _____ de la patience.

ACTIVITÉ K Qu'est-ce qu'il faut faire?

Étape 1. Dites à un(e) ami(e) les activités qu'il faut faire dans chaque ville.

Modèle: à Pittsburgh, PA
Visite le Heinz History Center, va à un match de hockey de l'équipe des Pittsburgh Penguins et mange un sandwich au restaurant Primanti Brothers.

1. à New York, NY
2. à Washington D.C.
3. à La Nouvelle-Orléans, LA
4. à Chicago, IL
5. à Seattle, WA

6. à Las Vegas, NV
7. à Los Angeles, CA
8. à Miami, FL
9. à ???

Étape 2. Et chez vous? Préparez une liste de trois choses qu'il faut faire et une liste de trois choses qu'il ne faut pas faire dans votre ville ou sur votre campus. Ensuite, partagez vos listes avec un(e) partenaire. Avez-vous les mêmes idées?

ACTIVITÉ L **Suggestions** Faites des suggestions aux différents camarades de classe. Parlez avec plusieurs *(several)* étudiants. Quelles suggestions est-ce que vous allez essayer *(try)*?

Modèle: É1: **Je ne sais pas toujours quoi faire le vendredi soir.**
É2: **Va à un restaurant Appleby's avec tes amis.**

1. Je ne sais pas où faire du sport.
2. Je grossis.
3. Je maigris.
4. Je ne sais pas quoi faire dans le quartier.

5. J'ai besoin d'une coupe de cheveux *(haircut)*.
6. Je ne réussis pas à mon cours de français.
7. Je ne sais pas où louer un appartement.
8. Mon colocataire ne range pas ses affaires.

ACTIVITÉ M **Erreurs à éviter** Quelles sont les erreurs à éviter dans ces différents endroits, à votre avis *(in your opinion)*?

Modèle: à la banque   **Ne soyez pas difficile!**

1. au centre-ville
2. dans le cours de français
3. dans un hôpital
4. chez vous
5. dans la rue

6. dans un amphithéâtre
7. au restaurant universitaire
8. dans un parking
9. dans un stade
10. dans une résidence universitaire

ACTIVITÉ N **Boîte à commentaires** Préparez quatre suggestions d'activités pour votre cours de français.

Modèle: **Allons à un restaurant français.**

ACTIVITÉ O **Le plan du campus de l'Université Laval**

Étape 1. À l'aide du *(With the help of the)* plan du campus de l'Université Laval (Québec), trouvez la destination pour chaque série d'indications suivantes.

Pavillons

7 Maison Omer-Gingras	19 Maison Eugène Roberge
8 Pavillon des Services	20 Maison Marie-Sirois
9 Pavillon Ferdinand-Vandry	21 Pavillon Agathe-Laserte
11 Pavillon Alexandre-Vachon	22 Pavillon Ernest-Lemieux
12 Pavillon Adrien-Pouliot	23 Pavillon Alphonse-Desjardins
13 Pavillon Charles-de-Korinck	26 Pavillon J.-A.-De Sève
14 Pavillon Jean-Charles-Bonenfant	27 Pavillon La Laurentienne
15 Pavillon des Sciences de l'éducation	30 Pavillon de l'Envirotron
16 Pavillon Félix-Antoine-Savard	31 Pavillon d'Optique Photonique
17 Pavillon Louis-Jacques-Casault	33 Édifice logeant Héma Québec
18 Pavillon Paul-Comtois	

Services

A Bibliothèque	D Arrêt Métrobus
B Caisse populaire Desjardins	P Parking
C Sécurité	? Information

1. Quittez *(Leave)* le parking par la rue de l'Agriculture. Tournez à droite et puis suivez la rue de l'Agriculture jusqu'au bout. Ensuite, traversez l'autoroute Robert-Bourassa et c'est le bâtiment juste en face.

2. Quittez la bibliothèque. D'abord, tournez à droite dans la rue des Archives. Suivez la rue des Archives et passez le Pavillon Félix-Antoine-Savard. Ensuite, au coin, tournez à gauche sur l'avenue du Séminaire et enfin, allez jusqu'au premier bâtiment à gauche.

Étape 2. Choisissez une destination sur ce campus et écrivez des indications pour arriver à cette destination. Vous quittez l'arrêt Métrobus.

Étape 3. Lisez vos indications à un(e) partenaire. Il/Elle va deviner *(guess)* la destination.

ACTIVITÉ P **Donnez des indications** Choisissez un lieu sur le campus ou en ville et écrivez une série d'indications. Ensuite, échangez vos indications avec un(e) partenaire et essayez de deviner le lieu de votre partenaire.

Modèle: D'abord, quitte la bibliothèque. Ensuite, tourne à droite et va jusqu'au parking. Puis, tourne à gauche et continue tout droit. C'est à côté du restaurant universitaire, à gauche. On arrive où?

ACTIVITÉ Q **Quelques projets pour le professeur** Avec un(e) partenaire, suggérez quatre projets pour votre professeur ce week-end.

Modèle: D'abord, cherchez un bon livre à la bibliothèque. Puis, allez au café pour lire.

1. D'abord, _____.
2. Puis, _____.
3. Ensuite, _____.
4. Enfin, _____.

La parole est à vous!

Les toilettes sont-elles seulement pour les clients du café?

Il y a une règle non-dite° en France que les toilettes d'un café sont réservées aux clients du café. Autrement dit°, si vous désirez utiliser les toilettes, il est nécessaire de prendre quelque chose à boire° en premier°. Est-ce que c'est normal, à votre avis?

- Émilie de Paris (France): «Mais oui! C'est complètement normal. Utiliser les toilettes sans être client du café est un manque de respect envers les employés du café. Il faut prendre quelque chose à boire par° politesse et par courtoisie°.»

- Paul de Montréal (Canada): «Non. Pourquoi ce besoin d'être client d'un café pour utiliser ses toilettes? Si j'ai besoin d'utiliser les W.-C. et j'ai soif°, je vais prendre quelque chose à boire. Sinon°, j'utilise simplement les W.-C. du café. Ce n'est pas nécessaire d'être client.»

non-dite *unspoken* **Autrement dit** *In other words* **prendre quelque chose à boire** *to have something to drink* **en premier** *first* **par** *out of* **courtoisie** *courtesy* **soif** *thirsty* **Sinon** *Otherwise*

Et vous? Qu'en pensez-vous?

Est-ce qu'il faut être client d'un établissement pour utiliser ses toilettes, à votre avis?

Les **espaces verts**

Green spaces

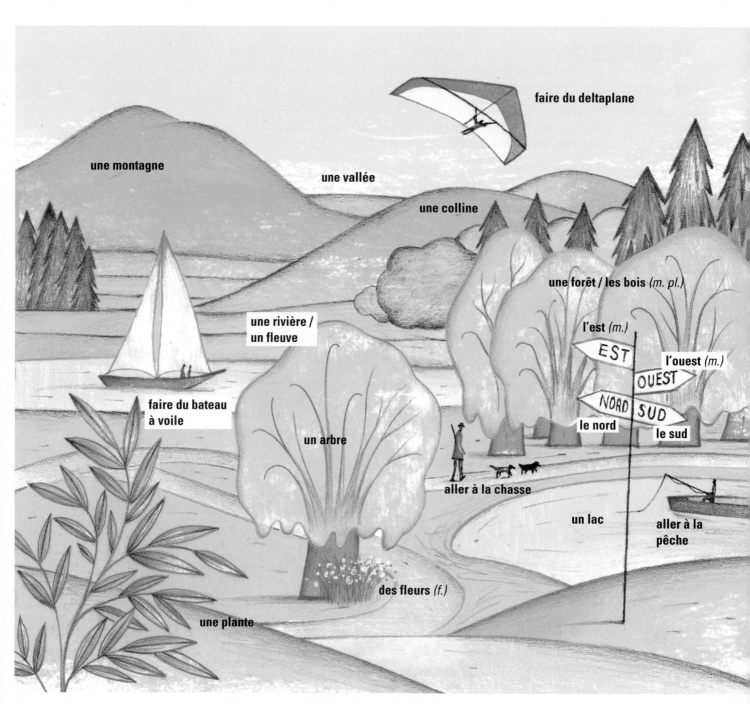

faire du deltaplane

une montagne

une vallée

une colline

une forêt / les bois *(m. pl.)*

une rivière /
un fleuve

l'est *(m.)*

EST

l'ouest *(m.)*

OUEST

NORD SUD

faire du bateau
à voile

le nord

le sud

un arbre

aller à la chasse

un lac

aller à la
pêche

des fleurs *(f.)*

une plante

Un après-midi à la campagne

Vocabulaire complémentaire

la campagne *the country(side)*	**la plage** *the beach*
un champ *field*	**une prairie** *meadow, grassland,*
un étang *pond*	*prairie*
une ferme *farm*	
un jardin *garden, lawn*	**faire de la randonnée** *to go hiking*
la mer *the sea*	**faire du jardinage** *to garden*

Les numéros plus grands que 100

100	**cent**	1 100	**mille cent**
105	**cent cinq**	1 300	**mille trois cents**
135	**cent trente-cinq**	1 550	**mille cinq cent cinquante**
200	**deux cents**	1 999	**mille neuf cent quatre-vingt-dix-neuf**
250	**deux cent cinquante**	2 000	**deux mille**
300	**trois cents**	2 780	**deux mille sept cent quatre-vingts**
375	**trois cent soixante-quinze**	1 000 000	**un million**
400	**quatre cents**	1 500 000	**un million cinq cent mille**
500	**cinq cents**	2 000 000	**deux millions**
600	**six cents**	2 555 000	**deux millions cinq cent**
700	**sept cents**		**cinquante-cinq mille**
800	**huit cents**	1 000 000 000	**un milliard**
900	**neuf cents**	2 000 000 000	**deux milliards**
1000	**mille**		

- **Cent** and **vingt** take an **s** if preceded by a number greater than one, but do not take an **s** if another number follows. **Cent** is never preceded by **un** to mean *one/a hundred.*

deux cents	**cinq cents**	**sept cent trente**
quatre-vingts	**quatre-vingt-un**	

- **Mille** never takes an **s** and is never preceded by **un** to mean *one/a thousand.*

mille étoiles	**mille huit cents personnes**	**quatre mille personnes**

- The number **un** is used before **million** to express *one/a million.* **Million(s)** is followed by **de/d'** before a noun.

un million de personnes	**trois millions de fleurs**	**dix millions d'arbres**

- In French, commas are used to denote decimals, and periods or a space are used after thousands, millions, etc. Read a comma as **virgule** and a period as **point.**

12,98 euros	Il y a **10 000 (10.000)** étudiants sur le campus.

🔊
CD2-9
ACTIVITÉ A **Qu'est-ce que c'est?** Associez chaque élément de la nature que vous allez entendre à son site naturel.

1. a. le Grand Canyon   b. le mont Everest
2. a. le Mississippi   b. Death Valley
3. a. Sherwood   b. les chutes du Niagara
4. a. l'Hudson   b. l'Erie
5. a. le Rio Grande   b. la Méditerranée
6. a. Daytona   b. les Rocheuses

🔊
CD2-10
ACTIVITÉ B **Où va-t-on?** Où est-ce qu'on fait chaque activité que vous allez entendre?

1. a. dans un arbre   b. dans un étang   4. a. dans une vallée   b. au soleil
2. a. à la montagne   b. à la mer   5. a. sur un nuage   b. dans le ciel
3. a. dans une ferme   b. sur une rivière   6. a. dans un champ   b. sur une colline

🔊
CD2-11
ACTIVITÉ C **Nombre de visiteurs approximatif** Vous allez entendre des phrases sur le nombre de visiteurs de sites touristiques en France. Choisissez le nombre correct.

1. les étangs de la Camargue (par mois)   a. 245 000   b. 1 245 000
2. le lac de Gérardmer (par année)   a. 2 000   b. 200 000
3. les jardins du château de Versailles (par année)   a. 1 000 000   b. 10 000 000
4. la vallée de la Loire (par année)   a. 400 000   b. 4 000 000

🔊
CD2-12
ACTIVITÉ D **Moments historiques**

Note de grammaire
You will learn how to say historical dates and years in **Chapitre 8**.

Étape 1. Choisissez la date historique que vous entendez.

1. a. 1799   b. 1789   5. a. 1066   b. 1166
2. a. 1944   b. 1844   6. a. 1271   b. 1211
3. a. 1929   b. 1829   7. a. 1940   b. 1914
4. a. 1669   b. 1609   8. a. 1777   b. 1767

Étape 2. Associez les dates de l'Étape 1 aux événements historiques appropriés.

1. __1799__ Napoléon 1er explore la Vallée des Rois (Kings) en Égypte.
2. _____ Les premières batailles de la Première Guerre mondiale (WWI) commencent dans les montagnes d'Alsace.
3. _____ René de La Salle, explorateur-voyageur français, explore le fleuve Mississippi.
4. _____ Les forces alliées attaquent les plages de Normandie.
5. _____ La fleur de lys devient le symbole de la noblesse (nobility) française.
6. _____ L'établissement des Prairies françaises dans l'État d'Oregon.
7. _____ La conquête de la campagne anglaise par Guillaume, duc de Normandie.
8. _____ Le Marquis de Lafayette traverse la mer atlantique pour soutenir (support) les rebelles américains et leur Révolution.

Étape 3. Écrivez les dates de l'Étape 2 en toutes lettres.

Modèle: (496) **quatre cent quatre-vingt-seize**

ACTIVITÉ E **Et si Abia... ?** Complétez chaque phrase avec le mot de vocabulaire qui convient.

1. Et si Abia désire dire: «Je suis désolée» à quelqu'un, elle envoie *(sends)* _____.

2. Et si Abia a un(e) ami(e) avec une nouvelle maison, elle offre souvent _____.

3. Et si Abia fête *(celebrates)* le Jour de la Terre *(Earth)*, elle plante souvent _____.

4. Et si Abia a envie de trouver des fruits bien frais *(fresh)*, elle va à _____.

5. Et si Abia désire aller à la pêche, elle passe beaucoup de temps sur _____.

6. Et si Abia fait du jardinage, elle passe du temps dans _____.

Et vous? Est-ce que vous aimez mieux *(better)* les espaces verts ou la ville?

© Heinle/Cengage Learning

ACTIVITÉ F **Les activités et les espaces verts** Dans quel espace vert est-ce qu'on fait normalement ces activités?

Modèle: faire un pique-nique

On fait un pique-nique à la campagne.

1. faire du deltaplane
2. faire du jardinage
3. aller à la chasse
4. faire du bateau à voile
5. faire de la randonnée
6. aller à la pêche

ACTIVITÉ G **Dans quelle partie des États-Unis?** Complétez chaque phrase avec deux ou trois activités populaires dans la région.

Modèle Dans le nord des États-Unis en été, on **va à la chasse.**

1. Dans le nord des États-Unis au printemps, on...
2. Dans le nord-est des États-Unis en automne, on...
3. Dans l'ouest des États-Unis en été, on...
4. Dans le sud des États-Unis en hiver, on...
5. Dans le Midwest des États-Unis en hiver, on...
6. Dans le sud-ouest des États-Unis en été, on…

Et vous? Vous êtes de quelle région? Quelles activités faites-vous en été et en hiver dans cette région?

✈ Si vous y allez

© sinephot/Shutterstock.com

Si vous allez dans les Hautes-Vosges—la chaîne de montagnes en Lorraine et en Alsace (France)—allez à la ferme-auberge du Kastelberg pour goûter *(taste)* la cuisine fermière traditionnelle de la région.

ACTIVITÉ H Qu'est-ce que c'est?

Étape 1. Avec un(e) partenaire, décrivez chaque site naturel suivant en une phrase.

Modèle: **Le Rio Grande est un fleuve entre le Mexique et les États-Unis.**

1. le lac Huron
2. les Alpes
3. la Seine
4. la jungle amazonienne
5. la Méditerranée
6. Venice (en Californie)
7. le Saint-Laurent
8. le Mississippi
9. le lac Supérieur

Étape 2. Toujours avec votre partenaire, préparez une liste de tous les sites naturels dans votre région qui valent le détour *(worth the trip)*.

ACTIVITÉ I Un hôtel de rêves

Étape 1. Préparez une description de quatre ou cinq phrases dans laquelle vous décrivez le bel hôtel *(resort)* et le forfait-vacances *(vacation package)* de vos rêves *(dreams)*. N'oubliez pas de mentionner en détail: le lieu *(setting)*, les activités et le prix *(price)*!

Modèle: **Pour l'hôtel et le forfait-vacances de mes rêves, je suis à la plage en Martinique. Ma chambre d'hôtel est face à l'océan et il y a des fleurs et des plantes aux belles couleurs partout. Il y a beaucoup d'activités possibles: faire du bateau à voile, faire une promenade sur la plage la nuit et faire de la randonnée dans les montagnes toutes proches. Il y a un spa et des cocktails exceptionnels. Le prix est mille trois cents dollars par personne.**

Étape 2. Montrez vos descriptions à un(e) partenaire. Désirez-vous aller à l'hôtel de votre partenaire? Quel bel hôtel est-ce que votre prof va préférer?

Un mot sur la culture

RÉSEAU Sépaq ⚜

Sépaq du Québec

Un des stéréotypes des Canadiens en général, et des Québécois en particulier, c'est qu'ils adorent la nature et les espaces verts. En fait, on appelle le Québec «la Belle Province» à cause de sa beauté naturelle. Au Québec, il existe la Société des établissements de plein air du Québec (Sépaq) qui a pour mission de respecter les espaces verts canadiens et de protéger° les territoires naturels au bénéfice° du peuple et des touristes ainsi qu'au° bénéfice des régions du Québec et des générations futures.

protéger *to protect* **au bénéfice** *to the benefit* **ainsi que** *as well as*

• Est-ce que les espaces verts sont un sujet sérieux chez vous?

◀)) **Liaisons avec les mots et les sons**

Les voyelles nasales

You were introduced to nasal vowels in **Chapitre 3.** Nasal vowels usually end in **m** or **n** in a single syllable. There are three basic nasal vowel sounds in French as illustrated by these words.

vin	vent	vont	bain	banc	bon

Nasal vowel sounds may have different spellings. The sound **bon** may be spelled **on** or **om.**

blond	maison	salon	micro-ondes	bombe

The nasal sound in **fin** may be spelled **ien, ain, aim, in,** or **im.**

bien	invitation	faim	important	mexicain

The nasal sound in **an** may be spelled **an, am, en,** or **em.**

quand	banque	restaurant	comment	temps	champ

Pratique A. Écoutez et répétez ces mots.

1. la chambre
2. la salle de bains
3. une lampe
4. les plantes
5. un voisin
6. l'arrondissement
7. la banlieue
8. un amphithéâtre
9. un jardin
10. un centre sportif
11. au coin de
12. devant

Pratique B. Écoutez et répétez ces répliques de la Séquence 2 du film *Liaisons.* Ensuite, relisez et écoutez les répliques. Encerclez toutes les voyelles nasales.

© Heinle/Cengage Learning

CLAIRE Oui. Je m'appelle Claire Gagner. Vous avez une réservation à mon nom?... Cette fin de semaine... Oui, samedi et dimanche... Ah, bon. Qui a fait la réservation, s'il vous plaît?... OK. Merci.

◀)) **À vos stylos! C'est l'heure de la dictée!**
CD2-14 Vous allez entendre trois phrases deux fois. La première fois, écoutez bien. La deuxième fois, écrivez les phrases.

Sujet Citations célèbres

Pour poser des questions

Les mots d'interrogation

DU FILM *LIAISONS*

Un coup d'œil sur la grammaire

Look at this photo from the film *Liaisons* and its caption, paying special attention to the question words.

© Heinle/Cengage Learning

CLAIRE Qui ferait *(would make)* une réservation pour moi? Et pourquoi?

What two question words do you recognize?

❖ The following words are commonly used in French to ask questions (**poser des questions**) aimed at obtaining specific information. These question words may be used with **est-ce que** or with inversion.

où *where*	**combien de** *how many, how much*
quand *when*	**comment** *how*
que / qu' *what*	**pourquoi** *why*
qui *who(m)*	**quel(le)(s)** *which*

Combien de vélos est-ce que vous avez?　　*How many bikes do you have?*

Que faites-vous ici?　　*What are you doing here?*

❖ When **qui** is the subject of a question, it is immediately followed by a singular verb. When **qui** is the direct object, it may be used with **est-ce que** or inversion.

Qui va à la campagne?　　*Who is going to the countryside?*

Qui est-ce que tu regardes?　　*Whom are you looking at?*

Qui aimez-vous?　　*Who do you like?*

❖ **Qui** may also be the object of prepositions like **à, avec, de,** and **pour.** In these cases, **qui** is equivalent to the English *whom*.

Avec qui est-ce que tu parles?　　*With whom are you speaking?*

De qui parlez-vous?　　*About whom are you speaking?*

❖ Informational question words (except **que**) may also be used alone.

—J'ai envie d'aller au lac.	—*I feel like going to the lake.*
—**Quand?**	—*When?*

—J'ai envie d'aller quelque part.	—*I feel like going somewhere.*
—**Où?**	—*Where?*

❖ Both **quand** and **à quelle heure** can mean *when*. Use **quand** to inquire about a day, date, season, or year. Use **à quelle heure** to inquire about a particular time or hour of day.

—**Quand** allez-vous faire du ski cette année?	—*When are you going skiing this year?*
—Nous allons en février.	—*We're going in February.*
—**À quelle heure** est-ce que nous partons?	—*At what time are we leaving?*
—À dix heures du matin.	—*At ten o'clock in the morning.*

❖ You answer questions asked with **pourquoi** with **parce que/qu'**.

—Je vais téléphoner à ma mère.	—*I am going to call my mother.*
—**Pourquoi?**	—*Why?*
—**Parce que** c'est son anniversaire.	—*Because it's her birthday.*

❖ You have already seen and used **quel/quelle/quels/quelles** in previous chapters. It is an adjective that agrees in number and gender with the noun it modifies. It can also appear in front of the verb **être**.

Quel âge as-tu?	*How old are you?*
Quelle est ta spécialisation?	*What is your major?*
Quels sont tes cours favoris?	*What are your favorite courses?*
Quelles sont les bonnes plages?	*Which are the good beaches?*

Pour aller plus loin
Quoi?!

To ask *What?* in French, you have a few options: **Quoi?, Comment?,** or **Pardon?** It is acceptable to use **Quoi?** with family and friends, but it is considered impolite in more formal contexts. In those instances, you want to use **Comment?** or **Pardon?**

Essayez! Dites-vous **Quoi?, Comment?,** or **Pardon?** dans ces situations?

1. Ton/Ta colocataire te demande *(asks you)* si tu as un stylo.
2. Ton professeur te pose une question.

ACTIVITÉ J **Comment répond-on?** Vous allez entendre une série de

CD2-15 questions. Choisissez la réponse logique.

1. a. Je sors avec mon frère et ma sœur.   b. J'ai un frère et une sœur.
2. a. Parce que j'adore la langue.   b. Avec mes collègues français.
3. a. Je travaille dans mon bureau.   b. Je travaille huit heures par jour.
4. a. Mon cours est dans le laboratoire.   b. Mon professeur est Mme Simard.
5. a. J'arrive sur le campus en voiture.   b. J'arrive sur le campus vers 7h30 du matin.
6. a. Parce que j'adore sortir le soir.   b. Je vais souvent au cinéma.

ACTIVITÉ K **Questions-Réponses** Faites correspondre les questions et leurs réponses.

1. _____ Quand parlez-vous souvent au téléphone?   a. Avec ma famille.
2. _____ Combien d'heures travaillez-vous par jour?   b. Avec mes camarades du cours de français.
3. _____ Avec qui sortez-vous?
4. _____ Pourquoi n'êtes-vous pas à la maison le vendredi soir?   c. Huit heures par jour.
    d. Le soir.
5. _____ Avec qui parlez-vous français?   e. Vers 7h30 du matin.
6. _____ À quelle heure arrivez-vous sur le campus?   f. Parce que j'adore sortir.

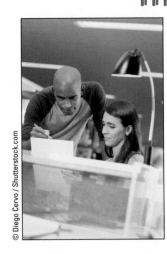

ACTIVITÉ L **La préparation du cours** Complétez chaque question et puis posez les questions à deux étudiants différents. N'oubliez pas de jouer les deux rôles. Avez-vous les mêmes habitudes de travail?

1. _____ étudiez-vous: dans le silence, devant la télé, sérieusement, avec des amis, etc.?
   a. Comment   b. Combien de   c. Quoi
2. _____ commencez-vous vos devoirs: dans l'après-midi, dans la soirée, etc.?
   a. Pourquoi   b. Qui   c. Quand
3. _____ temps passez-vous sur vos devoirs: trente minutes par jour, une heure par jour, deux heures par jour, plus de (more than) trois heures par jour, etc.?
   a. Quoi   b. Combien de   c. Où
4. _____ finissez-vous vos devoirs: avant 19h, vers 20h, vers 22h, après minuit, etc.?
   a. Quand   b. Comment   c. Pourquoi

ACTIVITÉ M **Détecteur de mensonges** Répondez aux questions. Mais **une** des réponses doit être **fausse**. Vous allez partager vos réponses en petits groupes et votre groupe va détecter le mensonge (lie).

1. **Combien de** camarades de chambres / colocataires avez-vous?
2. **Que** pensez-vous du restaurant universitaire sur votre campus?
3. **Avec qui** aimez-vous sortir?
4. **Où** allez-vous normalement le week-end?
5. **Quel** est votre film préféré?

ACTIVITÉ **N** **Êtes-vous fans de quiz?** Complétez chaque phrase et puis essayez *(try)* de répondre à toutes les questions.

1. Sur _____ ferme de fiction est-ce qu'on trouve Fern, Charlotte et Wilbur?
   a. quel   b. quelle   c. quels   d. quelles

2. Dans _____ lac légendaire habite Viviane, la Dame du Lac?
   a. quel   b. quelle   c. quels   d. quelles

3. Dans _____ bois habitent Robin des Bois et ses hommes?
   a. quel   b. quelle   c. quels   d. quelles

4. Dans _____ mer le dieu *(god)* grec Poséidon habite-t-il?
   a. quel   b. quelle   c. quels   d. quelles

5. _____ montagnes sont le lieu de naissance *(birthplace)* de Davy Crockett?
   a. Quel   b. Quelle   c. Quels   d. Quelles

ACTIVITÉ **O** **Personnages célèbres** Complétez chaque phrase et puis essayez *(try)* de deviner *(guess)* qui sont les personnages *(characters)*.

1. _____ qui est-ce que Jill va en haut *(on top)* de la colline?
   a. Chez   b. Avec   c. De

2. _____ qui est-ce que les gens de la Vallée endormie *(sleepy)* ont peur?
   a. De   b. Pour   c. Selon

3. _____ qui est-ce que le père cueille *(picks)* une rose du jardin de la Bête *(Beast)*?
   a. À   b. Avec   c. Pour

4. _____ qui est-ce que la pionnière *(pioneer)* Laura habite dans la prairie américaine?
   a. Avec   b. Selon   c. Après

5. _____ qui est-ce que Hansel et Gretel mangent des bonbons?
   a. Chez   b. Selon   c. Après

ACTIVITÉ **P** **Meneurs de jeu *(Quiz Masters)*** C'est votre tour *(turn)* maintenant de préparer un quiz! Utilisez le vocabulaire de ce chapitre et préparez quatre questions que vous allez poser à vos camarades de classe.

Modèle: **Quel fleuve traverse la ville de Paris?** (la Seine)
Combien de pièces la Maison Blanche a-t-elle? (132 pièces)

ACTIVITÉ **Q** **Former un groupe d'études**

Étape 1. C'est une bonne idée de former un petit groupe pour étudier le français ensemble en dehors du *(outside)* cours. Utilisez des mots d'interrogation pour écrire trois ou quatre questions que vous voudriez *(would like)* poser pour recruter *(recruit)* des membres.

Étape 2. Posez vos questions aux autres étudiants du cours. Notez leurs prénoms et leurs réponses. Qui voudriez-vous inviter à rejoindre *(join)* votre groupe d'études? Pourquoi?

ACTIVITÉ (R) **Chiche!** Chiche! est une association française de «jeunes écologistes alternatifs solidaires». Ils ont comme but *(goal)* la protection de l'environnement et des espaces verts. Voici un extrait d'une interview d'un membre. Quelles sont peut-être les questions posées pendant l'interview?

Modèle: Question: **Combien de membres avez-vous?**

Réponse: Nous avons au moins 200 membres.

1. Question: _____

   Réponse: Nous désirons organiser des actions de sensibilisation à la protection de l'environnement et de critique de la société de consommation.

2. Question: _____

   Réponse: Notre slogan est: «Tu crois que tu vas changer le monde? Chiche!»

3. Question: _____

   Réponse: Nous avons des groupes à Amiens, à Bordeaux, à Lille, à Rennes et à Toulouse.

4. Question: _____

   Réponse: On travaille souvent avec des membres de la fédération politique Jeunes Verts.

ACTIVITÉ (S) **Enthousiastes de la nature?** Vous allez faire un sondage *(survey)* pour trouver des enthousiastes de la nature dans le cours. Préparez au moins trois questions et puis posez vos questions aux étudiants.

Modèle: **Combien de fois par an est-ce que tu fais de la randonnée?**
Quelle(s) plage(s) est-ce que tu visites et avec quelle fréquence?
Quand est-ce que tu vas à la campagne et pour faire quoi?

ACTIVITÉ (T) **Artistes de paysages**

Étape 1. *Dessinez* individuellement une image d'un paysage *(landscape)*.

Étape 2. Posez des questions à votre partenaire sur son paysage et essayez de *(try to)* le dessiner. Utilisez les prépositions que vous avez apprises *(you learned)* dans le **Vocabulaire 2.**

> **D'AUTRES EXPRESSIONS UTILES**
>
> **au centre** *in the middle, center* **en bas** *on bottom* **en haut** *on top*

Modèle: É1 (artiste): **Qu'est-ce qu'on trouve dans ton image?**
É2: **Une colline, une rivière, quelques nuages et un arbre.**
É1: **Où est l'arbre?**
É2: **À côté de la rivière. À droite.**
É1: **Combien de nuages est-ce qu'il y a?**
É2: **Trois gros nuages.**
É1: **Comment est la colline?**
É2: **Petite.**

Que / Qu' vs. Quoi

Choosing between **que/qu'** and **quoi** depends on the structure of the question and sometimes the verb. Compare the differences.

Qu'est-ce que nous mangeons?	*What are we eating?*
On mange **quoi**?	*We are eating what?*
Que mangeons-nous?	*What are we eating?*
De quoi est-ce que vous parlez?	*What are you talking about?*
Vous parlez **de quoi**?	*You are talking about what?*
De quoi parlez-vous?	*What are you talking about?*

Qu'est-ce que is commonly used in spoken French. When used in written French, it is less formal than **que** used with inversion.

Que is used with inversion in both written and oral forms. In oral French, **que** plus inversion is more common in Quebec than in France.

Quoi is used with intonation and prepositions. With intonation, it is considered very informal and is used when speaking with friends. It is seldom written.

Essayez! Complétez chaque phrase avec **que/qu'** ou **quoi**.

1. _____ est-ce que tu penses de la langue française?
2. _____ fais-tu normalement après le cours de français?
3. De _____ est-ce que tu as besoin pour réussir dans le cours de français?

Liaisons musicales

© Pierre Guibert/Visual Press Agency/Photoshot

La musique d'Alister mélange *(mixes)* la chanson française avec le rock. Sa célèbre chanson, *Qu'est-ce qu'on va faire de toi?* (2008), est la première chanson de son premier album. Cherchez les paroles de cette chanson. Quelle action choisissez-vous parmi *(among)* les possibilités présentées dans la chanson? 🌐

La parole est à vous!

La vie est-elle meilleure à la campagne ou en ville?

Certains disent que la vie à la campagne est meilleure *(better)*. D'autres disent que la vie en ville est meilleure. Qu'en pensez-vous?

- Samuel de Lyon (France): «Surtout en ville. Il y a de la culture et toujours beaucoup de choses à faire. La vie est beaucoup plus intéressante en ville.»
- Sophie de Champagne (France): «C'est certainement la vie à la campagne qui est meilleure. Il n'y a pas de pollution. C'est plus beau et plus calme. La vie à la campagne est toujours tranquille et agréable.»

Et vous? Qu'en pensez-vous?

Est-ce que la vie est meilleure à la campagne ou en ville?

DEUXIÈME
PROJECTION

Avant de visionner

ACTIVITÉ A Vous rappelez-vous? Vous rappelez-vous (*Do you remember*) qui a dit ces phrases dans la Séquence 2 du film *Liaisons*?

	Claire	Abia	Michel
1. Émile? Où es-tu?	☐	☐	☐
2. Qui a fait la réservation, s'il vous plaît?	☐	☐	☐
3. Va à Québec, Claire. Pour la famille…	☐	☐	☐
4. … cet homme qui t'a fait la réservation, c'est peut-être un meurtrier, un psychopathe…	☐	☐	☐
5. Tu es sûre de ta décision?	☐	☐	☐
6. Il était là, près de la sortie (*exit*).	☐	☐	☐

ACTIVITÉ B Une scène du film Vous rappelez-vous cette scène? Claire dit à Abia qu'elle veut aller au Château Frontenac. Complétez les phrases avec les mots qui manquent (*are missing*).

ABIA Tu es (1) _____?

CLAIRE Abia, c'est peut-être une (2) _____.

ABIA Aventure? Un homme (3) _____—un homme que tu ne connais pas—il te fait une (4) _____ pour le Frontenac (5) _____ Québec, et tu ne sais pas qui a payé (6) _____.

© Heinle/Cengage Learning

Regarder la séquence

Vous allez regarder la Séquence 2 du film *Liaisons* deux fois. La première fois, vérifiez vos réponses à l'Activité A et à l'Activité B. La deuxième fois, faites attention à l'appartement de Claire et prenez des notes.

SUGGESTIONS: Son appartement est petit ou grand? Quels meubles y a-t-il dans l'appartement? Comment est la décoration: moderne, traditionnelle? L'appartement est propre, rangé, en désordre?

Après le visionnage

ACTIVITÉ C L'appartement de Claire

1. Faites une description de l'appartement de Claire avec vos notes.

2. Décrivez la personnalité de Claire avec trois adjectifs.

3. On dit que notre espace personnel reflète notre personnalité. Voyez-vous (*Do you see*) des liaisons entre l'appartement de Claire et sa personnalité?

ACTIVITÉ **D** **Claire et Abia**

Étape 1. Notez des similarités et des différences entre Claire et Abia. Pensez à leurs traits physiques et à leurs personnalités.

Similarités   **Différences**

_____   _____

_____   _____

_____   _____

_____   _____

Étape 2. Partagez vos notes avec un(e) camarade. Avec lui/elle, écrivez un profil de Claire et d'Abia pour la classe.

ACTIVITÉ **E** **Résumé de la Séquence 2** Voici un résumé de la Séquence 2 du film. Choisissez les mots qui manquent.

aller	Château Frontenac	famille	quart	en
appel	Hôtel Mont Royal	mystérieuse	Québec	son

Claire reçoit une enveloppe (1) _____. C'est une réservation anonyme pour deux nuits au (2) _____ à (3) _____. À trois heures et (4) _____ du matin, elle reçoit un (5) _____ de son oncle Michel (6) _____ France. Il dit qu'elle doit (7) _____ à Québec pour la (8) _____.

Abia	amie	bonne	cette	homme	mauvaise

Claire parle avec Abia au sujet de (9) _____ réservation. Elle dit à (10) _____ qu'elle va aller à Québec. Abia pense que c'est une (11) _____ idée. Abia a peur pour son (12) _____.

Dans les coulisses

You compared physical and personality profiles of Claire and Abia in **Activité D**. Abia comes from a large family and maintains close relationships with her relatives. Claire's family background is less clear. Her mother is in a psychiatric hospital, and her only other relative appears to be an uncle in France. Why do you think Claire and Abia are friends? What role does Abia play in Claire's life? What roles do secondary characters typically play in movies?

À DÉCOUVRIR: La Côte d'Ivoire et la ville d'Abidjan

À DÉCOUVRIR: La Côte d'Ivoire

Pays: La Côte d'Ivoire
Géographie: En Afrique occidentale sub-saharienne
Climat: Tropical sur la côte et semi-aride dans le nord; trois saisons: chaud et sec (novembre-mars), très chaud et sec (mars-mai), très chaud et pluvieux (juin-octobre).
Population: Plus de 20 millions
Capitale: Yamoussoukro

Activité Internet
La Côte d'Ivoire est un pays important dans la production et l'exportation de plusieurs *(several)* produits. Trouvez sur Internet quelques produits qu'exporte *(produces)* régulièrement la Côte d'Ivoire.

À DÉCOUVRIR: La ville d'Abidjan

Structure: Une mégalopole moderne
Région: Région des lagunes
Population: Plus de 3,5 millions
Réputation: La capitale économique de la Côte d'Ivoire; le carrefour culturel ouest-africain

Avant de lire

You will discover in this reading the city of Abidjan, the economic capital of **Côte d'Ivoire.**

Que savez-vous déjà?

1. Quels bâtiments sont normalement associés aux grandes villes?
2. Quelles activités est-ce qu'on fait normalement dans les grandes villes?
3. Quand vous voyez le mot **mégalopole**, qu'est-ce que vous imaginez?

OUTILS DE LECTURE
Using context to learn new nouns

Knowing the main idea of a text can help you guess what some unfamiliar nouns are. For example, if you know that the city of Abidjan is the economic capital of **Côte d'Ivoire,** what do you think the following words in bold mean in English?

1. Abidjan est un important **carrefour** commercial et culturel de l'Afrique de l'Ouest.
2. **le quartier des affaires**

Découvrir une mégalopole africaine

© Lonely Planet / SuperStock

Une des plus grandes villes francophones, Abidjan, avec 5,9 millions d'habitants dans l'agglomération°, est la capitale économique de la Côte d'Ivoire (Yamoussoukro est la capitale politique). Le français est la langue officielle. Parmi° les autres langues, on trouve le dioula, l'attié et le baoulé (il y a une soixantaine° de langues en Côte d'Ivoire).

Abidjan est un important carrefour° commercial et culturel de l'Afrique de l'Ouest. Le Plateau, le quartier des affaires, qui compte de nombreux immeubles° modernes, est quelquefois appelé «le Manhattan des tropiques». La ville est divisée en deux parties: Abidjan sud (au bord du° Golfe de Guinée) et Abidjan nord (de l'autre côté des° lagunes). Cette ville tropicale au bord de l'océan possède aussi des plages avec des palmiers et des cocotiers.

Comme beaucoup de villes africaines, elle a des quartiers d'habitation° «à l'européenne» (Cocody) et des quartiers traditionnels (Marcory ou Treichville) avec plusieurs logements construits autour de° cours collectives. Avec ses nombreuses discothèques et une vie nocturne particulièrement animée, Abidjan est un des centres de la musique africaine. Parmi les genres musicaux d'origine ivoirienne, il y a le zouglou et le mapouka. Avec des musiciens comme Alpha Blondy et Tiken Jah Fakoly, Abidjan est aussi le centre du reggae en Afrique.

agglomération *greater urban area* **Parmi** *Among* **soixantaine** *approximately sixty* **carrefour** *crossroads* **immeubles** *buildings* **au bord du** *at the edge of* **de l'autre côté des** *on the other side of* **quartiers d'habitation** *residential neighborhoods* **autour de** *around*

Après avoir lu

Compréhension

	Vrai	Faux
1. Abidjan n'est pas une grande ville francophone.	☐	☐
2. Le français est la langue officielle de la ville.	☐	☐
3. C'est une ville tropicale au bord de l'océan.	☐	☐
4. Il n'y a pas de vie nocturne à Abidjan.	☐	☐

Et vous?

1. Est-ce que tu viens d'une mégalopole?
2. Est-ce que le commerce est un aspect important de ta ville d'origine?
3. Est-ce qu'il y a une vie nocturne d'où tu viens? Qu'est-ce que les gens font?
4. Est-ce que la musique a une importance culturelle chez toi?

Activité Internet
Research one of the styles of music or one of the musicians mentioned in the reading. Summarize your findings in 2–3 sentences.

Descriptions of cities appear in many kinds of publications such as novels, magazines, travel guides, and study abroad brochures. Here is a description of the city of Abidjan in **Côte d'Ivoire,** Africa.

Abidjan, très grande ville francophone, compte 5,9 millions d'habitants avec le centre-ville et les banlieues. C'est la capitale économique de la Côte d'Ivoire. On trouve à Abidjan une importante industrialisation avec des industries diverses et une urbanisation rapide avec un nombre constant de personnes qui viennent vivre dans la région. Abidjan est à l'origine un petit village de pêcheurs mais aujourd'hui, avec son grand port, Abidjan est un carrefour commercial important pour tout le continent.

© Kambou Sia/Getty

Avant d'écrire

1. List the kinds of observations that appear in the description of Abidjan.

2. Answer the following questions to help you write your own **description d'une ville**.

a. De quelle ville voulez-vous faire une description?

b. Qu'est-ce que vous appréciez et/ou n'appréciez pas dans votre ville?

c. La ville a-t-elle certains traits physiques importants et/ou certaines activités préférées?

d. Comment décrivez-vous le caractère ou la personnalité de cette ville?

e. Cette ville change-t-elle selon les saisons, l'heure, le temps ou le jour de la semaine?

Écrire

Using information from **Avant d'écrire**, write your own description of 6–8 sentences in French.

Après avoir écrit

Exchange your **description d'une ville** with a partner. 1) Circle all the prepositions used with geographical location and verify that they are all correct. 2) Underline all verbs and verify that your partner correctly conjugated them. 3) Double-check that your partner made all of the adjectives agree in number and gender. 4) Put a * next to the key phrase or key idea that best communicates your partner's description. 5) How would you characterize your partner's description: **créative, amusante, banale, objective, imaginative, drôle, inspirante, neutre, ennuyeuse,** etc.? Discuss your reactions together and then write a second version of your **description d'une ville** taking into account your partner's comments and corrections.

PARTIE 1

LES LOGEMENTS

un appartement	apartment
un bail	lease
un(e) colocataire	roomate, housemate
le loyer	rent
une maison	house, home
le premier étage	second floor (USA)
le règlement (m.) de location	rental agreements, renter rules
le rez-de-chaussée	ground floor, first floor (USA)
les tâches ménagères (f.)	household chores
un(e) voisin(e)	neighbor

LES PIÈCES DE LA MAISON

la chambre	bedroom
le couloir	hallway
la cuisine	kitchen
le garage	garage
une pièce	room
la salle de bains	bathroom
la salle à manger	dining room
la salle de séjour	living room, family room
le salon	salon, formal living room
les W.-C. (m. pl.)	toilet (room), water closet

DANS LA MAISON

les affaires (f.)	things, stuff
un appareil audiovisuel	piece of audiovisual equipment
un appareil ménager	household appliance
une baignoire	bathtub
un balcon	balcony
un canapé	couch
les choses (f.)	things, stuff
une commode	chest of drawers
une console de jeux vidéo	videogame console
une cuisinière	stove
une douche	shower
l'escalier (m.)	staircase
les étagères (f.)	bookshelves
un fauteuil	armchair
un four	oven
une lampe	lamp
un lavabo	bathroom sink
un lecteur DVD	DVD player
un lit	bed
un meuble	piece of furniture
un (four à) micro-ondes	microwave
un miroir	mirror
un objet	object
un placard	closet
un réfrigérateur / un frigo	refrigerator / fridge
les rideaux (m.)	curtains
le sous-sol	basement
un tapis	rug
un téléviseur	television set

VERBES

choisir	to choose
faire la lessive	to do the laundry
faire le ménage	to do the housework
faire la poussière	to dust
faire la vaisselle	to do the dishes
finir	to finish
grandir	to grow up
grossir	to gain weight
louer	to rent
maigrir	to lose weight
obéir (à)	to obey
partager	to share
passer l'aspirateur (m.)	to vacuum
ranger	to pick up (the house), to put things away
réfléchir (à)	to reflect (upon), to consider
réussir (à)	to succeed (at, in)
salir	to dirty
sortir la poubelle	to take out the garbage, trash

ADJECTIFS

équipé(e)	equipped
propre	clean
sale	dirty

DIVERS

chez	at the home / place of
Il faut + *infinitive*	It is necessary . . . / One must . . . / to have to . . .
la loi	law
les règles (f.)	rules

PARTIE 2

LES LIEUX / ENDROITS

un amphithéâtre	lecture hall
la banlieue	suburbs
une banque	bank
un bâtiment	building
un bistro	café-restaurant
une boutique	store, boutique
un bureau de poste	post office
le centre commercial	shopping center / district
un centre sportif	recreation center
le centre-ville	downtown
le cinéma	movie theater
une église	church
un endroit	location, place
un hôpital	hospital
un institut de beauté	spa, beauty parlor
un kiosque à journaux	newsstand
un laboratoire	laboratory
une laverie automatique	laundromat
une librairie	bookstore
un lycée	high school
un magasin	store
une maison de la presse	newsstand
un musée	museum
un parking	parking lot
une pharmacie	pharmacy
la piscine (municipale)	(public) swimming pool
un quartier (résidentiel)	a (residential) neighborhood
une résidence universitaire	university / college residence hall

un restaurant universitaire	campus cafeteria
la rue	street
un stade	stadium
les toilettes (f. pl.) (publiques)	(public) restrooms
une ville	a city, a town
les W.-C. (m. pl.) (publics)	(public) restrooms

DANS LA VILLE

un magazine	magazine
un plan	map (of a city)

L'ORDRE DES ÉVÉNEMENTS

d'abord	first
ensuite / puis	next, then
plus tard	later
enfin	finally

PRÉPOSITIONS

à côté (de)	next (to)
au coin (de)	on the corner (of)
à droite (de)	to/on the right (of)
à gauche (de)	to/on the left (of)
derrière	behind
devant	in front (of)
en face (de)	across (from)
en ville	in town, in the city
entre	between
jusqu'à	until
jusqu'au bout	until the end
loin (de)	far (from)
près (de)	near
sur le campus	on campus
tout droit	straight ahead
vers	towards

LES INDICATIONS

tourner à droite / à gauche	to turn right / left
traverser la rue	to cross the street
aller / continuer tout droit	to go / to continue straight ahead
aller / continuer jusqu'à	to go / to continue until
aller jusqu'au bout	to go to the end
aller vers	to go towards

PARTIE 3

LES ESPACES VERTS

un arbre	tree
les bois (m. pl.)	woods
la campagne	the country(side)
un champ	field
une colline	hill
un étang	pond
une ferme	farm
une fleur	flower
une forêt	forest
un jardin	garden, lawn
un lac	lake
la mer	the sea

une montagne	mountain
la plage	the beach
une plante	plant
une prairie	meadow, grassland, prairie
une rivière / un fleuve	river
une vallée	valley

LES ACTIVITÉS

aller à la chasse	to go hunting, to hunt
aller à la pêche	to go fishing
faire du bateau (à voile)	to go (sail)boating
faire du deltaplane	to go hang-gliding, to hang-glide
faire du jardinage	to garden
faire de la randonnée	to go hiking, to hike

LES DIRECTIONS

l'est (m.)	east
le nord	north
l'ouest (m.)	west
le sud	south

LES NOMBRES

100 cent	1 550 mille cinq cent cinquante
105 cent cinq	1 999 mille neuf cent quatre-vingt-dix-neuf
135 cent trente-cinq	2 000 deux mille
200 deux cents	2 780 deux mille sept cent quatre-vingts
250 deux cent cinquante	
300 trois cents	1 000 000 un million
375 trois cent soixante-quinze	1 500 000 un million cinq cent mille
400 quatre cents	
500 cinq cents	2 000 000 deux millions
600 six cents	2 555 000 deux millions cinq cent cinquante-cinq mille
700 sept cents	
800 huit cents	
900 neuf cents	
1 000 mille	1 000 000 000 un milliard
1 100 mille cent	2 000 000 000 deux milliards
1 300 mille trois cents	

LES MOTS D'INTERROGATION

combien de	how many, how much
comment	how
où	where
pourquoi	why
quand	when
que / qu'	what
quel(le)(s)	which
qui	who(m)
quoi (informal)	what
parce que/qu'	because
poser des questions	to ask questions

DIVERS

un point	period/point
une virgule	comma

Les **plaisirs** de **la table**

En bref   In this chapter, you will:

- learn about food, beverages, meals, and nutrition

- learn the verbs **prendre, apprendre,** and **comprendre**

- learn partitive articles

- learn the verb **boire**

- learn vocabulary to discuss tastes and flavors, and learn expressions of quantity

- learn the **passé composé** with **avoir**

- learn the /r/ sound

- read about food, diet, and health in France and the Francophone world

 You will also watch **SÉQUENCE 3: À Québec** of the film *Liaisons.*

Ressources

 audio   http://www.cengagebrain.com

©Cultura /Alamy

🔊 ## Les **repas**

Meals

la confiture

le beurre

le café

un croissant

Le petit déjeuner français

le pain   le jus d'orange   le sucre

la crème

les œufs (m.)

les saucisses (f.)

Le (petit) déjeuner québécois

le poulet

la soupe à la tomate

l'eau minérale (f.)

une salade

les pâtes (f.)

Le déjeuner

un gâteau au chocolat

le vin

les haricots verts (m.)

une pomme de terre

le steak

Le dîner

Vocabulaire complémentaire

les plats (m.) *courses*
  un hors-d'œuvre / une entrée
    starter / appetizer
  un plat principal *main course, dish (kind of food)*
  un dessert *dessert*
  le goûter *snack*

la nourriture *food*
  un aliment *a particular food*
  les biscuits (m.) *cookies*
  des céréales (f.) *cereal*
  les chips (f.) *chips*
  les frites (f.) *French fries*
  le fromage *cheese*
  la glace *ice cream*
  une omelette *omelet*
  la pizza *pizza*
  le poisson *fish*
  le riz *rice*
  un sandwich (au fromage) *(cheese) sandwich*
  le yaourt *yogurt*

les boissons (f.) *drinks/beverages*
  la bière *beer*
  le citron pressé *lemonade*
  le Coca *Coca-Cola*
  le lait *milk*
  le thé *tea*

les fruits (m.) *fruits*
  une banane *banana*
  une orange *orange*
  une pomme *apple*

les légumes (m.) *vegetables*
  les carottes (f.) *carrots*
  les épinards (m.) *spinach*

la viande *meat*
  le bœuf *beef*
  le jambon *ham*
  un rôti (de porc) (m.) *(pork) roast*

ACTIVITÉ A **(Petit) déjeuner français ou québécois?** Vous allez
CD2-16 entendre le nom d'un aliment. Indiquez si l'aliment est associé **(a) au petit déjeuner français**, **(b) au déjeuner québécois** ou **(c) aux deux** *(both)*.

  1.   **2.**   **3.**   **4.**   **5.**   **6.**   **7.**   **8.**

Un mot sur la langue

Petit déjeuner ou déjeuner?

Est-ce qu'il y a une différence entre *dinner* et *supper* en anglais? La signification de ces mots varie selon la région ou le pays. En France, on prend **le petit déjeuner** le matin, **le déjeuner** à midi et **le dîner** le soir. Mais au Québec, en Belgique et en Suisse, **le déjeuner** est le repas du matin, **le dîner** le repas du midi et **le souper** le repas du soir.

• Complétez avec **le déjeuner, le dîner, le petit déjeuner** ou **le souper.**

  1. À 18h00 au Québec, on prend *(have, eat)*...
  2. À 9h00 en France, on prend...
  3. À midi en Belgique, on prend...
  4. À 20h00 en France, on prend...

🔊 **ACTIVITÉ B Les plats** Vous allez entendre le nom d'un aliment. Quels plats
CD2-17 associez-vous à chaque aliment: (**a**) **apéritif**, (**b**) **entrée / hors d'œuvre**, (**c**) **plat principal** ou (**d**) **dessert**?

1.   2.   3.   4.   5.   6.   7.   8.   9.   10.

🔊 **ACTIVITÉ C Associations**
CD2-18

Étape 1. Vous allez entendre le nom de plusieurs aliments. Quelle couleur associez-vous à chaque aliment?

1.   2.   3.   4.   5.   6.   7.   8.   9.   10.

Étape 2. Quels autres aliments associez-vous à ces couleurs?

1. rose   **2.** blanc   **3.** vert   **4.** jaune   **5.** rouge   **6.** orange

ACTIVITÉ D Les marques Pour chaque aliment, donnez une marque (*brand name*) populaire.

Modèle: le poulet   **Tysons / Kentucky's**

1. la glace
2. le citron pressé
3. les pommes de terre
4. les pâtes
5. la confiture
6. le jambon
7. la soupe
8. le thé
9. les biscuits
10. les céréales
11. le bœuf
12. l'eau minérale

Si vous y allez

Courtesy Café Krieghoff

Si vous allez à Québec, allez au Café Krieghoff pour un bon (petit) déjeuner québécois. Le café-bistro est également un gîte du passant* *(bed and breakfast)* bon marché pour les touristes. Cherchez le site officiel sur Internet pour voir les tarifs *(rates)*.

ACTIVITÉ E Quel aliment est bon pour… ? Créez des phrases selon *(according to)* le modèle.

Modèle: pour les cheveux   **Les œufs sont bons pour les cheveux.**

1. pour les yeux
2. pour l'estomac *(stomach)*
3. pour les muscles
4. pour le cerveau *(brain)*
5. pour les os *(bones)*
6. contre *(against)* le rhume *(cold)*

*The term **gîte du passant** is used in Quebec. In France, one would hear **chambre d'hôtes**.

ACTIVITÉ **F** **Votre opinion**

Étape 1. Indiquez ce que vous pensez de chaque aliment avec les adjectifs suivants ou d'autres: **délicieux, succulent, bon, mauvais, dégoutant.**

Modèle: la confiture   **La confiture est délicieuse.**

1. les céréales
2. le poisson
3. le yaourt
4. le steak
5. la pizza
6. les pâtes

Étape 2. Demandez à un(e) camarade de classe s'il/si elle aime ces aliments.

Modèle: É1: **Aimes-tu les céréales?**
É2: **Oui, les céréales sont délicieuses. / Non, les céréales sont mauvaises.**

ACTIVITÉ **G** **Pour le goûter** Quels aliments est-ce que la classe aime pour le goûter? Demandez à vos camarades s'ils aiment les aliments suivants et écrivez leurs noms et leurs réponses.

Modèle: É1: **Est-ce que tu aimes le Coca?**
É2: **Oui, j'aime le Coca.**

1. le lait
2. le citron pressé
3. les frites
4. les chips
5. les biscuits
6. le Coca
7. le fromage
8. l'eau minérale

ACTIVITÉ **H** **Un dîner élégant** Avec deux ou trois camarades de classe, préparez un menu pour un dîner élégant chez votre professeur. Qu'est-ce que vous allez servir *(serve)* en **entrée**, pour le **plat principal** et au **dessert**?

Modèle: **Entrée: soupe et pain**

Un mot sur la culture

De la frite belge à la poutine québécoise

Comme les Français, les Belges adorent les frites. Les Belges sont très fiers d'être les inventeurs de ce plat célèbre! En Belgique, on mange souvent des frites avec des moules°. En France, le steak-frites est un plat typique. Les Québécois ont aussi inventé un plat avec des frites: la poutine. On prépare la poutine avec des frites, du fromage en grains° et une sauce brune.

moules *mussels* **fromage en grains** *cheese curds*

- Qu'est-ce que vous aimez manger avec les frites?

© Lauri Patterson/Shutterstock.com

Pour parler de la nourriture

Le verbe **prendre** / Les articles partitifs

DU FILM *LIAISONS*
··
Un coup d'œil sur la grammaire

Look at this photo from the film *Liaisons* and its caption.

© Heinle/Cengage Learning

Claire **prend une petite salade** et **du café** dans **un** restaurant à Trois-Rivières.

1. What does **prend** mean?
   a. *to drink*   b. *to have*
2. Which article is used with nouns that are countable?
   a. **du**   b. **un/une**
3. Which article is used with mass nouns that are normally not counted?
   a. **du**   b. **un/une**

Les verbes-clés

Le verbe *prendre*

❖ The verb **prendre** *(to take)* is commonly used with food to mean *to have (food)*. It is irregular in the present tense.

prendre	
je **prends**	nous **prenons**
tu **prends**	vous **prenez**
il/elle/on **prend**	ils/elles **prennent**

—Qu'est-ce que vous **prenez**?   —*What are you having?*

—Je **prends** du pain.   —*I am having (some) bread.*

❖ Some common expressions with **prendre** include **prendre le déjeuner / le dîner** *(to have lunch / dinner)*, **prendre un verre** *(to have a drink)*, and **prendre son temps** *(to take one's time)*.

❖ Other verbs conjugated like **prendre** are **apprendre** *(to learn)* and **comprendre** *(to understand)*.

Marc et Lisa **apprennent** l'italien.   Nous **comprenons** le français.

❖ When an infinitive follows **apprendre,** the preposition **à** must be used.

Il **apprend à** faire la cuisine.   *He is learning (how) to cook.*

Les articles partitifs

In addition to definite and indefinite articles, French has partitive articles. Roughly equivalent to *some* or *any* in English, the **partitif** is used with mass nouns or things that are normally not counted and that you only take a part of like bread, cake, milk, butter, meat, fish, and sugar.

(m. sing.)	**du**	Vous prenez **du** pain?	*Are you having any/some bread?*
(f. sing.)	**de la**	**de la** viande?	*any/some meat?*
(m. / f. + vowel sound)	**de l'**	**de l'**eau?	*any/some water?*

Tu prends **de la** crème dans ton café?	*Do you take (any) cream in your coffee?*
Nous mangeons **du** poulet ce soir.	*We are eating (some) chicken tonight.*

With countable nouns, meaning those that are easily made plural and can be used with numbers (**un œuf, trois œufs**), the indefinite article (**un, une, des**) is used.

Je vais préparer **une** omelette.	*I am going to make an omelet.*
Je vais acheter **des** œufs.	*I am going to buy some eggs.*
Je vais faire **un** gâteau.	*I am going to make a cake.*

Un, une, and numbers may be used with mass nouns such as coffee and ice cream when referring to a fixed quantity. When the quantity is undetermined, use the **partitif.**

Nous prenons **du** café.	*We are having (some) coffee.*
Je prends **un** café.	*I'm having a coffee (a cup).*
Trois cafés, s'il vous plaît.	*Three coffees, please.*
On prend **de la** glace comme dessert.	*We're having (some) ice cream for dessert.*
Je prends **une** glace.	*I'm having an ice cream (a cone).*

As you learned in **Chapitre 1** and **Chapitre 2,** with negation, the partitive and indefinite articles become **de** or **d'.**

Tu ne manges pas **de** porc?	*You don't eat pork?*
Je n'ai pas **d'**œufs.	*I don't have any eggs.*
Elle ne prend pas **de** glace.	*She isn't having ice cream.*

Un mot sur la langue

La glace et la crème glacée

Au Québec on dit **la crème glacée** au lieu de *(instead of)* **la glace.** C'est parce que le Québec est en Amérique du Nord et donc influencé par les mots anglais *(ice cream).*

- Où trouve-t-on la meilleure *(best)* crème glacée dans votre ville?

ACTIVITÉ I Au gîte du passant

Étape 1. Les clients d'un gîte du passant *(bed and breakfast)* ont beaucoup d'activités. Utilisez les verbes pour déterminer le sujet de chaque phrase.

1. _____ **prennent** le goûter à 15h.   a. Émile   b. Émile et son frère

2. _____ **comprend** le russe.   a. Julie   b. Julie et Pierre

3. _____ **apprends à** jouer du piano.   a. J(e)   b. Claire

4. _____ **comprennent** le chinois.   a. Marthe   b. Marthe et Sarah

5. _____ **comprenons** l'allemand.   a. J(e)   b. Nous

6. _____ **apprenons à** jouer au rugby.   a. J(e)   b. Nous

7. _____ **prenez** du vin.   a. Nous   b. Vous

Étape 2. Et vous? Complétez les phrases.

1. Je comprends _____.   2. J'apprends (à) _____.

ACTIVITÉ J Qui prend… ? Est-ce que vous connaissez les préférences alimentaires de vos camarades de classe? Devinez qui prend ces aliments régulièrement.

> **SUGGESTIONS**
>
> Je   Le professeur   Nous   Mon/Ma camarade de classe _____

Modèle: _____ des escargots.   **Paul et Ben prennent** des escargots.

1. _____ des pâtes.   5. _____ de la glace.

2. _____ du café.   6. _____ du Coca.

3. _____ du fromage.   7. _____ une pomme.

4. _____ un sandwich.   8. _____ des croissants.

ACTIVITÉ K Qu'est-ce que ce touriste prend au petit déjeuner?
Utilisez les articles pour déterminer ce que le touriste prend au petit déjeuner.

1. Je prends **un…**   a. pain   b. croissant

2. Je prends **des…**   a. saucisses   b. pain

3. Je prends du café avec **de la…**   a. crème   b. lait

4. Je prends **un…**   a. biscuit   b. beurre

5. Je prends **une…**   a. confiture   b. omelette

6. Je prends **du…**   a. jus d'orange   b. œuf

7. Je prends **de l'…**   a. eau   b. œuf

8. Je prends **une…**   a. crème   b. petite baguette

Conclusion Pensez-vous que le touriste est en France ou au Québec?

ACTIVITÉ **L** **Qu'est-ce qu'elle prend?** Choisissez l'image qui correspond à chaque phrase.

1. Elle prend **du** thé.

a.   b.

2. Elle prend **un** Coca.

a.   b.

3. Elle prend **un** yaourt.

a.   b.

4. Elle prend **de la** glace.

a.   b.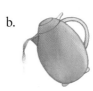

5. Elle prend **un** café.

a.   b.

6. Elle prend **du** gâteau.

a.   b.

ACTIVITÉ **M** **Robert mange bien?** Utilisez les articles pour déterminer si Robert prend ou ne prend pas chaque aliment. Utilisez **(a) Il prend** ou **(b) Il ne prend pas.**

© Heinle/Cengage Learning

Robert Levesque, gérant *(manager)* **de l'hôtel dans le film** *Liaisons*

1. ____ **de** beurre.

2. ____ **de** crème.

3. ____ **des** pommes

4. ____ **de** l'eau minérale.

5. ____ **de** sucre.

6. ____ **du** poisson.

7. ____ **une** salade.

8. ____ **de** biscuits.

9. ____ **des** haricots verts.

10. ____ **du** riz complet *(brown rice).*

11. ____ **de** bière.

12. ____ **de** chips.

Conclusion Est-ce que Robert mange bien? Pourquoi ou pourquoi pas?

Et vous? Et vous? Prenez-vous ces aliments? Vous êtes comme Robert?

ACTIVITÉ N Que mettez-vous sur la pizza?

Étape 1. Choisissez les ingrédients que vous mettez *(put)* sur la pizza.

☐ **du** fromage

☐ **du** bœuf

☐ **du** jambon

☐ **du** poulet

☐ **des** saucisses

☐ **de la** sauce tomate

☐ **des** oignons

☐ **des** olives

☐ **des** champignons *(mushrooms)*

☐ **des** ananas *(pineapple)*

☐ **des** anchois *(anchovies)*

☐ **???**

Étape 2. Demandez à un(e) camarade de classe s'il/si elle prend ces ingrédients pour décider si vous allez partager *(share)* une pizza avec lui/elle.

Modèle: É1: **Est-ce que tu prends du fromage?**
É2: **Oui, je prends du fromage. / Non, je ne prends pas de fromage.**

Conclusion Allez-vous partager une pizza avec lui/elle?

ACTIVITÉ O Mangez-vous bien?

Étape 1. Indiquez si vous prenez ou si vous ne prenez pas les aliments suivants.

Modèle: le beurre **Je prends du beurre. / Je ne prends pas de beurre.**

1. le bœuf
2. le lait
3. l'eau
4. les frites

5. les épinards
6. les chips
7. le Coca
8. les biscuits

9. le riz
10. le yaourt
11. le poisson
12. la bière

Étape 2. Montrez *(Show)* vos réponses à un(e) camarade de classe. Est-ce que votre camarade mange bien? Est-ce que vous mangez bien?

ACTIVITÉ P Un brunch

Étape 1. Qu'est-ce que vous prenez normalement au brunch?

Étape 2. Montrez votre réponse à un(e) camarade de classe. Quelle description est appropriée *(appropriate)* pour lui/elle? (Une personne qui apprécie la bonne nourriture ou qui aime manger est **gourmande.**)

Tu es raisonnable *(sensible).*

Tu es un peu gourmand(e).

Tu es très gourmand(e).

Liaisons musicales

© Lydie/SIPA/Newscom

Le chanteur-rappeur turc Lil' Maaz a eu beaucoup de succès avec *Mange du kebab* (2007). Cherchez les paroles *(lyrics)* et/ou un vidéo-clip de cette chanson sur Internet et identifiez les termes liés à *(related to)* la nourriture.🌐

Les expressions avec *avoir*

You already learned some expressions with **avoir** in **Chapitre 1.** Other expressions that use **avoir** include **avoir faim** *(to be hungry)* and **avoir soif** *(to be thirsty).*

Quand est-ce qu'on mange? J'**ai faim.**	*When are we eating? I'm hungry.*
Maman **a soif.** As-tu de l'eau?	*Mom is thirsty. Do you have some water?*

The adjectives **chaud** and **froid** are also used with **avoir** if you want to say that a person is hot or cold in the sense of temperature.

Anne **a chaud.** Elle va à la piscine.	*Anne is hot. She's going to the pool.*
Il neige et les filles **ont froid.**	*It's snowing and the girls are cold.*

When **faim, soif, chaud,** and **froid** refer to people and are used with **avoir,** agreement is not necessary. However, when **chaud** and **froid** do not refer to people and are used with **être,** agreement is necessary: **La soupe est froide.**

Essayez! Complétez les phrases avec **avoir chaud, avoir faim, avoir froid** ou **avoir soif.**

1. Mes amis mangent un steak. Ils…
2. Il fait 98° F (37° C). Laura…
3. Guy prend trois Coca. Il…
4. Il fait 12° F (–11° C). Jean et Yves…

La parole est à vous!

Est-ce qu'il faut éliminer la malbouffe°?

Les distributeurs automatiques° proposent trop facilement aux étudiants des chips, des bonbons, des biscuits et autres snacks trop sucrés ou trop salés. Pour manger plus sainement°, est-ce qu'il faut vider° nos distributeurs automatiques? Est-ce qu'il faut remplir° les distributeurs avec seulement° de la nourriture saine: des fruits, des yaourts, de l'eau?

- Leif de Chicoutimi (Québec): «Non, ce n'est pas nécessaire de vider les machines. Je suis adulte et je vais décider pour moi-même si je mange des chips ou une pomme.»

- Aude d'Arles (France): «C'est peut-être une bonne idée. S'il n'y a pas de cochonneries° dans le distributeur, je ne serai pas tentée° de prendre des chips!»

malbouffe *junk food* **distributeurs automatiques** *vending machines* **sainement** *healthily* **vider** *to empty* **remplir** *to fill* **seulement** *only* **cochonneries** *junk food* **ne serais pas tentée** *would not be tempted*

Et vous? Qu'en pensez-vous?

Est-ce qu'il faut éliminer les snacks trop sucrés ou trop salés qui sont dans nos distributeurs automatiques?

🔊 Une **alimentation** équilibrée

A balanced diet

les lentilles *(f.)*

les glucides *(m.)*
et les fibres *(f.)*

LENTILLES

la tarte

les matières *(f.)* grasses
et les sucres *(m.)*

l'huile *(f.)*
d'olive

les noix *(f.)*

LAIT

YAOURT

les produits *(m.)*
laitiers

un pain complet

les fruits *(m.)*
de mer

le tofu

le raisin *(m.)*

un avocat

le lait
de soja

les fraises *(f.)*

les protéines *(f.)*

les fruits *(m.)*
et les légumes *(m.)*

le brocoli

la dinde

les petits pois *(m.)*

Les portions idéales

Note de
vocabulaire
Noix refers to *walnuts*
only. The generic name for
nuts is **oléagineux**. Other
kinds of nuts include **les
amandes** *(f.) (almonds),*
les cacahuètes *(f.)*
(peanuts), and **les
noisettes** *(f.) (hazelnuts).*

Vocabulaire complémentaire

les bleuets *(m.)* blueberries
les framboises *(f.)* raspberries

les aliments frits *(m.)* fried foods
les aliments industriels *(m.)* processed foods
un bonbon candy
le fast-food fast food
un hamburger (ham)burger
le jus de canneberge cranberry juice

l'agneau *(m.)* lamb
le canard duck
le veau veal
la volaille poultry

être au régime to be on a diet
éviter (de + *infinitive)* to avoid (doing something)
faire attention (à) to pay attention (to)
fumer to smoke
grignoter to snack

alcoolisé(e) alcoholic
frais / fraîche fresh, cool
frit(e) fried
sain(e) healthy
la santé health
un(e) végétalien(ne) vegan
un(e) végétarien(ne) vegetarian

> **Note de vocabulaire**
> Not typically found in France, **les bleuets** of North America are a specialty of Quebec. In France, similar berries are called **les myrtilles** *(f.)*, and they are not typically found in North America. Because cranberries are not common outside of North America, the French may not be familiar with **les canneberges** like the Quebecois are.

ACTIVITÉ Ⓐ **Une protéine ou un fruit?** Dites si chaque aliment mentionné est **(a)** une protéine ou **(b)** un fruit.

1.   2.   3.   4.   5.   6.   7.   8.   9.   10.   11.   12.

Un mot sur la langue

Les mots étrangers au Québec

Étant donné° que le Québec est dans un pays anglophone, les Québécois ont tendance à **franciser** (donner un mot° français à un mot étranger) les mots étrangers, surtout les mots liés à la nourriture. En France, cette tendance est moins répandue° parce que le français dans l'Hexagone n'est pas menacé° par la langue anglaise. Par exemple, en France, on dit **hotdog** pour *hot dog* mais au Québec, on peut dire aussi **chien chaud**. En France, Kentucky Fried Chicken est **KFC** mais au Québec, c'est **PFK** qui signifie **Poulet frit du Kentucky**.

Étant donné *Given* **un mot** *word* **répandue** *widespread* **menacé** *threatened*

- Associez les mots étrangers utilisés en France aux mots étrangers utilisés au Québec.

En France	Au Québec
1. _____ chips	a. beignet
2. _____ sandwich	b. croustilles
3. _____ riz cantonais	c. riz frit chinois
4. _____ donut	d. sandwich sous-marin

ACTIVITÉ B Les catégories Quel aliment ne va pas avec les autres?

1. a. le brocoli   b. l'avocat   c. les noix   d. les petits pois
2. a. la dinde   b. le riz complet   c. le pain complet   d. les pâtes
3. a. le poulet   b. le canard   c. le steak   d. la dinde
4. a. l'agneau   b. le veau   c. les œufs   d. les bonbons
5. a. le lait   b. le lait de soja   c. le yaourt   d. la crème
6. a. l'huile   b. les aliments frits   c. le tofu   d. le beurre

ACTIVITÉ C Associations Associez les éléments de la première colonne aux éléments de la deuxième colonne.

1. _____ la volaille
2. _____ fumer
3. _____ être au régime
4. _____ grignoter
5. _____ un aliment industriel
6. _____ le fast-food

    a. le goûter
    b. grossir
    c. MacDo
    d. maigrir
    e. le canard
    f. le tabac
    g. la viande Spam

🔊 **ACTIVITÉ D Nommez-le!**

CD2-20

Étape 1. Nommez un aliment pour chaque catégorie que vous entendez.

1.   2.   3.   4.   5.   6.
7.   8.   9.   10.   11.   12.

Étape 2. Aimez-vous la pizza? La pizza représente *(represents)* quels groupes alimentaires?

© Lauri Patterson/Shutterstock.com

ACTIVITÉ E Quiz santé Quel aliment est meilleur pour la santé?

1. a. le poulet rôti   b. le poulet frit
2. a. un hamburger MacDo   b. un hamburger végétarien
3. a. le pain blanc   b. le pain complet
4. a. les noix   b. les chips
5. a. la volaille   b. la viande rouge
6. a. le tofu   b. le veau
7. a. l'agneau   b. les fruits de mer
8. a. le beurre   b. l'huile d'olive
9. a. le riz blanc   b. le riz complet
10. a. le Coca   b. le jus de canneberge
11. a. les lentilles   b. les frites
12. a. les pâtes au blé complet   b. la pizza au fromage

ACTIVITÉ **F** **Faites-vous attention à votre santé?** Prenez-vous les aliments suivants chaque jour? Qu'est-ce que vous prenez?

Modèle: Oui, je prends des épinards et des fraises.

1. des fruits et des légumes?
2. des glucides?
3. des protéines?
4. des produits laitiers?

ACTIVITÉ **G** **Les produits à éviter** Demandez à un(e) partenaire combien de fois par semaine il/elle prend ces produits.

Modèle: É1: Combien de fois par semaine est-ce que tu manges des aliments frits?
É2: Je mange des aliments frits une fois par semaine. / Jamais!

1. manger des aliments frits
2. prendre des boissons alcoolisées
3. prendre du tabac
4. manger de la viande rouge
5. prendre des aliments industriels
6. manger du fast-food

Conclusion Est-ce que ton/ta partenaire fait attention à sa santé?

ACTIVITÉ **H** **Les menus** Avec un(e) partenaire, préparez un menu équilibré pour quelqu'un qui est…

1. au régime
2. végétarien(ne)
3. végétalien(ne)
4. gourmand(e)

Si vous y allez

© Pascal Sittler/REA/Redux

Si vous allez à Paris, allez au restaurant Cojean pour sa cuisine rapide et saine. Allez sur le site officiel du restaurant pour voir le menu.

Un mot sur la culture

Le fast-food en France

©Pascal Sittler/REA/Redux

Le fast-food ou la restauration rapide, une invention américaine, a réussi à s'implanter en France et en Europe. On peut° trouver en France des chaînes déjà bien connues aux États-Unis comme McDo, KFC, Subway, Pizza Hut. Cependant, au cours des dernières années, ce mode de restauration a évolué avec un menu plus sain, des bars à salades et des jus de fruits naturels. Aujourd'hui en France, on peut trouver des restaurants qui servent de la nourriture rapide et plus saine. Le magasin Monoprix, par exemple, propose une gamme° de produits alimentaires plus sains en self-service. Les supermarchés vendent des repas préparés qu'on réchauffe° à la maison.

peut *can* **une gamme** *product line* **réchauffer** *to reheat*

• Avez-vous une chaîne de restauration rapide préférée?

Pour parler des boissons et exprimer ses préférences

Le verbe **boire** / Les articles définis et les articles partitifs

DU FILM *LIAISONS*
....

Un coup d'œil sur la grammaire

Look at these photos from the film *Liaisons* and their captions.

SERVEUSE Vous préférez **les** tartes peut-être? J'ai **la** tarte au sucre, **la** tarte aux bleuets...

CLAIRE Vous prenez quelque chose? Quelque chose à **boire**?

1. Why does the server use definite articles instead of indefinite or partitive articles with the food items?
   a. One typically only eats part of a pie.
   b. She is referring to pies in a general sense.
   c. She is referring to preferences.
   d. b and c
   e. a and c
   f. All of the above

2. What do you think **boire** means?
   a. *to drink*   b. *to eat*   c. *to take*

Les verbes-clés

Le verbe *boire*

•••❖ The verb **boire** (*to drink*) is irregular in the present tense.

boire	
je **bois**	nous **buvons**
tu **bois**	vous **buvez**
il/elle/on **boit**	ils/elles **boivent**

•••❖ Because liquids are typically mass nouns and not countable, **boire** is often used with partitive articles.

—Vous **buvez du** lait?   —*Do you drink milk?*

—Oui, je **bois du** lait.   —*Yes, I drink milk.*

—Non, nous **buvons du** vin.   —*No, we are drinking wine.*

- As with **prendre**, indefinite articles (**un, une, des**) may be used with **boire** if referring to a fixed quantity of a liquid.

—Qu'est-ce que Luc **boit**?	—*What is Luc drinking?*
—Il **boit un** thé vert.	—*He is drinking a (a cup of) green tea.*

- In negative statements with **boire,** partitive and indefinite articles become **de/d'.**

—Tu **bois du** vin rouge?	—*Do you drink red wine?*
—Non, je **ne bois pas de** vin rouge.	—*No, I don't drink red wine.*
—Vous **buvez de l'**eau minérale?	—*Do you drink mineral water?*
—Non, je **ne bois pas d'**eau minérale.	—*Non, I don't drink mineral water.*

Les préférences et l'article défini

- Because definite articles refer to nouns in a general sense, they are used to express (dis)likes with verbs like **aimer mieux, aimer bien, adorer,** and **détester.**

J'adore **les** biscuits!	*I adore cookies!*
Aimez-vous **la** viande rouge?	*Do you like red meat?*
Nous aimons mieux **le** poisson.	*We prefer fish.*
J'aime beaucoup **le** tofu et **les** lentilles.	*I like tofu and lentils a lot.*
Moi, je déteste **le** tofu.	*Me, I hate tofu.*

- Remember that, in negative sentences, the definite article does not change.

Je n'aime pas **la** friture.	*I don't like fried foods.*
Pierre n'aime pas **la** viande rouge.	*Pierre does not like red meat.*

ACTIVITÉ ❶ **Qui boit quoi?** Quand on fait la fête, on sert une variété de boissons. Trouvez le sujet de chaque phrase.

1. _____ **buvons** de l'eau minérale.   a. Je   b. Vous   c. Nous
2. _____ **bois** du vin rouge.   a. Tu   b. Il   c. Elles
3. _____ **boit** un Coca.   a. Elle   b. Tu   c. Ils
4. _____ **buvez** du jus de canneberge.   a. Nous   b. Vous   c. Elles
5. _____ **boivent** du thé glacé *(iced).*   a. Je   b. Il   c. Ils
6. _____ **bois** de la bière.   a. Je   b. Elle   c. Vous
7. _____ **buvons** du citron pressé.   a. Vous   b. Nous   c. On
8. _____ **buvez** du chocolat chaud.   a. Nous   b. Tu   c. Vous

Conclusion Que buvez-vous normalement aux fêtes?

ACTIVITÉ **J** **Les boissons**

Étape 1. Qui boit ces boissons? Regardez bien les verbes et complétez les phrases avec **(a) Le professeur** ou **(b) Les étudiants.**

1. _____ **boit** du thé vert.
2. _____ **boivent** du Coca.
3. _____ **boivent** du lait.
4. _____ **boit** du café.
5. _____ **boivent** de la bière.
6. _____ **boit** du champagne.

Étape 2. Et à votre université? Qui boit normalement ces boissons?

Modèle: **À mon université, les étudiants boivent du thé vert.**

ACTIVITÉ **K** **Les boissons et la santé** Utilisez les articles pour déterminer si ces étudiants boivent ou ne boivent pas ces boissons. Complétez les phrases avec **(a) Nous buvons** ou **(b) Nous ne buvons pas.**

1. _____ **de** l'eau minérale.
2. _____ **de** café.
3. _____ **du** jus de canneberge.
4. _____ **de** Mountain Dew.
5. _____ **du** thé vert.
6. _____ **de** bière.
7. _____ **de** Coca.
8. _____ **du** vin rouge.
9. _____ **du** lait du soja.
10. _____ **d'**espresso.

Conclusion Analysez *(Review)* les réponses. Est-ce que ces étudiants font attention à leur santé?

⋯ **Et vous?** Qu'est-ce que vous buvez et qu'est-ce que vous ne buvez pas? Est-ce que vous faites attention à votre santé?

ACTIVITÉ **L** **Qu'est-ce que vous buvez?**

Étape 1. Indiquez ce que vous buvez dans chaque situation suivante dans la colonne **Moi.**

	Moi	**Mon/Ma partenaire**
1. Quand il fait chaud	Je bois un Coca.	Il/Elle boit de l'eau.
2. Quand il fait froid		
3. Quand tu as sommeil		
4. Quand tu as très très soif		
5. Quand tu es nerveux(-euse)		
6. Quand tu es malade *(sick)*		

Étape 2. Posez les questions à un(e) partenaire. Notez ses réponses dans la colonne **Mon/Ma partenaire.**

Modèle: É1: **Qu'est-ce que tu bois quand il fait chaud?**
É2: **Je bois de l'eau.**

Pour aller plus loin
À ou *de*?

To say that juice is of a certain kind of fruit, the preposition **de** or **d'** is used followed by the fruit.

le jus **d'orange**   le jus **de canneberge**   le jus **de pomme**

To say that a dessert is made with a certain kind of fruit, the preposition **à** is usually used and contracted with the plural form of the fruit.

une tarte **aux pommes**   une tarte **aux bleuets**   un gâteau **aux fraises**

With mass nouns such as chocolate and cheese, the preposition **à** is contracted with the singular form of the noun.

les biscuits **au chocolat**   le gâteau **au chocolat**   le gâteau **au fromage**

Essayez! Donnez le noms de ces boissons et de ces desserts en français?

1. grape juice
2. strawberry juice
3. a raspberry pie
4. a chocolate pie
5. a strawberry cake
6. a banana cake

ACTIVITÉ M Proposer un restaurant

Étape 1. Complétez les phrases avec **Je déteste, Je n'aime pas, J'aime bien, J'aime beaucoup** ou **J'adore**.

1. _____ **les** fruits de mer.
2. _____ **les** pâtes.
3. _____ **la** nourriture chinoise.
4. _____ **la** pizza.
5. _____ **le** sushi.
6. _____ **la** cuisine végétarienne.
7. _____ **la** cuisine végétalienne.
8. _____ **le** fast-food.

Étape 2. Comparez vos réponses avec un(e) partenaire.

Modèle: É1: **Je n'aime pas les fruits de mer. Et toi?**
É2: **Moi, j'adore les fruits de mer. J'aime beaucoup les pâtes. Et toi?**
É1: **Moi aussi. J'aime beaucoup les pâtes.**

Étape 3. Proposez trois restaurants à votre partenaire.

Modèle: Pour toi, je propose les restaurants Red Lobster, Olive Garden et MacDo.

Liaisons musicales

© RA/Lebrecht Music & Arts

Les cornichons (1966) de Nino Ferrer est une chanson sur un pique-nique en famille. Cherchez les paroles *(lyrics)* et/ ou un vidéo-clip de la chanson sur Internet. Des articles partitifs et des articles indéfinis sont utilisés dans la première partie de la chanson et des articles définis dans la deuxième partie. Pourquoi? Et comment dit-on **un cornichon** en anglais?

ACTIVITÉ N Aimer ou prendre?

Étape 1. Utilisez les articles pour déterminer si cet étudiant **aime** ou s'il **prend** les aliments suivants. Complétez les phrases avec **(a) J'aime** ou **(b) Je prends.**

1. _____ **les** chips.

2. _____ **du** tofu.

3. _____ **des** haricots noirs.

4. _____ **le** steak.

5. _____ **le** poisson frit.

6. _____ **un** hamburger végétarien.

Étape 2. Et toi? Est-ce qu'il y a des aliments que **tu aimes** mais que **tu ne prends pas** parce qu'ils sont mauvais pour la santé? Donne des exemples.

Modèle: **J'aime le Coca mais je ne prends pas de Coca.**

ACTIVITÉ O Sont-ils difficiles? Utilisez les articles pour déterminer le verbe approprié pour chaque phrase.

1. _____ **les** oranges.	a. Édouard n'aime pas	b. Édouard prend
2. _____ **du** jus d'orange.	a. Bill boit	b. Bill ne boit pas
3. _____ **d'**agneau.	a. Stacey ne mange pas	b. Stacey n'aime pas
4. _____ **le** poulet frit.	a. Wynne ne prend pas	b. Wynne adore
5. _____ **le** fromage.	a. Édouard déteste	b. Édouard prend
6. _____ **du** gâteau au fromage.	a. Bill prend	b. Bill ne prend pas
7. _____ **le** café.	a. Stacey prend	b. Stacey adore
8. _____ **de** bière.	a. Édouard boit	b. Édouard ne boit pas

ACTIVITÉ P Êtes-vous difficile en ce qui concerne la nourriture?

Étape 1. Complétez les phrases suivantes à propos de vos préférences alimentaires. Vous devez mentionner au moins trois aliments pour chaque phrase.

Modèle: **Je n'aime pas l'huile d'olive, le pain complet et le sushi.**

Je prends souvent de la viande rouge, du riz et des légumes verts.

1. J'aime _____.

2. Je n'aime pas _____.

3. Je prends souvent _____.

4. Je ne prends pas _____.

5. Je ne mangerais *(would eat)* jamais _____.

6. Je mangerais _____ tous les jours.

Étape 2. Lisez vos phrases à un(e) partenaire. Votre partenaire va déterminer si vous êtes **très difficile, difficile, un peu difficile** ou **pas difficile.**

Étape 3. Préparez des questions pour votre professeur pour voir s'il/si elle est difficile.

Modèle: **Est-ce que vous aimez le poisson? Est-ce que vous prenez du fromage?**

ACTIVITÉ Q Repas équilibrés

Étape 1. Avec un(e) partenaire, décidez si les repas suivants sont des repas équilibrés. Si un repas n'est pas équilibré, expliquez pourquoi.

1. Repas A: yaourt, bleuets, œufs, pain complet, noix, jus d'orange
2. Repas B: banane, fraises, haricots verts, carottes, raisin, jus de pomme
3. Repas C: veau, épinards, agneau, avocat, poisson, vin
4. Repas D: tarte, frites, œufs, steak, gâteau, chocolat chaud
5. Repas E: dinde, petits pois, framboises, riz, gâteau, lait
6. Repas F: tofu, lentilles, avocat, fromage, pain, jus de canneberge

Étape 2. Écrivez ce que *(what)* vous avez mangé *(ate)* ce matin. Avec votre partenaire, décidez si votre petit déjeuner est équilibré ou pas équilibré.

© Ekaterina Pokrovsky / Shutterstock.com

ACTIVITÉ R Les étudiants de votre université

Étape 1. Avec un(e) partenaire, décrivez les habitudes alimentaires des étudiants typiques de votre université. Qu'est-ce ce qu'ils aiment? Qu'est-ce qu'ils n'aiment pas? Qu'est-ce qu'ils prennent au petit déjeuner? Qu'est-ce qu'ils prennent au dîner? Qu'est-ce qu'ils boivent le week-end? En général, est-ce que leurs repas sont équilibrés?

Étape 2. Proposez un menu équilibré pour **le petit déjeuner, le déjeuner** et **le dîner** pour ces étudiants.

La parole est à vous!
Est-ce que les portions sont trop grandes dans les restaurants américains?

Quand les Français voyagent aux États-Unis, ils sont souvent surpris de voir les grandes portions de nourriture dans les assiettes servies dans les restaurants. Les portions dans les restaurants français sont généralement plus petites qu'aux États-Unis. Pensez-vous que les portions sont trop grandes dans les restaurants américains?

- Mimi de Martinique: «Oui, les portions sont trop grandes aux États-Unis. Je ne finis jamais mon assiette°. C'est trop de nourriture. Ce n'est pas bon pour la santé de trop manger.»
- Frank de Calais (France): «Ça ne me dérange pas.° J'aime les grandes portions aux États-Unis. Si je ne finis pas mon assiette, je demande un *doggybag* comme les Américains le font chez eux.»

une assiette *plate* **Ça ne me dérange pas.** *It doesn't bother me.*

Et vous? Qu'en pensez-vous?
Pensez-vous que les portions sont trop grandes dans les restaurants américains?

La **cuisine**

Cooking

une poêle

le vinaigre

la farine

une casserole

la mayonnaise

la moutarde

des poivrons (m.)

un citron vert

un citron

l'ail (m.)

un oignon

le sel   le poivre

Faire la cuisine

Vocabulaire complémentaire

un ingrédient *ingredient*	**à la vapeur** *steamed*
une recette *recipe*	**au four** *baked*
(un steak) à point *medium-cooked (steak)*	**aigre** *sour*
bien cuit *well-done*	**amer / amère** *bitter*
saignant *medium rare*	**épicé(e)** *spicy*
bleu *rare*	**grillé(e)** *grilled*
	piquant(e) *hot*
ajouter *to add*	**salé(e)** *salty*
couper *to cut*	**sucré(e)** *sweet*
faire chauffer *to heat*	
trancher *to slice*	

Les expressions de quantité

une cuillère à café (de/d') *a teaspoon (of)*
une cuillère à soupe (de/d') *a table/soup spoon (of)*
une (demi-)tasse (de/d') *a (half) cup (of)*

une boîte (de/d') *a box (of)*
une bouteille (de/d') *a bottle (of)*
un sac (de/d') *a bag (of)*
un verre (de/d') *a glass (of)*

un gramme (de/d') *a gram (of)*
un kilo (de/d') *a kilogram (of)*
un litre (de/d') *a liter (of)*
une livre (de/d') *a pound (of)*

- After expressions of quantity and before a noun, **de/d'** is used instead of **du, de la, de l'** or **des.**

Je prends **un verre de** lait.	*I'm having **a glass of** milk.*
Elle a **un kilo d'**oranges.	*She has **a kilogram of** oranges.*

- Expressions of quantity you already know are **assez (de/d')**, **beaucoup (de/d')**, **(un) peu (de/d')**, and **trop (de/d').**

J'ai **beaucoup de** citrons.	*I have **a lot of** lemons.*
Nous avons mangé **trop d'**ail.	*We ate **too much** garlic.*

- In Quebec, as in the U.S., **une tasse de/d'** is used in recipes. In the rest of the Francophone world, recipes generally use measurements from the metric system like **grammes** and **kilos.**

Il faut 65 **grammes** de beurre.	*It is necessary to have 65 **grams** of butter.*
Préparez deux **kilos** de fraises.	*Prepare 2 **kilos** of strawberries.*

Pour aller plus loin
Quelque chose de sucré

Quelque chose means *something* in French. To say *something sweet, something salty, something spicy* and so forth, use the construction **quelque chose + de/d'** + the masculine form of the adjective.

quelque chose de sucré
something sweet

quelque chose d'épicé
something spicy

quelque chose de salé
something salty

quelque chose de délicieux
something delicious

Essayez! Quel est l'équivalent de ces expressions en français?

1. something cold
2. something hot
3. something good
4. something bad
5. something interesting
6. something cool (fresh)

CD2-21 **ACTIVITÉ A Les saveurs** Choisissez l'aliment qui va avec la description que vous entendez.

1. a. la moutarde   b. un biscuit   **4.** a. la mayonnaise   b. la moutarde

2. a. les oignons verts   b. le vinaigre   **5.** a. le chocolat noir   b. le sucre

3. a. le sel   b. un citron vert   **6.** a. le poivre   b. la farine

ACTIVITÉ B Quiz culinaire

Étape 1. Quel ingrédient n'appartient pas *(doesn't belong)* à la recette?

1. un gâteau   a. les œufs   b. la farine   c. l'ail

2. le steak-frites   a. les pommes de terre   b. le poulet   c. le bœuf

3. un sandwich   a. le pain   b. le fromage   c. les citrons

4. une omelette   a. la mayonnaise   b. les poivrons   c. les oignons

5. la sauce tomate   a. les tomates   b. l'ail   c. la moutarde

6. la vinaigrette   a. la farine   b. l'huile   c. le vinaigre

Étape 2. On utilise **une casserole** ou **une poêle** normalement pour préparer ces aliments?

7. la soupe   **9.** la sauce au chocolat   **11.** un œuf dur *(hard boiled)*

8. une omelette   **10.** le poisson frit   **12.** la sauce tomate

Si vous y allez

Si vous allez à Fresnoy-Le-Grand (France), visitez le dépôt d'usine *(factory outlet)* Le Creuset. Le Creuset fabrique des casseroles et des poêles d'une qualité exceptionnelle depuis 1925. Visitez le site officiel de Le Creuset pour voir la gamme des produits et des recettes.

CD2-22 **Étape 3.** Vous allez entendre le nom d'un ingrédient et une quantité. Quel aliment associez-vous à la quantité de chaque ingrédient?

13. a. une salade aux œufs   b. un hamburger

14. a. un sandwich   b. des macaronis au fromage

15. a. un gâteau   b. une tasse de café

16. a. une sangria   b. une fondue

Résultats du quiz

16: Bravo! Vous êtes le prochain Jacques Pépin!

13–15: Pas mal. Continuez.

10–12: Des cours de cuisine vous seraient *(would be)* utiles.

6–9: Attention! Vous êtes un peu dangereux/dangereuse dans la cuisine.

1–5: Quelle horreur! Vous êtes nul/nulle *(hopeless)* en cuisine!

ACTIVITÉ C C Livres, grammes et kilogrammes En Europe et au Québec, on utilise les **kilos** et les **grammes**. Convertissez le poids *(weight)* de ces aliments en kilos et en grammes.

1 livre = 0.45 kilos / 453.59 grammes

Note de vocabulaire

Note that **une livre** means *a pound* but **un livre** means *a book*. In practical terms, for instance in an open-air market, **une livre** means *half a kilo*.

1. 2 livres de fraises = _____ kilos   **3.** ½ livre de beurre = _____ grammes

2. 5 livres d'oranges = _____ kilos   **4.** ¼ livre de sel = _____ grammes

🔊 **ACTIVITÉ D** Les recettes

CD2-23

Étape 1. Vous allez entendre des extraits de recettes. Quel aliment associez-vous à chaque phrase?

1. a. un gâteau   b. une salade

2. a. les frites   b. une pomme de terre au four

3. a. la soupe   b. la glace

4. a. le thé glacé   b. la soupe

Étape 2. Décrivez comment vous préparez les aliments suivants. Utilisez les verbes **ajouter, faire chauffer, couper** ou **trancher.**

1. Je/J' _____ le pain pour faire un sandwich.

2. Je/J' _____ une poêle pour faire une omelette.

3. Je/J' _____ les fruits pour faire une salade.

4. Je/J' _____ du sel et du poivre dans la soupe.

ACTIVITÉ E Votre viande, comment l'aimez-vous? Quand vous commandez *(order)* un steak au restaurant, comment le commandez-vous: **bien cuit, à point, saignant** ou **bleu?**

Modèle: le steak   **J'aime mon steak bien cuit.**

1. le steak   **2.** le hamburger   **3.** l'agneau   **4.** la dinde   **5.** le porc

ACTIVITÉ F Quelle préparation?

Étape 1. Indiquez la préparation que vous aimez pour chaque aliment.

Modèle: le poulet   **J'aime le poulet rôti.**

1. le poulet   **4.** l'agneau   **7.** les pommes de terre

2. le poisson   **5.** le steak   **8.** les légumes

3. le canard   **6.** le porc

👥 **Étape 2.** Montrez vos réponses à un(e) partenaire. Est-ce que vous avez des préférences semblables? Qui a une alimentation plus saine?

ACTIVITÉ G Qu'est-ce que Claire Gagner prépare ce soir? Utilisez les articles pour déterminer si la première partie de chaque phrase est **(a) Elle prend…** ou **(b) Elle prend un kilo…**

1. _____ **de** l'emmental.   **3.** _____ **de** gruyère.   **5.** _____ **de** l'ail.

2. _____ **du** pain.   **4.** _____ **de** pommes vertes.   **6.** _____ **de** farine.

Conclusion Est-ce que Claire prépare **une tarte** ou **une fondue** avec ces ingrédients?

ACTIVITÉ H **Mme Saxton** Vous avez rencontré Madame Saxton dans la Séquence 1 du film *Liaisons.* Que prend Madame Saxton pour le goûter? Complétez chaque aliment avec une expression de quantité logique.

© Heinle/Cengage Learning

Modèle: _____ bonbons   **Madame Saxton prend un sac de** bonbons.

1. _____ lait   2. _____ Coca   3. _____ chips   4. _____ biscuits

ACTIVITÉ I **Vos habitudes alimentaires**

Étape 1. Complétez les phrases avec une expression de quantité: **jamais de/d', un peu de/d', assez de/d', beaucoup de/d'** ou **trop de/d'.**

Normalement, je (ne) prends…

1. _____ fruits et légumes   5. _____ matières grasses
2. _____ glucides   6. _____ produits sucrés
3. _____ produits laitiers   7. _____ alcool
4. _____ eau   8. _____ tabac

Étape 2. Comparez vos habitudes *(habits)* alimentaires avec un(e) partenaire. Qui a une alimentation plus saine?

Un mot sur la culture

© Vincent Besnault/Getty Images

La fondue suisse

Ingrédients: ½ kilo de gruyère, ½ kilo d'emmental, 1 ½ tasse de vin blanc, une gousse d'ail, 3 cuillères à soupe de Kirsch, du sel et du poivre

La fondue suisse est une fondue au fromage. Traditionnellement, on sert cette fondue avec des petits morceaux de pain piqués sur une fourchette°. Selon la tradition, la personne qui laisse tomber° son morceau de pain dans la casserole doit embrasser° son voisin de gauche ou lui payer une bouteille de vin!

fourchette *fork* **laisse tomber** *drops* **doit embrasser** *must kiss*

• Quels sont les ingrédients de ces autres types de fondue?

1. la fondue bourguignonne   2. la fondue au chocolat

🔊 Liaisons avec les mots et les sons

CD2-24 ## Le /r/ français

The French /r/ is a sound unique to French and is nothing like the English *r* or the Spanish *r*. Because the sound is made in the back of the throat, it is sometimes equated with the sound that one makes when you are about to gargle. The French /r/ is actually closer to an English *h* sound. To make the French /r/ sound, try replacing it with the English *h* sound and then push the air out gently as if you are about to gargle. Try practicing with the following words that have a similar sound.

Loch (Ness monster)	Bach (the composer)

Pratique A. Écoutez et répétez ces mots qui se terminent *(end)* par le son /r/.

1. beurre
2. verre
3. porc
4. boire
5. pour
6. canard

Pratique B. Écoutez et répétez ces mots qui commencent par le son /r/.

1. repas
2. rôti
3. raisin
4. riz
5. rester
6. Roger

Pratique C. Une voyelle précède le son /r/ dans ces mots. Écoutez et répétez les mots.

1. céréales
2. carotte
3. nourriture
4. hamburger
5. orange
6. haricots

Pratique D. Une consonne précède le son /r/ dans ces mots. Écoutez et répétez les mots.

1. fromage
2. croissant
3. trancher
4. brocoli
5. prendre
6. citron

Pratique E. Écoutez et répétez ces répliques de la Séquence 3 du film *Liaisons*.

CLAIRE Pardon. Asseyez-vous, je vous en prie. Vous prenez quelque chose? Quelque chose à boire?

🔊 **À vos stylos! C'est l'heure de la dictée!**

CD2-25 Vous allez entendre quatre phrases deux fois. La première fois, écoutez bien. La deuxième fois, écrivez les phrases.

Sujet Une serveuse *(waitress)* parle à Claire dans un café.

Pour parler du passé

Le passé composé

DU FILM *LIAISONS*

Un coup d'œil sur la grammaire

Look at these photos from the film *Liaisons* and their captions.

© Heinle/Cengage Learning

CLAIRE ... j'**ai cherché** votre nom dans le registre... mais je ne l'**ai pas trouvé**.

© Heinle/Cengage Learning

CLAIRE Alors, vous **avez fait** ma connaissance, Monsieur Prévost. Mission accomplie!

1. What four verbs do you recognize?
2. The verbs in bold are in the past tense. What verb is used to form the past tense?

> **Note de grammaire**
> Some verbs are also conjugated with **être** in the **passé composé**. You will learn these verbs in **Chapitre 6**.

❖ To indicate that an event or an action has been completed in the past, French uses the **passé composé**. The **passé composé** of most verbs is formed with the present tense of **avoir** (the auxiliary verb) plus a past participle.

passé composé du verbe *manger*	
j' **ai mangé**	nous **avons mangé**
tu **as mangé**	vous **avez mangé**
il/elle/on **a mangé**	ils/elles **ont mangé**

❖ The **passé composé** can express three meanings in English. For example, **j'ai mangé** can mean *I ate, I have eaten,* or *I did eat,* depending on the context.

❖ The past participle of **-er** verbs is formed by dropping the **-er** and replacing it with **é**.

J'**ai acheté** des fraises hier.	I **bought** some strawberries yesterday.
Nous **avons mangé** un gâteau au chocolat.	We **have eaten** a chocolate cake.
Il **a cuisiné** un poulet hier soir.	He **cooked** a chicken last night.
Vous **avez parlé** avec le cuisinier?	**Did** you **speak** with the cook?

To form the past participle of regular **-ir** verbs, drop the **r.**

J'**ai fini** mes devoirs la semaine passée.	*I **finished** my homework last week.*
Il **a choisi** une pomme verte.	*He **chose** a green apple.*
Nous **avons obéi** à la loi.	*We **have obeyed** the law.*
Tu **as réussi** à faire une omelette!	*You **succeeded** in making an omelette!*

The past participle of **prendre, apprendre**, and **comprendre** are **pris, appris,** and **compris.**

Vous **avez pris** des légumes hier?	***Did you have** any vegetables yesterday?*
J'**ai appris** le français l'année dernière.	*I **learned** French last year.*

The following verbs have irregular past participles.

avoir	**eu**	dire	**dit**	être	**été**
boire	**bu**	écrire	**écrit**	faire	**fait**
				lire	**lu**

> **Note de grammaire**
> The **passé composé** of **il y a** is **il y a eu**; that of **il faut** is **il a fallu.**

J'**ai eu** des cours difficiles.	*I **have had** difficult courses.*
Ils **ont bu** du thé vert.	*They **drank** (some) green tea.*
Qu'est-ce que vous **avez dit**?	*What **did** you **say**?*
Nous **avons été** au restaurant.	*We **have been** at the restaurant.*
Vous **avez fait** cette tarte?	*You **made** this pie?*
Tu **as lu** la recette?	***Did** you **read** the recipe?*

In negative sentences, **ne/n'... pas** and **ne/n'... jamais** go around the auxiliary verb **avoir.**

Je **n'ai pas bu** de café hier matin.	*I **didn't drink** any coffee yesterday morning.*
Nous **n'avons jamais pris** de vin.	*We **have never had** any wine.*

In questions with inversion, the subject pronoun and the conjugated form of **avoir** are inverted.

Avez-vous fini vos devoirs?	***Did you finish** your homework?*
Luc **a-t-il travaillé** hier?	***Did Luc work** yesterday?*
Les filles **ont-elles dansé** hier soir?	***Did the girls dance** last night?*

Short adverbs are placed between **avoir** and the past participle.

Il **a bien fait** ses devoirs.	*He **did** his homework **well**.*

These expressions are often used with the **passé composé.**

avant-hier	*the day before yesterday*	**l'année dernière / passée**	*last year*
hier	*yesterday*	**le mois dernier / passé**	*last month*
hier soir	*last night*	**la semaine dernière / passée**	*last week*

🔊 **ACTIVITÉ** Ⓙ **Aujourd'hui ou hier?** Écoutez les activités des étudiants.
CD2-26 Indiquez s'ils font les activités **(a) aujourd'hui** ou s'ils ont fait les activités **(b) hier.**

Modèle: Vous entendez: Nous avons fait nos devoirs.
Vous répondez: **hier**

1. **2.** **3.** **4.** **5.** **6.** **7.** **8.** **9.** **10.**

ACTIVITÉ Ⓚ **Ce soir ou la semaine dernière?** Utilisez les verbes pour déterminer si Abia fait ces activités ce soir ou si elle a fait ces activités la semaine passée. Complétez les phrases avec **(a) Ce soir** ou **(b) La semaine dernière.**

1. _____, j'**ai fait** un gâteau au fromage.

2. _____, j'**ai mangé** un steak.

3. _____, je **prends** du poulet rôti.

4. _____, j'**ai bu** un Coca.

5. _____, j'**ai** un cours de cuisine.

6. _____, j'**ai pris** des frites.

7. _____, je **prépare** du riz complet.

8. _____, j'**écris** à ma mère.

© Heinle/Cengage Learning

Conclusion Est-ce qu'Abia a été raisonnable (sensible) la semaine dernière? Et ce soir?

ACTIVITÉ Ⓛ **Céline Dion** Utilisez les verbes pour déterminer si Céline a fait ces activités **(a) l'année dernière** ou si elle fait ces activités **(b) aujourd'hui.**

1. _____ elle **chante** pour son mari.

2. _____ elle **fait** du shopping.

3. _____ elle **a dit** bonjour à ses fans.

4. _____ elle **finit** une tournée *(tour).*

5. _____ elle **a chanté** à Paris.

6. _____ elle **a lu** sa biographie.

7. _____ elle **a appris** une nouvelle langue.

8. _____ elle **mange** avec son fils René-Charles.

Conclusion Est-ce que la vie de Céline est plus calme aujourd'hui ou l'année passé?

ACTIVITÉ Ⓜ **Messagerie instantanée** Quelqu'un vous écrit par messagerie instantanée pour savoir si vous aimez la cuisine française. Répondez aux questions avec des phrases complètes.

Modèle: Avez-vous pris un steak-frites?
Non, je n'ai pas pris de steak-frites.

1. Avez-vous visité la France?

2. Avez-vous lu un livre de recettes en français?

3. Avez-vous appris à faire la cuisine française?

4. Avez-vous mangé des escargots?

5. Avez-vous bu du vin français?

6. Avez-vous fait un steak-frites?

7. Avez-vous pris du fromage français?

8. Avez-vous écrit à un chef français?

ACTIVITÉ N Connaissez-vous bien vos camarades de classe?

Étape 1. Qu'est-ce que vous avez fait hier? Écrivez cinq phrases complètes avec cinq verbes différents de la liste.

Modèle: J'ai étudié à la bibliothèque.

boire	être	naviguer
choisir	faire	parler
cuisiner	finir	prendre
danser	jouer	regarder
écouter	lire	
écrire	manger	

Étape 2. Devinez *(Guess)* ce que votre partenaire a fait hier. Écrivez cinq phrases.

Modèle: Il/Elle a lu le journal.

Étape 3. Demandez à votre partenaire s'il/si elle a fait les activités.

Modèle: É1: **Est-ce que tu as lu le journal hier?**
É2: **Oui, j'ai lu le journal. / Non, je n'ai pas lu le journal.**

© François Durand/Getty Images

Liaisons musicales

Benjamin Biolay (1973–) est un chanteur français et aussi l'ex-mari de Chiara Mastroianni, la fille de Catherine Deneuve. Sa chanson *Brandt rhapsodie* contient une petite recette. Cherchez les paroles *(lyrics)* et/ou un vidéo-clip de cette chanson sur Internet. Identifiez les termes liés à *(related to)* la nourriture et les verbes au passé composé.

La parole est à vous!
Manger régulièrement au restaurant, c'est mauvais pour la santé?

Les gens mangent de plus en plus° au restaurant parce qu'ils n'ont pas beaucoup de temps pour faire la cuisine à la maison. Malheureusement, la nourriture dans les restaurants contient normalement beaucoup de matières grasses, de sucre et de sel. Manger régulièrement au restaurant, c'est mauvais pour la santé?

- Samira de Tunis (Tunisie): «Oui, manger au restaurant, c'est mauvais pour la santé. Quand on fait la cuisine à la maison, on peut° choisir des ingrédients frais et sains. Les restaurants utilisent souvent trop de beurre et de sel.»

- Rochelle de Liège (Belgique): «Manger au restaurant, c'est pas nécessairement mauvais. La nourriture chez nous peut être aussi mauvaise pour la santé si on utilise de mauvais ingrédients. Il est plus sain de prendre une bonne salade au restaurant que de manger un hot dog à la maison. C'est une question de choix° et aussi d'argent. Les ingrédients frais coûtent cher au supermarché.»

de plus en plus *more and more* **peut** *can* **choix** *choice*

Et vous? Qu'en pensez-vous?
Manger régulièrement au restaurant, c'est mauvais pour la santé?

Avant de visionner

ACTIVITÉ Ⓐ Vous rappelez-vous? Vous rappelez-vous *(Do you remember)* ce qui s'est passé dans la Séquence 2 du film *Liaisons*? Pour chaque phrase, indiquez si c'est vrai ou faux.

	Vrai	Faux
1. Claire a téléphoné au Château Frontenac pour vérifier la réservation.	☐	☐
2. Claire a reçu un coup de téléphone de sa tante.	☐	☐
3. Claire a décidé d'aller à Québec.	☐	☐
4. Abia a eu peur pour Claire.	☐	☐
5. Claire a pensé avoir vu *(saw)* sa mère à l'hôtel.	☐	☐

ACTIVITÉ Ⓑ Mettez-les en ordre Mettez ces répliques entre Claire et Alexis en ordre (1-8). Vous allez vérifier vos réponses plus tard.

a. _____ A: Alexis Prévost. C'est un plaisir de vous revoir.

b. _____ A: Bonjour Mademoiselle! Excusez-moi. Je vous ai surprise.

c. _____ C: Je vais à Québec et je me suis arrêtée *(stopped)* pour manger quelque chose. Et vous?

d. _____ A: Moi aussi. Oui. Je viens de goûter la tarte aux bleuets d'ailleurs *(moreover)* ici. Elle est délicieuse. Puis-je?

e. _____ C: Monsieur Prévost, n'est-ce pas?

f. _____ C: Oui. Pardon. Asseyez-vous *(sit down)*. Je vous en prie.

g. _____ C: Pour moi aussi.

h. _____ A: Que faites-vous à Trois Rivières?

ACTIVITÉ Ⓒ Devinez Devinez *(Guess)* qui dit les phrases suivantes dans la Séquence 3: Claire **(C)** ou Alexis **(A)**? Vous allez vérifier vos réponses plus tard.

1. _____ Vous pouvez me demander ce que *(what)* vous voulez, sauf *(except)* mon âge et mon poids *(weight)*.

2. _____ ...j'ai cherché votre nom dans le registre... mais je ne l'ai pas trouvé.

3. _____ ... je n'étais pas un des clients de l'hôtel.

4. _____ Je voulais juste faire votre connaissance.

Regarder la séquence

Vous allez regarder la Séquence 3 du film *Liaisons*. Vérifiez vos réponses de l'Activité B et de l'Activité C.

Après le visionnage

ACTIVITÉ **D** **Avez-vous compris?**

1. D'où vient Alexis Prévost?
2. Pourquoi Alexis Prévost va-t-il à Québec?
3. Claire va loger dans quel hôtel à Québec?
4. Qui est-ce que Claire voit *(sees)* passer par la fenêtre du café?

ACTIVITÉ **E** **Utilisez le contexte** Regardez bien les mots en caractères gras *(boldface)* et répondez aux questions.

CLAIRE Alors, vous avez fait ma connaissance, Monsieur Prévost. Mission accomplie! Et maintenant? Que faites-vous ici? Vous me (1) **suivez**?

PRÉVOST Mademoiselle. (2) **Ce n'est pas mon genre**. ... Je ne suis pas un psychopathe. Non, c'est juste une belle coïncidence de vous rencontrer ici.

CLAIRE Hmmm... est-ce que je devrais *(should)* vous (3) **croire**?

1. Le mot suivez vient du verbe **suivre**. Que veut dire ce verbe?
   a. *to suggest*   b. *to follow*

2. Le mot **genre** veut dire *(means) kind, sort* ou *type*. Quand M. Prévost dit à Claire «Ce n'est pas mon genre», qu'est-ce qu'il veut dire?
   a. *I'm not that kind of person.*   c. *That's not my style.*
   b. *I'm not into that.*   d. a, b, c

3. Que veut dire le verbe **croire**?
   a. *to believe*   b. *to think*

Liaisons avec la culture

La cuisine traditionnelle du Québec

Les premier colons° français sont arrivés au Canada avec des traditions culinaires de la France et les ont adaptées à leur nouvel environnement. Souvent associée à une cuisine riche en calories, la cuisine traditionnelle québécoise intègre de grandes quantités de graisse animale dans sa préparation afin d'affronter° le climat hivernal et de fournir l'énergie nécessaire pour travailler dans les forêts et les champs. On trouve souvent des aliments du terroir comme le sirop d'érable°, le poisson, les viandes et les pommes de terre. Quelques exemples de recettes célèbres: la soupe aux pois, les tourtières, la tarte au sucre, la tarte aux bleuets, le pouding chômeur et le pâté chinois.

La tarte au sucre

colons *colonists* **afin d'affronter** *in order to face* **sirop d'érable** *maple syrup*

LIAISONS
CULTURELLES

La nourriture et la santé

OUTILS DE LECTURE
Learning adjectives by recognizing past participles

The past participle forms of verbs are not only used to form the **passé composé**. They may also function as adjectives. The following are taken from the texts you will read.

a. [...] le dîner **pris** en commun est un facteur d'équilibre du cercle familial.

b. Il est **adapté** aux grandes villes [...].

c. Le filet de poisson [...] est **mariné** pendant une demi-heure [...].

d. D'autres plats sont **influencés** par la cuisine chinoise [...].

1. What do the adjectives in bold mean?

2. What verbs do the adjectives come from?

L'importance des repas en famille au Maghreb

Dans trois pays arabophones du Maghreb (l'Algérie, le Maroc, la Tunisie), le français est une deuxième langue importante. Comme dans la plupart des° pays francophones, le repas reste un moment convivial privilégié. Manger ensemble, en famille ou avec des amis, c'est le moment de se détendre°, se retrouver° et discuter des événements de la journée. Rituel quotidien°, le déjeuner ou le dîner pris en commun est un facteur d'équilibre du cercle familial. La fonction sociale du repas est donc aussi importante (sinon plus) que la nourriture.

© Robert Fried / Alamy

la plupart des *most of* **se détendre** *relax* **se retrouver** *get together* **quotidien** *daily*

Vrai ou faux?

1. Le français est la première langue du Maroc.   V / F

2. La fonction sociale du repas est plus importante que la nourriture.   V / F

3. Dans les pays du Maghreb, chaque membre de la famille mange séparément.   V / F

4. Le moment du repas n'a pas beaucoup d'importance dans la structure familiale.   V / F

© Clive Streeter/Dorling Kindersley/Getty Images

Le fast-food et l'obésité en France

À la surprise générale, les entreprises américaines de restauration rapide ont réussi à s'implanter° en France. Les raisons de ce succès relatif sont connues: ce type de nourriture est économique et rapide. Il est adapté aux grandes villes et aux situations où on n'a pas le temps de faire la cuisine et on doit manger «sur le pouce»°. Cependant, comme aux États-Unis, ces changements d'habitudes alimentaires°, associés au manque° d'exercice physique, mènent° souvent à des conséquences semblables: les cas d'obésité augmentent chez les adultes. On peut même observer un nouveau phénomène d'obésité chez certains enfants.

s'implanter *establish* **manger «sur le pouce»** *eat in a hurry* **habitudes alimentaires** *eating patterns / customs* **manque** *lack* **mènent** *lead to*

Vrai ou faux?

1. Les entreprises de restauration rapide ont réussi à s'implanter en France. V / F
2. Les mauvaises habitudes alimentaires contribuent à l'augmentation de l'exercice physique. V / F
3. L'obésité chez les enfants est un problème en France. V / F

Les traditions et les nouvelles tendances en Polynésie

Tahiti est la plus connue° des îles° de la Polynésie française. Pour la plupart des Français, c'est le fantasme du paradis tropical par excellence. La cuisine polynésienne, à base de poissons, de crustacés° et de plantes locales (le taro, la patate douce), correspond à cette image d'exotisme. Voici un des plats les plus connus: le poisson cru° à la tahitienne. Le filet de poisson (généralement du thon°) est mariné pendant une demi-heure dans du jus de citron. Avant de servir, on ajoute du lait de noix de coco. D'autres plats sont influencés par la cuisine chinoise ou par celle de° la Métropole°.

© Douglas Peebles/Stock Connection/Aurora

connue *known* **une île** *island* **crustacés** *shellfish* **cru** *raw* **thon** *tuna* **celle de / celui de** *that of* **la Métropole** *the European part of France (roughly equivalent to the concept of the 48 contiguous states)*

Vrai ou faux?

1. Beaucoup de plats tahitiens sont influencés par la cuisine mexicaine. V / F
2. Beaucoup de Français sont attirés par le climat tropical de la Polynésie. V / F
3. La cuisine polynésienne est à base de viande rouge (du bœuf, de l'agneau). V / F

LIAISONS
CULTURELLES

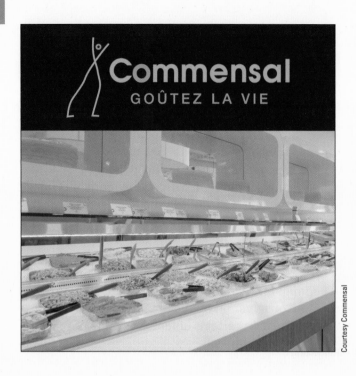

Courtesy Commensal

Les végétariens et les végétaliens en France et au Québec

Pour les anglophones, le terme **végétarien** est facile à comprendre. Mais, quand on est **végétalien,** on ne mange ni œufs ni° produits laitiers. Les Américains qui voyagent beaucoup à l'étranger° remarquent° souvent qu'il est relativement plus facile de trouver des plats végétariens ou végétaliens au Québec, qui est plus directement influencé par les habitudes alimentaires provenant des° États-Unis. Par contre, il est encore° rare de trouver des restaurants (ou des plats préparés) végétariens en France. Quant à° la cuisine végétalienne, c'est un phénomène récent et minoritaire en France.

ni... ni... *neither . . . nor . . .* **à l'étranger** *abroad* **remarquent** *notice* **provenant des** *originating from* **encore** *still* **Quant à** *As for*

Compréhension

1. Les végétaliens ne mangent pas de _____.
   a. fruits   b. produits laitiers

2. La cuisine _____ est un phénomène récent en France.
   a. végétalienne   b. végétarienne

3. Les Québécois sont influencés par les habitudes alimentaires des _____.
   a. Russes   b. Américains

🌐 Activités Internet

- Trouvez des recettes marocaines et des recettes polynésiennes sur Internet. Quels sont les plats les plus communs? Quels sont les ingrédients les plus souvent utilisés? Pensez-vous que vous aimeriez *(would like)* mieux la cuisine nord-africaine ou la cuisine polynésienne?

- Cherchez le menu d'un fast-food et le menu d'un restaurant végétarien en France ou au Québec. Est-ce qu'il y a des plats que vous trouvez intéressants? Quel menu préférez-vous?

- Cherchez des recettes végétaliennes sur Internet. Quels sont les plats les plus communs? Quels sont les ingrédients les plus souvent utilisés? Aimez-vous ce type de cuisine?

PARTIE 1

LES REPAS

le repas	meal
le petit déjeuner	breakfast
le déjeuner	lunch
le goûter	snack
le dîner	dinner

LES PLATS

le dessert	dessert
le hors-d'œuvre (m.) / l'entrée (f.)	starter / appetizer
le plat principal	main course, dish (kind of food)
les plats (m.)	courses (meals)

LA NOURRITURE

l'aliment (m.)	a particular food
la nourriture	food
le beurre	butter
la confiture	jam
la crème	cream
le sucre	sugar
les fruits (m.)	fruits
une banane	banana
une orange	orange
une pomme	apple
les légumes (m.)	vegetables
les carottes (f.)	carrots
les épinards (m.)	spinach
les haricots verts (m.)	green beans
une pomme de terre (f.)	potato
la viande	meat
le bœuf	beef
le jambon	ham
le poulet	chicken
un rôti (de porc)	(pork) roast
un biscuit	cookie
les céréales (f.)	cereal
les chips (f.)	chips
un croissant	croissant
les frites (f.)	fries
le fromage	cheese
un gâteau	cake
la glace	ice cream
les œufs (m.)	eggs
une omelette	omelet
le pain	bread
les pâtes (f.)	pasta
la pizza	pizza
le riz	rice
le poisson	fish
la salade	salad

un sandwich (au fromage)	(cheese) sandwich
les saucisses (f.)	sausages
la soupe (à la tomate)	(tomato) soup
le steak	steak
le yaourt	yogurt

LES BOISSONS

la bière	beer
le café	coffee
le citron pressé	lemonade
le Coca	Coca-Cola
l'eau minérale (f.)	mineral water
le jus d'orange	orange juice
le lait	milk
le thé	tea
le vin	wine

VERBES

avoir chaud	to be hot
avoir faim	to be hungry
avoid froid	to be cold
avoir soif	to be thirsty
apprendre (à)	to learn
comprendre	to understand
prendre	to take; to have food
prendre le déjeuner / le dîner	to have lunch / dinner
prendre un verre	to have a drink
prendre son temps	to take one's time

PARTIE 2

UNE ALIMENTATION ÉQUILIBRÉE

les fibres (f.)	fibers
les glucides (m.)	carbohydrates
les matières grasses (f.)	fats
les produits laitiers (m.)	dairy products
les protéines (f.)	proteins
les sucres (m.)	sugars

LA NOURRITURE

l'avocat (m.)	avocado
les bonbons (m.)	candies
les fraises (f.)	strawberries
les framboises (f.)	raspberries
les bleuets (m.)	blueberries
le raisin (m.)	grapes
le brocoli	broccoli
les petits pois (m.)	peas
l'agneau (m.)	lamb
le canard	duck
la dinde	turkey
le veau	veal
la volaille	poultry

les aliments industriels (m.)	processed foods
les aliments frits (m.)	fried foods
le fast-food	fast food
les fruits (m.) de mer	shellfish
un hamburger	hamburger
l'huile (f.) (d'olive)	(olive) oil
les lentilles (f.)	lentils
les noix (f.)	walnuts
le pain complet	whole grain bread
la tarte	pie
le tofu	tofu

LES BOISSONS

le jus de canneberge	cranberry juice
le lait de soja	soy milk

ADJECTIFS

alcoolisé(e)	alcoholic
frais / fraîche	fresh, cool
frit(e)	fried
sain(e)	healthy
végétalien(ne)	vegan
végétarien(ne)	vegetarian

VERBES

boire	to drink
être au régime	to be on a diet
éviter (de + infinitive)	to avoid (doing something)
faire attention (à)	to pay attention (to)
fumer	to smoke
grignoter	to snack

DIVERS

une portion (idéale)	(ideal) portion
la santé	health

PARTIE 3

LES INGRÉDIENTS ET LES RECETTES

l'ail (m.)	garlic
un citron	lemon
un citron vert	lime
la farine	flour
un ingrédient	ingredient
la mayonnaise	mayonnaise
la moutarde	mustard
un oignon	onion
le poivre	pepper
un poivron rouge / vert	red / green pepper
le sel	salt
une tomate	tomato
le vinaigre	vinegar

une casserole	saucepan
une poêle	fry pan, skillet
une recette	recipe
à point	medium
bien cuit	well-done
saignant	medium rare
bleu	rare
au four	baked
grillé(e)	grilled
à la vapeur	steamed
aigre	sour
amer / amère	bitter
épicé(e)	spicy
piquant(e)	hot
salé(e)	salty
sucré(e)	sweet
quelque chose de/d' + adjective	something + adjective

LES EXPRESSIONS DE QUANTITÉ

une cuillère à café (de/d')	a teaspoon (of)
une cuillère à soupe (de/d')	a table/soup spoon (of)
une (demi-)tasse (de/d')	a (half) cup (of)
un verre (de/d')	a glass (of)
une boîte (de/d')	a box (of)
une bouteille (de/d')	a bottle (of)
un sac (de/d')	a bag (of)
un gramme (de/d')	a gram (of)
un kilo (de/d')	a kilogram (of)
un litre (de/d')	a liter (of)
une livre (de/d')	a pound (of)

VERBES

ajouter	to add
couper	to cut
faire chauffer	to heat
trancher	to slice

EXPRESSIONS AVEC LE PASSÉ

l'année (f.) dernière / passée	last year
avant-hier	the day before yesterday
hier	yesterday
hier soir	last night
le mois dernier / passé	last month
la semaine dernière / passée	last week

Du **marché** à la **table**

En bref   In this chapter, you will:

- learn about types of grocery and food stores

- learn vocabulary related to restaurants and learn how to order food

- learn the verb **vendre** and other regular **-re** verbs

- learn the **passé composé** with the verb **être**

- learn direct object pronouns

- learn about final consonants that are pronounced

- read about the **marché de Belleville** in Paris

 You will also re-watch **SÉQUENCE 3: À Québec** of the film *Liaisons.*

Ressources

 audio http://www.cengagebrain.com

VOCABULAIRE 1

Les **grandes surfaces**

Large stores, shopping places

un pain de campagne

des madeleines *(f.)*

une brioche

du pain de mie *(m.)*

Le rayon boulangerie-pâtisserie

le saucisson

le rosbif

Le rayon charcuterie

le homard

les crevettes *(f. pl.)*

les moules *(f. pl.)*

le saumon

Le rayon poissons et fruits de mer

un téléviseur LCD

un mixeur

un service à fondue

une console wii

Le rayon audiovisuel

Le rayon électroménager

Dans un hypermarché

Vocabulaire complémentaire

le rayon boucherie *meat counter*
  le bœuf haché *ground beef*
  une côtelette d'agneau / de porc
    lamb / pork chop
le rayon maison-jardin *home and*
  garden aisle
  un barbecue *barbecue grill*
le rayon surgelés *frozen food aisle*
  les surgelés *(m. pl.)* *frozen foods*

l'argent *(m.)* *money*
une boîte (de conserves) *box, can*
  (canned goods)
un centime *cent*

un chariot *shopping cart*
un panier *basket*
le prix *price*
un supermarché *supermarket*

coûter *to cost*

Ça fait combien? *How much is it?*
Ça fait... euros. *That makes*
  (It costs) . . . euros.
C'est combien? *How much is it?*
Combien coûte(nt)...? *How much*
  is/are . . . ?

ACTIVITÉ A **Les rayons alimentaires** Indiquez le rayon alimentaire qui
CD2-27 est associé à chaque produit mentionné: **(a) boulangerie-pâtisserie, (b) boucherie,
(c) charcuterie, (d) poissons et fruits de mer.**

1.   2.   3.   4.   5.   6.   7.   8.   9.   10.   11.

ACTIVITÉ B **Les rayons non-alimentaires** Indiquez le rayon
CD2-28 non-alimentaire qui est associé à chaque produit mentionné: **(a) électroménager,
(b) audiovisuel, (c) maison-jardin.**

1.   2.   3.   4.   5.   6.   7.   8.   9.   10.   11.   12.

Un mot sur la langue

L'hypermarché et le supermarché

Un **supermarché** est un établissement qui vend *(sells)* des produits alimentaires. Un **hypermarché** est plus grand qu'un supermarché et vend des produits alimentaires et non-alimentaires comme les articles de maison et de jardin. On trouve souvent de bons prix et de bonnes promotions *(sales)* dans les hypermarchés.

• Quel est votre supermarché préféré?

• Avez-vous un hypermarché dans votre quartier?

© Meigneux/SIPA/Newscom

ACTIVITÉ C Associations Associez les éléments de la première colonne avec les éléments de la deuxième colonne.

1. _____ le rayon surgelés
2. _____ les centimes
3. _____ une boîte de conserves
4. _____ un chariot
5. _____ le rayon produits laitiers

a. les haricots verts Green Giant
b. la glace
c. un panier
d. l'argent
e. le lait

ACTIVITÉ D Ça fait combien? Quel produit associez-vous à chaque prix que vous entendez?

CD2-29

1. a. un homard
2. a. une côtelette de porc
3. a. un barbecue
4. a. une brioche
5. a. une pizza surgelée
6. a. un kilo de bœuf haché

b. du pain de mie
b. un téléviseur LCD
b. 2 kilos de moules
b. un service à fondue
b. une console wii
b. un mixeur

ACTIVITÉ E À l'hypermarché

> **Note de vocabulaire**
> You will learn more about the verb **acheter** *(to buy)* in **Vocabulaire 2.**

© Heinle/Cengage Learning

Étape 1. Indiquez à quel rayon Claire doit *(must)* aller pour acheter *(to buy)* ces produits.

Modèle: Elle va acheter des pommes et du bœuf haché.
Il faut aller au rayon fruits et légumes et au rayon boucherie.

1. Elle va acheter du pain de mie, du rosbif et du porc haché.
2. Elle va acheter un mixeur, du saumon et un barbecue.
3. Elle va acheter des fraises surgelées, une chaise de jardin et un lecteur DVD.
4. Elle va acheter du rosbif, des moules et des madeleines.
5. Elle va acheter une pizza surgelée, des haricots verts et du lait.
6. Elle va acheter un service à fondue, un pain de campagne et du fromage.

Étape 2. Qu'est-ce que vous allez acheter bientôt? Il faut aller à quels rayons?

Modèle: **Je vais acheter des pommes, du pain de mie et du saumon. Il faut aller au rayon fruits et légumes, au rayon boulangerie-pâtisserie et au rayon poissons et fruits de mer.**

ACTIVITÉ **F** **Faire les courses** Pour préparer un déjeuner, vous avez 25 € pour faire les courses au supermarché. Indiquez ce que vous allez acheter et combien ça vous coûte.

Modèle: J'achète un homard, un kilo de pommes de terre et une madeleine.
Ça coûte 24,59 €.

1,49 €

20 €

1kg 10,25 €

1 kg 15,50 €

1 kg 16,50 €

5,29 €

1kg 3,59 €

1,00 €

✈ ·····
Si vous y allez

Si vous allez en France, allez à l'hypermarché Carrefour pour acheter des cadeaux *(gifts)* ou des produits alimentaires. Visitez la boutique virtuelle sur le site officiel de Carrefour pour voir le choix de produits et les prix.

Un mot sur la culture

Les hypermarchés en France

Les Français ont créé leur premier hypermarché, Carrefour, en 1963 à Sainte-Geneviève-des-Bois, une banlieue parisienne. Les principales caractéristiques de l'hypermarché sont le libre-service°, l'usage des chariots, un vaste choix° de produits alimentaires et non-alimentaires à bas° prix et la présence d'un parking et d'une station-service°. Le nombre d'hypermarchés a beaucoup augmenté° depuis les années soixante. En 1966, il y avait seulement deux hypermarchés en France. Depuis 2008, on trouve plus de 1 400 hypermarchés français. Les principaux hypermarchés en France sont Carrefour, Leclerc, Casino, Cora et Hyper U.

libre-service *self-service* **choix** *choice* **bas** *low* **station-service** *gas station* **augmenté** *increased*

• Aimez-vous faire les courses dans les hypermarchés? Lesquels *(Which ones)*?

Pour parler des activités

Les verbes comme **vendre** / Le verbe **mettre**

DU FILM *LIAISONS*

Un coup d'œil sur la grammaire

Look at these photos from the film *Liaisons* and their captions.

© Heinle/Cengage Learning

Le café vend de très bons sandwichs et d'excellents desserts.

© Heinle/Cengage Learning

Elle met un verre d'eau sur la table.

1. Which word in the left photo caption is a verb? What does this verb mean?
2. Which word in the right photo caption is a verb? What does this verb mean?

Les verbes-clés

Note de **prononciation**
The **d** is not pronounced in the **je, tu** or **il/elle/on** forms of regular **-re** verbs in the present tense, but it is pronounced in the **nous, vous,** and **ils/elles** forms.

Vendre et les verbes réguliers en *-re*

The verb **vendre** is a regular **-re** verb that means *to sell*. It and other regular **-re** verbs like it follow a set pattern of endings in the present tense.

vendre		
je **vends**	nous **vendons**	
tu **vends**	vous **vendez**	PAST PARTICIPLE: **vendu**
il/elle/on **vend**	ils/elles **vendent**	

—Qu'est-ce que les supermarchés **vendent**?

—Ils **vendent** des produits alimentaires.

—Vous **vendez** des fleurs?

—Oui, nous **vendons** des roses.

—*What do supermarkets **sell**?*

—*They **sell** food products.*

—*Do you **sell** flowers?*

—*Yes, we **sell** roses.*

The past participle of regular **-re** verbs is formed by dropping the **-re** from the infinitive and adding an **u.**

J'ai vendu mes livres.

*I **sold** my books.*

❖❖ Here are some other verbs conjugated like **vendre**.

attendre *to wait, to wait for*	**rendre** *to give back, to return*
descendre *to go down (to), to get off*	**rendre visite à** *to visit (someone)*
entendre *to hear*	**répondre à** *to answer*
perdre *to lose*	

Elle **attend** Pierre à l'hypermarché.	She *is waiting for* Pierre at the hypermarket.
Ils **descendent** l'escalier.	They *are going down* the stairs.
Vous **entendez** la musique?	*Do* you *hear* the music?
Elle **rend** le livre à la bibliothèque.	She *is returning* the book at the library.
Nous **rendons visite à** notre mère.	We *are visiting* our mother.
J'**ai perdu** 25 centimes.	I *lost* 25 cents.
Il **a répondu** à la question.	He *answered* the question.

❖❖ To express *to visit people*, use the expression **rendre visite à,** not **visiter. Visiter** is only used with places or things.

À Québec, il **a visité** l'Université Laval et il **a rendu visite à** sa tante.

❖❖ As you encountered in **Séquence 3** of the film *Liaisons,* the expression **descendre à l'hôtel** means *to stay at the hotel (a specific hotel).* You can also say **descendre dans un hôtel** when you are not referring to any specific hotel.

Je **descends** toujours **à l'hôtel Delta.**	I always *stay at the Delta hotel.*
Luc **descend dans un hôtel de luxe.**	Luc *stays at a luxury hotel.*

Le verb *mettre*

Les verbes-clés

❖❖ The verb **mettre** is an irregular **-re** verb that means *to place* or *to put.* It does not follow the same pattern as **vendre** in the present tense.

mettre		
je **mets**	nous **mettons**	
tu **mets**	vous **mettez**	PAST PARTICIPLE: **mis**
il/elle/on **met**	ils/elles **mettent**	

Je **mets** une brioche dans mon panier.	I *put* a brioche in my shopping basket.
Elle **a mis** un mixeur dans son chariot.	She *placed* a blender in her shopping cart.
Mettez les pommes dans le panier.	*Put* the apples in the basket.

Note de prononciation: The **t** is not pronounced in the **je, tu** or **il/elle/on** forms of **mettre** in the present tense, but it is pronounced in the **nous, vous,** and **ils/elles** forms.

❖❖ **Mettre la table** is an idiomatic expression that means *to set the table.*

Jacques **met la table** pour sa mère.	Jacques *is setting the table* for his mother.

🔊 **ACTIVITÉ F** **eBay** Écoutez les verbes pour déterminer si c'est **Robert** qui
CD2-30 **vend** ces choses *(things)* sur eBay ou si ce sont **Robert et Abia** qui les **vendent**.

Modèle: Il vend des stylos.   **Robert**

1.   **2.**   **3.**   **4.**   **5.**   **6.**   **7.**   **8.**

Et vous? Est-ce que vous vendez des choses sur eBay? Quels produits?

🔊 **ACTIVITÉ G** **Il faut attendre** Utilisez les verbes pour déterminer si le sujet de
CD2-31 chaque phrase est **(a) Nous** ou **(b) Vous**.

Modèle: ...attendez vos parents. **b (Vous)**

1.   **2.**   **3.**   **4.**   **5.**   **6.**   **7.**   **8.**

Et vous? Qui est-ce que vous attendez souvent?

ACTIVITÉ H **Les activités de la famille d'Abia** Abia parle avec sa sœur
Nadia à propos de leurs activités et des activités de leur famille. Utilisez les verbes
pour déterminer le sujet de chaque phrase.

© Heinle/Cengage Learning

1. _____ descend**s** dans un hôtel.   a. Je   b. Maman et moi

2. _____ attend**ez** Maman.   a. Vous   b. Ils

3. _____ rend**s** visite à une amie.   a. Keesha   b. Je

4. _____ répond**ent** à mes questions.   a. Patrick et Aude   b. Aude

5. _____ entend**ons** la radio de Patrick.   a. Justin   b. Nous

6. _____ perd ses amis.   a. Xavier   b. Xavier et Patrick

ACTIVITÉ I **L'argent pour le Cercle français** Votre classe va vendre
des choses pour avoir de l'argent pour le Cercle français. Décidez qui va vendre les
choses suivantes.

SUGGESTIONS			
Je	**Le professeur**	**Nous**	**Noms des étudiants** _____

Modèle: _____ des stylos Bic   **Paul et Ben vendent** des stylos Bic.

1. _____ des madeleines.   **4.** _____ de la confiture.

2. _____ du camembert (fromage).   **5.** _____ des baguettes.

3. _____ des croissants.   **6.** _____ des biscuits.

Liaisons musicales

© Serge Dion/Images
Distribution/Newscom

Plume LaTraverse est un
chanteur-compositeur-
artiste-écrivain de
Montréal. Ses chansons,
comme par exemple *J'ai
vendu ma chèvre* (goat),
racontent *(tell)* souvent des
situations drôles. Trouvez
les paroles de cette
chanson sur Internet pour
savoir *(to know)* pourquoi il
a vendu sa chèvre. 🌐

ACTIVITÉ J Les étudiants du passé et d'aujourd'hui

Étape 1. Ces phrases décrivent-elles les étudiants des années soixante-dix, du 21ᵉ siècle ou les deux à la fois?

	années soixante-dix	21ᵉ siècle
1. ...rendent leurs livres à la bibliothèque.	☐	☐
2. ...attendent des lettres de leurs parents.	☐	☐
3. ...répondent aux courriels de leurs amis.	☐	☐
4. ...rendent visite à leur famille le week-end.	☐	☐
5. ...vendent leurs livres à la librairie.	☐	☐
6. ...perdent souvent leurs devoirs.	☐	☐
7. ...descendent dans un hôtel pendant les vacances.	☐	☐

Conclusion Les étudiants d'aujourd'hui sont-ils très différents des étudiants des années soixante-dix?

Étape 2. Demandez à votre partenaire s'il/si elle fait ces activités.

Modèle: É1: **Est-ce que tu rends tes livres à la bibliothèque?**
É2: **Non, je ne rends pas mes livres à la bibliothèque.**

Conclusion Votre partenaire et vous, êtes-vous similaires ou différent(e)s?

ACTIVITÉ K Qu'est-ce que vous perdez?

Étape 1. Répondez aux questions avec des phrases complètes. Est-ce que vous perdez souvent...

1. vos stylos?   3. vos livres?   5. vos CD?

2. vos devoirs?   4. vos clés (keys)?

Étape 2. Partagez vos réponses avec un(e) partenaire. Qui est plus distrait(e) (absent-minded)?

ACTIVITÉ L *Rendre visite* à ou *visiter*? Complétez chaque phrase avec **rendre visite à** ou **visiter** au présent.

1. Je _____ mes cousins à Paris.

2. Ma sœur _____ le Louvre ce matin.

3. Mes parents _____ leurs amis.

4. Mon frère _____ notre tante.

5. Nous _____ le Quartier latin à 13h00.

6. Nous _____ notre tante Marie ce soir.

7. Je vais _____ la tour Eiffel demain.

8. Nous allons _____ Marseille demain soir.

Et vous? Qu'est-ce que vous avez fait le mois dernier? À qui est-ce que vous avez rendu visite? Qu'est-ce que vous avez visité? Préparez des phrases au passé composé.

ACTIVITÉ (M) Qu'est-ce qu'ils mettent dans leurs sandwichs?

Étape 1. Utilisez les verbes pour déterminer le sujet de chaque phrase.

1. ...met des oignons.   a. Je   b. Mustapha   c. Claire et Anne
2. ...mett**ez** du jambon.   a. Luc et Paul   b. Nicole   c. Vous
3. ...met**s** de la mayonnaise.   a. Je   b. Vous   c. Alex
4. ...mett**ons** du rosbif.   a. Tu   b. Nous   c. Vous
5. ...mett**ent** des poivrons   a. Léon   b. Léon et Yves   c. Vous
   rouges.
6. ...met**s** de la dinde.   a. Tu   b. Michelle   c. On

Étape 2. Inventez un sandwich original. Quel est le nom de votre sandwich? Qu'est-ce que vous mettez dans le sandwich?

Modèle: **Mon sandwich s'appelle** *le club français.* **Je mets de la dinde, du brie, de la moutarde, des œufs et des oignons dans une baguette.**

Étape 3. Demandez à votre partenaire le nom de son sandwich et quels *(which)* ingrédients on met dans ce sandwich.

Modèle: **Comment s'appelle ton sandwich? Qu'est-ce que tu mets dans ton sandwich?**

ACTIVITÉ (N) Les sandwichs et les pizzas célèbres Qu'est-ce qu'on met dans ces sandwichs et ces pizzas célèbres?

Modèle: un croque-madame   **On met du jambon, du fromage et un œuf.**

1. un croque-monsieur   3. une pizza Margherita
2. un Philly cheesesteak   4. un burrito

ACTIVITÉ (O) Sondage Demandez à vos camarades de classe s'ils ont fait ces activités. Notez les noms des personnes qui répondent «oui». Utilisez le passé composé.

Modèle: **Est-ce que tu as jamais attendu le bus plus de trente minutes?**

1. (attendre) le bus plus de trente minutes
2. (entendre) les nouvelles *(news)* à la télé
3. (rendre) les DVD au club vidéo en retard
4. (rendre) visite à la famille de son (sa) petit(e) ami(e)
5. (vendre) des choses sur eBay
6. (vendre) son chien ou son chat
7. (répondre) à une petite annonce *(ad)* pour un appartement
8. (répondre) à une petite annonce pour trouver un(e) petit(e) ami(e)
9. (mettre) des posters dans son appartement
10. (mettre) des anchois *(anchovies)* sur une pizza

Il y a + expression de temps

You learned that **il y a** + *noun* means *there is* or *there are:* **Il y a un mixeur dans mon chariot.** However, when **il y a** is followed by a time expression, it conveys that something happened at a time *ago* in the past.

—Quand avez-vous fini vos devoirs?   — *When did you finish your homework?*

—**Il y a trente minutes.**   — ***Thirty minutes ago.***

Il a vendu ses livres **il y a deux semaines.**   *He sold his books **two weeks ago.***

Nous avons rendu visite à papa **il y a trois mois.**   *We visited Dad **three months ago.***

Il y a un an, j'ai perdu mon chat.   ***A year ago,** I lost my cat.*

Essayez! Utilisez **il y a** pour répondre à ces questions.

1. Quand avez-vous parlé avec votre camarade de chambre?
2. Quand avez-vous mangé au restaurant?
3. Quand avez-vous rendu visite à votre famille?
4. Quand avez-vous fait la cuisine?
5. Quand avez-vous pris du café?
6. Quand avez-vous regardé un film?

La parole est à vous!

L'hypermarché est-il une bonne ou une mauvaise chose?

Le nombre d'hypermarchés a augmenté° au cours des° années. Le nombre d'hypermarchés était° de deux en 1966 mais, depuis 2008, on trouve plus de 1 400 hypermarchés en France. L'hypermarché est-il une bonne ou une mauvaise chose?

- Christine de Paris: «Pour moi, l'hypermarché, c'est une bonne chose. À l'hypermarché, je trouve tous les produits dont j'ai besoin. C'est très pratique!»

- Sylvain de Saguenay-Lac-Saint-Jean (Québec): «Moi, je pense que l'hypermarché est une mauvaise idée°. Dans ma ville, beaucoup de petits magasins ont perdu leurs clients au profit des hypermarchés. Il faut protéger° les petits magasins.»

augmenté *increased* **au cours des** *over the course of* **était** *was* **idée** *idea* **protéger** *to protect*

Et vous? Qu'en pensez-vous?

L'hypermarché est-il une bonne ou une mauvaise chose?

🔊 Les **petits magasins** d'alimentation

Small food stores

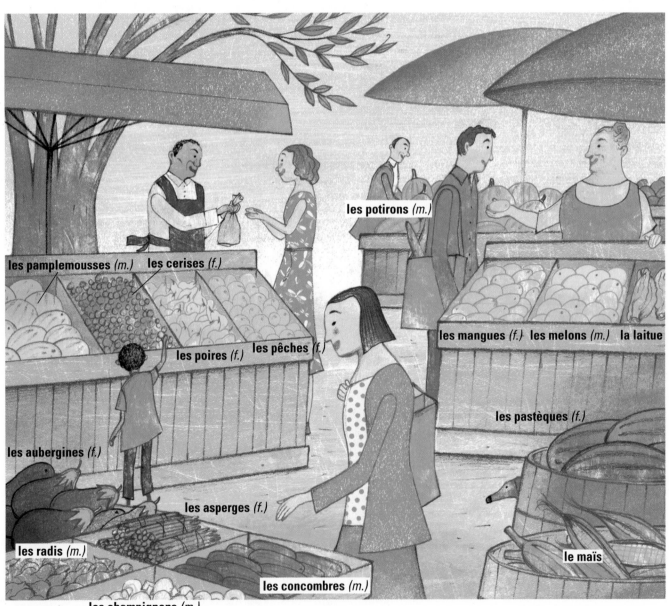

les potirons *(m.)*

les pamplemousses *(m.)*   les cerises *(f.)*

les poires *(f.)*   les pêches *(f.)*

les mangues *(f.)*   les melons *(m.)*   la laitue

les pastèques *(f.)*

les aubergines *(f.)*

les asperges *(f.)*

les radis *(m.)*

le maïs

les concombres *(m.)*

les champignons *(m.)*

Au marché

Note de **vocabulaire**
In Quebec, you can say **un melon d'eau** for **une pastèque.**

Vocabulaire complémentaire

une boucherie *butcher's shop*
une boulangerie *bread shop*
une charcuterie *deli shop*
une épicerie *small grocery store*
un magasin (de produits) bio *health / organic food store*
un marché (en plein air) *(open air) market*
une pâtisserie *pastry shop / pastry*
une poissonnerie *fish and seafood shop*

un chou à la crème *cream puff*
un éclair *éclair*
un pain au chocolat *croissant-type pastry filled with chocolate*

---

acheter *to buy*
amener *to bring someone*
apporter *to bring something*
préférer *to prefer*

---

biologique(s) / bio *organic*

> **Note de vocabulaire**
> **Une épicerie** is a small neighborhood grocery store that is usually family-owned.

> **Note de vocabulaire**
> To say *to bring something,* use **apporter.** To express *to bring someone,* use **amener: Nous apportons un gâteau à la fête. Nous amenons les enfants.**

Les verbes comme *acheter* et *préférer*

- Some regular **-er** verbs have spelling changes in their verb stems (that is, what remains when the final **-er** is dropped). For infinitives whose next-to-last syllable contains an **e** that has no accent, the **e** changes to **è** in all but the **nous** and **vous** forms of the present tense. **Acheter** and **amener** are verbs of this type.

acheter	
j'ach**è**te	nous ach**e**tons
tu ach**è**tes	vous ach**e**tez
il/elle/on ach**è**te	ils/elles ach**è**tent

amener	
j'am**è**ne	nous am**e**nons
tu am**è**nes	vous am**e**nez
il/elle/on am**è**ne	ils/elles am**è**nent

- For infinitives whose next-to-last syllable contains an **é**, the **é** changes to **è** in all but the **nous** and **vous** forms of the present tense. Verbs of this type are **célébrer** *(to celebrate),* **espérer** *(to hope),* **préférer** *(to prefer),* and **répéter** *(to repeat).*

espérer	
j'esp**è**re	nous esp**é**rons
tu esp**è**res	vous esp**é**rez
il/elle/on esp**è**re	ils/elles esp**è**rent

préférer	
je préf**è**re	nous préf**é**rons
tu préf**è**res	vous préf**é**rez
il/elle/on préf**è**re	ils/elles préf**è**rent

> **Note de vocabulaire**
> **Célébrer** is generally used in a religious or ceremonial context. The more common equivalent of *to celebrate* is **fêter** or **faire la fête.**

J'**amène** mon mari Luc chez mes parents.

Nous **célébrons** la première communion de ma sœur.

Luc **achète** une bouteille de vin.

J'**espère** être à l'heure chez mes parents.

🔊 **ACTIVITÉ A** **Qu'est-ce qu'on achète?** Vous allez entendre une série de
CD2-32 petits magasins. Qu'est-ce qu'on achète dans ces magasins?

1. a. du bœuf haché   b. un pain au chocolat
2. a. un pain de campagne   b. un saucisson
3. a. des crevettes   b. une côtelette de porc
4. a. un homard   b. un steak
5. a. une brioche   b. un chou à la crème
6. a. du poisson frit   b. des fruits biologiques
7. a. des fraises fraîches   b. des fraises congelées
8. a. un paquet de céréales   b. un téléviseur LCD

ACTIVITÉ B **Les catégories** Quel *(Which)* aliment ne va pas avec les autres?

1. a. la laitue   b. les asperges   c. les mangues   d. les concombres
2. a. les pêches   b. le maïs   c. les pamplemousses   d. les cerises
3. a. une tarte   b. une madeleine   c. du pain de mie   d. un éclair
4. a. un potiron   b. une pastèque   c. une aubergine   d. un radis
5. a. les champignons   b. les melons   c. les poires   d. les framboises

🔊 **ACTIVITÉ C** **Les fruits, les légumes et leurs couleurs** Nommez un
CD2-33 aliment qui correspond aux descriptions que vous allez entendre.

Modèle: un fruit rouge   **une fraise**

1.   2.   3.   4.   5.   6.   7.   8.   9.   10.   11.   12.

ACTIVITÉ D **Où va Claire?** Où est-ce que Claire doit *(must)* aller pour
acheter les aliments suivants?

Modèle: Elle achète des crevettes.   **Elle va à la poissonnerie.**

1. Elle achète des pains au chocolat.
2. Elle achète une baguette.
3. Elle achète des côtelettes d'agneau.
4. Elle achète un saucisson.
5. Elle achète des œufs biologiques.
6. Elle achète des boîtes de conserves.
7. Elle achète des fruits et des légumes.
8. Elle achète des moules.

✈ **Si vous y allez**

Si vous allez à Québec, allez
à l'épicerie J.A. Moisan,
la plus vieille épicerie en
Amérique du Nord. Allez sur
son site officiel pour voir la
sélection de produits.

ACTIVITÉ E **Qu'est-ce qu'il faut acheter à l'épicerie?** Nommez trois
ingrédients qu'il faut acheter pour préparer les plats suivants.

Modèle: un gâteau au chocolat   **On achète des œufs, de la farine et du chocolat.**

1. une tarte au potiron   2. une salade de fruits   3. une pizza

ACTIVITÉ **F** **Visites en famille** Déterminez la personne ou la chose qu'Abia amène ou apporte chez sa famille.

© Heinle/Cengage Learning

1. Abia **amène** _____ chez ses parents.   a. du chocolat   b. Claire

2. Elle **apporte** _____ chez sa grand-mère.   a. des éclairs   b. sa sœur

3. Elle **apporte** _____ chez sa nièce.   a. Claire   b. des madeleines

4. Finalement, elle **amène** _____ chez sa tante.   a. Claire   b. une pastèque

ACTIVITÉ **G** **Les occasions spéciales** Pour chaque occasion, indiquez qui vous amenez et ce que *(what)* vous apportez.

Modèle: le repas de Noël   **J'amène ma sœur. J'apporte des éclairs et du champagne.**

1. une fête d'anniversaire   **3.** un dîner de Thanksgiving

2. un pique-nique pour le 4 juillet   **4.** un déjeuner à la bonne franquette *(potluck)*

ACTIVITÉ **H** **Au buffet de salades**

Étape 1. Dites à un(e) partenaire ce que vous mettez normalement dans votre salade.

Modèle: É1: **Qu'est-ce que tu mets dans ta salade quand tu es au buffet de salades?**
É2: **Je mets de la laitue, des radis, des champignons, du jambon et des œufs.**

Étape 2. Avec votre partenaire, inventez une salade originale.

Modèle: **Notre salade s'appelle** *la salade César française.* **On met de la laitue, des œufs, du brie, de l'huile d'olive, des croûtons et des olives niçoises.**

Un mot sur la culture

© Tyler Olson/Shutterstock.com

La religion et la nourriture au Québec

L'Église catholique a eu une influence considérable dans la société québécoise avant les années soixante. Cette influence se reflète dans le français parlé au Québec par la présence de mots liés° à la religion catholique. Par exemple, une pâtisserie populaire qu'on trouve dans les épiceries québécoises s'appelle **les pets° de sœurs** ou **les pets de nonnes°**. Les Québécois apprécient aussi **les oreilles de crisse,** un plat constitué de lard salé frit qu'on mange avec du sirop d'érable°. Le mot **crisse** signifie **Christ**.

liés *tied* **pets** *farts* **nonnes** *nuns* **sirop d'érable** *maple syrup*

● Avez-vous envie de manger des pets de sœurs ou des oreilles de crisse?

Pour parler du passé

Le passé composé avec **être**

DU FILM *LIAISONS*

Un coup d'œil sur la grammaire

Look at these photos from the film *Liaisons* and their captions.

CLAIRE [...] quand **vous êtes parti,** j'ai cherché votre nom dans le registre *(registry)...*

ALEXIS J'habite à Paris. **Je suis arrivé** au Canada il y a une semaine.

In the captions, **partir, chercher,** and **arriver** are all in the past tense. What auxiliary verb do these verbs use to form the **passé composé**?

1. chercher   **2.** partir   **3.** arriver

⁂ You learned in **Chapitre 5, Grammaire 3** that most verbs form the **passé composé** with the auxiliary verb **avoir.** Some verbs, however, form the **passé composé** with **être.** You already know three of them: **aller, partir,** and **sortir.**

Note de grammaire

It is also accepted to use a plural past participle with **on** when it is meant as plural: **On est allés au restaurant** *(We went to the restaurant.).*

Passé composé of *aller*	
je **suis allé(e)**	nous **sommes allé(e)s**
tu **es allé(e)**	vous **êtes allé(e)(s)**
il/elle/on **est allé(e)**	ils/elles **sont allé(e)s**

⁂ In the **passé composé** with **être,** the past participle must agree with the subject in gender and number.

Monique **est partie** hier après le déjeuner.   *Monique **left** yesterday after lunch.*

Pierre et Guy **sont partis** il y a deux heures.   *Pierre and Guy **left** two hours ago.*

⁂ In negative sentences, **ne/n'... pas** goes around the auxiliary verb **être.**

Il **n'est pas allé** au marché.   *He did not go to the market.*

Elles **ne sont pas sorties** hier.   *They did not go out yesterday.*

⁂ In questions with inversion, the subject pronoun and the conjugated form of **être** are inverted.

Êtes-vous allés à l'épicerie?   ***Did you go** to the grocery store?*

Julie **est-elle partie** à 6h00?   ***Did Julie leave** at 6:00?*

Many of the verbs that take **être** in the **passé composé** deal with motion.

Infinitive	Past participle	English equivalent
aller	allé	*to go*
arriver	arrivé	*to arrive*
descendre	descendu	*to go down, to get off*
devenir	devenu	*to become*
entrer	entré	*to enter*
monter	monté	*to go up, to climb, to get on*
mourir	mort	*to die*
naître	né	*to be born*
partir	parti	*to leave*
passer (par)	passé	*to pass, to go by*
rentrer	rentré	*to return, to go home*
rester	resté	*to stay*
retourner	retourné	*to return, to go back*
revenir	revenu	*to come back*
sortir	sorti	*to go out*
tomber	tombé	*to fall*
venir	venu	*to come*

••❖ Note that **passer** can take either **avoir** or **être** depending on the intended meaning. To express *to pass by*, use **être.** To say *to pass / spend time*, use **avoir.**

Sara **est passée** par la bibliothèque ce matin.	*Sara **passed** by the library this morning.*
Sara **a passé** trois heures à la bibliothèque.	*Sara **spent** three hours at the library.*

••❖ **Partir** and **quitter** both mean *to leave*. **Partir** means *to leave* in a general sense (opposite of **arriver**) and cannot take a direct object. It may, however, be followed by a preposition, day, date, or time. **Quitter** means *to leave something or someone.* It takes **avoir** as its auxiliary verb and it must have a direct object.

Nous **sommes parties** jeudi matin.	*We **left** Thursday morning.*
Claire **est partie** pour Québec.	*Claire **left** for Quebec.*
Vous **avez quitté** la maison à 8h.	*You **left** the house at 8:00.*
Luc **a quitté** sa femme.	*Luc **left** his wife.*

••❖ If **descendre, monter,** and **sortir** are followed by a direct object, **avoir** is used in the **passé composé** instead of **être.**

Heidi **est descendue** de la montagne.	*Heidi **came down** from the mountain.*
Heidi **a descendu** l'horloge de sa chambre.	*Heidi **took** the clock **down** from her room.*
Les copains **sont sortis** hier soir.	*The friends **went out** last night.*
Ils **ont sorti** leur argent.	*They **took out** their money.*

ACTIVITÉ I Abia ou Robert?
Utilisez les participes passés pour déterminer quel(le) employé(e) de l'Hôtel Delta a dit les phrases suivantes: **(a) Abia** ou **(b) Robert, son patron** *(boss)*.

1. Je suis arrivée à l'hôtel à 7h00 ce matin.
2. Je suis allé au salon de beauté hier.
3. Je suis descendue à l'Hôtel Reine-Elizabeth.
4. Je suis retourné en Europe trois fois.
5. Je suis passé par le parc Lafontaine.
6. Je suis restée ici tout l'après midi.
7. Je suis passée vous voir à 15h00.
8. Je suis entrée dans le bar à 17h00.
9. Je suis sorti avec un client à 18h30.
10. Je suis partie avec un ami à 19h00.

ACTIVITÉ J Qui a fait quoi? Utilisez les participes passés pour déterminer qui a fait ces activités.

1. _____ est tombée à l'hypermarché hier.   a. Ève   b. Luc   c. Ève et Luc
2. _____ sont allés à la pâtisserie.   a. Yves   b. Tom et Yves   c. Anne et Alice
3. _____ est resté dans sa chambre.   a. Roger   b. Rose   c. Roger et Rose
4. _____ sont passées par un café.   a. Marc   b. Marc et Guy   c. Kim et Diane
5. _____ sont revenus du supermarché.   a. Frank   b. Lise et Anne   c. Frank et Anne
6. _____ est devenue célèbre.   a. Laura   b. Koffi   c. Laura et Joël

ACTIVITÉ K Où sont-ils nés? Quand sont-ils morts? Utilisez le participe passé pour déterminer le sujet de chaque phrase.

1. _____ sont nées en Suisse.   a. Colette   b. Colette et Luc   c. Colette et Sara
2. _____ est né au Canada.   a. Ahmed   b. Candice   c. Victor et Candice
3. _____ est morte en 2001.   a. Clara   b. Antoine   c. Clara et Antoine
4. _____ sont morts en 2002.   a. Georges   b. Georges et Luc   c. Anne et Clara

⁘ **Et vous?** Où êtes-vous né(e)?

ACTIVITÉ L Personnes célèbres Où et quand est-ce que ces personnes sont nées? Quand est-ce qu'elles sont mortes?

Modèle: Jackie Kennedy est née à Southhampton en 1929. Elle est morte en 1994.

POSSIBILITÉS

Jarnac, France (1916–1996)   Tampico, IL (1911–2004)

Dallas (1981–)   Vienne (1755–1793)

1. Marie-Antoinette
2. François Mitterrand
3. Barbara et Jenna Bush
4. Ronald Reagan

Liaisons musicales

Les Français et les Québécois admirent beaucoup James Dean. *Mourir comme lui* est une chanson de l'opéra rock de Michel Berger et Luc Plamondon *La légende de Jimmy,* un opéra sur la vie de James Dean. Écoutez la chanson sur un site Internet. 🌐

ACTIVITÉ Ⓜ **Qu'est-ce qu'ils sont devenus?** Qu'est-ce que ces personnes célèbres sont devenues?

Modèle: Marion Cotillard **Elle est devenue une actrice célèbre.**

1. Donald Trump et Bill Gates
2. Julia Child
3. Barack Obama
4. Justine Henin
5. Madonna et Céline Dion
6. Randy Pausch, Ph.D.

ACTIVITÉ Ⓝ **Vos activités d'hier**

Étape 1. Est-ce que vous avez fait ces activités hier?

Modèle: Êtes-vous parti(e) de chez vous tôt?
Oui, je suis parti(e) de chez moi tôt.

1. Êtes-vous parti(e) pour l'université le matin?
2. Êtes-vous allé(e) au restaurant pour manger?
3. Êtes-vous sorti(e) avec un(e) ami(e)?
4. Êtes-vous passé(e) par un supermarché ou une épicerie?
5. Êtes-vous rentré(e) chez vous très tard?
6. Est-ce que vos amis sont venus manger chez vous?

Étape 2. Posez les questions de l'Étape 1 à un(e) camarade de classe. Avez-vous fait des activités similaires?

Modèle: Mon/Ma partenaire et moi, nous sommes parti(e)s pour l'université le matin et nous sommes sorti(e)s avec une amie.

ACTIVITÉ Ⓞ **Avoir ou être?**

Étape 1. Utilisez les verbes pour compléter les phrases qui décrivent une journée de Claire Gagner.

1. Claire **est partie**   a. à 8h00.   b. son appartement à 8h00.
2. Claire **a sorti**   a. son livre.   b. avec Abia.
3. Claire **est descendue**   a. du métro.   b. une lampe.
4. Claire **a monté**   a. avec Robert.   b. l'escalier.
5. Claire **est sortie**   a. avec Abia.   b. ses livres de psychologie.
6. Claire **a descendu**   a. du train.   b. le fleuve Saint-Laurent en bateau.
7. Claire **est montée**   a. dans le train.   b. la colline à bicyclette.
8. Claire **a quitté**   a. l'hôtel à 17h00.   b. à 17h00.

Étape 2. Mettez les verbes au passé composé pour décrire une journée d'Abia.

1. Abia _____ (sortir) son argent.
2. Abia _____ (sortir) avec sa sœur.
3. Abia _____ (descendre) une photo de sa mère.
4. Abia _____ (monter) dans le métro.

ACTIVITÉ P **Le week-end dernier** Complétez les phrases avec (a) **Nous avons** ou (b) **Nous sommes**.

1. _____ **partis** à 11h.

2. _____ **allés** au supermarché.

3. _____ **acheté** des fruits biologiques.

4. _____ **passés** par un parc.

5. _____ **fait** un pique-nique.

6. _____ **mangé** des fruits et du fromage.

7. _____ **bu** de l'eau minérale

8. _____ **rentrés** chez nous à 16h.

ACTIVITÉ Q **La famille Brady** *La famille Brady* est une émission de télévision des années soixante-dix. Décrivez ce que les membres de la famille ont fait hier en utilisant les phrases suivantes.

POSSIBILITÉS

aller au cinéma	parler au téléphone	rendre visite à leurs amis
danser à la discothèque	partir pour Hawaii	sortir avec un intello *(nerd)*
faire les devoirs	prendre des côtelettes de porc	

Modèle: **Carol a fait la cuisine.**

1. Marcia _____

2. Jan et Marcia _____

3. Cindy et Bobby _____

4. Greg _____

5. Peter _____

6. Mike et Carol _____

ACTIVITÉ R **Avez-vous l'esprit jeune?** C'est quand la dernière fois *(time)* que vous avez fait ces activités? Répondez aux questions pour voir si vous avez l'esprit jeune *(young at heart)*.

Modèle: acheter du chewing-gum **J'ai acheté du chewing-gum il y a un mois.**

1. aller à Disneyland

2. faire un bonhomme de neige *(snowman)*

3. sortir pour prendre une glace

4. entrer dans une maison hantée

5. jouer à la marelle *(hopscotch)*

6. regarder un dessin animé *(cartoon)*

ACTIVITÉ S **Avons-nous une vie intéressante?** Posez ces questions à vos camarades de classe. Utilisez le passé composé.

Modèle: loger dans une auberge de jeunesse

É1: **Est-ce que tu as logé dans une auberge de jeunesse?**
É2: **Non, je n'ai jamais logé dans une auberge de jeunesse.**
É3: **Moi, si. J'ai logé dans une auberge de jeunesse.**

1. arriver en classe en pyjama

2. rencontrer quelqu'un de célèbre

3. tomber d'un arbre

4. retourner à ton lycée pour une fête

5. aller à la campagne

6. visiter une ville francophone

7. boire du champagne

8. rentrer chez toi après minuit

Pendant et *depuis*

Pendant + *a period of time* is used to say that something happened for a specific period of time that has ended. The verb in such sentences is usually in the **passé composé.**

J'ai travaillé **pendant huit heures.**	*I worked **for eight hours.***
Elle est restée chez elle **pendant deux jours.**	*She stayed at home **for two days.***

To ask for how long something happened, use **pendant combien de temps.**

—**Pendant combien de temps** avez-vous étudié hier?	—***(For) how long** did you study yesterday?*
—**Pendant cinq heures.**	—***For five hours.***

Remember from **Chapitre 2, Grammaire 3** that, if an event or action has not ended and continues into the present, **depuis** is used with a verb in the present tense.

—**Depuis quand** étudiez-vous?	—*(For) **how long** have you been studying?*
—J'étudie **depuis deux heures.**	—*I have been studying **for two hours.***

Essayez! Complétez les phrases avec **(a) pendant** ou **(b) depuis.**

1. Alexis **a habité** en France _____ vingt ans.
2. Il **visite** le Québec _____ une semaine.
3. Claire **étudie** à McGill _____ deux ans.
4. Elle **travaille** à l'hôtel _____ trois ans.
5. Abia **a étudié** à Montréal _____ quatre ans.
6. Elle **a travaillé** dans un café _____ deux mois.

La parole est à vous!

Faut-il informer le public sur les avantages des aliments biologiques?

Il est évident que les aliments biologiques sont plus sains. Les hormones dans nos viandes et les pesticides sur nos légumes sont mauvais pour la santé. Est-ce que le gouvernement devrait° informer le public sur les avantages° des aliments biologiques?

• Fatima d'Alger (Algérie): «Oui, on a besoin d'informations sur les avantages des aliments biologiques. Quand on mange plus sainement, on a moins° de problèmes de santé. Ça peut° aussi réduire° les frais de l'assurance médicale.»

• Fallou de Dakar (Senégal): «Non, parce que le problème n'est pas l'éducation. Le problème, c'est que les produits bio coûtent très cher. Un kilo de pommes bio coûte plus cher qu'un Big Mac chez MacDo!»

devrait *should* **avantages** *benefits* **moins** *fewer* **peut** *can* **réduire** *reduce*

Et vous? Qu'en pensez-vous?

Faut-il informer le public sur les avantages des aliments biologiques?

🔊 Les **arts** de la **table**

The art of the table

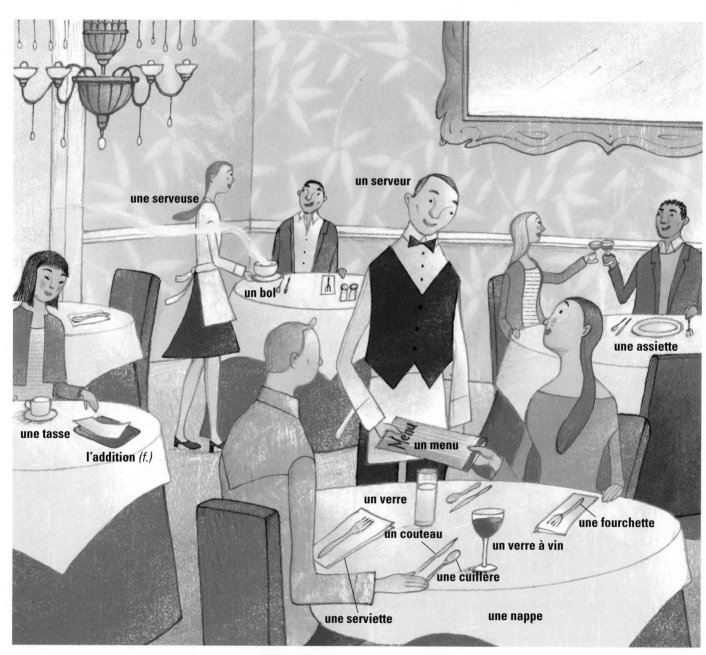

une serveuse · un serveur · un bol · une assiette · une tasse · l'addition *(f.)* · un menu · un verre · un couteau · un verre à vin · une fourchette · une cuillère · une serviette · une nappe

Samedi soir au restaurant

Vocabulaire complémentaire

les couverts *(m.)* *cutlery*
les doigts *(m.)* *fingers*
un repas à emporter *food to go*
une réservation *reservation*

---

au milieu (de) *in the middle (of)*
au-dessous (de) *below*
au-dessus (de) *above*

---

commander *to order*
débarrasser la table *to clear the table*
laisser (un pourboire) *to leave (a tip)*
payer (en liquide / par carte de crédit)
  to pay (in cash / with credit card)
payer chacun sa part *to go Dutch*
réserver (une table) *to reserve (a table)*

**Qu'est-ce que vous voulez
  prendre?** *What are you going to have?*
Vous désirez? *What would you like?*
  Je vais prendre... *I am going to have . . .*
  Je voudrais... *I would like . . .*
  Pour moi..., s'il vous plaît. *For me . . . ,
    please.*
Autre chose? *Anything else?*
  C'est tout! *That's all!*
C'est servi avec quoi? *What does this
  come with?*
C'est à votre goût? *Is it to your liking / taste?*
À table! *Let's eat! / The food is ready!*
À votre santé! *To your health!*
Bon appétit! *Enjoy (the meal)!*
Le service est compris. *The tip is
  included.*

Les verbes comme *payer*

- Payer *(to pay)* is an -**er** verb that has an optional spelling change in its verb stem (the **y** can change to **i**) in all forms of the present tense except the **nous** and **vous** forms. Another verb of this type is **essayer (de)** *(to try)*.

payer	
je pa**y**e (pa**i**e)	nous pa**y**ons
tu pa**y**es (pa**i**es)	vous pa**y**ez
il/elle/on pa**y**e (pa**i**e)	ils/elles pa**y**ent (pa**i**ent)

essayer	
j'essa**y**e (essa**i**e)	nous essa**y**ons
tu essa**y**es (essa**i**es)	vous essa**y**ez
il/elle/on essa**y**e (essa**i**e)	ils/elles essa**y**ent (essa**i**ent)

Je **paie** en liquide.   *I **am paying** in cash.*
Ils **essaient** les desserts.   *They **are trying** the desserts.*
Elle **a payé** par carte de crédit.   *She **paid** with her credit card.*
Il **n'a pas essayé** ce restaurant.   *He **didn't try** this restaurant.*

ACTIVITÉ A Qu'est-ce qu'on utilise? Qu'est-ce qu'on utilise normalement
CD2-34 pour manger chaque aliment mentionné?

1. a. une cuillère   b. une fourchette   c. un verre
2. a. un couteau   b. une fourchette   c. un bol
3. a. une tasse   b. une assiette   c. une fourchette
4. a. un bol   b. une fourchette   c. une cuillère
5. a. un bol   b. les doigts   c. un couteau
6. a. un verre   b. une assiette   c. une fourchette

ACTIVITÉ B Associations Associez les éléments de la première colonne aux
éléments de la deuxième colonne.

1. _____ un client   a. l'addition
2. _____ laisser un pourboire   b. commander
3. _____ une nappe   c. débarrasser / mettre la table
4. _____ payer   d. manger à la maison
5. _____ un repas à emporter   e. Le service n'est pas compris.
6. _____ un serveur   f. une serviette

ACTIVITÉ C Expressions Choisissez la bonne réponse pour chaque question
CD2-35 ou phrase que vous entendez.

1. a. À votre santé!   b. Je voudrais le steak-frites.
2. a. Avec des légumes.   b. Le service est compris.
3. a. Non, merci. C'est tout.   b. À table!
4. a. Bon appétit!   b. Oui, merci.
5. a. Je voudrais une omelette.   b. En liquide.
6. a. Oui, au nom de Tremblay.   b. Pour moi, un verre d'eau.
7. a. Une tarte, s'il vous plaît.   b. Un café, s'il vous plaît.
8. a. Bon appétit!   b. On paie chacun sa part.

Si vous y allez

©Ludovic/REA/Redux

Si vous allez à Paris, à New York ou à Las Vegas, visitez L'Atelier de Joël Robuchon, le restaurant du célèbre cuisinier français Joël Robuchon. Cherchez le site Web de son restaurant et regardez le menu. Qu'est-ce que vous avez envie de commander?

ACTIVITÉ D Les pourboires Avec un(e) partenaire, discutez du pourboire
que vous donnez aux personnes dans les situations suivantes aux États-Unis.

Modèle: un chauffeur de taxi
   É1: **Combien donnes-tu au chauffeur de taxi?**
   É2: **Je laisse 15 pourcent. / Je ne laisse pas de pourboire.**

1. au serveur quand le service est satisfaisant
2. au serveur quand le service n'est pas satisfaisant
3. au serveur dans un resto-rapide ou fast-food
4. au coiffeur *(hairdresser)*
5. au toiletteur *(dog groomer)*
6. au livreur *(delivery person)* de fleurs
7. au livreur de repas à emporter
8. à la femme de chambre dans un hôtel

ACTIVITÉ E Chez vous Quand vous mangez chez vous, quels couverts utilisez-vous pour les aliments suivants?

Modèle: le poulet frit   **J'utilise une assiette et mes doigts.**

1. les pâtes
2. le poulet rôti
3. la pizza
4. les frites
5. une côtelette de porc
6. la glace

Conclusion Avez-vous de bonnes manières *(manners)* chez vous?

ACTIVITÉ F Mettez la table Regardez le dessin and répondez aux questions.

1. Où est le couteau?	a. à gauche de l'assiette	b. à droite de l'assiette
2. Où est la fourchette?	a. à gauche de l'assiette	b. à droite de l'assiette
3. Où est la cuillère?	a. à côté de la fourchette	b. à côté du couteau
4. Où est l'assiette?	a. entre la fourchette et le couteau	b. à côté du bol
5. Où est la serviette?	a. sous la fourchette	b. sur la fourchette
6. Où est la bouteille?	a. au-dessous du verre	b. au milieu de la table
7. Où est le bol?	a. au-dessus de la tasse	b. au-dessous de la tasse
8. Où est le verre?	a. à côté de la bouteille	b. entre le vase et la bouteille

ACTIVITÉ G Les restaurants et les couverts Avec deux camarades de classe, décidez où on met les choses suivantes dans ces situations.

Modèle: à un pique-nique   **On met la fourchette et la cuillère sur l'assiette.**

1. dans un restaurant comme Denny's: cuillère, couteau, fourchette, serviette
2. au dîner chez vous: assiette, fourchette, couteau, cuillère, serviette, verre
3. dans un restaurant chic: assiette à salade, assiette pour le plat principal, serviette, verre à vin, verre à eau, fourchette principale, fourchette à salade, cuillère à café, cuillère à soupe, couteau, assiette à pain

L'art de mettre la table

ACTIVITÉ H Les situations

Étape 1. Dans quelles situations est-ce qu'on peut faire les choses suivantes? Discutez-en avec un(e) camarade de classe.

un rendez-vous romantique   un dîner avec des amis   un entretien *(interview)*

1. On arrive au restaurant en retard.
2. On paie chacun sa part.
3. On commande du vin.
4. On mange des frites avec les doigts.
5. On demande un *doggybag*.
6. On partage une assiette.

Étape 2. Choisissez une des situations de l'Étape 1 et préparez un sketch avec vos camarades de classe.

ACTIVITÉ I Questions personnelles Posez ces questions à un(e) ou deux camarade(s) de classe.

1. Chez vous, qui met la table? Qui débarrasse la table? Qui fait la cuisine et la vaisselle?
2. Vous laissez toujours un pourboire au restaurant? Combien?
3. Si le service est compris, vous laissez aussi un pourboire? Combien?
4. Vous préférez payer en liquide ou par carte de crédit?
5. Quel est votre restaurant préféré pour fêter une occasion spéciale?
6. Vous commandez souvent des repas à emporter? Dans quels restaurants?

> **Note de vocabulaire**
> La merguez est une saucisse épicée d'Afrique du Nord à base de viande de bœuf et d'agneau.

Un mot sur la culture

Les restaurants nord-africains en France

Un tajine d'agneau

La cuisine nord-africaine est très populaire en France. Parmi° les spécialités de la cuisine nord-africaine, on trouve les merguez (des saucisses), le couscous, le tajine et le thé à la menthe°. Un détail intéressant à noter est que les Nord-Africains mangent souvent avec les doigts. Par exemple, au lieu d'°une fourchette, on peut° utiliser un morceau de pain pour manger la viande dans un tajine. Les restaurants tunisiens et marocains sont nombreux, pas uniquement en France, mais aussi dans le monde francophone et même en Amérique du Nord.

Parmi *Among* **menthe** *mint* **au lieu d'** *instead of* **peut** *can*

• Avez-vous jamais mangé dans un restaurant nord-africain? Qu'avez-vous pris?

🔊 Liaisons avec les mots et les sons

CD2-36

Les consonnes finales

As you know from **Chapitre 2**, final consonants, except for **q, k, b, c, r, f,** and **l,** are usually silent in French. However, some words borrowed from other languages may have final consonants besides **q, k, b, c, r, f,** and **l** that are pronounced.

l'inde**x**	le foo**t**	le week-en**d**	le bu**s**

Numbers and geographical directions may have final consonants that are pronounced.

si**x**	sep**t**	su**d**	es**t**

Proper names are also some exceptions.

Agnè**s**	Anaï**s**	Maghre**b**	Viêt N**am**

Remember that a **liaison** occurs when a word that normally ends in a silent consonant (**s, t, x,** or **n**) is followed by a word that begins with a vowel sound.

Nous‿adorons ce restaurant.	Ils‿ont deux‿enfants.

There are also some cases where final consonants that are usually pronounced are not pronounced.

le dîne~~r~~	le pain blan~~c~~	le por~~c~~	le taba~~c~~

Pratique A. Écoutez bien et répétez ces mots dont les consonnes finales sont prononcées.

1. chic
2. lac
3. serveur
4. hiver
5. hôtel
6. bel
7. soif
8. huit
9. dix
10. ouest
11. Alfred
12. iPod

🔊 **À vos stylos! C'est l'heure de la dictée!**

CD2-37 Voici un extrait d'une petite conversation entre Claire et Alexis Prévost de la Séquence 3 du film *Liaisons.* Vous allez entendre les phrases de cette conversation deux fois. Écoutez bien et complétez les phrases. Ensuite, encerclez toutes les consonnes finales qui sont prononcées.

CLAIRE (1) Vous _____. (2) Votre accent... _____?

ALEXIS (3) _____. (4) _____. (5) _____ des affaires _____

qui exigent _____.

Pour parler des objets et des gens

Les pronoms compléments d'objet direct

DU FILM *LIAISONS*

Un coup d'œil sur la grammaire

Look at these photos from the film *Liaisons* and their captions.

© Heinle/Cengage Learning

ALEXIS J'ai vu une jeune femme charmante, avec un beau sourire *(smile)*... et j'ai voulu *(wanted)* **la** rencontrer.

1. What does **la** refer to in the photo caption?

a. une jeune femme b. un beau sourire

❖❖ Direct object pronouns allow you to substitute pronouns for direct object nouns. They may replace nouns that refer to people, places, objects, or situations.

J'aime **ces biscuits.** Je **les** achète.	*I like **cookies.** I am buying **them.***
Il adore **le musée.** On **le** visite aujourd'hui.	*He loves **the museum.** We are visiting **it** today.*
Il a **une sœur.** Il **la** garde aujourd'hui.	*He has **a sister.** He is looking after **her** today.*

Direct object pronouns			
Singular		Plural	
me/m'	*me*	**nous**	*us*
te/t'	*you*	**vous**	*you*
le/la/l'	*him/her/it*	**les**	*them*

❖❖ Direct object pronouns go before the conjugated verb. Note that **me, te, le,** and **la** become **m', t,'** and **l'** if they appear before a vowel or a vowel sound.

Nous **vous** entendons.	*We hear **you.***
Est-ce que tu **m'**aimes?	*Do you love **me?***
Je **t'**aime beaucoup.	*I love **you** very much.*
Je **l'**aime bien.	*I like **it.***

•••> **Ne... pas** goes around the direct object pronoun and the conjugated verb.

Tu sors avec Luc? Je **ne l'aime pas.**	*You're going out with Luc? I **don't like him.***
Ses livres? Elle **ne les lit pas.**	*Her books? She **is not reading them.***

•••> When an infinitive follows a conjugated verb, the direct object pronoun goes before the infinitive. In negative statements, **ne... pas** goes around the conjugated verb.

Les livres? Nicole va **les** acheter.	*The books? Nicole is going to buy **them.***
La télévision? J'aime **la** regarder.	*TV? I love to watch **it.***
J'aime **te** regarder danser.	*I like to watch **you** dance.*
Son vélo? Il **ne va pas le vendre.**	*His bike? He **is not going to sell it.***

•••> When a direct object pronoun is used with the **passé composé,** the past participle agrees in gender and number with the direct object. In negative statements, **ne... pas** goes around the direct object pronoun and the conjugated auxiliary verb.

—Tu as mis **la fourchette** sur la serviette?	*—You placed **the fork** on the napkin?*
—Oui, je **l'ai mise** sur la serviette.	*—Yes, I **placed it** on the napkin.*
—Vous avez regardé **les films** hier?	*—Did you watch **the movies** yesterday?*
—Non, nous **ne les avons pas regardés** hier.	*—No, we **did not watch them** yesterday.*
—Yves a écrit **les lettres?**	*—Did Yves write the letters?*
—Non, il **ne les a pas écrites.**	*—No, he **didn't write them.***

Pour aller plus loin

L'impératif et les pronoms compléments d'objet direct

Direct object pronouns are added to the end of affirmative commands separated by a hyphen. For the first and second persons, **moi** and **toi** are used.

Lisez **le journal.** Lisez-**le.**	*Read **the paper.** Read **it.***
Regardons **les films.** Regardons-**les.**	*Let's watch **the movies.** Let's watch **them.***
Regarde-**moi.**	*Look at **me.***

In negative commands, the pronoun precedes the verb. **Me** and **te** are used for the first and second persons. **Ne... pas** goes around the object pronoun and the verb.

Ne me regarde **pas.**	***Don't** look at **me.***
Ne le lisez **pas.**	***Don't** read **it.***

Essayez! Dites à un enfant de 5 ans de faire ou de ne pas faire ces activités.

Modèle: (lire) une lettre personnelle   **Ne la lis pas.**

1. (regarder) le film *Le Roi Lion*
2. (regarder) le film *Poltergeist*
3. (faire) tes devoirs
4. (lire) les livres de Stephen King

ACTIVITÉ J Qu'est-ce qu'elle vend?

Étape 1. Stéphanie, la cousine d'Abia, déménage *(is moving)* et elle vend des choses sur eBay. Regardez les pronoms pour déterminer les choses qu'elle vend.

Modèle: Elle le vend.   **son lit**

1. Elle **la** vend.   a. son téléviseur   b. sa table   c. ses rideaux
2. Elle **les** vend.   a. ses livres   b. sa poêle   c. sa lampe
3. Elle **le** vend.   a. son ordinateur   b. sa poubelle   c. ses tapis
4. Elle **les** vend.   a. sa table   b. sa console wii   c. ses assiettes
5. Elle **le** vend.   a. son service à fondue b. ses verres à vin   c. sa chaise
6. Elle **la** vend.   a. son mixeur   b. sa maison   c. ses affiches

Étape 2. Et vous? Indiquez si vous vendez les choses suivantes.

Modèle: votre lit   **Oui, je le vends. / Non, je ne le vends pas.**

1. vos livres   2. votre iPod   3. vos CD   4. votre maison

ACTIVITÉ K À l'hypermarché hier Utilisez les participes passés pour déterminer ce que Robert Levesque a acheté.

© Heinle/Cengage Learning

1. Il **l'**a acheté.   a. la glace Good Humor   b. le yaourt Yoplait
2. Il **l'**a achetée.   a. l'eau minérale Évian   b. le punch Kool-Aid
3. Il **l'**a achetée.   a. la moutarde Maille   b. le ketchup Walmart
4. Il **les** a achetées. a. les pâtes fraîches   b. les macaronis au fromage Kraft
5. Il **l'**a acheté.   a. la crème à 35%   b. le lait à 2%
6. Il **les** a achetés.   a. les fruits biologiques   b. les pizzas surgelées
7. Il **les** a achetées. a. les fromages Philadelphia b. les fraises Natural Choice
8. Il **l'**a acheté.   a. les hamburgers de Macdo   b. le poulet rôti de St. Hubert
9. Il **l'**a achetée.   a. la glace au lait de soja b. les pets de sœurs de Tim Horton
10. Il **les** a achetés.   a. les bières Budweiser   b. les jus biologiques POM

Conclusion Est-ce que Robert a acheté les produits qui sont bons pour la santé ou les produits qui sont mauvais pour la santé?

👥 **Étape 2.** Demandez à un(e) camarade de classe s'il/si elle a acheté les produits de l'Étape 1.

Modèle: É1: **Est-ce que tu as acheté la glace Good Humor?**
É2: **Oui, je l'ai achetée.**
É1: **Est-ce que tu as acheté le yaourt Yoplait?**
É2: **Non, je ne l'ai jamais acheté.**

✏️ **ACTIVITÉ L Questions personnelles** Répondez aux questions avec les pronoms compléments d'objet direct.

Modèle: Vous avez attendu <u>votre camarade</u>?

Oui, je l'ai attendu(e). / Non, je ne l'ai pas attendu(e).

1. Vous avez regardé <u>la télévision</u> hier?
2. Vous avez fait <u>vos devoirs</u> hier soir?
3. Vous avez mis <u>la table</u> hier soir?
4. Vous avez fait <u>la vaisselle</u> hier soir?
5. Vous avez lu <u>le journal</u> hier?
6. Vos amis <u>vous</u> ont invité chez eux?

👥👥 **ACTIVITÉ M Avez-vous envie de l'essayer?** Demandez à vos camarades de classe s'ils ont envie de goûter (*to try*) les aliments suivants. Notez les noms des personnes qui répondent «oui».

Modèle: **Est-ce que tu as envie de goûter le poulet frit?**

Oui, j'ai envie de le goûter. / Non, je n'ai pas envie de le goûter.

1. le couscous
2. le tajine
3. les merguez
4. les oreilles de crisse

5. les pets de sœurs
6. la poutine
7. la fondue au chocolat
8. les cuisses (*f.*) de grenouilles (*frog legs*)

La parole est à vous!
Est-ce qu'il faut laisser un pourboire supplémentaire?

En France on n'a pas besoin de laisser un pourboire parce que le service est compris. Les prix dans les menus incluent la taxe et le service (15%). Est-ce qu'il faut laisser un pourboire supplémentaire?

- Audrey d'Angers (France): «Oui, il faut laisser quelques° centimes ou quelques euros supplémentaires, surtout° si le service est bon. Dans un bon restaurant, je laisse normalement 5% supplémentaire. C'est un petit geste pour montrer° l'appréciation.»

- Alex de Tours (France): «Non, ce n'est pas nécessaire. Si le service est compris, je ne laisse jamais de pourboire supplémentaire. Mon pourboire est déjà° dans le prix de mon repas.»

quelques *a few* **surtout** *especially* **montrer** *to show* **déjà** *already*

Et vous? Qu'en pensez-vous?
Est-ce qu'il faut laisser un pourboire supplémentaire?

Liaisons musicales

© Philippe Lavieille/
Maxppp/Landov

Françoise Hardy (1944–) est une actrice et chanteuse française et aussi une icône culturelle depuis longtemps en France. Elle a écrit la chanson *Je te cherche* en 1974. Trouvez les paroles de cette chanson sur Internet. À votre avis (*opinion*), qui est «te» dans la chanson? 🌐

Avant de visionner

ACTIVITÉ A **Vous rappelez-vous?** Vous rappelez-vous (*Do you remember*) qui a dit ces phrases dans la Séquence 3 du film *Liaisons?*

	Claire	Alexis	La serveuse
1. ...encore du café, madame?	☐	☐	☐
2. ...j'ai cherché votre nom dans le registre... mais je ne l'ai pas trouvé.	☐	☐	☐
3. Non, je n'étais pas un des clients de l'hôtel.	☐	☐	☐
4. J'ai vu une jeune femme charmante... avec un beau sourire... et j'ai voulu la rencontrer.	☐	☐	☐
5. J'habite à Paris. Je suis arrivé au Canada il y a une semaine.	☐	☐	☐
6. ...attendez. Monsieur! S'il vous plaît.	☐	☐	☐

ACTIVITÉ B **Une scène du film** Vous rappelez-vous cette scène? Claire demande à Alexis s'il la suit (*follows*). Écrivez les mots qui manquent (*are missing*).

CLAIRE Alors, vous avez fait ma
(1) _____, Monsieur Prévost.
(2) _____ accomplie! Et maintenant?
Que faites-vous (3) _____? Vous
(4) _____ suivez?

ALEXIS (5) _____, ce n'est pas
mon (6) _____. Je ne suis pas un
psychopathe. Non, c'est juste une
belle (7) _____ de vous rencontrer.

© Heinle/Cengage Learning

Regarder la séquence

Vous allez regarder la Séquence 3 du film *Liaisons*. Vérifiez vos réponses à l'Activité A et à l'Activité B.

Après le visionnage

ACTIVITÉ C **Alexis Prévost**

Étape 1. Quelles nouvelles informations est-ce que Claire apprend sur Alexis Prévost au café à Trois-Rivières? Faites une liste d'au moins (*at least*) trois nouvelles informations.

Étape 2. Comparez votre liste avec la liste d'un(e) partenaire. Avez-vous écrit les mêmes choses?

ACTIVITÉ D **Est-ce que vous le croyez?** Pour chaque phrase, indiquez si vous croyez *(believe)* Alexis ou si vous ne le croyez pas.

Modèle: Alexis dit qu'il n'est pas descendu à l'hôtel. **Je le crois. / Je ne le crois pas.**

1. Il dit qu'il ne suit *(follows)* pas Claire.

2. Il dit qu'il avait besoin d'une brosse à dents.

3. Il dit qu'il est français.

4. Il dit qu'il n'est pas un homme dangereux.

5. Il dit qu'il est arrivé au Canada il y a trois semaines.

6. Il dit que sa famille a des affaires à Québec.

Conclusion Est-ce qu'Alexis Prévost est un homme honnête?

ACTIVITÉ E **Résumé de la séquence** Voici un résumé de la Séquence 3 du film. Choisissez les mots qui manquent.

l'addition   un croque-monsieur   manger   Québec   Trois-Rivières

En route pour (1) _____, Claire prend quelque chose à (2) _____ dans un café à (3) _____. Quand la serveuse apporte (4) _____, elle revoit Alexis Prévost.

aussi   café   famille   l'hôtel   mystérieux   Paris   pas   sa   salade

Claire apprend qu'Alexis n'est (5) _____ un client de (6) _____. Il voulait simplement faire (7) _____ connaissance. Alexis dit qu'il est de (8) _____ et qu'il va à Québec (9) _____ parce qu'il a des affaires de (10) _____. Après sa conversation avec Alexis au (11) _____, Claire voit l'homme (12) _____ qui lui a donné l'enveloppe par la fenêtre.

Dans les coulisses

In a **shot-reverse shot,** the director films one character looking at another, who is often off-screen, and then cuts to that second character who is shown looking back at the first character. This technique establishes a

© Heinle/Cengage Learning

© Heinle/Cengage Learning

character's point of view and is effective for filming conversations and exchanges of looks between two or more characters. A **shot-reverse shot** may have the following functions: a) to establish relationships between characters; b) to draw comparisons; or c) to make associations between characters.

   In which scenes can you observe this technique in **Séquence 3** and what do you think the function or functions were in using a **shot-reverse shot?**

LIAISONS AVEC LA LECTURE

À DÉCOUVRIR: La ville de Paris et son marché de Belleville

Courtesy of Stephen Hedge

À DÉCOUVRIR:
La ville de Paris

Importance: La ville la plus peuplée et la capitale de la France

Région: Île-de-France

Population: Plus de 2,2 millions à Paris intra-muros *(inner-Paris)*; plus de 10 millions à Paris métropole

Réputation: La capitale économique et commerciale de la France; la ville lumière *(light)*; la plus belle ville romantique du monde *(world)*; la capitale mondiale de l'industrie de la mode *(fashion)*

Climat: Un climat de type océanique avec des étés relativement frais, des hivers doux avec des pluies fréquentes en toute saison et un temps changeant

Activité Internet

La célèbre chanteuse française Édith Piaf est née et a grandi dans le quartier de Belleville. Beaucoup de scènes du film à succès international *La vie en rose* avec Marion Cotillard ont été filmées à Belleville. C'est un quartier parisien multiculturel et artistique. Cherchez sur Internet deux ou trois choses pour lesquelles ce quartier est connu *(known)*.

Avant de lire

You will discover in this reading the vibrant and dynamic outdoor market of Belleville.

Que savez-vous déjà?

1. Quels genres d'articles est-ce qu'on trouve typiquement dans un marché en plein air?

2. Quelles sont quelques différences entre un marché en plein air et un supermarché?

OUTILS DE LECTURE

Using adverbs and conjunctions to predict content

Some adverbs and conjunctions will help you predict what kind of information is in a sentence. When you see the conjunction **comme** *(like, as)*, expect to read about some kind of comparison. If you come across **pourtant** *(however)*, it is likely that the previously stated idea is being challenged. When you see **donc** *(thus, therefore)*, expect to read an example or idea that supports an earlier idea. If you see **mais**, expect to read an idea that may contradict an earlier statement. Guess what the rest of this French sentence might be about based on the beginning of the sentence.

　1. **Comme** toutes les grandes villes...　　a. a small city　　b. a large city

---

Découvrir le marché de Belleville

Paris a beaucoup de marchés en plein air. Le marché du boulevard de Belleville est un des plus connus. Il a aussi la réputation d'être un des moins chers°. Donc, on peut trouver des produits à bon prix.

Comme toutes les grandes villes, Paris est divisé en quartiers, qu'on appelle des arrondissements. Le marché de Belleville est dans le onzième arrondissement. C'est un quartier avec une histoire très riche. Le onzième arrondissement était le cœur° du Paris révolutionnaire au dix-huitième siècle et le site de plusieurs grandes révoltes ouvrières° du dix-neuvième siècle. Aujourd'hui, la vie dans le onzième arrondissement est plus calme. Pourtant, le quartier est toujours dynamique. En effet°, c'est un quartier multiculturel avec beaucoup de diversité ethnique. On trouve donc une grande variété de denrées° alimentaires au marché.

Le marché de Belleville est ouvert deux jours par semaine: le mardi et le vendredi. C'est principalement un marché alimentaire: des fruits, des légumes, de la viande. Pourtant, on peut aussi trouver des fleurs, des tissus°, des couverts et des ustensiles de cuisine. Le quartier est aussi un centre touristique où on trouve beaucoup de cafés, de pâtisseries et de restaurants. À cause du multiculturalisme du quartier, on y trouve une boucherie halal°, une pâtisserie casher°, un restaurant chinois et même un hammam°.

chers *expensive* **cœur** *heart* **ouvrières** *working class* **En effet** *In fact* **denrées** *food and food-related items* **tissus** *fabrics* **halal** *food deemed appropriate for Muslims* **casher** *kosher* **hammam** *Turkish bath*

Après avoir lu

Compréhension

1. Qu'est-ce qu'on peut acheter au marché de Belleville?
2. Nommez trois choses intéressantes à propos du onzième arrondissement de Paris.
3. Est-ce que les produits du marché coûtent cher ou est-ce qu'ils ne coûtent pas cher?
4. Donnez un exemple du multiculturalisme qu'on trouve dans le quartier.

Et vous?

1. Est-ce qu'il y a un marché en plein air dans votre quartier ou dans votre ville?
2. Avez-vous jamais acheté des produits dans un marché en plein air? Quels produits?
3. Préférez-vous faire vos courses au marché en plein air ou dans un supermarché?
4. Avez-vous envie de visiter le marché de Belleville?

Activité Internet
La fin de la lecture mentionne des genres d'épiceries, de restaurants et d'établissements différents. Utilisez Internet pour chercher trois magasins ou établissements du quartier de Belleville que vous trouvez intéressants.

La description d'un établissement d'alimentation

People often write descriptions of places that have impressed them and that they recommend others see. Here is a tourist's description of her visit to the **marché de Belleville.**

Il y a deux semaines, je suis allée au marché de Belleville dans le onzième arrondissement de Paris. Ce marché m'a impressionnée parce qu'il est dans un quartier multiculturel avec beaucoup de diversité ethnique. J'ai acheté beaucoup de choses intéressantes: de la confiture pour ma mère, des tissus pour ma grand-mère, des pâtisseries tunisiennes et des couverts pour la maison. J'ai aussi mangé dans un excellent restaurant marocain. J'ai pris des merguez, du couscous et du thé à la menthe. Si vous avez envie d'acheter des produits d'alimentation provenant de cultures différentes et de manger dans de bons restaurants, allez au marché de Belleville.

© Regis Duvignau/Reuters/Landov

Avant d'écrire

The chart displays information the tourist used in her description. Complete it with information that you would like to include in your description.

	La touriste	Vous
Nom de l'établissement	le marché de Belleville	_____
Où est cet établissement?	le onzième arrondissement de Paris	_____
Quand l'avez-vous visité?	il y a deux semaines	_____
Pourquoi l'aimez-vous?	C'est un marché multiculturel.	_____
Qu'est-ce que vous avez acheté ou mangé?	de la confiture, des tissus, des pâtisseries tunisiennes, des couverts, des merguez, du couscous, du thé à la menthe	_____ _____ _____

Écrire

Using information from **Avant d'écrire,** write your own description of a **supermarché, hypermarché, marché en plein air, restaurant,** or **café.** Write 6–8 sentences in French.

Après avoir écrit

Exchange your description with a partner. 1) Circle all the adjectives and verify that they all agree in number and gender. 2) Underline all of the verbs and verify that your partner correctly conjugated them, especially the verbs in the past tense. Did he/she use the correct auxiliary verb? Is past participle agreement correctly made if needed? 3) Put a * next to the sentence(s) that you think is (are) most interesting and explain why. 4) Does your partner's description make you want to go visit this place? Discuss your reactions together and then write a second version of your description, taking into account your partner's feedback.

PARTIE 1

À L'HYPERMARCHÉ

un hypermarché	*hypermarket*
un supermarché	*supermarket*
le rayon boucherie	*meat counter*
du bœuf haché *(m.)*	*ground beef*
une côtelette d'agneau / de porc	*lamb / pork chop*
le rayon boulangerie-pâtisserie	*bakery-pastry aisle*
une brioche	*round egg bread*
des madeleines *(f.)*	*madeleine cakes*
un pain de campagne	*country-style bread*
du pain de mie *(m.)*	*loaf of sliced bread*
le rayon charcuterie	*deli aisle*
le rosbif	*roast beef*
un saucisson	*dry salami type sausage*
le rayon poissons et fruits de mer	*fish and seafood aisle*
les crevettes *(f. pl.)*	*shrimp*
le homard	*lobster*
les moules *(f. pl.)*	*mussels*
le saumon	*salmon*
le rayon surgelés	*frozen food aisle*
les surgelés *(m. pl.)*	*frozen foods*
le rayon audiovisuel	*audio visual equipment aisle*
une console wii	*wii game box*
un téléviseur LCD	*flat screen tv*
le rayon électroménager	*household appliances aisle*
un mixeur	*blender*
un service à fondue	*fondue set*
le rayon maison-jardin	*home and garden aisle*
un barbecue	*barbecue grill*
l'argent *(m.)*	*money*
une boîte (de conserves)	*can (canned goods)*
un centime	*cent*
un chariot	*shopping cart*
un panier	*basket*
le prix	*price*

EXPRESSIONS

Ça fait combien?	*How much is it?*
Ça fait... euros.	*That makes (It costs) . . . euros.*
C'est combien?	*How much is it?*
Combien coûte(nt)... ?	*How much is/are . . . ?*

VERBES

attendre	*to wait (for)*
coûter	*to cost*
descendre	*to go down (to), to get off*
entendre	*to hear*
mettre (la table)	*to place, to put, to set (the table)*
perdre	*to lose*
rendre	*to give back, to return*
rendre visite à	*to visit (someone)*
répondre à	*to answer*
vendre	*to sell*
visiter	*to visit (something)*

DIVERS

il y a + *period of time*	*ago*

PARTIE 2

LES PETITS MAGASINS

une boucherie	*butcher's shop*
une boulangerie	*bread shop*
une charcuterie	*deli shop*
une épicerie	*small grocery store*
un magasin (de produits) bio	*health / organic food store*
un marché (en plein air)	*(open air) market*
une pâtisserie	*pastry shop / pastry*
un chou à la crème	*cream puff*
un éclair	*eclair*
un pain au chocolat	*croissant-type pastry filled with chocolate*
une poissonnerie	*fish and seafood shop*

LES FRUITS

les cerises *(f.)*	*cherries*
les mangues *(f.)*	*mangos*
les melons *(m.)*	*cantelopes*
les pamplemousses *(m.)*	*grapefruits*
les pastèques *(f.)*	*watermelons*
les pêches *(f.)*	*peaches*
les poires *(f.)*	*pears*

LES LÉGUMES

les asperges *(f.)*	*asparagus*
les aubergines *(f.)*	*eggplants*
les champignons *(m.)*	*mushrooms*
les concombres *(m.)*	*cucumbers*
la laitue	*lettuces*
le maïs	*corn*
les potirons *(m.)*	*pumpkins*
les radis *(m.)*	*radishes*

ADJECTIF

biologique (bio)	*organic*

VERBES

acheter	*to buy*
amener	*to bring someone*
apporter	*to bring something*
célébrer	*to celebrate*
espérer	*to hope*
préférer	*to prefer*

quitter	*to leave (a place / a person)*
répéter	*to repeat*

LES VERBES AU PASSÉ COMPOSÉ AVEC *ÊTRE*

aller	*to go*
arriver	*to arrive*
descendre	*to go down, to get off*
devenir	*to become*
entrer	*to enter*
monter	*to go up, to climb, to get on*
mourir	*to die*
naître	*to be born*
partir	*to leave*
passer (par)	*to pass (by), to go by*
rentrer	*to return, to go home*
rester	*to stay*
retourner	*to return, to go back*
revenir	*to come back*
sortir	*to go out*
tomber	*to fall*
venir	*to come*

DIVERS

depuis quand + *period of time*	*how long, since when*
pendant + *period of time*	*for*

PARTIE 3

AU RESTAURANT

l'addition *(f.)*	*check*
une assiette	*plate*
un bol	*bowl*
un couteau	*knife*
les couverts *(m.)*	*cutlery*
une cuillère	*spoon*
les doigts *(m.)*	*fingers*
une fourchette	*fork*
un menu	*menu*
une nappe	*table cloth*

un pourboire	*tip*
un repas à emporter	*food to go*
une réservation	*reservation*
un serveur / une serveuse	*waiter / waitress*
une serviette	*napkin*
un verre	*glass*
un verre à vin	*wine glass*

PRÉPOSITIONS

au-dessous (de)	*below*
au-dessus (de)	*above*
au milieu (de)	*in the middle (of)*

EXPRESSIONS

Qu'est-ce que vous voulez prendre?	*What are you going to have?*
Vous désirez?	*What would you like?*
Je vais prendre...	*I am going to have . . .*
Je voudrais...	*I would like . . .*
Pour moi..., s'il vous plaît.	*For me . . . please.*
Autre chose?	*Anything else?*
C'est tout!	*That's all.*
C'est servi avec quoi?	*What does this come with?*
C'est à votre goût?	*Is it to your liking / taste?*
À table!	*Let's eat! / The food is ready!*
À votre santé!	*To your health!*
Bon appétit!	*Enjoy (the meal)!*
Le service est compris.	*The tip is included.*

VERBES

commander	*to order*
débarrasser la table	*to clear the table*
essayer (de)	*to try (to)*
goûter	*to taste*
laisser un pourboire	*to leave a tip*
payer	*to pay*
chacun sa part	*to go Dutch*
en liquide	*in cash*
par carte de crédit	*with a credit card*
réserver	*to reserve*

DÉCOUVERTES CULTURELLES

L'art et l'architecture dans la France et la francophonie

Le Louvre: au cœur de l'art européen

Il y a beaucoup de musées à Paris. Le plus important et le plus grand, c'est évidemment le Louvre, avec 60 000 mètres carrés° consacrés aux expositions. Musée universaliste, avec des collections d'art égyptien, grec et romain, le Louvre contient 30 000 œuvres°, qui vont de la préhistoire au dix-neuvième siècle°. Les pièces les plus célèbres sont sans doute la *Vénus de Milo, La Victoire de Samothrace, La Joconde* de Léonard de Vinci et *La Liberté guidant le peuple* d'Eugène Delacroix.

mètre carré *square meter* **œuvres** *works* **siècle** *century*

© Laurie Chamberlain/Corbis

La tour Eiffel: symbole de Paris et de la France

Symbole de la capitale française, la tour Eiffel, surnommée° «la dame de fer°», est l'un des monuments les plus célèbres et les plus reconnus° au monde. Initialement nommée «tour de 300 mètres», la tour Eiffel est une tour de fer puddlé° construite par Gustave Eiffel et ses collaborateurs pour l'Exposition universelle de Paris de 1889. Ce monument est situé à l'extrémité du parc du Champ-de-Mars en bordure de la Seine. D'une hauteur de 313,2 mètres à l'origine, la tour Eiffel est restée le monument le plus élevé du monde pendant 41 ans.

surnommée *nicknamed* **fer** *iron* **reconnus** *recognized*
fer puddlé *puddled iron, form of wrought iron*

© Denis Pepin/Shutterstock.com

Marc Chagall: peintre français d'origine russe

Né en Russie, Marc Chagall part pour la France en 1910 pour étudier les arts plastiques et devient° l'un des plus célèbres artistes français du vingtième siècle. Son œuvre présente des caractéristiques du surréalisme et du néo-primitivisme. Inspiré par la tradition juive° et le folklore russe, il élabore° une iconographie très personnelle. La richesse poétique de son œuvre lui valent° beaucoup de commandes° telles que la décoration de l'Opéra de Paris. Le Musée national Marc Chagall à Nice est consacré à l'artiste.

devient *becomes* **juive** *Jewish* **élabore** *develops* **lui valent** *earned him*
commandes *commissions*

© ARS, NY. Erich Lessing/Art Resource, NY

Paul Gauguin: de la France à la Polynésie

L'œuvre de Gauguin constitue une transition entre la fin de l'impressionnisme et les différents mouvements qui caractérisent le modernisme du début du vingtième siècle, en particulier le fauvisme et le cubisme. Il a influencé les peintres° Picasso et Matisse. Il est particulièrement célèbre pour les tableaux qu'il a peints° pendant qu'il vivait° en Polynésie. Dans ces tableaux, il a produit des représentations idéalisées de la nature tropicale et de la culture polynésienne.

peintres *painters* **peints** *painted* **vivait** *was living*

Les Automatistes

Ce groupe d'artistes a été actif à Montréal pendant les années quarante et cinquante. Influencé par la psychanalyse et par le mouvement surréaliste, et en particulier par la théorie de l'écriture automatique, les Automatistes ont tenté de développer une forme de peinture intuitive, qui puisse° refléter les profondeurs° des sentiments inconscients, sans° passer par le filtre des processus intellectuels conscients. Le fondateur de ce groupe était Paul-Émile Borduas, qui était connu pour ses œuvres abstraites.

puisse *can* **profondeurs** *profoundness* **sans** *without*

Révision

1. Quel artiste a été influencé par la culture polynésienne?
2. Quel monument est le symbole de la France?
3. Quel musée est le plus célèbre au monde?
4. Quel groupe d'artistes a été influencé par le surréalisme?
5. Quel artiste est associé à la décoration de l'Opéra de Paris?

🌐 Activités Internet

- Cherchez les sites officiels du Louvre et du Musée national Marc Chagall sur Internet. Quelles sont les heures d'ouverture et les prix d'entrée? Nommez des expositions récentes de ces musées.

- Cherchez le site officiel de la tour Eiffel sur Internet. Nommez trois activités qu'on peut *(can)* faire à la tour Eiffel.

- Cherchez un tableau de Paul Gauguin ou un tableau de Paul-Émile Borduas que vous aimez bien sur Internet. Quel est le titre de ce tableau? Pourquoi l'aimez-vous?

La **vie professionnelle**

En bref   In this chapter, you will:

- learn vocabulary related to professions, jobs, schools, and degrees

- learn indirect object pronouns and the pronouns **y** and **en**

- learn the verbs **vouloir, pouvoir,** and **devoir**

- learn vocabulary for talking about personalities and abilities

- learn vocabulary related to banking and expenses

- learn how to make statements using comparisons and superlatives

- learn more about the vowel sound **o**

- read about work and school in France, Quebec, and Louisiana

 You will also watch **SÉQUENCE 4**: **La clé** of the film *Liaisons*.

Ressources

 audio   **iLrn** 🌐 http://www.cengagebrain.com

© Supernova/Getty Images

VOCABULAIRE 1

🔊 ## Les **professions**

Professions

un(e) agent(e)
de police

un avocat
(une avocate)

une chanteuse
(un chanteur)

un coiffeur
(une coiffeuse)

un commerçant
(une commerçante)

un comptable
(une comptable)

un cuisinier
(une cuisinière)

un dentiste
(une dentiste)

une enseignante
(un enseignant)

une infirmière
(un infirmier)

une femme médecin
(un médecin)

un musicien
(une musicienne)

un plombier
(une femme plombier)

un pompier
(une femme pompier)

Note de
vocabulaire
Un(e) enseignant(e) is a
general term for *teacher*
and may apply to any
education level.

Quelques professions

Vocabulaire complémentaire

un acteur / une actrice *actor, actress*

un(e) assistant(e) social(e) *social worker*

un(e) cadre *executive*

un(e) chef d'entreprise *company president*

un(e) employé(e) *employee*

un(e) gérant(e) *manager*

un homme / une femme d'affaires *businessman / businesswoman*

un(e) informaticien(ne) *computer specialist*

un ingénieur / une femme ingénieur *engineer*

un(e) journaliste *journalist*

un ouvrier / une ouvrière *(factory) worker*

un(e) patron(ne) *boss*

un(e) psychologue *psychologist*

un(e) secrétaire *secretary*

un vendeur / une vendeuse *salesperson*

---

un boulot *job (slang)*

une carrière *career*

un emploi *job*

une entreprise *company*

un métier *trade, vocation*

un poste *position*

une profession *profession*

un salaire *salary, pay, wages*

le travail *work*

gagner de l'argent *to earn money*

gagner sa vie *to earn a living*

Un mot sur la langue

La féminisation des professions en français

Beaucoup de professions ont longtemps été réservées aux hommes en France. Par conséquent, beaucoup de noms de professions sont longtemps restés exclusivement masculins; par exemple, **un médecin**. Quand des femmes ont commencé à obtenir des diplômes, en général on a d'abord ajouté le préfixe **femme** aux professions et plus tard une orthographe° féminine aux métiers. Cette dernière pratique est encore plus répandue° au Québec où on trouve des **professeurs** et des **professeures** à l'université.

une orthographe *spelling* **répandue** *widespread*

• Est-ce qu'il y a des exemples de la féminisation des professions en anglais?

🔊 **ACTIVITÉ** Ⓐ **Quel secteur d'activité?** À quel secteur d'activité associez-
CD2-38 vous chaque métier mentionné: **(a) médical, (b) technologie / bâtiment, (c) arts et
spectacles** ou **(d) commerce**?

1.   2.   3.   4.   5.   6.   7.   8.   9.   10.   11.   12.

ACTIVITÉ Ⓑ **Métiers correspondants** Quel métier ne correspond pas au
même secteur de travail que les deux autres?

1. a. une enseignante   b. une cuisinière   c. un assistant social

2. a. une journaliste   b. une femme médecin   c. une infirmière

3. a. un vendeur   b. une commerçante   c. un avocat

4. a. un musicien   b. un comptable   c. une chanteuse

5. a. une coiffeuse   b. une femme ingénieur   c. une plombière

6. a. un pompier   b. un agent de police   c. une secrétaire

🔊 **ACTIVITÉ** Ⓒ **Homme ou femme?** Qui exerce chaque métier mentionné:
CD2-39 **(a) un homme** ou **(b) une femme**?

1.   2.   3.   4.   5.   6.   7.   8.   9.   10.   11.   12.

ACTIVITÉ Ⓓ **Les objets et les métiers** Quel métier associez-vous aux
choses suivantes?

1. un évier   **4.** le feu *(fire)*   **7.** un revolver   **10.** un divan

2. une calculatrice   **5.** une poêle   **8.** l'addition   **11.** les cheveux

3. un ordinateur   **6.** les dents *(teeth)*   **9.** un hôpital   **12.** un manuel *(textbook)*
de français

ACTIVITÉ Ⓔ **Les personnes et les métiers** Quel métier associez-vous aux
personnes suivantes?

1. Anderson Cooper   **4.** Yo Yo Ma   **7.** Audrey Tautou

2. Homer Simpson   **5.** Donald Trump   **8.** Carla Bruni-Sarkozy

3. Robert Pattinson   **6.** Dr. Gregory House   **9.** Robert du film *Liaisons*

ACTIVITÉ Ⓕ **Les métiers et les salaires**

1. Nommez trois métiers qui rapportent *(bring in)* beaucoup d'argent.

2. Nommez trois métiers qui ne rapportent pas beaucoup d'argent.

3. Nommez un métier qui est très satisfaisant mais qui ne rapporte pas beaucoup
d'argent.

4. En général, les enfants aiment quels métiers?

ACTIVITÉ G **Les professions et la classe** Quelle profession suggérez-vous à chaque étudiant(e)?

Modèle: un étudiant doué *(gifted)* en mathématiques

comptable ou ingénieur

1. un étudiant doué en musique
2. une étudiante douée en biologie
3. un étudiant doué en informatique
4. une étudiante douée en communication
5. une étudiante douée en commerce
6. un étudiant doué pour l'accueil *(hospitality)*
7. une étudiante douée en droit *(law)*
8. un étudiant doué en bricolage *(maintenance)*

Si vous y allez

Si vous allez à Lyon (France), allez au Musée des métiers et des sciences pour des expositions sur l'histoire de quelques vieilles professions et vieux métiers en France.

© Lucas Dolega/epa/Corbis

ACTIVITÉ H **Pour quelle profession êtes-vous fait(e)?**

Étape 1. Complétez chaque phrase avec votre réponse personnelle.

	important	peu important	à éviter
1. Travailler pour une grande entreprise, c'est…	_____	_____	_____
2. Trouver facilement un emploi, c'est…	_____	_____	_____
3. Garder longtemps un poste, c'est…	_____	_____	_____
4. Avoir un bon patron, c'est…	_____	_____	_____
5. Avoir un gros salaire, c'est…	_____	_____	_____
6. Gagner suffisamment *(sufficiently)* bien sa vie, c'est…	_____	_____	_____

Étape 2. Échangez vos réponses avec un(e) camarade de classe. Quelles professions ou quels métiers lui suggérez-vous? Pourquoi?

Un mot sur la culture

© Lebrecht Music & Arts

Le travail comme sujet littéraire et poétique

Le travail figure souvent comme sujet principal dans la littérature française. Un traitement° bien connu du sujet est la fable *Le laboureur et ses enfants* (1679) de Jean de La Fontaine. Les fables sont de petites histoires souvent avec des animaux comme personnages et qui contiennent toujours une leçon de morale. Dans *Le laboureur et ses enfants*, un fermier° dit à ses fils qu'un trésor est caché dans leur champ. Le père sait que ses fils sont obsédés par l'argent et il utilise leur obsession pour leur faire travailler la terre°. C'est le fruit de leurs efforts qui va être leur trésor. La leçon de morale dans cette fable est que la richesse n'est pas forcément° matérielle et qu'elle résulte du travail.

traitement *treatment* **fermier** *farmer* **terre** *earth, ground* **forcément** *necessarily*

• Êtes-vous d'accord avec la morale de cette fable?

Pour décrire qui fait quoi à qui

Les pronoms compléments d'objet indirect

DU FILM *LIAISONS*

....

Un coup d'œil sur la grammaire

Look at these photos from the film *Liaisons* and their captions.

© Heinle/Cengage Learning

CLAIRE Je **t'**appellerai demain, d'accord?

© Heinle/Cengage Learning

ABIA D'accord. J'ai hâte que tu **me** racontes tout.

1. What does **t'** mean in the left caption? To whom does **t'** refer?
2. What does **me** mean in the right caption? To whom does **me** refer?

⟫ Indirect object pronouns replace indirect object nouns. Indirect objects answer the questions *to whom* or *for whom*.

—À qui Paul demande-t-il de l'argent?   —*Whom does Paul ask for money?*

—Il **me** demande de l'argent.   —*He asks **me** for money.*

⟫ Indirect object pronouns are identical in form to direct object pronouns except for the third-person forms **lui** and **leur**.

Note de **grammaire**
Me and **te** become **m'** and **t'** when they appear before a vowel or a vowel sound.

Indirect object pronouns			
Singular		**Plural**	
me/m'	*(to / for) me*	**nous**	*(to / for) us*
te/t'	*(to / for) you*	**vous**	*(to / for) you*
lui	*(to / for) him/her*	**leur**	*(to / for) them*

⟫ The placement of indirect object pronouns is identical to the placement of direct object pronouns. They usually precede the conjugated verb.

Je donne mon CV **à la secrétaire.**   Je **lui** donne mon CV.

Karim parle **à son patron.**   Il **lui** parle.

Guy donne des bonbons **à ses amis.**   Guy **leur** donne des bonbons.

- In negative statements, **ne... pas** goes around the indirect object pronoun and the conjugated verb.

—Tu téléphones souvent à ta mère?	—*You call your mother often?*
—Non, je **ne lui téléphone pas** souvent.	—*No, I **don't call her** often.*
—Il me donne le travail?	—*He is giving me the job?*
—Non, il **ne te donne pas** le travail.	—*No, he **is not giving you** the job.*

- When an infinitive follows a conjugated verb, the indirect object pronoun goes before the infinitive. In negative statements, **ne... pas** goes around the conjugated verb.

—Nicole **va me donner** ses livres?	—*Nicole **is going to give me** her books?*
—Oui, elle **va te donner** ses livres.	—*Yes, **she is going to give you** her books.*
—Elle désire parler à l'infirmière?	—*Does she want to speak to the nurse?*
—Non, elle **ne désire pas lui parler.**	—*No, she **does not want to speak to her.***

- Unlike direct object pronouns, when an indirect object pronoun is used with the **passé composé,** the past participle does *not* agree in gender and number with the indirect object.

Je **leur ai parlé** hier.	*I **spoke to them** yesterday.*
Ils **nous ont téléphoné** hier soir.	*They **called us** last night.*

- When statements in the **passé composé** are negative, **ne... pas** goes around the indirect object pronoun and the conjugated auxiliary verb.

Je **ne leur ai pas** parlé hier.	*I **didn't speak to them** yesterday.*
Ils **ne nous ont pas** téléphoné hier soir.	*They **didn't call us** last night.*

- If a sentence has an indirect object, it often also has a direct object. Verbs that often have both indirect and direct objects include:

demander à *to ask*	**montrer à** *to show to*
donner à *to give to*	**poser une question à** *to ask a question to*
écrire à *to write to*	**prêter à** *to lend to*
envoyer à *to send to*	**vendre à** *to sell to*

Note de grammaire
For infinitives that end in **-yer,** like **envoyer,** the **y** becomes an **i** in all forms of the present tense except the **nous** and **vous** forms: **j'envoie, tu envoies, il/ elle/on envoie** but **nous envoyons, vous envoyez.**

Je lui écris une lettre.	*I am writing him/her a letter.*
Elle me prête son livre.	*She is lending me her book.*
Ils nous ont montré la maison.	*They showed us the house.*
Il m'a vendu son vélo.	*He sold me his bike.*

- **Parler à,** **téléphoner à,** and **répondre à** are always used with indirect objects.

Le patron **va leur répondre** demain.	*The boss **is going to answer them** tomorrow.*

🔊 **ACTIVITÉ ① À qui est-ce qu'elle téléphone?** Abia parle souvent au
CD2-40 téléphone. Écoutez bien les pronoms compléments d'objet indirect pour déterminer à
qui elle téléphone.

Modèle: Elle leur téléphone.   **Antoine et David**

1. a. à Sarah et Marie   b. à Marie   c. à toi

2. a. à Karine   b. à moi   c. à Karine et David

3. a. à nous   b. à Éric   c. à Éric et Jean

4. a. à Luc   b. à toi   c. à nous

5. a. à moi   b. à nous   c. à toi

6. a. à Marc   b. à toi   c. à Tom et Damien

7. a. à Chloé   b. à Luc et Guy   c. à vous

8. a. à Maurice   b. à Hugo et Carole   c. à toi

⋯▶ **Et vous?** À qui téléphonez-vous souvent?

ACTIVITÉ ① À qui est-ce qu'il ne parle pas souvent? Utilisez les
pronoms compléments d'objet indirect pour déterminer à qui Robert Levesque du
film *Liaisons* ne parle pas souvent.

1. Il ne **lui** parle pas souvent.   a. à Frank   b. à nous   c. à Frank et Paul

2. Il ne **me** parle pas souvent.   a. à Julien   b. à moi   c. à nous

3. Il ne **leur** parle pas souvent.   a. à Céline   b. à toi   c. à Paul et Céline

4. Il ne **te** parle pas souvent.   a. à Stéphanie   b. à toi   c. à Anne et Paul

5. Il ne **nous** parle pas souvent.   a. à Carole   b. à moi   c. à nous

6. Il ne **lui** parle pas souvent.   a. à Véronique   b. à vous   c. à Sara et Nicole

⋯▶ **Et vous?** À qui est-ce que vous ne parlez pas souvent?

ACTIVITÉ ⓚ La communication Répondez aux questions avec un pronom
complément d'objet indirect.

Modèle: Est-ce que vous envoyez des textos <u>à votre sœur</u>?
           Oui, je lui envoie des textos. / Non, je ne lui envoie pas de textos.

1. Est-ce que vous envoyez des courriels <u>à votre professeur</u>?

2. Est-ce que vous envoyez des lettres <u>à vos parents</u>?

3. Est-ce que vous envoyez des textos <u>à votre meilleur(e) ami(e)</u>?

4. Est-ce que vous envoyez des messages instantanés <u>à vos camarades de classe</u>?

ACTIVITÉ **L** **Complément d'objet direct ou indirect?**

Étape 1. Utilisez les pronoms pour compléter les phrases.

1. M. Dupont **lui**…   a. parle tous les jours.   b. regarde tous les jours.
2. Carole **le**…   a. parle le matin.   b. lit le matin.
3. Michel **la**…   a. regarde souvent.   b. téléphone souvent.
4. Antoine **leur**…   a. étudie souvent   b. téléphone souvent.
5. Marc **les**…   a. fait le soir.   b. parle le soir.

Étape 2. Répondez aux questions en remplaçant les mots soulignés *(underlined)* par un pronom complément d'objet direct ou indirect.

Modèle: Lisez-vous souvent <u>vos courriels</u>?

           Oui, je les lis souvent. / Non, je ne les lis pas souvent.

1. Prêtez-vous vos livres <u>à vos camarades de classe</u>?
2. Regardez-vous souvent <u>les films de François Truffaut</u>?
3. Demandez-vous de l'argent <u>à votre camarade de chambre</u>?
4. Posez-vous des questions <u>à votre professeur</u>?
5. Faites-vous souvent <u>la cuisine</u>?
6. Lisez-vous souvent <u>le journal</u>?

ACTIVITÉ **M** **Les cadeaux et les métiers** Avez-vous des idées de cadeaux *(gifts)* pour les personnes suivantes?

Modèle: des journalistes   **On leur achète un portable.**

Idées			
argent liquide	calculatrice	fleurs	fruits
biscuits	chocolat	fromage	vin

1. une dentiste   3. des cuisiniers   5. des comptables
2. un secrétaire   4. une infirmière   6. un professeur de français

Et vous? Quels cadeaux aimez-vous recevoir?

ACTIVITÉ **N** **L'année dernière et l'année prochaine**

Étape 1. Qu'avez-vous acheté à ces personnes comme cadeaux l'année dernière?

Modèle: à votre mère   **Je lui ai acheté du chocolat.**

1. à votre (vos) camarade(s) de chambre   4. à votre frère ou votre sœur
2. à votre meilleur(e) ami(e)   5. à votre mère ou votre père
3. à votre petit(e) ami(e)   6. à votre cousin(e)

Étape 2. Qu'est-ce que vous allez acheter à ces personnes l'année prochaine?

Modèle: à votre mère   **Je vais lui acheter des fleurs.**

Étape 3. Demandez à un(e) partenaire ce qu'il/elle a acheté à ces personnes l'année dernière et ce qu'il/elle va leur acheter l'année prochaine.

ACTIVITÉ O Êtes-vous gentil(le)? Est-ce que vous allez prêter ces choses aux personnes suivantes?

Modèle: vos stylos <u>à votre sœur</u>   **Je (ne) vais (pas) lui prêter mes stylos.**

1. votre iPod <u>aux enfants</u>
2. votre ordinateur <u>à votre camarade de chambre</u>
3. votre vélo <u>à vos parents</u>
4. votre argent <u>à votre voisin(e)</u>
5. votre livre <u>aux camarades de classe</u>
6. votre brosse à dents *(toothbrush)* <u>à votre colocataire</u>

ACTIVITÉ P Des gestes généreux Par groupes de trois, dites qui s'est montré(e) généreux (généreuse) envers vous. Parlez de trois à cinq choses que quelqu'un a faites pour vous.

Modèle: É1: **Mon colocataire m'a prêté son livre.**

   É2: **Mes parents m'ont donné de l'argent pour mon loyer.**

   É3: **Mon petit ami m'a préparé un dîner romantique.**

Suggestions			
acheter	faire	argent	dîner
apporter	montrer	cadeaux	livres
donner	parler	chocolat	loyer
écrire	préparer	gâteau	ordinateur
envoyer	prêter	devoirs	soupe

ACTIVITÉ Q Encore des gestes généreux Avec un(e) partenaire, décidez quels gestes vous allez faire pour ces personnes.

Modèle: Un enfant est très triste.   **Nous allons lui acheter des bonbons.**

1. Une vieille femme est au marché. Il fait chaud et elle a soif.
2. La mère de votre ami(e) est à l'hôpital.
3. Un homme sans abri *(homeless)* a très faim.
4. Votre colocataire est très triste.
5. Votre petit(e) ami(e) est malade *(sick)*.
6. Les parents de votre ami(e) vous invitent à dîner chez eux.
7. Votre voisin(e) est déprimé(e) *(depressed)*.
8. Les enfants ont perdu *(lost)* leur chien.

Pour aller plus loin

L'impératif et les pronoms compléments d'objet indirect

Indirect object pronouns are added to the end of affirmative imperative commands separated by a hyphen. For the first and second person, **moi** and **toi** are used.

Donnez-moi dix minutes.	*Give me ten minutes.*
Achète-toi un ordinateur.	*Buy yourself a computer.*
Téléphonons-lui aujourd'hui.	*Let's phone him/her today.*

In negative commands, the pronouns precede the verb. Use **me** and **te** in negative commands. **Ne... pas** goes around the object pronoun and the verb.

Ne me posez pas de questions.	*Don't ask me any questions.*
Ne lui téléphonons pas aujourd'hui.	*Let's not phone him today.*
Ne lui donne pas plus de dix minutes.	*Don't give him/her more than ten minutes.*

Essayez! Indiquez trois choses qu'on donne et trois choses qu'on ne donne pas à un enfant de 3 ans.

Modèle: Donne-lui du lait.
Ne lui donne pas de couteau.

Liaisons musicales

Henri Salvador a écrit une chanson comique sur l'obsession du travail: *Le travail, c'est la santé* (1965). Cherchez les paroles de cette chanson sur Internet et identifiez les termes liés au *(related to)* travail.

La parole est à vous!

Est-ce qu'il faut surveiller les activités des employés?

Selon *BBC News*, plus de 50% des employés avouent° qu'ils naviguent sur Internet au travail pour des raisons personnelles. Est-ce qu'il faut surveiller° les activités des employés sur Internet?

- Kofi de Lomé (Togo): «Absolument pas! C'est une atteinte à la vie privée°! Je suis très productif au travail même si° parfois je navigue sur Internet.»

- Leif d'Ottawa: «Oui, c'est peut-être une bonne idée. Je gaspille° environ° une heure par jour sur Internet quand je suis au travail. Si mon patron surveille mes activités, je vais peut-être être plus productif.»

avouent *admit* **surveiller** *to monitor* **atteinte à la vie privée** *violation of privacy* **même si** *even if* **gaspille** *waste* **environ** *approximately*

Et vous? Qu'en pensez-vous?

Est-ce qu'il faut surveiller les activités des employés sur Internet?

🔊 # Les **atouts professionnels**

Professional skills

1. Avez-vous de bonnes capacités de communication?

oui   **non**

☐   ☐

6. Êtes-vous organisé(e)?

oui   **non**

☐   ☐

2. Êtes-vous bon(ne) avec les chiffres?

oui   **non**

☐   ☐

7. Êtes-vous jaloux (jalouse)?

oui   **non**

☐   ☐

3. Êtes-vous créatif (créative)?

oui   **non**

☐   ☐

8. Êtes-vous du matin?

oui   **non**

☐   ☐

4. Êtes-vous souvent de bonne humeur?

oui   **non**

☐   ☐

9. Êtes-vous du soir?

oui   **non**

☐   ☐

5. Êtes-vous souvent de mauvaise humeur?

oui   **non**

☐   ☐

🔊 **Test de personnalité et de caractère**

CD2-41

Vocabulaire complémentaire

acharné(e) *competitive, cutthroat*
antisocial(e) *anti-social*
autonome *independent*
coincé(e) *uptight*
déloyal(e) *disloyal*
drôle *funny, odd*
excentrique *eccentric*
exigeant(e) *demanding*
extraverti(e) *extroverted, extrovert*
farfelu(e) *scatter-brained*
flexible *flexible*
inflexible *inflexible*
introverti(e) *introverted, introvert*
loyal(e) *loyal, faithful*

professionnel(le) *professional*
sensible *sensitive*
solitaire *solitary, loner*
têtu(e) *stubborn*

---

avoir le goût du travail *to have a good work ethic*
avoir le sens de l'humour *to have a sense of humor*
être précis(e) *to be good with details*

les atouts *(m.)* **professionnels**
professional skills

Note de vocabulaire
Acharné(e) through **têtu(e)** are adjectives whereas **acharné(e)**, **excentrique, extraverti(e)**, **farfelu(e), introverti(e)**, **professionnel(le), solitaire** can be used either as nouns or adjectives.

Pour aller plus loin
Quelqu'un de...

To say *someone interesting, someone sensitive, someone funny* and so forth, use the construction **quelqu'un** + **de/d'** + the masculine form of the adjective.

Il y a **quelqu'un d'intéressant** dans la salle.

*There is **someone interesting** in the room.*

Il y a **quelqu'un de sensible** dans ma classe.

*There is **someone sensitive** in my class.*

J'ai rencontré **quelqu'un de drôle** à la fête.

*I met **someone funny** at the party.*

Essayez! Dites si vous voulez rencontrer ces types de personnes à une fête.

Modèle: quelqu'un d'exigeant   **Je (ne) veux (pas) rencontrer quelqu'un d'exigeant.**

1. quelqu'un d'acharné
2. quelqu'un d'antisocial
3. quelqu'un de coincé
4. quelqu'un d'excentrique
5. quelqu'un de farfelu
6. quelqu'un de solitaire

ACTIVITÉ **A** **Descriptions** Choisissez le mot qui complète le mieux *(the best)* chaque phrase que vous entendez.

CD2-42

1. a. antisocial   b. acharné   c. excentrique   d. autonome
2. a. déloyal   b. solitaire   c. farfelu   d. extraverti
3. a. têtu   b. flexible   c. sensible   d. exigeant
4. a. créatif   b. coincé   c. drôle   d. fidèle

ACTIVITÉ **B** **Traits de caractère et qualités** Qui a ces traits de caractère ou ces qualités?

Modèle: drôle   Margaret Cho et ma camarade de chambre sont drôles.

1. sensible
2. solitaire
3. coincé(e)
4. créatif / créative
5. têtu(e)

6. être bon(ne) avec les chiffres
7. farfelu(e)
8. être de mauvaise humeur
9. jaloux / jalouse
10. être du soir

ACTIVITÉ **C** **Les patrons agréables et détestables**

Étape 1. Décidez si les phrases décrivent un(e) patron(ne) agréable ou détestable. Puis partagez vos réponses avec un(e) partenaire. Avez-vous les mêmes opinions?

	Agréable	Détestable
1. Il/Elle a le sens de l'humour.	_____	_____
2. Il/Elle est exigeant(e) et inflexible.	_____	_____
3. Il/Elle a le goût du travail.	_____	_____
4. Il/Elle est du matin et souvent de bonne humeur.	_____	_____
5. Il/Elle est farfelu(e) et pas précis(e).	_____	_____
6. Il/Elle a de bonnes capacités de communication.	_____	_____

Étape 2. Robert est le patron de Claire et d'Abia. À votre avis, quelles phrases de l'Étape 1 décrivent Robert?

Étape 3. Avec votre partenaire, décrivez votre patron(ne) idéal(e).

© Heinle/Cengage Learning

ACTIVITÉ **D** **Et vous?**

Étape 1. Complétez le test de personnalité et de caractère à la page 278.

Étape 2. Partagez vos réponses avec un(e) camarade de classe. Lisez ses réponses. Quelle profession lui recommandez-vous? Pourquoi?

ACTIVITÉ **E** **Employés de l'entreprise** Complétez les évaluations de ces employés avec le mot qui convient.

Modèle: Cet employé travaille souvent tout seul.

Il est **solitaire.** / C'est **un solitaire.**

1. Cet employé ne parle pas beaucoup avec les autres. C'est _____.

2. Cette employée est très originale et même un peu bizarre. C'est _____.

3. Cet employé n'est pas très honnête. Il est _____.

4. Cette employée est très compétente et respectueuse. Elle est _____.

5. Cet employé travaille depuis longtemps pour cette entreprise. Il est

_____.

ACTIVITÉ **F** **Annonces d'emploi** Préparez une annonce d'emploi (*job ad*) de trois à quatre phrases pour les métiers suivants. Identifiez le profil idéal et les traits à éviter.

Modèle: un(e) comptable

Nous cherchons un(e) comptable. Il faut être bon avec les chiffres et bien organisé. Nous désirons un(e) employé(e) extraverti(e). Cette personne doit avoir le goût du travail. Nous ne désirons pas quelqu'un de solitaire.

1. un infirmier / une infirmière

2. un vendeur / une vendeuse

3. un(e) journaliste

4. un(e) secrétaire

Si vous y allez

Si vous allez à Avernes-Saint-Gourgon en Normandie, prenez un des cours de savoir-vivre et de bonnes manières de la Baronne Hargitay-Gran. Elle offre des cours sur la communication et le savoir-vivre en public et sur beaucoup d'autres thèmes similaires.

Un mot sur la culture

Le savoir-vivre

Les Français ont une expression très importante qu'on utilise aussi en anglais: **le savoir-vivre°.** Le sens de cette expression est, en effet, un peu philosophique. Il ne s'agit pas uniquement° de connaître et suivre «les règles de vie» (l'étiquette, la courtoisie et la politesse) mais de vivre bien, c'est-à-dire en équilibre et en profitant de la vie°. Par exemple, même si le travail joue un rôle important dans la culture et la société françaises, les Français réussissent en général à garder° le travail et ses obligations en harmonie avec d'autres aspects de leur vie, surtout avec «les plaisirs de la vie» comme la famille, les amis, les vacances, la cuisine et les passe-temps préférés.

savoir-vivre *to know how to live* **Il ne s'agit pas uniquement** *It's not only about* **profitant de la vie** *taking advantage of life* **garder** *to keep*

• Et vous? Quel rôle le travail joue-t-il dans votre vie? Avez-vous du savoir-vivre?

Pour parler des désirs, des capacités et des obligations

Les verbes **vouloir, pouvoir, devoir** / Les pronoms **y** et **en**

DU FILM _LIAISONS_ ·······································

Un coup d'œil sur la grammaire

Look at these photos from the film _Liaisons_ and their captions.

© Heinle/Cengage Learning

CLAIRE Je ne sais pas qui m'a offert ce séjour (_stay_).

RÉCEPTIONNISTE Si vous **voulez**, je **peux** demander à mon superviseur.

Claire a une clé pour un coffre-fort (_safety deposit box_). Mais c'est samedi et la banque est fermée. Donc, Claire ne peut pas **y** aller aujourd'hui.

1. In the left photo caption, which verb means _can_? Which verb means _want_?
2. In the right photo caption, what does the pronoun **y** refer to?

Les verbes-clés

Les verbes _vouloir, pouvoir, devoir_

The verbs **vouloir** (_to want_), **pouvoir** (_to be able to, can_), and **devoir** (_to have to, must, to owe_) are irregular. They often appear with infinitives, and they are conjugated with **avoir** in the **passé composé**.

vouloir	pouvoir	devoir
je **veux**	je **peux**	je **dois**
tu **veux**	tu **peux**	tu **dois**
il/elle/on **veut**	il/elle/on **peut**	il/elle/on **doit**
nous **voulons**	nous **pouvons**	nous **devons**
vous **voulez**	vous **pouvez**	vous **devez**
ils/elles **veulent**	ils/elle **peuvent**	ils/elles **doivent**
PAST PARTICIPLE: **voulu**	PAST PARTICIPLE: **pu**	PAST PARTICIPLE: **dû**

Voulez-vous voir la patronne?　　　_Do you **want** to see the boss?_
Pouvons-nous parler avec le gérant?　_**Can** we speak to the manager?_
Je **dois** travailler très tôt demain.　　_I **have to** work very early tomorrow._
Il **a pu terminer** son travail.　　　　_He **was able to** / **managed to** finish all his work._

Devoir means _to owe_ when used with a noun.

Je **dois six euros** à mon patron.　　_I owe my boss **six euros.**_

Les pronoms *y* et *en*

- The pronouns **y** and **en** replace phrases that contain previously mentioned ideas. **Y** replaces phrases that begin with a preposition (**à, chez, dans, en,** or **sur**), and **en** replaces phrases that begin with a partitive or indefinite article or phrases that begin with the preposition **de**.

Claire étudie **à l'université McGill**.	*Claire studies **at McGill University**.*
Claire **y** étudie.	*Claire studies **there**.*
Marc prend **du sucre** dans son café.	*Marc takes **sugar** in his coffee.*
Marc **en** prend dans son café.	*Marc takes **some** in his coffee.*

- Verbs used with **à** include **penser à, réussir à,** and **répondre à.** Verbs used with **de** include **penser de, parler de, avoir besoin de, avoir envie de,** and **avoir peur de.**

Karim pense **à son travail.** Il **y** pense.	*Karim thinks **about his work**. He thinks **about it**.*
Il a peur **des chiens.** Il **en** a peur.	*He is afraid **of dogs**. He is afraid **of them**.*

- The placement of **y** and **en** is identical to that of other object pronouns. In the **passé composé,** the past participle does not agree with **y** and **en**.

—Il a répondu **à la question**?	*—He answered **the question**?*
—Oui, il **y** a répondu.	*—Yes, he answered **it**.*
—Il a mis **de la** crème dans la soupe?	*—Did he put **any** cream in the soup?*
—Non, il n'**en** a pas mis.	*—No, he did not put **any**.*
—Tu vas manger **dans ton bureau**?	*—Are you going to eat **in your office**?*
—Oui, je vais **y** manger.	*—Yes, I am going to eat **there**.*
—Avez-vous besoin **de papier**?	*—Do you need **some paper**?*
—Non, nous n'**en** avons pas besoin.	*—No, we don't need **any**.*

- **En** is also used to replace a noun that is modified by a number or by an expression of quantity.

—Combien de biscuits allez-vous manger?	*—How many cookies are you going to eat?*
—Je vais **en** manger **trois**.	*—I am going to eat **three (of them)**.*
—Vous avez **beaucoup de** devoirs?	*—Do you have **a lot of** homework?*
—Non, je n'**en** ai pas **beaucoup**.	*—No, I don't have **much (a lot of it)**.*

- With some verbs, **y** and **en** cannot replace people. When referring to people, use a disjunctive pronoun after the preposition.

Je pense souvent **à Marc.**	Je pense souvent **à lui.**
Il parle **de Luc et de Marie.**	Il parle **d'eux.**

- In the imperative, add an **s** to the **tu** form of any **-er** verb before adding **y** or **en**.

Va **au bureau.**	Va**s**-**y**.	*Go **there**.*
Mange **du chocolat.**	Mange**s**-**en**.	*Eat **some**.*

ACTIVITÉ **G** **Qui le dit?** Qui dit les phrases suivantes?

1. Je **dois** mettre la table.	a. un client	b. un serveur
2. Je **veux** un nouveau look.	a. un client	b. un coiffeur
3. Je **ne peux pas** faire la cuisine.	a. un cuisinier	b. un enfant
4. Je **peux** nager.	a. un chat	b. un chien
5. Je **dois** de l'argent à mes parents.	a. un étudiant	b. un cadre
6. Je **ne veux pas** travailler avec les chiffres.	a. un comptable	b. un acteur
7. Je **veux** vendre un gâteau.	a. un client	b. une vendeuse
8. Je **dois** faire mes devoirs.	a. un étudiant	b. un professeur

ACTIVITÉ **H** **Désirs, compétences et obligations** Des gens parlent des désirs, des compétences et des obligations dans le monde du travail. Choisissez le sujet approprié pour chaque phrase.

1. _____ **veut** trouver un bon poste.	a. Je	b. Frank	c. Nous
2. _____ **veux** un bon salaire.	a. Marie	b. Marie et Luc	c. Je
3. _____ **veulent** des horaires flexibles.	a. Yin et Tran	b. Vous	c. Nous
4. _____ **pouvez** travailler le week-end.	a. Nous	b. Vous	c. Luc
5. _____ **peux** être organisée.	a. Je	b. Marie	c. Nous
6. _____ **pouvons** voyager souvent.	a. Vous	b. Pierre	c. Nous
7. _____ **dois** 10 euros au patron.	a. Tu	b. Michel	c. Vous
8. _____ **devez** être sociables.	a. Marc et Luc	b. Nous	c. Vous
9. _____ **doivent** travailler tard.	a. Sara et Anne	b. Mustapha	c. Tu
10. _____ **devons** être du matin.	a. Vous	b. Luc et Yves	c. Nous

Et vous? Complétez les phrases.

1. Je veux _____. **2.** Je peux _____. **3.** Je dois _____.

ACTIVITÉ **I** **Votre professeur** Devinez si chaque activité est un désir, une compétence ou une obligation pour votre professeur. Complétez chaque phrase avec **veut, peut** ou **doit.**

Mon professeur…

1. _____ parler français.

2. _____ regarder des films français.

3. _____ travailler le soir.

4. _____ faire la cuisine.

5. _____ manger dans un bistro français.

6. _____ faire du shopping.

7. _____ lire des courriels.

8. _____ rendre visite à sa famille.

Et vous? Refaites l'activité avec **Je veux, Je peux** ou **Je dois.** Est-ce que vous êtes comme votre professeur?

ACTIVITÉ J **Les personnalités, les compétences et les carrières**

Étape 1. Quelles compétences est-ce que ces personnes doivent avoir?

Modèle: Marc veut être professeur de français. **Il doit parler français.**

1. Jean veut être comptable.

2. Marie veut être baby-sitter.

3. Benoît et Ali veulent être artistes.

4. Émilie et Sara veulent être journalistes.

Étape 2. Quelle carrière est-ce que ces personnes peuvent avoir?

Modèle: Marie aime faire du shopping. **Elle peut devenir vendeuse.**

1. Claire Gagner aime la psychologie.

2. Antoine joue de la guitare.

3. Luc et Lise aiment faire la cuisine.

4. Nicole et Luce sont excentriques.

ACTIVITÉ K **Les talents** Demandez à un(e) partenaire s'il/si elle **peut** faire ces activités. Si votre partenaire répond «non», demandez s'il/si elle **veut** faire ces activités.

Modèle: É1: **Est-ce que tu peux jouer du piano?**
É2: **Non, je ne peux pas jouer du piano.**
Oui, je veux jouer du piano.

1. jouer de la guitare

2. chanter bien

3. faire du karaoké

4. dessiner bien

5. danser bien

6. écrire des poèmes

7. préparer un repas français

8. parler français

Conclusion Avez-vous les mêmes *(same)* talents? Voulez-vous faire les mêmes activités?

Modèle: **Nous pouvons parler français. Nous voulons bien chanter et danser.**

ACTIVITÉ L **Les contes de fées** Lisez-vous des contes de fées *(fairytales)*? Complétez chaque phrase avec les éléments suivants au passé composé.

(devoir) dormir pendant 100 ans	(ne pas pouvoir) dire des mensonges *(lies)*
(devoir) travailler dans la forêt	(ne pas vouloir) grandir
(ne pas pouvoir) aller au bal *(ball)*	(vouloir) être humain(e)

1. La petite sirène Arielle _____.

2. La Belle au bois dormant _____.

3. Cendrillon _____.

4. Peter Pan _____.

5. Pinocchio _____.

6. Les sept nains *(dwarfs)* _____.

ACTIVITÉ M **Les activités de Patrick, le neveu d'Abia** Utilisez les pronoms pour déterminer de quoi Patrick parle.

1. J'**y** joue.   a. au tennis   b. du violon
2. J'**en** joue.   a. au football   b. de la guitare
3. J'**en** prends.   a. au café   b. du thé
4. J'**y** mange.   a. au bistro   b. du pain
5. J'**y** ai réussi.   a. à mon examen   b. de ses devoirs
6. J'**y** ai pensé.   a. à Abia   b. à la fête

ACTIVITÉ N **Êtes-vous un(e) bon(ne) employé(e)?** Répondez aux questions en remplaçant les mots soulignés avec les pronoms **y** ou **en**.

Modèle: Avez-vous peur <u>de la compétition</u>?   **Non, je n'en ai pas peur.**

1. Avez-vous besoin <u>d'horaires flexibles</u>?
2. Travaillez-vous souvent <u>chez vous</u>?
3. Avez-vous <u>des enfants</u>?
4. Prenez-vous <u>de l'alcool</u>?
5. Allez-vous souvent <u>aux toilettes</u>?
6. Répondez-vous rapidement <u>aux courriels</u>?
7. Avez-vous envie <u>de travailler le week-end</u>?
8. Pensez-vous constamment <u>à votre travail</u>?

• Quelles questions sont normalement interdites *(forbidden)* dans une entrevue?

ACTIVITÉ O **Vous êtes bien équipés?** Posez ces questions à un(e) partenaire. Est-ce qu'il/elle est bien équipé(e)?

Modèle: É1: **Tu as combien de calculatrices?**
          É2: **J'en ai trois.**

1. Tu as combien de téléviseurs?
2. Tu as combien de téléphones?
3. Tu as combien d'iPods?
4. Tu as combien de CD?

ACTIVITÉ P **Les activités de Claire Gagner** Claire a-t-elle fait les activités suivantes dans le film *Liaisons*? Avec un(e) partenaire, répondez aux questions pour voir si vous avez une bonne mémoire.

Modèle: Claire a lu <u>son livre de psychologie</u>?   **Oui, elle l'a lu.**

1. Claire a mangé <u>des oranges</u> au café?
2. Claire a regardé <u>la télé</u> chez elle?
3. L'oncle Michel a téléphoné <u>à Claire</u>?
4. Claire est allée <u>à Québec</u>?
5. Elle a répondu <u>aux questions des clients</u>?
6. Claire a pensé <u>à Alexis Prévost</u>?
7. Claire a fait <u>ses devoirs</u>?
8. Claire a bu beaucoup <u>de bières</u>?

© Heinle/Cengage Learning

L'ordre des pronoms compléments d'objet

Use this sequence when a sentence contains two object pronouns.

me te nous vous	*before*	le la les	*before*	lui leur	*before*	y / en

Double object pronouns occupy the same position in sentences as single object pronouns.

Mon père (ne) m'achète (pas) les livres.	→ Il (ne) **me les** achète (pas).
Les voisins (ne) lui ont (pas) donné du (de) sucre.	→ Ils (ne) **lui en** ont (pas) donné.
Luc (ne) leur a (pas) montré les maisons.	→ Luc (ne) **les leur** a (pas) montré**es**.
Ne lui donne pas le couteau.	→ Ne **le lui** donne pas.

In affirmative commands, the direct object pronoun precedes the indirect object pronoun. Remember that **moi** and **toi** are used instead of **me** and **te**.

Montrez-moi les assiettes.	→ Montrez-**les-moi**.

Essayez! Répondez aux questions avec deux pronoms.

1. Vous montrez <u>les films</u> d'horreur de Wes Craven <u>aux enfants</u>?
2. L'an dernier, vous avez donné <u>des cadeaux</u> <u>à votre voisin</u>?
3. L'année prochaine, vous allez acheter <u>vos livres</u> <u>à la librairie universitaire</u>?

La parole est à vous!

Est-ce que les tests de personnalité sont une bonne idée?

Les conseillers° d'orientation donnent souvent des tests de personnalité aux étudiants pour déterminer les professions qui leur seraient° idéales. C'est une bonne idée?

- Anaïs de Genève: «Non, parce qu'il n'y pas de données° empiriques pour soutenir° leur validité. On risque de donner une mauvaise orientation à quelqu'un.»
- Maude de Québec: «Moi, je pense que ces tests sont un bon outil° pour découvrir nos atouts professionnels. Ce n'est pas le seul° outil mais c'est un bon début.»

conseillers *counselors* **seraient** *would be* **données** *data* **soutenir** *to support* **outil** *tool* **seul** *only*

Et vous? Qu'en pensez-vous?

Est-ce que les tests de personnalité sont une bonne idée pour déterminer le choix d'une profession?

🔊 La **formation** et les **dépenses**

Training and expenses

une **école de commerce**

une **faculté de médecine**

> **Note** de **vocabulaire**
> In France, **une faculté de sciences et technologie** may also be called **une école polytechnique.**

une **faculté de droit**

une **faculté de sciences et technologie**

une **faculté de lettres et de sciences humaines**

une **école professionnelle**

La formation

> **Note** de **vocabulaire**
> Students may study music, dance, or dramatic arts at a **conservatoire.**

🔊 **Vocabulaire complémentaire**

le baccalauréat *end-of-high-school exam*
un collège *junior high / middle school*
un conservatoire *conservatory*
un diplôme (universitaire) *(university) diploma*
un doctorat *doctorate, Ph.D.*
les études supérieures *(f.) higher education*
une formation *training*
une licence *equivalent of a bachelor's degree*

un lycée *high school*
un master *master's degree*
un MBA *MBA*
un stage de formation *internship*

une bourse d'études *scholarship*
une carte bancaire *debit card*
un compte-chèques *checking account*
un compte d'épargne *savings account*
les frais de scolarité *(m.) tuition*
un prêt étudiant *student loan*

Les dépenses

Vocabulaire complémentaire

dépenser (de l'argent) *to spend (money)*	**obtenir** *to obtain*
déposer (de l'argent) *to deposit (money)*	**payer en liquide** *to pay cash*
emprunter *to borrow*	**payer par chèque** *to pay by check*
épargner *to save up (in a bank account)*	**rembourser** *to pay back*
faire des économies *to save money*	**retirer de l'argent** *to withdraw money*

Note de **grammaire**
Obtenir is conjugated like **venir: j'obtiens, tu obtiens, il/elle/on obtient, nous obtenons, vous obtenez, ils/elles obtiennent.**

Un mot sur la langue

Différences lexicales: faculté vs U.F.R.

Il y a eu une évolution du mot **faculté** en France. Avec la loi Savary de 1984, l'appellation° **faculté** a été remplacée *(replaced)* par l'expression **unité de formation et de recherche** (U.F.R.). Pourtant, il y a des universités qui ont gardé l'ancienne appellation **faculté** par tradition et la plupart de° la population française dit toujours **faculté** par habitude. Il y a aussi quelques différences entre le français et le québécois par rapport aux appellations des institutions universitaires.

l'appellation *the name* **la plupart de** *the majority of*

- Lisez ces deux appellations québécoises et essayez de trouver leurs équivalents dans la liste de vocabulaire de cette leçon.

    1. l'école secondaire   2. un diplôme d'études secondaires

🔊 **ACTIVITÉ Ⓐ Les écoles et leurs diplômes** Dans quelle institution
CD2-43 obtient-on les diplômes mentionnés?

1. a. au lycée   b. dans une faculté de médecine
2. a. dans une école professionnelle   b. dans une faculté de sciences et technologie
3. a. au collège   b. dans une faculté de mathématiques
4. a. dans une faculté de lettres   b. au lycée
5. a. dans une école de commerce   b. dans une faculté de médecine
6. a. dans une faculté de lettres   b. dans une école professionnelle

🔊 **ACTIVITÉ Ⓑ Les professions et la formation** Quelle école ou faculté
CD2-44 associez-vous aux professions mentionnées?

1. a. une école de commerce   b. une faculté de sciences et technologie
2. a. une faculté de médecine   b. une faculté de lettres et de sciences humaines
3. a. une faculté de droit   b. un conservatoire
4. a. une école professionnelle   b. une faculté de sciences humaines et sociales

ACTIVITÉ Ⓒ Où ont-ils étudié? Où est-ce que ces personnes ont étudié?

Modèle: un comptable   **dans une école de commerce**

1. une actrice   3. un plombier   5. un ingénieur   7. une chanteuse
2. un médecin   4. une assistante sociale 6. un avocat   8. un cuisinier

ACTIVITÉ Ⓓ Qualifications nécessaires Quels diplômes sont nécessaires
pour ces professions et ces métiers?

Modèle: une assistante sociale   **Il faut une licence.**

1. une infirmière   3. un chef d'entreprise   5. un commerçant
2. un agent de police   4. un professeur   6. un ouvrier

ACTIVITÉ Ⓔ Claire Gagner Claire étudie la psychologie. Répondez à ces
questions au sujet de Claire.

1. Quelle profession Claire a-t-elle choisie?
2. Dans quelle école ou faculté est-ce que Claire étudie?
3. Claire prépare un MBA ou un doctorat à l'Université McGill?

© Heinle/Cengage Learning

ACTIVITÉ (F) **L'argent** Complétez chaque phrase logiquement.

1. Si tu paies avec **des billets** et **des pièces de monnaie,** tu…
   a. paies en liquide.   b. paies par chèque.

2. Si tu **retires de l'argent** de ton compte, tu…
   a. soustrais *(subtract)* de l'argent.   b. ajoutes *(add)* de l'argent.

3. Au **distributeur automatique,** il faut insérer *(insert)*…
   a. ta carte de crédit.   b. ta carte bancaire.

4. Si tu **paies par chèque,** la banque soustrait la somme d'argent de…
   a. ton compte-chèques.   b. ton compte d'épargne.

5. Si tu **déposes de l'argent** sur ton compte ou si tu **fais des économies,** tu…
   a. épargnes ton argent.   b. dépenses ton argent.

6. On paie typiquement les **frais de scolarité**…
   a. en liquide.   b. par chèque.

7. Il faut **rembourser**…
   a. un prêt étudiant.   b. une bourse d'études.

8. On **n'a pas besoin de rembourser**…
   a. un prêt étudiant.   b. une bourse d'études.

ACTIVITÉ (G) **Vos études**

Étape 1. Répondez aux questions.

1. Quelle est votre spécialisation à l'université? Quelle profession avez-vous choisie?

2. Dans quelle école ou faculté est-ce que vous étudiez?

3. Vous voulez obtenir un master? un doctorat? un MBA?

4. Qui paie vos frais de scolarité? Comment payez-vous vos frais? Avez-vous un prêt étudiant? une bourse d'études?

Étape 2. Posez ces questions à un(e) partenaire. Préparez un résumé de ses réponses.

   Modèle: La spécialisation de Luc est la comptabilité. Il veut être comptable…

ACTIVITÉ (H) **Votre partenaire et son argent** Posez ces questions à un(e) partenaire. Est-ce qu'il/elle gère *(manage)* bien son argent?

1. Tu préfères dépenser ou épargner ton argent?

2. Tu aimes payer en liquide, avec ta carte bancaire ou avec ta carte de crédit?

3. As-tu un compte d'épargne? As-tu un crédit en cours *(credit card/active loan)*?

Si vous y allez

Si vous allez à Paris, prenez des cours de français à l'Alliance Française Paris Île-de-France pour obtenir un Diplôme de Français Professionnel (en affaires) si ça vous intéresse!

ACTIVITÉ I **Descriptions de professions** Complétez le tableau pour chaque profession selon le système universitaire américain. Utilisez les **Vocabulaires 1, 2 et 3.**

Profession	Institution	Diplômes et années d'études	Compétences nécessaires
1. un(e) journaliste	une faculté de lettres	une licence, 4 années	intelligent, acharné, créatif, précis, extraverti
2. un(e) avocat(e)	_____	_____	_____
3. un(e) comptable	_____	_____	_____
4. un(e) musicien(ne)	_____	_____	_____
5. un homme / une femme d'affaires	_____	_____	_____

ACTIVITÉ J **Chasse au trésor** Posez des questions à des étudiants différents. Quand vous trouvez quelqu'un qui correspond à chaque action, notez son prénom.

Trouvez quelqu'un qui…

1. emprunte de l'argent de temps en temps.
2. a fait un stage de formation.
3. désire étudier dans une faculté de droit.
4. va obtenir une maîtrise.
5. n'a pas d'argent sur son compte-chèques.
6. a besoin de rembourser ses parents.
7. fait des économies.
8. a utilisé sa carte bancaire hier.
9. a envie d'obtenir un MBA.
10. a reçu une bourse d'études.

Un mot sur la culture

Après le bac

© Christophe Morin / Maxppp / Landov

Comme l'indique l'expression souvent répétée par les parents, «Passe ton bac d'abord», le baccalauréat est quelque chose de très important dans la vie des lycéens en France. Cependant, même si le bac ouvre les portes de l'université, tous les lycéens ne deviennent pas des étudiants. Certains choisissent d'entrer directement dans le monde du travail. Pour les personnes qui choisissent l'université, il est important de noter qu'en France, il n'y a pas de *major / minor.* Les cours généraux que les étudiants américains suivent la première année d'université correspondent à l'examen de baccalauréat à la fin du lycée français. Donc, quand les étudiants français entrent à l'université, ils choisissent tout de suite° leur spécialisation.

tout de suite *right away*

• Quels examens sont importants pour les lycéens aux États-Unis?

Liaisons avec les mots et les sons

🔊 Les voyelles ouvertes et fermées: o / au / eau

CD2-45

You have already seen how the **o** vowel sound can be written in different ways in French (**o / au / eau**). It is important to learn now that two sounds are associated with **o**.

The first sound is called an open **o**. This sound is often found in a syllable that ends with a pronounced consonant. This sound is more frequent in French.

| sport | prof | ad**o**re | **o**ffre | n**o**tre | téléph**o**ne | b**o**l | h**o**rloge |

The second sound is called a closed **o**. This sound is usually, but not always, the last sound of the syllable. It can be spelled **o, ô, au,** or **eau**.

| h**ô**tel | bat**eau** | f**au**te | bur**eau** | g**au**che | m**o**t | vél**o** | gr**o**s |

However, when the **o** is followed by the pronounced consonant **s**, which creates the **z** sound, it is pronounced as a closed **o**.

| cho_s_e | ro_s_e | propo_s_e | dépo_s_e | po_s_er | philo_s_ophie | prépo_s_itions |

Pratique A. Écoutez et répétez ces mots de vocabulaire.

Les voyelles ouvertes		Les voyelles fermées	
1. un compte-chèques	**4.** une informaticienne	**7.** un diplôme	**10.** un agent de police
2. une commerçante	**5.** un doctorat	**8.** déposer de l'argent	**11.** un boulot
3. un homme d'affaires	**6.** autonome	**9.** un assistant social	**12.** composé

Pratique B. Écoutez ces répliques de la Séquence 4 du film **Liaisons**. Soulignez *(Underline)* les mots avec des voyelles ouvertes et encerclez *(circle)* les mots avec des voyelles fermées.

© Heinle/Cengage Learning

CLAIRE Cet hôtel est un vrai château.

CLAIRE Oui. Je vous attendrai au rez-de-chaussée…

ALEXIS Bon après-midi…

🔊 À vos stylos! C'est l'heure de la dictée!

CD2-46

Vous allez entendre trois phrases deux fois. La première fois, écoutez bien. La deuxième fois, écrivez les phrases.

Sujet Citations célèbres

Pour faire des comparaisons

Les expressions de comparaison et les superlatifs

DU FILM *LIAISONS*

Un coup d'œil sur la grammaire

Look at these photos from the film *Liaisons* and their captions.

CLAIRE Cet hôtel est un vrai château. Il est encore **plus beau que** je l'avais imaginé.

RÉCEPTIONNISTE C'est **le plus célèbre** du Québec.

1. How do you say *more beautiful than* in French?

2. How do you say *the most famous* in French?

•••◇ To compare adverbs and adjectives in French, use **plus** *(more)*, **moins** *(less)*, and **aussi** *(as)* before the adverb or adjective and **que** *(than, as)* after them.

adverb
↓

Les Français parlent **plus** vite **que** les Américains.
The French speak faster than Americans.

adjective
↓

Les professeurs américains sont **moins** sévères **que** les professeurs français.
American professors are less strict than French professors.

adjective
↓

Les diplômes universitaires sont **aussi** importants en France **qu'**au Québec.
University diplomas are as important in France as in Quebec.

•••◇ The superlative form of adjectives is formed by adding the appropriate definite article (**le, la, les**) to the comparative form and placing it after the noun (when the noun is expressed). The preposition **de** is used to express *in* or *of*.

Les médecins sont les gens **les plus riches.**

Doctors are the richest people.

C'est l'hôtel **le plus cher de la ville.**

It's the most expensive hotel in the city.

Anne est **la moins payée** dans l'entreprise.

Anne is the least paid in the company.

- Adjectives that precede the noun such as **beau, grand, petit,** and **nouveau** may precede or follow the nouns they modify in the superlative form.

Paris, c'est **la plus belle** ville.	*Paris is the most beautiful city.*
Paris, c'est la ville **la plus belle.**	*Paris is the most beautiful city.*

- The article **le** is always used in the superlative of adverbs because adverbs do not have gender or number.

Les Français parlent **le plus vite.**	*The French speak **the fastest.***
Cette calculatrice coûte **le moins cher.**	*This calculator costs **the least.***

- Some adverbs and adjectives have irregular comparative and superlative forms.

Adjectif	Comparatif	Superlatif
bon(ne)(s)	meilleur(e)(s)	le/la/les meilleur(e)(s)
mauvais(es)	pire(s) *or*	le/la/les pire(s) *or*
	plus mauvais(es)	le/la/les plus mauvais(es)

Adverbe	Comparatif	Superlatif
bien	mieux	le mieux
mal	plus mal	le plus mal

Les oranges sont **meilleures que** les pommes.	*The oranges are **better than** the apples.*
Les examens sont **pires que** les devoirs.	*Exams are **worse than** homework.*
Tu chantes **mieux que** moi.	*You sing **better than** me.*
Luc danse **plus mal que** Marc.	*Luc dances **worse than** Marc.*
C'est **la meilleure** profession du monde!	*That's **the best** profession in the world!*
C'est **la plus mauvaise** histoire.	*That's **the worst** story.*
Il chante **le plus mal** dans le groupe.	*He sings **the worst** in the group.*

- To compare nouns or quantities of things, use the following expressions.

plus de/d'	+ *noun*	+ **que**	*(more . . . than)*
moins de/d'	+ *noun*	+ **que**	*(less . . . than)*
autant de/d'	+ *noun*	+ **que**	*(as much / many . . . as)*

Anne a **plus de** livres **que** Luc.	*Anne has **more books than** Luc.*
Koffi a moins d'enfants **que** Luc.	*Koffi has **fewer children than** Luc.*
J'ai **autant d'**argent que toi.	*I have as **much money as** you.*

🔊 **ACTIVITÉ K** **Vrai ou faux?** Vous allez entendre des phrases sur la
CD2-47 géographie. Sont-elles vraies ou fausses?

    1.   **2.**   **3.**   **4.**   **5.**   **6.**   **7.**   **8.**   **9.**   **10.**

ACTIVITÉ L **Le monde du travail** Complétez les phrases suivantes et puis
indiquez si vous êtes d'accord ou pas d'accord.

1. Les secrétaires sont _____ riches que leurs patrons.
    a. moins de   b. moins

2. Un journaliste passe _____ années à l'école qu'un médecin.
    a. moins d'   b. moins

3. Les comptables sont _____ bons avec les chiffres que les cadres.
    a. autant de   b. aussi

4. Les chanteurs gagnent _____ argent que les acteurs.
    a. autant d'   b. aussi

5. Être riche, c'est bien, mais être très riche, c'est encore _____.
    a. mieux   b. meilleur

6. Être solitaire n'est pas bien mais être antisocial, c'est _____.
    a. pire   b. mal

ACTIVITÉ M **Votre opinion** Donnez votre opinion sur les sujets suivants avec
les éléments donnés.

Modèle: cadre / cuisinier (gagner / argent)
                Un cadre gagne plus d'argent qu'un cuisinier.

1. étudiants / professeurs (être / riche)

2. les Français / les Anglais (cuisiner / bien)

3. pompier / enseignant (être / courageux)

4. Big Mac / pizza (avoir / calories)

5. Garfield / Bart Simpson (chanter / mal)

6. chocolat belge / chocolat suisse (être / bon)

ACTIVITÉ N **Comparaisons**

Étape 1. Posez ces questions à deux camarades de classe. Notez leurs réponses.

	É1	É2
1. Tu as quel âge?	_____	_____
2. Tu as combien d'argent sur ton compte-chèques?	_____	_____
3. Tu étudies pendant combien d'heures le week-end?	_____	_____
4. Tu as combien de frères et de sœurs?	_____	_____
5. Tu as combien de colocataires?	_____	_____

Étape 2. À partir des informations de l'Étape 1, écrivez quatre à cinq phrases pour
comparer vos deux camarades de classe.

Modèle: **Paul est plus jeune que Marc. Marc a moins de frères que Paul.**

ACTIVITÉ O **Êtes-vous d'accord?** Êtes-vous d'accord avec les phrases suivantes?

1. Andy Warhol est l'artiste le plus créatif.
2. Tom Cruise est l'acteur le moins beau.
3. Rachael Ray cuisine le moins bien.
4. Martha Stewart cuisine le mieux.

ACTIVITÉ P **Les personnes célèbres et nos opinions**

Étape 1. Répondez aux questions et écrivez vos réponses dans la colonne 1.

	Moi	É1	É2
1. Qui est l'actrice la plus belle?	_____	_____	_____
2. Qui est la chanteuse la plus farfelue?	_____	_____	_____
3. Qui est le chanteur le plus excentrique?	_____	_____	_____
4. Qui est l'acteur le plus drôle?	_____	_____	_____
5. Qui chante le mieux?	_____	_____	_____
6. Qui chante le plus mal?	_____	_____	_____

Étape 2. Posez les questions à deux personnes. Écrivez leurs réponses dans la colonne 2 et la colonne 3.

Étape 3. Faites un résumé de vos opinions et des opinions de vos camarades de classe.

Modèle: **Pour mes camarades de classe, les actrices les plus belles sont Natalie Portman et Keira Knightley. Pour moi, l'actrice la plus belle est Emma Watson.**

La parole est à vous!
Qu'est-ce qui compte le plus dans le monde du travail?

Il y a un débat très ancien dans le monde du travail. Qu'est-ce qui est le plus important sur le marché du travail, le diplôme et la connaissance ou bien l'expérience et la pratique? Qu'en pensez-vous?

- Anne-Sophie de Monte Carlo (Monaco): «À mon avis, je peux dire que le diplôme et la connaissance ont autant d'importance que l'expérience et la pratique. C'est impossible de donner la priorité à une seule de ces nécessités.»

- Maxime, Français expatrié à San Francisco: «Mes collègues américains disent que ce sont l'expérience et la pratique qui sont plus importantes mais à mon avis, au moins en France, ce sont le diplôme et la connaissance qui comptent le plus.»

Et vous? Qu'en pensez-vous?

Quels sont les avantages ou les désavantages d'avoir plus (ou moins) d'éducation ou de connaissance et moins (ou plus) d'expérience et de pratique?

Liaisons musicales

© Guibbaud Christophe/MCT/Newscom

Laure Milan, chanteuse française de musique R&B et hip-hop, vient de Toulouse. Dans sa chanson *La meilleure* (2006), son petit ami l'a quittée. Est-ce qu'elle veut redevenir un couple? Cherchez les paroles de cette chanson pour trouver la réponse à la question. 🌐

PREMIÈRE PROJECTION

Avant de visionner

ACTIVITÉ A Vous rappelez-vous? Vous rappelez-vous *(Do you remember)* ce qui s'est passé dans la Séquence 3 du film *Liaisons*? Pour chaque phrase, indiquez si c'est vrai ou faux.

	Vrai	Faux
1. Claire est partie pour la ville de Québec.	☐	☐
2. Claire a pris quelque chose à manger dans un café.	☐	☐
3. Claire a appris qu'Alexis Prévost est de Trois-Rivières.	☐	☐
4. Claire a un rendez-vous avec M. Prévost à Montréal.	☐	☐

ACTIVITÉ B Devinez Devinez ce qui va se passer dans la Séquence 4 du film *Liaisons*. Pour chaque phrase, indiquez si c'est vrai ou faux. Vous allez vérifier vos réponses plus tard.

	Vrai	Faux
1. Claire arrive à Québec.	☐	☐
2. Claire apprend qui a fait la réservation pour elle.	☐	☐
3. Claire revoit *(sees again)* Alexis Prévost.	☐	☐
4. Claire revoit l'homme mystérieux qui lui a donné l'enveloppe.	☐	☐
5. Un nouveau mystère attend Claire.	☐	☐

ACTIVITÉ C Un coup d'œil sur une scène Voici une scène de la Séquence 4 du film *Liaisons*. Claire est au Château Frontenac. Elle parle avec la réceptionniste de l'hôtel. Choisissez la lettre du mot qui correspond à chaque espace *(space)* dans le dialogue. Vous allez vérifier vos réponses plus tard.

RÉCEPTIONNISTE Voici votre
(1) _____. La (2) _____ 315. [...] Les
(3) _____ sont à votre gauche. Avez-vous (4) _____ d'aide *(help)* avec vos
(5) _____?

CLAIRE Non, ça va. Je n'en ai qu(e)
(6) _____.

© Heinle/Cengage Learning

1. a. chambre   b. clé *(key)*
2. a. chambre   b. clé
3. a. ascenseurs *(elevators)*   b. escaliers
4. a. besoin   b. envie
5. a. sacs   b. valises *(suitcases)*
6. a. deux   b. une

Note de grammaire

Ne... que/qu' means *only*. You will learn this construction in **Chapitre 10, Grammaire 3.**

Regarder la séquence

Vous allez regarder la Séquence 4 du film *Liaisons*. Vérifiez vos réponses à l'Activité B et à l'Activité C.

Après le visionnage

ACTIVITÉ D **Avez-vous compris?** Complétez les phrases.

1. Quelqu'un a remis _____ à la chambre de Claire.
   a. une clé dans une enveloppe   b. des fleurs et du chocolat

2. Claire parle avec _____ avant de sortir de l'hôtel.
   a. le concierge   b. sa mère

3. Claire prend une tasse de thé dans un café et lit un livre sur _____.
   a. la psychose   b. la ville de Québec

4. Claire apprend qu'Alexis Prévost va _____.
   a. rester à Québec pendant une semaine   b. partir pour la France lundi

ACTIVITÉ E **Utilisez le contexte**
Regardez bien les mots en caractères gras *(boldface)* et répondez aux questions.

CONCIERGE C'est une clé (1) **coffre-fort**.

CLAIRE Comme dans une banque?

CONCIERGE Oui, c'est ça. [...] [Ma mère] avait une clé (2) **semblable**. Elle avait un **coffre-fort** à la Banque Nationale.

© Heinle/Cengage Learning

1. Le mot **coffre-fort** veut dire *(means)*...
   a. safety deposit box.   b. jewelry box.

2. Le mot **semblable** veut dire...
   a. différent.   b. similaire.

ACTIVITÉ F **Les personnages du film** Répondez aux questions par **Abia, Claire, Alexis Prévost** ou **Simone Gagner**. Puis, posez ces questions à un(e) partenaire pour voir si vous avez les mêmes opinions.

1. Qui est le/la plus autonome dans le film?
2. Qui est le/la plus drôle dans le film?
3. Qui est le/la plus sensible dans le film?
4. Qui est le/la plus solitaire?
5. Qui est le/la plus loyal(e)?
6. Qui est le/la plus mystérieux (mystérieuse)?

Liaisons avec la culture

Le Château Frontenac

Le Château Frontenac, situé dans le quartier du Vieux-Québec, est l'une des attractions les plus populaires de la ville. Son architecture est inspirée des châteaux français de l'époque de la Renaissance. On lui a donné le nom Frontenac en l'honneur de Louis de Buade, comte de Frontenac, qui a été gouverneur de la Nouvelle-France de 1672 à 1682 et de 1689 à 1698. Selon le journal *Le Soleil*, le Château Frontenac est l'hôtel le plus photographié au monde et le monument le plus associé à la ville de Québec.

© Robert F. Bukaty / AP Photo

LIAISONS CULTURELLES

Au boulot!

Les universités et les grandes écoles

Contrairement à la plupart des pays comparables, la France a un double système d'études supérieures: les universités et les grandes écoles. Les grandes écoles sont des instituts d'études spécialisées: les affaires, l'administration, le génie, etc. Pour s'inscrire à l'université, il faut réussir aux examens du baccalauréat. Par contre°, pour entrer dans une grande école, il faut non seulement avoir son bac, mais aussi faire des études préparatoires (2 ou 3 ans) et passer un examen de sélection.

© Loïc Venance/AFP/Getty Images

Par contre *By contrast*

Vrai ou faux?

1. Il faut avoir le baccalauréat pour entrer à l'université.   V / F

2. Les universités sont généralistes, mais les grandes écoles sont spécialisées.   V / F

3. Il est plus facile d'entrer à l'université que dans une grande école.   V / F

Courtesy Codofil

Conseil pour le développement du français en Louisiane

D'après le dernier recensement°, il y a plus de 198 784 francophones en Louisiane. Le Conseil pour le développement du français en Louisiane (CODOFIL) a été créé en 1968 pour promouvoir° le français dans les écoles et dans la société louisianaises. Aujourd'hui, plus de 57 000 élèves apprennent le français en Louisiane. De nombreuses bourses d'études sont financées par cette fondation. Il y a plus de 360 enseignants, non seulement de Louisiane et des autres états des États-Unis, mais aussi de France, de Belgique, du Canada, d'Afrique et de Haïti.

recensement *census* **promouvoir** *promote*

Vrai ou faux?

1. Il n'y pas beaucoup de francophones en Louisiane.   V / F
2. CODOFIL donne des bourses aux étudiants pour étudier le français.   V / F
3. Tous les enseignants de français en Louisiane sont de France.   V / F

Ressources humaines: film de Laurent Cantet

La particularité du film réalisé par Laurent Cantet en 1999, *Ressources humaines,* c'est que l'essentiel de l'intrigue° est situé dans le monde du travail. Le personnage° principal, Franck, est un brillant étudiant dans une grande école de commerce à Paris. Avant de terminer ses études, il fait un stage de formation° au service des ressources humaines à l'usine° où son père est ouvrier depuis trente ans. Quand il y a un conflit du travail entre les employés et la direction° de l'entreprise, Franck doit décider s'il va soutenir° les ouvriers en grève° ou les cadres.

intrigue *plot* **personnage** *character* **un stage de formation** *internship* **usine** *factory* **la direction** *the management* **soutenir** *support* **en grève** *on strike*

Courtesy Everett Collection

Compréhension

1. *Ressources humaines* est un film _____.
   a. romantique   b. réaliste
2. Franck, le personnage principal, est le fils d'un _____.
   a. cadre   b. ouvrier
3. Les ouvriers sont en grève à cause d'un conflit _____.
   a. amoureux   b. du travail

© Courtesy Service des communications et Liaison cégep-entreprises, Cégep de Sherbrooke

Les CÉGEP au Québec

Après leurs études secondaires, les étudiants québécois doivent aller au CÉGEP (collège d'enseignement général et professionnel). Ces collèges offrent deux types de programmes. Les programmes techniques durent trois ans et mènent° au marché du travail et à certains programmes universitaires. Les programmes pré-universitaires durent deux ans et mènent à l'université. Ce système a été créé° pour faciliter l'accès à l'université et au marché du travail ainsi que° la transition entre l'école secondaire et l'université. Le Québec est la seule° province au Canada à posséder le système de CÉGEP.

mènent *lead to* **créé** *created* **ainsi que** *as well as* **seule** *only*

Vrai ou faux?

1. Les étudiants vont au CÉGEP après l'université.   V / F
2. Les CÉGEP facilitent l'accès à l'université.   V / F
3. Les programmes techniques mènent au marché du travail.   V / F
4. La province d'Alberta a aussi le système de CÉGEP.   V / F

Activités Internet

- Cherchez une grande école célèbre (par exemple: l'ENA, Polytechnique, HEC, l'ENS) sur Internet. Est-ce qu'elles sont semblables aux *graduate schools* américaines?

- Cherchez le site officiel du Conseil pour le développement du français en Louisiane sur Internet. Quelles sont les conditions requises *(requirements)* pour demander une bourse pour étudier le français en Louisiane?

- Cherchez une scène du film *Ressources humaines* sur Internet. Est-ce que vous avez envie de le voir?

- Cherchez le nom d'un CÉGEP à Montréal sur Internet. Nommez trois programmes techniques et trois programmes pré-universitaires de ce CÉGEP.

PARTIE 1

LES PROFESSIONS

un acteur / une actrice	actor, actress
un(e) agent(e) de police	police officer
un(e) assistant(e) social(e)	social worker
un(e) avocat(e)	lawyer
un(e) cadre	executive
un chanteur / une chanteuse	singer
un(e) chef d'entreprise	company president
un coiffeur / une coiffeuse	hairdresser
un(e) commerçant(e)	shopkeeper
un(e) comptable	accountant
un cuisinier / une cuisinière	cook
un(e) dentiste	dentist
un(e) employé(e)	employee
un(e) enseignant(e)	instructor, teacher
un(e) gérant(e)	manager
un homme / une femme d'affaires	businessman / businesswoman
un infirmier / une infirmière	nurse
un(e) informaticien(ne)	computer specialist
un ingénieur / une femme ingénieur	engineer
un(e) journaliste	journalist
un médecin / une femme médecin	doctor
un(e) musicien(ne)	musician
un ouvrier / une ouvrière	(factory) worker
un(e) patron(ne)	boss
un plombier / une femme plombier	plumber
un pompier / une femme pompier	firefighter
un(e) psychologue	psychologist
un(e) secrétaire	secretary
un vendeur / une vendeuse	salesperson

NOMS

un boulot	job (slang)
une carrière	career
un emploi	job
une entreprise	company
un métier	trade, vocation
un poste	position
une profession	profession
un salaire	salary, pay, wages
le travail	work

VERBES

demander (à)	to ask
donner (à)	to give
envoyer (à)	to send
gagner de l'argent	to earn money
gagner sa vie	to earn a living
montrer (à)	to show
poser (une question) (à)	to ask (a question)
prêter (à)	to lend

PRONOMS COMPLÉMENTS D'OBJET INDIRECT

me/m'	(to / for) me
te/t'	(to / for) you
lui	(to / for) him, her
nous	(to / for) us
vous	(to / for) you
leur	(to / for) them

PARTIE 2

ADJECTIFS

antisocial(e)	anti-social
autonome	independent
coincé(e)	uptight
créatif / créative	creative
déloyal(e)	disloyal
drôle	funny, odd
exigeant(e)	demanding
flexible	flexible
inflexible	inflexible
jaloux / jalouse	jealous
loyal(e)	loyal, faithful
organisé(e)	organized
sensible	sensitive
têtu(e)	stubborn

ADJECTIFS OU NOMS

acharné(e)	competitive, cutthroat
excentrique	eccentric
extraverti(e)	extroverted, extrovert
farfelu(e)	scatter-brained
introverti(e)	introverted, introvert
professionnel(le)	professional
solitaire	solitary, loner

EXPRESSIONS

avoir de bonnes capacités de communication	to have good communication skills
avoir le goût du travail	to have a good work ethic
avoir le sens de l'humour	to have a sense of humor
être bon / bonne avec les chiffres	to be good with numbers
être de bonne humeur	to be in a good mood
être de mauvaise humeur	to be in a bad mood
être du matin	to be a morning person
être précis(e)	to be good with details
être du soir	to be a night person

VERBES

devoir	*to have to, must, to owe*
pouvoir	*to be able, can*
vouloir	*to want*

PRONOMS

en	*of them/it, some*
y	*there, of / about it*

DIVERS

quelqu'un de/d' + adjectif	*someone + adjective*

PARTIE 3

LES DIPLÔMES ET LES ÉTUDES

le baccalauréat	*end-of-high-school exam*
un collège	*junior high / middle school*
un diplôme (universitaire)	*(university) diploma*
un doctorat	*doctorate, Ph.D.*
les études supérieures *(f.)*	*higher education*
une licence	*equivalent of a bachelor's degree*
un lycée	*high school*
un master	*master's degree*
un MBA	*MBA*
un stage de formation	*internship*

LES INSTITUTIONS

un conservatoire	*conservatory*
une école de commerce	*business school*
une école professionnelle	*professional / vocational school*
une faculté de droit	*law school*
une faculté de lettres et de sciences humaines	*liberal arts college*
une faculté de médecine	*medical school*
une faculté de sciences et de technologie	*science and technology college*

LES FINANCES

les billets *(m.)*	*bills, banknotes*
une bourse d'études	*scholarship*

une carte bancaire	*debit card*
une carte de crédit	*credit card*
un compte-chèques	*checking account*
un compte d'épargne	*savings account*
un distributeur automatique	*ATM*
les frais de scolarité *(m.)*	*tuition*
les pièces de monnaie *(f.)*	*coins*
un prêt étudiant	*student loan*

VERBES

dépenser (de l'argent)	*to spend (money)*
déposer (de l'argent)	*to deposit (money)*
emprunter	*to borrow*
épargner	*to save up (in a bank account)*
faire des économies	*to save money*
obtenir	*to obtain*
payer en liquide	*to pay cash*
payer par chèque	*to pay by check*
rembourser	*to pay back*
retirer de l'argent	*to withdraw money*

COMPARATIFS

aussi… que	*as . . . as*
autant de… que	*as many, as much . . . as*
meilleur(e)(s) *(adj.)*	*better*
mieux *(adv.)*	*better*
moins (de)… que	*less, fewer . . . than*
pire *(adj.)*	*worse*
plus (de)… que	*more . . . than*
plus mal *(adv.)*	*worse*
plus mauvais *(adj.)*	*worse*

SUPERLATIFS

le/la/les meilleur(e)(s) *(adj.)*	*the best*
le mieux *(adv.)*	*the best*
le/la/les moins	*the least*
le/la/les pire(s) *(adj.)*	*the worst*
le/la/les plus	*the most*
le plus mal *(adv.)*	*the worst*
le/la/les plus mauvais(es) *(adj.)*	*the worst*

Les **événements marquants**

En bref In this chapter, you will:

- talk about parties, holidays, personal events, and historical events

- learn the imperfect past tense of regular verbs

- learn vocabulary to talk about the different stages of life

- learn when to use the **passé composé** and the **imparfait**

- learn about important historical events in the Francophone world

- learn more about the vowel sound **eu**

- read about Canada and **les Fêtes de la Nouvelle-France**

- write about a memorable holiday or party

 You will also re-watch **SÉQUENCE 4: La clé** of the film *Liaisons*.

Ressources

 audio http://www.cengagebrain.com

© Michael Blann/Getty Images

🔊 Les **événements historiques**

Historical events

Célébrez le patrimoine français et francophone!

Hommage à douze personnes qui ont influencé la France et le monde francophone

Charlemagne (768–814) est devenu **Roi** des Francs en 768 et **Empereur** d'Occident en 800.

Jeanne d'Arc (1412–1431), **une héroïne** nationale dans la culture française, **a aidé** l'armée française à **gagner la guerre contre** l'Angleterre.

Jacques Cartier (1497–1557), **un explorateur** français, a pris possession du Canada (la Nouvelle-France) au nom de la France en 1534.

Samuel de Champlain (1580–1635), **un soldat** et un explorateur français, **a fondé** la ville de Québec le 3 juillet 1608.

Louis XIV (1654–1715), appelé *le Roi-Soleil,* a imposé **la grandeur** de la langue française et sa culture en Europe.

Napoléon 1ᵉʳ (1769–1821), **un général** ambitieux, est devenu *Empereur des Français* en 1804 et a organisé beaucoup de **réformes** de la société française.

Charles de Gaulle (1890–1970), militaire et **homme politique français**, a été **Président** de la République.

Léopold Senghor (1906–2001), homme politique et **écrivain** sénégalais, est le symbole de la coopération entre la France et ses anciennes **colonies.**

Félix Leclerc (1914–1988), **poète,** chanteur et **écrivain,** est le «père» de la *chanson québécoise* et un symbole important du **nationalisme** québécois.

René Lévesque (1922–1987), **Premier Ministre** du Québec de 1976 à 1985, a encouragé le désir d'**indépendance** du Québec par des efforts **pacifiques.**

Assia Djebar (1936–), **une écrivaine** algérienne d'expression française, traite souvent des thèmes de **la guerre** et de **la liberté humaine.**

Patrick Chamoiseau (1953–), **écrivain** français originaire de la Martinique et associé au **mouvement** de la *Créolité,* écrit aussi pour le théâtre et le cinéma.

Pour parler de l'affiche

un empereur / une impératrice *emperor / empress*

un explorateur / une exploratrice *explorer*

un général *general (military)*

un héros / une héroïne *hero / heroine*

un homme / une femme politique *politician*

un poète / une femme poète *poet*

(Madame/Monsieur) le Premier Ministre *Prime Minister*

(Madame/Monsieur) le Président *President (of a country)*

le roi / la reine *king / queen*

un soldat / une femme soldat *soldier*

la colonie *colony*

la grandeur *greatness*

la guerre (contre) *war (against)*

l'indépendance *(f.) independence*

la liberté *freedom*

le mouvement *(political) movement*

le nationalisme *nationalism*

la réforme *reform*

aider *to help*

fonder *to found, to constitute*

gagner *to win*

pacifique *peaceful*

Note de vocabulaire side box

Note de vocabulaire
Un général has no feminine form.

Note de vocabulaire
Madame le Président is the President of a country.
Madame la Présidente is the wife of the President.

Vocabulaire complémentaire

la colonisation *colonization*

la décolonisation *decolonization*

l'époque contemporaine *(f.) contemporary time*

la monarchie *monarchy*

la paix *peace*

une révolution *revolution*

la tolérance *tolerance*

marquant(e) *(adj.) memorable, important*

- There are three ways to say the date in French. There is no real difference in meaning among the three.

  C'est le 28 avril 2010.   **On est le 28 avril 2010.**   **Nous sommes le 28 avril 2010.**

- There are two ways to say years before 2000 and one way for years after 2000.

  1999 **mille neuf cent quatre-vingt-dix-neuf / dix-neuf cent quatre-vingt-dix-neuf**

  2001 **deux mille un**   2010 **deux mille dix**   2050 **deux mille cinquante**

- To express the sixties, the seventies, and so forth, use **les années** with the decade.

  Les années 60 marquent la Révolution tranquille au Québec.

Un mot sur la culture

Quelques événements historiques importants

Les événements suivants ont déterminé l'histoire de la France et du Québec.

1759: La France a perdu la Nouvelle-France dans une bataille sur les Plaines d'Abraham.

1789: La Révolution française (la fin de la monarchie française)

1830: La France a commencé à établir son empire colonial en Afrique.

1960: La Révolution tranquille au Québec (la séparation de l'Église catholique et de l'État)

1977: Le français est devenu la seule langue officielle du Québec avec la Loi 101.

🔊 **ACTIVITÉ A Qui c'est?**

CD2-48

Étape 1. Quel(s) personnage(s) correspond(ent) aux mots que vous entendez?

1. a. Jacques Cartier   b. Patrick Chamoiseau

2. a. Léopold Senghor   b. René Lévesque

3. a. Jeanne d'Arc   b. Félix Leclerc

4. a. Napoléon 1er   b. Charles de Gaulle

5. a. Charlemagne   b. Louis XIV

6. a. Charles de Gaulle   b. Charlemagne

7. a. Jeanne d'Arc   b. Assia Djebar

8. a. Jeanne d'Arc   b. Assia Djebar

Étape 2. Nommez une personne qui correspond aux mots que vous entendez.

Modèle: Vous entendez: un homme politique

Vous dites: **Bill Clinton**

1.   **2.**   **3.**   **4.**   **5.**   **6.**

🔊 **ACTIVITÉ B Associations** Quelle(s) association(s) faites-vous avec chaque

CD2-49 nom de personnage historique que vous allez entendre?

1. a. la guerre contre l'Angleterre   b. la fondation du Québec

2. a. la grandeur de la culture française   b. le mouvement de la Créolité

3. a. l'indépendance du Québec   b. la Révolution française

4. a. la décolonisation   b. la Nouvelle-France

5. a. les réformes égalitaires   b. le Roi-Soleil

6. a. la colonisation   b. le père de la chanson québécoise

ACTIVITÉ C Personnages célèbres Identifiez ces personnages célèbres.

Modèle: John McCain **est homme politique.**

1. Winston Churchill _____.

2. Elizabeth II d'Angleterre _____.

3. Barack Obama _____.

4. Hillary Clinton _____.

5. Jessica Lynch (la guerre d'Irak) _____.

6. Juan Carlos 1er _____.

🔊 **ACTIVITÉ D Quelle année dans l'histoire de la France?** Complétez

CD2-50 chaque phrase avec l'année que vous entendez.

Modèle: Vous entendez: La ville de Québec a été fondée en **mille six cent huit.**

Vous écrivez: La ville de Québec a été fondée en __1608.__

1. Clovis, premier roi chrétien de France, est baptisé à Reims en _____.

2. La Réforme protestante provoque des guerres de religions qui commencent en _____.

3. Napoléon 1er vend la Louisiane aux États-Unis en _____.

4. La Révolution tranquille au Québec a commencé en _____.

ACTIVITÉ E **Les anniversaires** Quand est-ce que ces personnes sont nées?

Modèle: R. Lévesque: 24/08/22

Il est né le vingt-quatre août mille neuf (dix-neuf) cent vingt-deux.

1. Assia Djebar: 30/06/36
2. Patrick Chamoiseau: 03/12/53
3. Félix Leclerc: 02/08/14
4. Sasha Obama: 10/06/01

ACTIVITÉ F **Événements marquants**

Étape 1. Écrivez le premier exemple qui vient à l'esprit *(comes to mind)* pour chaque événement mentionné. Écrivez aussi la date et l'année si possible.

Modèle: une exploration **Christophe Colomb en 1492**

1. une élection
2. une guerre
3. une révolution
4. un attentat terroriste *(terrorist attack)*
5. un ouragan
6. un tremblement de terre *(earthquake)*

Étape 2. Comparez vos exemples avec deux camarades de classe. Est-ce qu'il y a des exemples qui sont les mêmes *(same)* pour tout le monde? Si oui, expliquez pourquoi ces exemples sont marquants pour tout le monde.

Étape 3. Comparez vos exemples avec la classe. Quels événements sont les plus marquants pour votre classe?

Si vous y allez

© Paul A. Souders/Corbis

Si vous allez à Québec, allez au Parc-des-Champs-de-Bataille, l'endroit où la France a perdu la Nouvelle-France dans la bataille de 1759.

Un mot sur la culture

PLC

La Révolution tranquille au Québec

La Révolution tranquille des années 60 est une période caractérisée par une véritable séparation entre l'Église catholique et l'État et la construction d'une identité québécoise. Cette rupture avec la tradition marque l'entrée du Québec dans la modernité. C'est une révolution «tranquille» parce que c'est une révolution sans violence. Avec la Révolution tranquille, «les Canadiens-Français» sont devenus officiellement «les Québécois» et maîtres° de leur destin.

maîtres *masters*

• Pouvez-vous nommer d'autres révolutions dans l'histoire?

Pour décrire et parler des événements habituels

L'imparfait

DU FILM *LIAISONS*

Un coup d'œil sur la grammaire

Look at these photos from the film *Liaisons* and their captions.

© Heinle/Cengage Learning

© Heinle/Cengage Learning

CLAIRE Cet hôtel est un vrai château. [...] Quand j'**étais** petite fille, je **voulais** toujours descendre au Château Frontenac.

CONCIERGE [Ma mère] **avait** une clé semblable. Elle **avait** un coffre à la Banque Nationale.

1. What are the infinitive forms of the verbs **étais, voulais,** and **avait**?
2. What do the verbs **étais, voulais,** and **avait** mean?

❖❖❖ The **passé composé** is used to talk about actions that occurred at a specific time in the past such as yesterday, last week, and last year. To talk about repeated, habitual, or ongoing events or activities in the past or to express how things used to be, French uses the **imparfait** (*imperfect*). The **imparfait** has several equivalents in English: **je dansais** (*I danced, I was dancing, I used to dance, or I would dance.*)

Quand j'**étais** petit, je **chantais** à l'église le dimanche.

*When I **was** a child, I **used to sing** at church on Sundays.*

Mustapha **sortait** avec sa grand-mère le samedi soir.

*Mustapha **would go out** with his grandmother Saturday evenings.*

❖❖❖ With the exception of **être**, the **imparfait** of all verbs is formed by dropping the **-ons** from the **nous** form of the present tense and adding the **imparfait** endings.

Note de prononciation

The imperfect endings of the singular forms and the **ils/elles** forms are all pronounced alike. The **nous** and **vous** forms, **-ions** and **-iez,** are distinguished from the present tense forms by the **i** sound in their endings.

avoir	parler	prendre
av~~ons~~ → av-	parl~~ons~~ → parl-	pren~~ons~~ → pren-
j'**avais**	je **parlais**	je **prenais**
tu **avais**	tu **parlais**	tu **prenais**
il/elle/on **avait**	il/elle/on **parlait**	il/elle/on **prenait**
nous **avions**	nous **parlions**	nous **prenions**
vous **aviez**	vous **parliez**	vous **preniez**
ils/elles **avaient**	ils/elles **parlaient**	ils/elles **prenaient**

- The imperfect stem of **être** is **ét-**: j'**étais**, tu **étais**, il/elle/on **était**, nous **étions**, vous **étiez**, ils/elles **étaient**.

- Verbs like **étudier,** which have an imperfect stem that ends in **i (étudi-),** have a double **i** in the first- and second- person plural forms of the **imparfait: nous étudiions, vous étudiiez.**

- Verbs whose infinitives end in -**ger** add an **e** before all endings of the **imparfait** except the **nous** and **vous** forms. Verbs whose infinitives end in -**cer** change **c** to **ç** before all endings except the **nous** and **vous** forms.

tu **mang**e**ais**	*but*	nous **mangions**
elles **commen**ç**aient**	*but*	vous **commenciez**

- Here are some words and expressions associated with habitual or recurring events.

à cette époque-là	*at that time, in those days*	le lundi, le samedi...
autrefois	*in the past, long ago*	souvent
chaque année / mois	*each year / month*	toujours
d'habitude	*usually*	tous les jours

Le dimanche, nous **prenions** l'apéritif à 18h00.

*Every Sunday we **would have** a drink at 6:00 pm.*

Quand j'**étais** jeune, je **n'allais pas** toujours à mes cours.

*When I **was** young, I **did not** always **go** to my classes.*

- The **imparfait** is also often used to talk about age and states of mind or to provide descriptions in the past.

Guy **était** mince quand il **avait** 5 ans.

*Guy **was** thin when he **was** five years old.*

Il **faisait** du soleil pendant nos vacances.

*It **was** sunny during our vacation.*

Il y **avait** un étudiant français dans mon cours.

*There **was** a French student in my class.*

- **Devoir, pouvoir,** and **vouloir** are often used in the **imparfait** to talk about the past.

Tu **voulais** être pompier?

*You **wanted** to be a fireman?*

Je **devais** faire mes devoirs.

*I **had to do** my homework.*

Nous ne **pouvions** pas dormir.

*We **could** not sleep.*

- The following expressions are also helpful to learn in the **imparfait.**

Il pleuvait et **il neigeait.**

It was raining and snowing. / It rained and snowed.

Il fallait rendre les livres.

It was necessary to return the books.

ACTIVITÉ G Aujourd'hui ou quand nous étions plus jeunes? Les cousins d'Abia parlent de leurs activités. Utilisez les verbes pour déterminer s'ils font ces activités aujourd'hui ou s'ils faisaient ces activités quand ils étaient plus jeunes.

	Aujourd'hui	Quand ils étaient plus jeunes
1. Nous **regardons** *Les Simpson*.	☐	☐
2. Nous **faisions** la vaisselle.	☐	☐
3. Nous **lisions** le journal.	☐	☐
4. Nous **dansons** dans les fêtes.	☐	☐
5. Nous **allions** à l'église.	☐	☐
6. Nous **jouons** au poker.	☐	☐
7. Nous **étudiions** tous les jours.	☐	☐
8. Nous **n'étudions** jamais.	☐	☐

Conclusion Sont-ils plus sérieux aujourd'hui ou quand ils étaient plus jeunes?

🔊 **ACTIVITÉ H Aujourd'hui ou dans leur enfance?** Écoutez bien les verbes
CD2-51 pour déterminer si les étudiants font ces activités **(a) aujourd'hui** ou s'ils faisaient ces activités **(b) dans leur enfance** *(childhood)*.

1.   2.   3.   4.   5.   6.   7.   8.

ACTIVITÉ I Quand Madame Gagner était petite

Étape 1. Simone Gagner, la mère de Claire Gagner, est à l'hôpital psychiatrique. Comment imaginez-vous sa vie quand elle était petite? Complétez les phrases.

1. Elle **habitait** _____.
2. Elle **allait** _____ le dimanche.
3. Elle **pouvait** _____.
4. Elle **était** souvent _____.
5. Elle **parlait** toujours avec _____.
6. Elle **désirait** _____.

© Heinle/Cengage Learning

Étape 2. Comment imaginez-vous la vie de Claire et d'Abia quand elles étaient plus jeunes? Complétez les phrases.

1. Elles **étudiaient** _____.
2. Elles **faisaient** _____.
3. Elles **devaient** _____.
4. Elles **buvaient** _____.
5. Elles **sortaient** _____.
6. Elles **réussissaient** _____.

Étape 3. Et quand vous étiez jeune?

1. Je **regardais** _____.
2. Je **dormais** _____.
3. Je **lisais** _____.
4. Je **finissais** _____.
5. Je **jouais** _____.
6. Je **voulais** _____.

ACTIVITÉ Ⓙ **Quand vous étiez petit(e)**

Étape 1. Répondez à ces questions sur votre enfance *(childhood)*.

Quand vous étiez petit(e), vous...

1. **jouiez** aux Lego?
2. **buviez** du lait?
3. **aviez** peur des orages?
4. **dormiez** avec un animal en peluche *(stuffed animal)*?
5. **aimiez** les épinards?
6. **regardiez** *Sesame Street*?
7. **étiez** scout / éclaireuse *(boy scout / girl scout)*?
8. **faisiez** du camping?

Étape 2. Posez les questions de l'Étape 1 à un(e) partenaire.

Modèle: É1: **Quand tu étais petit(e), tu jouais aux Lego?**
          É2: **Oui, je jouais aux Lego. / Non, je ne jouais pas aux Lego.**

Conclusion Votre enfance et l'enfance de votre partenaire étaient typiques?

ACTIVITÉ Ⓚ **Quand votre professeur était petit(e)** Que faisait votre professeur quand il/elle était petit(e)? Préparez cinq questions avec les verbes suivants. Posez les questions à votre professeur.

Modèle: **Quand vous étiez petit(e), vous regardiez des films français?**

aimer chanter en français	pouvoir parler français
écouter des chansons françaises	regarder des films français
étudier le français à l'école	vouloir être professeur de français
lire des livres français	voyager dans un pays francophone
manger des pets de sœurs	????

Conclusion Votre professeur était destiné à être professeur de français?

Et vous? Quelle profession aimiez-vous quand vous étiez petit(e)?

ACTIVITÉ Ⓛ **Quel âge aviez-vous?** Quel âge aviez-vous quand vous avez fait ces activités pour la première fois? Vous pouvez répondre **jamais** si vous n'avez jamais fait ces activités.

Modèle: boire un Coca   **J'avais 5 ans.**

1. faire la cuisine
2. aller au lycée
3. faire du vélo
4. pouvoir parler
5. pouvoir marcher
6. boire du champagne

ACTIVITÉ **M** **Quel temps faisait-il?** Quel temps faisait-il pendant ces journées? Répondez aux questions.

Modèle: la fête du Travail   **Il pleuvait.**

1. Noël dernier
2. Halloween dernier
3. votre dernier anniversaire

4. votre dernier pique-nique ou barbecue
5. lundi dernier
6. hier

ACTIVITÉ **N** **Au lycée** Quand vous étiez au lycée, que faisiez-vous…

1. tous les jours?
2. le week-end?
3. le samedi matin?

4. le lundi soir?
5. chaque Noël ou Hanoukka?
6. pendant les vacances de printemps?

Conclusion Est-ce que vos activités aujourd'hui sont différentes de vos activités au lycée?

ACTIVITÉ **O** **La première scène du film _Liaisons_**

Étape 1. Écrivez une description de cette scène en répondant aux questions suivantes. Utilisez votre imagination.

C'était quelle année? Quel temps faisait-il? Quels meubles étaient dans la chambre?

Qui était dans la chambre? Qui écrivait? Qu'est-ce que la personne écrivait?

© Heinle/Cengage Learning

Étape 2. Montrez votre description à un(e) partenaire. Avez-vous écrit les mêmes détails?

ACTIVITÉ **P** **La société québécoise d'autrefois**

Étape 1. Choisissez le verbe et complétez chaque phrase à l'imparfait.

La vie au Québec (1) _____ (avoir / être) très différente avant les années 60.

L'Église catholique (2) _____ (avoir / être) une influence considérable sur la

société québécoise. Les femmes (3) _____ (devoir / faire) avoir beaucoup d'enfants,

parfois douze enfants. Les filles (4) _____ (aller / faire) rarement à l'école parce

qu'elles (5) _____ (faire / rester) les tâches ménagères à la maison. Les fils

(6) _____ (étudier / vouloir) pour devenir prêtres _(priests)._ Les hommes

(7) _____ (étudier / travailler) souvent dans les forêts ou dans les bois. Ils ne

(8) _____ (devenir / pouvoir) pas avoir de bons emplois parce qu'ils ne

(9) _____ (faire / parler) pas anglais, la langue dominante au Québec avant la Loi 101.

Étape 2. Écrivez trois à quatre phrases pour décrire votre société avant les années 60. Comment était la vie? Que faisaient les femmes? Que faisaient les hommes? Qu'est-ce qu'ils ne pouvaient pas faire?

ACTIVITÉ Q La vie avant les ordinateurs

Étape 1. Pouvez-vous imaginer votre vie sans (*without*) ordinateur? Notre société n'avait pas d'ordinateurs avant 1975. Écrivez un paragraphe de cinq à six phrases pour parler de ce que (*what*) les gens faisaient quand il n'y avait pas d'ordinateurs.

> **Questions possibles à discuter**
>
> • Comment est-ce que les étudiants faisaient leurs devoirs?
>
> • Que faisaient les étudiants s'ils devaient trouver la définition d'un mot?
>
> • Comment est-ce que les étudiants communiquaient avec leurs professeurs? Avec leurs amis? Avec leur famille?
>
> • Que faisaient les gens s'ils avaient besoin d'une recette ou d'une réservation?
>
> • Que faisaient les gens s'ils voulaient retirer de l'argent de leur compte d'épargne?
>
> • Que faisaient les gens s'ils voulaient regarder un film?
>
> • Que faisaient les gens s'ils voulaient trouver un(e) petit(e) ami(e)?

Étape 2. Montrez vos phrases à un(e) partenaire. Avez-vous écrit des phrases similaires? Voulez-vous modifier vos phrases? Voulez-vous ajouter (*add*) des phrases?

Étape 3. Vous préférez la vie d'aujourd'hui ou la vie d'autrefois? Est-ce qu'il y a des avantages associés à une vie sans ordinateur?

Liaisons musicales

Avec la Loi 101, le français est devenu langue officielle du Québec. Michel Rivard (1951–) a écrit *Le cœur de ma vie* pour célébrer la langue française des Québécois. Il chante: *C'est une langue de France aux accents d'Amérique.* Cherchez les paroles de cette chanson sur Internet. Quelles sont d'autres caractéristiques de la langue française au Québec?

La parole est à vous!

Est-ce que les étudiants sont nuls en histoire aujourd'hui?

On dit que les étudiants aujourd'hui sont très faibles° en histoire. Certains pensent que les programmes d'histoire dans les lycées et les universités sont moins rigoureux qu'autrefois. Qu'en pensez-vous? Est-ce que les étudiants sont nuls° en histoire? Ils ont besoin de suivre plus de cours d'histoire?

• Pierre de Louisiane (USA): «Absolument! Je suis professeur et j'étais surpris d'apprendre que mes étudiants ne savaient° pas qui était le Roi-Soleil! Il faut bien comprendre l'histoire pour pouvoir comprendre notre société actuelle°.»

• Maude de Tadoussac (Québec): «Mais non! Je suis étudiante en biologie et je n'ai pas besoin d'avoir beaucoup de cours en histoire. Si j'ai besoin d'informations, je peux toujours en trouver sur Internet.»

faibles *weak* **nuls** *hopeless, lousy* **savaient** *know* **actuelle** *present*

Et vous? Qu'en pensez-vous?

Les étudiants sont nuls en histoire? Ils ont besoin de suivre plus de cours d'histoire?

VOCABULAIRE **2**

🔊 Les **occasions spéciales**

Special occasions

l'anniversaire

la fête des Mères

la fête des Pères

la fête nationale

Hanoukka

Pâques

le 1er Avril / le poisson d'Avril

Mardi gras

la Saint-Valentin

le jour de l'Action de Grâce

Noël

le jour de l'An

Note de vocabulaire
L'Action de Grâce is used in Quebec. Because this holiday is not celebrated in France, the French call it **Thanksgiving**.

Quelques grands jours de festivités

Vocabulaire complémentaire

l'anniversaire *(m.)* **de mariage** *wedding anniversary*
la fête du Travail *Labor Day*
la Saint-Sylvestre *New Year's Eve*
la veille de Noël *Christmas Eve*

un jour férié *legal holiday*
une journée de congé *day-off*

un cadeau *gift*
une carte de vœux *greeting card*
une fête *holiday, party, celebration*
un hôte / une hôtesse *host / hostess*
un(e) invité(e) *guest*

un potluck *potluck party*
une soirée *(evening) party*
un vœu *wish*

Bon / Joyeux anniversaire! *Happy birthday!*
Bonne année! *Happy New Year!*
Félicitations! *Congratulations!*
Meilleurs vœux! *Best wishes!*

fêter *to celebrate*
organiser une fête *to throw / organize a party*

> **Note de vocabulaire**
> In France, **manger à la bonne franquette** or **faire un repas à la fortune du pot** is used for **un potluck**.

Les nombres ordinaux

premier (1ᵉʳ) / première (1ᵉʳᵉ)
  first (1st)
quatrième (4ᵉ) *fourth (4th)*
cinquième (5ᵉ) *fifth (5th)*
neuvième (9ᵉ) *ninth (9th)*
vingt-et-unième (21ᵉ)
  twenty-first (21st)

trente-et-unième (31ᵉ)
  thirty-first (31st)
soixante-quinzième (75ᵉ)
  seventy-fifth (75th)
centième (100ᵉ) *hundredth (100th)*

- Used to rank people or things, ordinal numbers are formed by adding **-ième** to a cardinal number. If a number ends in **e,** the final **e** is dropped before adding **-ième.** The exception is **un** whose ordinal numbers are **premier/première.**

- **Cinq** and **neuf** have spelling changes in their ordinal forms: **cinquième, neuvième.**

- Ordinal numbers have two possible abbreviations.

    3ᵉ / 3ᵉᵐᵉ   12ᵉ / 12ᵉᵐᵉ   51ᵉ / 51ᵉᵐᵉ   80ᵉ / 80ᵉᵐᵉ

- To say the century in French, use **au** + ordinal number + **siècle** *(century).*

    Nous sommes au vingt-et-unième siècle. / Nous sommes au 21ᵉ siècle.

ACTIVITÉ A Fête ou jour férié?

Étape 1. Les fêtes suivantes sont quel genre de fête: **(a) une fête religieuse, (b) une fête laïque** *(secular)*, **(c) un jour férié, (d) une combinaison d'une fête et d'un jour férié**?

1. la fête nationale   **3.** Hanoukka   **5.** le Poisson d'avril   **7.** le jour du Nouvel An

2. Mardi gras   **4.** la fête du Travail   **6.** Noël   **8.** la fête des Mères

ACTIVITÉ B Traditions

Étape 1. Nommez au moins *(at least)* une fête qui correspond à chaque tradition suivante.

Modèle: On mange des latkes.   ➔   **Hanoukka**

1. On donne des cadeaux.

2. On apporte un plat à partager.

3. On envoie une carte de vœux.

4. On mange des œufs au chocolat.

5. On dit «Bonne année!»

6. On mange du gâteau.

7. On décore la maison avec des cœurs *(hearts)* rouges.

8. On boit du champagne.

9. On fait des farces *(tricks / pranks)* à quelqu'un.

10. On fête avec des feux d'artifice *(fireworks)*.

Étape 2. Demandez à un(e) partenaire comment il/elle fête…

1. Halloween   **2.** l'Action de Grâce   **3.** la Saint-Sylvestre   **4.** son anniversaire

ACTIVITÉ C Quel étage?   Notez les étages mentionnés. Et vous, à quel étage habitez-vous?

CD2-52

Modèle: Vous entendez: J'habite au troisième étage.

Vous écrivez: _____3ᵉ_____

1.   **2.**   **3.**   **4.**   **5.**   **6.**   **7.**   **8.**   **9.**   **10.**   **11.**   **12.**

ACTIVITÉ D Personnages historiques

Étape 1. Avec un(e) partenaire, décidez à quel siècle ces personnes sont nées.

Modèle: George Washington   **Il est né au dix-huitième siècle.**

1. Assia Djebar   **3.** Marco Polo   **5.** Napoléon 1ᵉʳ   **7.** Charlemagne

2. Sasha Obama   **4.** Louis XIV   **6.** Jeanne d'Arc   **8.** Charles de Gaulle

Étape 2. À quel siècle les personnages du film *Liaisons* sont nés?

1.

© Heinle/Cengage Learning
Claire Gagner

2.

© Heinle/Cengage Learning
Alexis Prévost

ACTIVITÉ E **Les traditions d'autrefois et d'aujourd'hui**

Étape 1. Avec un(e) partenaire, décidez si les phrases suivantes décrivent une tradition d'**autrefois**, d'**aujourd'hui** ou **les deux** *(both)*.

1. On préfère dire «meilleurs vœux» et pas «joyeux Noël».
2. Il faut aller à la messe *(mass)* de minuit la veille de Noël.
3. Il faut échanger des cadeaux le jour du Nouvel An.
4. Il ne faut pas porter *(wear)* de blanc après la fête du Travail.
5. Il ne faut pas porter de noir à un mariage *(wedding)*.
6. Les hommes ne peuvent pas voir *(see)* la robe de mariée *(bride)* avant la cérémonie du mariage.

Étape 2. Discutez avec votre partenaire au sujet des traditions de l'Étape 1 que vous respectez. Est-ce qu'il y a d'autres *(other)* traditions que vous respectez?

ACTIVITÉ F **Une fête nationale mémorable**

Étape 1. Écrivez un petit paragraphe pour décrire une fête nationale mémorable. Utilisez l'imparfait.

Questions à discuter		
Vous aviez quel âge?	Vous étiez avec qui?	Que buviez-vous?
Quel temps faisait-il?	Que mangiez-vous?	Que faisiez-vous?

 Étape 2. Lisez votre description à un(e) partenaire. Qui a passé une meilleure fête nationale?

Liaisons musicales

© Jacques Morell/Kipa/Corbis

La chanson *Gens du pays* de Gilles Vigneault est l'hymne national du Québec: *Gens du pays // c'est à ton tour* (turn) *// de te laisser parler d'amour.* Pour fêter l'anniversaire de quelqu'un, on chante cette chanson aussi mais on remplace *gens du pays* avec *mon/ma cher/chère ami(e)*. Trouvez cette chanson sur Internet pour découvrir sa mélodie.

Un mot sur la culture
Variations de la fête nationale

© Dimitrios Papadopoulos/The Quebec Press/Newscom

En France, on appelle le 14 juillet «le jour de la prise de la Bastille» pour commémorer le 14 juillet 1789 quand le peuple de Paris a pris la Bastille. La fête nationale au Québec, «la Saint-Jean», est le 24 juin parce que cette date est la fête de Saint-Jean-Baptiste, le saint patron du Québec. La Saint-Jean est associée aux célébrations du solstice d'été et donne l'occasion aux Québécois de fêter leur héritage français et leur identité québécoise. Aux États-Unis, on appelle la fête nationale américaine «le jour de l'Indépendance» pour commémorer la déclaration d'indépendance des États-Unis par rapport à l'Angleterre en 1776. Même s'il y a des différences, la fête nationale représente la naissance de son pays ou de sa communauté.

• Est-ce que vous fêtez les fêtes nationales des autres pays?

Pour parler du passé

L'imparfait et le passé composé

DU FILM *LIAISONS*

....

Un coup d'œil sur la grammaire

Look at these photos from the film *Liaisons* and their captions.

RÉCEPTIONNISTE L'hôtel **a ouvert** ses portes en 1893.

CONCIERGE Quand ma mère est morte, il fallait qu'on s'occupe *(take care)* de ses affaires. Elle avait une clé semblable.

1. Identify the verb(s) in the **passé composé** and the verb(s) in the **imparfait**.

2. Which verb tense is used to talk about events that have been completed at a specific point in the time in the past? And to describe continuous actions or states?

❖ As you know from **Grammaire 1**, the **imparfait** is used to express how things used to be and to describe repeated or habitual actions that do not have a beginning or end. If an event began or ended at a specific time in the past, the **passé composé** is used. Expressions like **hier, la semaine dernière, il y a trois ans,** and **à 14h00** are often used with the **passé composé**.

Je **lisais** un livre chaque semaine.	*I read (was reading) a book each week.*
Hier, j'**ai lu** ce livre.	*Yesterday I read this book.*
Avant les ordinateurs, on **écrivait** des lettres.	*Before computers, we used to write letters.*
La semaine dernière, Luc **a écrit** une lettre.	*Last week Luc wrote a letter.*

❖ In **Grammaire 1**, you also learned that the **imparfait** is used to give background information, to describe a scene, weather, physical or mental states, and to express age in the past. To describe a sequence of events, however, the **passé composé** is used.

Imparfait

Claire **avait** 8 ans. Il **neigeait** mais il **faisait** du soleil. Claire **était** heureuse parce que c'**était** son anniversaire.
Claire was eight. It was snowing, but it was sunny. Claire was happy because it was her birthday.

Passé composé

Claire **a préparé** le déjeuner. Puis, elle **a fait** la vaisselle et elle **a sorti** la poubelle.
Claire prepared lunch. Then she did the dishes and took out the trash.

❖ The **imparfait** and the **passé composé** may also be used together. In fact, it is often difficult to tell a story in the past without using both. The **imparfait** describes an activity or condition that was in progress (background information) while the **passé composé** expresses an interruption of that activity or condition to move the story along in time.

Quand je **suis entré** dans le bar, Guy **chantait.**	*When I entered the bar, Guy was singing.*
J'**écoutais** Guy quand le serveur **est arrivé.**	*I was listening to Guy when the waiter arrived.*
Guy **était** content parce que je **suis venu** à son spectacle.	*Guy was happy because I came to his show.*

❖ To indicate a change of state in a narration, the **passé composé** is used. Words like **soudain** (suddenly), **tout d'un coup** (all of a sudden), **une fois** (once), **un jour,** and **un matin** often denote a change of state.

Je **dormais** quand **tout d'un coup** j'**ai entendu** le tonnerre.	*I was sleeping when all of a sudden I heard the thunder.*
Carole **buvait toujours** du café américain. **Un jour**, elle **a essayé** le café français et elle l'**a adoré**! Aujourd'hui, elle boit toujours du café français.	*Carole always drank American coffee. One day she tried French coffee and she loved it! Today she always drinks French coffee.*

❖ The chart summarizes the basic uses of the **imparfait** and the **passé composé.**

Uses of *imparfait*	Uses of *passé composé*
1. To communicate that an event occurred repeatedly in the past (how things used to be) • Events without reference to a beginning or end • Habitual or continuous actions of unspecified duration	1. Events that happened at a particular point in time • Events that are confined by time limits • Completed actions of specific duration
2. To describe or provide background information in the past • Scene or setting • Weather, age, and mental or physical states	2. Sequence of actions in the past
3. To communicate that an event was in progress	3. To communicate actions interrupting something in progress or changes in states

🔊 **ACTIVITÉ G** **Les activités de Nadia, la sœur d'Abia** Écoutez bien les
CD2-53 verbes pour déterminer si Nadia faisait l'activité **(a) souvent** (imparfait) ou si elle a
fait l'activité **(b) la semaine dernière** (passé composé).

1.   2.   3.   4.   5.   6.   7.   8.   9.   10.

ACTIVITÉ H **Le père d'Abia**

Étape 1. Adelai Ndono, le père d'Abia,
parle de ses activités. Décidez s'il faisait
l'activité quand il était jeune ou s'il a fait
l'activité hier.

	quand j'étais jeune	hier
1. J'**écoutais** la radio.	☐	☐
2. Je **jouais** aux jeux de société.	☐	☐
3. J'**ai fait** du jogging.	☐	☐
4. Je **lisais** des livres d'histoire.	☐	☐
5. J'**ai joué** au tennis.	☐	☐
6. Je **faisais** la grasse matinée	☐	☐
7. J'**ai dansé** le tango.	☐	☐
8. Je **suis allé** au centre sportif.	☐	☐

Conclusion Adelai était plus actif quand il était jeune ou hier?

Étape 2. Et vous?

1. Écrivez trois activités que vous faisiez quand vous étiez plus jeune.

2. Écrivez trois activités que vous avez faites hier.

Conclusion Vous étiez plus actif (active) hier ou quand vous étiez plus jeune?

ACTIVITÉ I **Nos activités du passé** Complétez les phrases avec l'imparfait
ou le passé composé.

1. **La semaine dernière,** je _____.

2. **Halloween passé,** mes amis _____.

3. **D'habitude,** mes camarades et moi, nous _____.

4. **Pendant la dernière classe,** nous _____.

5. Je _____ **tous les jours.**

6. Mon/Ma colocataire _____ **tous les soirs.**

ACTIVITÉ J **Une Saint-Sylvestre mémorable**

Étape 1. Décrivez une Saint-Sylvestre mémorable en répondant aux questions.

1. C'était quelle année? Vous aviez quel âge? Quel temps faisait-il?

2. Quelles sont trois activités que vous avez faites ce soir-là?

Étape 2. Écrivez un petit paragraphe avec les informations de l'Étape 1.

ACTIVITÉ **K** **Les séquences du film *Liaisons***

Étape 1. Choisissez les bonnes réponses.

1. Dans le Prologue, Claire **attendait** le bus et elle…
   a. **lisait** un livre de psychologie.
   b. **lisait** un journal.

2. Dans la Séquence 1, quand l'oncle Michel a **téléphoné**, Claire…
   a. **mangeait.**
   b. **dormait.**

3. Dans la Séquence 2, quand Claire **a dit** à Abia qu'elle **allait** à Québec, Abia…
   a. **était** contente.
   b. **était** surprise.

4. Dans un café à Trois-Rivières, Claire **lisait** son livre quand…
   a. Abia **est entrée** dans le café.
   b. Alex Prévost **est passé** par la fenêtre.

Étape 2. Décrivez ces scènes du film *Liaisons* avec les éléments donnés.

Modèle: parler / poser

> **Claire parlait au téléphone quand Mme Saxton lui a posé une question.**

1.

arriver / parler

3.

donner une enveloppe / travailler

2.

entrer / jouer

4.

travailler / demander une brosse à dents

Liaisons musicales

© Alexandra Boulat/VII/Corbis

Un événement tragique qui a beaucoup affecté la société américaine est l'acte terroriste du 11 septembre 2001. Médine Zaouiche, un rappeur français d'origine algérienne, a écrit une chanson à propos de cet événement tragique intitulée *11 septembre*. Écoutez et regardez le clip de cette chanson sur Internet. 🌐

ACTIVITÉ L Des événements historiques

Étape 1. Associez les situations de la colonne A avec les événements de la colonne B.

A

1. La France **était** une monarchie quand...
2. Autrefois, le Canada **était** un territoire français mais...
3. Autrefois, la Louisiane **était** un territoire français mais...
4. Abraham Lincoln **était** au théâtre *Ford* quand...
5. Les gens de La Nouvelle-Orléans **avaient** peur quand...
6. George W. Bush **lisait** un livre aux enfants quand...

B

a. un groupe de terroristes **a attaqué** New York le 11 septembre 2001.
b. les Français **ont perdu** ce territoire pendant la guerre de Sept Ans en 1763.
c. le peuple de Paris **a pris** la Bastille en 1789.
d. l'ouragan Katrina **est arrivé** le 28 août 2008.
e. la France **a perdu** ce territoire face aux Britanniques après la bataille de 1759.
f. un assassin **l'a tué** *(killed)* le 15 avril 1865.

Étape 2. Répondez aux questions à propos d'un événement marquant.

1. Quel événement du passé était le plus marquant *(memorable)* pour vous?
2. Quelle est la date de cet événement? Qu'est-ce qui s'est passé *(What happened)*?
3. Vous étiez où? Vous étiez avec qui?
4. Qu'est-ce que vous faisiez?
5. Quelles étaient vos émotions?

Étape 3. Posez les questions de l'Étape 2 à un(e) partenaire pour savoir quel événement était le plus marquant pour lui/elle.

ACTIVITÉ M Les histoires de suspense

Étape 1. Aimez-vous les films à suspense ou les films d'horreur? Créez des situations avec du suspense avec les éléments donnés.

Mots utiles		
un assassin *assassin, killer*	**frapper** *to knock*	**une sorcière** *witch*
attaquer *to attack*	**hurler** *to howl, to yell*	**un vampire** *vampire*
attentat *attack*	**un loup-garou** *werewolf*	**un voleur** *robber*
crier *to scream*	**un monstre** *monster*	
un extraterrestre *alien*	**pleurer** *to cry*	

Modèle: Une fille _____ quand **soudain** _____.
　　　　Une fille regardait un film quand soudain son voisin a crié.

1. Les enfants _____ quand **soudain** _____.
2. Une princesse _____ quand **tout d'un coup** _____.
3. La baby-sitter _____. **Soudain,** _____.
4. L'homme _____. **Tout d'un coup,** _____.

Étape 2. Montrez vos situations à un(e) partenaire. Qui est le/la meilleur(e) scénariste *(screen writer)*? Vous ou votre partenaire?

Étape 3. Choisissez une situation de votre partenaire et continuez son histoire avec deux autres phrases.

ACTIVITÉ N L'histoire d'une rencontre

CD2-54

Étape 1. Vous allez écouter une histoire qui raconte comment Nadia, la sœur d'Abia, a rencontré son conjoint. Vous allez entendre l'histoire deux fois. Pendant que vous écoutez l'histoire, prenez notes des détails de l'histoire mais n'écrivez pas de phrases complètes. Vous allez comparer vos notes avec vos camarades de classe plus tard.

Étape 2. Montrez vos notes à deux camarades de classe. Avec toutes vos notes, essayez de raconter l'histoire que vous avez écoutée.

Étape 3. Lisez votre histoire à la classe. Écoutez les histoires de vos camarades de classe. Est-ce qu'il vous manque *(missing)* des détails?

Étape 4. Et vous? Est-ce que quelqu'un dans votre famille a rencontré l'âme sœur *(soulmate)*? Comment? Avez-vous rencontré l'âme sœur? Comment?

La parole est à vous!

Est-ce qu'il faut acheter un cadeau si on ne va pas à la fête?

Si on est invité à un mariage ou à une petite fête pour célébrer une future naissance, il est poli d'acheter un cadeau pour la future mariée° ou maman. Et si on ne va pas à la fête? Il faut acheter un cadeau quand même°?

- Sadia de Hoh Chi Minh (Vietnam): «Oui, surtout si la personne est une bonne amie. J'achète toujours un cadeau pour montrer mon appréciation même si je ne vais pas à la fête.»
- Christophe de Lafayette (Louisiane): «Non, ce n'est pas nécessaire. On offre un cadeau seulement° si on va aller à la fête. Si c'est un bon ami, on peut lui donner une carte de vœux.»

mariée *bride* **quand même** *anyway* **seulement** *only*

Et vous? Qu'en pensez-vous?

Est-ce qu'il faut acheter un cadeau si on ne va pas à la fête?

Les **événements personnels**

Personal events

la naissance de Luce

le baptême

Luce à l'âge de 5 ans
l'enfance *(f.)*

Luce à l'âge de 13 ans
l'adolescence *(f.)*

Luce à l'âge de 16 ans
la jeunesse

Luce à l'âge de 18 ans
la cérémonie de remise
des diplômes

Luce à l'âge de 22 ans
l'âge adulte *(m.)*

Luce à l'âge de 24 ans
les fiançailles *(f.)*

Luce à l'âge de 25 ans
le mariage

Luce à l'âge de 65 ans
la retraite

Luce à l'âge de 75 ans le
troisième âge / la vieillesse

Luce à l'âge de 84 ans
l'enterrement *(m.)*

Les étapes de la vie de Luce

Vocabulaire complémentaire

un banquet *banquet*
un coup de foudre *love at first sight*
un décès *death*
un divorce *divorce*
une étape (de la vie) *stage (of life)*
une réception *(formal) reception*
un vin d'honneur *punch, cocktail reception*
un voyage de noces *honeymoon*

un(e) adolescent(e) *adolescent*
un(e) adulte *adult*
un couple *couple*
un époux / une épouse *spouse*
des nouveaux mariés *newly weds*
une relation *relationship*
un rendez-vous *date, appointment*

Bonne chance! *Good luck!*
Au bonheur de (qqn)! *To the happiness of (someone)!*
Mes condoléances. *My condolences.*
Bonne retraite! *Happy retirement!*
Au succès de (qqn, qqch)! *To the success of (someone, something)!*
À la réussite de (qqn, qqch)! *To the success of (someone, something)!*

avoir de l'avancement *(m.)* *to get a promotion, to advance (in a job)*
prendre sa retraite *to retire (from a job)*
rêver (de) *to dream (of, about)*
tomber amoureux / amoureuse (de) *to fall in love (with)*

> **Note de vocabulaire**
> Note that **qqn** and **qqch** are abbreviations for **quelqu'un** and **quelque chose**.

ACTIVITÉ A **Les étapes de la vie** À quelle(s) étape(s) de la vie ces grands événements arrivent-ils *(do they happen)* typiquement à une personne? Indiquez vos réponses. Anticipez-vous un grand événement personnel cette année?

a. pendant l'enfance **b. pendant l'adolescence** **c. à l'âge adulte** **d. au troisième âge**

1. la retraite
2. un divorce
3. un rendez-vous
4. un baptême
5. les fiançailles
6. un coup de foudre
7. un décès
8. un mariage
9. une naissance
10. la remise des diplômes
11. un voyage de noces
12. avoir de l'avancement

Un mot sur la langue

Courtesy Aristile

Laissez les bons temps rouler

En Louisiane, surtout à La Nouvelle-Orléans, on entend souvent l'expression **Laissez les bons temps rouler!** Les Français ne comprennent pas nécessairement cette phrase parce que cette expression est calquée° sur l'anglais *Let the good times roll*. En France, on dit plutôt **Que la fête commence!** *(Let the party begin!)* Le français en Louisiane, le cajun, a des caractéristiques particulières. Quand la France a perdu la Louisiane au début du dix-neuvième siècle, la langue française a évolué de manières° différentes en Louisiane et en France.

calquée *calqued, directly and literally translated* **manières** *manners*

• Est-ce qu'il y a des mots ou des expressions que les anglophones utilisent qui sont calqués sur le français?

ACTIVITÉ B Ça fait penser à... ? À quelle étape de la vie est-ce que chaque phrase vous fait penser?

1. On joue à la marelle *(hopscotch)*.
2. On a une relation romantique.
3. On a peur de perdre son époux / épouse.
4. On est des nouveaux mariés.
5. On rêve du coup de foudre.
6. On habite avec ses parents.
7. On rêve de devenir pompier.
8. On prend sa retraite.
9. On cherche à avoir de l'avancement.
10. On est fiancé à quelqu'un.

ACTIVITÉ C Les gens célèbres

Étape 1. Donnez un exemple pour chaque description.

Modèle: Nommez le couple le plus célèbre aux États-Unis.
Barack et Michelle Obama

Nommez…

1. le couple le plus célèbre du monde francophone
2. le mariage le plus célèbre d'Hollywood
3. le décès le plus tragique
4. le divorce le plus scandaleux
5. l'adolescent(e) le/la plus célèbre
6. la retraite la plus méritée *(deserved)*
7. l'époux / l'épouse le/la plus fidèle
8. un couple du troisième âge célèbre

Étape 2. Montrez vos réponses à un(e) partenaire. Avez-vous les mêmes opinions? Voulez-vous modifier vos réponses?

ACTIVITÉ D Les grands événements personnels À quel grand événement personnel est-ce que chaque phrase vous fait penser?

1. On entend «Mes condoléances».
2. Il y a une séparation du couple.
3. On dit «Oui» *(I do)*.
4. Quelqu'un vous dit «Bonne chance!»
5. On dit «C'est une fille!»
6. Un bébé crie.
7. On dit «Bonne retraite!»
8. Un homme présente une bague *(ring)*.
9. Quelqu'un vous dit «À ta réussite!»
10. On entend «Au bonheur des nouveaux mariés!»

ACTIVITÉ **E** **Les endroits pour des événements exceptionnels**

Étape 1. Répondez aux questions.

Où est le meilleur endroit pour…

Modèle: Un parc est le meilleur endroit pour un premier rendez-vous.

1. un premier rendez-vous?
2. un mariage?
3. un voyage de noces?
4. une réception?
5. un vin d'honneur?
6. un banquet?

 Étape 2. Posez les questions à un(e) partenaire. Notez ses réponses.

Étape 3. Regardez vos réponses et les réponses de votre partenaire.

1. Qui est plus romantique? 2. Qui est plus extravagant(e)? 3. Qui est plus pratique?

ACTIVITÉ **F** **Comment fêter?**

Étape 1. Comment aimez-vous fêter les événements suivants? Avec un banquet? une réception? un vin d'honneur? Avez-vous d'autres suggestions?

1. un mariage
2. une cérémonie de remise de diplômes
3. une retraite
4. une naissance

 Étape 2. Posez les questions à un(e) partenaire pour savoir *(know)* ses préférences.

ACTIVITÉ **G** **Les endroits pour quels événements?**

Étape 1. Les endroits suivants sont bons pour quels événements? Notez vos réponses.

© Heinle/Cengage Learning

Étape 2. Posez des questions à deux camarades de classe et notez leurs réponses. Ensuite, décidez si vous êtes plus comme l'Étudiant(e) 1 ou comme l'Étudiant(e) 2.

Modèle: Vous: **Un stade est un bon endroit pour quel événement?**
É1: **Un stade est un bon endroit pour les fiançailles.**
É2: **Pour moi, un stade est un bon endroit pour un anniversaire.**

	Moi	É1	É2
1. un stade	_____	_____	_____
2. une église	_____	_____	_____
3. un parc	_____	_____	_____
4. le restaurant *Chucky Cheese*	_____	_____	_____
5. l'hôtel Ritz Carlton	_____	_____	_____
6. une maison	_____	_____	_____
7. un cimetière *(cemetery)*	_____	_____	_____
8. une école	_____	_____	_____

Étape 3. Dans le film *Liaisons*, Claire descend au Château Frontenac. À votre avis, cet hôtel est idéal pour quels événements?

ACTIVITÉ H **On est un groupe de romantiques?** Faites un sondage *(poll)* pour savoir combien d'étudiant(e)s dans votre classe…

Noms des étudiant(e)s

1. ont un rendez-vous ce week-end. _____

2. sont tombé(e)s amoureux / amoureuses de quelqu'un. _____

3. pensent que le coup de foudre existe. _____

✈ **Si vous y allez**

Si vous allez dans le Val de Loire en France, cherchez des couples américains qui se marient dans cette région. La France et ses châteaux sont un choix très populaire!

© Ghislain & Marie David de Lossy/ Photolibrary

Pour aller plus loin

Depuis quand… ?

As you know, to ask *how long* someone has been doing something, you ask **depuis combien de temps** and you answer with **depuis** + the length of time. To ask *since when* someone has been doing something, form your question with **depuis quand** and answer with **depuis** + a precise moment, for example, a day, a month, a date, or a year.

Depuis combien de temps habitez-vous à Paris? **Depuis** trois ans.
(For) how long have you been living in Paris? *For three years.*

Depuis quand habitez-vous à Paris? **Depuis** 2010.
Since when have you been living in Paris? *Since 2010.*

Essayez! Répondez à ces questions.

1. **Depuis combien de temps** étudiez-vous le français? Depuis _____.
2. **Depuis quand** étudiez-vous à cette université? Depuis _____.

Un mot sur la culture

Les unions en France

© SGM/Photolibrary

Il y a plusieurs moyens° pour un couple en France de former une union. Premièrement, il y a le mariage qui est considéré comme un acte civil et religieux. Les couples doivent se présenter en premier à la mairie° pour être mariés par un officier d'état civil°. Le mariage civil est la seule forme reconnue par l'État français. Après la mairie, le couple peut choisir de faire un mariage religieux à l'église mais c'est facultatif°. Une deuxième forme d'union civile en France s'appelle le Pacte civil de solidarité (PACS). Le PACS est un partenariat contractuel entre deux personnes qui veulent organiser leur vie ensemble. Contrairement au mariage, le PACS est ouvert aux couples de même sexe.

moyens *ways* **mairie** *city / town hall* **officier d'état civil** *civil officer* **facultatif** *optional*

• Quels sont les moyens pour les couples de former une union dans votre culture?

Liaisons avec les mots et les sons

🔊 Les voyelles ouvertes et fermées: eu

CD2-55 You were introduced to open and closed vowels in **Chapitre 7** through the **o** vowel sound. French also has the **eu** vowel sound that can be open or closed.

If the last sound of a syllable is **eu** or if **eu** is followed by a **z** sound, it is closed.

| série**u**x | mie**u**x | vend**eu**se | serv**eu**se | d**eu**x | p**eu** | heur**eu**x |

If a pronounced consonant follows **eu,** it is open.

| b**eu**rre | project**eu**r | j**eu**ne | ordinat**eu**r | chant**eu**r | déj**eu**ner |

The vowel combination **œu** is also typically pronounced as an open **eu** sound.

| belle-s**œu**r | **œu**f | b**œu**f | c**œu**r |

Pratique A. Écoutez et répétez ces mots de vocabulaire.

Les voyelles ouvertes		**Les voyelles fermées**	
1. un explorateur	4. un chanteur	7. tu peux	10. eux
2. un empereur	5. ils peuvent	8. deuxième	11. une chanteuse
3. la grandeur	6. meilleurs	9. je veux	12. curieux

Pratique B. Écoutez ces répliques de la Séquence 4 du film *Liaisons*. Ensuite, encerclez toutes les voyelles **eu** ouvertes et soulignez (*underline*) toutes les voyelles **eu** fermées.

© Heinle/Cengage Learning

RÉCEPTIONNISTE Ah voilà. Claire Gagner. C'est pour deux nuits?

RÉCEPTIONNISTE Voici votre clé. La chambre 315. Les ascenseurs sont à votre gauche.

🔊 À vos stylos! C'est l'heure de la dictée!

CD2-56 Vous allez entendre trois phrases deux fois. La première fois, écoutez bien. La deuxième fois, écrivez les phrases. Ensuite, encerclez toutes les voyelles **eu** ouvertes et soulignez toutes les voyelles **eu** fermées.

Sujet Citations célèbres

Pour parler des gens et des informations
Les verbes **connaître** et **savoir**

DU FILM *LIAISONS*

Un coup d'œil sur la grammaire

Look at these photos from the film ***Liaisons*** and their captions.

CLAIRE Je ne **sais** pas qui m'a offert ce séjour.

CLAIRE [...] je ne **connais** pas très bien la ville.

1. Which verb means *to know* or *to be familiar with a place*?
2. Which verb means *to know information*?

Les verbes-clés

› Both **connaître** and **savoir** mean *to know*, but they are used differently.

connaître		savoir	
je **connais**	nous **connaissons**	je **sais**	nous **savons**
tu **connais**	vous **connaissez**	tu **sais**	vous **savez**
il/elle/on **connaît**	ils/elles **connaissent**	il/elle/on **sait**	ils/elles **savent**
PAST PARTICIPLE: **connu**		PAST PARTICIPLE: **su**	

› **Connaître** means *to know* or *to be familiar with people, places or things* and is followed by a direct object.

Je **connais** très bien Abia Ndono.	*I **know** Abia Ndono very well.*
Nous ne **connaissons** pas cet adolescent.	*We **don't know** this adolescent.*
Claire **connaît** bien Montréal.	*Claire **knows** Montreal well.*
Vous **connaissez** cette chanson?	*Do you **know** / Are you **familiar with** this song?*

› **Savoir** means *to know facts, information, or how to do something* and may be followed by:

- an infinitive

Nous **savons parler** français.	*We **know how to speak** French.*
Nicole **sait jouer** de la flûte.	*Nicole **knows how to play** the flute.*

- a clause introduced by **que**

Je **sais qu**'il est tombé amoureux d'elle.   *I **know (that)** he fell in love with her.*

Elles **savent que** Pierre est beau.   *They **know (that)** Pierre is handsome.*

- a clause introduced by a question word or **si**

Tu **sais pourquoi** Anouk est triste?   *Do you **know why** Anouk is sad?*

Savez-vous **si** Sadia est jolie?   *Do you **know if** Sadia is pretty?*

•❖ To talk about the past, **connaître** and **savoir** are usually used in the **imparfait.**

Tu **connaissais** Madame Leclerc?   ***Did you know*** *Madame Leclerc?*

Il **savait** jouer de la flûte.   ***He knew*** *how to play the flute.*

•❖ When used in the **passé composé**, **connaître** means *to have met someone,* and **savoir** means *to have found out* or *discovered.*

J'**ai connu** ma femme à une fête.   *I **met / came to know** my wife at a party.*

Claire **a su** qu'Alexis n'était pas un client.   *Claire **found out** that Alexis was not a client.*

Pour aller plus loin

Connaître ou *savoir* un poème?

To talk about things that can be known, either **connaître** or **savoir** may be used, but there is a subtle difference in meaning. **Savoir** implies you know something by heart. **Connaître** suggests you are familiar with something, but do not necessarily know it by heart.

Je **sais** la chanson.   *(You can sing or recite the song by heart.)*

Je **connais** la chanson.   *(You've heard of the song before but can't necessarily recite it.)*

Je **sais** son adresse.   *(You know the address by heart).*

Je **connais** son adresse.   *(You know the address but not necessarily by heart.)*

Essayez! Complétez les phrases avec **Je connais** ou **Je sais.**

1. _____ le courriel de mon professeur.
2. _____ mon numéro de téléphone.
3. _____ l'hymne (*anthem*) national.
4. _____ la chanson *Jingle Bells.*

ACTIVITÉ ❶ **Les personnes et les événements dans nos vies**

Répondez à chaque question avec «oui» ou «non».

1. Connaissez-vous quelqu'un qui a pris sa retraite?
2. Connaissez-vous des nouveaux mariés?
3. Savez-vous qui va être votre époux ou épouse?
4. Savez-vous quand est votre cérémonie de remise des diplômes?

ACTIVITÉ **J** **À l'hôtel Delta** Les clients de l'hôtel Delta parlent avec Abia et Claire. Choisissez le sujet.

1. _____ **connaissez** la rue Sainte-Catherine?	a. Nous	b. Vous	c. Ils
2. _____ **sais** que le café ferme à minuit.	a. Ils	b. Je	c. Elle
3. _____ **savons** parler anglais.	a. Nous	b. Ils	c. Vous
4. _____ **connaissent** bien la ville.	a. Elles	b. Vous	c. Je
5. _____ **savez** parler français?	a. Ils	b. Nous	c. Vous
6. _____ **connais** ce client?	a. Tu	b. Elle	c. Ils
7. _____ **savent** où est la boutique?	a. Je	b. On	c. Elles
8. _____ **connaît** le parc La Fontaine?	a. Il	b. Tu	c. Elles

Et vous? Vous connaissez l'hôtel Delta? Vous savez où sont les hôtels Delta aux États-Unis?

ACTIVITÉ **K** **Claire et Abia**

Étape 1. Décidez si Claire et Abia du film *Liaisons* connaissent ou savent les choses suivantes. Complétez les phrases avec **(a) Elles connaissent** ou **(b) Elles savent**.

1. _____ les poèmes de Félix Leclerc.
2. _____ parler anglais.
3. _____ quelqu'un d'excentrique.
4. _____ les livres de Victor Hugo.
5. _____ qu'on parle français en Louisiane.
6. _____ faire la fête.
7. _____ la ville de Montréal.
8. _____ où est le Château Frontenac.

Étape 2. Refaites l'Étape 1 avec **Je (ne) connais (pas)** ou **Je (ne) sais (pas)**.

ACTIVITÉ **L** **Les choses en commun**

Étape 1. Vous savez / connaissez les choses et les informations suivantes?

Modèle: les films *Twilight*   **Je ne connais pas les films *Twilight*.**

1. les films *Harry Potter*
2. qui était le/la *American Idol* l'année dernière
3. Paris
4. les chansons de Lady Gaga
5. faire la cuisine
6. les livres de *Stephen King*
7. qui est l'épouse du président Obama
8. étudier le français

Étape 2. Posez les questions à un(e) partenaire.

Étape 3. Indiquez ce que vous et votre partenaire avez en commun (*in common*).

Modèle: **Nous connaissons Paris. Nous savons qui est l'époux de Katie Holmes.**

Liaisons musicales

© Richard Melloul/
Sygma/Corbis

Félix Leclerc (1914–1988) est connu comme le père de la chanson québécoise. Un poète engagé pour la souveraineté du Québec et pour la langue française, il avait une influence considérable sur la culture québécoise. Sa chanson *Le petit bonheur* parle de la situation des Canadiens-Français avant la Révolution tranquille. Écoutez la chanson sur Internet.

ACTIVITÉ M Saviez-vous…?

Étape 1. Écrivez cinq informations que vous avez apprises de la télévision, d'Internet ou du journal de votre ville ou de votre campus.

Modèle: La mort de Michael Jackson. L'ouragan à Miami. La visite de Michelle Obama sur notre campus.

Étape 2. Demandez à deux camarades de classe s'il/si elle savait les informations que vous avez écrites.

Modèle: É1: **Saviez-vous que Michael Jackson était mort?**
É2: **Oui, je le savais.**

Étape 3. Répondez aux questions de vos camarades de classe. Indiquez trois à cinq choses que vous avez apprises d'eux.

Modèle: J'ai appris qu'il allait neiger. J'ai appris que Keira Knightley avait un nouveau film.

ACTIVITÉ N Une personne que vous admirez Décrivez quelqu'un que vous connaissez et que vous admirez mais qui n'est pas un membre de votre famille. Traitez *(Treat)* des questions suivantes.

- Qui est cette personne?
- Comment avez-vous rencontré cette personne?
- Depuis quand / combien de temps le/la connaissez-vous?
- Pourquoi l'admirez-vous?
- Est-ce que cette personne a des talents spéciaux?
- Qu'est-ce qu'il/elle sait faire?

La parole est à vous!

Est-ce qu'il faut augmenter l'âge légal pour la consommation de boissons alcoolisées?

L'âge légal pour la consommation de boissons alcoolisées est 18 ans au Québec et en France. Faut-il passer° l'âge légal à 21 ans comme aux États-Unis?

- Yannick de Gaspé (Québec): «Mais non! C'est ridicule! Si je peux voter à 18 ans, je peux prendre un verre aussi!»
- Francine d'Arles (France): «Oui. Le *binge drinking* est en augmentation rapide chez les adolescents depuis longtemps. L'alcool est la première cause de décès chez les jeunes hommes en France.»

passer *to raise*

Et vous? Qu'en pensez-vous?

Est-ce qu'il faut augmenter l'âge légal pour la consommation de boissons alcoolisées?

DEUXIÈME
PROJECTION

LIAISONS **SÉQUENCE 4:**
La clé

Avant de visionner

ACTIVITÉ A **Qu'est-ce qui s'est passé?** Qu'est-ce qui s'est passé *(What happened)* dans la Séquence 4 du film **Liaisons**? Mettez les événements en ordre.

a. _____ Claire a trouvé une clé.

b. _____ Claire lisait un livre dans un café.

c. _____ Claire savait que des clients célèbres étaient descendus au Château Frontenac.

d. _____ Claire a trouvé une enveloppe dans sa chambre.

e. _____ Claire a téléphoné à Abia.

f. _____ Claire savait que la clé était pour un coffre-fort.

g. _____ Claire admirait un tableau d'art.

h. _____ Claire a vu *(saw)* Alexis Prévost.

ACTIVITÉ B **Une scène du film** Vous rappelez-vous *(Do you remember)* cette scène? Claire téléphone à Abia dans sa chambre. Écrivez les mots qui manquent *(are missing)*.

CLAIRE Oh (1) _____, aujourd'hui j'ai reçu une (2) _____ pour un coffre-fort.

ABIA (3) _____?

CLAIRE C'est (4) _____. Je t'expliquerai tout ça plus tard, mais je (5) _____ aller à la Banque Nationale (6) _____. Donc, je ne (7) _____ pas si je serai (8) _____ pour le travail...

© Heinle/Cengage Learning

Regarder la séquence

Vous allez regarder la Séquence 4 du film **Liaisons**. Vérifiez vos réponses à l'Activité A et à l'Activité B.

Après le visionnage

ACTIVITÉ C Qu'est-ce qu'on sait?

Étape 1. On a regardé quatre séquences du film *Liaisons*. Avec deux camarades de classe, décidez si on sait maintenant les informations suivantes à propos du film.

1. On sait pourquoi la mère de Claire est à l'hôpital psychiatrique?

2. On sait qui est l'homme qui a donné à Claire l'enveloppe avec la réservation?

3. On sait pourquoi quelqu'un a payé une réservation pour Claire au Château Frontenac?

4. On sait qui est Alexis Prévost?

5. On sait pourquoi Alexis Prévost est au Québec?

6. On sait qui a remis une enveloppe à la chambre de Claire à l'hôtel?

7. On sait ce qui *(what)* était dans l'enveloppe que Claire a trouvée dans sa chambre?

8. On sait ce qui est dans le coffre-fort à la Banque Nationale?

Étape 2. Avec vos deux camarades, faites une liste des choses de l'Étape 1 qu'on ne sait pas encore. Spéculez sur ce que les réponses pourraient *(could)* être.

> **Modèle:** **On ne sait pas qui sont les deux personnes dans le Prologue.**
> **É1: L'homme est peut-être la personne qui a donné l'enveloppe à Claire.**
> **É2: Oui. Il écrivait quelque chose. Peut-être que c'était la réservation?**
> **É3: Ou peut-être que c'était l'oncle Michel?**

ACTIVITÉ D Résumé de la Séquence 4 Si vous deviez raconter la Séquence 4 à quelqu'un, qu'est-ce que vous diriez *(would say)*? Complétez le résumé.

Claire est arrivée à Québec. Elle est allée au Château Frontenac et elle a cherché la clé de sa chambre. Claire était dans la salle de bains quand quelqu'un a remis...

Dans les coulisses

After Claire leaves the concierge, the camera shows her strolling through different streets and sights of Old Quebec without dialogue. The scene ends with Claire stopping to admire an artist's painting. When a filmmaker includes city or scenery shots without dialogue, he/she may want to draw a parallel between the character and scenery in some way. The places can comment on the character's psychology: inner thoughts, fears, dreams, and so forth. What do you think these scenes reveal about Claire?

© Heinle/Cengage Learning

LIAISONS AVEC LA LECTURE

À DÉCOUVRIR: Le Canada et ses Fêtes de la Nouvelle-France

À DÉCOUVRIR: Le Canada

Pays: Le Canada
Géographie: L'Amérique du Nord
Climat: Varié: tempéré dans le sud, subarctique et arctique dans le nord
Population: Plus de 33 millions
Capitale: Ottawa

Activité Internet

Le Canada est le premier partenaire commercial des États-Unis. C'est-à-dire que, parmi tous les pays-partenaires commerciaux, les États-Unis font le plus de commerce avec le Canada. Trouvez sur Internet quelques secteurs industriels importants du commerce canadien.

À DÉCOUVRIR: La ville de Québec

Structure: La ville capitale de la province de Québec
Région: Capitale-Nationale
Population: Plus de 700 000
Réputation: «La Vieille Capitale»; la communauté métropolitaine de Québec

Avant de lire

You will discover in this reading the summer Festival of New France in Old Quebec.

Que savez-vous déjà?

1. Quels genres d'activités est-ce qu'on fait typiquement dans une fête d'été?
2. Quels genres de spectacles ou d'attractions font partie d'une fête d'été?
3. Quels sont plusieurs thèmes populaires pour les fêtes d'été en général?
4. Pourquoi aime-t-on souvent faire revivre (relive) l'histoire sous forme de fêtes?

OUTILS DE LECTURE
Visualizing a text as you read

Visualizing a text as you read can help you better understand the various pieces of information and better "see" how they fit together. Read the following sentence about the Festival of New France and try to picture the details in your mind. Share and compare your visualizations with a partner. What do you see in your "mind's eye?"

> **Pendant les Fêtes, les rues du Vieux-Québec sont pleines d'acteurs, de musiciens, d'artisans et de touristes portant des costumes des dix-septième et dix-huitième siècles.**

Découvrir les Fêtes de la Nouvelle-France

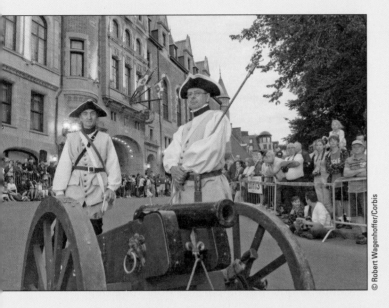

© Robert Wagenhoffer/Corbis

Les premières Fêtes de la Nouvelle-France ont eu lieu en 1997 mais ce que les Québécois fêtent pendant cet événement annuel (au début du mois d'août) est beaucoup plus ancien. Les Fêtes de la Nouvelle-France sont surtout consacrées à l'histoire du Québec, et en particulier aux débuts historiques de la présence française en Amérique du Nord. Elles fournissent° une occasion aux participants de faire revivre quelques événements historiques ainsi que de réanimer de vieilles traditions culinaires, culturelles et festives.

Parmi leurs activités, les premiers colons cultivaient la terre, faisaient le marché, tressaient° des paniers et forgeaient des pièces en fer°. Et pour des réjouissances°, ils dansaient, jouaient de la musique et rôtissaient un cochon au feu de bois°. Pendant les Fêtes de la Nouvelle-France aujourd'hui, les visiteurs peuvent voir des illustrations de toutes ces activités.

Pendant les Fêtes, les rues du Vieux-Québec sont pleines d'acteurs, de musiciens, d'artisans et de touristes portant des costumes des dix-septième et dix-huitième siècles. Une des particularités de cet événement, c'est la présence de plusieurs «géants», des statues ambulantes° qui sont portées° à travers la ville. L'origine de ces géants, chacun représentant un personnage historique ou un aspect de l'histoire du Québec, remonte au Moyen Âge° en France. Le défilé° des géants, hauts de quatre ou cinq mètres, dans les rues de Québec constitue un spectacle impressionnant.

fournissent *provide* **tressaient** *wove* **forgeaient des pièces en fer** *worked metal* **réjouissances** *festivities* **rôtissaient un cochon au feu de bois** *roasted a pig* **statues ambulantes** *parading statues* **portées** *carried* **remonte au Moyen Âge** *dates back to the Middle Ages* **défilé** *parade*

Après avoir lu

Compréhension

	Vrai	Faux
1. Les Fêtes de la Nouvelle-France ont lieu à Montréal.	☐	☐
2. Les débuts historiques de la présence française sont fêtés.	☐	☐
3. L'origine des «géants» remonte au Moyen Âge en France.	☐	☐

Et vous?

1. Est-ce qu'il y a des fêtes intéressantes ou amusantes dans votre région?
2. Est-ce que votre ville d'origine est connue pour une certaine tradition festive?
3. Est-ce qu'il y a quelque chose que vous voudriez voir fêté(e) l'été?

Activité Internet
Vous avez lu un texte sur la tradition des statues ambulantes qui remonte au Moyen Âge en France. Cherchez les «défilés géants» sur Internet pour trouver d'autres endroits où les gens pratiquent toujours cette tradition dans le monde francophone.

People often write about memorable occasions from their childhood. Here is an example of **une fête mémorable.**

© Britt Erlanson/Getty

J'avais 11 ou 12 ans et ma famille et moi, nous sommes allés chez mes grands-parents maternels un samedi soir pour le dîner. Toutes mes tantes et tous mes oncles et cousins étaient aussi invités. Nous étions vingt personnes. Après le dîner (tous les adultes dans la salle à manger et tous les enfants dans la cuisine), ma sœur, mes six cousins et moi avions envie de faire quelque chose d'amusant. Comme c'était le mois d'octobre et que nous avions la fête d'Halloween à l'esprit, on a décidé d'organiser «un château hanté» au sous-sol pour nos parents et grands-parents. On a emprunté des vêtements de nos grands-parents pour faire des déguisements et on a utilisé des décorations d'Halloween pour décorer le sous-sol. On a créé des «scènes monstrueuses»! C'était une fête mémorable chez nos grands-parents.

Avant d'écrire

Complete the chart with information about a memorable occasion you experienced.

	L'auteur	Vous
Âge du narrateur	11 ou 12 ans	_____
Endroit de la fête	Chez ses grands-parents	_____
Invités à la fête	Parents, sœur, tantes, oncles, cousins	_____
Saison ou raison pour la fête	Dîner chez grand-mère un samedi soir autour d'Halloween	_____
Événement(s) mémorable(s)	Les enfants ont organisé «un château hanté».	_____

Écrire

Using information from **Avant d'écrire,** write your own description of **une fête mémorable** in 6–8 French sentences.

Après avoir écrit

Exchange your memorable holiday or party story with a partner. (1) Underline all the adjectives and verify that they all agree in number and gender. (2) Circle all of the verbs in the **imparfait** and verify that your partner correctly conjugated them. Did he/she correctly use the **imparfait**? (3) Put a * next to the sentence(s) that you think create the best visualization or image of the story and explain why. (4) Are you able to picture the entire story clearly in your mind's eye? Discuss your reactions together and then write a second version of your description, taking into account your partner's feedback.

PARTIE 1

LES TITRES

un écrivain / une écrivaine	*writer*
un empereur / une impératrice	*emperor / empress*
un explorateur / une exploratrice	*explorer*
un général	*general*
un héros / une héroïne	*hero / heroine*
un homme / une femme politique	*politician*
un poète / une femme poète	*poet*
(Madame / Monsieur) le Premier Ministre	*Prime Minister*
(Madame / Monsieur) le Président	*President (country)*
un roi / une reine	*king / queen*
un soldat / une femme soldat	*soldier*

NOMS

la colonie	*colony*
un empire	*empire*
la grandeur	*greatness*
une guerre (contre)	*war (against)*
l'indépendance *(f.)*	*independence*
la liberté	*freedom*
une monarchie	*monarchy*
un mouvement	*(political) movement*
le nationalisme	*nationalism*
la paix	*peace*
des réformes *(f.)*	*reforms*
une révolution	*revolution*
la tolérance	*tolerance*

LES MOMENTS HISTORIQUES

la colonisation	*colonization*
la décolonisation	*decolonization*
l'époque contemporaine *(f.)*	*contemporary time*

VERBES

aider	*to help*
fonder	*to found*
gagner	*to win*

DIVERS

à cette époque-là	*at that time, in those days*
autrefois	*in the past, long ago*
chaque	*each*
d'habitude	*usually*
marquant(e)	*memorable, important*
pacifique	*peaceful*

PARTIE 2

LES FÊTES

l'anniversaire *(m.)*	*birthday*
l'anniversaire de mariage	*wedding anniversary*
la fête des Mères	*Mother's Day*
la fête des Pères	*Father's Day*
la fête du Travail	*Labor Day*
la fête nationale	*National Holiday*
Hanoukka	*Hanukah*
le jour de l'Action de Grâce	*Thanksgiving*
le jour de l'An	*New Year's Day*
Mardi gras	*Mardi Gras*
Noël	*Christmas*
Pâques	*Easter*
le 1er Avril / le poisson d'Avril	*April 1st / April Fools' Day*
la Saint-Sylvestre	*New Year's Eve*
la Saint-Valentin	*St. Valentine's Day*
la veille de Noël	*Christmas Eve*

NOMS

un cadeau	*gift*
une carte de vœux	*greeting card*
une fête	*holiday, party, celebration*
un hôte / une hôtesse	*host / hostess*
un(e) invité(e)	*guest*
un jour férié	*legal holiday*
une journée de congé	*day-off*
un potluck	*potluck party*
une soirée	*(evening) party*
un vœu	*wish*

EXPRESSIONS

Bon / Joyeux anniversaire!	*Happy birthday!*
Bonne année!	*Happy New Year!*
Félicitations!	*Congratulations!*
Meilleurs vœux!	*Best wishes!*

VERBES

fêter	*to celebrate*
organiser une fête	*to throw / organize a party*

LES NOMBRES ORDINAUX

premier (1er) / première (1ère)	*first (1st)*
quatrième (4e)	*fourth (4th)*
cinquième (5e)	*fifth (5th)*
neuvième (9e)	*ninth (9th)*
vingt-et-unième (21e)	*twenty-first (21st)*
trente-et-unième (31e)	*thirty-first (31st)*
soixante-quinzième (75e)	*seventy-fifth (75th)*
centième (100e)	*hundredth (100th)*

RÉSUMÉ DE VOCABULAIRE

DIVERS

une fois	*once*
soudain	*suddenly*
tout d'un coup	*all of a sudden*

PARTIE 3

LES ÉTAPES DE LA VIE

l'adolescence *(f.)*	*adolescence*
l'âge adulte *(m.)*	*adulthood*
l'enfance *(f.)*	*childhood*
une étape (de la vie)	*stage (of life)*
la jeunesse	*youth*
la vieillesse / le troisième âge	*old age, the elderly*

LES ÉVÉNEMENTS PERSONNELS

un baptême	*baptism*
la cérémonie de remise des diplômes	*graduation ceremony*
un décès	*death*
le divorce	*divorce*
un enterrement	*burial, funeral*
les fiançailles *(f.)*	*engagement*
le mariage	*marriage*
une naissance	*birth*
la retraite	*retirement*
un voyage de noces	*honeymoon*
un(e) adolescent(e)	*adolescent*
un(e) adulte	*adult*
le coup de foudre	*love at first sight*
un couple	*couple*

un époux / une épouse	*spouse*
les nouveaux mariés	*newly weds*
une relation	*relationship*
un rendez-vous	*date, appointment*

LES FÊTES

un banquet	*banquet*
une réception	*(formal) reception*
un vin d'honneur	*punch, cocktail reception*

EXPRESSIONS

Bonne chance!	*Good luck!*
Au bonheur de (qqn)!	*To the happiness of (someone)!*
Mes condoléances.	*My condolences.*
Bonne retraite!	*Happy retirement!*
Au succès de (qqn, qqch)!	*To the success of (someone, something)!*
À la réussite de (qqn, qqch)!	*To the success of (someone, something)!*

VERBES

avoir de l'avancement *(m.)*	*to get a promotion, to advance (in a job)*
connaître	*to know, to be familiar with*
prendre sa retraite	*to retire (from a job)*
rêver (de)	*to dream (of, about)*
savoir	*to know, to know how to, to know by heart*
tomber amoureux / amoureuse (de)	*to fall in love (with)*

Les **arts** et les **médias**

En bref In this chapter, you will:

- learn about visual arts, literature, film, and television

- learn the present conditional tense

- talk about possibilities, expectations, and hypothetical situations

- learn the demonstrative pronouns **celui, celle, ceux, celles**

- learn about the sounds **qu / ph / th / gn / ch**

- read about visual arts and popular media in France and the Francophone world

 You will also watch **SÉQUENCE 5**: **Une rencontre** of the film *Liaisons.*

Ressources

 audio   🌐 http://www.cengagebrain.com

🔊 Les **arts visuels**

Visual arts

faire de la sculpture (Elle fait de la sculpture.)

une tapisserie

un sculpteur /
une sculptrice

une sculpture

faire de la peinture (Il fait de la peinture.)

un tableau pop art

un(e) peintre

un tableau

faire un portrait (Elle fait un portrait.)

prendre une (des)
photo(s) (Il prend
une photo.)

un paysage

un portrait

un(e) artiste

photographier (Il photographie)

une nature
morte

un(e) photographe

Les ateliers d'art

Note de **vocabulaire**

A painting is usually referred to as **un tableau,** but it can also mean any other kind of framed art that hangs on a wall. The plural is **des tableaux.**

La peinture can also mean *paint* as in the *paint* on an artist's palette or *painting* as in the art form an artist practices.

The verb **photographier** means *to photograph* in the artistic sense. **Prendre une (des) photo(s)** is commonly used in everyday speech to express *to take a photo (photos).*

Vocabulaire complémentaire

une aquarelle *a watercolor*
un atelier *art studio, workshop*
les beaux-arts *(m.)* *fine arts*
un chef-d'œuvre *a masterpiece*
un dessin *a drawing*
une exposition *an exhibition*
une galerie d'art *an art gallery*
une œuvre d'art *a work of art*
**une photographie / une
    photo** *photograph*

le style *the style*
le sujet *the subject*
abstrait(e) *abstract*
cubiste *cubist*
impressionniste *impressionist*
primitif / primitive *primitive,
    amateur art*
sombre *somber, dark*
surréaliste *surrealist*
vif / vive *bright, lively, colorful*

 ACTIVITÉ Ⓐ **Qui fait quoi?** Quelle œuvre peut produire chaque artiste

CD3-2 mentionné?

1. a. une nature morte
   b. un dessin
   c. une photographie
   d. une sculpture

2. a. une aquarelle
   b. une sculpture
   c. un paysage
   d. un portrait

3. a. une sculpture
   b. une photographie
   c. un tableau
   d. une tapisserie

4. a. un paysage
   b. une sculpture
   c. une nature morte
   d. une aquarelle

Un mot sur la langue

Le sens culturel du mot artiste

**Sculpture de l'artiste américain Jeff Koons
au Château de Versailles (2008)**

On peut distinguer deux sens culturels au mot **«artiste»**
en français. Le premier sens décrit une personne qui
pratique un des beaux-arts. Le deuxième sens se réfère à
une personne qui pratique à un niveau supérieur un des
arts appliqués; par exemple, les personnes qui dessinent
l'espace (architecture d'intérieur), la mode (vêtements,
accessoires), les produits (objets industriels) et la
communication (multimédia, publicité).

● Les gens qui pratiquent ces professions sont aussi considérés des **artistes** en France.
Êtes-vous d'accord?

1. acteur
2. architecte
3. cinéaste
4. créateur *(designer)*
5. danseur
6. écrivain
7. jongleur *(juggler)*
8. musicien

ACTIVITÉ B Découvrir trois musées importants à Paris Il y a beaucoup de musées à Paris mais les trois principaux sont: **le musée du Louvre** (un musée universaliste des œuvres d'art de la préhistoire jusqu'au 19ᵉ siècle), **le musée d'Orsay** (qui rassemble la peinture et la sculpture occidentale de 1848 à 1914) et **le Centre Pompidou** (qui possède une des plus importantes collections d'art moderne et contemporain au monde). Dans lequel de ces trois musées trouveriez-vous *(would you find)* probablement les œuvres d'art suivantes?

© Jorge Felix Costa / Shutterstock.com

1. des tableaux pop art
2. des tableaux impressionnistes
3. des antiquités gréco-romaines
4. des sculptures primitives
5. des tableaux cubistes
6. des tableaux de la Renaissance

Et vous? Quels genres d'œuvres d'art pouvez-vous trouver sur votre campus?

 ACTIVITÉ C Des artistes et des chefs-d'œuvre célèbres

CD3-3

Étape 1. Vous allez entendre des phrases qui parlent de genres artistiques ou qui mentionnent les noms d'œuvres d'art. Quelle œuvre d'art ou quel(le) artiste associez-vous à chaque genre ou œuvre mentionné(e)?

Modèle: Vous entendez: une photographie
Vous dites: **Anne Geddes**

1.   2.   3.   4.   5.   6.   7.   8   9.   10.

Étape 2. Dans la Séquence 4 du film *Liaisons,* Claire parle avec un artiste à propos d'un tableau. Quel est le genre, le sujet et le style de ce tableau?

© Heinle/Cengage Learning

ACTIVITÉ D Pensées et préférences Nommez quelque chose ou quelqu'un qui correspond à chaque description.

1. un tableau sombre
2. un artiste cubiste célèbre
3. un chef-d'œuvre impressionniste
4. un sculpteur bien connu
5. une exposition d'art intéressante
6. votre musée préféré
7. votre peintre préféré
8. votre genre de peinture préféré
9. votre style d'art préféré
10. votre sujet d'art préféré

ACTIVITÉ **E** **Quelques outils nécessaires** Quels genres d'œuvres d'art peuvent être créés avec les outils (*tools*) suivants?

1. des crayons
2. de la pierre (*stone*)
3. de la peinture
4. une toile (*canvas*)
5. un stylo
6. du tissu (*fabric*)
7. un appareil photo
8. de l'eau

•••▸ **Et vous?** Travaillez-vous avec ces outils pour créer des œuvres d'art?

ACTIVITÉ **F** **Chez Christie's** Christie's est une société de commissaires-
CD3-4 priseurs (*auction company*). La société a organisé des enchères (*auctions*) à Paris.
Notez les informations que vous allez entendre pour décrire ces trois chefs-d'œuvre
de l'art français.

1. *Femme accroupie* (squatting) de Henri Laurens (1885–1954)

   a. Genre: _____   c. Sujet: _____

   b. Style: _____   d. Prix: _____

2. *La montagne Sainte-Victoire vue des Lauves* de Paul Cézanne (1838–1906)

   a. Genre: _____   c. Sujet: _____

   b. Style: _____   d. Prix: _____

3. *Composition, dans l'usine* (factory) de Fernand Léger (1881–1955)

   a. Genre: _____   c. Sujet: _____

   b. Style: _____   d. Prix: _____

ACTIVITÉ **G** **Catalogue d'une galerie d'art**

Étape 1. Complétez ces descriptions selon vos impressions de chaque œuvre d'art.

Au bord du fleuve (2002) de Pierre Bédard

La tour Eiffel, Paris (2010) de Neal Turner

1. a. Genre: _____
   b. Style: _____
   c. Sujet: _____
   d. Couleurs: _____
   e. Valeur (*value*): _____

2. a. Genre: _____
   b. Style: _____
   c. Sujet: _____
   d. Couleurs: _____
   e. Valeur: _____

Étape 2. Parlez de vos réponses aux questions suivantes avec deux étudiants.

1. Est-ce qu'il y a une galerie d'art sur votre campus ou dans votre ville? Si oui, quels genres d'œuvres d'art est-ce qu'on y trouve?

2. Est-ce qu'il y a une exposition d'art sur votre campus ou dans votre ville en ce moment? Si oui, quel est (sont) le(s) sujet(s) de l'exposition?

ACTIVITÉ H Quatre artistes contemporains à découvrir

Étape 1. Écoutez ces descriptions de quatre artistes contemporains québécois et
CD3-5 français et décidez quel artiste a créé chaque tableau: **M.A.J. Fortier, Denis Nolet, Patrick Rodrigue** ou **Neal Turner.**

a.

_____

c.

_____

b.

d.

_____

_____

Étape 2. Regardez bien les quatre tableaux. Écrivez une petite description de chaque tableau, puis inventez et donnez un titre à chaque tableau.

Modèle: C'est un paysage. Il y a une maison. Le style est un peu abstrait. Il y a beaucoup de couleurs sombres. Le titre est _Souvenirs de Québec._

Étape 3. Montrez vos descriptions et vos titres à un(e) partenaire.

1. Qui a les descriptions et les titres les plus intéressants, vous ou votre partenaire?

2. Qui ferait (would make) un(e) meilleur(e) rédacteur / rédactrice (writer) de catalogues d'art?

3. Lequel (Which one) de ces tableaux préférez-vous? Et votre partenaire?

Étape 4. Notez le nom de l'artiste et le titre de chaque tableau de l'Étape 1. Vérifiez vos réponses. Préférez-vous les vrais titres ou vos titres inventés?

ACTIVITÉ Ⓘ **Qu'est-ce que l'art?**

Étape 1. Est-ce que ces objets sont des œuvres d'art pour vous? Indiquez oui ou non.

1. un tableau de Claude Monet
2. une aquarelle d'un enfant de 10 ans
3. un pastel d'Edgar Degas
4. une sculpture en neige de l'Arc de Triomphe
5. une sculpture en Spam de la tour Eiffel
6. une photographie d'Ansel Adams
7. une photographie d'un arbre prise par votre mère
8. un vase de Christian Dior
9. un vase en papier mâché qu'un enfant a fait
10. des graffitis

Étape 2. Demandez à deux camarades de classe ce qu'*(what)* ils pensent.

Modèle: Un tableau de Claude Monet est une œuvre d'art pour toi?

Conclusion Qui a une définition de l'art plus rigide? Qui a une définition de l'art plus libre?

ACTIVITÉ Ⓙ **Votre premier projet d'art** Décrivez l'un de vos premiers projets d'art. Considérez les questions suivantes.

- C'était quoi: un dessin, une sculpture, une peinture faite avec les doigts?
- Quel était le sujet?
- Quels matériaux avez-vous utilisés: de la peinture, du papier, des bâtonnets en bois *(popsicle sticks),* de la céramique, de la pâte à modeler *(modeling clay)*?
- Qu'est-ce que vous avez fait de votre projet d'art?

Si vous y allez

Si vous allez à Miami, allez au musée Haitian Heritage Museum pour voir des spectacles de danse et de musique et des œuvres d'art haïtiennes.

Un mot sur la culture

L'art haïtien

Haïti est bien connu à travers le monde pour son art distinctif, notamment sa peinture et sa sculpture. On y trouve des couleurs très vives. Parmi les sujets préférés des artistes haïtiens, on compte la nourriture luxuriante et des paysages riches. Faire le marché est aussi un sujet très répandu°. La peinture haïtienne est caractérisée par ses sources d'inspiration environnementales et spirituelles et a été source d'inspiration de plusieurs écrivains et poètes français, tels que° André Breton et André Malraux.

répandu *widespread* **tels que** *such as*

- Savez-vous quelle forme d'art populaire ces artistes haïtiens pratiquent?

1. Raoul Peck
2. Jacques Roumain
3. Wyclef Jean
4. Emeline Michel

Market Scene by Andre Pierre, 1977

Pour parler des désirs, des possibilités et des suggestions

Le conditionnel

DU FILM *LIAISONS*

Un coup d'œil sur la grammaire

Look at these photos from the film *Liaisons* and their captions.

ALEXIS Il y a des choses que j'**aimerais** vous dire, *[pause]* mais...

CLAIRE **Pourriez**-vous me donner les indications pour retourner à l'hôtel Frontenac s'il vous plaît?

Aimerais and **pourriez** are verb forms that make requests and suggestions sound more polite.

1. In the left photo caption, what do you think **aimerais** means?
2. What do you think **pourriez** in the right photo caption means?

❖ The conditional form is used to express wishes and possibilities, to give advice, and to make polite requests and suggestions.

J'**aimerais** aller en France cet été.	I **would like** to go to France this summer.
Nous **pourrions** voir l'exposition en ville.	We **could see** the exhibition in town.
Ils **devraient** faire leurs devoirs.	They **should do** their homework.
Voudriez-vous faire une promenade?	**Would** you **like** to take a walk?
Est-ce que je **pourrais** avoir un verre d'eau?	**Could** I **have** a glass of water?

❖ To form the conditional of regular verbs, add the **imparfait** endings to the infinitive. If the infinitive ends in **-e**, drop the **-e** before adding the endings.

manger	partir	dire
je manger**ais**	je partir**ais**	je dir**ais**
tu manger**ais**	tu partir**ais**	tu dir**ais**
il/elle/on manger**ait**	il/elle/on partir**ait**	il/elle/on dir**ait**
nous manger**ions**	nous partir**ions**	nous dir**ions**
vous manger**iez**	vous partir**iez**	vous dir**iez**
ils/elles manger**aient**	ils/elles partir**aient**	ils/elles dir**aient**

Tu **préférerais** ce dessin?					*Would* you **prefer** this drawing?
Vous **diriez** toujours la vérité.					*You* **would** always **tell** the truth.
Je **sortirais** avec toi.					*I* **would go out** with you.
L'artiste **vendrait**-il cette aquarelle?					*Would* the artist **sell** this watercolor?

* For irregular verbs, add the **imparfait** endings to the irregular stems.

aller	ir-	devoir	devr-	pouvoir	pourr-
avoir	aur-	faire	fer-	savoir	saur-
envoyer	enverr-	mourir	mourr-	venir	viendr-
être	ser-	obtenir	obtiendr-	vouloir	voudr-

À ta place, j'**irais** chez le dentiste.	*In your place, I* **would go** to the dentist's.
Auriez-vous assez de patience?	*Would* you **have** enough patience?

* Verbs conjugated in the present like **venir** (**devenir** and **revenir**) have similar stems in the conditional.

Ils **deviendraient** artistes.	*They* **would become** artists.
Il a dit qu'il **reviendrait** aujourd'hui.	*He said he* **would come back** today.

* Some verbs have a spelling change in the stems of the conditional.

appeler	acheter	essayer
j'**appellerais**	j'**achèterais**	j'**essaierais**
tu **appellerais**	tu **achèterais**	tu **essaierais**
il/elle/on **appellerait**	il/elle/on **achèterait**	il/elle/on **essaierait**
nous **appellerions**	nous **achèterions**	nous **essaierions**
vous **appelleriez**	vous **achèteriez**	vous **essaieriez**
ils/elles **appelleraient**	ils/elles **achèteraient**	ils/elles **essaieraient**

Liaisons musicales

Indochine est un groupe de rock français de style *new wave*. Leur chanson *J'ai demandé à la Lune* (2002) est un mélange de métal industriel et de musique pop électronique. Cherchez les paroles de la chanson dans laquelle ils parlent d'une aventure. Pourquoi cette aventure ne durerait-elle pas? 🌐

* Verbs with **é** in the stem like **préférer** and **répéter** are regular in the conditional. They do not change spelling.

Je **préférerais** une pizza.	*I* **would prefer** a pizza.
On **espérerait** qu'il a étudié.	*One* **would hope** that he studied.
Est-ce que tu le **répéterais**?	*Would* you **repeat** it?

* To say that one *should* do something, use the conditional of **devoir** + infinitive.

Je **devrais** faire plus de sport.	*I* **should exercise** more.
Elle **devrait** écouter le professeur.	*She* **should listen** to the professor.
Nous **devrions** partir tout de suite.	*We* **should leave** right away.

* To say that one *could* do something, use the conditional of **pouvoir** + infinitive.

Tu **pourrais** me faire un dessin.	*You* **could** draw me a picture.
Nous **pourrions** aller au musée.	*We* **could** go the museum.
Je **pourrais** prendre un café.	*I* **could have** a coffee.

ACTIVITÉ K Les personnages du film *Liaisons*

Étape 1. Claire du film *Liaisons* parle des goûts artistiques des personnages. Utilisez les verbes pour déterminer le sujet de chaque phrase.

1. ____ **aimerait** avoir une aquarelle.   a. Ma mère   b. Les clients

2. ____ **choisirait** un tableau cubiste pour le restaurant.   a. Je/J'   b. Robert

3. ____ **préféreraient** un tableau impressionniste.   a. Abia   b. Les clients

4. ____ **choisirions** un portrait.   a. Alexis   b. Abia et moi

5. ____ **achèterais** une nature morte.   a. Je/J'   b. Vous

Et vous? Quel genre de tableau aimeriez-vous avoir?

Étape 2. Qu'est-ce que les clients de l'hôtel Delta devraient dire pour être plus polis?

Modèle: Je veux du lait!

J'aimerais avoir du lait, s'il vous plaît. / Pourriez-vous m'apporter du lait?

1. Je veux un verre d'eau.

2. Nous avons besoin de plus d'eau minérale.

3. Vous devez fermer la fenêtre.

4. Nous voulons écouter de la musique.

ACTIVITÉ L Actions variées

Étape 1. Que feraient-ils? Complétez les phrases avec des noms de célébrité(s).

1. Entre Los Angeles ou New York, _____ et _____ **travailleraient** à New York.

2. Entre faire un film ou un album, _____ et _____ **feraient** un film.

3. Entre chanter de la pop ou du rap, _____ **chanterait** de la pop.

4. Entre adopter un bébé ou un chien, _____ **adopterait** un chien.

Étape 2. Que feriez-vous? Que feraient les gens que vous connaissez?

Modèle: Entre Détroit et Chicago, ma colocataire (habiter) **habiterait à Chicago.**

1. Entre New York et Paris, ma/mon colocataire (habiter) _____.

2. Entre Toronto et Québec, mes camarades de classe (aller) _____.

3. Entre le fromage français et le fromage américain, j(e) (acheter) _____.

4. Entre le vin californien et le vin français, mon professeur (prendre) _____.

5. Entre une pizza ou des escargots, mes amis et moi, nous (choisir) _____.

6. Entre un Coca et un Perrier, mon/ma colocataire (boire) _____.

Étape 3. Posez les questions de l'Étape 2 à un(e) partenaire pour savoir ce qu'il/elle ferait.

Modèle: É1: **Est-ce que tu habiterais à New York ou à Paris?**
É2: **J'habiterais à New York.**

Conclusion Est-ce que votre partenaire est francophone?

ACTIVITÉ M Suggestions Quelques étudiants ont besoin de conseils. Qu'est-ce qu'on pourrait suggérer?

Modèle: Je suis en retard.

Tu devrais marcher plus vite. / Tu pourrais partir plus tôt.

1. J'étais absent(e) le jour d'un examen.

2. Mon ami a perdu son livre.

3. Mes amis veulent voir un film.

4. Nous avons faim.

ACTIVITÉ N Êtes-vous audacieux / audacieuse?

Étape 1. Indiquez votre réponse à chaque question pour savoir si vous êtes quelqu'un d'audacieux *(daring)*.

	Oui	Non
1. Seriez-vous un(e) modèle nu(e) pour un cours d'art?	☐	☐
2. Feriez-vous du saut en parachute *(skydiving)*?	☐	☐
3. Mangeriez-vous des insectes?	☐	☐
4. Prendriez-vous un repas dans un restaurant tout(e) seul(e) *(alone)*?	☐	☐
5. Iriez-vous à une plage nudiste?	☐	☐
6. Sortiriez-vous avec quelqu'un que vous rencontrez sur Internet?	☐	☐
7. Loueriez-vous une maison hantée?	☐	☐
8. ???	☐	☐

Étape 2. Posez les questions de l'Étape 1 à un(e) partenaire. Préparez une question pour le numéro 8.

La parole est à vous!

Est-ce que l'État devrait soutenir° les arts?

Dans certaines cultures les arts et l'État sont liés° et dans d'autres cultures les arts et l'État sont séparés. Qu'en pensez-vous? Est-ce que l'État devrait soutenir les arts?

- Marie-Élise de Port-au-Prince (Haïti): «L'art est la voix du peuple et l'État représente le peuple. Donc, l'État devrait toujours respecter et soutenir les arts.»

- Henri-Georges de Compiègne (France): «Pas forcément. Oui, l'art fait partie de la culture mais il est décoratif. L'État ferait mieux de soutenir les entreprises.»

soutenir *support* **liés** *linked*

Et vous? Qu'en pensez-vous?

Est-ce que l'État devrait soutenir les arts?

🔊 La **littérature** et les **spectacles**

Literature and shows, performances

un(e) dramaturge *(m./f.)*

une pièce de théâtre

un orchestre   un concert

un ballet

un opéra

une danseuse / un danseur

un chœur

un auteur / une femme auteur

un compositeur /
une femme
compositeur /
une compositrice

Célébrons l'art théâtral et les arts du spectacle

Note de
vocabulaire

In Quebec, **une auteure** is
used instead of **une femme
auteur.**

Vocabulaire complémentaire

une chanson *a song*
une comédie musicale *a musical (stage, film)*
un conte (de fées) *a tale (fairytale)*
un(e) critique *a reviewer, critic*
une critique *a review, critique*
le début *the beginning*
la fin *the end, ending*
un genre *a genre*

une troupe (de théâtre) *a theatre company, troop*

littéraire *literary*
poétique *poetic*
récent(e) *recent*

applaudir *to applaud*
publier *to publish*

La musique

le blues / le R'n'B
le hip-hop
le jazz
la musique alternative
la musique classique
la (musique) country
les musiques du monde

la musique folk (contemporaine) / le folk
la musique new age
la pop
le rap
le rock

Un mot sur la langue

© Yellowj/Shutterstock.com

Mon coup de cœur

(Avoir un) coup de cœur est une expression idiomatique qu'on utilise pour exprimer une passion personnelle ou une admiration pour quelque chose ou quelqu'un. Cette expression n'existe pas en anglais mais elle est semblable à *favorite pick, personal favorite, heart stopper,* and *falling in love with something*. Quand on tombe amoureux d'un livre, d'un film, d'un acteur, d'une nourriture ou d'une autre chose, on peut dire **J'ai eu un coup de cœur!** or **C'est mon coup de cœur du moment!** Regardez ces exemples.

En littérature, mes **coups de cœur** sont *L'étranger* d'Albert Camus et *Gigi* de Colette.

Bénabar, c'est mon **coup de cœur** de l'année!

J'ai eu un **coup de cœur** pour la chanson *L'amour existe encore* de Céline Dion.

Mes parents ont eu un **coup de cœur** pour cette maison.

• Quels sont vos coups de cœur actuels dans les catégories suivantes?

   1. art   2. musique   3. cinéma

🔊 **ACTIVITÉ A Qui écrit quoi?** Qui écrit chaque genre de texte mentionné?

CD3-6

1. a. un critique   b. un auteur   c. un compositeur

2. a. un compositeur   b. un poète   c. un dramaturge

3. a. un poète   b. un auteur   c. un critique

4. a. une dramaturge   b. une femme compositeur   c. une femme poète

5. a. une critique   b. une femme auteur   c. une compositrice

6. a. un dramaturge   b. un auteur   c. un critique

ACTIVITÉ B Associations artistiques Associez les mots de la première colonne aux mots de la deuxième colonne.

Si vous y allez

Si vous allez à New York, trouvez La Comédie-Française New York qui propose des cours de comédie *(acting)* en français.

© Ingram Publishing/ Photolibrary

1. _____ *Roméo et Juliette* de Shakespeare   a. un opéra

2. _____ *Cats* d'Andrew Lloyd Webber   b. une pièce de théâtre

3. _____ *Le Corbeau (The Raven)* d'Edgar Allen Poe   c. un roman

4. _____ *Cendrillon* de Charles Perrault   d. un poème

5. _____ *Carmen* de Georges Bizet   e. une chanson

6. _____ *Love Story* de Taylor Swift   f. une comédie musicale

7. _____ Le Philharmonique de Londres   g. un orchestre

8. _____ *Twilight* de Stephenie Meyer   h. un conte de fées

9. _____ Le cirque du soleil   i. un ballet

10. _____ *Le Lac des Cygnes (Swan Lake)* de Tchaïkovski   j. une troupe

ACTIVITÉ C Les artistes célèbres

Étape 1. Quelle(s) personne(s) célèbre(s) est-ce que vous associez aux mots suivants?

1. un chœur   **3.** un orchestre   **5.** un dramaturge

2. un auteur   **4.** un compositeur   **6.** une critique

Étape 2. Quel artiste (musique, littérature, théâtre ou poésie) aimeriez-vous être?

Modèle: chanteur / chanteuse   **J'aimerais être Taylor Swift.**

1. chanteur / chanteuse   **2.** auteur / femme auteur   **3.** danseur / danseuse

ACTIVITÉ D Les spectacles Dans la Séquence 5 du film *Liaisons* que vous allez regarder, Claire a un rendez-vous avec Alexis Prévost. À votre avis, quel type de spectacle de l'Activité B Claire préférerait-elle? Quel type de spectacle préférerait Alexis Prévost?

© Heinle/Cengage Learning

Et vous? Quels types de spectacles est-ce que vous aimez et n'aimez pas?

◀))) **ACTIVITÉ E** **Caractéristiques importantes** Donnez les titres des œuvres

CD3-7 qui correspondent à chaque caractéristique mentionnée.

    1.   **2.**   **3.**   **4.**   **5.**   **6.**   **7.**   **8.**

⋯⋮ **Et vous?** Quels genres d'histoire ou quelles caractéristiques appréciez-vous dans les œuvres?

ACTIVITÉ F **Testez vos connaissances**

Étape 1. Avec un(e) partenaire, complétez les phrases avec les mots qui manquent *(missing)*.

Modèle: Émile Nelligan est **un poète québécois.**

  1. Claude Debussy est _____.   **5.** *Chant d'automne* est _____.

  2. Félix Leclerc est _____.   **6.** *Notre-Dame de Paris* est _____.

  3. Charles Baudelaire est _____.   **7.** *Le Roi Soleil* est _____.

  4. Simone de Beauvoir est _____.   **8.** *Le Misanthrope* et *Tartuffe* sont _____.

Étape 2. Votre professeur va vous donner les réponses. Avez-vous bien réussi au quiz?

ACTIVITÉ G **Résister à l'épreuve du temps**

Étape 1. Parlez avec un(e) partenaire des œuvres ou des personnes qui ont résisté à l'épreuve du temps *(withstood the test of time)*. Notez vos réponses.

	Nous	Autre paire
1. un écrivain français	_____	_____
2. une pièce de théâtre américaine	_____	_____
3. un conte de fées allemand	_____	_____
4. un opéra italien	_____	_____
5. une écrivaine anglaise	_____	_____

Étape 2. Interviewez une autre paire d'étudiants et notez leurs réponses.

Modèle: É1: **À votre avis, quel écrivain français a résisté à l'épreuve du temps?**
           É2: **Nous avons dit Jean-Paul Sartre.**

Étape 3. Est-ce que les œuvres suivantes vont résister à l'épreuve du temps, à votre avis?

  1. la série *Harry Potter*

  2. les romans de Stephen King

  3. les comédies musicales d'Andrew Lloyd Webber

  4. les chansons de Britney Spears

  5. les poèmes de Maya Angelou

  6. les romans de la saga *Twilight*

Étape 4. Défendez vos prédictions de l'Étape 3 dans votre petit groupe.

ACTIVITÉ H **Associations musicales**

Étape 1. Quel artiste associez-vous aux mots suivants?

1. le blues / le R'n'B
2. le jazz
3. le hip-hop
4. la musique classique
5. le folk contemporain
6. la musique alternative
7. le rock
8. la pop
9. les musiques du monde
10. la country
11. le rap
12. la musique new age

Étape 2. Quels sont vos coups de cœur en musique? Nommez-en trois.

Étape 3. Montrez vos réponses de l'Étape 1 à deux camarades de classe. Connaissez-vous les artistes ou compositeurs que vos camarades ont mentionnés?

Modèle: É1: **Pour le blues, j'ai mis John Lee Hooker. Et vous?**
É2: **Moi, je ne connais pas bien le blues mais j'ai mis Usher pour le R'n'B.**
É3: **Moi, j'ai mis Billie Holiday.**

Étape 4. Partagez vos coups de cœur avec deux autres camarades de classe.

Modèle: **Mes coups de cœur sont Taylor Swift, Norah Jones et Lady Gaga. Taylor Swift est une chanteuse de musique country. Norah Jones fait de la musique jazz. Lady Gaga est une chanteuse de musique pop.**

ACTIVITÉ I **Goûts musicaux** Quels genres musicaux est-ce que les personnes suivantes écoutent? Que pensez-vous de leurs goûts musicaux? C'est cool? C'est nul? C'est moyen? C'est bien?

1. votre camarade de chambre
2. vos grands-parents
3. votre meilleur(e) ami(e)
4. vos parents
5. votre prof de français
6. vos amis
7. votre frère / votre sœur
8. vos voisins

Et vous? Quel(s) genre(s) musical (musicaux) écoutez-vous?

ACTIVITÉ J **La musique et nos activités**

Étape 1. Quel genre de musique aimez-vous écouter quand vous faites ces activités?

Modèle: étudier   **Quand j'étudie, j'aime écouter du jazz.**

1. étudier
2. faire le ménage
3. faire la fête
4. faire un pique-nique
5. aller à un dîner élégant
6. faire de la gym

Étape 2. Posez les questions à un(e) partenaire. Êtes-vous similaires ou différent(e)s?

ACTIVITÉ K Une île déserte

Étape 1. Imaginez que vous êtes naufragé(e) *(marooned)* sur une île déserte. Posez ces questions à un(e) partenaire et notez ses réponses.

1. Quels cinq romans est-ce que tu voudrais avoir avec toi?
2. Quels cinq albums musicaux est-ce que tu voudrais avoir avec toi?

Étape 2. Aimez-vous les choix de votre partenaire? Voudriez-vous être naufragé(e) sur la même île que votre partenaire ou préféreriez-vous être naufragé(e) sur votre propre *(own)* île déserte?

Étape 3. Avec votre partenaire, devinez *(guess)* les réponses de votre professeur. Quels romans ou albums musicaux votre professeur aimerait avoir avec lui/elle s'il/elle est naufragé(e) sur une île déserte? Ensuite, demandez à votre professeur ses réponses.

ACTIVITÉ L Ou peut-être une critique?

Préparez une critique de cinq ou six phrases d'un roman récent que vous avez lu, d'une pièce de théâtre que vous avez vue *(seen)*, d'une nouvelle chanson que vous avez entendue ou d'un concert auquel *(which)* vous avez assisté *(attended)*.

Modèle: Je viens de terminer le dernier roman de Stephenie Meyer, *Révélation*. C'est le quatrième roman de sa série *Twilight*. Je dois dire que je n'ai pas du tout aimé cette histoire. Meyer a écrit avec le même style de langue captivant et j'applaudis ses efforts pour essayer de développer les personnages mais la fin est mauvaise. J'ai envie de donner le livre au magasin Goodwill.

Un mot sur la culture

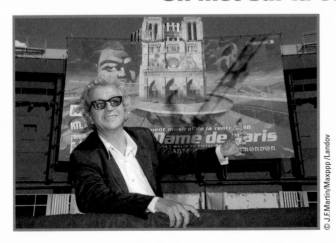

Les comédies musicales

La comédie musicale est un genre de spectacle qui combine la comédie ou la tragédie, le chant et généralement la danse. On a tendance à associer ce genre à la culture américaine mais, en fait, elle a une longue histoire européenne aussi. En Europe, le théâtre musical date du temps des Grecs anciens. Shakespeare a plusieurs scènes chantées dans beaucoup de ses pièces de théâtre et Molière a ajouté des chansons et des danses à plusieurs de ses farces. Dans le monde francophone aujourd'hui, c'est à Montréal (Québec) et à Paris (France) qu'on a le plus de chance de voir une comédie musicale française, telle que *Notre-Dame de Paris*, *Le Roi Soleil*, *Les Dix Commandements*, *Roméo et Juliette* et *Mozart: l'opéra rock*.

- Avez-vous déjà vu *(seen)* une comédie musicale?
- Avez-vous peut-être joué dans une comédie musicale? Quel(s) rôle(s)?
- Est-ce que vous aimeriez jouer dans une comédie musicale? Laquelle?

Pour parler des situations hypothétiques

Le conditionnel dans les phrases avec *si*

DU FILM *LIAISONS*

Un coup d'œil sur la grammaire

Look at these photos from the film *Liaisons* and their captions.

Si Alexis Prévost **n'avait pas besoin** de retourner à Paris, il **pourrait** passer plus de temps avec Claire.

Si Abia **n'avait pas besoin** de travailler, elle **irait** à Québec pour rejoindre *(to join)* Claire.

Sentences that express hypothetical situations often begin with **si** *(if)*.

1. What two verb tenses or moods are in boldface in the captions?
2. Which tense or mood is used with **si** to express a hypothetical situation?

⋙ In addition to conveying possibilities, offering suggestions, and making requests more polite, the present conditional is also used to express ideal or hypothetical, contrary-to-fact situations. In this usage, the **conditionnel présent** is used to express what *would happen* if a hypothetical situation in a **si** clause *were to occur*. The verb in the **si** clause is in the **imparfait**.

Si j'**avais** plus d'argent, j'**achèterais** une nouvelle voiture.
*If I **had** more money, I **would buy** a new car.*

Nous **réussirions** notre examen **si** nous **faisions** attention pendant le cours.
*We **would pass** our exam **if** we **paid** attention in class.*

Si Anne **pouvait** manger dans un restaurant français tous les jours, elle **serait** très contente.
*If Anne **could eat** at a French restaurant everyday, she **would be** very happy.*

⋙ Notice that **si** + **il/ils** contract to become **s'il** and **s'ils**.

S'ils voulaient parler avec le professeur, ils **iraient** le voir dans son bureau.
*If they **wanted** to speak with the professor, they **would go** see him in his office.*

The **si** clause can begin the sentence or appear in the second half. Note that if the **si** clause begins the sentence, it is followed by a comma. If the **si** clause occurs in the second half of the sentence, there is no comma.

Si elle **prenait** son temps, elle **ferait** mieux ses devoirs.
*If she **took** her time, she **would do** her homework better.*

Vous **auriez** plus de chance dans la vie **si** vous **travailliez** plus dur.
*You **would have** more luck in life **if** you **worked** harder.*

A **si** clause may be used alone with the **imparfait** to express a wish or to make a suggestion.

Si on **allait** au cinéma?
How about going to the movies?

Si seulement il y **avait** moins de monde ici!
If only there were fewer people here!

Pour aller plus loin

Le verbe *vivre*

Like the verb **habiter,** the verb **vivre** means *to live.* Its present tense forms are **je vis, tu vis, il/elle/on vit, nous vivons, vous vivez, ils/elles vivent.** Its past participle is **vécu.**

Habiter and **vivre** can be used interchangeably to express *to reside in / at a place.*

Si je pouvais, j'**habiterais** à Paris.	*If I could, I **would live** in Paris.*
Si je pouvais, je **vivrais** à Paris.	*If I could, I **would live** in Paris.*

To express *a moment in time when you have lived or are living,* a *lifestyle* or *to live for someone / something,* use **vivre.**

Ils **vivent** pour l'art et la musique.	*They **live** for art and music.*
Je **vivais** sans meubles quand j'étais petit.	*I **lived** without furniture when I was little.*
Elle veut **vivre** jusqu'à l'âge de 100 ans.	*She wants **to live** till she's 100.*
Mes grands-parents **ont vécu** la guerre.	*My grandparents **lived** through the war.*

Vivre is also used idiomatically to mean *long live.*

Vive la France!	*Long live France!*

Essayez! Complétez les phrases avec le nom de personnes que vous connaissez.

Modèle: _____ vit au Canada.　　**Ma tante vit au Canada.**

1. _____ **vit** pour les livres.

2. _____ **vivent** dans une petite ville.

3. _____ **vivait** simplement.

4. _____ **ont vécu** une situation difficile.

ACTIVITÉ **M** **Que feriez-vous?**

Étape 1. Indiquez ce que vous feriez dans chaque situation.

1. **Si** je **pouvais** acheter un tableau d'art d'un musée, j'…
   a. **achèterais** *La Joconde (Mona Lisa)*.
   b. **achèterais** un tableau surréaliste de Salvador Dali.
   c. **achèterais** un portrait d'Elvis Presley.
   d. **???**

2. **Si** je **devais** lire un roman, je…
   a. **lirais** *Les Misérables* de Victor Hugo.
   b. **lirais** *Crime et Châtiment* de Fiodor Dostoïevski.
   c. **lirais** *Harry Potter* de J.K. Rowling.
   d. **???**

3. **Si** je **voulais** écouter de la musique, j'…
   a. **écouterais** des chansons d'artistes français ou francophones.
   b. **écouterais** de la musique classique.
   c. **écouterais** de la musique country.
   d. **???**

4. **Si** j'**avais** envie d'aller à un spectacle, j'…
   a. **irais** à un opéra.
   b. **irais** à une comédie musicale.
   c. **irais** à un concert de blues.
   d. **???**

5. **Si** je **pouvais** vivre dans un autre pays, je…
   a. **vivrais** en France.
   b. **vivrais** en Angleterre.
   c. **vivrais** au Canada.
   d. **???**

Liaisons musicales

© ZICH/SIPA/Newscom

Willy Denzey est un chanteur / rappeur français d'origine laotienne qui est inspiré par la musique R'n'B et la soul. Cherchez les paroles de sa chanson *Et si tu n'existais pas* et trouvez une *suite (ending)* pour Willy à «si tu n'existais pas».

Étape 2. Montrez vos réponses à un(e) partenaire. Dans quelles situations avez-vous les mêmes réponses?

Étape 3. Avec votre partenaire, devinez *(guess)* comment votre professeur répondrait.

Modèle: **Si notre professeur pouvait acheter un tableau d'art d'un musée, il/elle achèterait *La Joconde*.**

ACTIVITÉ **N** **Connaissez-vous bien votre famille et vos amis?** Complétez les conditions et situations suivantes.

1. Si mon/ma colocataire devait étudier une langue étrangère, il/elle _____.

2. Mes parents seraient très contents si _____.

3. Si mon ami(e) et moi avions beaucoup d'argent, nous _____.

4. Le petit ami de mon amie irait à un opéra si _____.

5. Si mon ami(e) et moi trouvions une grosse somme d'argent dans la rue, nous _____.

ACTIVITÉ O Les cours sont annulés!

Étape 1. Que feriez-vous si les cours étaient annulés *(cancelled)*? Notez vos réponses.

1. réviser pour un autre cours ou regarder la télé?
2. chatter sur Internet ou lire la prochaine leçon du livre de français?
3. terminer les devoirs ou envoyer des textos?
4. lire un roman ou faire du shopping sur Internet?
5. dormir ou faire le ménage?

Étape 2. Posez les questions à un(e) partenaire. Qui profiterait *(would take advantage)* davantage *(more)* des cours annulés? Vous ou votre partenaire?

ACTIVITÉ P Des situations hypothétiques

Étape 1. Répondez aux questions. Inventez une situation hypothétique pour le numéro 6.

1. Si vous n'étudiiez pas à cette université, où étudieriez-vous?
2. Si le français n'était pas proposé, quelle langue choisiriez-vous?
3. Si vous pouviez vivre dans une ville francophone, où vivriez-vous?
4. Si vous pouviez rencontrer une personne célèbre, qui aimeriez-vous rencontrer?
5. Si vous vouliez avoir des enfants, combien d'enfants auriez-vous?
6. ???

Étape 2. Posez ces questions à deux camarades de classe. Est-ce que leurs réponses sont similaires ou différentes?

La parole est à vous!

Est-ce que la littérature et le cinéma sont sur le déclin aujourd'hui?

On entend dire de plus en plus que la littérature et le cinéma sont sur le déclin; c'est-à-dire, qu'ils sont maintenant moins populaires que dans le passé. Qu'en pensez-vous?

- Dominique, expatrié à Austin (USA): «Si seulement ce n'était pas vrai! Il y a aujourd'hui trop de concurrence°. Entre les DVD et les home-cinémas et toutes les émissions de télé°, les gens ne lisent pas et ne vont pas au cinéma».
- Carole de Genève (Suisse): «Pas du tout! Il y a toujours de longues queues° pour les sorties de nouveaux films à minuit. Et en ce qui concerne° la littérature, elle est encore° une expression culturelle très importante. Les deux sont encore intéressants!»

concurrence *competition* **émissions de télé** *TV programs* **queues** *lines*
en ce qui concerne *regarding, concerning* **encore** *still*

Et vous? Qu'en pensez-vous?

Est-ce que la littérature est sur le déclin aujourd'hui? Et le cinéma?

La **télévision** et le **cinéma**

Television and movies

un film d'horreur

un film de science-fiction

un western

un policier

Au ciné

un match télévisé

une émission de téléachat

1-888-555-6781

BBC AMERICA

les informations / les infos *(f.)*

un jeu télévisé

À la télé

une émission *a broadcast, TV show*
une histoire *a story*
les nouvelles *(f.)* *news, news items*
un personnage *a character*
un programme *a TV program*
une publicité / une pub *a commercial*
un réalisateur / une réalisatrice *a director (TV or movie)*
un rôle *a role*

D'autres genres de films
une comédie *comedy*
un documentaire *documentary*
un drame (psychologique) *(psychological) drama*
un film d'action *action film*
un film romantique *romance film*
un film à suspense *suspense film*

D'autres émissions de télé
une causerie *talk show*
un dessin animé / un film d'animation *(animated) cartoon / animated film*
une émission sportive *sports (talk) show*
une émission de téléréalité *reality TV show*
une émission de variétés *variety show*
un feuilleton *soap opera*
une série *a serial sitcom or TV drama*
un téléfilm *made-for-TV film*

> **Note de vocabulaire**
> **Un dessin animé** may also refer to an animated film.

Un mot sur la langue

Prépositions avec la radio et la télé

In French, you can use the prepositions **à** and **sur** with both television and radio, but the meanings are very different. Compare the differences.

J'ai vu un chat tout mignon *à* la télé.	*I saw a really cute cat **on** TV.*
J'ai vu un chat tout mignon *sur* la télé.	*I saw a really cute cat **on (top)** of the TV.*

- Répondez aux questions avec des informations personnelles.
    1. Quelle émission regardez-vous souvent **à la télé**?
    2. Avez-vous quelque chose **sur la télé** chez vous?

🔊 **ACTIVITÉ** Ⓐ **Quel genre d'émission de télé?** À quel genre d'émission de
CD3-8 télé appartiennent *(belong)* les titres mentionnés?

1. a. un jeu télévisé	b. un dessin animé	c. un feuilleton
2. a. les infos	b. une série	c. un téléfilm
3. a. une émission sportive	b. une émission de téléréalité	c. une série
4. a. une publicité	b. une série	c. un jeu télévisé
5. a. les infos	b. une émission de téléachat	c. un feuilleton
6. a. un téléfilm	b. un dessin animé	c. un match télévisé

🔊 **ACTIVITÉ** Ⓑ **Quel genre de film?** Quel film appartient *(belongs)* au genre
CD3-9 cinématographique mentionné?

a. _____ *Halloween* de John Carpenter

b. _____ *Public Enemy* de Michael Mann

c. _____ *Capitalism: A Love Story* de Michael Moore

d. _____ *Pirates of the Caribbean* de Gore Verbinski

e. _____ *Ratatouille* de Brad Bird

f. _____ *Avatar* de James Cameron

g. _____ *A Fistful of Dollars* de Sergio Leone

h. _____ *Psycho* d'Alfred Hitchcock

👥 **ACTIVITÉ** Ⓒ **Vos préférences personnelles**

Étape 1. Parlez avec un(e) partenaire des films ou des émissions de télé que vous
adorez et que vous **détestez** pour chaque genre mentionné ici. Donnez deux ou trois
titres pour chaque numéro.

1. un film d'action	**4.** une émission de téléréalité	**7.** une comédie
2. un film à suspense	**5.** un dessin animé	**8.** un jeu télévisé
3. un feuilleton	**6.** un film romantique	**9.** une série

Étape 2. Vous connaissez un peu les personnalités de Claire et d'Abia du film
Liaisons. Quels genres de films ou d'émissions de télé imaginez-vous qu'elles
aimeraient et détesteraient? Pourquoi?

ACTIVITÉ Ⓓ **Cinéphile du cinéma français?** Faites correspondre les
phrases suivantes.

1. L'œuvre du réalisateur François
Truffaut est...

2. *Les Enfants du paradis* (Carné, 1945)
a été voté...

3. On compare souvent les films de
Jean Renoir...

4. Jean Reno est une star française...

5. Comparé souvent à Hitchcock,...

a. aux tableaux de son père Auguste
Renoir.

b. Claude Chabrol est réputé *(known)*
pour ses films à suspense.

c. caractérisée par des personnages
intéressants.

d. connue pour ses films d'action et ses
policiers.

e. «Meilleur film du siècle» par des
critiques français.

⁘ **Et vous?** Connaissez-vous les réalisateurs, le film ou l'acteur mentionnés ici?

ACTIVITÉ **E** **Films et personnages classiques**

Étape 1. Nommez un personnage, un acteur ou une actrice classique qui, selon vous *(according to you)*, est typique pour chaque genre de film.

1. un policier
2. un film d'horreur
3. un film de science-fiction
4. un western
5. un drame psychologique

6. un film romantique
7. un film à suspense
8. une comédie musicale
9. un film d'action

Étape 2. Quel est le genre de ces films? Quels films sont de grands classiques?

1. *Superman*
2. *Star Wars*
3. *Friday the 13th*
4. *Gone with the Wind*
5. *Pirates of the Caribbean*

6. *Ace Ventura*
7. *High Noon*
8. *Mary Poppins*
9. *Alien*

 Étape 3. Comparez vos réponses de l'Étape 1 et de l'Étape 2 avec celles *(those)* d'un(e) autre camarade de classe. Êtes-vous d'accord avec toutes ses réponses? Qui est plus cinéphile *(film enthusiast)*?

ACTIVITÉ **F** **Le programme de télé** Quelles émissions passent *(air)* typiquement à la télé à ces moments de la journée?

Modèle: à 10h **des causeries**

1. le samedi matin
2. tous les après-midi
3. à midi
4. après l'école

5. le vendredi soir
6. tous les soirs
7. le samedi après-midi
8. à 18h

9. le dimanche soir
10. le dimanche après-midi
11. tard la nuit
12. à 21h

Et vous? Quelles émissions de télé regardez-vous et à quelles heures?

ACTIVITÉ **G** **Petit quiz!**

Étape 1. Utilisez un mot de chaque colonne ou d'autres mots pour préparer une petite description d'un film ou d'une émission de télé. Ne donnez pas le titre!

Modèle: **C'est une série télévisée. Les personnages sont un groupe d'amis et une famille qui habitent à Point Place dans l'état du Wisconsin.**

un dessin animé	les spectateurs	montrer
une émission de téléréalité	les personnages	raconter *(to tell)*
une série télévisée	les participants	jouer
un film de science-fiction	les rôles	être sur
un film romantique	l'histoire	avoir pour vedette *(to star)*
???	???	???

Étape 2. Échangez votre description avec un(e) partenaire. Essayez de deviner le titre.

Modèle: C'est *That 70s Show.*

 ACTIVITÉ H Si tu pouvais…

Étape 1. À tour de rôle *(taking turns),* posez les questions à un(e) partenaire et notez ses réponses.

Modèle: jouer un rôle de série de télé

> É1: **Si tu pouvais jouer un rôle de série de télé, quel rôle est-ce que tu aimerais jouer?**
> É2: **J'aimerais jouer le rôle de Jack Bauer de la série *24*. Et toi?**

1. faire un numéro *(number, act)* pour une émission de variétés
2. être l'animateur / l'animatrice *(host)* d'un jeu télévisé ou d'une causerie
3. commenter un match sportif ou une émission sportive
4. dessiner pour un dessin animé
5. être un(e) participant(e) dans une émission de téléréalité

Étape 2. Discutez de vos réponses à ces questions avec votre partenaire.

1. Quelles réponses vous ont surpris(e)?
2. Avez-vous maintenant une nouvelle impression de votre camarade de classe?
3. Qui pourrait jouer votre personnage si un réalisateur voulait tourner *(to make)* un film sur vous?

Si vous y allez

Si vous allez à Paris, allez au Musée de Radio-France pour visiter les premiers studios de radio et de télévision en France et pour voir *(to see)* une belle collection de «machines à son et images» de 1898 à aujourd'hui.

© Stefan Ataman/ Shutterstock.com

Un mot sur la culture

Les émissions de variétés

En général, les Français sont fous de° leurs émissions de variétés. Il y en a normalement au moins une par semaine. Ces émissions accueillent typiquement des artistes de spectacles de tous les coins du monde. Il y a des acrobates, des magiciens, des transformistes°, des illusionnistes, des humoristes, des chanteurs et des danseurs. Les numéros de musique sont souvent nostalgiques avec des reprises contemporaines de vieilles chansons françaises. Les spectateurs participent très souvent et chantent en salle avec les artistes en scène°.

© Jean-Marc Haedrich/Visual Press/Photoshot

fous de *crazy about / for* **transformistes** *quick-change artists* **en scène** *on stage*

- La culture française a une longue tradition des arts du spectacle dans la rue, au théâtre, dans les cabarets, aux music-halls et à la télé. Est-ce que c'est similaire dans votre culture?

Liaisons avec les mots et les sons

🔊 CD3-10 qu / ph / th / gn / ch

Some consonant combinations have a relatively constant pronunciation in French.

The combination **qu** is pronounced like the English *k* and the combination **th** like *t*.

criti**que**	cho**que**	**qu**and	**th**éâtre	**th**é	sympa**th**ique

The combination **ph** is pronounced like the English *f* and the combination **gn** like the *n* sound in *onion*.

photogra**ph**ie	télé**ph**one	cinématogra**ph**ie	compa**gn**e	ga**gn**er	Espa**gn**e

The combination **ch** is usually pronounced like the English *sh*, as in *shush*. When the **ch** appears in a word that is borrowed from another language, pronounce it like *k*.

Examples of the *sh* sound:	blan**ch**e	**ch**ose	**ch**anson
Examples of the *k* sound:	psy**ch**ologie	**ch**œur	or**ch**estre

Pratique A. Écoutez et répétez ces mots de vocabulaire.

1. **qu**el
2. **qu**oi
3. une **ph**oto
4. la **ph**ilosophie
5. une pièce de **th**éâtre
6. les ma**th**s
7. l'Allema**gn**e
8. l'espa**gn**ol
9. une **ch**anson
10. une dou**ch**e
11. un psy**ch**ologue
12. la te**ch**nologie

Pratique B. Écoutez ces répliques du film *Liaisons*. Ensuite, encerclez toutes les combinaisons de consonnes de cette leçon.

CLAIRE Ne dramatise pas Abi. [...] mon oncle a téléphoné ce matin...

CLAIRE Bon, quand vous êtes parti, j'ai cherché votre nom dans le registre... mais je ne l'ai pas trouvé.

ALEXIS Claire Gagner. Vous attendez quelqu'un? À une prochaine fois, j'espère.

✒ **À vos stylos! C'est l'heure de la dictée!**
🔊 Vous allez entendre deux citations *(quotations)* deux fois. La première fois, écoutez bien. La deuxième fois, écrivez les phrases.

CD3-11 **Sujet** Citations célèbres

Pour parler de nos observations et nos sentiments

Les verbes **croire, recevoir** et **voir** / Les pronoms démonstratifs

DU FILM *LIAISONS*

Un coup d'œil sur la grammaire

Look at these photos from the film *Liaisons* and their captions.

Claire **voit** encore une fois l'homme mystérieux qui lui a donné l'enveloppe.

Abia dit à Claire qu'elle **a reçu** un message d'une femme de France.

1. What do you think **voit** means in the left caption?
2. What do you think **a reçu** means in the right caption?

Les verbes *croire, voir* et *recevoir*

Les verbes-clés

⟫⟫⟫ **Croire** *(to believe)*, **voir** *(to see)*, and **recevoir** *(to receive)* are irregular verbs. They take **avoir** in the **passé composé,** and they have irregular conditional stems.

Note de grammaire
The verb **revoir** *(to see again)* is conjugated like **voir: Ils ont revu leurs amis.** *They saw their friends again.*

croire *(to believe)*	voir *(to see)*	recevoir *(to receive)*
je **crois**	je **vois**	je **reçois**
tu **crois**	tu **vois**	tu **reçois**
il/elle/on **croit**	il/elle/on **voit**	il/elle/on **reçoit**
nous **croyons**	nous **voyons**	nous **recevons**
vous **croyez**	vous **voyez**	vous **recevez**
ils/elles **croient**	ils/elles **voient**	ils/elles **reçoivent**
PAST PARTICIPLE: **cru**	PAST PARTICIPLE: **vu**	PAST PARTICIPLE: **reçu**
CONDITIONAL STEM: **croir-**	CONDITIONAL STEM: **verr-**	CONDITIONAL STEM: **recevr-**

S'il pouvait, il **verrait** l'opéra *Carmen.*   *If he could, he **would see** the opera* Carmen.

Je **n'ai pas reçu** votre message.   *I **didn't receive** your message.*

To express *to believe in something or someone*, use **croire à**. To express *to believe someone or something*, **à** is not used.

> Les enfants **croient au** Père Noël. *Children **believe in** Santa Claus.*
> Il **croit** Anne. *He **believes** Anne.*
> Nous ne **croyons** pas les hommes politiques. *We **do** not **believe** politicians.*

Note de **vocabulaire**
To express *to believe in God*, use **croire en: Ma famille croit en Dieu.**

Les pronoms démonstratifs

Demonstrative pronouns are used to refer to a person, thing, or idea that has already been mentioned. They agree in gender and number with the noun to which they refer.

	Singular	Plural
Masculine	celui	ceux
Feminine	celle	celles

Demonstrative pronouns are often used with prepositional phrases.

> Quelles pommes voulez-vous? **Celles de** Provigo ou **celles du** marché?
> *Which apples do you want? **The ones from** Provigo or **the ones from** the market?*

> Est-ce que nous suivons les conseils de Marc ou **ceux du** professeur?
> *Are we following Marc's advice or **the professor's**?*

> Quel film voyons-nous? **Celui avec** Gérard Depardieu ou **celui avec** Beyoncé?
> *Which film are we seeing? **The one with** Gérard Depardieu or **the one with** Beyoncé?*

> Est-ce que tu préfères l'émission sur le Québec ou **celle sur** la Guadeloupe?
> *Do you prefer the program on Quebec or **the one on** Guadeloupe?*

ACTIVITÉ I Les choix

Étape 1. Répondez aux questions.

1. **Quel concert** aimeriez-vous **voir**? **Celui** de Carrie Underwood ou **celui** de Sarah McLaughlin. J'aimerais **voir celui** de _____.

2. **Quel livre** aimeriez-vous **recevoir**? **Celui** de Victor Hugo ou **celui** de Kurt Vonnegut? J'aimerais **recevoir celui** de _____.

3. **Quelle sculpture** aimeriez-vous **recevoir**? **Celle** de Rodin ou **celle** de Picasso? J'aimerais **recevoir celle** de _____.

4. **Quels films** aimeriez-vous **voir**? **Ceux** de Steven Spielberg ou **ceux** de Quentin Tarantino? J'aimerais **voir ceux** de _____.

5. **À quelles** promesses *(promises)* **croyez**-vous? **À celles** de votre patron ou **à celles** de votre professeur? Je crois **à celles** de _____.

6. **Quels films** aimeriez-vous **revoir**? J'aimerais **revoir ceux** de _____.

7. **Quel CD** aimeriez-vous **recevoir**? J'aimerais **recevoir celui** de _____.

8. **À quel** discours *(speech)* présidentiel **croyez**-vous? Je **crois à celui** de _____.

Étape 2. Posez les questions à un(e) partenaire. Avez-vous les mêmes réponses?

ACTIVITÉ J De quoi parle-t-on? Choisissez la bonne réponse pour chacune des questions suivantes.

1. Préféreriez-vous voir **celui** sur les pingouins ou **celui** sur la nourriture biologique?

   a. l'émission culturelle   b. le documentaire

2. Aimeriez-vous **celle** avec Kiefer Sutherland ou **celle** avec Patrick Dempsey?

   a. la série   b. le téléfilm

3. Verriez-vous **ceux** de Tim Burton ou **ceux** de Steven Spielberg?

   a. les films   b. le film

4. Choisiriez-vous **celles** sur NBC ou **celles** sur ABC?

   a. la série télévisée   b. les séries télévisées

ACTIVITÉ K Vos chaînes de télé préférées?

Étape 1. Complétez chaque phrase avec le pronom démonstratif approprié et votre chaîne de télé (*TV channel*) préférée pour chaque genre d'émission de télévision suivant.

Modèle: Pour les dessins animés, je préfère **ceux** de **la chaîne Fox.**

1. Pour les informations, je préfère _____ de _____.

2. Pour les jeux télévisés, je préfère _____ de _____.

3. Pour les séries, je préfère _____ de _____.

4. Pour les causeries, je préfère _____ de _____.

5. Pour les émissions de téléréalité, je préfère _____ de _____.

6. Pour les feuilletons, je préfère _____ de _____.

7. Pour les dessins animés, je préfère _____ de _____.

8. Pour les téléfilms, je préfère _____ de _____.

Étape 2. Montrez vos réponses à un(e) partenaire. Pouvez-vous regarder la télé ensemble?

ACTIVITÉ L Moments mémorables Formulez des phrases avec un mot de chaque colonne ou d'autres mots pour raconter (*to tell about*) quelques moments mémorables que vous et des gens que vous connaissez avez vécus.

Modèle: É1: **J'ai reçu mon premier vélo comme cadeau de Noël quand j'avais 8 ans.**
    É2: **Mes parents m'ont vu danser une fois à la télé.**

je	voir	cadeau(x)
mon/ma meilleur(e) ami(e)	croire	à la télé
nous	recevoir	dans un film / dans un match
mes amis	revoir	l'histoire / le mensonge (*lie*)
???	???	???

👤👤 **ACTIVITÉ Ⓜ Croyez-vous toujours?** Posez des questions à un(e) partenaire. Inventez un sujet pour le numéro 8.

Modèle: É1: **Est-ce que tu crois tes parents?**
É2: **Oui, je crois mes parents. / Oui, je les crois.**
É1: **Est-ce que tu crois aux promesses de ton/ta colocataire?**
É2: **Oui, je crois à ses promesses. / Oui, j'y crois.**

1. aux promesses du président

2. tes professeurs

3. au Père Noël

4. au karma

5. tes amis

6. ton/ta colocataire

7. au coup de foudre

8. ???

👤👤👤 **ACTIVITÉ Ⓝ Fanatiques** Posez ces questions à trois étudiants différents. Notez leurs réponses.

Modèle: É1: **Quelles comédies est-ce que tu verrais si tu étais triste?**
É2: **Je verrais celles de Will Ferrell.**

1. Quelle musique est-ce que tu écouterais si tu avais envie de danser?

2. Quelles publicités te donnent envie d'acheter le(s) produit(s) présenté(s)?

3. Quelles œuvres d'art t'impressionnent beaucoup?

4. Quels films est-ce que tu verrais si tu étais de mauvaise humeur?

La parole est à vous!

Est-ce que la télévision est un média de masse (trop) puissant?

Il y a de plus en plus d'émissions et de chaînes de télé et tout le monde semble passer de plus en plus de temps devant le téléviseur. Qu'en pensez-vous? Est-ce que la télévision est une drogue puissante qui crée une dépendance°?

• Amadou de Kinshasa (République démocratique du Congo): «La télé a certainement beaucoup de pouvoir et d'influence sociale. Mais nous avons aussi beaucoup de pouvoir. On peut simplement l'éteindre°.»

• Marie-Laure de Témiscamingue (Québec): «Absolument! Je passe trop de temps devant mon téléviseur. Je devrais passer plus de temps à lire ou même en dehors de° la maison. Mais je ne peux pas me passer de° mes émissions préférées!»

qui crée une dépendance *addictive* **éteindre** *to turn off* **en dehors de** *outside of*
me passer de *to go / live without*

Et vous? Qu'en pensez-vous?

Est-ce que la télévision est un média de masse (trop) puissant?

Avant de visionner

ACTIVITÉ ⓐ Vous rappelez-vous? Vous rappelez-vous *(Do you remember)* qui a dit ces phrases dans la Séquence 4 du film *Liaisons*?

	Claire	Alexis	Abia
1. [...] quelqu'un a déposé une enveloppe pour moi à ma chambre	☐	☐	☐
2. Oui, c'est dommage mais mon pays m'attend.	☐	☐	☐
3. C'est simplement une coïncidence.	☐	☐	☐
4. Ne t'en fais pas *(don't worry)*. Je m'occuperai *(will take care)* de Robert.	☐	☐	☐
5. J'ai hâte *(look forward)* que tu me racontes tout...	☐	☐	☐
6. [...] j'ai reçu une clé pour un coffre-fort.	☐	☐	☐

ACTIVITÉ ⓑ Devinez Devinez *(Guess)* ce qui va se passer dans la Séquence 5 du film *Liaisons*. Pour chaque phrase, indiquez si c'est vrai ou faux. Vous allez vérifier vos réponses plus tard.

	Vrai	Faux
1. Claire et Alexis visitent la ville de Québec.	☐	☐
2. Claire découvre ce qui est dans le coffre-fort.	☐	☐
3. Alexis Prévost dit un grand secret à Claire.	☐	☐
4. Claire revoit l'homme mystérieux qui lui a donné l'enveloppe.	☐	☐
5. Claire fait un voyage en France.	☐	☐

ACTIVITÉ ⓒ Un coup d'œil sur une scène Voici une scène de la Séquence 5 du film *Liaisons*. Claire parle au téléphone avec une femme, Mme Papillon. Avec un(e) partenaire, devinez le mot qui correspond à chaque espace *(space)* dans le dialogue. Vous allez vérifier vos réponses plus tard.

© Heinle/Cengage Learning

© Heinle/Cengage Learning

MME PAPILLON Oui, Mademoiselle Gagner. C'est (1) _____. Une (2) _____. (3) _____ était encore jeune.

CLAIRE Pardon? Mais qu'est-ce qui s'est passé *(happened)*?

MME PAPILLON Ah, ma pauvre petite. J'ai une (4) _____ nouvelle à vous annoncer. Votre (5) _____ est (6) _____.

1. a. merveilleux	b. terrible	4. a. bonnes	b. mauvaise
2. a. comédie	b. tragédie	5. a. oncle	b. mère
3. a. Il	b. Elle	6. a. mort	b. morte

Regarder la séquence

Vous allez regarder la Séquence 5 du film *Liaisons*. Vérifiez vos réponses à l'Activité B et à l'Activité C.

Après le visionnage

ACTIVITÉ D L'avez-vous compris? Complétez les phrases.

1. Alexis dit à Claire qu'il espère qu'elle pourra *(will be able to)* _____ quelqu'un.
   a. aimer
   b. pardonner

2. Dans l'église, Claire voit _____ qui pleurait.
   a. une petite fille
   b. une vieille dame

3. Mme Papillon dit à Claire qu'elle a trouvé son oncle dans _____.
   a. un restaurant vers 3h00
   b. son appartement vers 3h00.

Note de grammaire
Pleurer *(to cry)* is a regular **-er** verb.

ACTIVITÉ E Utilisez le contexte Regardez bien les mots en caractères gras *(boldface)* et répondez aux questions.

AGENT DE POLICE Ça va madame? Vous êtes **blessée**?

CLAIRE Non. Ça va.

AGENT DE POLICE Vous êtes sûre? Je vous **emmène** à l'hôpital?

1. L'adjectif **blessée** veut dire *(means)*... a. *blessed* b. *hurt*
2. Le verbe **emmener** veut dire... a. *to take (someone) somewhere* b. *to emulate*

ACTIVITÉ F Une scène mystérieuse

Étape 1. Dans cette séquence, il y avait une scène mystérieuse dans une église. Faites une liste des détails de cette scène dont *(that)* vous vous souvenez *(you remember)*.

© Heinle/Cengage Learning

Étape 2. Montrez votre liste à un(e) partenaire. Avez-vous écrit les mêmes choses? Quelles questions est-ce qu'on peut poser à propos de cette scène?

Liaisons avec la culture

Les plaines d'Abraham: parc historique

Le 13 septembre 1759, l'armée française menée par le Général Montcalm a perdu la Nouvelle-France face à l'armée anglaise sur *Les plaines d'Abraham.* Cette bataille marque le début de la conquête britannique et la fin du régime français en Nouvelle-France. Aujourd'hui, *Les plaines* est un parc d'une valeur inestimable au cœur de la ville de Québec.

Wynne Wong

LIAISONS CULTURELLES

L'expression culturelle

La bande dessinée franco-belge

Souvent appelée le «neuvième art», en Belgique et à travers le monde francophone, la bande dessinée constitue une forme d'expression artistique populaire, tout comme le cinéma ou la chanson. En même temps, la bande dessinée (la «BD» ou «bédé») a acquis° dans le monde francophone un statut culturel qui est différent de celui des *comics strips* aux États-Unis. Les albums de BD sont souvent lus par des adultes, et certains auteurs de BD sont plus connus que les romanciers°. Les BD sont donc plus comparables aux *graphic novels,* qui peuvent être analysées et critiquées comme les romans. La BD franco-belge est peut-être la tradition la plus célèbre avec ses personnages mondialement connus, comme Tintin ou Astérix.

a acquis *has acquired, taken on* **romanciers** *novelists*

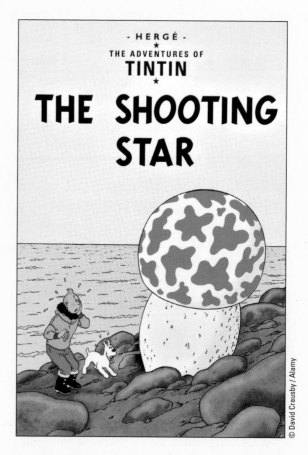

Vrai ou faux?

1. La bande dessinée est une forme d'art en France et en Belgique. V / F

2. Ce sont seulement les enfants qui lisent les BD. V / F

3. Quelques personnages de la BD franco-belge sont mondialement connus. V / F

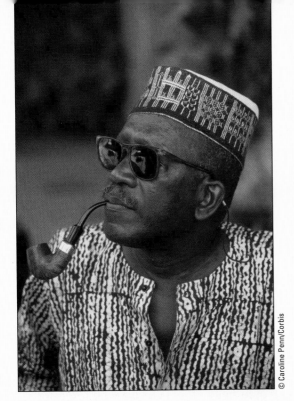

© Caroline Penn/Corbis

Un cinéaste sénégalais: Ousmane Sembène

Voici un des plus grands cinéastes° du cinéma africain. Ousmane Sembène (1923–2007) a acquis à travers ses films et ses romans un statut exceptionnel dans le patrimoine° culturel du Sénégal moderne. En 1966, il a réalisé le premier long-métrage° de l'Afrique sub-saharienne, un film qui s'appelle *La Noire de...* Dans son œuvre cinématographique, il traite souvent de sujets difficiles, comme la critique de la colonisation française, certains aspects de la société sénégalaise et la condition des femmes au Sénégal.

cinéastes *filmmakers* **patrimoine** *heritage*
long-métrage *full-length film*

Compréhension

1. Ousmane Sembène est un réalisateur _____.　　a. typique　　b. important
2. *La Noire de...* est le _____ film de l'Afrique sub-saharienne.　　a. premier　　b. dernier
3. Dans son œuvre, Sembène traite de sujets _____.　　a. comiques　　b. sérieux

La Comédie-Française

En France, la Comédie-Française, fondée en 1680 à Paris, est le théâtre national le plus ancien et le seul° avec une troupe permanente de comédiens°. C'est pourquoi on l'appelle aussi le Théâtre-Français ou le théâtre de la République. La Comédie-Française est le plus souvent associée au dramaturge français Molière (1622–1673). Même si on a tendance à considérer la Comédie-Française comme «la

© Philippe Lavieille/Maxppp/Landov

maison de Molière», la troupe d'aujourd'hui monte° en fait beaucoup de pièces de théâtre variées. Située dans le 1er arrondissement dans la salle Richelieu à côté du Palais Royal, la troupe a un répertoire de plus de 3 000 pièces de théâtre à sa disposition.

le seul *the only one* **comédiens** *stage actors* **monte** *puts on*

Vrai ou faux?

1. La Comédie-Française est une nouvelle salle de théâtre à Paris. V / F
2. La troupe de la Comédie-Française est composée d'acteurs intérimaires. V / F
3. La Comédie-Française a un répertoire de pièces de théâtre très limité. V / F

© Toby Adamson/Photolibrary

Un héritage culturel: la Louisiane et sa musique

On connaît la Louisiane pour beaucoup de choses mais c'est peut-être sa musique qu'on apprécie le plus. La musique de la Louisiane est très diverse. Dans le sud, on reconnaît la musique cadienne°, la musique créole, le *swamp blues* et le zydeco. Mais, dans le nord, on entend plus de musique du style country ou country rock. Pourtant°, c'est à La Nouvelle-Orléans qu'on trouve la plus grande diversité de musique louisianaise. On peut y entendre surtout le jazz *Dixieland* et le blues aux influences afro-antillaises mais aussi la musique *gospel,* le rap et le *heavy metal.* Et on note toujours une présence de la langue française dans la musique louisianaise, comme dans la musique du groupe Beausoleil.

cadienne *cajun* **Pourtant** *However*

Vrai ou faux?

1. La musique de la Louisiane est très diverse. V / F
2. C'est dans le nord qu'on entend le zydeco. V / F
3. On peut entendre le *heavy metal* à La Nouvelle-Orléans. V / F
4. Toutes les chansons louisianaises sont en anglais. V / F

🌐 Activités Internet

- Cherchez des images et des textes correspondant à une série d'albums de BD (par exemple: *Les passagers du vent* de François Bourgeon) sur Internet. Est-ce que ce genre de narration complexe dans un format visuel vous intéresse?

- Cherchez des renseignements sur Ousmane Sembène et ses films sur Internet. Combien de films a-t-il réalisés? Quelle a été son influence sur le cinéma francophone?

- Cherchez le site officiel de la Comédie-Française. Citez une pièce que la troupe monte actuellement *(presently)* ou va monter cette année.

- Cherchez le site officiel du groupe Beausoleil sur Internet et regardez des vidéo-clips. Lisez quelques titres de leurs chansons en français. Quels sont quelques sujets communs dans leur musique?

PARTIE 1

LES ARTS VISUELS

une aquarelle	*watercolor*
les beaux-arts *(m.)*	*fine arts*
un chef-d'œuvre	*masterpiece*
un dessin	*drawing*
une nature morte	*still life*
une œuvre d'art	*work of art*
un paysage	*landscape*
une photographie / une photo	*photograph*
le pop art	*pop art*
un portrait	*portrait*
une sculpture	*sculpture*
un tableau	*painting*
une tapisserie	*tapestry*

LES ARTISTES

un(e) artiste	*artist*
un(e) peintre	*painter*
un(e) photographe	*photographer*
un sculpteur / une sculptrice	*sculptor*

NOMS

un atelier	*art studio*
une exposition	*exhibition*
une galerie d'art	*art gallery*
le sujet	*subject*
le style	*style*

VERBES

faire de la peinture	*to paint*
faire de la sculpture	*to sculpt*
photographier	*to photograph*
prendre une (des) photo(s)	*to take a (some) photo(s)*

ADJECTIFS

abstrait(e)	*abstract*
cubiste	*cubist*
impressionniste	*impressionist*
moderne	*modern*
primitif / primitive	*primitive, amateur art*
sombre	*somber, dark*
surréaliste	*surrealist*
vif / vive	*bright, lively, colorful*

PARTIE 2

LES ARTS DU THÉÂTRE ET DU SPECTACLE

un ballet	*ballet*
une chanson	*song*
un chœur, une chorale	*choir*
une comédie musicale	*musical (stage, film)*
un compositeur / une femme compositeur / une compositrice	*composer*
un concert	*concert*
un danseur / une danseuse	*dancer*
un(e) dramaturge	*playwright*
un opéra	*opera*
un orchestre	*orchestra*
une pièce de théâtre	*play*
un spectacle	*show, performance*
une troupe (de théâtre)	*company, troop*

LES ARTS DE LA PAGE

un auteur / une femme auteur	*author*
un conte (de fées)	*tale (fairytale)*
un(e) critique	*reviewer, critic*
une critique	*review, critique*
le début	*beginning*
la fin	*end, ending*
un genre	*genre*

LES GENRES DE MUSIQUE

le blues / le R'n'B	*blues, R&B*
le hip-hop	*hip-hop*
le jazz	*jazz*
la musique alternative	*alternative*
la musique classique	*classical*
la (musique) country	*country*
la musique folk (contemporaine) / le folk	*folk*
les musiques du monde	*world music*
la musique new age	*new age music*
la pop	*pop*
le rap	*rap*
le rock	*rock*

ADJECTIFS

littéraire	*literary*
poétique	*poetic*
récent(e)	*recent*

VERBES

applaudir	*to applaud*
publier	*to publish*
vivre	*to live*

PARTIE 3

LE CINÉMA

une comédie	*comedy*
un documentaire	*documentary*
un drame (psychologique)	*(psychological) drama*
un film d'action	*action film*
un film d'horreur	*horror film*

un film romantique	*romance film*
un film à suspense	*suspense film*
un film de science-fiction	*sci-fi film*
un policier	*crime / detective film*
un western	*western*

LA TÉLÉVISION

une causerie	*talk show*
un dessin animé / un film d'animation	*(animated) cartoon / animated film*
une émission	*broadcast; TV show*
une émission sportive	*sports (talk) show*
une émission de téléachat	*shopping network show*
une émission de téléréalité	*reality TV show*
une émission de variétés	*variety show*
un feuilleton	*soap opera*
les informations / les infos *(f.)*	*news broadcast*
un jeu télévisé	*game show*
un match télévisé	*televised game*
les nouvelles *(f.)*	*news, news items*
un programme	*TV program*

une publicité / une pub	*commercial*
une série	*serial sitcom or TV drama*
un téléfilm	*made-for-TV film*

NOMS

une histoire	*story*
un personnage	*character*
un réalisateur / une réalisatrice	*director (TV or movie)*
un rôle	*role*

VERBES

croire	*to believe*
recevoir	*to receive*
revoir	*to see again*
voir	*to see*

LES PRONOMS DÉMONSTRATIFS

celui *(m.)*	*this one, that one*
ceux *(m. pl.)*	*these (ones), those (ones)*
celle *(f.)*	*this one, that one*
celles *(f. pl.)*	*these (ones), those (ones)*

Le cinéma francophone

Denys Arcand

Un des réalisateurs québécois les plus connus, Denys Arcand, a obtenu deux grand succès critiques et commerciaux avec *Le déclin de l'empire américain* (1986) et sa suite, filmée dix-huit ans plus tard, *Les invasions barbares* (2003). Ses autres films sont en général très enracinés° dans la réalité sociale du Québec moderne. L'œuvre° d'Arcand est un bon exemple de la réussite du cinéma québécois, le second cinéma francophone par le nombre de films produits. Il a travaillé avec beaucoup d'acteurs et d'actrices célèbres tels que Johanne Marie Tremblay (Simone Gagner) du film **Liaisons.**

enracinés *rooted* **œuvre** *(artistic) work*

Madame Brouette

Ce film sénégalais a été réalisé en 2002 par Moussa Sène Absa. Le récit est situé dans un quartier populaire de la capitale, Dakar. Construit autour d'une enquête policière sur un meurtre°, le film décrit la lutte quotidienne de Mati, une commerçante qu'on appelle «Madame Brouette», pour gagner sa vie et assurer un avenir° à sa fille. Rythmé par de très beaux morceaux musicaux, par des images aux couleurs vives et par un mélange d'humour et de critique sociale, ce film rappelle que le cinéma sénégalais n'est pas limité à l'œuvre d'Ousmane Sembène (1923–2007) et que c'est un cinéma très riche et divers.

une enquête policière sur un meurtre *police murder investigation* **un avenir** *future*

Le cinéma d'elles

L'industrie cinématographique française est bien connue dans le monde pour sa diversité, surtout de sujets et de styles mais aussi pour sa diversité de réalisatrices. La France est peut-être le pays avec le plus grand nombre de femmes qui tournent des films°. Malgré le fait° que «le cinéma d'elles» reste minoritaire dans l'industrie, beaucoup de femmes ont eu un grand succès en France. Parmi les réalisatrices les plus connues, on compte Agnès Varda, Claire Denis, Diane Kurys, Coline Serreau, Martine Dugowson, Catherine Breillat, Laetitia Masson, Yamina Benguigui, Chantal Akerman, Raja Amari et Anne Fontaine.

tournent des films *to make movies* **Malgré le fait** *Despite the fact*

Les frères Dardenne

Les frères Jean-Pierre et Luc Dardenne ont largement contribué à faire connaître le cinéma franco-belge, qui a connu de grands succès au niveau international. Les deux frères belges travaillent toujours ensemble sur un film. Ils ont renouvelé le cinéma social, qui était autrefois° un élément caractéristique du cinéma français. Leurs films ont obtenu plusieurs prix au Festival de Cannes, le grand festival de cinéma qui a lieu en France chaque année en mai.

autrefois *formerly, in the past*

Merzak Allouache

Un célèbre réalisateur émigré° d'origine algérienne qui tourne des films en France et en Algérie, Merzak Allouache a produit une œuvre variée *(Bab El-Oued City, Salut Cousin!, Chouchou, Bal el web),* avec des films aux dialogues à la fois° en arabe et en français. Observateur critique de la société algérienne et de la société française, Allouache a surtout réalisé des comédies acides qui jouent parfois sur les conflits et les influences réciproques entre les réalités culturelles en Algérie et en France.

émigré *emigrant* **à la fois** *at the same time*

Révision

1. Quel est le second cinéma francophone par le nombre de films produits?
2. Quel réalisateur est connu pour ses images aux couleurs vives?
3. Quels réalisateurs travaillent toujours ensemble sur un film?
4. Quel pays est connu pour son cinéma de femmes?
5. Quelles langues est-ce que Merzak Allouache utilise dans ses films?

🌐 Activités Internet

- Trouvez la filmographie de Merzak Allouache ou de Denys Arcand sur Internet. Quel est le dernier film qu'Allouache ou Arcand a tourné? Semble-t-il intéressant? Pourquoi ou pourquoi pas?

- Cherchez le site officiel du film *Rosetta* (1999) ou du film *L'enfant* (2005) des frères Dardenne. Quels prix est-ce qu'ils ont gagné au Festival de Cannes? D'après les descriptions des deux films, est-ce que les prix vous semblent mérités *(deserved)*?

- Cherchez un portrait d'une des réalisatrices mentionnées dans le petit texte sur «le cinéma d'elles». Sur quels thèmes ou quels sujets tourne-t-elle des films?

Les **relations interpersonnelles**

En bref In this chapter, you will:

- learn how to express how you feel

- learn negative and affirmative adverbs and pronouns

- talk about values, lifestyles, relationships, and personal characteristics

- learn about reflexive verbs like **s'aimer, se marier, se respecter,** and **se rappeler**

- learn about semi-vowels

- read about changing family structures and relationships in Togo

- write about relationships

 You will also re-watch **SÉQUENCE 5: Une rencontre** of the film *Liaisons*.

Ressources

 audio   ⊕ http://www.cengagebrain.com

🔊 Les **caractéristiques personnelles**

Personal characteristics

une femme au foyer

un homme au foyer

les fanas de la santé *(m., f.)*

les retraités

les bourreaux de travail

les écologistes / les écolos

les membres de la jet-set

les accros du shopping

les babas cool / les hippies

Les modes *(m.)* **de vie**

Vocabulaire complémentaire

les célibataires *(m., f.) single people*
une mère active / un père actif
   a working mom / a working dad
une mère célibataire / un père célibataire *a single mother / a single father*

l'amitié *(f.) friendship*
l'amour *(m.) love*
le bonheur *happiness*
l'environnement *(m.) environment*
la fidélité / l'infidélité *(f.) loyalty / disloyalty*
la moralité *morality*
le prestige *prestige*
la spiritualité *spirituality*
le succès *success*

avare *miserly, stingy*
bavard(e) *talkative, gossipy*
bête *stupid, idiotic*
bien habillé(e) / mal habillé(e) *well-dressed / poorly-dressed*
égoïste *selfish*
fidèle / infidèle *loyal / disloyal*
gracieux / gracieuse *graceful, gracious*
grossier / grossière *crude, crass*
indiscret / indiscrète *indiscreet*
jaloux / jalouse *jealous*
maladroit(e) *clumsy*
mou / molle *soft, no backbone, wimpy*
orgueilleux / orgueilleuse *(very) proud*
prétentieux / prétentieuse *pretentious*
simple *simple*
soigné(e) *well-groomed, fancy, spiffy*

être bien dans sa peau *to have confidence in / to feel good about oneself*

ACTIVITÉ A **Antonymes** Choisissez l'antonyme de chaque adjectif mentionné.

CD3-12

1. a. beau   b. gracieux   c. difficile   d. égoïste
2. a. poli   b. prétentieux   c. grand   d. avare
3. a. intelligent b. jaloux   c. idiot   d. vieux
4. a. jeune   b. honnête   c. difficile   d. fidèle
5. a. nouveau   b. facile   c. soigné   d. dur
6. a. fière   b. charmante   c. meilleure   d. célèbre
7. a. brillant   b. nerveux   c. indiscret   d. délicieux
8. a. nombreuse   b. pessimiste   c. silencieuse   d. active

🔊 **ACTIVITÉ** Ⓑ **Quelles valeurs?** Quelle valeur associez-vous à chaque mode
CD3-13 de vie mentionné?

Modèle: les babas cool   **l'amour, la paix, le bonheur**

1.   2.   3.   4.   5.   6.   7.   8.   9.   10.

👥 **ACTIVITÉ** Ⓒ **À qui cela vous fait penser?**

Étape 1. À quelle personne connue est-ce que chaque mot de vocabulaire vous fait
penser? Partagez vos idées avec un(e) partenaire. Pensez-vous de la même manière?

1. intelligent   9. bête
2. prétentieuse   10. gracieux
3. infidèle   11. avoir beaucoup de succès
4. grossier   12. être bien habillé
5. bavard   13. être bien dans sa peau
6. jalouse   14. avoir beaucoup de prestige
7. grossière   15. avoir beaucoup d'esprit (to be witty)
8. égoïste

Étape 2. Quelles caractéristiques utiliseriez-vous pour décrire ces personnages du
film *Liaisons*?

1. Claire Gagner   2. Abia Ndono   3. Alexis Prévost

ACTIVITÉ Ⓓ **Les priorités**

Étape 1. Classez (*Classify*) ces valeurs par ordre d'importance pour les personnes
suivantes.

| l'amour | l'environnement | la famille | la spiritualité | le succès |

Modèle: les fanas de la santé
    **Pour les fanas de la santé, la spiritualité vient en premier, l'environnement
    en deuxième, l'amour en troisième, la famille en quatrième et le succès en
    cinquième.**

1. les pères actifs   5. les femmes au foyer
2. les mères célibataires   6. les bourreaux de travail
3. les retraités   7. les écologistes
4. les accros du shopping   8. les hommes au foyer

Étape 2. Classez les valeurs de l'Étape 1 par ordre d'importance pour vous. Y a-t-il
d'autres valeurs que vous voudriez ajouter (*add*)?

👥 **Étape 3.** Montrez vos réponses de l'Étape 1 et de l'Étape 2 à un(e) partenaire.
Décidez pour quel mode de vie votre partenaire est fait(e).

ACTIVITÉ E Les stéréotypes Quels sont les stéréotypes pour chacun *(each one)* de ces modes de vie?

Modèle: Les célébrités sont **indiscrètes et bien habillées. Elles apprécient la liberté.**

1. Les hommes au foyer sont _____.
2. Les membres de la jet-set sont _____.
3. Les mères actives sont _____.
4. Les écologistes sont _____.
5. Les célibataires sont _____.
6. Les pères célibataires sont _____.

ACTIVITÉ F La question des caractéristiques Comment considéreriez-vous ces caractéristiques?

	Toujours positif	Toujours négatif	Ça dépend.
1. être mou / molle	_____	_____	_____
2. être bavard(e)	_____	_____	_____
3. être avare	_____	_____	_____
4. être bien dans sa peau	_____	_____	_____
5. être grossier / grossière	_____	_____	_____

ACTIVITÉ G Les pages de Facebook Préparez une description pour votre page d'accueil de Facebook.

Modèle: **Je suis un jeune homme célibataire de 23 ans et un grand joueur de foot. L'amitié est très importante pour moi et je cherche des amis aussi passionnés par le foot que moi. Je déteste les gens orgueilleux et je préfère vivre une vie active.**

Si vous y allez

Si vous allez à Saint-Tropez en France, allez au Café Le Sénéquier sur le port pour regarder les gens passer, surtout des célébrités ou des membres de la jet-set!

Un mot sur la culture

Les supermamans

© Images.com/Corbis

Les modes de vie en transformation

Les tendances de la consommation° d'un peuple aident à créer des modes de vie. En France, comme ailleurs, il y a une transformation constante des modes de vie. Prenons le cas *des femmes actives / des hommes actifs*. Dans le passé récent, les Français ne croyaient pas forcément à la possibilité d'avoir à la fois° une carrière professionnelle et une vie familiale. Aujourd'hui on constate° une transformation dans le développement du mode de vie «actif»: une famille heureuse et une carrière réussie. Les médias en parlent assez souvent et on trouve de plus en plus de produits et de magazines à acheter pour mieux réussir sa vie familiale et professionnelle.

consommation *consumption* **à la fois** *at the same time* **constate** *observes*

• Quelles transformations constatez-vous dans les modes de vie de votre culture?

Pour parler de nos rapports

Les verbes réfléchis

DU FILM *LIAISONS*

Un coup d'œil sur la grammaire

© Heinle/Cengage Learning

© Heinle/Cengage Learning

Claire et Alexis **se parlent** après leur rendez-vous.

Claire **se parle** après le départ d'Alexis.

1. What do you think the verb **se parlent** means in the left caption?
2. What do you think the verb **se parle** means in the right caption?

❖ A reflexive construction is one in which the subject and object of a verb are the same. In English, this is generally rendered with *-self / -selves*. Compare the following.

> I know myself. (I am both the subject and the object of *know*.)
>
> I know him. (I am the subject but someone else—a male—is the object.)
>
> They know themselves. (*They* is both the subject and the object of *know*.)
>
> They know him. (*They* is the subject but someone else is the object of *know*.)

❖ French uses reflexive pronouns for this kind of construction.

Je **me connais.**	*I **know myself.***
Je le connais.	*I know him.*
Ils **se connaissent.**	*They **know themselves.***
Ils le connaissent.	*They know him.*

❖ The reflexive pronouns are the same as direct object pronouns with the exception of the third-person which uses **se.**

je **me connais**	nous **nous connaissons**
tu **te connais**	vous **vous connaissez**
il/elle/on **se connaît**	ils/elles **se connaissent**

❖ Just about any verb that can take a direct object can be reflexive, including **aimer / s'aimer, connaître / se connaître, détester / se détester, parler / se parler, regarder / se regarder,** and **voir / se voir.**

When the subject and object of a verb are plural and are the same, the English equivalent can be *-selves* or *each other*. Context determines which is meant.

Ils **se voient** (dans le miroir).	*They **see themselves** (in the mirror).*
Ils **se voient** tous les jours.	*They **see each other** everyday.*
Elles **se connaissent** bien.	*They **know themselves** well.*
Elles sont amies et **se connaissent** bien.	*They are friends and **know each other** well.*

Some verbs in French use reflexive pronouns, but do not normally translate into English as *-self / -selves* or *each other*. One group deals with emotions and psychological states. When used reflexively, the English translation often uses *get / become* + adjective.

s'amuser	*to have a good time*	**se fâcher**	*to get angry*
s'ennuyer	*to get bored*	**s'inquiéter**	*to worry*
s'énerver	*to get upset*	**se sentir**	*to feel*

Note de **grammaire**

S'ennuyer is a spelling-changing verb like **payer**: je m'ennuie, nous nous ennuyons. S'inquiéter is like **espérer**: je m'inquiète, nous nous inquiétons.

Another group of verbs almost never occurs without the reflexive pronoun. You have to memorize their meanings and their typical English translations.

se disputer	*to argue*	**se rendre compte** (**que / de**)	*to realize*
se marier	*to get married*	**se souvenir de**	*to remember*

Jean et Luce **se marient**.	*Jean and Luce **are getting married**.*
Je **me marie** aujourd'hui.	*I'm **getting married** today.*
Est-ce que Yves et Guy **se disputent** souvent?	*Do Yves and Guy **argue** often?*
Nous **nous disputons** avec nos voisins.	*We **argue** with our neighbors.*

Note de **grammaire**

Se souvenir is conjugated like venir (je me souviens, nous nous souvenons, ils se souviennent).

The English equivalent of some French verbs may change depending on whether the verb uses a reflexive pronoun or not. This is because English does not have this construction.

aller / s'en aller	*to go / to leave, to go away*
demander / se demander	*to ask / to wonder*
entendre / s'entendre	*to hear / to get along*
mettre / se mettre (à)	*to put / to begin (to)*
quitter / se quitter	*to leave / to break up*
trouver / se trouver	*to find / to be located*

Je **m'en vais** ce soir.	*I'm **going away** tonight.*
Est-ce que tu **te demandes** pourquoi il est triste?	*Are you **wondering** why he is sad?*

Note de **grammaire**

You will learn more reflexive verbs in **Vocabulaire 2**.

In the infinitive, the reflexive pronoun precedes the infinitive and agrees with the subject of the verb. Place **ne** before the reflexive pronoun and **pas** after the verb in negative constructions.

Nous allons **nous marier** demain.	*We are getting married tomorrow.*
Ils aimeraient **s'entendre** bien.	*They would like to get along (with each other).*
Vous **ne vous détestez pas**.	*You don't hate each other.*

ACTIVITÉ H **Les couples** À votre avis, les phrases suivantes décrivent quels types de couple?

1. Ils ne **se voient** pas souvent.
   a. une femme au foyer et un bourreau de travail
   b. un mari et une femme retraités

2. Ils **se connaissent** bien.
   a. des jeunes mariés
   b. un mari et une femme retraités

3. Ils **se parlent** souvent.
   a. un homme au foyer et une femme jet-set
   b. un homme et une femme au foyer

4. Ils **se disputent** souvent.
   a. une femme jet-set et un baba cool
   b. un baba cool et une écologiste

Liaisons musicales

Ancien participant de l'émission de télé *Star Academy,* Patxi Garat est un auteur-compositeur-interprète *(singer-songwriter)* du pays basque français. Connu maintenant sous le nom de Patxi, il a sorti la chanson *S'embrasser* en 2006. Cherchez les paroles de cette chanson. Qu'est-ce qu'ils pourraient faire ensemble?

© AFP/Getty Images

ACTIVITÉ I **Les valeurs et les modes de vie** Choisissez un verbe pour chaque phrase.

1. Les gens bavards ____ constamment.   a. se connaissent b. se parlent
2. Je ____ quand je suis avec des gens infidèles. a. m'amuse   b. me fâche
3. Un bourreau de travail ____ sans   a. se sent   b. s'ennuie
   (*without*) travail.
4. Les parents ____ les anniversaires de   a. se rappellent   b. se sentent
   leurs enfants.
5. Je ____ que la famille est importante.   a. me rends compte b. m'énerve
6. Un bourreau de travail ____ à travailler à 7h00. a. se met   b. met
7. Les hommes célibataires ____ ma fille belle.   a. se trouvent   b. trouvent
8. Les couples infidèles ____ souvent.   a. se quittent   b. quittent
9. Les couples fidèles ____ bien.   a. s'entendent   b. entendent
10. On ____ aux employés d'être bien habillés.   a. se demande   b. demande

ACTIVITÉ J **Les gens bavards au Château Frontenac** Les clients du Château Frontenac se parlent au bar. Choisissez le sujet de chaque verbe.

1. ____ **me souviens de** son premier mari.   a. Je   b. Caroline
2. ____ **se voient** souvent.   a. Mon copain   b. Mes enfants
3. ____, **nous nous disputons** parfois.   a. Mon mari et moi b. Mes voisins
4. ____ **s'amuse** avec sa copine.   a. Nous   b. Mon neveu
5. ____ **te maries** avec Mustapha?   a. Caroline   b. Tu
6. ____ ne **vous sentez pas** bien? Buvez du thé. a. Vous   b. Vos enfants
7. ____ **me** demande si mon voisin est infidèle. a. Je   b. Mes amis
8. ____ **s'énerve** parce que son copain est jaloux. a. Tu   b. Ma fille

❖ **Et vous?** Vous êtes bavard(e)?

ACTIVITÉ **K** **Abia et Nadia** Abia du film *Liaisons* et sa sœur Nadia se parlent. Complétez les phrases avec la forme appropriée du verbe qui convient.

NADIA Abia, est-il difficile d'être célibataire? Je (1) _____ souvent pour toi.

    a. s'énerver   b. s'inquiéter   c. se disputer   d. se souvenir

NADIA Est-ce que tu (2) _____ seule *(lonely)* Abia?

    a. s'ennuyer   b. se fâcher   c. se sentir   d. s'entendre

ABIA Mais non! J'ai de bons amis comme Claire et nous (3) _____ souvent.

    a. s'amuser   b. s'ennuyer   c. s'énerver   d. se fâcher

NADIA Mais tu ne veux pas trouver un copain? Est-ce que tu veux (4) _____ un jour?

    a. s'aimer   b. se disputer   c. se quitter   d. se marier

ABIA Si, mais c'est difficile. Je (5) _____ quand je parle avec des hommes grossiers.

    a. se fâcher   b. se sentir   c. se trouver   d. s'en aller

NADIA Je comprends. Ce n'est pas toujours facile de (6) _____ la bonne personne.

    a. trouver   b. se trouver   c. entendre   d. s'entendre

ABIA C'est vrai que parfois je (7) _____ le week-end quand je ne sors pas.

    a. s'en aller   b. s'ennuyer   c. se trouver   d. se souvenir

ABIA Mais je (8) _____ aujourd'hui qu'il est plus important d'être bien dans sa peau.

    a. se sentir   b. s'énerver   c. s'inquiéter   d. se rendre compte

ABIA Et toi Nadia, est-ce que tu (9) _____ parfois si tu préférerais être célibataire?

    a. demander   b. se demander   c. aller   d. s'en aller

NADIA Non, jamais. François et moi, nous (10) _____ très bien. Je l'adore.

    a. mettre   b. se mettre   c. entendre   d. s'entendre

NADIA Je (11) _____ de la naissance de Patrick. Ma famille est ma vie.

    a. se souvenir   b. se sentir   c. se fâcher   d. se demander

ABIA Bon! Je vais (12) _____ à chercher l'homme de ma vie aujourd'hui!

    a. mettre   b. se mettre   c. demander   d. se demander

Et vous? Préférez-vous être célibataire ou en couple?

ACTIVITÉ **L** **Vos sentiments**

Étape 1. Comment compléteriez-vous les phrases suivantes?

Modèle: Je m'amuse quand **je joue avec mon chien.**

1. Je m'amuse quand _____.
2. Je m'ennuie quand _____.
3. Je m'énerve quand _____.
4. Je me fâche quand _____.
5. Je m'inquiète quand _____.
6. Je me sens triste quand _____.

Ï†Ï Étape 2. Posez les questions à un(e) partenaire.

Modèle: É1: **Quand est-ce que tu t'amuses?**
É2: **Je m'amuse quand je joue avec mon chien. Et toi?**
É1: **Moi, je m'amuse quand mes parents me rendent visite.**

Étape 3. Est-ce que vous et votre partenaire avez des réponses qui sont similaires? Si oui, lesquelles?

Modèle: **Mon partenaire et moi, nous nous fâchons quand nous parlons avec des gens bêtes.**

ACTIVITÉ M Les célébrités

Étape 1. Quelle personne célèbre associez-vous à chaque description suivante?

Modèle: Il/Elle s'aime beaucoup. **Paris Hilton s'aime beaucoup.**

1. Il/Elle se regarde souvent dans le miroir.
2. Il/Elle se connaît bien.
3. Il/Elle s'aime beaucoup.
4. Il/Elle ne s'aime pas bien.
5. Il/Elle ne se connaît pas bien.
6. Il/Elle se parle parfois.

Étape 2. Quelles descriptions de l'Étape 1 vous décrivent aussi?

Modèle: **Je me regarde souvent dans le miroir aussi. Je me connais bien.**

Ï†Ï Étape 3. Demandez à un(e) partenaire si les descriptions de l'Étape 1 le/la décrivent.

Modèle: É1: **Est-ce que tu te regardes souvent dans le miroir?**
É2: **Non, je ne me regarde pas souvent dans le miroir.**

Conclusion Est-ce que votre partenaire et vous êtes similaires ou différent(e)s?

ACTIVITÉ N Dans votre famille

Étape 1. Répondez aux questions au sujet des membres de votre famille.

Modèle: Quelles personnes s'aiment? **Mon frère et moi, nous nous aimons beaucoup.**

1. Quelles personnes s'aiment beaucoup?
2. ... se disputent souvent?
3. ... se voient souvent?
4. ... se connaissent bien?
5. ... se parlent souvent?
6. ... s'entendent bien?
7. ... se fâchent parfois?
8. ... se détestent parfois?
9. ... ne se parlent pas souvent?
10. ... se voient rarement?

Étape 2. Posez les questions à un(e) partenaire.

Modèle: É1: **Quelles personnes dans ta famille s'aiment beaucoup?**
É2: **Mes grands-parents s'aiment beaucoup.**

Étape 3. Écrivez trois choses que vous avez apprises de votre partenaire.

Modèle: **Ses sœurs s'aiment beaucoup. Sa tante et sa mère se disputent souvent. Elles ne s'entendent pas bien.**

Pour aller plus loin
Les verbes réfléchis et les questions

To ask a question using inversion with a reflexive verb, invert the verb and the subject pronoun and place the reflexive pronoun before it.

Nicole **se marie-t-elle** bientôt?	*Is Nicole getting married soon?*
Pourquoi **vous fâchez-vous**?	*Why are you getting angry?*

However, in spoken French, **est-ce que** and intonation are more frequently used.

Nicole **se marie** bientôt?	Pourquoi **est-ce que** vous **vous fâchez**?

Essayez! Posez les questions suivantes à votre professeur avec l'inversion.

Modèle: (se disputer) avec les voisins **Vous disputez-vous avec vos voisins?**

1. (s'amuser) dans le cours de français
2. (s'entendre) bien avec les voisins

La parole est à vous!

Est-ce que les nouveaux moyens de communication changent les interactions entre les gens?

Certaines personnes pensent que les nouveaux moyens de communication (le courriel, les messages instantanés et les textos) changent la façon dont on se comporte *(the way one behaves)* avec les autres. Qu'en pensez-vous?

- Martine de Lomé (Togo): «Un petit peu sans doute. On est peut-être moins formel dans nos relations les uns avec les autres mais on est plus souvent en contact.»
- Justin de Zurich (Suisse): «Absolument! Oui, avec ces nouveaux moyens de communication on devient de plus en plus distant.»

Et vous? Qu'en pensez-vous?

Est-ce que les nouveaux moyens de communication changent les interactions entre les gens? Qu'est-ce qu'on gagne ou perd dans les relations aujourd'hui?

🔊 Les rapports personnels
CD3-14

Personal relationships

Un couple s'installe dans sa nouvelle maison. (s'installer dans / à)

Ils se détendent dans le salon. (se détendre)

Elle se dépêche parce qu'elle est en retard. (se dépêcher)

Il se promène avec son chien dans le parc. (se promener)

Ils s'arrêtent. (s'arrêter)

Ils s'embrassent. (s'embrasser)

Ils se perdent parce que l'homme ne veut pas regarder le plan. (se perdre)

Ils s'excusent. (s'excuser)

Ils se réconcilient. (se réconcilier)

La vie d'un jeune couple

Vocabulaire complémentaire

s'appeler *to be named / called*
se fiancer *to get engaged*
s'intéresser (à) *to be interested (in)*
se méfier (de) *to be suspicious (of)*
s'occuper (de) *to take care (of)*
se passer *to happen*
se rappeler *to remember*
se reposer *to rest*
se téléphoner *to téléphone*
se tromper (de) *to be mistaken (about)*

À mon (votre) avis *In my (your) opinion*
À propos de *About / Speaking of*
Selon *According to*

- **S'appeler, se rappeler,** and **se promener** are spelling-change verbs.

s'appeler	je m'appelle, nous nous appelons
se rappeler (like **s'appeler**)	je me rappelle, nous nous rappelons
se promener (like **acheter**)	je me promène, nous nous promenons

- **Se rappeler** means approximately the same thing as **se souvenir,** and many people use them interchangeably in everyday speech. However, **se rappeler** can be used more often with facts that one recalls and **se souvenir** with memories one remembers. The important difference is grammatical: **on se rappelle quelque chose** *but* **on se souvient <u>de</u> quelque chose.**

- Note the meaning of these verbs when they are used reflexively and non-reflexively.

s'appeler	*to be named / called*
se rappeler	*to remember*
se tromper (de)	*to be mistaken (about)*
appeler	*to call*
rappeler	*to call back*
tromper	*to cheat on (someone)*

Si vous allez à Québec, visitez la promenade des Gouverneurs. La construction de ces planches *(boardwalk)* a débuté en 1958 pour commémorer le 350ᵉ anniversaire de la fondation de Québec par Samuel de Champlain en 1608. 200 000 personnes empruntent chaque année la promenade des Gouverneurs. La vue est vraiment spectaculaire!

Un mot sur la langue

Mon chum et ma blonde

Dans le français parlé au Québec, on peut aussi dire **mon chum** pour **mon petit ami/mon copain** et **ma blonde** pour **ma petite amie/ma copine.**

Luc se promène avec **sa blonde.**

Carole se fiance avec **son chum.**

- Comment s'appelle votre chum ou votre blonde?

ACTIVITÉ A Qui l'a dit? Vous vous rappelez qui a dit les phrases suivantes dans le film *Liaisons*?

1. De temps en temps, **il s'occupe** des réservations spéciales.
   a. Abia   b. Claire   c. Alexis   d. Réceptionniste

2. La chambre 315, c'est la suite présidentielle. Elle **se trouve** au 14ᵉ étage…
   a. Abia   b. Claire   c. Alexis   d. Réceptionniste

3. Quand ma mère est morte, il fallait qu'on **s'occupe de** ses affaires.
   a. Abia   b. Claire   c. Alexis   d. Concierge

4. Vous êtes à Québec pour **vous occuper d'**affaires de famille.
   a. Abia   b. Claire   c. Alexis   d. Concierge

5. C'est l'homme qui m'a donné l'enveloppe avec la réservation au Frontenac.
   Il **s'appelle** Tremblay.
   a. Abia   b. Claire   c. Alexis   d. Robert

6. Je dois **m'en aller**. J'ai beaucoup de choses à faire très tôt demain.
   a. Abia   b. Claire   c. Alexis   d. Concierge

7. Pas de problème. Je vais **m'occuper** de Robert.
   a. Abia   b. Claire   c. Alexis   d. Concierge

8. Je **me rappelle** quand Michel parlait de vous.
   a. Abia   b. Claire   c. Alexis   d. Mme Papillon

ACTIVITÉ B Quelqu'un qui est… Choisissez un verbe pour chaque phrase.

1. Quelqu'un qui est fana de la santé _____ les conseils de son entraîneur *(trainer)*.
   a. se promène   b. se rappelle   c. se fiance   d. se trompe

2. Quelqu'un qui est bourreau de travail ne _____ pas assez.
   a. se passe   b. se réconcilie   c. s'intéresse   d. se détend

3. Quelqu'un qui est célèbre _____ souvent des paparazzi.
   a. se dépêche   b. se promène   c. se méfie   d. se passe

4. Une mère célibataire _____ de ses enfants.
   a. s'occupe   b. s'arrête   c. se téléphone   d. se repose

5. Les retraités _____ plus que les bourreaux de travail.
   a. se trompent   b. se reposent   c. s'installent   d. se passent

6. Les écologistes _____ à l'environnement.
   a. s'intéressent   b. s'embrassent   c. s'appellent   d. se détendent

7. Les gens bavards _____ pas de bavarder *(to gossip)*.
   a. se méfient   b. se rappellent   c. n'arrêtent   d. se réconcilient

8. Les membres de la jet-set _____ toujours dans une suite d'un bel hôtel en vacances.
   a. s'installent   b. s'occupent   c. se méfient   d. se trompent

ACTIVITÉ C La famille d'Abia

Étape 1. Abia décrit ce que les membres de sa famille font ou disent pendant la fête d'anniversaire de sa nièce Aude. Choisissez un verbe pour chaque phrase.

1. Aude _____ son chat Fifi.
   a. appelle   b. s'appelle

2. Xavier _____ en route pour la fête.
   a. perd   b. se perd

3. Papa et l'oncle Kofi _____ leurs clés *(keys)*.
   a. perdent   b. se perdent

4. Aude demande à Patrick «Qu'est-ce qui _____?»
   a. passe   b. se passe

5. Keesha annonce que Jerome va nous _____ plus tard.
   a. rappeler   b. se rappeler

6. Adelai dit qu'il pense que son voisin _____ sa femme.
   a. trompe   b. se trompe

7. Abia pense que son père _____ parce que le voisin est un homme fidèle.
   a. trompe   b. se trompe

Étape 2. Et vous? Complétez les phrases.

1. Je m'appelle _____.

2. Je perds souvent _____.

3. Je me perds parfois _____.

4. Je me rappelle _____.

ACTIVITÉ D L'ami de Robert Levesque Robert, le patron de Claire dans le film *Liaisons* parle de son ami Yves. Complétez les phrases avec la forme appropriée des verbes qui conviennent.

1. Mon ami Yves _____ à Montréal. Il est vendeur dans une boutique.
   a. se passer   b. se dépêcher   c. se rappeler   d. s'installer

2. Nous sommes de bons amis. Nous _____ au parc Lafontaine le week-end.
   a. se promener   b. se tromper   c. se dépêcher   d. se passer

3. Yves _____ de sa sœur Sarah qui a 15 ans.
   a. s'occuper   b. se téléphoner   c. s'arrêter   d. se reposer

4. Ce soir, nous _____ parce que nous allons à un concert.
   a. s'intéresser   b. se passer   c. s'occuper   d. se dépêcher

5. Je _____ souvent donc il faut partir très tôt.
   a. se fiancer   b. se méfier   c. se perdre   d. s'excuser

6. Yves _____ souvent d'adresse aussi.
   a. s'appeler   b. s'intéresser   c. s'embrasser   d. se tromper

7. Mais ce soir on n'a pas besoin de _____ pour demander notre chemin *(to ask for directions)*.
   a. se méfier   b. s'arrêter   c. se tromper   d. se passer

8. Nous arrivons au concert. Nous _____ en écoutant *(while listening)* de la musique.
   a. se détendre   b. se fiancer   c. s'excuser   d. s'installer

⋯ **Et vous?** Est-ce que vous vous perdez facilement?

ACTIVITÉ **E** **Questionnaire: Mode de vie**

Étape 1. Répondez aux questions suivantes.

	Oui	Non
1. Est-ce que vous vous méfiez de l'amitié ou de l'amour?	_____	_____
2. Est-ce que vous vous occupez de votre santé?	_____	_____
3. Est-ce que vous vous intéressez plus au travail qu'aux vacances?	_____	_____
4. Est-ce que vous vous rappelez toujours qu'il faut économiser de l'énergie?	_____	_____
5. Est-ce que vous vous intéressez à l'amour?	_____	_____
6. Est-ce que vous vous reposez souvent?	_____	_____

Étape 2. Posez les questions de l'Étape 1 à un(e) partenaire. Notez ses réponses.

Modèle: Est-ce que tu te méfies de l'amitié ou de l'amour?

Étape 3. À partir de vos réponses aux questions de l'Étape 1 et des réponses de votre partenaire aux questions de l'Étape 2, pour quel(s) mode(s) de vie êtes-vous fait(e)s?

ACTIVITÉ **F** **Interview avec Michel Cymes et Marina Carrère d'Encausse** Michel Cymes et Marina Carrère d'Encausse sont les présentateurs du *Magazine de la santé* sur la chaîne *(channel)* de télévision France 5. Voici un extrait d'une interview avec Audrey Aveaux, fana de la santé, diététicienne et auteur célèbre de livres de cuisine. Inventez une réponse logique pour chaque question.

Modèle: Question: À votre avis, on doit se méfier des matières grasses?
Réponse: **Oui, il faut arrêter de manger des matières grasses et du sucre.**

1. Question: Selon vous, il faut manger des produits bio. Est-ce que vous vous méfiez des produits non biologiques?

   Réponse: _____

2. Question: À votre avis, est-ce qu'on peut trop se reposer?

   Réponse: _____

3. Question: Est-ce que vos ami(e)s s'occupent de leur santé comme vous?

   Réponse: _____

4. Question: À quoi est-ce que vous allez vous intéresser l'année prochaine?

   Réponse: _____

Et vous? Répondez aux questions.

1. Est-ce que vous vous méfiez des produits non biologiques?

   Réponse: _____

2. Est-ce que vous vous reposez assez?

   Réponse: _____

3. Est-ce que vous vous occupez bien de votre santé?

   Réponse: _____

ACTIVITÉ **G** **Sondage: À propos de la communication en public**

Posez les questions suivantes à trois étudiants pour découvrir leurs opinions.

1. Que pensez-vous des gens qui s'embrassent en public?
2. Que pensez-vous des gens qui se fiancent en public?
3. Que pensez-vous des gens qui se disputent en public?
4. Selon vous, est-ce qu'on devrait s'excuser en public?
5. À votre avis, est-ce qu'on devrait se réconcilier en public?

Un mot sur la langue

C'est le fun!

Une expression populaire qu'on entend souvent au Québec est **C'est le fun!** En français standard, cette expression veut dire **C'est amusant!** ou **C'est génial!** *(That's great!)* Les Québécois disent parfois aussi **J'ai du fun** pour **Je m'amuse bien.** Donc, **avoir du fun** est un peu comme le verbe **s'amuser** en français standard.

J'ai du fun chez toi!	Je **m'amuse** chez toi!
On va **avoir du fun** ce soir!	On va **s'amuser** ce soir!
C'est le fun d'avoir vos amis ici.	**C'est amusant** d'avoir vos amis ici.
Le Carnaval de Québec, **c'est le fun**!	Le Carnaval de Québec, **c'est amusant**!

• Êtes-vous d'accord avec cette phrase? **Apprendre le français, c'est le fun!**

Un mot sur la culture

© Jane September/Shutterstock.com

L'espace privé et l'espace public en France

En Amérique du Nord, quand on rencontre une personne pour la première fois, on a l'habitude de lui poser des questions telles que «Comment vous appelez-vous?» ou «Qu'est-ce que vous faites dans la vie?». Cependant, si vous posez ces mêmes° questions en France, on va vous trouver impoli(e). Les Français ont une conception de l'espace° privé et de l'espace public qui est différente de celle des Américains. En France, le nom de quelqu'un ainsi que° sa profession appartiennent°

à l'espace privé. Les Français se demandent souvent pourquoi les Américains s'intéressent tellement° à la vie privée des gens, surtout la vie privée des hommes et des femmes politiques. Par contre°, c'est tout à fait° normal pour les Français d'exprimer° leurs sentiments ou de se montrer affectueux en public. On peut aussi voir les Français se disputer et s'embrasser en public.

mêmes *same* **l'espace** *space* **ainsi que** *as well as* **appartiennent** *belongs* **tellement** *so much* **Par contre** *On the contrary*
tout à fait *entirely* **exprimer** *to express*

• Posez-vous la question «Qu'est-ce que vous faites dans la vie?»?

Pour parler du passé
Les verbes réfléchis au passé composé

DU FILM *LIAISONS*

···

Un coup d'œil sur la grammaire

Look at these photos from the film *Liaisons* and their captions.

CLAIRE Merci, Alexis. Je **me suis bien amusée** aujourd'hui.

CLAIRE Pardon? Mais qu'est-ce qui **s'est passé**?

1. What two reflexive verbs do you recognize in the two photo captions?
2. Is the auxiliary verb **avoir** or **être** used in the photo captions?
3. Why is there an **e** at the end of **amusée** in the left caption?

❖❖❖ Reflexive verbs always take **être** in the **passé composé.** The reflexive pronoun goes before the verb **être** and there is usually agreement between the past participle and the subject pronoun.

Ils **se sont excusés.**	*They apologized.*
Nous **nous sommes occupés** du problème.	*We took care of the problem.*
Vous **vous êtes mariés** en 2002.	*You got married in 2002.*
Elle **s'est mise à** faire ses devoirs.	*She began to do her homework.*

❖❖❖ The past participle *does not* agree with the subject pronoun when the reflexive pronoun is an indirect object. If the non-reflexive form of the verb takes **à** + *indirect object*, the reflexive pronoun is an indirect object.

téléphoner à quelqu'un: Ils **se sont téléphoné** hier.	*They **called each other** yesterday.*
parler à quelqu'un: Elles **se sont parlé** hier.	*They **spoke to each other** yesterday.*

❖❖❖ The past participle of **se rendre compte** also never agrees with its subject pronoun.

Elles **se sont rendu compte** de l'heure.	*They realized the time.*

Note de grammaire

The conditionnel and **imparfait** of reflexive verbs are formed just like for non-reflexive verbs: **je me perdrais, on s'amusait.**

To form negative statements with reflexive verbs in the **passé composé,** put **ne** before the reflexive pronouns and **pas** after the conjugated auxiliary verb **être.**

Ils **ne se sont pas disputés** hier soir.　　*They **didn't fight** with each other last night.*

Elle **ne s'est pas installée** dans la maison.　　*She **didn't move** into the house.*

To ask a question using inversion with a reflexive verb in the **passé composé,** invert the auxiliary verb **être** and the subject pronoun. Place the reflexive pronoun before the auxiliary verb.

Luc **s'est-il perdu** à Montréal?　　*Did Luc get lost in Montreal?*

In spoken French, intonation and **est-ce que** are more frequently used to ask questions with reflexive verbs than inversion.

Est-ce que tu t'es fâché avec lui?　　*Did you get angry with him?*

Vous vous êtes mis à travailler à 20h00?　　*You began to work at 8 pm?*

Liaisons musicales

© POL Emile/SIPA/Newscom

Richard Anthony est un chanteur français connu pour ses reprises *(covers)* françaises des chansons étrangères des années 60, surtout de style twist et rock. Cherchez les paroles de sa chanson *Je me suis souvent demandé* (1965) et trouvez ce qu'il s'est souvent demandé. ⊕

ACTIVITÉ H Couples célèbres Complétez ces phrases avec la (les) célébrité(s) qui rend(ent) chaque phrase vraie.

Possibilités: A. Banderas, C. Cox et D. Arquette, A. Jolie et B. Pitt, J. Lopez et B. Affleck

1. _____ se sont rencontrés en jouant dans *(while acting in) Mr. et Mrs. Smith* (2005).
2. _____ se sont mariés en 1999 après avoir joué *(after acting)* dans *Scream 2* (1997).
3. _____ s'est marié avec Melanie Griffiths en 1996.
4. _____ se sont quittés en 2004 pour Marc Anthony et Jennifer Garner, respectivement.

ACTIVITÉ I Comment sont ces étudiants? Complétez ces phrases avec le participe passé qui convient.

1. Ils ne se sont pas _____. 　　a. excusé　　b. excusés.
2. Elles ne se sont pas _____. 　　a. réconcilié　　b. réconciliées
3. Nous ne nous sommes pas _____ aux études. 　　a. intéressé　　b. intéressés
4. Elles se sont _____ à cause des problèmes au prof. 　　a. mis　　b. mises
5. Nous nous sommes _____ pendant le cours. 　　a. disputé　　b. disputés
6. Ils se sont _____ pendant que le prof parlait. 　　a. parlé　　b. parlés

Conclusion Ces étudiants sont-ils de bons ou de mauvais étudiants?

ACTIVITÉ J Les cousins d'Abia

Étape 1. Les cousins d'Abia parlent de leurs activités. Indiquez qui a dit chaque phrase: **(a) Jerome** ou **(b) Cindy.**

Jerome

Cindy

1. Je me suis détendu chez moi.
2. Je me suis détendue chez Stéphanie.
3. Je ne me suis pas occupé de mon chien.
4. Je me suis promenée dans le parc.
5. Je me suis amusée avec mes amis.
6. Je ne me suis pas occupée de Fifi
7. Je me suis disputée avec Nadia.
8. Je me suis amusé avec Patrick.

Étape 2. Et vous? Répondez aux questions avec des phrases complètes.

Modèle: Est-ce que vous vous êtes amusé(e) avec votre voisin hier?
Non, je ne me suis pas amusé(e) avec mon voisin hier.

1. Est-ce que vous vous êtes amusé(e) avec vos amis hier?
2. Est-ce que vous vous êtes occupé(e) de votre linge *(laundry)* hier?
3. Est-ce que vous vous êtes disputé(e) avec un professeur hier?
4. Est-ce que vous vous êtes détendu(e) devant la télévision hier?

Étape 3. Posez les questions à un(e) partenaire. Avez-vous fait les mêmes choses hier?

Modèle: Est-ce que tu t'es amusé(e) avec tes amis hier?

ACTIVITÉ K Quand ils étaient petits Que faisaient régulièrement vos camarades de classe quand ils étaient petits? Posez ces questions à deux camarades de classe.

1. Comment est-ce que vous vous amusiez le samedi matin?
2. Vous vous entendiez bien avec qui?
3. Vous vous méfiiez de qui?
4. Vous vous disputiez souvent avec qui?
5. Qu'est-ce que vous faisiez quand vous vous ennuyiez?

Conclusion Les deux camarades de classe étaient-ils similaires ou différents quand ils étaient petits?

ACTIVITÉ L Des rêves bizarres Faites-vous parfois des rêves bizarres sur des célébrités? Inventez des rêves (au passé composé).

Modèle: Angelina Jolie s'est rendu compte que Brad Pitt n'est pas un bon mari.

Suggestions			
s'amuser	s'embrasser	s'intéresser à	(se) quitter
(se) demander	se fâcher	se marier	se réconcilier
se détester	se fiancer	se méfier de	se rendre compte de / que
se disputer	s'installer	se parler	(se) tromper

1. Johnny Depp…
2. Lindsay Lohan…
3. Miley Cyrus…
4. Les frères Jonas…
5. Kristen Stewart et Robert Pattinson…
6. Venus et Serena Williams…
7. Tom Cruise et _____…
8. Mon professeur…
9. Moi, je…
10. _____ et moi, nous…

Pour aller plus loin

Les verbes réfléchis à l'impératif

The imperative of reflexive verbs is formed as it is for non-reflexive verbs. In affirmative commands, the reflexive pronoun follows the verb with a hyphen; **toi** is used instead of **te/t'**. In negative commands, the reflexive pronoun precedes the verb.

Amuse-**toi** bien!	*Have a good time!*
Dépêchez-**vous**!	*Hurry up!*
Téléphonons-**nous** ce soir.	*Let's phone each other tonight.*
Ne **t'**inquiète pas.	*Don't worry.*
Ne **vous** sentez pas mal.	*Don't feel bad.*
Ne **nous** téléphonons pas.	*Let's not phone each other.*

··

Essayez! Que diriez-vous aux personnes suivantes?

Modèle: (s'inquiéter) Un ami a perdu son emploi. **Ne t'inquiète pas.**

1. (se reposer) Votre ami est très fatigué aujourd'hui. _____
2. (se dépêcher) Votre ami est en retard pour son cours de français. _____
3. (se perdre) Votre ami doit aller à une ville qu'il ne connaît pas bien. _____
4. (s'amuser) Vos amis vont aller à une fête ce soir. _____
5. (s'inquiéter) Vos amis ont un examen et ils sont nerveux. _____
6. (se disputer) Vous devez étudier mais vos colocataires se disputent. _____

La parole est à vous!

Est-ce que les jeunes aujourd'hui ont moins de respect pour leurs aînés?

On entend souvent dire aujourd'hui que les jeunes ont moins de respect qu'autrefois° pour leurs aînés°. Qu'en pensez-vous?

- Henri-Georges de Paris (France): «C'est certainement le cas où je travaille, peut-être moins dans la vie en général. Les jeunes qui sortent des universités pensent qu'on leur doit tout, même depuis le début. C'est difficile pour eux de respecter la hiérarchie.»

- Louise de Bruxelles (Belgique): «Je crois que ça dépend de l'individu. J'ai quelques jeunes collègues qui se rendent compte qu'ils ont des choses à apprendre des anciens comme moi. Du coup°, ils nous respectent. Mais ce n'est pas toujours le cas.»

autrefois *in the past* **aînés** *elders* **Du coup** *Thus*

Et vous? Qu'en pensez-vous?

Est-ce que les jeunes aujourd'hui ont moins de respect pour leurs aînés qu'autrefois?

🔊 L'expression personnelle

Personal expression

Les médias

Vocabulaire complémentaire

un article *article*

un hebdomadaire / un hebdo *a weekly (magazine, newspaper) publication*

un (magazine) mensuel *a monthly (magazine) publication*

la messagerie instantanée *instant messaging*

un message instantané *an instant message*

un (journal) quotidien *a daily (newspaper) publication*

un réseau social *a social network*

un site Web *a website*

un fait *a fact*

une idée *an idea*

une pensée *a thought*

les potins / un potin *a gossip / a piece of gossip*

un sentiment *a feeling*

déranger *to bother, to upset*

écœurer *to sicken, to gross out*

exprimer *to express*

faire plaisir à quelqu'un *to please someone*

pleurer *to cry*

raconter *to tell (about), to narrate*

regretter *to regret, to be sorry about*

rendre quelqu'un (heureux) *to make someone (happy)*

ressentir *to feel (emotion—sadness)*

toucher *to touch, to deeply move*

C'est dommage! *That's too bad!*

Enfin! *Finally!*

Formidable! / Génial! *Great! / Awesome!*

Je regrette. / Je suis désolé(e). *I'm sorry.*

Merveilleux! / Super! *Marvelous! Wonderful! Super!*

d'autres fois *other times*

de temps en temps *from time to time*

parfois / quelquefois *sometimes, at times*

la plupart du temps *most of the time*

Note de vocabulaire

Note that **s'ennuyer** means *to be bored,* but **ennuyer** means *to bore:* **Je m'ennuie.** *(I am bored.)* **Les potins m'ennuient.** *(Gossip bores me.)*

Pour aller plus loin
Les adjectifs à partir des verbes

You can make adjectives out of most regular and irregular verbs in French by dropping the **-ons** ending from the **nous** form of the verb conjugated in present tense and adding **-ant(e)(s)**.

Anne est vraiment **énervante** aujourd'hui.   *Anne is really irritating today.*

C'est **bouleversant**.   *That's overwhelming.*

Les deux lettres sont très **touchantes**.   *The two letters are very touching.*

Essayez! Qu'est-ce que vous pensez des sujets suivants? Sont-ils **inquiétants, ennuyants, troublants, amusants, écœurants, reposants,** etc.?

1. la politique
2. le climat économique
3. les films de Ron Howard
4. Fox News

◀)) **ACTIVITÉ A** **C'est quelle publication?** Identifiez le genre de publication
CD3-15 pour chaque exemple mentionné.

1. a. un journal intime
   b. un quotidien
   c. un hebdomadaire
2. a. un quotidien
   b. un blog
   c. une revue
3. a. un microblogging
   b. un magazine
   c. un blog
4. a. un quotidien
   b. un journal intime
   c. un magazine de mode
5. a. un article
   b. un mensuel
   c. un hebdomadaire
6. a. un blog
   b. un réseau social
   c. une messagerie instantanée
7. a. un réseau social
   b. une revue
   c. un journal intime
8. a. un article
   b. un microblogging
   c. un hebdomadaire

Si vous y allez

Si vous allez à Paris, allez voir les bouquinistes *(booksellers)* sur le bord de la Seine entre le pont Marie et le quai du Louvre.

© Ekaterina Pokrovsky / Shutterstock.com

◀)) **ACTIVITÉ B** **Exclamations** Quelle phrase déclenche logiquement chaque
CD3-16 exclamation que vous entendez?

1. a. Tu me déranges là.
   b. Ça me rend très heureux.
2. a. C'est bouleversant.
   b. Comment tu te sens?
3. a. J'ai perdu mon chien.
   b. Je me sens très bien.
4. a. Tu m'énerves!
   b. Ça me fait très plaisir.
5. a. Ça me rend triste.
   b. Je ressens de la joie.
6. a. Ça m'écœure.
   b. Ça me touche beaucoup.

ACTIVITÉ C **Vous êtes discrets / discrètes?**

Étape 1. Indiquez les publications dans lesquelles vous exprimeriez les choses ci-dessous *(below)*: **dans un blog, dans un microblog, dans un journal intime, dans un message instantané** ou **dans un courriel.**

1. raconter votre journée
2. raconter vos projets
3. raconter des potins
4. exprimer vos pensées intimes
5. exprimer vos sentiments personnels
6. exprimer vos idées sur la vie

Étape 2. Formulez et posez des questions à un(e) partenaire. Est-ce que vous êtes discret / discrète?

Modèle: Dans quel genre de publication est-ce que tu raconterais ta journée?

ACTIVITÉ D **Langue des textos** Faites correspondre les abréviations avec leur signification.

1. _____ A+
2. _____ MDR
3. _____ mr6
4. _____ SQZ
5. _____ OQP
6. _____ NRV

a. Mort de rire
b. À plus tard
c. Merci
d. Occupé
e. Énervé
f. Excuse-moi!

ACTIVITÉ Ⓔ **État d'esprit**

CD3-17 **Étape 1.** Indiquez votre état d'esprit *(state of mind)* pour chaque activité mentionnée.

Ça me dérange.	Ça m'ennuie.	Ça me fait plaisir.	Ça m'énerve.
1. _____	_____	_____	_____
2. _____	_____	_____	_____
3. _____	_____	_____	_____
4. _____	_____	_____	_____

Étape 2. Répondez à ces questions et puis montrez vos réponses à un(e) camarade de classe. Avez-vous des tendances similaires ou bien différentes?

1. Qui ou qu'est-ce qui *(What)* vous dérange le plus dans la vie?
2. Qui ou qu'est-ce qui vous écœure le plus dans la vie?
3. Qui ou qu'est-ce qui vous plaît le plus dans la vie?
4. Qui ou qu'est-ce qui vous touche le plus dans la vie?
5. Qui ou qu'est-ce qui vous fait pleurer?

ACTIVITÉ Ⓕ **Émoticônes** Indiquez *le smiley* qui correspond à chaque émotion suivante.

Possibilités

a. :-)   b. :-(c. :-| d. :'-)   e. xP   f. :-<

1. _____ Ça me rend heureux / heureuse.
2. _____ Je m'ennuie.
3. _____ Ça ne me fait pas plaisir.
4. _____ Je veux pleurer
5. _____ Ça me touche vraiment.
6. _____ Je suis écœuré(e).

Et vous? Quels *smileys* utilisez-vous pour exprimer vos émotions?

ACTIVITÉ Ⓖ **Moyens de communication et d'expression** Indiquez les moyens de communication d'**il y a 20 ans** et ceux d'**aujourd'hui** pour ces besoins.

	Il y a 20 ans	Aujourd'hui
1. Pour rester en contact avec des amis	_____	_____
2. Pour parler des activités de la journée	_____	_____
3. Pour poser une question à un collègue	_____	_____
4. Pour exprimer ses pensées intimes	_____	_____
5. Pour se renseigner au sujet *(to become informed about)* des actualités	_____	_____
6. Pour apprendre ce qui s'est passé dans un cours qu'on a séché *(skipped)*	_____	_____
7. Pour se renseigner sur les nouvelles tendances de la mode	_____	_____
8. Pour connaître les gens	_____	_____

Conclusion Est-ce que les moyens de communication ont changé pour le meilleur ou le pire?

ACTIVITÉ Ⓗ **Répliques attendues**

Quelles expressions est-ce que Claire utiliserait pour répondre si Abia lui disait ces phrases?

Modèle: J'ai réussi à mon examen.   **Formidable!**

1. La pizza m'a rendue malade hier.

2. Je me suis beaucoup dérangée pour venir.

3. Je me sentais mieux ce matin.

4. Je m'ennuie. Et si on allait au cinéma?

© Heinle/Cengage Learning

Et vous? Comment répondriez-vous à votre meilleur(e) ami(e)?

ACTIVITÉ Ⓘ **Vos télécommunications**

Étape 1. Faites trois ou quatre phrases qui expriment vos expériences et/ou pratiques de télécommunication.

Modèle: **Parfois, j'exprime mes sentiments dans un blog. La plupart du temps, je fais du microblogging. De temps en temps, je mets des photos sur mon réseau social.**

Possibilités

parfois	exprimer	des faits	un appareil photo numérique
d'autres fois	lire / écrire	des idées	la messagerie instantanée
de temps en temps	mettre	des pensées	le microblogging
la plupart du temps	publier	des photos	un réseau social
toujours	regretter	des potins	un site Web / un blog

Étape 2. Lisez vos phrases à deux ou trois camarades de classe. Demandez-leur si vous pratiquez du «bon sens» sur Internet ou pas! Si c'est non, ont-ils des conseils pour vous?

Un mot sur la culture

© Marlene Awaad/Maxppp / Landov

Les réseaux sociaux en France

Les réseaux sociaux sont tellement populaires en France qu'il y a plusieurs classements°. On compte des réseaux sociaux *pro* (à but° professionnel: trouver des postes), *perso* (à but personnel: rester en contact avec des amis ou la famille) et *fun* (à but récréatif: partager des informations sur les loisirs). D'après une étude française réalisée en 2010, les internautes° français appartiennent° aux réseaux sociaux suivants, par ordre de popularité: Copainsdavant.com (49%), Windows Live (46%), Facebook (37%), MySpace (8%) et Twitter (5%).

classements *classifications* **buts** *goals* **internautes** *Internet users* **appartiennent** *belong*

◀)) Liaisons avec les mots et les sons

CD3-18
Les semi-voyelles

French has three semi-vowels, which are letter combinations that sound like vowels that glide from or into an accompanying vowel sound.

A semi-vowel sound occurs with **u** when it is pronounced like the vowel sound in **tu**. The sound then glides into the following vowel.

intellect**uel**	s**ui**s	biling**ui**sme	l**ui**	spirit**ua**lité	mens**uel**

A semi-vowel sound occurs with **y, i,** or **ill** when they are pronounced like the English *ee*. The sound then glides into the following sound.

fam**ille**	nat**io**nal	b**ie**n	ch**ie**n	**pay**er	br**ill**ant	b**ill**ets

A semi-vowel sound occurs with **o** or **ou** when they are pronounced like the English *w* as in **soif.** The sound then glides into the following sound.

oui	m**oi**	b**oî**te	framb**oi**se	b**oi**re	Lou**i**s XIV	b**oi**s

Pratique A. Écoutez et répétez ces mots. Soulignez *(Underline)* les semi-voyelles **u.** Encerclez *(Circle)* les semi-voyelles **y, i, ill.** Cochez *(check)* les semi-voyelles **o** et **ou.**

1. d'autres f**ois**
2. parf**ois**
3. se v**oir**
4. merve**ill**eux
5. se **pay**er
6. orgue**ill**euse
7. enn**uy**er
8. intellect**uel**
9. j**ui**n
10. fianç**aill**es
11. j**uill**et
12. m**ois**

Pratique B. Écoutez et répétez ces répliques de la Séquence 5 du film *Liaisons.* Soulignez *(Underline)* les mots avec des semi-voyelles.

ALEXIS [...] cette fois-ci, ce n'est pas une coïncidence. Nous avons rendez-vous.

CLAIRE Oui. Allons-y?

ALEXIS Allons voir ce que cette belle capitale nous propose.

© Heinle/Cengage Learning

◀)) **À vos stylos! C'est l'heure de la dictée!**
CD3-19 Vous allez entendre trois phrases deux fois. La première fois, écoutez bien. La deuxième fois, écrivez les phrases.

Sujet Citations célèbres

Pour exprimer la négation

Les expressions négatives

DU FILM *LIAISONS*

···

Un coup d'œil sur la grammaire

Look at these photos from the film ***Liaisons*** and their captions, focusing on the negative expressions.

© Heinle/Cengage Learning

RÉCEPTIONNISTE Avez-vous besoin d'aide avec vos valises *(suitcases)*?

CLAIRE Non. Ça va. Je **n'**en ai **qu'**une.

CLAIRE Mon oncle Michel? Et la personne qui a téléphoné, c'était qui?

ABIA Je **n'**en ai **aucune** idée.

1. In the left caption, what does **Je n'en ai qu'une** mean?
2. In the right caption, what do you think **Je n'ai aucune idée** means?

⁖ You already know how to make sentences negative using **ne... pas.** Here are some other common negative expressions and their affirmative counterparts. The placement of these negative expressions is the same as **ne... pas.**

AFFIRMATIVE	NEGATIVE
toujours *always*	**ne... jamais** *never*
encore *still*	**ne... plus** *no longer, no more*
déjà *already*	**ne... pas encore** *not yet*

Je suis **toujours** en retard. — *I am **always** late.*

Je **ne** suis **jamais** en retard. — *I am **never** late.*

Guy parle **encore** avec ses amis de lycée. — *Guy **still** speaks with his high school friends.*

Marie **ne** parle **plus** avec ses amis. — *Marie **no longer** speaks to her friends.*

⁖ The following are additional useful negative expressions.

ne... aucun(e)	*none, not any*	**ne... pas du tout**	*not at all*
ne... personne	*nobody, no one*	**ne... que**	*only*
ne... rien	*nothing, not anything*	**ne... ni... ni**	*neither ... nor*

Je **ne** vois **personne**.	*I don't see **anyone**.*
Il **n'**y a **rien** dans le frigo!	*There's **nothing** in the fridge!*
Elle **n'**aime **pas du tout** étudier.	*She does not like to study **at all**.*
Ils **n'**ont **que** trois euros.	*They **only** have three euros.*
Guy **ne** fait **que** m'ennuyer.	*Guy does **nothing but** bore me.*

- **Aucun(e)** is an adjective and must agree with the noun it modifies.

Elle **n'**a **aucune** idée.	*She does **not** have **any** idea.*
On **ne** trouve **aucun** livre ici.	*We can't find **any** book here.*

- Note that three negative words are required to express *neither . . . nor*: **ne... ni... ni.** Partitive and indefinite articles are not used.

Je **n'**ai **ni** le temps **ni** la patience.	*I have neither the time nor the patience.*
Elle **n'**a **ni** stylo **ni** papier.	*She has neither pen nor paper.*

- The placement of these negative expressions in the **passé composé** is similar to **ne... pas** with the exceptions of **ne... personne** and **ne...aucun(e)**, which surround the entire verb.

—Vous avez **déjà** vu le spectacle?	*—You've **already** seen the show?*
—Non, nous **ne** l'avons **pas encore** vu.	*—No, we have **not** seen it **yet**.*
Je **n'**ai **rien** trouvé aujourd'hui.	*I didn't find **anything** today.*
Elle **n'**a **plus** parlé de Jean.	*She didn't speak about Jean **anymore**.*
Tu **n'**as écouté **personne**.	*You did not listen to **anyone**.*
Il **n'**a eu **aucune** réponse.	*He didn't get a **single** response.*

- **Rien** and **personne** can also be the subject of a sentence.

—Que se passe-t-il ici?	*—What's going on here?*
—**Rien ne** se passe ici.	*—Nothing's going on here.*
—**Rien.**	*—Nothing.*
—Qui est là?	*—Who's there?*
—**Personne n'**est là.	*—Nobody / No one is here.*
—**Personne.**	*—Nobody / No one.*

- You can double up **jamais, personne, plus, aucun(e)**, and **rien** with **ne**.

Vous **ne** travaillez **jamais** avec **personne**.	*You never work with anyone.*
Il **n'**y a **plus rien** à dire.	*There's nothing more to say.*
Elles **ne** font **jamais rien**.	*They never do anything.*
Aucun blog **ne** m'intéresse **jamais**.	*No blog ever interests me.*

- Like **quelque chose** and **quelqu'un, personne**, and **rien** can be modified with a masculine adjective after **de**.

Il n'y avait **personne d'intéressant** à la fête.	*There was **no one interesting** at the party.*
Je ne trouve **rien de nouveau** ici.	*I am not finding **anything new** here.*

- **Moi non plus** (*Me neither*) is the negative form of the common expression **moi aussi** (*me too*).

—**Moi aussi.**	—**Moi non plus.**

ACTIVITÉ J Qui le dirait? À votre avis, qui dirait chaque phrase suivante: **(a) un adolescent de 15 ans, (b) un adulte de 75 ans** ou **(c) tous les deux?**

1. Je **n**'aime **pas du tout** le microblogging.

2. Je **n**'ai lu **rien d'intéressant** sur mon réseau social aujourd'hui.

3. Je **n**'ai **pas encore** d'appareil photo numérique.

4. Je **ne** vois **plus** mes amis.

5. Je **ne** lis **jamais** le magazine *Reader's Digest*.

6. Je **n**'ai **ni** enfant **ni** petit-enfant.

7. Je **n**'ai reçu **aucun** message instantané aujourd'hui.

ACTIVITÉ K Comment était votre week-end?

Étape 1. Complétez chaque phrase avec **(a) Quelqu'un** ou **(b) Personne.** Puis, indiquez si la phrase est vraie ou fausse pour vous.

1. _____ m'a rendu visite.

2. _____ **ne** m'a téléphoné.

3. _____ **ne** m'a envoyé de courriel.

4. _____ **ne** m'a invité(e) à dîner.

5. _____ m'a invité(e) à aller au cinéma.

6. _____ **n**'a étudié avec moi.

Étape 2. Demandez à un(e) partenaire si quelqu'un a fait ces activités avec ou pour lui/elle. Est-ce que votre partenaire était sociable ou solitaire le week-end dernier?

Modèle: É1: **Est-ce que quelqu'un t'a rendu visite le week-end dernier?**
É2: **Non, personne ne m'a rendu visite.**

ACTIVITÉ L Moi aussi! Moi non plus! Avec un(e) partenaire, indiquez si vous aimez ou si vous n'aimez pas ces choses.

Modèle: les revues
É1: **Moi, j'aime les revues. / Moi, je n'aime pas les revues.**
É2: **Moi aussi! / Moi non plus!**

1. les magazines de mode

2. le microblogging

3. les textos

4. le magazine *Sports Illustrated*

5. les réseaux sociaux

6. les potins

ACTIVITÉ M Les célébrités et vous Comparez votre vie avec celle des célébrités.

Modèle: Bill Gates a plus de dix maisons.   **Moi, je n'ai qu'une maison.**

1. Martha Stewart a plus de cinq frigos.

2. Kelly Ripa a plus de trois iPods.

3. Régis Philbin a plus de huit téléphones.

4. Ashton Kutcher a plus de six téléviseurs.

Liaisons musicales

© AFP/Getty Images

Chanteur de raï et de pop et acteur français d'origine algérienne, Faudel chante en arabe et en français. Cherchez les paroles de sa chanson *Je n'ai que mon cœur* (2003) et trouvez une raison pour laquelle il n'a que son cœur à offrir à son amour. 🌐

ACTIVITÉ N **Kofi et Marie-Claire**

Étape 1. Kofi (l'oncle d'Abia du film *Liaisons*) et sa conjointe Marie-Claire se sont quittés parce qu'ils sont trop différents. Kofi est une personne positive et sociable mais Marie-Claire est très négative. Décrivez Marie-Claire.

Modèle: Kofi s'amuse souvent avec ses amis.

Marie-Claire ne s'amuse jamais avec ses amis.

1. Kofi va souvent au cinéma.
2. Kofi voit encore ses amis de lycée.
3. Kofi aime danser et chanter.
4. Kofi a beaucoup d'amis.
5. Kofi adore faire la fête.
6. Kofi a toujours quelque chose de positif à dire.

Étape 2. Posez les questions à un(e) partenaire. Est-ce qu'il/elle est comme Kofi ou comme Marie-Claire?

Modèle: É1: **Est-ce que tu vas souvent au cinéma?**
É2: **Oui, je vais souvent au cinéma. / Non, je ne vais jamais au cinéma.**

ACTIVITÉ O **La vie d'étudiant**

Étape 1. Écrivez quatre à cinq raisons de se plaindre de *(complain about)* sa vie d'étudiant en utilisant des expressions négatives.

Modèle: **Je n'ai jamais le temps de sortir avec mes amis.**

Étape 2. Montrez votre liste à un(e) partenaire. Êtes-vous d'accord avec les raisons de votre partenaire?

La parole est à vous!

Est-ce que la vie privée n'existe plus dans la société contemporaine?

Avec toutes les nouvelles technologies de communication qui sortent chaque année et la tendance des jeunes à raconter toute leur vie sur Internet, on commence à se poser la question: «La vie privée n'existe-t-elle plus dans la société contemporaine?» Qu'en pensez-vous?

• Delphine de Carnoux (France): «Si, la vie privée existe toujours— même chez les jeunes. Je peux toujours garder un secret. Je ne raconte pas tous les détails de ma vie.»

• Loïc d'Ottawa (Canada): «Je crois que non. Avec la prolifération des textos, du microblogging et des messages instantanés en vue d'humilier les autres, les gens—et surtout les jeunes—ne savent plus les limites entre la vie publique et la vie privée.»

Et vous? Qu'en pensez-vous?

Est-ce que la vie privée n'existe plus dans la société contemporaine?

DEUXIÈME
PROJECTION

LIAISONS SÉQUENCE 5:
Une rencontre

Avant de visionner

ACTIVITÉ Ⓐ **Vous rappelez-vous?** Vous rappelez-vous ce qui s'est passé dans la Séquence 5 du film *Liaisons*? Pour chaque phrase, indiquez si c'est vrai ou faux.

	Vrai	Faux
1. Claire et Alexis se sont embrassés après leur rendez-vous.	☐	☐
2. Claire a vu un petit garçon qui pleurait dans une église.	☐	☐
3. Claire a appris que son oncle est mort.	☐	☐
4. Claire doit aller en France pour un enterrement.	☐	☐

ACTIVITÉ Ⓑ **Une scène du film** Vous rappelez-vous cette scène? Claire et Alexis sont devant le Château Frontenac après leur rendez-vous. Écrivez les mots qui manquent *(are missing)*.

© Heinle/Cengage Learning

ALEXIS Il y a des choses que (1) _____ vous dire, (pause) mais...

CLAIRE (2) _____?

ALEXIS C'est que... (3) _____ que vous pourrez nous pardonner.

CLAIRE Pardonner? Pardonner à (4) _____? Alexis, que voulez-vous (5) _____?

ALEXIS (6) _____ moi. Ce n'est (7) _____. Je... La fatigue. Je divague *(am rambling).* Bon. Je dois (8) _____. J'ai beaucoup de choses à faire très tôt demain.

> ### Regarder la séquence
>
> Vous allez regarder la Séquence 5 du film *Liaisons*. Vérifiez vos réponses à l'Activité A et à l'Activité B.

Après le visionnage

ACTIVITÉ C Avez-vous une bonne mémoire?

Étape 1. Répondez aux questions pour voir si vous avez une bonne mémoire. Après, montrez vos réponses à un(e) partenaire. Avez-vous les mêmes réponses?

1. Est-ce que vous vous rappelez l'adresse de l'église où Claire a vu la petite fille?
2. La petite fille dans le rêve de Claire, elle avait environ *(approximately)* quel âge?
3. Comment s'appelle la femme qui a trouvé le corps *(body)* de l'oncle Michel?
4. Vers quelle heure l'oncle Michel est-il mort?

Étape 2. Avec votre partenaire, répondez à la question suivante: À votre avis, qu'est-ce qu'Alexis voulait dire à Claire devant le Château Frontenac après leur rendez-vous?

ACTIVITÉ D Résumé de la Séquence 5 Voici un résumé de la Séquence 5 du film. Choisissez les mots qui manquent.

Alexis   allé   Claire   devant   l'enveloppe   l'homme   rien   voulait

Après leur rendez-vous, Alexis (1) _____ dire quelque chose à (2) _____ mais il n'a (3) _____ dit. Quand Alexis s'en est (4) _____, Claire a vu l'homme qui lui a donné (5) _____. Claire a couru après (6) _____ et elle s'est retrouvée (7) _____ une église.

chambre   l'enterrement   Française   mort   petite   plus   rendu   rêve

Dans l'église Claire a vu une (8) _____ fille qui pleurait. Claire s'est (9) _____ compte plus tard que ce n'était qu'un (10) _____. Plus tard dans sa (11) _____ d'hôtel, Claire a appris d'une (12) _____ que son oncle était (13) _____ à Paris. Claire doit aller à Paris pour (14) _____. Mais d'abord, elle doit aller à la Banque Nationale lundi.

Dans les coulisses

Directors use dream sequences to create a brief interlude from the main story. Dreams may be used to reveal information to viewers or to shed light on a character's psyche or thought processes. Can you think of films you've seen that included dream sequences? What was the purpose of those sequences? What do you think is the significance of the dream sequence in **Séquence 5** of the film *Liaisons*?

À DÉCOUVRIR: Le Togo et ses structures familiales

© Claude Marchal/ Photolibrary

À DÉCOUVRIR: Le Togo

Pays: Le Togo
Géographie: L'Afrique occidentale; entre le Bénin et le Ghana
Climat: Tropical; chaud et humide dans le sud; semi-aride dans le nord
Population: Plus de 6 millions
Capitale: Lomé

Activité Internet

Les Togolais sont connus pour leurs statuettes folkloriques qui s'appellent des **fétiches**. Cherchez des photos de fétiches sur Internet et trouvez des informations sur leur(s) signification, histoire, traditions et rôle(s) dans la culture ou la société.

À DÉCOUVRIR: La ville de Lomé

Structure: Une grande ville moderne
Région: Région maritime
Population: Plus de 800 000
Réputation: La capitale économique, administrative et industrielle du Togo

© Agostino Pacciani/Anzenberger/Redux

Avant de lire

You will discover in this reading the issues of urbanization and family structures in Togo.

Que savez-vous déjà?

1. Que veut dire le terme «l'urbanisation»?
2. Quels sont quelques avantages ou désavantages de l'urbanisation pour un pays?
3. Quels effets l'urbanisation a-t-elle souvent sur la culture ou la société d'un pays?

OUTILS DE LECTURE
Using titles to predict content

You will increase your reading comprehension when you use a text's title as a clue to predicting its content. For example, try to predict some of the content of this reading based on its title: **Les structures et relations familiales changeantes.**

Les structures et relations familiales changeantes

© Godong Godong/ Photolibrary

Le Togo est l'un des plus petits pays de l'Afrique (environ la superficie° de la Virginie-Occidentale). C'est aussi un pays où on constate° une évolution des structures et relations familiales comme à travers° une grande partie du continent africain. Le processus d'urbanisation croissante° est en train de modifier les structures et parfois les relations familiales traditionnelles. Beaucoup de Togolais ont quitté leurs villages pour aller vivre dans les grandes villes, en particulier dans la capitale Lomé. Lors de° l'indépendance du pays en 1960, Lomé ne comptait qu'environ 100 000 habitants. Depuis, la population de la capitale a été multipliée par huit.

Ayant° quitté un mode de vie rural pour aller chercher du travail dans un milieu urbain, les nouveaux citadins° trouvent des conditions de logement très différentes. La famille élargie des sociétés traditionnelles de l'Afrique sub-saharienne, qui faisait cohabiter trois ou même quatre générations, a été progressivement transformée par les nouvelles réalités économiques et sociales des grandes villes. Au lieu de° vivre tous ensemble dans une concession°, aujourd'hui on trouve de plus en plus de familles nucléaires vivant séparément.

Au niveau des relations familiales, le respect pour les aînés° reste primordial, même dans les familles divisées entre la ville et la campagne. Ce respect représente toujours le facteur déterminant pour les liens° entre les générations. Donc, au lieu d'une transformation totale, il y a eu une diversification des modèles familiaux, et en particulier une augmentation° du nombre de familles monoparentales, dans lesquelles la mère est le chef de famille. Mais le contact quotidien avec la famille élargie a diminué°.

superficie *surface area* **constate** *observe* **à travers** *throughout* **croissante** *increasing* **Lors de** *At the time of* **Ayant** *Having* **citadins** *city-dwellers*
Au lieu de *Instead of* **concession** *compound* **aînés** *elders* **liens** *links* **augmentation** *increase* **a diminué** *has decreased*

Après avoir lu

Compréhension

	Vrai	Faux
1. Cette situation de l'urbanisation est limitée au Togo.	☐	☐
2. La population de Lomé a triplé depuis 1960.	☐	☐
3. De plus en plus de familles nucléaires vivent séparément.	☐	☐
4. Le respect pour les aînés est toujours très important.	☐	☐

Et vous?

1. Est-ce que vous venez d'une région touchée par l'urbanisation?
2. Est-ce que vous avez grandi dans une maison multi-générationnelle?
3. Est-ce que le respect pour les aînés est important dans votre famille?
4. Est-ce que vous avez beaucoup de contact avec votre famille élargie?

Activité Internet

Quelles industries importantes existent à Lomé qui pourraient inciter des gens à s'y installer? Faites une recherche sur Internet.

LIAISONS AVEC LA LECTURE ET L'ÉCRITURE Une description des relations interpersonnelles

Descriptions of human relationships appear often in journalism, especially in human-interest stories. Here is a description of interpersonal relations in Togo from the perspective of Mawuli, a college student.

Dans la culture togolaise et surtout dans ma famille, les relations interpersonnelles sont toujours très importantes et parfois compliquées. Nous avons des règles à respecter. Respecter les aînés (surtout les grands-parents), c'est important dans toute la société. Quand on reçoit des invités à la maison, ma mère leur offre toujours de l'eau et mon père leur pose des questions sur leur famille et leur santé. Mes parents s'entendent bien avec le copain de ma sœur aînée. Mon père organise ses visites à la maison mais mes parents ne croient plus au mariage arrangé. En général, aucune démonstration publique d'affection n'est pratiquée. Par exemple, ma sœur et son copain ne s'embrassent pas en public.

© Danita Delimont / Alamy

Avant d'écrire

1. What kinds of details appear in the description of Togolese interpersonal relations?

2. Answer the following questions to help you write your own description **des relations interpersonnelles.**

   a. Les rapports entre quelles deux (ou plus de deux) personnes voulez-vous décrire?

   b. Quels exemples de leur comportement *(behavior)* ensemble voulez-vous citer?

   c. Voulez-vous tirer *(draw)* une conclusion ou porter un jugement sur leurs relations interpersonnelles?

Écrire

Using information from **Avant d'écrire,** write your own description of a personal relationship you have with someone in 6–8 French sentences.

Après avoir écrit

Exchange your description with a partner. (1) Circle all the reflexive verbs and verify that your partner correctly conjugated them. (2) Underline all negative expressions and verify that they are all correct. (3) Double-check that your partner made all of the adjectives agree in number and gender. (4) Put a * next to the key phrase or key idea that best communicates your partner's description. (5) How would you characterize your partner's description: **perspicace** *(insightful)*, **objective, ennuyeuse, touchante, dérangeante, imaginative, drôle**? Discuss your reactions together and then write a second version of your description taking into account your partner's comments and corrections.

PARTIE 1

LES MODES DE VIE

les accros du shopping	shopaholics
les babas cool / les hippies	hippies
les bourreaux de travail	workaholics
les célibataires (m., f.)	single people
les écologistes / les écolos	ecologists, environmentalists
les fanas de la santé	health nuts
les femmes / les hommes au foyer	housewives, househusbands
les membres de la jet-set	jet setters
une mère active / un père actif	working mom / working dad
une mère célibataire / un père célibataire	single mother / single father
les retraités	retired people, retirees

NOMS

l'amitié (f.)	friendship
l'amour (m.)	love
le bonheur	happiness
l'environnement (m.)	environment
la fidélité / l'infidélité (f.)	loyalty / disloyalty
la moralité	morality
le prestige	prestige
la spiritualité	spirituality
le succès	success

ADJECTIFS

avare	stingy, miserly
bavard(e)	talkative, gossipy
bête	stupid, idiotic
bien habillé(e) / mal habillé(e)	well-dressed / poorly-dressed
égoïste	selfish
fidèle / infidèle	loyal / disloyal
gracieux / gracieuse	graceful, gracious
grossier / grossière	crude, crass
indiscret / indiscrète	indiscreet
jaloux / jalouse	jealous
maladroit(e)	clumsy
mou / molle	soft, no backbone, wimpy
orgueilleux / orgueilleuse	(very) proud
prétentieux / prétentieuse	pretentious
simple	simple
soigné(e)	well-groomed, fancy

VERBES

s'aimer	to like / love oneself / each other
se connaître	to know oneself / each other
se détester	to hate oneself / each other
se disputer	to argue with (each other)
s'embrasser	to kiss each other
s'énerver	to get upset
se fiancer	to get engaged to (each other)
se marier	to marry (each other)
se parler	to talk to oneself / each other
se quitter	to leave each other
se réconcilier	to make up with each other
se regarder	to look at oneself / each other
se rencontrer	to meet each other
se téléphoner	to telephone each other
se voir	to see oneself / each other

EXPRESSION

être bien dans sa peau	to have confidence in / to feel good about oneself

PARTIE 2

VERBES

s'appeler	to be named / called
appeler	to call
s'en aller	to go away
s'amuser	to have a good time
se demander	to wonder
se dépêcher	to hurry
se détendre	to relax, to take it easy
s'ennuyer	to be bored
s'entendre (bien / mal avec quelqu'un)	to get along (well / badly with someone)
s'excuser	to be sorry, to apologize
se fâcher	to get angry
s'inquiéter (de)	to worry
s'installer (dans / à)	to move into, to settle into
s'intéresser (à)	to be interested (in)
se méfier (de)	to be suspicious (of)
se mettre (à)	to begin (to)
s'occuper (de)	to take care of
se passer	to happen
se perdre	to get lost
se promener	to take a walk, to stroll
se rappeler	to remember
rappeler	to call back
se rendre compte (de / que)	to realize
se reposer	to rest
se sentir	to feel
se souvenir (de)	to remember
se trouver	to be located
se tromper (de)	to be mistaken (about)
tromper	to cheat on (someone)

DIVERS

À mon (votre) avis	In my (your) opinion
À propos de	About / Speaking of
Selon	According to

RÉSUMÉ DE VOCABULAIRE

PARTIE 3

LA COMMUNICATION

un appareil photo numérique (APN)	digital camera
un article	article
un blog	blog
un hebdomadaire	weekly (magazine, newspaper) publication
un journal intime	diary
un magazine (de mode)	magazine (fashion magazine)
un (magazine) mensuel	monthly (magazine) publication
un message instantané	instant message
la messagerie instantanée	instant messaging
le microblogging	Twitter-like messages
un (journal) quotidien	daily (newspaper) publication
un réseau social	social network
une revue	magazine
un site Web	website
un Smartphone	Smartphone

NOMS

un fait	fact
une idée	idea
une pensée	thought
les potins / un potin	gossip / piece of gossip
un sentiment	feeling

VERBES

déranger	to bother, to upset
écœurer	to sicken, to gross out
exprimer	to express
pleurer	to cry
raconter	to tell (about), to narrate
regretter	to regret, to be sorry about
rendre quelqu'un (heureux)	to make someone (happy)
ressentir	to feel (emotion—sadness)
toucher	to touch, to deeply move

EXPRESSIONS

C'est dommage!	That's too bad!
Enfin!	Finally!
faire plaisir à quelqu'un	to please someone
Formidable! / Génial!	Great! / Awesome!
Je regrette. / Je suis désolé(e).	I'm sorry.
Merveilleux! / Super!	Marvelous! Wonderful! Super!

ADVERBES

d'autres fois	other times
de temps en temps	from time to time
parfois / quelquefois	sometimes, at times
la plupart du temps	most of the time

LES EXPRESSIONS AFFIRMATIVES

déjà	already
encore	still
toujours	always

LES EXPRESSIONS NÉGATIVES

ne… aucun(e)	none, not any
ne… jamais	never
ne… ni… ni	neither . . . nor
ne… pas du tout	not at all
ne… pas encore	not yet
ne… personne	nobody, no one
ne… plus	no longer, no more
ne… que	only
ne… rien	nothing, not anything

La **vie** en **action**

En bref   In this chapter, you will:

- talk about transportation, the post office, traveling, clothing, and lifestyles

- learn the **futur simple** form

- learn the relative pronouns **qui, que,** and **dont**

- learn some indefinite adjectives and pronouns

- learn about the sounds /z/ and /s/

- read about transportation, the post office, and travel in the France and the Francophone world

You will also watch SÉQUENCE **6**: Une découverte of the film *Liaisons.*

Ressources

 audio iLrn 🌐 http://www.cengagebrain.com

🔊 Les **modes de vie** et les **transports**

Lifestyles and transportation

un avion

un train

un (auto)bus

faire des courses à pied

LA POSTE

un taxi

LA POSTE — un camion

une boîte à lettres

un colis

une moto

une camionnette

une voiture

un 4x4 *(quatre-quatre)*

un facteur/une factrice

le courrier

Ça bouge!

Vocabulaire complémentaire

une carte postale *postcard*
une enveloppe *envelope*
un timbre *stamp*

le covoiturage *carpooling*
le métro *subway*
les moyens *(m.)* de transport *means of transportation*
un scooter *moped*

bouger *to move*
conduire *to drive*
envoyer quelque chose en express
　to send something express
faire le trajet (entre) *to travel, to commute (between)*
livrer *to deliver goods / groceries*
transporter *to transport*

- The prepositions **en** and **à** are used to express that you travel by a specific means of transportation. If you travel *in* this means of transportation, use **en.** If it's a means of transportation that you cannot be inside of, use **à.**

Ils voyagent souvent **en avion.**	*They often travel **by plane.***
Elle va à l'université **à pied.**	*She goes to the university **by foot.***
Il va au marché **à moto.**	*He goes to the market **by motorcycle.***

- Note that to express that you are sending something by a specific means of transportation, you use the preposition **par.**

| Je veux envoyer cette lettre **par avion.** | *I want to send this letter **by air.*** |

Pour aller plus loin
Le verbe *conduire*

conduire *(to drive)*	
je **conduis**	nous **conduisons**
tu **conduis**	vous **conduisez**
il/elle/on **conduit**	ils/elles **conduisent**
PAST PARTICIPLE: **conduit**	

Other verbs conjugated like **conduire** are **construire** *(to construct)*, **détruire** *(to destroy)*, and **traduire** *(to translate)*.

Essayez! Complétez chaque phrase avec les formes appropriées des verbes **conduire, construire, détruire** ou **traduire** au présent.

1. L'orage _____ notre jardin.
2. Mon professeur _____ trop vite sa voiture.
3. Nous _____ ces phrases en anglais.
4. Mes frères _____ une nouvelle maison.

Si vous y allez

Si vous allez à Paris, découvrez la ville à bord d'un bateau-mouche. Vous pourrez découvrir les plus beaux monuments de Paris dans l'un des plus célèbres bateaux au monde. Le bateau-mouche vous offre aussi la possibilité d'un déjeuner ou d'un dîner élégant.

ACTIVITÉ A Les marques Quelle marque (*brand name*) associez-vous à chaque moyen de transport mentionné? CD3-20

Modèle: un bateau **le bateau-mouche**

1.   2.   3.   4.   5.   6.   7.   8.

ACTIVITÉ B Comment font-ils le trajet? CD3-21

Étape 1. Quel moyen de transport associe-t-on typiquement à chaque mode de vie mentionné?

1. a. à scooter   b. en camionnette   6. a. à moto   b. en autobus
2. a. en camionnette b. en avion   7. a. en 4X4   b. en métro
3. a. à moto   b. en taxi   8. a. en taxi   b. en covoiturage
4. a. à pied   b. en voiture   9. a. en camionnette b. en autobus
5. a. en camionnette b. en avion   10. a. en taxi   b. à moto

Étape 2. Complétez la phrase à propos de Claire Gagner du film *Liaisons*.

Claire a fait le trajet entre Montréal et Québec _____.

ACTIVITÉ C Les services de la poste Connaissez-vous bien les services de la poste? Répondez aux questions.

1. Combien coûte un timbre pour envoyer une carte postale du Texas à la Floride?
2. Combien coûte un timbre pour envoyer une lettre des États-Unis à la France?
3. Ça coûte combien pour envoyer une grande enveloppe en express aux États-Unis?
4. Combien coûte la location (*rental*) d'une boîte à lettres à la poste?

ACTIVITÉ D Comment les transporter?

Étape 1. Comment transporteriez-vous les objets suivants?

Modèle: une commode de Paris à Québec   **Je la transporterais par bateau.**

1. un divan de Detroit à New York   5. une guitare de Toronto à Montréal
2. un petit chien de Chicago à Paris   6. cinq chats de Boston à New York
3. cinq colis de Miami à Rome   7. dix tableaux d'art de Québec à Nice
4. un piano de New York à Paris   8. un téléviseur de Dallas à Austin

Étape 2. À tour de rôle, posez des questions à un(e) partenaire. Après, décidez qui serait un(e) expéditionnaire (*shipping clerk*). Qui a répondu chaque fois avec un moyen de transport plus efficace?

ACTIVITÉ **E** **Quel moyen de transport?**

Étape 1. Quel moyen de transport choisiriez-vous dans chaque situation?

Modèle: pour faire le trajet entre votre maison et le café   **Je prendrais l'autobus.**

1. votre maison et l'université
2. votre maison et le supermarché
3. votre maison et le cinéma
4. votre maison et la salle de sports
5. le cours de français et la bibliothèque
6. votre maison et une fête au centre-ville

Étape 2. Posez les questions à deux camarades de classe. Qui est le plus écologique? Qui est le plus paresseux/paresseuse?

ACTIVITÉ **F** **Les habitudes de conduite**

Étape 1. Comment classifieriez-vous chaque situation? **(a) Pas de problème,** **(b) Ce n'est pas une bonne idée mais parfois c'est nécessaire** ou **(c) C'est dangereux et stupide.**

1. On conduit et on mange.
2. On conduit et on boit du café.
3. On conduit et on parle au téléphone.
4. On conduit et on écrit des textos.
5. On conduit quand on a sommeil.
6. On boit de l'alcool et on conduit.
7. On conduit quand il fait mauvais.
8. On conduit et on écoute de la musique.

Étape 2. Montrez vos réponses à un(e) partenaire pour voir si vous êtes d'accord. Puis, demandez à votre partenaire s'il/si elle fait ces activités pour déterminer s'il/si elle est un conducteur/une conductrice *(driver)* prudent(e) ou dangereux/dangereuse.

Modèle: **Est-ce que tu conduis et tu manges en même temps** *(at the same time)*?

Un mot sur la culture

Le TGV en France

Le train est un moyen de transport beaucoup plus répandu° en France qu'aux États-Unis. C'est un moyen de voyager pratique et économique pour les Français. En 1981, la S.N.C.F. (Société nationale des chemins de fer° français) a mis en service son premier train à grande vitesse°, le TGV. Avec le TGV, aujourd'hui on peut faire le trajet entre Paris et Lyon en deux heures et entre Paris et Londres en trois heures.

répandu *widespread* **chemins de fer** *railroad* **vitesse** *speed*

© G. Bowater/Corbis

• Aimez-vous voyager en train? Quels avantages associez-vous à un voyage en train?

Pour parler de l'avenir

Le futur

DU FILM *LIAISONS*

Un coup d'œil sur la grammaire

Look at these photos from the film *Liaisons* and their captions.

CLAIRE Je t'appeller**ai** demain, d'accord?

ABIA Bon voyage. [...] Je m'occuper**ai** de Monsieur Émile.

1. What does **Je t'appellerai demain** mean?

2. What is the tense of the verb **appellerai** in the left caption?

3. What does **Je m'occuperai de Monsieur Émile** mean in the right caption?

•◦• You learned how to express future events that *are going to happen* with the **futur proche** (the verb **aller** plus the infinitive form of a verb). To express future events that *will happen*, use the **futur simple**.

> Marie **prendra** l'avion pour aller en Espagne.
>
> *Marie **will take** the plane to Spain.*

•◦• To form the **futur simple,** add the future endings to the future stem. The future verb stems are identical to the conditional verb stems.

> **Note** de **grammaire**
>
> Note that, with the exception of the **nous** and **vous** forms, the future endings are identical to the present tense forms of the verb **avoir.**

s'amuser	sortir	prendre
je m'amuser**ai**	je sortir**ai**	je prendr**ai**
tu t'amuser**as**	tu sortir**as**	tu prendr**as**
il/elle/on s'amuser**a**	il/elle/on sortir**a**	il/elle/on prendr**a**
nous nous amuser**ons**	nous sortir**ons**	nous prendr**ons**
vous vous amuser**ez**	vous sortir**ez**	vous prendr**ez**
ils/elles s'amuser**ont**	ils/elles sortir**ont**	ils/elles prendr**ont**

•◦• The irregular future stem forms are identical to the irregular conditional stem forms.

> Luc **fera** le trajet en train.
>
> *Luc **will make** the trip/commute by train.*
>
> Elles n'**iront** pas en France l'été prochain.
>
> *They **will** not **go** to France next summer.*

- **-Er** verbs with spelling changes in the conditional form have the same spelling changes in the **futur simple.**

Nous **achèterons** une maison l'année prochaine.

*We **will buy** a house next year.*

- The choice between the **futur proche** and the **futur simple** depends on how certain you are that the event will occur. If you think that the event will definitely occur, use the **futur proche.** If there is less certainty about the event occurring, use the **futur simple.** Compare the following sentences:

Je **ferai** mes devoirs ce soir.

*I **will do** my homework tonight (maybe).*

Je **vais faire** mes devoirs ce soir.

*I **am going to do** my homework tonight (you're sure).*

Il **étudiera** le chinois un jour.

*He **will study** Chinese one day (thinks he will).*

Il **va étudier** le chinois en mai.

*He **is going to study** Chinese in May (definitely).*

- You learned in **Chapitre 9** that **si** clauses using the imperfect and conditional forms can be used to express hypothetical situations. You can also use **si** clauses to express events and conditions that are possible or likely to happen. In these cases, the **si** clause that expresses the condition is in the present tense and the main clause that expresses the possible outcome is in the **futur proche** or the **futur simple.**

Si tu ne **conduis** pas, je **prendrai** un taxi.

*If you're not **driving**, **I'll take** a taxi.*

Si je **vais** à Paris, j'**irai** au Louvre.

*If I **go** to Paris, **I will go** to the Louvre.*

- In French, if a clause begins with **quand, lorsque** *(when),* **dès que** *(as soon as)* or **aussitôt que** *(as soon as),* and a future event is implied, use the future tense. In English, the present tense is used.

Quand il **quittera** Paris, il **sera** triste.

When he leaves Paris, he'll be sad.

Dès que j'**aurai** un chien, je l'**appellerai** Fido.

As soon as I get a dog, I'll call it Fido.

- If future time is not implied in clauses with **quand** or **dès que,** the verb may be in another tense.

Quand avez-vous étudié l'anglais?

***When did you study** English?*

Dès qu'il est arrivé, on s'est mis à manger.

***As soon as he arrived,** we began to eat.*

- Note that **le futur** refers to the grammatical future only. If you are referring to future events that have not occured, you must use **l'avenir** *(m.).*

Claude s'inquiète de son **avenir.**

*Claude is worried about his **future.***

On a étudié **le futur** en classe aujourd'hui.

*We studied the **future tense** in class today.*

ACTIVITÉ G **Les prédictions pour les modes de vie** À votre avis, est-ce que chaque prédiction sera vraie ou fausse?

Dans vingt ans…	Vrai	Faux
1. les mères célibataires **pourront** avoir une carrière plus facilement.	☐	☐
2. les bourreaux de travail **voudront** avoir plus d'enfants.	☐	☐
3. les fanas de la santé **vivront** moins longtemps	☐	☐
4. les retraités **seront** plus pauvres.	☐	☐
5. il y **aura** moins de femmes au foyer.	☐	☐
6. les babas cool **n'existeront** plus.	☐	☐
7. il y **aura** plus de pères célibataires.	☐	☐
8. tout le monde **deviendra** plus écologiste.	☐	☐

ACTIVITÉ H **Dans dix ans** Un étudiant parle avec ses deux colocataires de ses prédictions pour l'avenir (dans dix ans). Choisissez le sujet de chaque phrase. Puis, indiquez si vous êtes d'accord avec les prédictions de cet étudiant.

1. _____ sera uniquement électronique.   a. Le courrier   b. Les cartes postales
2. _____ n'ir**ons** plus à la poste.   a. Vous   b. Nous
3. _____ coûter**a** plus cher.   a. Un timbre   b. Les enveloppes
4. _____ coûter**ont** moins cher.   a. L'autobus   b. Les taxis
5. _____ pourr**ons** conduire plus vite.   a. On   b. Nous
6. _____ devr**ai** payer plus pour l'essence *(gas).*   a. Je   b. Tu
7. _____ attend**rez** le bus moins longtemps.   a. Les étudiants   b. Vous
8. _____ ne voudr**as** plus voyager en avion.   a. On   b. Tu

ACTIVITÉ I **Les prédictions pour les célébrités d'Hollywood**

Étape 1. Est-ce que chaque prédiction est probable ou pas probable? Si la prédiction n'est pas probable, faites une prédiction que vous pensez probable pour la célébrité.

1. Michael Jordan **achètera** un stade de baseball.
2. Miley Cyrus **gagnera** un grammy.
3. Oprah **tombera** enceinte *(pregnant).*
4. Martha Stewart **ira** en prison encore une fois.
5. Leonardo DiCaprio **aura** une nouvelle copine.
6. Daniel Radcliffe et Emma Watson **se marieront**.
7. Sarah Jessica Parker et Matthew Broderick **se quitteront**.
8. Tom Cruise et Katie Holmes **auront** un autre enfant.

Étape 2. Demandez à un(e) partenaire ce qu'il/elle pense de ces prédictions.

Modèle: É1: **Michael Jordan achètera un stade. C'est probable ou pas probable?**
É2: **Ce n'est pas probable. Je pense qu'il achètera un restaurant.**

Le week-end du professeur

Étape 1. Avec un(e) partenaire, devinez *(guess)* si votre professeur fera les activités suivantes ce week-end.

Notre professeur…

1. **ira** au cinéma.
2. **fera** du shopping.
3. **conduira** à la campagne
4. **s'amusera** avec des amis.

5. **verra** un spectacle.
6. **louera** un film français
7. **prendra** un repas gastronomique.
8. **sortira** avec sa famille.

Étape 2. Votre professeur va vous donner ses réponses. Avez-vous bien deviné?

Étape 3. Demandez à votre partenaire s'il/si elle fera ces activités.

Modèle: Est-ce que tu iras au cinéma ce week-end?

Conclusion Qui aura un week-end plus intéressant? Votre professeur ou votre partenaire?

ACTIVITÉ K **Les événements possibles pour notre classe de français** Complétez chaque phrase avec un verbe au futur.

1. Si je ne peux pas conduire demain, je…
2. Si notre classe de français fait une excursion, nous…
3. Si mes camarades de classe veulent étudier ensemble, ils…
4. Si je veux apprendre une autre langue étrangère, je…
5. Si les cours sont annulés *(cancelled),* mon professeur…
6. Si notre professeur nous demande si nous voulons voir un film en classe, nous…
7. Si nous devons écouter de la musique française en classe, nous…
8. Si on invite quelqu'un de célèbre dans notre cours de français, on…

ACTIVITÉ L **Les événements personnels possibles**

Étape 1. Complétez les phrases avec un verbe au présent ou au futur selon le cas pour décrire votre avenir.

1. Dès que je terminerai mes études,…
2. Je ferai un master si…
3. Je voyagerai en France si…
4. J'achèterai une maison quand…
5. Aussitôt que j'aurai un bon emploi…
6. J'achèterai une nouvelle voiture dès que…
7. Je me marierai si…
8. J'aurai des enfants si…

Étape 2. Montrez vos réponses à un(e) partenaire. Vos avenirs seront-ils similaires ou différents?

ACTIVITÉ Ⓜ **L'avenir des modes de vie** Décrivez l'avenir de ces modes de vie dans dix ans en utilisant les phrases suivantes.

Possibilités

s'amuser plus/moins	gagner plus/moins d'argent
avoir des enfants plus tôt/tard	manger plus/moins de produits bio
avoir plus/moins d'enfants	se marier plus tôt/tard
avoir plus/moins de temps libre	s'occuper plus/moins facilement de ses enfants
dépenser plus/moins d'argent	
devoir retourner au travail	prendre plus/moins de journées de congé
s'ennuyer plus/moins	retourner à l'université
être plus/moins heureux/heureuse	travailler plus/moins
être plus/moins riche	voyager plus/moins facilement en avion
faire plus/moins de lessive	????

Modèle: Les fanas de la santé seront moins heureux.

1. Les mères actives _____
2. Les pères célibataires _____
3. Les mères célibataires _____
4. Les membres de la jet-set _____
5. Les accros du shopping _____
6. Les babas cool _____
7. Les bourreaux de travail _____
8. Les écologistes _____
9. Les femmes au foyer _____
10. Les retraités _____

ACTIVITÉ Ⓝ **L'histoire de Roland**

Étape 1. Roland consulte un voyant *(fortune teller)* à propos de son avenir. Avec deux camarades de classe, écrivez une histoire de cinq à six phrases sur l'avenir de Roland à l'aide des dessins suivants.

© Photodisc/Photolibrary

Étape 2. Lisez votre histoire à un autre groupe. Qui a une meilleure histoire?

ACTIVITÉ O Les péchés mignons

Étape 1. Décrivez trois péchés mignons (*guilty pleasures*) ou trois mauvaises habitudes (*habits*) que vous avez.

Modèle: J'achète beaucoup de chaussures (*shoes*). **Je mange beaucoup de chips. Je fais la grasse matinée le samedi.**

Étape 2. Lisez vos péchés mignons ou vos mauvaises habitudes à un(e) partenaire. Écoutez ceux/celles de votre partenaire. Dites à votre partenaire ce qui pourra se passer s'il/si elle n'a plus ces péchés mignons ou ces mauvaises habitudes.

Modèle: **Si tu n'achètes plus de chaussures, tu auras plus d'argent pour acheter des choses plus importantes comme la nourriture. Si tu ne manges pas de chips, tu maigriras et tu seras en bonne santé. Si tu ne fais plus la grasse matinée, tu pourras finir tes devoirs plus tôt.**

ACTIVITÉ P Quand les hommes vivront d'amour

Quand les hommes vivront d'amour est une chanson québécoise composée par Raymond Lévesque en 1956. Le refrain, *Quand les hommes vivront d'amour // il n'y aura plus de misère*, appelle à la paix et est resté populaire jusqu'à aujourd'hui. Décrivez comment notre monde pourra être quand les hommes vivront d'amour. Écrivez au moins (*at least*) quatre phrases.

Modèle: Quand les hommes vivront d'amour, **il n'y aura plus de violence. Les enfants ne s'inquiéteront plus. Le monde sera plus beau.**

La parole est à vous!

Est-ce qu'il faut changer l'âge minimum pour conduire?

En Amérique du Nord, on peut conduire à l'âge de 16 ans. En France, il faut avoir 18 ans pour obtenir un permis de conduire. Faut-il changer l'âge minimum en France à 16 ans?

- Martin de Salon-de-Provence (France): «Oui! Si les jeunes peuvent conduire à l'âge de 16 ans aux États-Unis, nous devrions pouvoir le faire aussi.»

- Marthe de Paris (France): «Non, c'est une mauvaise idée. Les jeunes ont tendance à avoir plus d'accidents que les adultes. Ils ne sont pas responsables à 16 ans.»

Et vous? Qu'en pensez-vous?

Est-ce qu'il faut changer l'âge minimum pour conduire en France à 16 ans?

🔊 Partons en vacances!

Let's go on vacation!

débarquer de l'avion

une porte d'embarquement

PORTE 23

un(e) agent(e) de la sécurité

un(e) agent(e) de bord

embarquer dans l'avion

la carte d'embarquement

BA

un billet d'avion

une valise

une voyageuse (un voyageur)

un passeport

enregistrer les bagages

À l'aéroport

Note de vocabulaire

Un scanner corporel is a body scanner, **un appareil de radiographie** is an x-ray machine; and **un détecteur de métaux** is a metal detector.

Vocabulaire complémentaire

à l'étranger *abroad/overseas*
un billet aller-retour *round-trip ticket*
un billet aller simple *one-way ticket*
un permis de conduire *driver's license*
une pièce d'identité *a form of identification*
un siège (côté couloir) *(aisle) seat*
un vol direct/une correspondance *direct/connecting flight*

la première classe *first-class*
la classe affaires *business class*
la classe économique *economy class*

une agence de voyages *travel agency*
un(e) agent(e) de voyages *travel agent*
un arrêt d'autobus *bus stop*
une auberge de jeunesse *youth hostel*
une chambre fumeurs/non-fumeurs *smoking/nonsmoking rom*
une chambre individuelle/double *single/double room*
une clé *key*
un(e) client(e) *client, guest*

une croisière *cruise*
une gare *(bus/train) station*
un gîte du passant *bed and breakfast*
un hôtel (trois/quatre/cinq étoiles) *(three/four/five star) hotel*
un hôtel de luxe *luxury hotel*
un lit simple/double *single/double bed*
le logement *lodging*
un motel *motel*
le service de chambre *room service*
une tente *tent*

aller en vacances *(f.)* *to go on vacation*
attacher la ceinture de sécurité *to fasten the seatbelt*
déclarer (vos achats) *to declare (your purchases)*
faire les valises *to pack*
passer à la douane *to go through customs*
passer au contrôle de sécurité *to go through security*
payer des frais *(m.)* supplémentaires *to pay extra fees*

Si vous y allez

Si vous allez à Québec, visitez la Gare du Palais, une gare construite dans le même style que le Château Frontenac qui est desservi par *Via Rail Canada* et les autobus *Orléans Express*.

Pour aller plus loin
Dans l'avion ou sur l'avion?

In French, to say that you are *on the plane, on the train,* or *on the bus,* you must use the preposition **dans. Sur l'avion** means there is something *on top of* the plane.

Je lis **dans** l'avion.	*I'm reading **on** the plane.*
Il y a un oiseau **sur** l'avion.	*There is a bird **on (top of)** the plane*

Essayez! Répondez aux questions.

1. Qu'aimez-vous faire dans l'avion?

2. Qu'aimez-vous faire dans l'autobus?

🔊 **ACTIVITÉ Ⓐ C'est où?** Complétez chaque phrase que vous entendez avec
CD3-22 **(a) l'aéroport, (b) l'arrêt d'autobus** ou **(c) la gare.**

1.   2.   3.   4.   5.   6.

ACTIVITÉ Ⓑ Les modes de vie et les voyages

Étape 1. Qu'est-ce que vous associez à chaque mode de vie?

1. une retraitée	a. une auberge de jeunesse	b. un gîte du passant
2. un fana de la santé	a. une chambre fumeurs	b. une chambre non-fumeurs
3. une femme de la jet-set	a. un hôtel cinq étoiles	b. une tente
4. un homme d'affaires	a. la classe économique	b. la classe affaires
5. un baba cool	a. une tente	b. un hôtel de luxe
6. une mère et un père actifs	a. un lit simple	b. un lit double
7. une femme célibataire	a. une chambre double	b. une chambre individuelle
8. un étudiant	a. un motel	b. un hôtel cinq étoiles

Étape 2. Le Château Frontenac, c'est quel genre
de logement *(accommodation)*?

© Maridav /Shutterstock.com

🔊 **ACTIVITÉ Ⓒ À l'agence de voyages** La sœur d'Abia, Nadia, et leur cousin,
CD3-23 Jerome, veulent partir en vacances. Écoutez ce qu'ils disent à l'agent de voyages pour
déterminer le meilleur vol et hébergement pour eux.

Voyage 1: Nadia

1. a. billet aller simple	b. billet aller-retour
2. a. vol national	b. vol international
3. a. première classe	b. classe économique
4. a. besoin d'enregistrer des valises	b. pas besoin d'enregistrer les bagages
5. a. motel	b. hôtel 4 ou 5 étoiles
6. a. chambre fumeur	b. chambre non-fumeur
7. a. lit simple	b. lit double

Voyage 2: Jerome

1. a. billet aller-simple	b. billet aller-retour
2. a. vol national	b. vol international
3. a. première classe	b. classe économique
4. a. besoin d'enregistrer des valises	b. pas besoin d'enregistrer les bagages
5. a. motel	b. hôtel 4 ou 5 étoiles
6. a. chambre fumeur	b. chambre non-fumeur
7. a. lit simple	b. lit double

ACTIVITÉ D **Savez-vous quoi faire à l'aéroport?**

Étape 1. Que devez-vous faire pour voyager en avion? Mettez les événements dans l'ordre.

a. _____ Vous donnez la carte d'embarquement à l'agent de bord.

b. _____ Vous attendez le vol à la porte d'embarquement.

c. _____ Vous débarquez de l'avion.

d. _____ Vous réservez un billet d'avion.

e. _____ Vous passez au contrôle de sécurité.

f. _____ Vous présentez une pièce d'identité et la carte d'embarquement à l'agent de sécurité.

g. _____ Vous embarquez dans l'avion.

h. _____ Vous confirmez votre vol.

i. _____ Vous mettez votre sac sous le siège devant vous et vous attachez votre ceinture de sécurité pour le décollage.

j. _____ L'agent de bord vous demande de vous préparer pour l'atterrissage *(landing)*.

k. _____ Vous enregistrez vos valises.

l. _____ L'agent de bord vous sert une boisson.

Étape 2. Complétez les phrases.

1. S'il n'y a pas de vol direct,…   **3.** Si vous avez trois valises,…

2. Si vous voyagez à l'étranger,…   **4.** Si vous voulez transporter un couteau,…

 Étape 3. Montrez vos réponses à un(e) partenaire pour voir si vous êtes d'accord.

ACTIVITÉ E **Voyager à l'étranger**

Étape 1. Savez-vous quoi faire quand vous voyagez à l'étranger? Avec un(e) partenaire, décidez si chaque phrase est vraie ou fausse. Corrigez *(Correct)* les phrases qui sont fausses.

1. Il faut arriver à l'aéroport 30 minutes en avance.

2. On peut utiliser un permis de conduire comme pièce d'identité.

3. On peut fumer dans la section fumeurs de l'avion.

4. Il faut passer à la douane.

5. On peut rapporter *(bring back)* trois litres de vin ou de bière.

6. On peut rapporter du chocolat et des bonbons.

7. On peut rapporter du jambon et des steaks.

8. On ne déclare pas les produits qu'on achète au magasin hors taxe *(duty-free)*.

9. Il faut payer les frais de douane si on achète plus de 800 dollars U.S. de produits.

10. On peut aller en prison si on ment *(lie)* à l'agent de douane.

Étape 2. Discutez ces questions avec votre partenaire.

1. Avez-vous voyagé à l'étranger? Où?

2. Avez-vous jamais menti à l'agent de douane?

👥 **ACTIVITÉ** **F** **Comment voyagez-vous?**

Étape 1. Comment voyagez-vous typiquement? Notez vos réponses.

	Moi	Mon partenaire
1. Vous voyagez en première classe ou en classe économique?	_____	_____
2. Vous utilisez une agence de voyages ou Internet?	_____	_____
3. Vous préférez un siège près du hublot (window) ou un siège côté couloir?	_____	_____
4. Quel type de logement choisissez-vous?	_____	_____
5. Vous préférez une chambre fumeurs ou non-fumeurs?	_____	_____
6. Vous perdez souvent votre clé d'hôtel?	_____	_____
7. Vous utilisez souvent le service de chambre?	_____	_____

Étape 2. Posez les questions à un(e) partenaire et notez ses réponses dans la deuxième colonne. Êtes-vous similaires ou différent(e)s? Pouvez-vous voyager ensemble?

Étape 3. Avec votre partenaire, devinez (guess) ce que (what) dirait votre professeur.

👥 **ACTIVITÉ** **G** **Êtes-vous un(e) bon(ne) agent(e) de voyages?**

Étape 1. Avec un(e) partenaire, discutez quel type de voyage serait idéal pour les personnes suivantes.

Nom: Mimi

Occupation: mère célibataire et secrétaire

Domicile: Tampa, FL.

Nombre de voyageurs: cinq (moi, mes trois enfants et ma sœur)

Durée du voyage: trois à cinq jours pour nous amuser

Argent à dépenser: 1000 dollars

Nom: Claude

Occupation: homme d'affaires célibataire et stressé

Domicile: Montréal, Québec

Nombre de voyageurs: un

Durée du voyage: une semaine pour me détendre et rencontrer une femme

Argent à dépenser: sans limite

Suggestions

aller à Disney	faire du camping	louer une voiture
descendre dans un hôtel de luxe	faire une croisière	louer un châlet

Questions à considérer

• Quel type de voyage proposez-vous? Où est-ce que les voyageurs iront?

• S'ils prennent l'avion, quel type de billets proposez-vous?

• Quel type de logement proposez-vous? Quels types d'activités sont possibles?

Étape 2. Avec votre partenaire, préparez un itinéraire pour Mimi et pour Claude.

Modèle: **Mimi peut faire du camping avec sa sœur et ses enfants à Wisconsin Dells...**

Étape 1. Indiquez si chaque situation s'applique *(apply)* au passé avant le 11 septembre 2001, au présent ou à l'avenir. Vous pouvez cocher *(check)* plus d'une catégorie.

	Le passé	Le présent	L'avenir
1. On peut passer au contrôle de sécurité sans carte d'embarquement.	_____	_____	_____
2. On peut apporter du vin dans les vols nationaux.	_____	_____	_____
3. On peut passer au contrôle de sécurité avec une bouteille d'eau.	_____	_____	_____
4. Il faut enlever *(remove)* les chaussures *(shoes)* au contrôle de sécurité.	_____	_____	_____
5. Il faut passer au scanner corporel au contrôle de sécurité.	_____	_____	_____
6. On ne paie pas de frais supplémentaires pour enregistrer les valises.	_____	_____	_____
7. On peut utiliser des couteaux en plastiques dans l'avion.	_____	_____	_____
8. Les vols ont souvent du retard.	_____	_____	_____

Étape 2. Montrez vos réponses à un(e) partenaire pour voir si vous avez mis les mêmes choses. À votre avis, comment est-ce que les voyages en avion seront à l'avenir? Discutez la question avec votre partenaire.

Étape 3. Parlez avec votre partenaire d'un mauvais voyage en avion que vous avez fait.

Un mot sur la culture

© Vivafilm/courtesy Everett Collection

Les snowbirds en Floride

Savez-vous qu'il existe des villages québécois en Floride? En hiver, plus de cinq cent mille Québécois s'en vont en Floride pour s'y installer. On appelle ces Floriquébécois, dont la plupart° sont des retraités, des *snowbirds*. On peut trouver en Floride des publications en français et on peut être servi en français dans plusieurs restaurants, épiceries et hôtels. L'âge moyen° des snowbirds est de 70 ans. En 1993, le cinéaste québécois George Mihalka a tourné° un film comique, *La Florida*, sur les snowbirds québécois.

plupart *most part* **moyen** *average* **a tourné** *produced*

• Connaissez-vous des quartiers québécois ou français aux États-Unis?

Pour relier deux idées

Les pronoms relatifs **qui, que, dont** et **où**

DU FILM *LIAISONS*

Un coup d'œil sur la grammaire

Look at these photos from the film *Liaisons* and their captions.

CLAIRE C'est l'homme **qui** m'a donné l'enveloppe avec la réservation au Frontenac.

CLAIRE Et ici... c'est l'homme **que** j'ai rencontré...

1. What follows the relative pronoun **qui**? A verb or a subject?
2. What follows the relative pronoun **que**? A verb or a subject?
3. What do you think the two captions mean?

❖❖ Relative pronouns allow you to combine two ideas together into one sentence. Relative pronouns may be omitted in English, but they cannot be omitted in French.

La femme **qui** parle est ma tante. *The woman **who** is speaking is my aunt.*

Le livre **que** j'ai lu était drôle. *The book (**that**) I read was funny.*

Les pronoms relatifs	
qui *who, that, which*	**dont** *that, (of) which, (of) whom, whose*
que *that, which*	**où** *where, when*

Note de **grammaire**
Qui may be also followed by a conjugated verb that has an object pronoun in front of it: **C'est l'homme qui m'a donné l'enveloppe.**

❖❖ **Qui** may refer to people or things and is used as the subject of a dependent clause. Because **qui** acts as the subject, it is always followed by a conjugated verb.

Tu vois l'homme **qui voyage** avec son chien?
*Do you see the man **who is traveling** with his dog?*

L'agente **qui a enregistré** mes valises est belle.
*The agent **who checked** (in) my bags is beautiful.*

❖❖ **Que** also refers to people or things and is used as the direct object of a dependent clause so **que** is always followed by a subject (not a verb). Note that **que** becomes **qu'** if the subject begins with a vowel.

C'est l'homme **qu'elle** a vu à l'hôtel! *That's the man (**that**) **she** saw at the hotel!*

J'ai lu le livre **que Luc** m'a donné. *I read the book (**that**) **Luc** gave me.*

⋯⟫ Note that in the **passé composé,** the past participle after **que** agrees in number and gender with the direct object.

La clé que Claire a trouvé**e** est pour un coffre-fort.

The key that Claire found is for a safety deposit box.

⋯⟫ **Dont** replaces **de** plus a noun and can refer to people or things. Some expressions that contain **de** include **parler de, avoir besoin de, avoir peur de,** and **se souvenir de.**

Voici la femme **dont** tu parlais.　　*Here is the woman **whom** you were talking about.*

Voici les livres **dont** j'ai besoin.　　*Here are the books (**that**) I need.*

⋯⟫ **Dont** can also be used to refer to possessions. In this case, **dont** is followed by a definite article.

Voici les gens **dont la** maison est grande.
*Here are the people **whose** house is big.*

J'ai rencontré une femme **dont le** mari est agent de bord.
*I met a woman **whose** husband is a flight attendant.*

⋯⟫ Use **où** to refer to a place or a time.

Je me rappelle le moment **où** il m'a dit qu'il m'aimait.
*I remember the moment **when** he told me he loved me.*

C'est une ville **où** il y a beaucoup de Français.
*It's a city **where** there are lots of French people.*

ACTIVITÉ ① **Les films, les émissions et les personnes**

Étape 1. Quel film ou quelle personne associez-vous à chaque description?

C'est un film…

1. **qui** est très drôle.
2. **qui** a gagné un Oscar.
3. **qui** est très mauvais.
4. **qui** vient de sortir.

C'est une personne…

5. **qui** voyage en première classe.
6. **qui** boit beaucoup d'alcool.
7. **qui** est très intelligente.
8. **qui** parle bien français.

Étape 2. Quelle émission ou quelle personne associez-vous à chaque description?

C'est une émission de télévision…

1. **que** les enfants aiment beaucoup.
2. **que** les gens aimaient dans les années 80.
3. **que** je regarderai cette semaine.
4. **que** je déteste.

C'est une personne…

5. **que** j'admire beaucoup.
6. **que** les adolescents aiment.
7. **que** j'aimerais rencontrer.
8. **que** tout le monde connaît.

Liaisons musicales

© YP B0/Images Distribution/Newscom

Éric Lapointe (1969–) est un rockeur québécois dont les chansons se trouvent dans beaucoup de bandes sonores *(soundtracks)* de films populaires québécois comme *Les Boys* et *Bon cop, bad cop.* Cherchez une chanson d'Éric Lapointe sur Internet et décrivez son style. 🌐

ACTIVITÉ J **Les livres, les personnes et les villes** Quel livre ou quelle personne associez-vous à chaque description?

C'est un livre…

1. **dont** tout le monde **parle.**
2. **dont** les étudiants **ont besoin.**
3. **dont** les enfants **ont peur.**

C'est quelqu'un…

1. **dont** la maison est à Beverly Hills.
2. **dont** les cheveux sont blonds.
3. **dont** le mari est beau.

C'est une personne…

4. **dont** les journaux **parlent.**
5. **dont** je **me souviens** bien.
6. **dont** j'ai peur.

C'est une ville …

5. **où** on trouve les meilleurs restaurants.
6. **où** on peut parler français.
7. **où** il y a un aéroport international.

ACTIVITÉ K **Aimez-vous lire?**

Étape 1. Complétez les phrases avec **qui** ou **que** et indiquez si vous êtes d'accord avec chaque phrase.

J'aime les livres…

1. _____ J.K. Rowling écrit.
2. _____ parlent des extra-terrestres.
3. _____ le *New York Times* recommande.
4. _____ sont en français.
5. _____ ont beaucoup de dessins.
6. _____ mes amis aiment.
7. _____ je dois lire pour mes cours.
8. _____ ne coûtent pas cher.

Étape 2. Demandez à un(e) partenaire s'il/si elle aime ces livres.

Modèle: Est-ce que tu aimes les livres que J.K. Rowling écrit?

ACTIVITÉ L **Les femmes**

Étape 1. Complétez chaque phrase avec **que** ou **dont**. Ensuite, donnez le nom d'une femme qui correspond à chaque description.

Voici la femme…

1. _____ la mère est célèbre. _____
2. _____ le monde entier *(entire)* admire. _____
3. _____ les hommes adorent. _____
4. _____ les journaux parlent. _____
5. _____ la voix est très belle. _____
6. _____ les hommes ont peur. _____
7. _____ les parents détestent. _____
8. _____ on se souviendra toujours. _____

Étape 2. Posez les questions suivantes à un(e) partenaire.

1. Est-ce que tu connais quelqu'un que tous les parents adorent?
2. Est-ce que tu connais quelqu'un dont les enfants ont peur?
3. Est-ce que tu connais quelqu'un dont la voiture coûte très cher?

ACTIVITÉ M **Quel objet?** Utilisez les participes passés pour déterminer l'objet de chaque phrase. Puis, demandez à un(e) partenaire de vous donner un exemple de chaque chose qu'il/elle a lue, qu'il/elle a vue et qu'il/elle a essayée.

1. Nomme _____ que tu as lue.　　a. une revue　　b. un journal　　c. des livres
2. Nomme _____ que tu as vus.　　a. une émission　　b. un spectacle　　c. des films
3. Nomme _____ que tu as essayé.　　a. une boisson　　b. un dessert　　c. des fruits

ACTIVITÉ N **L'agent de voyages** Nommez trois villes que vous trouvez intéressantes. Si vous étiez l'agent(e) de voyages, comment décririez-vous ces villes à votre partenaire? Utilisez le pronom relatif **où**. Décidez si vous voulez visiter les villes que votre partenaire a décrites.

Modèle: **Québec est une ville où on peut manger de la poutine. C'est aussi l'endroit où se trouve le Château Frontenac.**

ACTIVITÉ O **Les potins et les opinions** Créez des potins ou exprimez votre opinion sur ces sujets en utilisant les pronoms relatifs **qui, que, dont** et **où**. Dites vos potins/opinions à un(e) partenaire.

Modèle: **Ashton Kutcher est un acteur que ma sœur trouve stupide.** *Austin Powers* **est le plus mauvais film qui vient de sortir au cinéma. Boston est la ville où je suis né.**

1. Lindsey Lohan / actrice
2. Mon/Ma voisin(e) / personne
3. Mon ex / personne
4. Las Vegas / ville
5. Le français / cours
6. Central Park / parc
7. Alan Lambert / chanteur
8. ??? / film
9. ???

La parole est à vous!

Est-ce que les scanners corporels sont nécessaires à l'aéroport?

Il existe un nouveau système de détection dans les aéroports: le scanner corporel. À votre avis, est-ce que ces scanners sont nécessaires?

- Ève de Dijon (France): «Non! Ces scanners sont une intrusion excessive dans la vie privée. L'administration de la sécurité des transports va trop loin.»

- Luc de Québec (Canada): «Je n'aime pas ces scanners mais je pense qu'ils sont nécessaires. Le monde a changé depuis le 11 septembre 2001. Il faut l'accepter.»

Et vous? Qu'en pensez-vous?

Est-ce que les scanners corporels sont nécessaires à l'aéroport?

Que **porter?**

What to wear?

- une écharpe
- un smoking
- un bracelet
- une robe du soir
- un sweat (à capuche)
- un tee-shirt
- un chapeau
- un manteau
- des gants
- un jean
- un jogging
- une casquette
- un chemisier
- un pull à col roulé
- un costume
- un foulard
- une chemise
- un tailleur
- une robe
- une (mini) jupe
- une mallette
- un pantalon
- un short
- les chaussettes *(f.)*
- des bottes *(f.)*
- des sandales *(f.)*

La réunion des anciens du lycée Gatineau

Note de **grammaire**

The plural forms of **chapeau** and **manteau** are **chapeaux** and **manteaux.**

Vocabulaire complémentaire

un anorak *anorak*

des baskets *(f.)* tennis shoes

un blouson *windbreaker*

des chaussures *(f.)* à talon *high heel shoes*

un collier *necklace*

une cravate *tie*

un gilet *cardigan*

un imperméable *raincoat*

des lunettes *(f.)* (de soleil) *glasses (sunglasses)*

un maillot (de bain) *swimsuit*

une montre *watch*

un pantalon à pattes d'éléphant *bell bottom pants*

un pull-over *sweater*

un pyjama *pyjama*

un sous-vêtement *underwear*

une tenue *outfit*

un vêtement / les vêtements *an article of clothing / clothing*

à la mode *stylish, fashionable*

ancien / ancienne *former*

bon marché *inexpensive*

cher / chère *expensive*

confortable *comfortable*

démodé(e) *old fashioned, out-of-date*

en solde *on sale*

porter *to wear*

Quelle est votre taille *(f.)*? *What size do you wear?*

Je fais du 32. *I'm a size 32.*

Quelle est votre pointure *(f.)*? *What is your shoe size?*

Je chausse du 36. *I wear a size 36 shoe.*

Ça vous va très bien. *That looks good on you.*

ACTIVITÉ A Classifiez les vêtements

CD3-24

Étape 1. Indiquez si chaque vêtement mentionné est normalement pour **(a) une femme, (b) un homme** ou **(c) une femme ou un homme.**

1.   2.   3.   4.   5.   6.   7.   8.   9.   10.   11.   12.

Étape 2. Indiquez si chaque vêtement mentionné est **(a) un haut** *(top)* ou **(b) un bas** *(bottom)*.

1.   2.   3.   4.   5.   6.   7.   8.   9.   10.   11.   12.

Étape 3. Indiquez si chaque vêtement mentionné est normalement pour **(a) l'hiver, (b) l'été** ou **(c) l'hiver et l'été.**

1.   2.   3.   4.   5.   6.   7.   8.   9.   10.   11.   12.

🔊 **ACTIVITÉ** Ⓑ **Quel magasin?**

CD3-25

Étape 1. Quel est votre magasin préféré pour acheter les choses mentionnées?

Modèle: des chaussettes **Kmart**

1. 2. 3. 4. 5. 6. 7. 8. 9. 10. 11. 12.

ACTIVITÉ Ⓒ **Au magasin** Associez les éléments de la première colonne aux éléments de la deuxième colonne.

1. _____ Ça vous va très bien.
2. _____ Je fais du 36.
3. _____ Je chausse du 34.
4. _____ Oui, j'aimerais l'essayer.

a. Quelle est votre pointure?
b. Que pensez-vous?
c. Je peux vous aider?
d. Quelle est votre taille?

👥 **ACTIVITÉ** Ⓓ **Est-ce que l'habit fait le moine?**

Étape 1. Est-ce que l'habit *(clothing)* fait le moine *(monk)*? Quels vêtements associez-vous aux personnes suivantes?

Modèle: un professeur **une chemise, un gilet, un pantalon et une cravate**

1. un acteur/une actrice
2. un(e) artiste
3. un(e) baba cool
4. un(e) bourreau de travail
5. un(e) écologiste
6. un(e) fana de la santé

7. un(e) femme active
8. un homme d'affaires
9. une femme au foyer
10. un(e) retraité(e)
11. un sportif/une sportive
12. un homme au foyer

Note de vocabulaire

Est-ce que l'habit fait le moine? is an idiomatic expression that means *Do the clothes make the man?*

👥 **Étape 2.** Regardez le dessin de la réunion des anciens du lycée Gatineau au début du **Vocabulaire 3** et répondez aux questions avec votre partenaire. Justifiez votre réponse.

Modèle: Qui pourrait être un homme au foyer? **Éric parce qu'il porte des vêtements confortables. Il porte des chaussettes avec un short et un pull-over.**

1. Qui pourrait être un baba cool?
2. Qui pourrait être une femme au foyer?
3. Qui pourrait être un sportif?
4. Qui pourrait être un bourreau de travail?
5. Qui pourrait être un fana de la santé?
6. Qui pourrait être artiste?

Si vous y allez

© Charles Platiau/Reuters/Corbis

Si vous allez à Paris, allez au grand magasin *Galeries Lafayette*. Situé sur le boulevard Haussmann dans le neuvième arrondissement, ce grand magasin a une sélection de vêtements à la mode pour hommes et femmes.

Étape 3. Dans le film *Liaisons*, Claire attend Alexis pour un rendez-vous. Qu'est-ce qu'ils portent? Est-ce que leurs vêtements sont à la mode ou démodés?

© Heinle/Cengage Learning

Étape 1. Que mettriez-vous dans votre valise pour les événements suivants? Vous ne pouvez mettre que dix choses dans votre valise.

1. faire une croisière à la Martinique
2. aller au carnaval de Québec en février
3. aller à un mariage à Paris en mars
4. faire du ski en Suisse
5. faire du camping au Canada
6. fêter le Mardi gras à La Nouvelle-Orléans

 Étape 2. Montrez vos réponses à un(e) partenaire. Qui fait mieux ses valises?

ACTIVITÉ **F** **Que porteriez-vous?**

Étape 1. Que porteriez-vous dans les situations suivantes?

1. pour faire de la gym
2. pour aller à un restaurant élégant
3. pour aller à un mariage
4. pour aller à un entretien (*interview*)
5. pour passer au contrôle de sécurité à l'aéroport
6. pour aller à la plage
7. pour aller à une réunion d'anciens élèves du lycée
8. pour dormir

 Étape 2. Dites à un(e) partenaire ce que vous porteriez pour les situations de l'Étape 1 mais ne lui dites pas la situation. Votre partenaire va deviner (*guess*) la situation.

Modèle: É1: **Je porterais un tee-shirt, un short et des baskets.**
É2: **Tu vas à la plage?**

ACTIVITÉ **G** **Qu'est-ce qu'on porte en classe aujourd'hui?**

Étape 1. Notez combien de femmes et combien d'hommes dans la classe portent les vêtements suivants aujourd'hui.

1. un jean
2. un tee-shirt
3. une casquette
4. une cravate
5. une jupe
6. un sweat
7. un jogging
8. des bottes
9. des baskets
10. un pull-over
11. un foulard
12. un chemisier
13. un gilet
14. une chemise
15. des sandales
16. ???

Étape 2. Pour chaque vêtement, notez environ (*approximately*) combien vous en avez chez vous.

Étape 3. Avec un(e) partenaire, comparez vos chiffres et répondez aux questions.

1. Y a-t-il une tenue typique pour les étudiants de notre classe? Décrivez-la.
2. Y a-t-il une différence entre ce que (*what*) les femmes et les hommes portent? Quelle est la différence?
3. Y a-t-il une différence entre les vêtements que vous avez chez vous et les vêtements que votre partenaire a chez lui/elle? Quelle est la différence?

ACTIVITÉ **H** **Avez-vous bon goût?**

Étape 1. Que porteriez-vous avec ces vêtements pour compléter la tenue?

Modèle: une mini-jupe noire

Je porterais une mini-jupe noire avec un tee-shirt blanc, des chaussures à talon noires et une ceinture.

1. un pull à col roulé rouge
2. des bottes noires
3. un pull-over orange Gap
4. un chemisier/une chemise jaune
5. un pantalon à pattes d'éléphant
6. un gilet vert
7. un blouson noir
8. des chaussettes blanches

© Signed model release filed with Shutterstock Images LLC

Étape 2. Posez les questions à un(e) partenaire. À votre avis, est-ce que votre partenaire est à la mode ou démodé(e)? Il/Elle a bon ou mauvais goût?

Étape 3. Toujours avec votre partenaire, décrivez une jolie tenue et une tenue laide que vous avez vue. Qui portait ces tenues?

Modèle: **J'ai vu une très jolie tenue à la télévision aux Oscars. Kate Winslet portait une robe du soir violette avec des talons hauts, un collier et un bracelet. Mon voisin portait une tenue très laide. Il portait un tee-shirt jaune, un gilet marron, un short rouge, des baskets, des chaussettes blanches et une casquette des Dallas Cowboys.**

Un mot sur la culture

© Hulton Archive/ Getty Images

Coco Chanel

Quand on pense à la mode française, on pense immédiatement à Chanel. Née à Saumur (Maine-et-Loire), Gabrielle «Coco» Chanel (1883–1971) a commencé sa carrière dans la confection de chapeaux où elle a rapidement connu le succès avant de se lancer dans la couture. On doit à Chanel le pantalon pour femmes et le tailleur très pratique qui porte son nom. Chanel a contribué à l'émancipation des femmes avec des vêtements féminins confortables qui étaient traditionnellement réservés aux hommes. Son parfum, Chanel N° 5, reste l'un des parfums les plus célèbres au monde. Chanel est le symbole du goût et de l'élégance des maisons de mode.

- Avez-vous des produits Chanel? Quels produits Chanel aimeriez-vous avoir?
- Est-ce que vous avez vu le film «Coco avant Chanel» avec Audrey Tautou?

Liaisons avec les mots et les sons

CD3-26
Les sons /z/ et /s/

You already learned that the **s** sound in a **liaison** is pronounced /**z**/.

très occupé	deux écharpes	trois imperméables	vous aidez

An **s** is also pronounced /**z**/ when it occurs between two vowels.

un blouson	une chemise	Isabelle	un magasin

An **s** is pronounced /**s**/ when it occurs at the beginning of a word.

un sac	des sandales	un smoking	un siège

An **s** is pronounced /**s**/ before or after a pronounced consonant.

une casquette	un costume	transporter	Mustapha

A double **ss** is pronounced /**s**/.

les chaussures	les chaussettes	un passeport	les tissus

The following spellings also have the sound /**s**/: **ç**, **c** followed by **i** or **e**, and **t** in **-tion**.

Ça va	un bracelet	une ceinture	la natation

Pratique A. Écoutez et répétez ces mots de vocabulaire.

Le son /z/
1. deux agents
2. trois étoiles
3. vos achats
4. un chemisier
5. une croisière
6. une valise

Le son /s/
7. en solde
8. un sweat
9. passer
10. je chausse
11. une agence
12. un centime

Pratique B. Écoutez et répétez ces répliques de la Séquence 5 du film *Liaisons*. Relisez les répliques. Encerclez (*Circle*) tous les sons /z/ et soulignez (*underline*) tous les sons /s/.

MME PAPILLON C'est si triste. Mourir comme ça, tout seul, sans personne. Le médecin a dit qu'il était mort vers neuf heures du matin.

CLAIRE Vous..., vous avez dit vers neuf heures? Ça fait trois heures du matin au Québec. Mais il m'a appelé à cette heure. C'est pas possible...

CD3-27
À vos stylos! C'est l'heure de la dictée!
Vous allez entendre six phrases deux fois. La première fois, écoutez bien. La deuxième fois, écrivez les phrases.

Sujet Claire et Mme Papillon parlent au téléphone.

Pour parler des personnes et des choses non-spécifiées

Les adjectifs et les pronoms indéfinis

DU FILM *LIAISONS*

Un coup d'œil sur la grammaire

Look at these photos from the film *Liaisons* and their captions.

MME LEGRAND Hier j'ai égaré (*misplaced*) **toutes** mes cartes de crédit et maintenant ma clé.

MME LEGRAND À bientôt, Marie. À bientôt... Bonne journée à **tous**!

1. In the left caption, what is **toutes** referring to? And **tous** in the right caption?
2. What do you think **toutes** and **tous** mean in the captions?

Liaisons musicales

Luce Dufault (1966–) est une chanteuse québécoise de R'n'B qui a joué aussi dans des comédies musicales. *Tous ces mots* (1998) est une belle chanson sur un chagrin d'amour (*break-up*). Écoutez la chanson sur Internet.

- Indefinite adjectives and pronouns allow you to refer to people, things, or qualities that are not specified. They also allow you to express sameness.

- **Tout** (*all*) may be used as an adjective or a pronoun. As an adjective, it must agree in number and gender with the noun it modifies and it can be followed by an article, a possessive adjective (**mon, ses...**), or a demonstrative adjective (**ce, cette...**).

J'ai vu **tous** mes amis.	*I saw **all** my friends.*
J'ai mangé **toute** la tarte.	*I ate **all** of the pie.*
Nous avons bu **tout** le café.	*We drank **all** the coffee.*
Toutes ces jupes sont belles.	***All** these skirts are beautiful.*

- The masculine form **tout** may be used as a pronoun to mean *all* or *everything*.

Tout va bien.	***Everything** is going well.*
Tout ça me fait peur.	***All** this scares me.*
J'aime **tout**.	*I like **everything**.*

- The pronouns **tous** and **toutes** mean *everyone, every one (of them)*, or *all (of them)*.

Tu vois ces robes? **Toutes** sont jolies.	*Do you see these dresses. **All** of them are pretty.*
Ces enfants veulent **tous** aller au parc.	*These children **all** want to go to the park.*

> Use the pronoun **tous** to refer to a group that includes at least one male. Use **toutes** to refer to a group that consists only of females.

| Merci à **tous**! | *Thank you **everyone** (men only or men and women)!* |
| **Toutes** veulent venir. | ***All of them** (only women) want to come.* |

> To say *everyone*, use the expression **tout le monde.**

| **Tout le monde** est arrivé. | ***Everyone** has arrived.* |

> Here are other common expressions that may be used as adjectives or pronouns:

d'autres *(some) other(s)*	**certain(e)s (de)** *certain (of)*
l'autre/les autres *the other(s)*	**le/la/les même(s)** *the same*
un(e) autre *another*	**plusieurs (de)** *several (of)*

Les questions? **D'autres** sont plus faciles.	*The questions? **Some others** are easier.*
Il préfère **l'autre** chapeau.	*He prefers **the other** hat.*
Certaines chemises sont confortables.	***Certain** shirts are comfortable.*
Ces tee-shirts? **Certains** sont chers.	*These t-shirts? **Certain (ones)** are expensive.*
Les mêmes viennent toujours.	***The same ones** always come.*
Elle a acheté **plusieurs** bracelets.	*She bought **several** bracelets.*

> Some indefinites have different forms when used as adjectives and pronouns.

Adjectives	Pronouns
chaque *(+ noun) each, every*	**chacun/chacune (de)** *each (one) (of)*
quelques *(+ noun) some*	**quelques-uns/quelques-unes (de)** *some, a few (of)*

Chaque femme ici est belle.	***Every** woman here is beautiful.*
Chacune de ces femmes est française.	***Each one** of these women is French.*
J'ai **quelques** chemisiers.	*I have **some** blouses.*
Les chemisiers? **Quelques-uns** sont verts.	*The blouses? **A few of them** are green.*

ACTIVITÉ ① À la réunion des anciens étudiants du lycée Gatineau

Étape 1. Complétez les conversations des anciens élèves du lycée Gatineau avec un adjectif ou avec un pronom indéfinis.

1. ____ de mes copains est ici.	a. Chaque	b. Chacun	c. Chacune
2. ____ cours était intéressant.	a. Chaque	b. Chacun	c. Chacune
3. ____ de mes amis sont mariés.	a. Quelques	b. Quelques-uns	c. Quelques-unes
4. ____ camarades sont en Europe.	a. Quelques	b. Quelques-uns	c. Quelques-unes
5. Les femmes? ____ ont un MBA.	a. Quelques	b. Quelques-uns	c. Quelques-unes
6. Bonjour Mireille! ____ va bien?	a. Tout	b. Toute	c. Tous
7. Éric a perdu ____ ses cheveux.	a. tout	b. toutes	c. tous
8. Je suis sorti avec ____ les filles.	a. tout	b. toutes	c. tous

ACTIVITÉ **J** **Un potin à la réunion du lycée Gatineau** Complétez l'histoire avec la forme appropriée des mots suivants.

d'autres   l'autre   un(e) autre

(1) _____ jour, je suis allée à la réunion des anciens élèves du lycée Gatineau. Je n'ai pas vu mon professeur préféré, Monsieur Painchaud, mais j'ai parlé avec (2) _____ anciens professeurs. (3) _____ étudiante, Sandrine, voulait le voir aussi mais il n'est jamais venu.

certain(e)s   le/la/les même(s)   plusieurs   tout/toutes/tous/toutes

(4) _____ amis ont dit qu'ils ont entendu un potin de (5) _____ étudiants: la femme de M. Painchaud vient de le quitter. Mon amie Anne a dit qu'elle a entendu (6) _____ chose. C'est dommage. (7) _____ mes anciens camarades de classe sont tristes pour lui.

ACTIVITÉ **K** **Les confessions d'un accro du shopping**

Étape 1. Un accro du shopping achète tout. Et vous? Utilisez les adjectifs indéfinis.

Modèle: Je veux acheter toutes les montres de Macy's.
Moi, j'achèterais toutes les montres de Macy's aussi. / J'achèterais certaines montres de Macy's. / Je n'achèterais aucune montre de Macy's.

Je veux acheter tous/toutes…

1. les livres de Barnes and Noble
2. les chocolats Godiva
3. les glaces Ben & Jerry's
4. les écharpes de Kmart
5. les montres de T.J. Maxx
6. les iPods d'Apple

ACTIVITÉ **L** **Votre opinion**

Étape 1. Quelle est votre opinion sur les vêtements de ces magasins? Utilisez des adjectifs et des pronoms indéfinis.

Modèle: les pantalons de Walmart
Certains pantalons de Walmart sont à la mode mais d'autres sont démodés. Tous leurs pantalons sont bon marché.

1. les lunettes de soleil de Target
2. les manteaux de Macy's
3. les chaussettes de T.J. Maxx
4. les chaussures de Sears
5. les jeans de Gap
6. les tee-shirts d'Urban Outfitters

Étape 2. Montrez vos réponses à un(e) partenaire. Êtes-vous d'accord avec les descriptions de votre partenaire?

Le pronom *lequel*

Lequel (laquelle, lesquels, lesquelles) means *which.* The different forms of **lequel** may be used as interrogative pronouns and must agree with the nouns they modify. They may also be used with prepositions. Note that **à** and **de** contract with **lequel.**

Laquelle de ces robes préférez-vous? La robe Chanel ou la robe Dior?

Which of these dresses do you prefer? The dress by Chanel or the dress by Dior?

Lesquels de ces tee-shirts aimez-vous? Les tee-shirts bleus ou les tee-shirts noirs?

Which of these t-shirts to you like? The blue t-shirts or the black t-shirts?

À laquelle pensez-vous? La cravate Burberry ou la cravate Dior?

Which tie are you thinking of? The Burberry tie or the Dior tie?

Vous parlez **duquel**? Du jean Gap ou du jean Calvin Klein?

Which one are you talking about? The Gap jeans or the Calvin Klein jeans?

Essayez! Complétez les phrases avec une forme de **lequel.**

1. _____ de ces jupes aimez-vous? Les jupes courtes ou les jupes longues?

2. _____ de ces pyjamas aimez-vous? Les pyjamas roses ou les pyjamas blancs?

3. _____ de ces chapeaux aimez-vous? Le chapeau noir ou le chapeau orange?

4. _____ de ces montres aimez-vous? La montre Cartier ou la montre Swatch?

5. _____ parlez-vous? De la chemise courte ou de la chemise longue?

La parole est à vous!

Est-ce que les magasins doivent pouvoir vous rembourser les vêtements vendus en solde?

Certains magasins ne remboursent° pas les vêtements qui sont soldés. Êtes-vous d'accord?

- Annick de Rimouski (Québec): «Non. Si j'ai toujours mon reçu°, je devrais pouvoir être remboursée si le vêtement ne me va pas bien, même si c'est en solde.»
- Marc d'Aptes (France): «Moi, je suis d'accord avec cette politique°. Les vêtements vendus en soldes sont les vêtements hors saison° et les magasins ne peuvent plus les vendre.»

remboursent *refund* **reçu** *receipt* **politique** *policy* **hors saison** *off-season*

Et vous? Qu'en pensez-vous?

Est-ce que vous devriez pouvoir vous faire rembourser les vêtements vendus en soldes?

PREMIÈRE PROJECTION

Avant de visionner

ACTIVITÉ A **Vous rappelez-vous?** Vous rappelez-vous qui a dit ces phrases dans la Séquence 5 du film *Liaisons:* Claire, Alexis ou Mme Papillon?

Note de vocabulaire

The expression **être de passage** means *to pass through*.

1. _____ La prochaine fois que vous êtes de passage […] au Québec, vous me le direz?

2. _____ Il y a des choses que j'aimerais vous dire, [pause] mais...

3. _____ C'est que... J'espère que vous pourrez nous pardonner...

4. _____ Ah, ma pauvre petite. J'ai une mauvaise nouvelle... Votre oncle est mort.

5. _____ Vous...vous avez dit neuf heures? […] C'est pas possible...

6. _____ Ah, ma pauvre petite. On se parlera quand vous arriverez...

ACTIVITÉ B **Devinez** Dans la Séquence 6 du film *Liaisons,* Claire va à la Banque Nationale avec sa clé mystérieuse. Devinez ce qui se passera. Complétez les phrases au futur simple avec les verbes donnés.

1. (parler) Claire _____.
2. (voir) Claire _____.
3. (trouver) Claire _____.
4. (apprendre) Claire _____.
5. (retourner) Claire _____.
6. (s'en aller) Claire _____.

ACTIVITÉ C **Un coup d'œil sur une scène** Voici une scène de la Séquence 6 du film *Liaisons.* Claire parle avec un employé de banque à la Banque Nationale. Avec un(e) partenaire, devinez le mot qui correspond à chaque espace *(space)* dans le dialogue. Vous allez vérifier vos réponses plus tard.

CLAIRE (1) _____

EMPLOYÉ Bonjour Madame.

CLAIRE J'ai reçu cette (2) _____ et je voulais savoir si elle ouvre (3) _____ ici.

EMPLOYÉ Avez-vous (4) _____ du coffre?

CLAIRE Non. J'ai pas (5) _____, j'ai reçu (6) _____ avant-hier.

© Heinle/Cengage Learning

1. a. Bonjour   b. Excusez-moi
2. a. clé   b. enveloppe
3. a. un coffre-fort   b. une porte
4. a. la clé   b. le numéro
5. a. le numéro   b. une pièce d'identité
6. a. la clé   b. l'enveloppe

Regarder la séquence

Vous allez regarder la Séquence 6 du film *Liaisons*. Vérifiez vos réponses à l'Activité B et à l'Activité C.

Après le visionnage

ACTIVITÉ D **L'avez-vous compris?** Pour chaque phrase, indiquez si c'est vrai ou faux.

	Vrai	Faux
1. Claire trouve des photos dans le coffre-fort.	☐	☐
2. Les documents dans le coffre-fort datent des années 90.	☐	☐
3. Claire trouve une autre clé dans le coffre-fort.	☐	☐
4. Claire s'en va en France.	☐	☐

ACTIVITÉ E **Un chiffre important**

Étape 1. Faites une liste des événements dans lesquels vous vous rappelez le chiffre 315.

Étape 2. Montrez votre liste à un(e) partenaire. Avez-vous écrit les mêmes choses? Aimeriez-vous ajouter d'autres détails à votre liste? À votre avis, quelle est la signification du chiffre 315 dans le film?

ACTIVITÉ F **Utilisez le contexte**

© Heinle/Cengage Learning

Regardez bien le mot en caractère gras *(boldface)* et répondez à la question.

CLIENTE Bruno, je ne trouve pas ma clé. Où est-ce que je l'ai mise? **Cibole!**

- On utilise l'expression «Cibole!» quand on est calme ou quand on est énervé?

Liaisons avec la culture

La langue et les objets religieux au Québec

© Bill Greenblatt/UPI/Landov

Ciboire et calice

L'Église catholique a eu une influence considérable dans la société québécoise avant la Révolution tranquille. Pour cette raison, les noms de certains objets utilisés lors de la messe catholique peuvent avoir un double sens. Par exemple, à l'église, un ciboire° est un vase° où on met les hosties° consacrées° pendant la communion et un calice° est le vase pour le vin consacré. Pourtant, quand on est énervé et que l'on dit ces mots avec un point d'exclamation, ils peuvent représenter des gros mots°! D'autres termes religieux qui peuvent être des gros mots sont **baptême**, **hostie** et **tabernacle**. Il est donc très important de faire attention au contexte quand on utilise ces mots au Québec. Le mot «cibole!», que Madame LeGrand a utilisé, est un euphémisme du mot **ciboire** qui veut dire «darn it!» en anglais.

ciboire *ciborium* **vase** *vessel* **hosties** *holy bread* **consacrées** *holy* **calice** *chalice* **gros mots** *curse words*

La mode: du transport à la haute couture

OUTILS DE LECTURE

Identifying previously learned vocabulary

When you read, it can be helpful to identify vocabulary you have already learned. Identifying previously learned words and expressions helps you remember their meanings better. In turn, these words can help you to guess the meaning of new words in a text and to predict a text's content.

1. Skim the text **La Poste et les services bancaires** and jot down the vocabulary words you have learned in this and previous chapters.

2. Look at your list of words. What do you think this text is about?

La Poste et les services bancaires

La Poste n'est pas uniquement un lieu où on achète des timbres et d'où on envoie des lettres et des colis. En France et dans plusieurs pays francophones, La Poste fonctionne également° comme une banque. Ouvrir un compte-chèques, un compte d'épargne, un plan-épargne-logement°, obtenir une carte bleue (carte de crédit) ou un prêt immobilier°, tout cela est possible au bureau de poste, ce qui fait de La Poste une des plus grandes banques françaises. Dans

©Jerome CHATIN/EXPANSION-REA

plusieurs pays africains, comme au Bénin ou au Cameroun, La Poste joue un rôle crucial dans l'économie, par exemple, en facilitant les transferts de fonds à travers les mandats° postaux.

également *also* **un plan-épargne-logement** *mortgage savings account* **un prêt immobilier** *mortgage* **un mandat** *money order*

Vrai ou faux?

1. La Poste ne joue aucun rôle dans l'économie.   V / F

2. On peut acheter des timbres dans une banque.   V / F

3. On peut transférer des fonds en envoyant un mandat postal.   V / F

Le métro de Paris

Le métro de Paris est un système populaire de transports desservant° la ville de Paris et son agglomération°. Le métro transporte plus de 3,9 millions de voyageurs par jour. Il dessert° 300 stations avec 384 points d'arrêt. Devenu un des symboles de Paris, il se caractérise par la densité de son réseau° au cœur de Paris et par son style architectural influencé par l'Art nouveau. La première ligne du métro de Paris a été inaugurée quelques mois après le début de l'Exposition universelle de 1900. Le métro parisien se classe, pour le nombre de voyageurs transportés, en quatrième position derrière Tokyo (3,2 milliards), Moscou (2,4 milliards) et Séoul (2 milliards).

desservant *serving* **agglomération** *neighboring areas* **dessert** *serves* **réseau** *network*

Vrai ou faux?

1. Le métro de Paris a moins de 300 points d'arrêt.   V / F
2. Le métro parisien est un des symboles de Paris.   V / F
3. La première ligne du métro a été inaugurée en 1900.   V / F

La Belgique: destination populaire pour les vacances

La Belgique est une destination populaire pour les vacances, surtout pour les Européens parce qu'elle est facile d'accès. Bruxelles, sa capitale, est une ville cosmopolite et l'un des sièges° de l'Union européenne. C'est également à Bruxelles qu'on trouve le siège de l'OTAN° (Organisation du traité de l'Atlantique Nord). Bruxelles est le lieu privilégié de beaucoup de manifestations culturelles et de lieux célèbres tels que la Grand-Place, les Galeries royales Saint-Hubert, la fontaine Manneken pis et le Festival Couleur-Café. En gastronomie, la Belgique est connue pour son chocolat et ses gaufres°.

sièges *headquarters* **OTAN** *NATO* **gaufres** *waffles*

Vrai ou faux?

1. Les Européens n'aiment pas voyager en Belgique.   V / F
2. L'un des sièges de l'OTAN est à Bruxelles.   V / F
3. Bruxelles a beaucoup de manifestations culturelles.   V / F

© WireImage/ Getty Images

La Fédération Française de la Couture

La Fédération Française de la Couture, du Prêt-à-Porter des couturiers et des créateurs de Mode, a été établie en 1973. Les missions importantes de la fédération sont d'établir les critères de la haute couture et de déterminer le calendrier des collections Printemps-Été et Automne-Hiver en ce qui concerne° la haute couture et le prêt-à-porter masculin et féminin. Paris accueille° chaque année, en janvier et en juillet, une trentaine de défilés° durant la semaine de la Haute Couture, et en mars et octobre plus d'une centaine de défilés de Prêt-à-Porter féminin. Parmi° les maisons membres les plus célèbres en France, on trouve Chanel, Chloé, Christian Dior, Hermès, Jean-Paul Gaultier, Louis Vuitton et Yves Saint-Laurent, entre autres.

en ce qui concerne *concerning* **accueille** *welcomes* **défilés** *fashion shows* **Parmi** *Among*

Vrai ou faux?

1. Chaque maison de mode décide de ses critères pour la haute couture.   V / F

2. La Fédération Française de la Couture établit le calendrier pour les collections.   V / F

3. La semaine de la Haute Couture est à Paris.   V / F

🌐 Activités Internet

• Cherchez sur Internet le site Web de La Poste en France. Nommez trois services intéressants.

• Cherchez un plan du métro de Paris sur Internet. Quelle station de métro est près du musée du Louvre?

• Cherchez sur Internet un musée célèbre à Bruxelles. Qu'est-ce qu'on peut voir dans ce musée?

• Cherchez le site officiel de la Fédération Française de la Couture sur Internet. Quelle est la date du prochain défilé de mode? Nommez trois maisons de mode qui vont participer au défilé.

PARTIE 1

LES TRANSPORTS

un (auto)bus	*bus*
un avion	*plane*
un camion	*truck*
une camionnette	*van, mini van*
le covoiturage	*carpooling*
le métro	*subway*
une moto	*motorcycle*
les moyens (*m.*) de transport	*means of transportation*
à pied	*on foot*
un 4X4 (quatre-quatre)	*SUV*
un scooter	*moped*
un taxi	*taxi*
un train	*train*
une voiture	*car*

À LA POSTE

une boîte à lettres	*mailbox*
une carte postale	*postcard*
un colis	*package*
le courrier	*mail*
une enveloppe	*envelope*
un facteur/une factrice	*mail carrier*
la poste	*post office*
un timbre	*stamp*

VERBES

bouger	*to move*
conduire	*to drive*
construire	*to construct*
détruire	*to destroy*
envoyer quelque chose en express	*to send something express*
faire le trajet (entre)	*to travel, to commute (between)*
livrer	*to deliver goods/groceries*
traduire	*to translate*
transporter	*to transport*

PARTIE 2

À L'AÉROPORT

un aéroport	*airport*
un(e) agent(e) de bord	*flight attendant*
un(e) agent(e) de la sécurité	*security agent*
un billet d'avion	*plane ticket*
un billet aller-retour	*round-trip ticket*
un billet aller simple	*one-way ticket*
une carte d'embarquement	*boarding pass*
à l'étranger	*abroad, overseas*
un passeport	*passport*
un permis de conduire	*driver's license*
une pièce d'identité	*a form of identification*
une porte d'embarquement	*departure gate*
un siège (côté couloir)	*(aisle) seat*
une valise	*suitcase*
un vol direct/une correspondance	*direct/connecting flight*
un voyageur/une voyageuse	*traveler*
la première classe	*first-class*
la classe affaires	*business class*
la classe économique	*economy class*

LES VOYAGES

une auberge de jeunesse	*youth hostel*
une chambre fumeur/non-fumeur	*smoking/nonsmoking rom*
une chambre individuelle/double	*single/double room*
une clé	*key*
un(e) client(e)	*client, guest*
un gîte du passant	*bed and breakfast*
un hôtel (trois/quatre/cinq étoiles)	*(three/four/five star) hotel*
un hôtel de luxe	*luxury hotel*
un lit simple/double	*single/double bed*
un motel	*motel*
le logement	*lodging*
le service de chambre	*room service*
une agence de voyages	*travel agency*
un(e) agent(e) de voyages	*travel agent*
un arrêt d'autobus	*bus stop*
une croisière	*cruise*
une gare	*(bus/train) station*
une tente	*tent*

VERBES

aller en vacances (*f.*)	*to go on vacation*
attacher la ceinture de sécurité	*to fasten the seatbelt*
débarquer de l'avion	*to get off the plane*
déclarer (vos achats)	*to declare (your purchases)*
embarquer dans l'avion	*to board the plane*
enregistrer (les valises)	*to check in (luggage)*
faire les valises	*to pack*
passer au contrôle de sécurité	*to go through security*
passer à la douane	*to go through customs*
payer des frais supplémentaires	*to pay extra fees*

LES PRONOMS RELATIFS

dont	*that, (of) which, (of) whom*
où	*where, when*
que	*that, which*
qui	*who, that, which*

PARTIE 3

LES VÊTEMENTS

un anorak	*parka*
des baskets *(f.)*	*sports shoes*
un blouson (en cuir)	*(leather) windbreaker*
des bottes *(f.)*	*boots*
un bracelet	*bracelet*
une casquette	*baseball cap*
un chapeau	*hat*
des chaussettes *(f.)*	*socks*
des chaussures *(f.)* (à talon)	*(high-heeled) shoes*
une chemise	*shirt*
un chemisier	*blouse*
un collier	*necklace*
un costume	*man's suit*
une cravate	*tie*
une écharpe	*scarf*
un foulard	*silk scarf*
des gants *(m.)*	*gloves*
un gilet	*cardigan sweater*
un imperméable	*raincoat*
un jean	*jeans*
un jogging	*sweatpants*
des lunettes *(f.)* de soleil	*sunglasses*
un maillot (de bain)	*swimsuit*
une mallette	*briefcase*
un manteau	*overcoat*
une (mini-)jupe	*(mini) skirt*
une montre	*watch*
un pantalon	*slacks*
un pantalon à pattes d'éléphant	*bell bottom pants*
un pull à col roulé	*turtle neck sweater*
un pull-over	*pullover sweater*
un pyjama	*pyjama*
une robe	*dress*
une robe du soir	*evening dress*
des sandales *(f.)*	*sandals*
un short	*shorts*
un smoking	*tuxedo*
un sous-vêtement	*underwear*
un sweat (à capuche)	*(hooded) sweatshirt*
un tailleur	*woman's suit*
un tee-shirt	*t-shirt*
une tenue	*outfit*
un vêtement / les vêtements	*an article of clothing / clothing*

ADJECTIFS

à la mode	*stylish, fashionable*
ancien/ancienne	*former*
bon marché	*inexpensive*
cher/chère	*expensive*
confortable	*comfortable*
démodé(e)	*old fashioned, out-of-date*

EXPRESSIONS

Quelle est votre taille *(f.)*?	*What size do you wear?*
Je fais du 32.	*I'm a size 32.*
Quelle est votre pointure *(f.)*?	*What is your shoe size?*
Je chausse du 36.	*I wear a size 36 shoe.*
Ça vous va très bien.	*That looks good on you.*

ADJECTIFS/PRONOMS INDÉFINIS

une autre/d'autres	*another/(some) other(s)*
l'autre/les autres	*the other(s)*
certain(e)s (de)	*certain (of)*
chacun/chacune (de)	*each (one) (of)*
chaque *(+ noun)*	*each, every*
le/la/les même(s)	*the same*
lequel/laquelle/ lesquels/lesquelles	*which*
plusieurs (de)	*several (of)*
quelques *(+ noun)*	*some*
quelques-uns/ quelques-unes (de)	*some, a few (of)*
tout/tous/toute/toutes	*all (of them)/everyone*
tout le monde	*everyone*

DIVERS

en solde	*on sale*
porter	*to wear*

La santé

En bref In this chapter, you will:

- learn vocabulary to talk about health and hygiene

- learn parts of the body for humans and animals

- talk about similarities and differences between humans and animals

- learn reflexive verbs that pertain to hygiene and daily routines

- learn the present subjunctive

- learn expressions of volition, necessity, and emotions that take the subjunctive

- learn about the sounds **e caduc, e muet, and h**

- read about medical tourism in Tunisia

- write about your reaction to medical tourism

You will also re-watch **SÉQUENCE 6: Une découverte** of the film *Liaisons*.

Ressources

 audio http://www.cengagebrain.com

🔊 L'hygiène **personnelle**

Personal hygiene

les sourcils *(m.)*
les oreilles *(f.)*
les joues *(f.)*
le cou
la crème à raser
un rasoir
la main
le genou
le pied
la bouche
le savon
le dentifrice
un sèche-cheveux
un peigne
une brosse (à cheveux)
la tête
les épaules *(f.)*
le dos
le bras
la taille
le coude
une serviette
la jambe

Dans le vestiaire du centre sportif

Vocabulaire complémentaire

la cheville *ankle*	**la poitrine** *chest*	**la crème solaire** *sunscreen*
le corps *body*	**le ventre** *abdomen, belly*	**le maquillage** *makeup*
les dents *(f.) teeth*	**le visage / la figure** *face*	**un rouge a lèvres** *lipstick*
la gorge *throat*		**le shampooing** *shampoo*
la langue *tongue*	**une brosse a dents** *toothbrush*	
les lèvres *(f.) lips*	**l'hygiène** *(f.) hygiene*	**un vestiaire** *a locker, locker room*
la nuque *nape of the neck*	**les produits** *(m.)* **de soin personnel**	
les orteils *(m.) toes*	*personal care products*	**utiliser** *to use*
le poignet *wrist*	**la crème hydratante** *moisturizer*	

ACTIVITÉ A **Des vêtements** Quel vêtement associez-vous à la partie du
CD3-28 corps mentionnée?

1.   2.   3.   4.   5.   6.   7.   8.

ACTIVITÉ B **Les produits et les parties du corps**

Étape 1. Quelle partie du corps associez-vous aux produits suivants?

1. une brosse à dents	a. le dos	b. la cheville	c. la bouche
2. la crème à raser	a. les joues	b. la langue	c. le ventre
3. le dentifrice	a. le coude	b. le genou	c. les dents
4. un rouge à lèvres	a. les sourcils	b. les lèvres	c. la poitrine
5. le shampooing	a. le visage	b. la tête	c. les mains

Étape 2. De quel produit de soin personnel est-ce qu'Alexis avait besoin à l'hôtel?

© Heinle/Cengage Learning

ACTIVITÉ C **Quelle partie du corps?**

Étape 1. Sur quelle partie du corps utilisez-vous ces produits ou appareils?

1. la crème hydratante	**4.** une serviette	**7.** le shampooing
2. la crème solaire	**5.** le savon	**8.** un peigne
3. un sèche-cheveux	**6.** le maquillage	**9.** le déodorant

Étape 2. Posez les mêmes questions à deux camarades de classe, si possible un étudiant et une étudiante.

Étape 3. Est-ce que vos réponses et celles de vos camarades de classe sont semblables ou différentes? S'il y a des différences, décrivez-les.

ACTIVITÉ D Les activités

Étape 1. Quelles parties du corps est-ce qu'on utilise pour les activités suivantes?

Modèle: le bowling **On utilise les mains, les doigts, les bras et les jambes.**

1. écouter de la musique
2. regarder un film
3. manger un steak
4. faire de l'aérobic
5. jouer du violon
6. jouer au tennis
7. faire de la danse du ventre
8. faire du surf

Étape 2. Quelle est votre activité physique préférée? Quelles parties du corps utilisez-vous pour faire cette activité?

ACTIVITÉ E Les produits de soin personnel

Étape 1. Quels produits trouvez-vous…

1. chez un dentiste?
2. chez un coiffeur?
3. chez un coiffeur pour hommes?
4. chez le toiletteur *(dog groomer)*?
5. dans un institut de beauté?
6. dans une chambre d'hôtel?

© Cristi Matei/Shutterstock.com

Étape 2. Demandez à un(e) partenaire quels produits de soin personnel il/elle apporte au vestiaire du centre sportif.

Conclusion Est-ce que votre partenaire est **propre, très propre** ou **obsessionnel(le)?**

ACTIVITÉ F Vos marques préférées

Étape 1. Quelle est votre marque *(brand)* préférée pour les produits suivants?

1. le dentifrice
2. le shampooing
3. le savon
4. le déodorant
5. le maquillage
6. les brosses à dents
7. la crème hydratante
8. la crème solaire

Étape 2. Posez les questions à un(e) partenaire. Avez-vous choisi les mêmes marques? Quelles marques avez-vous en commun?

Étape 3. Avec votre partenaire, essayez de nommer une marque française pour chaque produit de l'Étape 1.

Étape 4. Si vous pouviez seulement emporter *(take)* trois produits de soin personnel pour faire du camping dans la forêt, lesquels emporteriez-vous?

ACTIVITÉ G Lady Gaga ou Adam Lambert?

Étape 1. Avec un(e) partenaire, indiquez si ces traits décrivent Lady Gaga, Adam Lambert ou ni l'un ni l'autre *(neither)*.

	Lady Gaga	Adam Lambert	Ni l'un ni l'autre
1. un gros ventre	_____	_____	_____
2. une taille fine *(slender)*	_____	_____	_____
3. les épaules larges *(broad)*	_____	_____	_____
4. les dents blanches	_____	_____	_____
5. un long cou	_____	_____	_____
6. de grands pieds	_____	_____	_____
7. une poitrine musclée	_____	_____	_____
8. les sourcils broussailleux *(bushy)*	_____	_____	_____
9. un dos poilu *(hairy)*	_____	_____	_____
10. les oreilles percées *(pierced)*	_____	_____	_____
11. les jambes longues	_____	_____	_____
12. les cheveux parfois bleus	_____	_____	_____

© Helfa Esteb/Shutterstock.com

Note de vocabulaire
Note that **cheveux** only refers to human hair on the head. To refer to human hair not on the head and animal hair or fur, use **les poils** *(hair)* or the adjective **poilu(e)(s)**.

Étape 2. Décrivez les traits physiques d'une autre personne célèbre.

© Gleb Garanich/Reuters/Landov

Un mot sur la culture

Les critères de beauté

Dans les cultures occidentales°, être mince est à la mode. Pour être un top-modèle, il faut avoir une petite taille et un ventre plat. Pourtant, dans certaines cultures africaines et asiatiques, on considère une femme charnue° belle. C'est un symbole de la fortune et de la prospérité. Par exemple, en Mauritanie, un pays saharien de l'Afrique de l'Ouest, certaines femmes désirent grossir pour se préparer au mariage. Au Sénégal et en Côte d'Ivoire, il existe des concours de beauté° pour les femmes charnues. Pourtant, à cause des influences internationales comme la mode occidentale et la télévision française, cette tradition devient moins populaire chez certaines jeunes filles.

occidentales *western* **charnue** *plump* **concours de beauté** *beauty contests*

• Aimeriez-vous voir des concours de beauté pour les hommes?
• À votre avis, est-ce que les top-modèles des cultures occidentales sont trop minces?

Pour parler de l'hygiène personnelle et de la routine

Encore des verbes réfléchis

 DU FILM *LIAISONS*

Un coup d'œil sur la grammaire

Look at these photos from the film *Liaisons* and their captions.

MME LEGRAND Je dois **m'habiller** [...] **me maquiller**...

MME LEGRAND Je dois rentrer chez moi pour **me préparer.**

1. What do the verbs **s'habiller** and **se maquiller** mean in the left caption?
2. What does the verb **se préparer** mean in the right caption?

❖❖ In **Chapitre 10,** you learned about reflexive verbs. Many verbs used to express daily routines are also reflexive verbs since they convey what people do to or for themselves.

se brosser	*to brush*	**se laver**	*to wash (oneself)*
se coucher	*to go to bed*	**se lever**	*to get up*
se couper	*to cut (oneself)*	**se maquiller**	*to put on make-up*
se doucher	*to (take a) shower*	**se préparer**	*to get ready, to prepare*
s'endormir	*to go, fall asleep*	**se raser**	*to shave (oneself)*
s'habiller	*to get dressed*	**se réveiller**	*to wake up*
se déshabiller	*to (get) undress(ed)*	**se sécher**	*to dry (oneself)*

❖❖ Many of these verbs can be used reflexively and non-reflexively. When the subject and object of the verb are the same, the verb is used reflexively. When the subject and the object of the verb are different, the verb is used non-reflexively.

Mme Loubard s'habille.	*Mme Loubard is getting dressed.*
Mme Loubard habille sa fille.	*Mme Loubard is dressing her daughter.*
Je me lave.	*I am washing up.*
Je lave mon chien.	*I am washing my dog.*

When a part of the body is used with a reflexive verb, it is usually preceded by the definite article, not the possessive adjective as in English.

Il se brosse les dents.	*He is brushing his teeth.*
Nous nous lavons les mains.	*We are washing our hands.*

As you learned in **Chapitre 10,** reflexive verbs always take **être** in the **passé composé,** and there is usually agreement between the past participle and the subject pronoun.

Nous nous sommes endormis.	*We fell asleep.*
Anne s'est habillée?	*Did Anne get dressed?*
Elles se sont réveillées à 8h30.	*They woke up at 8:30.*

If a reflexive verb in the **passé composé** is followed by a direct object, the past participle does not agree with the subject.

Elle s'est rasé les jambes.	*She shaved her legs.*
Ils se sont lavé les mains.	*They washed their hands.*
Nous nous sommes coupé les cheveux.	*We cut our hair.*

Remember that, if a verb is used non-reflexively instead of reflexively, it uses **avoir**—not **être**—as the auxiliary verb in the **passé composé.**

Marie s'est lavé les mains.	*but*	**Marie a lavé la vaisselle.**
Marie washed her hands.		*Marie washed the dishes.*

> **Note de grammaire**
> Remember that the past participle does not agree with verbs like **se parler** and **se téléphoner** that take indirect objects.

ACTIVITÉ Ⓗ **Votre routine**

Étape 1. Dans quel ordre est-ce que vous faites ces activités le matin?

_____ Je me brosse les dents.   _____ Je me maquille.

_____ Je me douche.   _____ Je me rase.

_____ Je m'habille.   _____ Je me réveille.

_____ Je me lave le visage.   _____ Je me sèche les cheveux.

Étape 2. Est-ce qu'il y a des activités de l'Étape 1 que vous ne faites pas? Pourquoi pas?

ACTIVITÉ Ⓘ **Les parties du corps** Complétez chaque phrase avec un verbe réfléchi au présent.

Modèle: les yeux   **Je me maquille les yeux.**

1. _____ les dents.
2. _____ les jambes.
3. _____ le visage.
4. _____ les cheveux.
5. _____ les pieds.
6. _____ les mains.

ACTIVITÉ **J** **Qu'est-ce qu'ils font?** Décrivez les images suivantes avec une phrase complète au présent.

1. a.

b.

2. a.

b.

3. a.

b.

ACTIVITÉ **K** **Les activités d'Abia et de Nadia** Abia et sa sœur Nadia décrivent ce qu'elles ont fait hier. Complétez les phrases.

1. Nous nous sommes lavées _____.   a. avant de partir   b. les mains

2. Nous nous sommes rasées _____.   a. les jambes   b. avec un nouveau rasoir

3. Nous nous sommes séché _____.   a. les cheveux   b. après la douche

4. Nous nous sommes brossé _____.   a. les dents   b. le chat de Patrick

5. Nous avons lavé _____.   a. les cheveux   b. la voiture de papa

Et vous? Quelles activités de l'Étape 1 avez-vous faites hier?

ACTIVITÉ L **Qu'est-ce qu'ils ont fait?** Décrivez les images de l'Activité J au passé composé.

ACTIVITÉ M **Votre routine**

Étape 1. Répondez aux questions à propos de votre routine.

1. Est-ce que vous vous préparez rapidement ou lentement?
2. Est-ce que vous vous lavez les mains avant de manger?
3. Est-ce que vous vous brossez les dents tous les jours?
4. Est-ce que vous vous douchez tous les jours?
5. Est-ce que vous vous réveillez tôt ou tard?
6. Est-ce que vous vous endormez souvent devant la télé?
7. Est-ce que vous vous déshabillez avant de vous coucher?
8. Est-ce que vous vous couchez tôt ou tard?

Étape 2. Posez les questions à deux camarades de classe. Notez leurs réponses. Avec qui pourriez-vous partager un appartement?

ACTIVITÉ N **Un jeu de charades** En groupes de trois à quatre personnes, vous allez jouer aux charades. Votre professeur va vous donner des expressions avec des verbes de cette leçon. Vous devez mimer vos expressions. Les autres personnes de votre groupe vont deviner votre expression. Qui sont les meilleurs acteurs de votre classe?

La parole est à vous!

Est-ce que votre chef a son mot à dire sur votre coiffure?

Des chefs d'entreprises disent que certains employés ont des coiffures° qui ne sont pas convenables° professionnellement. Est-ce que les entreprises devraient avoir le droit d'interdire° les coiffures non conventionnelles telles que° les crêtes°?

- Pascal de Tadoussac (Québec): «Absolument pas! Personne n'a le droit de réglementer° ma coiffure. Une coiffure c'est un choix personnel.»
- Guy de Nîmes (France): «Oui. J'ai eu un employé qui s'est teint° les cheveux en vert. Ça a donné une très mauvaise image de mon entreprise.»

coiffures *hairstyles* **convenables** *appropriate* **interdire** *to ban, to forbid* **telles que** *such as* **crêtes** *mohawks* **réglementer** *to regulate* **s'est teint** *dyed*

Et vous? Qu'en pensez-vous?

Est-ce que votre chef a son mot à dire sur votre coiffure?

🔊 Toutes les créatures

All creatures

un aigle

un serpent

les humains *(m.)*

un lion

un tigre

un ours

un hamster

une chèvre

un oiseau

un lapin

un rat

un cochon

un coq

une grenouille

L'homme et ses amis

Vocabulaire complémentaire	
une animalerie *pet store*	**les poils** *(m.) animal hair, fur*
une créature *creature*	**un refuge** *(animal) shelter*
les moustaches *(f.) whiskers*	**un requin** *shark*
une patte *paw*	

ACTIVITÉ **A** **Testez vos connaissances**

🔊 **Étape 1.** Indiquez si chaque animal que vous entendez **(a) a une queue, (b) a des**
CD3-29 **ailes** *(wings)* ou **(c) n'a ni l'un ni l'autre.**

1.   2.   3.   4.   5.   6.   7.   8.   9.   10.   11.   12.

Étape 2. Quel animal habite dans l'eau?

1. a. un hamster   b. un poisson
2. a. un lapin   b. un requin
3. a. un canard   b. une chèvre
4. a. une grenouille b. un ours

Étape 3. Quel animal a des pattes?

1. a. un lion   b. un poisson
2. a. une chèvre   b. un humain
3. a. un aigle   b. un lapin
4. a. un chien   b. un chat
5. a. un ours   b. un serpent
6. a. un requin   b. un tigre

Étape 4. Quel animal est plus féroce *(ferocious)*?

1. a. un oiseau   b. un serpent
2. a. une chèvre   b. un requin
3. a. un tigre   b. un chat
4. a. un rat   b. un hamster
5. a. un lapin   b. un ours
6. a. un humain   b. un lion

Étape 5. À quel pays associez-vous les animaux suivants?

1. le coq   2. le lion   3. l'aigle   4. le panda   5. la grenouille

ACTIVITÉ **B** **Les animaux et les caractéristiques humaines**

Étape 1. Dans les fables de l'écrivain français Jean de La Fontaine,
les animaux ont des caractéristiques humaines. Quels traits et caractéristiques
associez-vous aux animaux suivants?

Modèle: une chèvre   **Elle est têtue.**

1. un rat   3. un aigle   5. un cochon
2. un requin   4. un ours   6. un serpent

👥 **Étape 2.** Montrez vos réponses à un(e) partenaire. Est-ce que vous êtes
d'accord avec ses réponses?

Si vous y allez

Si vous allez à Anvers en
Belgique, visitez le zoo
d'Anvers. Créé *(Created)* au
19e siècle, le zoo d'Anvers
est un des plus anciens et
des plus célèbres en Europe.
Plus de 5 000 animaux vous
y attendent.

Le coq et le renard
de Jean de La Fontaine

ACTIVITÉ C **Le zodiaque chinois**

Étape 1. Décrivez votre caractère avec cinq adjectifs.

Modèle: **Je suis intelligent(e), patient(e), excentrique, optimiste et têtu(e).**

Étape 2. Lisez les descriptions des animaux du zodiaque chinois. Quel animal est associé à votre année de naissance? Êtes-vous d'accord avec la description?

 Les rats (né[é] en 1936, 48, 60, 72, 84, 96) sont ambitieux et honnêtes. Ils aiment dépenser beaucoup d'argent. Rats célèbres: Shakespeare, Mozart.

 Les vaches *(cows)* (1937, 49, 61, 73, 85, 97) sont travailleuses, intelligentes, patientes et exigeantes. Vaches célèbres: Napoléon, Van Gogh.

 Les tigres (1938, 50, 62, 74, 86, 98) sont agressifs, courageux, passionnés et sensibles. Tigres célèbres: Marco Polo, Marilyn Monroe.

 Les lapins (1939, 51, 63, 75, 87, 99) sont talentueux, articulés et timides. Ils aiment faire la paix. Lapins célèbres: Confucius, Albert Einstein.

 Les dragons (1940, 52, 64, 76, 88, 2000) sont excentriques, extravertis, intelligents, indiscrets, exigeants et sains. Dragons célèbres: Jeanne d'Arc, Freud.

 Les serpents (1941, 53, 65, 77, 89, 2001) sont sages *(wise),* romantiques, beaux et ont le sens de l'humour. Ils sont aussi avares. Serpents célèbres: Darwin, A. Lincoln.

 Les chevaux (1942, 54, 66, 78, 90, 2002) sont populaires, beaux, intelligents et travailleurs mais aussi impatients et égoïstes. Chevaux célèbres: Rembrandt, Chopin.

 Les chèvres (1943, 55, 67, 79, 91, 2003) sont élégantes, créatives et timides. Parfois elles sont pessimistes. Chèvres célèbres: Michelangelo, Mark Twain.

 Les singes *(monkeys)* (1944, 56, 68, 80, 92, 2004) sont intelligents et ambitieux mais ils peuvent être facilement découragés *(discouraged).* Singe célèbre: Jules César.

 Les coqs (1945, 57, 69, 81, 93, 2005) sont créatifs, fiers, égoïstes et excentriques. Ils sont dévoués *(devoted)* à leur travail. Coq célèbre: Rudyard Kipling.

 Les chiens (1946, 58, 70, 82, 94, 2006) sont fidèles, honnêtes, têtus, idéalistes et parfois égoïstes. Ils s'inquiètent souvent. Chiens célèbres: Socrate, Benjamin Franklin.

 Les cochons (1947, 59, 71, 83, 95, 2007) sont intellectuels, sincères, optimistes et tolérants. Ils s'amusent et ils ont la joie de vivre. Cochon célèbre: Ernest Hemingway.

Étape 3. Décrivez votre caractère à deux camarades de classe et écoutez leurs descriptions. Devinez *(Guess)* quel animal est associé à leurs années de naissance. Avez-vous bien deviné?

Étape 4. Quel animal est associé aux enfants nés cette année? Quel animal sera associé aux enfants nés l'année prochaine?

Étape 4. Dans votre groupe, discutez de quel animal vous associez aux modes de vie et aux carrières suivants. Justifiez vos choix.

1. un gérant
2. un avocat
3. un écrivain
4. un homme politique
5. un baba cool
6. un bourreau de travail
7. un acteur
8. un accro du shopping
9. un professeur

ACTIVITÉ D Les animaux et les humains Avec un(e) partenaire, dites en quoi les animaux suivants sont similaires ou différents des humains.

Modèle: les chats **Les chats et les humains ont deux oreilles, deux yeux, un nez, une bouche et une langue. Les chats sont différents des humains parce qu'ils ont quatre pattes, des poils, des moustaches et une queue.**

1. les singes (monkeys)
2. les tigres
3. les chiens
4. les oiseaux

Conclusion À quel animal est-ce ques les humains ressemblent (resemble) le plus?

ACTIVITÉ E Les animaux et vous Posez ces questions à un(e) partenaire.

1. Est-ce que tu as des animaux chez toi? Est-ce que tu as un(e) ami(e) qui a des animaux chez lui/elle? Quel animal ou quels animaux?
2. Est-ce que tu (ou ton ami[e]) as (a) acheté l'animal dans une animalerie ou est-ce que tu l'as (il/elle l'a) adopté dans un refuge pour animaux abandonnés?
3. À ton avis, quels animaux sont parfaits pour les étudiants?

Un mot sur la culture

Les animaux de Jean de La Fontaine

© The Art Archive / Private Collection / Marc Charmet

Jean de La Fontaine (1621–1695) est un écrivain français de la période classique. Il est célèbre pour ses fables dans lesquelles il personnifie les animaux pour donner des leçons de morale. Quelques-unes de ses fables les plus connues sont: *La cigale°* et *la fourmi,°* *Le corbeau°* et *le renard, La grenouille et le rat, Le singe et le chat, Le cochon, La chèvre et le mouton* et *Le chat et le vieux rat.*

cigale *grasshopper* **fourmi** *ant* **corbeau** *crow*

• Cherchez une fable de La Fontaine sur Internet. Quels animaux sont dans cette fable? Quelle est la leçon de morale de cette fable?

LE LOUP ET L'AGNEAU

Pour exprimer les désirs et les obligations

Les verbes réguliers au subjonctif

DU FILM *LIAISONS*

Un coup d'œil sur la grammaire

Look at these photos from the film ***Liaisons*** and their captions.

© Heinle/Cengage Learning

© Heinle/Cengage Learning

CLIENTE [...] **il faut** donc **que** je **sorte** quelques bijoux *(jewels)* de mon coffre.

CLAIRE Quelqu'un **voulait que** je les **trouve.**

1. What verb follows **il faut que** in the left caption? What does the caption mean?
2. What verb follows **voulait que** in the right caption? What does the caption mean?

Note de **grammaire**
The subjunctive is not often used in English: *It's important that you not **be** sick. I wish that I **were** healthier.*

⋯ You have used the indicative mood to state facts and ideas and to ask questions. You have used the imperative mood to express commands and the conditional mood to make suggestions and to express hypothetical situations. When you want to express will and influence (volition), desires, opinions, and obligations, you need to use the subjunctive mood, **le subjonctif.** The subjunctive is used quite frequently in French.

   Il faut que je sorte avec Florian.   *It is necessary that I go out with Florian.*

   Je veux que tu finisses tes devoirs.   *I want you to finish your homework.*

⋯ The present subjunctive of most verbs is formed by dropping the -**ent** from the third person plural form (**ils/elles**) of the present indicative and adding the subjunctive endings -**e, -es, -e, -ions, -iez,** and -**ent.**

Note de **grammaire**
The **nous** and **vous** forms of the present subjunctive are identical to those of the imperfect.

Infinitive				
Stem	**regarder**	**vendre**	**choisir**	**connaître**
	(ils) regard~~ent~~	(ils) vend~~ent~~	(ils) choisiss~~ent~~	(ils) connaiss~~ent~~
... que je	regard**e**	vend**e**	choisiss**e**	connaiss**e**
... que tu	regard**es**	vend**es**	choisiss**es**	connaiss**es**
... qu'il/elle/on	regard**e**	vend**e**	choisiss**e**	connaiss**e**
... que nous	regard**ions**	vend**ions**	choisiss**ions**	connaiss**ions**
... que vous	regard**iez**	vend**iez**	choisiss**iez**	connaiss**iez**
... qu'ils/elles	regard**ent**	vend**ent**	choisiss**ent**	connaiss**ent**

- Some verbs have two stems in the subjunctive: one stem for the **nous** and **vous** form and another stem for the **je, tu, il/elle/on,** and **ils/elles** forms.

	acheter	boire	prendre	venir
… que je/j'	ach**è**te	boive	prenn**e**	vienn**e**
… que tu	ach**è**tes	boives	prenn**es**	vienn**es**
… qu'il/elle/on	ach**è**te	boive	prenn**e**	vienn**e**
… que nous	achet**ions**	buv**ions**	pren**ions**	ven**ions**
… que vous	achet**iez**	buv**iez**	pren**iez**	ven**iez**
… qu'ils/elles	ach**è**t**ent**	boiv**ent**	prenn**ent**	vienn**ent**

- Other verbs that have two stems in the subjunctive include the following:

  appeler: que j'appelle, que nous appelions

  comprendre: que je comprenne, que nous comprenions

  croire: que je croie, que nous croyions

  devenir: que je devienne, que nous devenions

  devoir: que je doive, que nous devions

  essayer: que j'essaie, que nous essayions

  payer: que je paie, que nous payions

  préférer: que je préfère, que nous préférions

  recevoir: que je reçoive, que nous recevions

  voir: que je voie, que nous voyions

- The subjunctive almost always occurs in sentences that contain a main clause and a dependent clause *and* in which the subject of the main clause is different from the subject of the dependent clause. The expression or verb in the main clause causes the subjunctive to be used in the dependent clause. The dependent clause begins with **que** *(that).*

  Il faut **que vous lisiez** ce livre.　　*It is necessary that you read this book.*

  Il veut **que nous dormions** plus.　　*He wants us to sleep more.*

- The subjunctive commonly occurs after these verbs and expressions of volition, opinion, and obligation.

Il (ne) faut (pas) que	**aimer mieux que**
Il vaut mieux que	**désirer que**
Il (n') est (pas) nécessaire que	**préférer que**
Il (n') est (pas) important que	**vouloir que**

Il vaut mieux que vous payiez l'addition.
It's better that you pay the bill.

Il est important que tu te brosses les dents.
It's important for you to brush your teeth.

Je préfère que tu ne te lèves pas à midi.
I prefer that you don't get up at noon.

L'enfant veut que sa mère l'habille.
The child wants his mother to dress him.

ACTIVITÉ F Les désirs des activistes pour les droits des animaux

Indiquez si chaque phrase est vraie ou fausse.

Un activiste pour les droits des animaux…

	Vrai	Faux
1. **préfère que nous achetions** les chats dans une animalerie.	☐	☐
2. **désire que nous respections** les oiseaux.	☐	☐
3. **aime mieux que nous adoptions** les animaux d'un refuge.	☐	☐
4. **veut que vous apportiez** les chiens abandonnés à un refuge.	☐	☐
5. **désire que vous vendiez** des lapins pour la recherche (research).	☐	☐
6. **préfère que vous portiez** des manteaux de fourrure (fur).	☐	☐
7. **aime mieux qu'on abandonne** les vieux chevaux.	☐	☐
8. **veut qu'on vive** en paix avec les animaux.	☐	☐

Et vous? Êtes-vous un(e) activiste pour les droits des animaux?

ACTIVITÉ G Les animaux et les humains

Étape 1. Complétez les phrases avec le verbe approprié.

1. Il est important qu'un ours _____ beaucoup.　　a. dorme　　b. dort
2. Il ne faut pas qu'un chien _____ du chocolat.　　a. prend　　b. prenne
3. Il ne faut pas que nous _____ les animaux.　　a. abandonnons　　b. abandonnions
4. Il faut qu'on _____ les droits des animaux.　　a. reconnaisse　　b. reconnaît
5. Il ne faut pas que vous _____ du requin.　　a. mangiez　　b. mangez
6. Il vaut mieux que vous ne _____ pas avec les rats.　　a. jouez　　b. jouiez

Étape 2. Complétez les phrases avec (a) Il faut, (b) Il ne faut pas, (c) Il vaut mieux, (d) Il n'est pas nécessaire ou (e) Il est important.

1. _____ qu'un humain se brosse les dents.
2. _____ qu'on brosse les dents des chiens et des chats.
3. _____ qu'un humain prenne de la viande rouge.
4. _____ qu'une vache prenne de la viande rouge.
5. _____ qu'un humain boive de l'eau.
6. _____ qu'un canard boive de l'eau.
7. _____ qu'un humain se lave tous les jours.
8. _____ qu'un cochon se lave tous les jours.
9. _____ qu'un humain dorme le soir.
10. _____ qu'un rat dorme le soir.

Étape 3. Comparez vos réponses avec un(e) partenaire. Avez-vous les mêmes réponses? Avec votre partenaire, nommez deux similarités et deux différences entre un humain et un animal.

Liaisons musicales

© Jean Yves DesFoux/Maxppp/Landov

Née Béatrice Martin (1989), Cœur de Pirate est une chanteuse et pianiste québécoise qui joue du piano depuis l'âge de trois ans. Elle a gagné le prix Félix de la Révélation de l'année avec son premier album *Cœur de pirate* (2008). *Corbeau,* une chanson de cet album, utilise la métaphore des oiseaux, (des corbeaux *[crows]*) pour décrire une rupture *(breakup)*. Écoutez cette chanson sur Internet.

ACTIVITÉ **H** **Les désirs de Patrick et d'Aude**

Étape 1. Le neveu et la nièce d'Abia du film *Liaisons*, Patrick et Aude, parlent de leurs désirs et de ceux des membres de leur famille. Complétez les phrases avec la forme appropriée du verbe qui convient.

1. Il vaut mieux que maman _____ un spectacle avec papa.
   a. chanter   b. danser   c. voir
2. Il faut que papa _____ «Je t'aime» à maman plus souvent.
   a. dire   b. écouter   c. parler
3. Patrick, il est important que tu _____ la lettre de l'oncle Jerome.
   a. entendre   b. lire   c. réussir
4. Aude, il ne faut pas que tu _____ les Cocas de papa.
   a. boire   b. manger   c. mettre
5. Il faut que l'oncle Xavier _____ ses études bientôt.
   a. étudier   b. finir   c. sortir
6. Je désire que nous _____ plus souvent avec notre chat.
   a. s'amuser   b. se perdre   c. se demander
7. Je veux qu'on _____ bien avec l'ex-femme de l'oncle Kofi.
   a. s'entendre   b. se méfier   c. se mettre à
8. Nous préférons qu'Abia nous _____ des bonbons.
   a. acheter   b. manger   c. parler
9. Nous préférons que grand-mère nous _____ visite plus souvent.
   a. jouer   b. finir   c. rendre
10. J'aime mieux que l'oncle Xavier _____ nous voir ce soir.
    a. partir   b. prendre   c. venir
11. Papa ne veut pas que grand-maman _____ avec nous.
    a. connaître   b. essayer   c. vivre
12. Maman et papa veulent que nous _____ à nos examens.
    a. jouer   b. lire   c. réussir

Étape 2. Qu'est-ce que vous désirez de la part des personnes suivantes? Complétez les phrases avec les verbes donnés.

1. Je veux que mon/ma camarade de chambre (écouter) _____.
2. J'aime mieux que mes voisins (s'entendre) _____.
3. Il vaut mieux que mon ami(e) (sortir) _____.
4. Je préfère que mon/ma colocataire (dormir) _____.
5. Je veux que ma famille (se sentir) _____.
6. Je désire que mon professeur (donner) _____.
7. Il vaut mieux que mes camarades de classe et moi, nous (regarder) _____.
8. Il est important que la classe et moi, nous (parler) _____.

Étape 3. Comparez vos réponses avec un(e)partenaire. Qui est plus exigeant(e) envers *(toward)* les autres? Vous ou votre partenaire?

ACTIVITÉ I **Les personnages du film *Liaisons*** Décrivez les photos avec les éléments donnés.

Modèle: Mme Gagner / Claire / rendre visite
Mme Gagner veut que Claire lui rende visite plus souvent.

1. Claire / la serveuse / servir

3. Claire / l'homme mystérieux / dire

2. la voisine de l'oncle Michel / Claire / venir

4. l'employé de la banque / Claire / donner

ACTIVITÉ J **Les chefs**

Étape 1. Que veulent les chefs? Choisissez un type de chef et complétez les phrases selon ses désirs. Utilisez le subjonctif.

Possibilités: le président de notre pays, un cadre d'entreprise, un président d'une chaîne de télé, un chef de cuisine, un professeur, le président de notre université, un membre de la clergé, un parent, … veut…?

1. que nous (prendre) _____.

2. que nous (aider) _____.

3. que les enfants (obéir) _____.

4. que les jeunes (obtenir) _____.

5. qu'on (apprendre) _____.

6. qu'on (connaître) _____.

7. qu'on (essayer) _____.

8. qu'on (vivre) _____.

Conclusion Est-ce que votre partenaire est comme son chef choisi?

Étape 2. Demandez à un(e) partenaire s'il/si elle veut les choses que vous avez écrites dans l'Étape 1.

Modèle: É1: **Est-ce que tu veux que nous prenions plus de vacances?**
É2: **Oui, je veux que nous prenions plus de vacances.**

Conclusion Est-ce que votre partenaire est comme le président de votre pays?

Les demandes des étudiants Avez-vous des demandes *(requests)* ou des suggestions pour votre professeur? Avec un(e) partenaire, écrivez une lettre de cinq à sept phrases à votre professeur avec les verbes donnés. Utilisez chaque verbe seulement *(only)* une fois.

Verbes possibles

acheter	écouter	lire	revenir
s'amuser	écrire	manger	sortir
apprendre	enseigner	prendre	travailler
boire	goûter	réfléchir	venir
commander	inviter	regarder	visiter
donner	jouer	répondre	voir

Modèle: Cher Monsieur/Chère Madame
Il est nécessaire que vous nous écoutiez. Il faut que nous nous amusions plus en classe. Nous voulons que vous organisiez une fête pour la classe de français.

La parole est à vous!

Faut-il interdire aux chiens d'entrer dans les restaurants en France?

Les Français aiment beaucoup les animaux, surtout° les chiens. Les touristes sont souvent surpris d'apprendre qu'on peut manger sur les terrasses des restaurants avec son chien. On peut même° trouver des restaurants qui permettent aux chiens d'entrer à l'intérieur. Pourtant, certains touristes pensent que cette pratique constitue un risque pour la santé. Qu'en pensez-vous? Faut-il que la France interdise° aux chiens d'entrer dans les restaurants?

- Sarah de Rivière-du-Loup (Québec): «Je pense que oui. J'aime les animaux mais on ne peut pas amener un chien dans un restaurant. Les chiens pourraient avoir des maladies. C'est un risque pour la santé.»

- Yves-Antoine de Paris (France): «Absolument pas! Les Français apprécient beaucoup leurs animaux de compagnie. Nos chiens sont des membres de notre famille et ils ont le droit de manger avec nous, même dans les restaurants. Ça fait partie de notre culture.»

surtout *especially* **même** *even* **interdise** *ban*

Et vous? Qu'en pensez-vous?
Faut-il interdire aux chiens d'entrer dans les restaurants en France?

🔊 Rester en forme

Staying healthy

un(e) patient(e)

le cœur

prendre la tension (artérielle)

faire une prise de sang

avoir mal au ventre

un pansement

des points *(m.)* de suture

prendre la température

avoir de la fièvre

éternuer

une allergie

un kleenex

être allergique à

Les maladies et les soins

 Vocabulaire complémentaire

l'assurance-maladie *(f.) health insurance*
une blessure *wound*
un comprimé *tablet*
la grippe *flu*
l'hypertension *(f.) high blood pressure*
une intervention chirurgicale *surgery*
une maladie *illness*

un médicament *medication*
une radiographie *X-ray*
un rhume *cold*
le stress *stress*
un symptôme *symptom*
un traitement *treatment*
les urgences *(f.) emergency room*

tousser

le sirop contre la toux

une ordonnance

un(e) pharmacien(ne)

un cachet d'aspirine

ASPIRINE

un(e) vétérinaire

faire une piqûre

se gratter

les béquilles *(f.)*

un plâtre

D'autres maladies et soins

Vocabulaire complémentaire

aller aux urgences *to go to the emergency room*

avoir mal à (la tête) *to hurt (to have a headache)*

avoir mal au cœur *to be nauseated*

se casser (le bras) *to break one's (arm)*

conseiller *to advise*

donner son sang *to give one's blood*

être en bonne/mauvaise santé *to be in good/bad health*

être en forme *to be in good shape*

être / tomber malade *to be / to get sick*

fatigué(e) *tired*

grave *serious*

Qu'est-ce qui ne va pas? *What's wrong?*

🔊 **ACTIVITÉ** Ⓐ **Qui le dit?** Indiquez qui dit chaque phrase que vous entendez:
CD3-30 **(a) un médecin** ou **(b) un(e) patient(e).**

1.   2.   3.   4.   5.   6.   7.   8.   9.   10.   11.   12.

ACTIVITÉ Ⓑ **C'est grave ou ce n'est pas grave?** À votre avis, est-ce que chaque traitement suivant est pour une maladie qui **est très grave, peut-être un peu grave** ou **pas grave?**

Modèle: Prenez deux aspirines. **Ce n'est pas grave.**

1. Voici un pansement.
2. On va faire une radiographie.
3. Il faut faire une intervention chirurgicale.
4. Allez aux urgences!
5. Prenez du sirop pour votre toux.
6. Il faut faire dix points de suture.
7. Voici des comprimés pour vos allergies.
8. On va vous mettre le bras dans un plâtre.

⋯▶ **Et vous?** Avez-vous jamais reçu ces soins?

ACTIVITÉ Ⓒ **Quelle activité?**

Étape 1. Indiquez quelles activités ou situations vous associez aux symptômes de ces patients.

Modèle: Il est stressé.   **Il travaille trop.**

1. Il a un rhume.
2. Il a mal à la tête.
3. Il a de l'hypertension.
4. Il est toujours fatigué.
5. Il se gratte et éternue beaucoup.
6. Il a une blessure au genou.
7. Il a la grippe.
8. Il s'est cassé le bras.

👥 **Étape 2.** Montrez vos réponses à un(e) partenaire. Avez-vous les mêmes réponses?

ACTIVITÉ Ⓓ **Les examens médicaux pour les animaux et pour nous**

Étape 1. Indiquez qui dit chaque phrase: **(a) un médecin, (b) un vétérinaire** ou **(c) tous les deux.**

1. Est-ce qu'il a l'assurance-maladie?
2. Est-ce qu'il se gratte souvent?
3. Il faut lui donner du sirop contre la toux.
4. Il a des puces *(fleas).*
5. Je vais lui faire une piqûre.
6. Il a besoin de béquilles.
7. Il a de la fièvre.
8. On va prendre sa tension.
9. Voudriez-vous donner votre sang?
10. Voici des comprimés.

👥 **Étape 2.** Comparez vos réponses avec un(e) partenaire pour voir si vous êtes d'accord.

✈ ⋯⋯
Si vous y allez

Si vous voyagez au Québec et si vous avez besoin d'aspirines ou de médicaments, allez à la pharmacie Brunet dont le slogan est: **En santé depuis 150 ans.**

© Jeff Greenberg / Alamy

Étape 3. Avec votre partenaire, comparez en quoi un examen médical est semblable et différent pour les humains et pour les animaux.

ACTIVITÉ E Les maladies

Étape 1. Quels problèmes pourraient avoir ces personnages du film *Liaisons* s'ils faisaient les activités suivantes?

Modèle: Robert a fait du vélo toute la journée. **Il va avoir mal aux jambes.**

1. Abia ne s'est pas séché les cheveux avant de sortir en hiver.
2. Robert est tombé du balcon de son appartement.
3. Claire a donné son sang à la Croix-Rouge *(Red Cross)*.
4. Claire a fait une nuit blanche *(all-nighter)* pour étudier pour ses examens.
5. Abia a bu du lait périmé *(expired)*.
6. Robert a mangé deux pizzas et a bu trois bouteilles de vin.

Étape 2. Quelle maladie associez-vous à ces symptômes?

1. Abia éternue et elle se gratte.
2. Claire a mal à la gorge, elle tousse et elle éternue.
3. Robert a mal à la tête, il a de la fièvre, il a froid et il a mal au ventre.

Étape 3. Montrez vos réponses à un(e) partenaire. Qui est le meilleur médecin? Avez-vous jamais eu ces symptômes?

ACTIVITÉ F Les remèdes de grand-mère

Étape 1. La grand-mère d'Abia connaît de bons remèdes *(remedies)*. Quelle maladie associez-vous à ces remèdes?

Il faut que tu…

1. boives du jus d'orange.
2. prennes de la soupe au poulet.
3. dormes beaucoup.
4. évites de prendre du sel.
5. boives de la tisane *(herbal tea)*.
6. te gargarises *(gargle)* avec de l'eau salée.

Étape 2. Montrez vos réponses à un(e) partenaire pour voir si vous êtes d'accord. Connaissez-vous de bons remèdes aussi?

ACTIVITÉ G Si vous étiez médecin Si vous étiez médecin, que suggéreriez-vous à ces patient(e)s?

1. J'ai de la fièvre.
2. J'ai mal à la gorge.
3. J'ai mal au cœur.
4. Mon nez est trop grand.
5. Je me suis coupé le doigt.
6. Je tousse beaucoup.

ACTIVITÉ H Le dossier médical

Étape 1. Préparez le dossier médical (*medical history*) d'une personne célèbre. Répondez aux questions à sa place. **Suggestions:** Bart Simpson, Eric Cartman, Tom Cruise, Lindsay Lohan, Betty White, Sean Penn, Oprah Winfrey, David Beckham

1. Est-ce que vous fumez? À quelle fréquence (*frequency*)? Avez-vous jamais fumé?

2. Est-ce que vous buvez de l'alcool? À quelle fréquence?

3. Mangez-vous très gras? À quelle fréquence?

4. Avez-vous jamais subi (*undergo*) une intervention chirurgicale? Pour quelle raison?

5. Avez-vous jamais eu une chirurgie esthétique (*plastic surgery*)? Pour quelle raison?

6. Prenez-vous des médicaments? Lesquels?

7. Avez-vous des allergies? Quelles allergies?

8. Avez-vous jamais été hospitalisé(e)? Pour quelle raison?

Étape 2. Comparez votre dossier médical avec ceux de deux camarades de classe.

ACTIVITÉ I Êtes-vous en bonne santé cette année?

Étape 1. Avez-vous eu ces problèmes de santé cette année? Répondez aux questions.

1. Vous avez eu mal à la tête?
2. Vous avez eu mal au cœur?
3. Vous avez eu mal à la gorge?
4. Vous avez eu un rhume?

5. Vous avez eu de la fièvre?
6. Vous avez eu un plâtre?
7. Vous avez eu des points de suture?
8. Vous avez eu la grippe?

Étape 2. Posez ces questions à un(e) partenaire. Qui est en meilleure forme cette année: vous ou votre partenaire?

Un mot sur la culture

L'assurance-maladie en France

En France, l'assurance-maladie fait partie de la Sécurité Sociale. Tous les salariés, français ou étrangers, peuvent bénéficier de la Sécurité Sociale pour la couverture des frais médicaux et dentaires (consultation de médecins généralistes et spécialistes, radiologie), des médicaments et des frais d'hospitalisation (chirurgie, maternité). Si vous êtes salarié(e), vous recevrez automatiquement votre carte d'assuré(e) social(e). La France a l'un des meilleurs systèmes d'assurance maladie au monde.

• Aimez-vous le système d'assurance-maladie de votre pays?

© J-C&D. Pratt/ Photononstop/ Photolibrary

◀)) Liaisons avec les mots et les sons

CD3-31

La lettre *h,* le *e* caduc et le *e* muet

As you have seen, the **h** in French is usually silent and treated as a vowel.

l'homme	s'habiller	les humains	des heures

Some words have an **h aspiré.** This means the **h** is not treated as vowel, so it is not preceded by **l'** and there is no **liaison.**

le hockey	les haricots verts	le huit novembre	les héros

An unaccented **e** is usually pronounced like the **e** in the following words. This sound is called an *e* **caduc.**

ce	de	le	me	se regarder	cheveux

An *e* **caduc** is sometimes called *e* **muet** *(mute)* when it is silent. An *e* **muet** occurs at the end of words and when it is preceded by only one consonant.

coude	singe	tête	vache	logement	traitement

The *e* **caduc** sound is often dropped in spoken French.

Je ne sais pas.	Il ne se brosse pas les dents.	Je ne suis pas certain.

Pratique A. Écoutez et répétez ces mots de vocabulaire.

1. l'hygiène
2. hydratante
3. s'habiller
4. l'hypertension
5. le hamster
6. les hors-d'œuvre
7. se lever
8. le refuge
9. le requin
10. la brosse
11. un tigre
12. un rouge à lèvres

Pratique B. Écoutez ces répliques *(lines)* du film **Liaisons.** Ensuite, lisez-les et barrez *(cross out)* tous les *e* **muets.**

1. **EMPLOYÉ** Ça va bien, mon petit toutou *(doggy)*?
2. **MME LEGRAND** Je dois rentrer chez moi pour me préparer.
3. **CLAIRE** Je ne suis pas tombée sur ces documents par hasard.

◀)) **À vos stylos! C'est l'heure de la dictée!**

CD3-32 Vous allez entendre cinq phrases deux fois. La première fois, écoutez bien. La deuxième fois, écrivez les phrases.

Sujet Claire décrit à Abia les photos qu'elle a trouvées.

Pour exprimer la volonté et les émotions

Le subjonctif des verbes irréguliers

DU FILM *LIAISONS*

Un coup d'œil sur la grammaire

Look at these photos from the film *Liaisons* and their captions.

MICHEL (V.O.) Il faut que tu **ailles** à Québec.

CLAIRE Il faut que je **fasse** mes valises.

1. What is the infinitive form of **ailles** in the left caption? What does the caption mean?
2. What is the infinitive form of **fasse** in the right caption? What does the caption mean?

•❖• Some verbs have irregular subjunctive stems. With the exception of **avoir** and **être,** the endings themselves are regular.

	avoir	être	aller	faire
... que je/j'	**aie**	**sois**	**aille**	**fasse**
... que tu	**aies**	**sois**	**ailles**	**fasses**
... qu'il/elle/on	**ait**	**soit**	**aille**	**fasse**
... que nous	**ayons**	**soyons**	**allions**	**fassions**
... que vous	**ayez**	**soyez**	**alliez**	**fassiez**
... qu'ils/elles	**aient**	**soient**	**aillent**	**fassent**

	pouvoir	savoir	vouloir
... que je/j'	**puisse**	**sache**	**veuille**
... que tu	**puisses**	**saches**	**veuilles**
... qu'il/elle/on	**puisse**	**sache**	**veuille**
... que nous	**puissions**	**sachions**	**voulions**
... que vous	**puissiez**	**sachiez**	**vouliez**
... qu'ils/elles	**puissent**	**sachent**	**veuillent**

Il faut que j'**aille** aux urgences.   *I must go to the emergency room.*

Le médecin veut que je **boive** de l'eau.   *The doctor wants me to drink some water.*

⋰⋰ Here are some other verbs and expressions of volition, opinion, and obligation after which the subjunctive commonly occurs.

conseiller que *to advise that*	**souhaiter que** *to wish that*
demander que *to ask that*	**Il est essentiel que** *It is essential that*
exiger que *to demand that*	**Il est préférable que** *It is preferable that*

Mon mari **souhaite que je sois** plus heureuse.

*My husband **wishes that I were** happier.*

Je **demande que tu ailles** à l'hôpital.

*I **ask that you go** to the hospital.*

Il est préférable qu'on ait une voiture ici.

*It is **preferable that we have** a car here.*

Il est essentiel que vous fassiez attention!

*It is **essential that you pay** attention!*

⋰⋰ The subjunctive is also used after verbs and expressions of emotion when there is a change in subject between the main clause and the dependent clause.

aimer que	**être heureux/heureuse que**
avoir peur que	**être surpris(e) que**
être content(e) que	**être triste que**
être désolé(e) que	**regretter que**
être furieux/furieuse que	

Je **regrette que tu sois** malade.

*I'm **sorry you are** sick.*

Anne **est surprise que nous ne sachions pas** parler anglais.

*Anne **is surprised that we don't know** how to speak English.*

Nous **sommes heureux que tu veuilles** donner ton sang.

*We **are happy that you want** to give blood.*

Liaisons musicales

© bo-Yp/Images Distribution/ Newscom

Kevin Parent est un chanteur québécois bilingue de la Gaspésie. Sa chanson «Seigneur» *(Lord)* lui a remporté le Félix de chanson de l'année en 1996: Seigneur, Seigneur // Qu'est-ce qu' tu veux que j' te dise? …//Mon rôle dans la vie n'est pas encore défini//Pourtant je m'efforce pour qu'il soit accompli//Je le sais, faut tout que je recommence// Mais Seigneur j'ai pas envie… Cherchez un vidéoclip de cette chanson sur Internet. 🌐

ACTIVITÉ J Un bon ou un mauvais médecin? Indiquez qui dit chaque phrase: **(a)** un bon médecin ou **(b)** un mauvais médecin.

1. Je conseille que vous **alliez** manger à MacDo.

2. Il est préférable que vous **soyez** plus stressé(e).

3. Je recommande qu'on vous **fasse** une piqûre contre la grippe.

4. Je souhaite que vous **soyez** en bonne santé.

5. Je suis content que vous n'**ayez** pas d'assurance-maladie.

6. Il est préférable que vous **sachiez** prendre la tension.

7. Je suis heureux que vous **veuillez** fumer. Continuez.

8. Je suis content que vous **puissiez** donner votre sang. Merci.

⋰⋰ **Et vous?** Vous avez un bon ou un mauvais médecin?

ACTIVITÉ K Si vous étiez médecin ou parent...

Étape 1. Que diriez-vous à vos patients si vous étiez médecin? Complétez les phrases suivantes.

Expressions utiles		
aimer que	être désolé(e) que	exiger que
avoir peur que	être furieux/furieuse que	souhaiter que
conseiller que	être heureux/heureuse que	regretter que
demander que	être surpris(e) que	Il est essentiel que
être content(e) que	être triste que	Il est préférable que

Modèle: (faire) de la gym   **Je conseille que vous fassiez de la gym.**

1. (être) allergique au chocolat
2. (faire) du yoga
3. (pouvoir) vous reposer plus
4. (savoir) bien manger
5. (vouloir) manger du poulet frit
6. (avoir) beaucoup de stress
7. (aller) souvent au centre sportif
8. (vouloir) éviter les matières grasses

Étape 2. Si vous étiez parent, que diriez-vous à votre enfant?

Modèle: (aller) à l'école   **J'exige que tu ailles à l'école.**

1. (pouvoir) réciter l'alphabet
2. (aller) dans ta chambre
3. (savoir) parler une langue étrangère
4. (vouloir) manger tes légumes
5. (avoir) beaucoup de bon(ne)s ami(e)s
6. (faire) la vaisselle
7. (être) impoli(e) avec tes ami(e)s
8. (avoir) une mauvaise note à l'examen

Étape 3. Montrez vos réponses à un(e) partenaire. Qui est le meilleur parent ou médecin?

ACTIVITÉ L Vous êtes en forme? Posez ces questions à un(e) partenaire. Ensuite, donnez votre réaction à sa réponse.

Modèle: É1: **Est-ce que tu es allergique aux chiens?**
É2: **Non, je ne suis pas allergique aux chiens.**
É1: **Je suis content que tu ne sois pas allergique aux chiens.**

1. (être) allergique aux chats
2. (avoir) mal à la tête maintenant
3. (avoir) mal au cœur avant un examen
4. (prendre) des vitamines
5. (aller) souvent aux urgences avec vos amis
6. (se brosser) les dents chaque jour
7. (boire) de l'alcool
8. (dormir) bien le soir
9. (se reposer) assez le week-end
10. (devoir) avoir une piqûre

Conclusion Qui est en meilleure forme? Vous ou votre partenaire?

ACTIVITÉ M Les professeurs de français

Étape 1. Quelles sont les pensées des professeurs de français? Complétez les phrases.

Modèle: Ils veulent que les étudiants **soient intelligents.**

1. Ils veulent que les étudiants…
2. Ils exigent que nous…
3. Ils ont peur que nous…
4. Ils sont parfois surpris que la classe…
5. Ils sont furieux que certains étudiants…
6. Ils sont contents que je…

Étape 2. Posez les questions à votre professeur.

Modèle: Vous voulez que les étudiants soient intelligents?

ACTIVITÉ N Les personnages du film *Liaisons* Complétez les phrases à propos des personnages du film *Liaisons.*

1. Claire regrette que sa mère…
2. Claire souhaite qu'Alexis…
3. Abia a peur que Claire…
4. Robert exige que Claire et Abia…
5. Robert est content que les clients…
6. Alexis est heureux que Claire…

ACTIVITÉ O Un membre de ma famille Faites une liste de cinq à six choses qu'un membre de votre famille fait que vous aimez ou que vous n'aimez pas.

Modèle: J'aime que ma sœur aille à l'église. Je regrette qu'elle soit paresseuse.

La parole est à vous!

Est-ce que les articles médicaux sur Internet sont une bonne idée?

L'Internet nous donne accès à beaucoup d'informations médicales. À votre avis, est-ce une bonne ou une mauvaise idée d'avoir accès aux articles médicaux sur Internet?

- Michel de Paris (France): «C'est une mauvaise idée. Je suis médecin et je lis beaucoup d'articles sur Internet qui donnent de mauvaises informations aux patients.»

- Nadine de Tours (France): «C'est une bonne idée. J'apprends beaucoup sur Internet à propos des différentes maladies. Je n'ai pas toujours besoin de consulter un médecin.»

Et vous? Qu'en pensez-vous?

Est-ce que les articles médicaux sur Internet sont une bonne idée ou une mauvaise idée?

DEUXIÈME
PROJECTION

LIAISONS **SÉQUENCE 6:**
Une découverte

Avant de visionner

ACTIVITÉ A Vous rappelez-vous? Vous rappelez-vous ce qui s'est passé dans la Séquence 6 du film *Liaisons*? Choisissez la bonne réponse pour chaque phrase.

1. Le numéro du coffre-fort était _____. a. 513 b. 315
2. Il y avait des photos et un _____ dans le coffre-fort. a. testament b. livre
3. L'une des personnes sur les photos ressemblait (*ressembled*) à _____. a. Abia b. Alexis
4. Claire devait aller à _____ de son oncle. a. la fête b. l'enterrement

ACTIVITÉ B Une scène du film Vous rappelez-vous cette scène? Claire et Abia se parlent à propos des photos que Claire a trouvées. Écrivez les mots qui manquent (*are missing*).

© Heinle/Cengage Learning

CLAIRE Et regarde cette (1) _____. C'est l'homme qui m'a donné (2) _____ avec la réservation au Frontenac. Il s'appelle Tremblay. Et ici... c'est (3) _____ que j'ai rencontré le soir où Tremblay m'a (4) _____ l'enveloppe, (5) _____.

ABIA Seigneur! Claire. C'est pas (6) _____. Cette photo date de (7) _____. Et tu m'avais dit qu'il était jeune et (8) _____.

CLAIRE Je (9) _____, je sais, Abia. Ça n'a aucun sens. C'est (10) _____ un mystère.

ABIA Mais si cette photo date de 1959, il devrait avoir 80 ans ou plus maintenant!

> **Regarder la séquence**
> Vous allez regarder la Séquence 6 du film *Liaisons.* Vérifiez vos réponses à l'Activité A et à l'Activité B.

Après le visionnage

ACTIVITÉ C Qu'est-ce qui n'a pas de sens?

Étape 1. Dans la Séquence 6, Claire découvre des choses dans le coffre-fort qui sont encore plus mystérieuses et qui n'ont pas de sens. Avec un(e) partenaire, faites une liste des choses qui sont mystérieuses ou qui n'ont pas de sens.

Modèle: Claire a trouvé une photo de l'homme mystérieux qui lui a donné l'enveloppe à l'hôtel. La date sur la photo était 1936.

Étape 2. Montrez votre liste à une autre paire d'étudiant(e)s. Voulez-vous ajouter d'autres choses à votre liste?

Étape 1. Voici le testament que Claire a trouvé. Choisissez les mots qui manquent.

1930	15 mars	mort	dit	donné
fille	l'île d'Orléans	m'appelle	mariage	partager
pouvais	Québec	a épousé	six	sœurs

«Je (1) _____ Rémy Tremblay, frère et employé de Madeleine Tremblay, et je jure

(swear) que ce testament repose sur la vérité...»

«Madeleine Tremblay a épousé Henri Prévost en (2) _____...»

«M. Prévost avait une (3) _____ adoptive d'un premier (4) _____.

Elle s'appelait Claire-Angèle...»

«Née le (5) _____...»

«À la (6) _____ de M. Prévost, en 1933, Mme Prévost ne voulait pas (7) _____ ses

biens *(assets)* avec Claire-Angèle et m'a (8) _____ l'ordre de la tuer *(kill)*...»

«... mais je ne (9) _____ pas le faire. La pauvre petite n'avait que (10) _____ ans...»

«Je suis venu à (11) _____ et j'ai amené la petite avec moi. Les bonnes (12) _____

de l'Église Notre-Dame-des-Victoires l'ont gardée...»

«Je ne lui ai rien (13) _____ sur son passé, pour la protéger...»

«Claire-Angèle (14) _____ un garçon de (15) _____ et ils ont eu un fils, Michel

et une fille, Simone...»

Étape 2. Montrez vos réponses à un(e) partenaire et devinez les réponses aux questions suivantes.

1. Qui est Rémy Tremblay?
2. Qui est Madeleine Tremblay-Prévost?
3. Qui est Henri Prévost?
4. Qui est Claire-Angèle?

Dans les coulisses

In mystery genres, directors leave clues throughout a film to lead viewers to a discovery. The number 315 in the film is symbolic and is a clue that leads Claire to the testament and photos in the safety deposit box. Did you pick up on this clue in earlier segments of this film? What other films do you know that use numbers as clues?

© Heinle/Cengage Learning

À DÉCOUVRIR: La Tunisie

Pays: La Tunisie
Géographie: L'Afrique du Nord (le Maghreb); entre l'Algérie et la Libye
Climat: Méditerranéen dans le nord; désertique dans le sud
Population: Plus de 10 millions
Capitale: Tunis

Activité Internet
La ville de Carthage en Tunisie est le site d'une ancienne civilisation qui s'est développée dans la région méditerranéenne. Trouvez sur Internet des informations sur son histoire, ses antiquités, ses personnages historiques importants et son statut actuel.

À DÉCOUVRIR: La ville de Tunis

Structure: Une grande ville moderne
Région: Bab el Bahr / Porte de France (dans le nord)
Population: Plus de 1 200 000 (en ville)
Réputation: La capitale administrative et politique de la Tunisie; le centre commercial et culturel

Avant de lire

You will discover in this reading the topic of medical tourism in Tunisia.

Que savez-vous déjà?

1. Qu'est-ce que le tourisme médical?
2. Quels sont quelques avantages ou désavantages du tourisme médical?
3. Pour quelles raisons est-ce qu'on s'intéresse au tourisme médical?

OUTILS DE LECTURE
Preparing a summary of a text

You can have an easier time comprehending a text when you prepare a summary. To get started, skim the text **Le tourisme médical: la chirurgie esthétique** and jot down a few notes about its overall or general meaning.

Le tourisme médical: la chirurgie esthétique

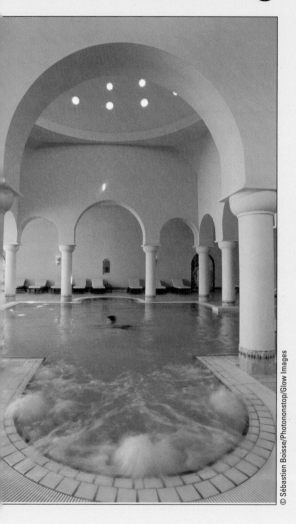

© Sébastien Boisse/Photononstop/Glow Images

Le «tourisme médical» est un phénomène récent. La raison de son développement est simple: certains services médicaux—en particulier la chirurgie esthétique°—sont moins chers en dehors de l'Europe de l'Ouest. La Tunisie, pays ensoleillé et relativement proche de la France, est devenue une des premières destinations de ces touristes européens d'un nouveau genre.

De nombreux sites Web de cliniques tunisiennes proposent des formules «tous frais compris» (le voyage, l'hôtel, les repas et... l'intervention chirurgicale) qui, compte tenu du taux de change° de l'euro, sont (beaucoup) moins chères qu'une simple procédure médicale équivalente en France. Par exemple, une augmentation mammaire° et un *easy lift* coûteraient environ 9 000 euros en Tunisie tandis qu°'en Europe les deux mêmes opérations coûteraient approximativement 30 000 euros.

La majorité des médecins et chirurgiens tunisiens ont fait leurs études médicales en Europe ou aux États-Unis. Par conséquent, le niveau des soins médicaux dans certaines cliniques en Tunisie est à présent comparable à celui de la France, mais la période de récupération immédiate est bien différente. Les patients-touristes peuvent récupérer, après une liposuccion ou une rhinoplastie°, au bord de la piscine ou sur la plage de sable fin d'un hôtel quatre étoiles. Le phénomène du tourisme médical reste cependant minoritaire et concerne essentiellement les interventions chirurgicales à caractère purement esthétique (par opposition à la chirurgie réparatrice, par exemple après un accident), qui ne sont pas remboursées par la Sécurité Sociale en France.

la chirurgie esthétique *cosmetic surgery* **le taux de change** *exchange rate*
une augmentation mammaire *breast augmentation* **tandis qu'** *whereas*
une rhinoplastie *"nose job"*

Après avoir lu

Compréhension

	Vrai	Faux
1. La Tunisie est déjà une destination touristique importante pour le tourisme médical.	☐	☐
2. Les procédures médicales sont moins chères en Tunisie.	☐	☐
3. Le tourisme médical concerne la chirurgie esthétique.	☐	☐

Et vous?

1. Est-ce que le tourisme médical est une bonne idée, à votre avis?
2. Est-ce que vous êtes pour ou contre la chirurgie esthétique?
3. Est-ce que vous auriez peur de recevoir des soins médicaux à l'étranger?
4. Est-ce que vous voudriez combiner des soins médicaux avec des vacances?

🌐 Activité Internet
Cherchez sur Internet des sites Web de cliniques ou d'hôpitaux privés en Tunisie avec les mots-clés «cliniques esthétiques tunisiennes». Préparez un petit rapport des informations que vous trouvez.

LIAISONS AVEC LA LECTURE ET L'ÉCRITURE Les réactions personnelles

The ability to express your personal reaction to a topic in an articulate manner is an important life skill. Here is a personal reaction to the topic of medical tourism.

À mon avis, la question du tourisme médical à caractère esthétique est très complexe. Premièrement, c'est une question personnelle. Si des gens veulent changer une partie de leur corps, c'est leur choix. Il est préférable qu'ils soient heureux. Mais deuxièmement, c'est aussi une question de santé. Il faut que les gens qui s'intéressent au tourisme médical réfléchissent beaucoup. Toutes les chirurgies, esthétiques ou réparatrices, sont dangereuses et une chirurgie à l'étranger pourrait avoir de plus grandes complications. Cette question du tourisme médical exige qu'un patient-touriste fasse attention.

Avant d'écrire

1. What kinds of statements appear in the personal reaction?
2. Answer the following questions to help you write your own **réaction personnelle.**

   a. Quelle est votre position au sujet du tourisme médical? Êtes-vous pour ou contre?

   b. Quelles sont deux ou trois raisons pour lesquelles vous avez cette position?

   c. Quel est votre «dernier mot»? Que voudriez-vous que les autres pensent du tourisme médical à la fin?

Écrire

Using information from **Avant d'écrire**, write you own personal reaction of 6–8 sentences in French.

Après avoir écrit

Exchange your **réaction personnelle** with a partner. (1) Underline any subjunctive expressions you see and verify that your partner correctly used them. (2) Circle all the subjunctive verbs and verify that they are all correctly conjugated. (3) Double-check that your partner correctly conjugated all other verbs and used infinitives when necessary. (4) Put a * next to the key phrase or key idea that best communicates your partner's personal reaction. (5) How would you characterize your partner's personal reaction: **neutre, forte, faible** (weak), **typique, unique,** etc.? Discuss your reactions together. Do you share the same personal reaction? Write a second version of your **réaction personnelle** taking into account your partner's comments and corrections.

PARTIE 1

LES PARTIES DU CORPS

la bouche	mouth
le bras	arm
la cheville	ankle
le corps	body
le cou	neck
le coude	elbow
les dents (f.)	teeth
le dos	back
les épaules (f.)	shoulders
le genou	knee
la gorge	throat
la jambe	leg
les joues (f.)	cheeks
la langue	tongue
les lèvres (f.)	lips
la main	hand
les oreilles (f.)	ears
les orteils (m.)	toes
le pied	foot
le poignet	wrist
la poitrine	chest
les sourcils (m.)	eyebrows
la tête	head
le ventre	abdomen, belly
le visage / la figure	face

LES PRODUITS DE SOIN

une brosse (à cheveux)	hairbrush
une brosse à dents	toothbrush
la crème à raser	shaving cream
la crème hydratante	moisturizer
la crème solaire	sunscreen
le dentifrice	toothpaste
l'hygiène (f.)	hygiene
le maquillage	makeup
un peigne	comb
les produits (m.) de soin personnel	personal care products
un rasoir	razor
un rouge à lèvres	lipstick
le savon	soap
un sèche-cheveux	hairdryer
une serviette	towel
le shampooing	shampoo

VERBES

se brosser	to brush
se coucher	to go to bed
se couper	to cut (oneself)
(se) déshabiller	to (get) undress(ed)
se doucher	to shower
s'endormir	to fall asleep
(s')habiller	to (get) dress(ed)
se laver	to wash
se lever	to get up
se maquiller	to put on makeup
se préparer	to get ready, to prepare
se raser	to shave
se réveiller	to wake up
se sécher	to dry
utiliser	to use

DIVERS

un vestiaire	locker, locker room

PARTIE 2

LES ANIMAUX

un aigle	eagle
une chèvre	goat
un cochon	pig
un coq	rooster
une grenouille	frog
un hamster	hamster
un lapin	rabbit
un lion	lion
les moustaches (f.)	whiskers
un oiseau	bird
un ours	bear
un rat	rat
un requin	shark
un serpent	snake
un tigre	tiger

DIVERS

une animalerie	pet store
une créature	creature
les humains (m.)	humans
une patte	paw
les poils (m.)	animal hair, fur
la queue	tail
un refuge	(animal) shelter

LES EXPRESSIONS AVEC LE SUBJONCTIF

aimer mieux que	to like better that
désirer que	to desire that
préférer que	to prefer that
vouloir que	to want that
Il (ne) faut (pas) que	It is (not) necessary that
Il vaut mieux que	It is better that
Il (n')est (pas) nécessaire que	It is (not) necessary that
Il (n')est (pas) important que	It is (not) important that

PARTIE 3

LES SOINS MÉDICAUX

les béquilles *(f.)*	*crutches*
un cachet d'aspirine	*aspirin*
un comprimé	*tablet*
un examen médical	*medical exam*
une intervention chirurgicale	*surgery*
un médicament	*medication*
une ordonnance	*prescription*
un pansement	*bandage*
un plâtre	*cast*
un point de suture	*stitch, suture*
une radiographie	*X-ray*
le sirop contre la toux	*cough syrup*
un traitement	*treatment*
les urgences *(f.)*	*emergency room*
aller aux urgences	*to go to the emergency room*
donner son sang	*to give one's blood*
faire une piqûre	*to give a shot*
faire une prise de sang	*to take one's blood*
prendre la température	*to take one's temperature*
prendre la tension (artérielle)	*to take one's blood pressure*

LES MALADIES

une allergie	*allergy*
une blessure	*wound*
la fièvre	*fever*
la grippe	*flu*
l'hypertension *(f.)*	*high blood pressure*
une maladie	*illness*
un rhume	*cold*
le stress	*stress*
un symptôme	*symptom*
avoir mal à (la tête)	*to hurt (to have a headache)*
avoir mal au cœur	*to be nauseated*

avoir mal au ventre	*to have a stomach ache*
se casser (le bras)	*to break one's (arm)*
éternuer	*to sneeze*
être allergique à	*to be allergic to*
être en bonne/mauvaise santé	*to be in good/bad health*
être en forme	*to be in shape*
être / tomber malade	*to be / to get sick*
se gratter	*to scratch*
tousser	*to cough*

DIVERS

l'assurance-maladie *(f.)*	*health insurance*
le cœur	*heart*
un kleenex	*tissue*
un(e) patient(e)	*patient*
un(e) vétérinaire	*vet*
fatigué(e)	*tired*
grave	*serious*
conseiller	*to advise*
Qu'est-ce qui ne va pas?	*What's wrong?*

LES EXPRESSIONS AVEC LE SUBJONCTIF

aimer que	*to love that*
avoir peur que	*to be afraid that*
conseiller que	*to advise that*
demander que	*to ask that*
être content(e) que	*to be happy that*
être désolé(e) que	*to be sorry that*
être furieux/furieuse que	*to be furious that*
être heureux/heureuse que	*to be happy that*
être surpris(e) que	*to be surprised that*
être triste que	*to be sad that*
exiger que	*to demand that*
regretter que	*to regret, to be sorry that*
souhaiter que	*to wish that*
Il est essentiel que	*It is essential that*
Il est préférable que	*It is preferable that*

Les sciences et la technologie dans la francophonie

Eurocopter

C'est en 1907, en Normandie, que le premier décollage° d'un hélicoptère a eu lieu°. Depuis, les hélicoptères ont connu beaucoup de progrès technologiques. Puisqu'ils peuvent effectuer des vols° stationnaires et atterrir° presque n'importe où°, les hélicoptères sont particulièrement adaptés aux missions de secours ou d'aide médicale d'urgence. Cependant, ces appareils sont aussi utilisés pour des fonctions militaires. Eurocopter est le plus grand fabricant° mondial d'hélicoptères. Son siège° est à Marignane (près de Marseille).

le décollage *take-off* **a eu lieu** *took place, occurred* **un vol** *flight* **atterrir** *to land* **n'importe où** *anywhere* **un fabricant** *manufacturer* **le siège** *headquarters*

Les cartes à puce

Contrairement aux cartes en plastique équipées d'une bande ou piste magnétique, les cartes à puce° contiennent au moins un circuit intégré (la «puce» électronique). Les premières versions de ces cartes ont été créées par l'inventeur français Roland Moreno au milieu des années 70. Depuis, les nouvelles versions des cartes à puce ont progressivement remplacé les cartes à piste magnétique, en particulier dans le domaine des cartes bancaires, qui nécessitent un niveau° de sécurité élevé.

une carte à puce *smart card* **un niveau** *level*

L'énergie solaire en Afrique

Le développement économique en Afrique passe par l'accès à des sources d'énergie nouvelles, moins coûteuses° et moins polluantes. Par son climat et son niveau d'ensoleillement, la plus grande partie du continent africain est un lieu particulièrement approprié au développement de l'énergie solaire. En 2011, le Sénégal, avec l'aide d'une société° suisse et d'une société allemande, est devenu le premier pays sub-saharien à construire une usine de fabrication de panneaux solaires. Mais en dehors des° panneaux solaires, il y a aussi de nouveaux produits adaptés aux réalités économiques africaines, par exemple des lampes qui fonctionnent la nuit grâce à l'énergie solaire qu'elles ont captée° pendant la journée.

coûteuses *costly* **une société** *a company* **en dehors de** *aside from* **captée** *captured*

© SGM/ Photolibrary

Ariane

Le centre spatial en Guyane est situé près de la ville de Kourou. C'est de ce centre spatial que les fusées de l'Agence spatiale européenne sont lancées°, depuis une quarantaine° d'années. La Guyane, un département d'outre-mer français en Amérique du Sud, est proche de l'équateur, ce qui permet de lancer à plus bas prix des fusées transportant de gros satellites géostationnaires de télécommunications ou d'observation météorologique. Plusieurs centaines° de fusées Ariane ont été lancées du centre spatial guyanais.

lancées *launched* **quarantaine** *about 40* **centaines** *several hundreds*

Le viaduc de Millau

Inauguré en 2004, le pont le plus haut du monde (270 mètres à son point culminant; presque aussi haut que la tour Eiffel) fait partie de l'autoroute A75, qui permet de relier° les villes de Clermont-Ferrand et de Béziers. Ce pont traverse° la vallée de la rivière Tarn et offre un panorama magnifique aux voyageurs. Puisque le vent peut souffler° à 200 kilomètres à l'heure à cette hauteur, le pont est équipé d'écrans brise-vent° spécifiquement conçus° pour protéger les véhicules et leurs passagers.

relier *link* **traverse** *crosses* **souffler** *to blow* **d'écrans brise-vent** *windscreens* **conçus** *designed*

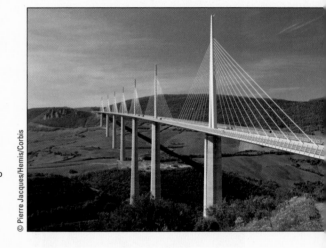

© Pierre Jacques/Hemis/Corbis

Révision

1. Où est-ce que le premier décollage d'un hélicoptère a eu lieu?
2. Qui a inventé la carte à puce?
3. Pourquoi est-ce que l'énergie solaire est adaptée au continent africain?
4. Où se trouve la Guyane?
5. Pourquoi le viaduc de Millau est-il équipé d'écrans brise-vent?

🌐 Activités Internet

- Cherchez le site officiel de l'Agence internationale de l'énergie renouvelable. Quels sont quelques projets que cette agence est en train de développer? Voyez-vous une promotion des énergies renouvelables similaire dans votre région?

- Cherchez «les grandes inventions» sur Internet. Quelles inventions qui ont révolutionné le monde ont été inventées en France ou par des scientifiques ou inventeurs français? Pourriez-vous imaginer un monde sans ces inventions?

- Cherchez «Eurocopter Group» sur Internet. Dans quels pays peut-on trouver des hélicoptères Eurocopter en service? Trouvez des images des hélicoptères Eurocopter sur Internet. Avez-vous vu un hélicoptère Eurocopter en service dans votre région?

Les innovations

En bref   In this chapter, you will:

- learn about science, technology, and medical inventions

- learn expressions of opinion that take the subjunctive

- learn vocabulary for environmental and social concerns

- learn expressions of doubt that take the subjunctive

- distinguish between uses of the subjunctive and the indicative moods

- read about humanitarians in France and in the Francophone world

 You will also watch **SÉQUENCE 7: Un nouveau chapitre** of the film *Liaisons.*

Ressources

 audio   http://www.cengagebrain.com

🔊 La **technologie**

Technology

une imprimante

un moniteur

un écran

un lecteur de cédéroms, de DVD

un disque dur   une webcam

un clavier

une souris

Mon ordinateur

une navette spatiale

un satellite

une antenne parabolique

l'énergie solaire *(f.)*

D'autres innovations technologiques

....

le clonage *cloning*

un cœur artificiel *artificial heart*

une connexion Internet à haut débit *high speed Internet connection*

une découverte *discovery*

un fichier *file*

un hybride *hybrid animal or plant*

une invention *invention*

un logiciel *software, program*

un mot de passe *password*

la réalité virtuelle *virtual reality*

un réseau (sans fil) *(wireless) network*

le traitement de texte *word processing program*

————————————————

démarrer *to start up*

effacer *to delete, erase*

être en ligne (avec) *to be online (with)*

fermer / éteindre *to close / to shut off*

imprimer *to print*

sauvegarder *to save*

taper *to type*

télécharger *to download*

> **Note de grammaire**
> The present tense conjugation of **éteindre** is **j'éteins, tu éteins, il/elle/on éteint, nous éteignons, vous éteignez, ils/elles éteignent.** Its past participle is **éteint.**

🔊 **ACTIVITÉ A Un ordinateur ou un iPhone?** Décidez si on trouve chaque
CD3-33 chose mentionnée sur **(a) un ordinateur, (b) un iPhone** ou **(c) les deux** *(both)*.

1.   2.   3.   4.   5.   6.   7.   8.   9.   10.   11.   12.

Conclusion Est-ce qu'un ordinateur est semblable à un iPhone ou est-ce que c'est très différent?

ACTIVITÉ B L'ordinateur

Étape 1. Est-ce que vous utilisez l'ordinateur pour faire vos devoirs? Mettez les étapes dans l'ordre.

a. _____ Choisissez un traitement de texte.

b. _____ Imprimez votre document.

c. _____ Éteignez l'ordinateur.

d. _____ Démarrez l'ordinateur.

e. _____ Tapez votre devoir sur le clavier.

f. _____ Sauvegardez votre document.

Étape 2. Répondez aux questions. Ensuite, posez les questions à un(e) partenaire.

1. Est-ce que vous avez une imprimante chez vous?

2. Quel logiciel utilisez-vous pour le traitement de texte?

3. Qu'est-ce que vous avez téléchargé récemment?

4. Est-ce que vous effacez les documents dont vous n'avez plus besoin?

5. Est-ce que votre ordinateur est sur un réseau sans fil?

Conclusion Vous servez-vous de *(Do you use)* l'ordinateur de la même manière que votre partenaire ou faites-vous des choses différemment?

ACTIVITÉ C Classez

Étape 1. Classez les découvertes et les inventions par ordre d'importance. Utilisez les chiffres 1–10.

_____ les animaux hybrides
_____ l'antenne parabolique
_____ le clonage
_____ le cœur artificiel
_____ l'énergie solaire

_____ une connexion Internet à haut débit
_____ la navette spatiale
_____ la réalité virtuelle
_____ le satellite
_____ la voiture hybride

Étape 2. Comparez vos réponses avec un(e) partenaire.

Modèle: **J'ai mis le satellite en premier, l'antenne parabolique en deuxième, la voiture hybride en troisième…**

Étape 3. Posez les questions suivantes à deux camarades de classe. Ensuite, comparez les réponses de ces deux personnes.

1. Est-ce que tu as une antenne parabolique?

2. Est-ce que tu as des gadgets qui utilisent l'énergie solaire? Lesquels?

3. Est-ce que tu as une voiture hybride? Est-ce que tu aimerais en avoir une?

4. Est-ce que tu aimerais avoir un chien hybride? Si oui, quel type de chien?

5. Est-ce que tu joues aux jeux de réalité virtuelle?

Si vous y allez

© Christophe Lehenaff / Photononstop / Glow Images

Si vous allez à Paris, allez à la Cité des sciences et de l'industrie dans le XIXe arrondissement. La Cité des sciences est un musée spécialisé dans la diffusion de la culture scientifique et technique. Les expositions permanentes sont organisées autour de thèmes: les mathématiques, l'océan, l'énergie, l'automobile, les étoiles et les galaxies.

ACTIVITÉ D Une publicité pour un ordinateur

Étape 1. Décrivez quatre à cinq points forts de cet ordinateur que vous aimez.

© Rick Wilking/Reuters/Landov

Sony - VAIO VPC-EB1M1E - Ordinateur Portable

- Intel Core i3 330M / 2.13 GHz
- Mémoire cache: 3 Mo - L3
- RAM: 4 Go (installé) / 8 Go (maximum)
- Lecteur de carte: Oui
- Disque dur: 500 Go - Serial ATA-150 - 5400 tours/min
- DVD±RW (±R DL) / DVD-RAM – integré
- Écran 15.5" TFT 1366 × 768 (WXGA)
- ATI Mobility Radeon HD 5650
- Mémoire vidéo: 1 Go
- Adaptateur réseau - Ethernet, Fast Ethernet, Gigabit Ethernet, IEEE 802.11b
- Webcam: Intégrée - 0,3 Mégapixel
- Clavier, touchpad/ 4 ports USB
- Système d'exploitation: Microsoft Windows 7 Édition Familiale Premium 64 bits
- Microphone/Dolby Home Theater/ Carte son
- Carte Mémoire SD, Memory Stick, Memory Stick PRO-HG Duo

Étape 2. Comparez votre ordinateur avec l'ordinateur Sony dans la publicité. (Écrivez deux à trois comparaisons.) Quel ordinateur préférez-vous?

ACTIVITÉ E Devant l'ordinateur

Étape 1. Pendant combien de temps avez-vous fait ces activités hier devant l'ordinateur?

Modèle: lire des courriels **Hier, j'ai lu mes courriels pendant quarante minutes.**

1. lire des courriels
2. être en ligne avec des amis
3. faire les devoirs
4. télécharger de la musique
5. imprimer des documents
6. naviguer sur Internet
7. jouer aux jeux vidéo
8. regarder un film

Étape 2. Posez les questions à deux camarades de classe.

Modèle: Pendant combien de temps est-ce que tu as lu tes courriels hier?

Conclusion Qui a passé le plus de temps devant l'ordinateur hier? Quelles activités étaient les plus populaires hier?

ACTIVITÉ F Entretien: les innovations Posez les questions à un(e) partenaire.

1. Quelles technologies ou quelles innovations pourraient sauver *(save)* des vies?
2. Quelles technologies ou quelles innovations sont controversées?
3. Quelle nouvelle découverte ou invention aimerais-tu voir dans l'avenir?

Un mot sur la culture

La greffe de visage: innovation médicale française

La France n'est pas seulement reconnue pour sa culture; on lui doit aussi beaucoup d'innovations médicales. Une innovation que les médias ont rendue célèbre est la greffe° de visage. En 2005, des chirurgiens français ont réalisé la première greffe partielle de visage au monde sur une femme de 38 ans, Isabelle Dinoire. Selon un communiqué de presse BBC, un an après l'opération, la patiente pouvait manger, parler, sourire° et sortir en public sans attirer l'attention. La greffe et ses suites° sont racontées dans un livre de Noëlle Châtelet, *Le Baiser d'Isabelle.*

greffe *transplant* **sourire** *smile* **suites** *after-effects*

• Connaissez-vous d'autres innovations médicales françaises?

© Fayolle/epa/Corbis

Pour exprimer les opinions

Le subjonctif et les opinions

DU FILM *LIAISONS*

Un coup d'œil sur la grammaire

Look at these photos from the film *Liaisons* and their captions.

© Heinle/Cengage Learning

MME PAPILLON C'est triste qu'il **soit** mort comme ça.

© Heinle/Cengage Learning

MME PAPILLON C'est dommage qu'on ne **puisse** pas parler plus longtemps.

1. Are the verbs **soit** and **puisse** in the subjunctive or the indicative?
2. Do the captions express opinions or facts?

In **Chapitre 12,** you learned that the subjunctive is used after verbs and expressions of volition, obligation, necessity, and emotion in a dependent clause that begins with **que.** The subjunctive is also similarly used after expressions of opinion.

<table>
<tr><td>Il est bizarre que</td><td>Il est merveilleux que</td></tr>
<tr><td>Il est bon que</td><td>Il est normal que</td></tr>
<tr><td>Il est dommage que</td><td>Il est possible que</td></tr>
<tr><td>Il est essentiel que</td><td>Il est stupide que</td></tr>
<tr><td>Il est juste (fair) / injuste (unfair) que</td><td>Il est triste que</td></tr>
<tr><td>Il est indispensable que</td><td>Il est utile / inutile que</td></tr>
</table>

Note de grammaire

These expressions are called *impersonal expressions* because they begin with **Il** *(It)*. Note that, in spoken French, **ce/c'** is often used instead of **il: c'est bizarre que, c'est dommage que, c'est triste que.**

Il est bizarre que tu ne **saches** pas utiliser un ordinateur.
*It's strange that you don't **know** how to use a computer.*

Il est bon qu'il **fasse** du soleil ce week-end.
*It's good that **it's** sunny this weekend.*

Il n'est pas bon que tu **sois** célibataire.
*It's not good that you **are** single.*

Il est injuste que nous ne **puissions** pas sortir ce soir.
It's unfair that we can't go out tonight.

ACTIVITÉ G Qu'en pensez-vous?

Étape 1. Indiquez si vous êtes d'accord ou pas d'accord avec les phrases suivantes.

1. Il est essentiel qu'on utilise l'énergie solaire.
2. Il est bon que les étudiants aient une antenne parabolique dans leur résidence.
3. Il est indispensable que le FBI nous surveille *(to keep watch on)* avec des satellites.
4. Il est inutile que les astronautes fassent des voyages en navette spatiale.
5. Il est stupide qu'on ait des voitures hybrides.
6. Il est injuste qu'on vende des chiens hybrides.
7. Il est dommage qu'on ait inventé la réalité virtuelle.
8. Il est utile que les scientifiques *(scientists)* fassent du clonage.
9. Il est bizarre que tout le monde n'ait pas une connexion Internet à haut débit.
10. Il est merveilleux qu'on puisse sauver des vies avec un cœur artificiel.

Étape 2. Demandez à un(e) partenaire s'il/si elle est d'accord avec ces phrases.

Modèle: É1: **Est-ce qu'il est essentiel qu'on utilise l'énergie solaire?**

É2: **Non, à mon avis, il est utile mais pas essentiel qu'on utilise l'énergie solaire. Et toi?**

É1: **À mon avis, oui, il est essentiel qu'on utilise l'énergie solaire.**

ACTIVITÉ H Deux camarades de chambre et un ordinateur

Étape 1. Deux camarades de chambre vont partager un ordinateur. Complétez les phrases avec une expression de nécessité ou d'opinion.

Modèle: _____ que nous (ne pas être) _____ en ligne trop souvent.

Il est indispensable que nous ne soyons pas en ligne trop souvent.

1. _____ que nous (imprimer) _____ tous nos documents.
2. _____ que nous (acheter) _____ un bon traitement de texte.
3. _____ que nous (penser) _____ à un mot de passe qui soit facile à retenir *(retain)*.
4. _____ que nous (avoir) _____ les meilleurs logiciels.
5. _____ que nous (installer) _____ un réseau sans fil.
6. _____ que nous (effacer) _____ les documents dont nous n'avons plus besoin.
7. _____ que nous (garder) *(keep)* _____ le clavier et le moniteur propre.
8. _____ que nous (sauvegarder) _____ les documents importants.
9. _____ que nous (ne pas télécharger) _____ trop de musique.
10. _____ que nous (éteindre) _____ l'ordinateur quand nous ne l'utilisons pas.

Étape 2. Montrez vos réponses à un(e) partenaire. Aimeriez-vous partager un ordinateur avec cette personne?

Liaisons musicales

© THE CANADIAN PRESS/ Graham Hughes

Luc De Larochellière (1966–) est un chanteur québécois. Plusieurs de ses chansons sont devenues des classiques québécois tels que *La machine est mon amie*, une chanson qui parle des effets de la technologie sur la société. Cherchez les paroles de cette chanson sur Internet. Quelles machines sont mentionnées dans la chanson?

ACTIVITÉ I La santé et vos opinions

Étape 1. Complétez les phrases suivantes.

Modèle: Cette patiente a mal à la tête. Il est indispensable qu'elle **se repose.**

1. Cette patiente a un rhume. Il est normal qu'elle _____.
2. Cette patiente a la grippe. Il est utile qu'elle _____.
3. Cette patiente a de la fièvre. Il est bon qu'elle _____
4. Cette patiente est allergique aux chats. Il est dommage qu'elle _____.
5. Cette patiente est allergique au chocolat. Il est stupide qu'elle _____.
6. Cette patiente a de l'hypertension artérielle. Il n'est pas bon qu'elle _____.
7. Cette patiente est stressée. Il est indispensable qu'elle _____.
8. Cette patiente s'est cassé la jambe. Il est dommage qu'elle _____.
9. Cette patiente est en bonne santé. Il est merveilleux qu'elle _____.
10. Cette patiente est pauvre. Il est injuste qu'elle _____.

Étape 2. Complétez les phrases à propos des personnages du film *Liaisons.*

© Heinle/Cengage Learning

© Heinle/Cengage Learning

1. La mère de Claire souffre d'hallucinations. Il est normal qu'elle _____.
2. Robert, le patron de Claire et d'Abia, est allergique aux chiens. Il est bon qu'il _____.

ACTIVITÉ J Entretien

Étape 1. Répondez aux questions. Indiquez vos réponses dans la colonne **Moi.** Ensuite, posez les questions à deux camarades de classe. Notez leurs réponses.

	Moi	É1	É2
1. Est-ce que vous mangez trois repas par jour?	___	___	___
2. Est-ce que vous dormez huit heures par nuit?	___	___	___
3. Est-ce que vous mangez beaucoup de matières grasses?	___	___	___
4. Est-ce que vous buvez assez d'eau chaque jour?	___	___	___
5. Est-ce que vous mangez assez de fruits et de légumes?	___	___	___
6. Est-ce que vous achetez des plats préparés?	___	___	___
7. Est-ce que vous faites de la gym régulièrement?	___	___	___
8. Est-ce que vous consultez votre médecin régulièrement?	___	___	___

Étape 2. Écrivez un paragraphe de cinq à six phrases pour donner votre opinion à propos des réponses de vos deux camarades de classe.

Modèle: **Il est bon que Marc et André mangent trois repas par jour. Il est merveilleux que Marc dorme huit heures par jour. Il est dommage qu'André ne dorme pas assez. Il est indispensable qu'André dorme plus…**

L'infinitif ou le subjonctif?

When sentences with verbs of volition, emotion, or opinion have only one subject, the infinitive is used without **que**. With **avoir peur, regretter,** and expressions with **être,** use **de/d'** before the infinitive.

Je suis surpris que tu ne **viennes** pas.	***I'm surprised** that **you're** not **coming.***
Je suis surpris de voir Anne ce soir.	***I'm surprised to see** Anne tonight.*
Je regrette que tu sois malade.	***I'm sorry that you are** sick.*
Je regrette d'être en retard.	***I'm sorry to be** late.*

When impersonal expressions of emotion, opinion, or necessity do not specify a particular person or thing, they are followed by the infinitive without **que**. Add **de/d'** before the infinitive if the expression contains **être**.

Il est essentiel qu'il ait un ordinateur.	***It's essential that he has** a computer.*
Il est essentiel d'avoir un ordinateur.	***It's essential to have** a computer.*
Il faut qu'on lise les courriels.	***We must read** the e-mails.*
Il faut lire les courriels.	***We must read** the e-mails.*

Essayez! Complétez les phrases avec l'infinitif ou le subjonctif.

Modèle: Il est merveilleux d'**avoir une voiture hybride.**

1. Il est dommage **que les étudiants** _____.
2. Il est important **de/d'**_____.
3. Il est indispensable **que nous** _____.
4. Il faut _____.
5. Je suis content(e) **que mon professeur** _____.
6. J'ai peur **de/d'**_____.

La parole est à vous!
Est-ce que la réalité virtuelle est utile ou dangereuse?

On utilise la réalité virtuelle (RV) dans beaucoup de domaines aujourd'hui tels que la chirurgie, l'éducation et l'armée. La RV est-elle utile ou dangereuse?

- Cheikh de Touba (Sénégal): «C'est très utile. On peut utiliser la RV dans la formation des pilotes et des médecins. Les médecins peuvent s'entraîner sur des modèles virtuels avant d'opérer des opérations sur de vrais sujets.»

- Pierre de Nîmes (France): «C'est dangereux. Il existe trop de jeux violents. On risque de passer plus de temps dans un monde imaginaire que dans la réalité.»

Et vous? Qu'en pensez-vous?
Est-ce que la réalité virtuelle est utile ou dangereuse?

L'environnement et la **société**

The environment and society

les déchets domestiques *(m.)*

la déforestation

les déchets industriels *(m.)*

les espèces menacées *(f.)*

Quelques préoccupations écologiques et sociales

 Vocabulaire complémentaire

une ampoule basse consommation *energy saving lightbulb*

l'assistance sociale *(f.)* *social aid*

une association humanitaire *humanitarian association*

le chômage *unemployment*

l'effet de serre *(m.)* *greenhouse effect*

l'énergie renouvelable *(f.)* *renewable energy*

la faim *hunger*

la pauvreté *poverty*

une préoccupation (sociale) *(social) concern*

la préservation *preservation, protection*

un problème *problem*

une ressource naturelle *natural resource*

la société *society*

une solution *solution*

> **Note** de **vocabulaire**
> Use **être au chômage** to express *to be unemployed.* An unemployed person is **un chômeur / une chômeuse.**

la pollution

un sans-abri / un SDF
(sans domicile fixe)

le réchauffement climatique

le recyclage

la surpopulation

les organismes *(m.)* génétiquement
modifiés (OGM)

D'autres préoccupations écologiques et sociales

Note de
grammaire
There is never an **s** at the
end of **OGM: les OGM.**

Vocabulaire complémentaire

écologique *ecological*
non biodégradable *nonbiodegradable*

conserver *to conserve*
faire du compost *to compost*
gaspiller *to waste*
interdire *to forbid*

jeter *to throw (out)*
polluer *to pollute*
préserver *to preserve*
protéger *to protect*
protester *to protest*
recycler *to recycle*
sauver *to save, protect*

Note de
grammaire
The verb **interdire** is
conjugated like **dire:**
**j'interdis, tu interdis,
il/elle/on interdit,
nous interdisons, vous
interdisez, ils/elles
interdisent.** Its past
participle is **interdit.**

ACTIVITÉ A **Un problème ou une solution?** Indiquez si chaque mot ou expression que vous entendez est (a) **un problème** ou (b) **une solution.**

CD3-34

1.   2.   3.   4.   5.   6.   7.   8.   9.   10.   11.   12.   13.   14.

❖ **Et vous?** À votre avis, est-ce qu'il y a plus de problèmes ou plus de solutions dans notre société?

ACTIVITÉ B **Une préoccupation écologique ou sociale?** Indiquez si chaque préoccupation mentionnée est (a) **une préoccupation écologique,** (b) **une préoccupation sociale** ou (c) **les deux.**

CD3-35

1.   2.   3.   4.   5.   6.   7.   8.   9.   10.   11.   12.

❖ **Et vous?** À votre avis, quelles préoccupations sont plus importantes? Les préoccupations écologiques ou les préoccupations sociales?

ACTIVITÉ C **Classez!**

Étape 1. Classez les préoccupations par ordre d'importance pour vous. Utilisez les chiffres 1–10.

_____ le chômage   _____ la pauvreté

_____ la déforestation   _____ la pollution

_____ l'effet de serre   _____ le réchauffement climatique

_____ les espèces menacées   _____ les sans-abri / les SDF

_____ la faim   _____ la surpopulation

Étape 2. Comparez vos réponses avec un(e) partenaire. Avec lui/elle, décidez quelles sont les trois préoccupations qui sont les plus importantes pour notre société aujourd'hui.

ACTIVITÉ D **Êtes-vous écologiste?**

Étape 1. Indiquez si chaque phrase est vraie ou fausse pour vous.

1. J'éteins la lumière quand je quitte la pièce.

2. J'utilise des produits biodégradables.

3. J'éteins le moniteur de mon ordinateur quand je ne l'utilise pas.

4. Je ferme le robinet *(faucet)* quand je me brosse les dents.

5. Je recycle.

6. Je ne mange pas d'espèces menacées.

7. J'utilise des ampoules basse consommation.

8. Je fais du compost.

Conclusion Si vous avez dit **vrai** à plus de six phrases, vous êtes écologiste!

Si vous y allez

© Jeff Presnail / Alamy

Si vous voyagez à Ottawa, visitez le parc Omega où vous pouvez découvrir de nombreux animaux vivant dans leur habitat naturel en toute liberté sur le parcours *(tour)* en voiture.

Étape 2. Demandez à un(e) partenaire s'il/si elle fait les choses de l'Étape 1.

Modèle: Est-ce que tu éteins la lumière quand tu quittes la pièce?

Conclusion Qui est le/la plus écologiste? Vous ou votre partenaire?

ACTIVITÉ E Les meilleures solutions

Étape 1. Décidez si chaque solution donnée est une bonne ou une mauvaise idée *(idea)* pour le problème indiqué.

	bonne idée	mauvaise idée
1. le chômage: On donne aux gens plus d'assistance sociale.	_____	_____
2. la surpopulation: On interdit aux gens d'avoir plus de deux enfants.	_____	_____
3. les espèces menacées: On interdit aux gens d'aller à la chasse.	_____	_____
4. le réchauffement climatique: On n'a besoin de rien faire.	_____	_____
5. les déchets domestiques: On jette les déchets dans la mer.	_____	_____
6. la faim: Les gens pauvres peuvent manger plus d'aliments OGM.	_____	_____
7. la pollution: On exige que les gens fassent du compost.	_____	_____
8. la pauvreté: On paie plus d'impôts *(taxes)*.	_____	_____

Étape 2. Montrez vos réponses à un(e) partenaire. Avez-vous les mêmes réponses? Pour chaque réponse où vous avez mis **mauvaise idée,** décidez quelle est la meilleure solution au problème avec votre partenaire.

Modèle: la pollution
On peut exiger que les gens recyclent. Nous pouvons faire du compost.

Un mot sur la culture

Greenpeace

Greenpeace est une organisation internationale présente sur tous les continents et sur tous les océans. Elle compte près de trois millions d'adhérents° à travers le monde. Selon son site Web officiel, Greenpeace est une organisation non-violente qui est indépendante des pouvoirs politiques et économiques. Sa mission est de dénoncer les atteintes° à l'environnement et d'apporter des solutions qui contribuent à la protection de l'environnement et à la promotion de la paix. Une préoccupation récente de Greenpeace France est la campagne° contre la dissémination des organismes génétiquement modifiés (OGM). Greenpeace France a réussi à obtenir plus de 100 000 signatures pour défendre l'interdiction du maïs OGM dans plusieurs pays européens.

adhérents *members* **atteintes** *attacks* **campagne** *campaign*

• Dans quels autres pays trouve-t-on l'organisation Greenpeace?

Pour exprimer le doute et la certitude
Le subjonctif et l'indicatif

DU FILM *LIAISONS*

Un coup d'œil sur la grammaire

Look at these photos from the film *Liaisons* and their captions.

ALEXIS Je **crois que** vous **comprenez**…

ABIA Hmm… je **ne suis pas certaine que** tu me **dises** la vérité…

1. Is the verb **comprenez** in the subjunctive or the indicative? Is Alexis expressing a belief or is he expressing a doubt?
2. Is the verb **dises** in the subjunctive or the indicative? Is Abia expressing certainty or doubt?

You learned that when you express desires, obligations, emotions, and opinions in a clause with **que,** you use the subjunctive. The subjunctive is also used to express doubt, uncertainty, and disbelief, and this is often conveyed by the following verbs and expressions.

douter que *to doubt that*	**ne pas être sûr(e) que** *not to be sure that*
ne pas croire que *not to believe that*	**Il est impossible que** *It is impossible that*
ne pas penser que *not to think that*	**Il n'est pas évident que** *It is not obvious that*
ne pas être certain(e) que *not to be certain that*	**Il n'est pas vrai que** *It is not true that*

On **ne pense pas** que Luc **fasse** du compost.

We **don't think** Luc **composts.**

Anne **n'est pas sûre** que Guy **comprenne.**

Anne **is not sure** that Guy **understands.**

Il **est impossible** qu'ils **aillent à** la chasse.

It **is impossible** that they go **hunt.**

The indicative is used after verbs and expressions that indicate certainty (**la certitude**) and beliefs such as the following.

croire que *to believe that*	**être sûr(e) que** *to be sure that*
penser que *to think that*	**Il est clair que** *It is clear that*
savoir que *to know that*	**Il est évident que** *It is obvious that*
être certain(e) que *to be certain that*	**Il est vrai que** *It is true that*

Note de **grammaire**
Note that is it not possible to say **Il n'est pas clair que**…

Je **crois** qu'il **a** faim.	*I **believe** he **is** hungry.*
Sara **sait** que tu **as** raison.	*Sara **knows** you **are** right.*
Il **est clair** que le chômage **est** un problème.	*It is **clear** that unemployment **is** a problem.*
Il **est vrai** qu'elle **fait** du compost.	*It **is true** that she **composts**.*

•••❖ A speaker may choose to use the subjunctive when asking a question with expressions of belief and certainty to indicate that he/she is unsure of the response.

> **Croyez-vous** que le réchauffement climatique **soit** un gros problème?
> *Do **you believe** that global warming **is** a big problem?*

Liaisons musicales

La chanson *L'hymne à la beauté du monde* de Luc Plamondon nous demande d'être plus écologiques: *Ne tuons pas la beauté du monde // Faisons de la terre un grand jardin // pour ceux qui viendront après nous.* La chanson a été rendue célèbre par la chanteuse québécoise Isabelle Boulay. Écoutez la chanson sur Internet. 🌐

🔊 **ACTIVITÉ F** **Le doute ou la certitude?** Un écologiste parle à un groupe
CD3-36 d'étudiants. Vous allez entendre la première partie de chaque phrase. Choisissez la deuxième partie de chaque phrase.

1. a. … **recyclez** régulièrement.   b. … **recycliez** régulièrement.
2. a. … **faites** du compost.   b. … **fassiez** du compost.
3. a. … **achetez** des produits biodégradables.   b. … **achetiez** des produits biodégradables.
4. a. … **éteignez** la lumière quand il faut.   b. … **éteigniez** la lumière quand il faut.
5. a. … **conservez** l'eau.   b. … **conserviez** l'eau.
6. a. … **protégez** les espèces menacées.   b. … **protégiez** les espèces menacées.
7. a. … **prenez** des OGM.   b. … **preniez** des OGM.
8. a. … **gaspillez** les ressources naturelles.   b. … **gaspilliez** les ressources naturelles.

•••❖ **Et vous?** Quelles activités écologiques faites-vous?

🔊 **ACTIVITÉ G** **Le maire d'une ville** Un maire *(mayor)* parle aux habitants
CD3-37 de sa ville. Décidez s'il exprime le doute ou s'il exprime la certitude à propos des préoccupations de ses concitoyens *(fellow citizens)*.

1. a. Il est clair que…   b. Il est impossible que…
2. a. Je crois que…   b. Je ne crois pas que…
3. a. Il est certain que…   b. Il n'est pas certain que…
4. a. Il est évident que…   b. Il n'est pas évident que…
5. a. Je suis sûr que…   b. Je ne suis pas sûr que…
6. a. Je sais que…   b. Je doute que…
7. a. Je pense que…   b. Je ne pense pas que…
8. a. Il est vrai que…   b. Il n'est pas vrai que…

Conclusion Est-ce que ce maire est informé des préoccupations de ses concitoyens?

ACTIVITÉ H Les personnages du film *Liaisons*

Étape 1. Décidez si chaque phrase exprime une opinion, un doute ou une certitude à propos des personnages du film *Liaisons*.

1. … **aille** en France pour l'enterrement de son oncle.
   a. Il est évident que Claire   b. Il est bon que Claire

2. … **soit** une amie de Claire.
   a. Il est merveilleux qu'Abia   b. On sait qu'Abia

3. … **fait** ses devoirs avant de travailler à l'hôtel.
   a. Il est évident que Claire   b. Il n'est pas certain que Claire

4. … **doive** rester à l'hôpital.
   a. Il est dommage que Simone Gagner   b. Il est clair que Simone Gagner

5. … ne **prend** pas d'OGM.
   a. Il n'est pas vrai que Robert Levesque   b. On sait que Robert Levesque

6. … **est** français.
   a. Il n'est pas sûr qu'Alexis   b. Il est sûr qu'Alexis

7. … **ait** beaucoup d'amis à Montréal.
   a. Il est important qu'Abia   b. On pense qu'Abia

8. … **sache** faire la cuisine.
   a. Il est vrai que Claire   b. Il est utile que Claire

Étape 2. Complétez les phrases logiquement.

1. Je pense que Claire _____.   3. Il est bizarre qu'Alexis _____.

2. Je doute que Claire _____.   4. Il est évident qu'Abia _____.

Étape 3. Montrez vos réponses de l'Étape 2 à un(e) partenaire. Avez-vous écrit les mêmes choses?

ACTIVITÉ I Le chat de Claire

Étape 1. Monsieur Émile, le chat de Claire, est un chat spécial. Utilisez les verbes pour déterminer si chaque phrase exprime un fait *(fact)* (**Il est vrai que**) ou une opinion (**Il est bizarre que**) à propos de Monsieur Émile.

© Heinle/Cengage Learning

	Il est vrai que M. Émile…	Il est bizarre que M. Émile...
1. **sait** ouvrir la porte.	☐	☐
2. **fait** du jogging dans l'appartement.	☐	☐
3. **veuille** jouer avec les chiens.	☐	☐
4. **boive** du lait biologique.	☐	☐
5. **comprenne** le français.	☐	☐
6. **puisse** dormir sur la table de la cuisine.	☐	☐
7. **sache** danser.	☐	☐
8. **va** parfois voir Mme Gagner avec Claire.	☐	☐

Étape 2. Complétez les phrases suivantes. Écrivez deux faits et deux opinions.

1. Il est vrai que je _____.

2. Il est vrai que mes amis et moi _____.

3. Il est bizarre que ma famille _____.

4. Il est bizarre que les étudiants _____.

ACTIVITÉ J Votre camarade de classe Dites à un(e) camarade de classe si vous croyez ou si vous ne croyez pas qu'il/elle fait (fasse) les activités suivantes. Votre camarade de classe va vous dire si vous avez raison ou si vous avez tort.

Modèle: (vouloir) recycler
   É1: **Je ne crois pas que tu veuilles recycler.**
   É2: **Tu as tort. Je veux recycler.**

1. (faire) du compost

2. (prendre) le temps de recycler

3. (avoir) des ampoules basse consommation

4. (savoir) conserver l'énergie

5. (donner) de l'argent aux associations humanitaires

6. (vouloir) manger des OGM

7. (avoir) envie de sauver les espèces menacées

8. (gaspiller) l'eau

Conclusion Est-ce que votre camarade de classe est écologique?

ACTIVITÉ K Je sais ou je doute?

Étape 1. Connaissez-vous bien votre professeur? Complétez chaque phrase avec **Je sais que mon professeur** ou **Je doute que mon professeur.** Mettez les verbes à l'indicatif ou au subjonctif.

Modèle: (sortir) le lundi soir **Je doute que mon professeur sorte le lundi soir.**

1. (savoir) parler français

2. (prendre) du fromage français

3. (boire) du café italien

4. (faire) bien la cuisine

5. (comprendre) le chinois

6. (aller) en France chaque été

7. (devoir) travailler ce week-end

8. (avoir) un chat qui comprend le français

Étape 2. Montrez vos réponses à un(e) partenaire. Avez-vous écrit les mêmes choses?

Étape 3. Votre professeur va vous donner ses réponses. Écrivez quatre phrases pour donner votre opinion sur les activités de votre professeur.

Modèle: Il est dommage que mon professeur ne sorte pas le lundi soir.

ACTIVITÉ L Les potins

Étape 1. Vous êtes journaliste d'un magazine à potins. Écrivez huit phrases avec les éléments donnés à propos des vedettes d'Hollywood.

Il est bon que	avoir beaucoup de petit(e)s ami(e)s
Il n'est pas certain que	s'aimer beaucoup
Il est clair que	comprendre le français
Il est dommage que	connaître leurs fans
Il est évident que	écrire de belles chansons
Il est (im)possible que	être fidèle(s)/infidèle(s)
Il est nécessaire que	être heureux/heureuse
Il est stupide que	faire bien la cuisine
Il est sûr que	pouvoir chanter
Il est triste que	savoir danser
Je crois que	sortir avec quelqu'un de nouveau
Je doute	vouloir avoir un chien hybride
Je sais que	???
Je veux que	???

Modèle: Kristin Stewart **Je veux que Kristin Stewart sorte avec Robert Pattinson.**

1. Paris Hilton
2. Lady Gaga
3. Tom Cruise et Katie Holmes
4. Brad Pitt et Angelina Jolie
5. Justin Timberlake
6. Tony Parker
7. ?
8. ?

Étape 2. Montrez vos phrases à deux camarades de classe. Qui est le/la meilleur(e) journaliste?

ACTIVITÉ M Votre université

Étape 1. Qu'avez-vous à dire à propos de votre université? Complétez les phrases.

1. Il est évident que les cours…
2. Je veux que la nourriture…
3. Je doute que les étudiants…
4. Il est important que les professeurs…
5. Je pense que le campus…
6. Il faut que les frais de scolarité…
7. Je désire que le président…
8. Je crois que la bibliothèque…

Étape 2. Montrez vos réponses à un(e) partenaire. Êtes-vous d'accord avec les réponses de votre partenaire?

Espérer et *souhaiter*

The subjunctive is used after the verb **souhaiter** *(to wish)* in a clause with **que**.

Je **souhaite** que vous **puissiez** aller en France.
*I **wish** that you **could** go to France.*

Est-ce que tu **souhaites** que nous ne **gaspillions** pas nos ressources naturelles?
*Do you **wish** that we didn't **waste** our natural resources?*

The future indicative is used after the verb **espérer** in a clause with **que**.

J'**espère** que vous **pourrez** aller en France un jour.
*I **hope** you **will be able** to go to France one day.*

Nous **espérons** que tout le monde **recyclera** ses bouteilles.
*We **hope** that everyone **will recycle** their bottles.*

....

Essayez! Complétez les phrases avec le futur ou le subjonctif.

1. J'espère que mon professeur (faire) _____.

2. Mon professeur souhaite que nous (pouvoir) _____.

3. J'espère que mes amis _____.

4. Je souhaite que mon/ma camarade de chambre _____.

© Suzanne Tucker/Shutterstock.com

La parole est à vous!
Les OGM: un problème ou une solution?

Les organisations écologiques européennes protestent activement depuis longtemps contre les organismes génétiquement modifiés (OGM). Pourtant, certains scientifiques pensent que les OGM peuvent être une solution aux problèmes liés à la surpopulation. Les OGM sont-ils un problème ou une solution pour la société?

- Sadia de Bruxelles (Belgique): «C'est un problème. Les OGM comportent des risques pour la santé et menacent les équilibres économiques et sociaux.»

- Marcel de Papeete (Tahiti): «Je pense que les OGM présentent plus d'avantages que de risques. Les OGM pourraient être une solution à la faim dans le monde.»

Et vous? Qu'en pensez-vous?

Les OGM sont-ils un problème ou une solution pour la société?

Avant de visionner

ACTIVITÉ A Devinez Dans la Séquence 7 du film *Liaisons,* la dernière séquence, Claire va à Paris pour l'enterrement de son oncle. Devinez ce qui va se passer à Paris. Complétez les phrases.

1. Je pense que Claire _____.

3. Je ne pense pas que Claire _____.

2. Je crois que Claire _____.

4. Je ne crois pas que Claire _____.

ACTIVITÉ B Un coup d'œil sur une scène Voici une scène de la Séquence 7 du film *Liaisons.* Claire est à Paris chez Madame Papillon, la voisine de l'oncle Michel. Avec un(e) partenaire, devinez le mot qui correspond à chaque espace *(space)* dans le dialogue. Vous allez vérifier vos réponses plus tard.

CLAIRE Est-ce que (1) _____ vous parlait de la famille, de (2)_____, par exemple? Je (3) _____ que vous étiez son amie...

MME PAPILLON Je suis désolée, (4) _____. Michel était très (5) _____, vous savez. Il n'aimait pas parler (6) _____.

© Heinle/Cengage Learning

1. a. ma mère   b. mon oncle

2. a. ses amis   b. ses parents

3. a. doute   b. sais

4. a. Claire   b. mademoiselle

5. a. réservé   b. timide

6. a. avec moi   b. de sa vie privée

Regarder la séquence

Vous allez regarder la Séquence 7 du film *Liaisons.* Vérifiez vos réponses à l'Activité A et à l'Activité B.

Après le visionnage

ACTIVITÉ C Liaisons familiales Dans la Séquence 7, Alexis parle de sa famille à Claire. Complétez les phrases.

1. Madeleine et Henri Prévost sont les parents _____.
a. d'Alexis   b. de Tremblay

2. Claire-Angèle est la fille _____.
a. biologique de Madeleine   b. adoptive d'Henri

3. Rémy Tremblay est _____.
a. le frère d'Alexis   b. le frère et l'employé de Madeleine

4. Simone Gagner est la fille de _____.
a. Claire-Angèle Prévost   b. Madeleine Prévost

5. Claire Gagner est la petite-fille de _____.
a. Madeleine   b. Claire-Angèle

ACTIVITÉ D L'avez-vous compris?

Étape 1. Avec un(e) partenaire, indiquez si chaque phrase est vraie ou fausse.

1. Madeleine Prévost voulait tuer *(kill)* Claire-Angèle pour garder la fortune familiale.
2. Claire-Angèle est la sœur adoptive d'Alexis Prévost.
3. Henri a emmené la petite Claire-Angèle à Québec pour lui sauver la vie.
4. Claire-Angèle est la sœur de Simone Gagner.
5. Madeleine a fait une confession à son fils Alexis avant sa mort.
6. Claire est l'héritière de la fortune familiale de la famille Prévost.

ACTIVITÉ E Utilisez le contexte
Lisez bien ces répliques *(lines)* d'Alexis et de Claire. Que veulent dire les mots en caractères gras *(boldface)*?

ALEXIS Claire, vous êtes (1) **la petite-fille** de cette (2) **fillette** abandonnée, (3) **l'héritière** légitime de sa fortune. [...]

ALEXIS Voilà, à présent (4) **vous êtes au courant** de tout. (5) **Quant à moi**, j'ai accompli ma mission.

CLAIRE Maman... ses hallucinations... Elle me parlait toujours des (6) **voix**, des visions... moi, je croyais que c'était à cause de à sa (7) **folie**. De sa (8) **psychose**.

© Heinle/Cengage Learning

ACTIVITÉ F Vous souvenez-vous de l'ordre de ces répliques?
Avec un(e) partenaire, mettez ces répliques entre Claire (C) et Alexis (A) dans le bon ordre.

a. **A** Qu'en pensez-vous? ___

b. **A** Ne soyez pas triste, Claire. On se reverra un jour. [...] ___

c. **A** Non, ce n'est pas un rêve, Claire. [...] ___

d. **A** Je sais que c'est difficile à comprendre. Je reviens du passé. ___

e. **C** Je ne sais pas... ___

f. **C** Vous allez me quitter maintenant? ___

g. **C** C'est pas possible. C'est un rêve. ___

h. **C** Alexis... et vous? Vous êtes un ange? Un esprit? ___

Et vous? Qu'en pensez-vous? Qui est Alexis? Un ange? Un esprit? Un rêve?

Dans les coulisses

In **Séquence 7**, when Claire discovers the tombstone, she is overcome by a startling revelation. Alexis tells her: "Je reviens du passé." What clues or hints surrounding the character of Alexis were provided throughout the movie to foreshadow this revelation?

© Heinle/Cengage Learning

LIAISONS
CULTURELLES

Ceux et celles qui travaillent pour l'humanité

OUTILS DE LECTURE
Recognizing related words

Recognizing words that are related to each other when you read can help you guess the meaning of words and improve reading comprehension. For example, a verb may have an adjective or a noun that is related. In the text *Une Française découvre le virus du sida,* the words **chercheuse** and **chercheur** appear. You have not learned these words but you do know the verb **chercher** which means *to look for*. Based on the meaning of the verb **chercher,** what do you think the nouns **chercheuse** and **chercheur** mean? Can you find other examples of related words in these texts?

Une Française découvre le virus du sida

Françoise Barré-Sinoussi est la troisième femme Nobel en France. Avec Luc Montaigner, elle a été récompensée par le prix Nobel de médecine pour l'identification du virus de l'immunodéficience humaine (VIH). Madame Barré-Sinoussi obtient son doctorat en 1974 à la Faculté des sciences de Paris. Chercheuse à l'Institut Pasteur à partir de 1975, elle mène° des travaux sur des thèmes liés au sida° (syndrome immunodéficitaire acquis). Depuis 2008, sa recherche se tourne vers les régulations congénitales des infections par le VIH. En 2012, elle sera Présidente de l'International Aids Society, première société internationale indépendante de chercheurs et de médecins contre le VIH/sida.

mène *leads, directs* **sida** *Aids*

Vrai ou faux?

1. Françoise Barré-Sinoussi est la première Française à obtenir le prix Nobel.   V / F

2. Françoise Barré-Sinoussi a travaillé à l'Institut Pasteur.   V / F

3. Madame Barré-Sinoussi sera Présidente de la première société internationale indépendante de médecins contre le sida.   V / F

© Sergio Gaudenti / Kipa / Corbis

Aimé Césaire: fondateur de la négritude

Aimé Césaire (1913–2008) est un poète et homme politique français de Martinique. Il est l'un des fondateurs du mouvement littéraire de la négritude et un anticolonialiste résolu. La négritude, un concept forgé par Aimé Césaire en réaction à l'oppression culturelle du système colonial français de l'époque, vise° à rejeter le projet français d'assimilation culturelle et à promouvoir° l'Afrique et sa culture. La pensée et la poésie de Césaire ont également marqué les intellectuels africains et noirs américains en lutte° contre la colonisation et l'acculturation.

vise *aims* **promouvoir** *promote* **en lutte** *struggling*

Vrai ou faux?

1. Aimé Césaire est de Paris.   V / F

2. La négritude rejette la colonisation française.   V / F

3. La poésie de Césaire influence aussi les noirs américains.   V / F

La Fondation France Libertés

La Fondation France Libertés a été créée° en 1986 par Danielle Mitterrand, la veuve de l'ancien président de la République française, François Mitterrand. La fondation s'engage activement dans les grands combats tels que le soutien° au peuple tibétain et participe aux grands projets d'aide aux pays du Sud comme la reconstruction du système éducatif au Cambodge ou la lutte° contre le sida en Afrique. Aujourd'hui, la défense des droits fondamentaux demeure° au cœur de l'action de la fondation. Le droit pour tous à disposer d'une eau potable°, libre et gratuite est devenu un de leurs premiers combats.

créée *created* **soutien** *support* **lutte** *struggle* **demeure** *remains* **potable** *drinkable*

© Christophe Lartige / SIPA / Newscom

Vrai ou faux?

1. Danielle Mitterrand est la fille de François Mitterrand.   V / F

2. La Fondation France Libertés a été créée par François Mitterrand.   V / F

3. Une préoccupation importante de France Libertés est d'assurer l'accès à l'eau potable pour tout le monde.   V / F

UN DOCUMENTAIRE CHOC
de Richard Desjardins et Robert Monderie

L'Erreur boréale

« Un film de légitime défense. » — Richard Desjardins

Courtesy ACPAV Association coopérative de productions audiovisuelles

Richard Desjardins: chanteur et cinéaste pour l'environnement

Originaire de l'Abitibi-Témiscamingue (Québec), Richard Desjardins (1948–) est humaniste, chanteur et cinéaste. Son film (réalisé avec Robert Moderie), *L'Erreur boréale* (1999), expose le problème de la déforestation au Québec et lui a valu le prix Jutra du meilleur documentaire. Ce film a questionné la responsabilité citoyenne° face à la destruction de l'environnement. Aujourd'hui, le gouvernement reconnaît en partie le bien-fondé de ce documentaire et l'importance d'une gestion° plus responsable des forêts. En 2009, l'Université du Québec à Montréal lui décerne un doctorat honoris causa pour souligner son apport° exceptionnel en tant qu'artiste engagé dans la lutte pour la justice sociale et sa contribution essentielle à l'avènement° d'une éco-société.

citoyenne *citizen* **gestion** *management* **apport** *contribution* **l'avènement** *arrival*

Vrai ou faux?

1. Richard Desjardins est un cinéaste québécois.   V / F

2. *L'Erreur boréale* est un film sur les sans-abri / les SDF au Québec.   V / F

3. Desjardins a reçu un doctorat honoris causa pour son travail pour l'environnement.   V / F

🌐 Activités Internet

- À part *(Other than)* Françoise Barré-Sinoussi, qui sont d'autres lauréat(e)s *(winners)* français(e)s ou francophones du prix Nobel? Cherchez des informations sur Internet.

- Cherchez des poèmes d'Aimé Césaire sur Internet. Donnez le titre de l'un de ses poèmes qui traite de la négritude.

- Cherchez le site officiel de la Fondation France Libertés. Nommez un projet récent de la fondation.

- Cherchez le site officiel de Richard Desjardins. À part le prix Jutra, quels autres prix et distinctions a-t-il reçus?

PARTIE 1

L'ORDINATEUR

un clavier	*keyboard*
une connexion Internet à haut débit	*high speed Internet connection*
un disque dur	*hard drive*
un écran	*computer screen*
un fichier	*file*
une imprimante	*printer*
un lecteur de cédérom	*CD-ROM drive*
un lecteur de DVD	*DVD drive*
un logiciel	*software, program*
un moniteur	*monitor*
un mot de passe	*password*
un réseau (sans fil)	*(wireless) network*
une souris	*mouse*
le traitement de texte	*word processing program*
une webcam	*webcam*

LA TECHNOLOGIE ET LES INNOVATIONS

une antenne parabolique	*satellite dish*
le clonage	*cloning*
un cœur artificiel	*artificial heart*
une découverte	*discovery*
l'énergie solaire *(f.)*	*solar energy*
un hybride	*hybrid animal or plant*
une invention	*invention*
une navette spatiale	*space shuttle*
la réalité virtuelle	*virtual reality*
un satellite	*satellite*

VERBES

démarrer	*to start up*
effacer	*to delete, erase*
être en ligne (avec)	*to be online (with)*
fermer / éteindre	*to close, to shut off*
imprimer	*to print*
sauvegarder	*to save*
taper	*to type*
télécharger	*to download*

LES EXPRESSIONS D'OPINION

Il est bizarre que	*It is bizarre that*
Il est bon que	*It is good that*
Il est dommage que	*It is too bad that*
Il est essentiel que	*It is essential that*
Il est indispensable que	*It is indispensable that*
Il est juste / injuste que	*It is fair / unfair that*
Il est merveilleux que	*It is wonderful that*
Il est normal que	*It is normal that*
Il est possible que	*It is possible that*
Il est stupide que	*It is stupid that*
Il est triste que	*It is sad that*
Il est utile / inutile que	*It is useful / not useful that*

PARTIE 2

LES PRÉOCCUPATIONS ÉCOLOGIQUES

les déchets domestiques *(m.)*	*domestic waste*
les déchets industriels *(m.)*	*industrial waste*
la déforestation	*deforestation*
l'effet de serre *(m.)*	*greenhouse effect*
l'énergie renouvelable *(f.)*	*renewable energy*
les espèces menacées *(f.)*	*endangered species*
les organismes génétiquement modifiés (OGM) *(m.)*	*genetically modified foods*
la pollution	*pollution*
le réchauffement climatique	*global warming*

LES PRÉOCCUPATIONS SOCIALES

le chômage	*unemployment*
la faim	*hunger*
la pauvreté	*poverty*
une préoccupation (sociale)	*(social) concern*
un sans-abri / un SDF (sans domicile fixe)	*homeless person*
la surpopulation	*overpopulation*

NOMS

une ampoule basse consommation	*energy saving lightbulb*
l'assistance sociale *(f.)*	*social aid*
une association humanitaire	*humanitarian association*
la préservation	*preservation, protection*
un problème	*problem*
le recyclage	*recycling*
une ressource naturelle	*natural resource*
la société	*society*
une solution	*solution*

VERBES

conserver	*to conserve*
faire du compost	*to compost*
gaspiller	*to waste*
interdire	*to forbid*
jeter	*to throw (out)*
polluer	*to pollute*
préserver	*to preserve*
protéger	*to protect*
protester	*to protest*
recycler	*to recycle*
sauver	*to save, protect*

ADJECTIFS

écologique	*ecological*
non biodégradable	*nonbiodegradable*

RÉSUMÉ DE VOCABULAIRE

LES EXPRESSIONS DE DOUTE

douter que	*to doubt that*
ne pas croire que	*not to believe that*
ne pas être certain(e) que	*not to be certain that*
ne pas être sûr(e) que	*not to be sure that*
ne pas penser que	*not to think that*
Il est impossible que	*It is impossible that*
Il n'est pas évident que	*It is not obvious that*
Il n'est pas vrai que	*It is not true that*

LES EXPRESSIONS DE CERTITUDE

croire que	*to believe that*
être certain(e) que	*to be certain that*
être sûr(e) que	*to be sure that*
penser que	*to think that*
savoir que	*to know that*
Il est clair que	*It is clear that*
Il est évident que	*It is obvious that*
Il est vrai que	*It is true that*

I. L'alphabet phonétique

Voyelles

[a] madame	[i] qui	[œ] sœur
[e] thé	[o] eau	[u] vous
[ɛ] être	[ɔ] porte	[y] sur
[ə] que	[ø] peu	

Semi-voyelles

[j] bien	[ɥ] puis	[w] oui

Voyelles nasales

[ɑ̃] quand	[ɛ̃] vin	[ɔ̃] non

Consonnes

[b] bleu	[l] lire	[s] sur
[d] dormir	[m] marron	[ʃ] chat
[f] faire	[n] nouveau	[t] triste
[ɥ] gris	[ɳ] enseigner	[v] vers
[ǰ] jaune	[p] parler	[z] rose
[k] quand	[ʀ] rester	

II. Les verbes réguliers

A. Conjugaison régulière

INFINITIF	PRÉSENT	PASSÉ COMPOSÉ	IMPARFAIT	PLUS-QUE-PARFAIT
		INDICATIF		
Verbes en -er **parler**	je parle tu parles il/elle/an parle nous parlons vous parlez ils/elles parlent	j'ai parlé tu as parlé il a parlé nous avons parlé vous avez parlé ils ont parlé	je parlais tu parlais il parlait nous parlions vous parliez ils parlaient	j'avais parlé tu avais parlé il avait parlé nous avions parlé vous aviez parlé ils avaient parlé
Verbes en -ir **finir**	je finis tu finis il/elle/on finit nous finissons vous finissez ils/elles finissent	j'ai fini tu as fini il a fini nous avons fini vous avez fini ils ont fini	je finissais tu finissais il finissait nous finissions vous finissiez ils finissaient	j'avais fini tu avais fini il avait fini nous avions fini vous aviez fini ils avaient fini
Verbes en -re **répondre**	je réponds tu réponds il/elle/on répond nous répondons vous répondez ils/elles répondent	j'ai répondu tu as répondu il a répondu nous avons répondu vous avez répondu ils ont répondu	je répondais tu répondais il répondait nous répondions vous répondiez ils répondaient	j'avais répondu tu avais répondu il avait répondu nous avions répondu vous aviez répondu ils avaient répondu
Verbes pronominaux **se laver**	je me lave tu te laves il/on se lave elle se lave nous nous lavons vous vous lavez ils se lavent elles se lavent	je me suis lavé(e) tu t'es lavé(e) il s'est lavé elle s'est lavée nous nous sommes lavé(e)s vous vous êtes lavé(e)(s) ils se sont lavés elles se sont lavées	je me lavais tu te lavais il se lavait elle se lavait nous naus lavions vous vous laviez ils se lavaient elles se lavaient	je m'étais lavé(e) tu t'étais lavé(e) il s'était lavé elle s'était lavée nous nous étions lavé(e)s vous vous étiez lavé(e)(s) ils s'étaient lavés elles s'étaient lavées

B. Verbes à modification orthographique

INFINITIF	PRÉSENT	INDICATIF PASSÉ COMPOSÉ	IMPARFAIT	PLUS-QUE-PARFAIT
acheter	j'achète tu achètes il/elle/on achète nous achetons vous achetez ils/elles achètent	j'ai acheté	j'achetais	j'avais acheté
préférer	je préfère tu préfères il/elle/on préfère nous préférons vous préférez ils/elles préfèrent	j'ai préféré	je préférais	j'avais préféré
payer	je paie tu paies il/elle/on paie nous payons vous payez ils/elles paient	j'ai payé	Je payais	j'avais payé
appeler	j'appelle tu appelles il/elle/on appelle nous appelons vous appelez ils/elles appellent	j'ai appelé	j'appelais	j'avais appelé

INFINITIF		PRÉSENT	INDICATIF PASSÉ COMPOSÉ	IMPARFAIT	PLUS-QUE-PARFAIT
amener	j'	amène	ai amené	amenais	avais amené
	tu	amènes	as amené	amenais	avais amené
	il/elle/on	amène	a amené	amenait	avait amené
	nous	amenons	avons amené	amenions	avions amené
	vous	amenez	avez amené	ameniez	aviez amené
	ils/elles	amènent	ont amené	amenaient	avaient amené

		CONDITIONNEL PRÉSENT	PASSÉ	FUTUR SIMPLE	IMPÉRATIF
	j'	amènerais	aurais amené	amènerai	
	tu	amènerais	aurais amené	amèneras	amène!
	il/elle/on	amènerait	aurait amené	amènera	
	nous	amènerions	aurions amené	amènerons	amenons!
	vous	amèneriez	auriez amené	amènerez	amenez!
	ils/elles	amèneraient	auraient amené	amèneront	

		SUBJONCTIF	PARTICIPE PRÉSENT	PARTICIPE PASSÉ
	que j'	amène	amenant	amené
	que tu	amènes		
	qu'il/elle/on	amène		
	que nous	amenions		
	que vous	ameniez		
	qu'ils/elles	amènent		

célébrer

INFINITIF		PRÉSENT	PASSÉ COMPOSÉ	IMPARFAIT	PLUS-QUE-PARFAIT
célébrer	je	**célèbr**e	ai célébré	célébrais	avais célébré
	tu	**célèbr**es	as célébré	célébrais	avais célébré
	il/elle/on	**célèbr**e	a célébré	célébrait	avait célébré
	nous	célébrons	avons célébré	célébrions	avions célébré
	vous	célébrez	avez célébré	célébriez	aviez célébré
	ils/elles	**célèbr**ent	ont célébré	célébraient	avaient célébré

		CONDITIONNEL PRÉSENT	PASSÉ	FUTUR SIMPLE	IMPÉRATIF
	je	célébrerais	aurais célébré	célébrerai	
	tu	célébrerais	aurais célébré	célébreras	**célèbr**e!
	il/elle/on	célébrerait	aurait célébré	célébrera	
	nous	célébrerions	aurions célébré	célébrerons	célébrons!
	vous	célébreriez	auriez célébré	célébrerez	célébrez!
	ils/elles	célébreraient	auraient célébré	célébreront	

		SUBJONCTIF	PARTICIPE PRÉSENT	PARTICIPE PASSÉ
	que je	**célèbr**e	célébrant	célébré
	que tu	**célèbr**es		
	qu'il/elle/on	**célèbr**e		
	que nous	célébrions		
	que vous	célébriez		
	qu'ils/elles	**célèbr**ent		

espérer

INFINITIF		PRÉSENT	PASSÉ COMPOSÉ	IMPARFAIT	PLUS-QUE-PARFAIT
espérer	j'	**espèr**e	ai espéré	espérais	avais espéré
	tu	**espèr**es	as espéré	espérais	avais espéré
	il/elle/on	**espèr**e	a espéré	espérait	avait espéré
	nous	espérons	avons espéré	espérions	avions espéré
	vous	espérez	avez espéré	espériez	aviez espéré
	ils/elles	**espèr**ent	ont espéré	espéraient	avaient espéré

		CONDITIONNEL PRÉSENT	PASSÉ	FUTUR SIMPLE	IMPÉRATIF
	j'	espérerais	aurais espéré	espérerai	
	tu	espérerais	aurais espéré	espéreras	**espèr**e!
	il/elle/on	espérerait	aurait espéré	espérera	
	nous	espérerions	aurions espéré	espérerons	espérons!
	vous	espéreriez	auriez espéré	espérerez	espérez!
	ils/elles	espéreraient	auraient espéré	espéreront	

		SUBJONCTIF	PARTICIPE PRÉSENT	PARTICIPE PASSÉ
	que j'	**espèr**e	espérant	espéré
	que tu	**espèr**es		
	qu'il/elle/on	**espèr**e		
	que nous	espérions		
	que vous	espériez		
	qu'ils/elles	**espèr**ent		

INFINITIF		PRÉSENT	PASSÉ COMPOSÉ	IMPARFAIT	PLUS-QUE-PARFAIT
répéter	je	**répèt**e	ai répété	répétais	avais répété
	tu	**répèt**es	as répété	répétais	avais répété
	il/elle/on	**répèt**e	a répété	répétait	avait répété
	nous	répétons	avons répété	répétions	avions répété
	vous	répétez	avez répété	répétiez	aviez répété
	ils/elles	**répèt**ent	ont répété	répétaient	avaient répété

		CONDITIONNEL			
		PRÉSENT	PASSÉ	FUTUR SIMPLE	IMPÉRATIF
	je	répéterais	aurais répété	répéterai	
	tu	répéterais	aurais répété	répéteras	**répèt**e!
	il/elle/on	répéterait	aurait répété	répétera	
	nous	répéterions	aurions répété	répéterons	répétons!
	vous	répéteriez	auriez répété	répéterez	répétez!
	ils/elles	répéteraient	auraient répété	répéteront	

		SUBJONCTIF	PARTICIPE PRÉSENT	PARTICIPE PASSÉ	
	que je	**répèt**e	répétant	répété	
	que tu	**répèt**es			
	qu'il/elle/on	**répèt**e			
	que nous	répétions			
	que vous	répétiez			
	qu'ils/elles	**répèt**ent			

INFINITIF		PRÉSENT	PASSÉ COMPOSÉ	IMPARFAIT	PLUS-QUE-PARFAIT
ennuyer	j'	**ennui**e	ai ennuyé	ennuyais	avais ennuyé
	tu	**ennui**es	as ennuyé	ennuyais	avais ennuyé
	il/elle/on	**ennui**e	a ennuyé	ennuyait	avait ennuyé
	nous	ennuyons	avons ennuyé	ennuyions	avions ennuyé
	vous	ennuyez	avez ennuyé	ennuyiez	aviez ennuyé
	ils/elles	**ennui**ent	ont ennuyé	ennuyaient	avaient ennuyé

		CONDITIONNEL			
		PRÉSENT	PASSÉ	FUTUR SIMPLE	IMPÉRATIF
	j'	**ennui**erais	aurais ennuyé	**ennui**erai	
	tu	**ennui**erais	aurais ennuyé	**ennui**eras	**ennui**e!
	il/elle/on	**ennui**erait	aurait ennuyé	**ennui**era	
	nous	**ennui**erions	aurions ennuyé	**ennui**erons	ennuyons!
	vous	**ennui**eriez	auriez ennuyé	**ennui**erez	ennuyez!
	ils/elles	**ennui**eraient	auraient ennuyé	**ennui**eront	

		SUBJONCTIF	PARTICIPE PRÉSENT	PARTICIPE PASSÉ	
	que j'	**ennui**e	ennuyant	ennuyé	
	que tu	**ennui**es			
	qu'il/elle/on	**ennui**e			
	que nous	ennuyions			
	que vous	ennuyiez			
	qu'ils/elles	**ennui**ent			

INFINITIF		PRÉSENT	PASSÉ COMPOSÉ	IMPARFAIT	PLUS-QUE-PARFAIT
essayer	j'	**essaie, essaye**	ai essayé	essayais	avais essayé
	tu	**essaies, essayes**	as essayé	essayais	avais essayé
	il/elle/on	**essaie, essaye**	a essayé	essayait	avait essayé
	nous	essayons	avons essayé	essayions	avions essayé
	vous	essayez	avez essayé	essayiez	aviez essayé
	ils/elles	**essaient, essayent**	ont essayé	essayaient	avaient essayé

CONDITIONNEL

		PRÉSENT	PASSÉ	FUTUR SIMPLE	IMPÉRATIF
	j'	**essaierais, essayerais**	aurais essayé	**essaierai, essayerai**	
	tu	**essaierais, essayerais**	aurais essayé	**essaieras, essayeras**	**essaie, essaye!**
	il/elle/on	**essaierait, essayerait**	aurait essayé	**essaiera, essayera**	
	nous	**essaierions, essayerions**	aurions essayé	**essaierons, essayerons**	essayons!
	vous	**essaieriez, essayeriez**	auriez essayé	**essaierez, essayerez**	essayez!
	ils/elles	**essaieraient, essayeraient**	auraient essayé	**essaieront, essayeront**	

		SUBJONCTIF	PARTICIPE PRÉSENT	PARTICIPE PASSÉ
	que j'	**essaie, essaye**	essayant	essayé
	que tu	**essaies, essayes**		
	qu'il/elle/on	**essaie, essaye**		
	que nous	essayions		
	que vous	essayiez		
	qu'ils/elles	**essaient, essayent**		

INFINITIF		PRÉSENT	PASSÉ COMPOSÉ	IMPARFAIT	PLUS-QUE-PARFAIT
envoyer	j'	**envoi**e	ai envoyé	envoyais	avais envoyé
	tu	**envoi**es	as envoyé	envoyais	avais envoyé
	il/elle/on	**envoi**e	a envoyé	envoyait	avait envoyé
	nous	envoyons	avons envoyé	envoyions	avions envoyé
	vous	envoyez	avez envoyé	envoyiez	aviez envoyé
	ils/elles	**envoi**ent	ont envoyé	envoyaient	avaient envoyé

CONDITIONNEL

		PRÉSENT	PASSÉ	FUTUR SIMPLE	IMPÉRATIF
	j'	**enverrais**	aurais envoyé	**enverrai**	
	tu	**enverrais**	aurais envoyé	**enverras**	envoie!
	il/elle/on	**enverrait**	aurait envoyé	**enverra**	
	nous	**enverrions**	aurions envoyé	**enverrons**	envoyons!
	vous	**enverriez**	auriez envoyé	**enverrez**	envoyez!
	ils/elles	**enverraient**	auraient envoyé	**enverront**	

		SUBJONCTIF	PARTICIPE PRÉSENT	PARTICIPE PASSÉ
	que j'	**envoi**e	envoyant	envoyé
	que tu	**envoi**es		
	qu'il/elle/on	**envoi**e		
	que nous	envoyions		
	que vous	envoyiez		
	qu'ils/elles	**envoi**ent		

INFINITIF		PRÉSENT	PASSÉ COMPOSÉ	IMPARFAIT	PLUS-QUE-PARFAIT
jeter	je	**jett**e	ai jeté	jetais	avais jeté
	tu	**jett**es	as jeté	jetais	avais jeté
	il/elle/on	**jett**e	a jeté	jetait	avait jeté
	nous	jetons	avons jeté	jetions	avions jeté
	vous	jetez	avez jeté	jetiez	aviez jeté
	ils/elles	**jett**ent	ont jeté	jetaient	avaient jeté

—— CONDITIONNEL ——

		PRÉSENT	PASSÉ	FUTUR SIMPLE	IMPÉRATIF
	je	**jett**erais	aurais jeté	**jett**erai	
	tu	**jett**erais	aurais jeté	**jett**eras	**jett**e!
	il/elle/on	**jett**erait	aurait jeté	**jett**era	
	nous	**jett**erions	aurions jeté	**jett**erons	jetons!
	vous	**jett**eriez	auriez jeté	**jett**erez	jetez!
	ils/elles	**jett**eraient	auraient jeté	**jett**eront	

		SUBJONCTIF	PARTICIPE PRÉSENT	PARTICIPE PASSÉ	
	que je	**jett**e	jetant	jeté	
	que tu	**jett**es			
	qu'il/elle/on	**jett**e			
	que nous	jetions			
	que vous	jetiez			
	qu'ils/elles	**jett**ent			

INFINITIF		PRÉSENT	PASSÉ COMPOSÉ	IMPARFAIT	PLUS-QUE-PARFAIT
se promener	je	me **promè**ne	me suis promené(e)	me promenais	m'**étais** promené(e)
	tu	te **promè**nes	t'es promené(e)	te promenais	t'**étais** promené(e)
	il/elle/on	se **promè**ne	s'est promené(e)	se promenait	s'**était** promené(e)
	nous	nous promenons	nous sommes promené(e)s	nous promenions	nous **étions** promené(e)s
	vous	vous promenez	vous êtes promené(e)(s)	vous promeniez	vous **étiez** promené(e)(s)
	ils/elles	se **promè**nent	se sont promené(e)s	se promenaient	s'**étaient** promené(e)s

—— CONDITIONNEL ——

		PRÉSENT	PASSÉ	FUTUR SIMPLE	IMPÉRATIF
	je	me **promè**nerais	me **serais** promené(e)	me **promè**nerai	–
	tu	te **promè**nerais	te **serais** promené(e)	te **promè**neras	**promè**ne-toi!
	il/elle/on	se **promè**nerait	se **serait** promené(e)	se **promè**nera	–
	nous	nous **promè**nerions	nous **serions** promené(e)s	nous **promè**nerons	promenons-nous!
	vous	vous **promè**neriez	vous **seriez** promené(e)(s)	vous **promè**nerez	promenez-vous!
	ils/elles	se **promè**neraient	se **seraient** promené(e)s	se **promè**neront	–

		SUBJONCTIF	PARTICIPE PRÉSENT	PARTICIPE PASSÉ	
	que je	me **promè**ne	promenant	promené	
	que tu	te **promè**nes			
	qu'il/elle/on	se **promè**ne			
	que nous	nous promenions			
	que vous	vous promeniez			
	qu'ils/elles	se **promè**nent			

se rappeler

INDICATIF				
INFINITIF	PRÉSENT	PASSÉ COMPOSÉ	IMPARFAIT	PLUS-QUE-PARFAIT
se rappeler je	me **rappelle**	me **suis** rappelé(e)	me rappelais	m'**étais** rappelé(e)
tu	te **rappelles**	t'**es** rappelé(e)	te rappelais	t'**étais** rappelé(e)
il/elle/on	se **rappell**e	s'**est** rappelé(e)	se rappelait	s'**était** rappelé(e)
nous	nous rappelons	nous **sommes** rappelé(e)s	nous rappelions	nous **étions** rappelé(e)s
vous	vous rappelez	vous **êtes** rappelé(e)(s)	vous rappeliez	vous **étiez** rappelé(e)(s)
ils/elles	se **rappell**ent	se **sont** rappelé(e)s	se rappelaient	s'**étaient** rappelé(e)s

CONDITIONNEL				
	PRÉSENT	PASSÉ	FUTUR SIMPLE	IMPÉRATIF
je	me **rappell**erais	me **serais** rappelé(e)	me **rappell**erai	–
tu	te **rappell**erais	te **serais** rappelé(e)	te **rappell**eras	**rappell**e-toi!
il/elle/on	se **rappell**erait	se **serait** rappelé(e)	se **rappell**era	–
nous	nous **rappell**erions	nous **serions** rappelé(e)s	nous **rappell**erons	rappelons-nous!
vous	vous **rappell**eriez	vous **seriez** rappelé(e)(s)	vous **rappell**erez	rappelez-vous!
ils/elles	se **rappell**eraient	se **seraient** rappelé(e)s	se **rappell**eront	–

SUBJONCTIF	PARTICIPE PRÉSENT	PARTICIPE PASSÉ
que je me **rappelle**	rappelant	rappelé
que tu te **rappell**es		
qu'il/elle/on se **rappell**e		
que nous nous rappelions		
que vous vous rappeliez		
qu'ils/elles se **rappell**ent		

se lever

INDICATIF				
INFINITIF	PRÉSENT	PASSÉ COMPOSÉ	IMPARFAIT	PLUS-QUE-PARFAIT
se lever je	me **lève**	me **suis** levé(e)	me levais	m'**étais** levé(e)
tu	te **lèv**es	t'**es** levé(e)	te levais	t'**étais** levé(e)
il/elle/on	se **lèv**e	s'**est** levé(e)	se levait	s'**était** levé(e)
nous	nous levons	nous **sommes** levé(e)s	nous levions	nous **étions** levé(e)s
vous	vous levez	vous **êtes** levé(e)(s)	vous leviez	vous **étiez** levé(e)(s)
ils/elles	se **lèv**ent	se **sont** levé(e)s	se levaient	s'**étaient** levé(e)s

CONDITIONNEL				
	PRÉSENT	PASSÉ	FUTUR SIMPLE	IMPÉRATIF
je	me **lèv**erais	me **serais** levé(e)	me **lèv**erai	–
tu	te **lèv**erais	te **serais** levé(e)	te **lèv**eras	**lèv**e-toi!
il/elle/on	se **lèv**erait	se **serait** levé(e)	se **lèv**era	–
nous	nous **lèv**erions	nous **serions** levé(e)s	nous **lèv**erons	levons-nous!
vous	vous **lèv**eriez	vous **seriez** levé(e)(s)	vous **lèv**erez	levez-vous!
ils/elles	se **lèv**eraient	se **seraient** levé(e)s	se **lèv**eront	–

SUBJONCTIF	PARTICIPE PRÉSENT	PARTICIPE PASSÉ
que je me **lève**	levant	levé
que tu te **lèv**es		
qu'il/elle/on se **lèv**e		
que nous nous levions		
que vous vous leviez		
qu'ils/elles se **lèv**ent		

III. Les verbes auxiliaires

INFINITIF	PRÉSENT	INDICATIF		
		PASSÉ COMPOSÉ	IMPARFAIT	PLUS-QUE-PARFAIT
être	je suis tu es il/elle/on est nous sommes vous êtes ils/elles sont	j'ai été	j'étais	j'avais été
avoir	j'ai tu as il/elle/on a nous avons vous avez ils/elles ont	j'ai eu	j'avais	j'avais eu

IV. Les verbes irréguliers

INFINITIF	PRÉSENT	INDICATIF	PASSÉ COMPOSÉ	IMPARFAIT	PLUS-QUE-PARFAIT
aller	je vais tu vas il/elle/on va	nous allons vous allez ils/elles vont	je suis allé(e)	j'allais	j'étais allé(e)
s'asseoir	je m'assieds tu t'assieds il/elle/on s'assied	nous nous asseyons vous vous asseyez ils/elles s'asseyent	je me suis assis(e)	je m'asseyais	je m'étais assis(e)
boire	je bois tu bois il/elle/on boit	nous buvons vous buvez ils/elles boivent	j'ai bu	je buvais	j'avais bu
conduire	je conduis tu conduis il/elle/on conduit	nous conduisons vous conduisez ils/elles conduisent	j'ai conduit	je conduisais	j'avais conduit
connaître	je connais tu connais ill/elle/on connaît	nous connaissons vous connaissez ils/elles connaissent	j'ai connu	je connaissais	j'avais connu
courir	je cours tu cours il/elle/on court	nous courons vous courez ils/elles courent	j'ai couru	je courais	j'avais couru
croire	je crois tu crois il/elle/on croit	nous croyons vous croyez ils/elles croient	j'ai cru	je croyais	j'avais cru
devoir	je dois tu dois il/elle/on doit	nous devons vous devez ils/elles doivent	j'ai dû	je devais	j'avais dû
dire	je dis tu dis il/elle/on dit	nous disons vous dites ils/elles disent	j'ai dit	je disais	j'avais dit
écrire	j'écris tu écris il/elle/on écrit	nous écrivons vous écrivez ils/elles écrivent	j'ai écrit	j'écrivais	j'avais écrit

INFINITIF	PRÉSENT		PASSÉ COMPOSÉ	IMPARFAIT	PLUS-QUE-PARFAIT
envoyer	j'envoie tu envoies il/elle/on envoie	nous envoyons vous envoyez ils/elles envoient	j'ai envoyé	j'envoyais	j'avais envoyé
faire	je fais tu fais il/elle/on fait	nous faisons vous faites ils/elles font	j'ai fait	je faisais	j'avais fait
falloir	il faut		il a fallu	il fallait	il avait fallu
lire	je lis tu lis il/elle/on lit	nous lisons vous lisez ils/elles lisent	j'ai lu	je lisais	j'avais lu
mettre	je mets tu mets il/elle/on met	nous mettons vous mettez ils/elles mettent	j'ai mis	je mettais	j'avais mis
ouvrir	j'ouvre tu ouvres il/elle/on ouvre	nous ouvrons vous ouvrez ils/elles ouvrent	j'ai ouvert	j'ouvrais	j'avais ouvert
partir	je pars tu pars ill/elle/on part	nous partons vous partez ils/elles partent	je suis parti(e)	je partais	j'étais parti(e)
pleuvoir	il pleut		il a plu	il pleuvait	il avait plu
pouvoir	je peux tu peux il/elle/on peut	nous pouvons vous pouvez ils/elles peuvent	j'ai pu	je pouvais	j'avais pu
prendre	je prends tu prends il/elle/on prend	nous prenons vous prenez ils/elles prennent	j'ai pris	je prenais	j'avais pris
recevoir	je reçois tu reçois il/elle/on reçoit	nous recevons vous recevez ils/elles reçoivent	j'ai reçu	je recevais	j'avais reçu
savoir	je sais tu sais il/elle/on sait	nous savons vous savez ils/elles savent	j'ai su	je savais	j'avais su
suivre	je suis tu suis il/elle/on suit	nous suivons vous suivez ils/elles suivent	j'ai suivi	je suivais	j'avais suivi
venir	je viens tu viens il/elle/on vient	nous venons vous venez ils/elles viennent	je suis venu(e)	je venais	j'étais venu(e)
vivre	je vis tu vis il/elle/on vit	nous vivons vous vivez ils/elles vivent	j'ai vécu	je vivais	j'avais vécu
voir	je vois tu vois il/elle/on voit	nous voyons vous voyez ils/elles voient	j'ai vu	je voyais	j'avais vu
vouloir	je veux tu veux il/elle/on veut	nous voulons vous voulez ils/elles veulent	j'ai voulu	je voulais	j'avais voulu

The column header "INDICATIF" spans PRÉSENT, PASSÉ COMPOSÉ, IMPARFAIT, PLUS-QUE-PARFAIT.

INFINITIF		PRÉSENT	INDICATIF			
			PASSÉ COMPOSÉ	IMPARFAIT	PLUS-QUE-PARFAIT
sortir	je	**sors**	**suis** sorti(e)	sortais	étais sorti(e)
	tu	**sors**	**es** sorti(e)	sortais	étais sorti(e)
	il/elle/on	**sort**	**est** sorti(e)	sortait	était sorti(e)
	nous	sort**ons**	**sommes** sorti(e)s	sortions	étions sorti(e)s
	vous	sort**ez**	**êtes** sorti(e)(s)	sortiez	étiez sorti(e)(s)
	ils/elles	sort**ent**	**sont** sorti(e)s	sortaient	étaient sorti(e)s

		CONDITIONNEL			
		PRÉSENT	PASSÉ	FUTUR SIMPLE	IMPÉRATIF
	je	sortirais	**serais** sorti(e)	sortirai	–
	tu	sortirais	**serais** sorti(e)	sortiras	**sors**!
	il/elle/on	sortirait	**serait** sorti(e)	sortira	–
	nous	sortirions	**serions** sorti(e)s	sortirons	sort**ons**!
	vous	sortiriez	**seriez** sorti(e)(s)	sortirez	sort**ez**!
	ils/elles	sortiraient	**seraient** sorti(e)s	sortiront	–

		SUBJONCTIF	PARTICIPE PRÉSENT	PARTICIPE PASSÉ
	que je	sort**e**	sortant	sorti
	que tu	sort**es**		
	qu'il/elle/on	sort**e**		
	que nous	sort**ions**		
	que vous	sort**iez**		
	qu'ils/elles	sort**ent**		

INFINITIF		PRÉSENT	INDICATIF			
			PASSÉ COMPOSÉ	IMPARFAIT	PLUS-QUE-PARFAIT
sentir	je	**sens**	ai senti	sent**ais**	avais senti
	tu	**sens**	as senti	sent**ais**	avais senti
	il/elle/on	**sent**	a senti	sent**ait**	avait senti
	nous	sent**ons**	avons senti	sent**ions**	avions senti
	vous	sent**ez**	avez senti	sent**iez**	aviez senti
	ils/elles	sent**ent**	ont senti	sent**aient**	avaient senti

		CONDITIONNEL			
		PRÉSENT	PASSÉ	FUTUR SIMPLE	IMPÉRATIF
	je	sentirais	aurais senti	sentirai	–
	tu	sentirais	aurais senti	sentiras	**sens**!
	il/elle/on	sentirait	aurait senti	sentira	–
	nous	sentirions	aurions senti	sentirons	sent**ons**!
	vous	sentiriez	auriez senti	sentirez	sent**ez**!
	ils/elles	sentiraient	auraient senti	sentiront	–

		SUBJONCTIF	PARTICIPE PRÉSENT	PARTICIPE PASSÉ
	que je	sent**e**	sentant	senti
	que tu	sent**es**		
	qu'il/elle/on	sent**e**		
	que nous	sent**ions**		
	que vous	sent**iez**		
	qu'ils/elles	sent**ent**		

INFINITIF		PRÉSENT	PASSÉ COMPOSÉ	IMPARFAIT	PLUS-QUE-PARFAIT
vendre	je	vends	ai vendu	vendais	avais vendu
	tu	vends	as vendu	vendais	avais vendu
	il/elle/on	vend	a vendu	vendait	avait vendu
	nous	vendons	avons vendu	vendions	avions vendu
	vous	vendez	avez vendu	vendiez	aviez vendu
	ils/elles	vendent	ont vendu	vendaient	avaient vendu

CONDITIONNEL

		PRÉSENT	PASSÉ	FUTUR SIMPLE	IMPÉRATIF
	je	vendrais	aurais vendu	vendrai	–
	tu	vendrais	aurais vendu	vendras	vends!
	il/elle/on	vendrait	aurait vendu	vendra	–
	nous	vendrions	aurions vendu	vendrons	vendons!
	vous	vendriez	auriez vendu	vendrez	vendez!
	ils/elles	vendraient	auraient vendu	vendront	–

		SUBJONCTIF	PARTICIPE PRÉSENT	PARTICIPE PASSÉ
	que je	vende	vendant	vendu
	que tu	vendes		
	qu'il/elle/on	vende		
	que nous	vendions		
	que vous	vendiez		
	qu'ils/elles	vendent		

INFINITIF		PRÉSENT	PASSÉ COMPOSÉ	IMPARFAIT	PLUS-QUE-PARFAIT
mourir	je	**meurs**	**suis mort(e)**	mou**rais**	**étais mort(e)**
	tu	**meurs**	**es mort(e)**	mou**rais**	**étais mort(e)**
	il/elle/on	**meurt**	**est mort(e)**	mou**rait**	**était mort(e)**
	nous	mou**rons**	**sommes mort(e)s**	mou**rions**	**étions mort(e)s**
	vous	mou**rez**	**êtes mort(e)(s)**	mou**riez**	**étiez mort(e)(s)**
	ils/elles	**meurent**	**sont mort(e)s**	mou**raient**	**étaient mort(e)s**

CONDITIONNEL

		PRÉSENT	PASSÉ	FUTUR SIMPLE	IMPÉRATIF
	je	mou**rrais**	**serais mort(e)**	mou**rrai**	–
	tu	mou**rrais**	**serais mort(e)**	mou**rras**	**meurs**!
	il/elle/on	mou**rrait**	**serait mort(e)**	mou**rra**	–
	nous	mou**rrions**	**serions mort(e)s**	mou**rrons**	mou**rons**!
	vous	mou**rriez**	**seriez mort(e)(s)**	mou**rrez**	mou**rez**!
	ils/elles	mou**rraient**	**seraient mort(e)s**	mou**rront**	–

		SUBJONCTIF	PARTICIPE PRÉSENT	PARTICIPE PASSÉ
	que je	**meure**	mourant	mort
	que tu	**meures**		
	qu'il/elle/on	**meure**		
	que nous	mou**rions**		
	que vous	mou**riez**		
	qu'ils/elles	**meurent**		

INFINITIF		PRÉSENT	PASSÉ COMPOSÉ	IMPARFAIT	PLUS-QUE-PARFAIT
				INDICATIF	
obtenir	j'	**obtiens**	ai obtenu	obten**ais**	avais obtenu
	tu	**obtiens**	as obtenu	obten**ais**	avais obtenu
	il/elle/on	**obtient**	a obtenu	obten**ait**	avait obtenu
	nous	obten**ons**	avons obtenu	obten**ions**	avions obtenu
	vous	obten**ez**	avez obtenu	obten**iez**	aviez obtenu
	ils/elles	**obtiennent**	ont obtenu	obten**aient**	avaient obtenu

		CONDITIONNEL			
		PRÉSENT	**PASSÉ**	**FUTUR SIMPLE**	**IMPÉRATIF**
	j'	**obtiendrais**	aurais obtenu	**obtiendrai**	–
	tu	**obtiendrais**	aurais obtenu	**obtiendras**	**obtiens**!
	il/elle/on	**obtiendrait**	aurait obtenu	**obtiendra**	–
	nous	**obtiendrions**	aurions obtenu	**obtiendrons**	obten**ons**!
	vous	**obtiendriez**	auriez obtenu	**obtiendrez**	obten**ez**!
	ils/elles	**obtiendraient**	auraient obtenu	**obtiendront**	–

		SUBJONCTIF	PARTICIPE PRÉSENT	PARTICIPE PASSÉ
	que j'	**obtienne**	obtenant	obtenu
	que tu	**obtiennes**		
	qu'il/elle/on	**obtienne**		
	que nous	obten**ions**		
	que vous	obten**iez**		
	qu'ils/elles	**obtiennent**		

INFINITIF		PRÉSENT	PASSÉ COMPOSÉ	IMPARFAIT	PLUS-QUE-PARFAIT
				INDICATIF	
éteindre	j'	**étein**s	ai **éteint**	**éteign**ais	avais **éteint**
	tu	**étein**s	as **éteint**	**éteign**ais	avais **éteint**
	il/elle/on	**éteint**	a **éteint**	**éteign**ait	avait **éteint**
	nous	**éteign**ons	avons **éteint**	**éteign**ions	avions **éteint**
	vous	**éteign**ez	avez **éteint**	**éteign**iez	aviez **éteint**
	ils/elles	**éteign**ent	ont **éteint**	**éteign**aient	avaient **éteint**

		CONDITIONNEL			
		PRÉSENT	**PASSÉ**	**FUTUR SIMPLE**	**IMPÉRATIF**
	j'	éteindrais	aurais **éteint**	éteindrai	–
	tu	éteindrais	aurais **éteint**	éteindras	**étein**s!
	il/elle/on	éteindrait	aurait **éteint**	éteindra	–
	nous	éteindrions	aurions **éteint**	éteindrons	**éteign**ons!
	vous	éteindriez	auriez **éteint**	éteindrez	**éteign**ez!
	ils/elles	éteindraient	auraient **éteint**	éteindront	–

		SUBJONCTIF	PARTICIPE PRÉSENT	PARTICIPE PASSÉ
	que j'	**éteign**e	éteignant	éteint
	que tu	**éteign**es		
	qu'il/elle/on	**éteign**e		
	que nous	**éteign**ions		
	que vous	**éteign**iez		
	qu'ils/elles	**éteign**ent		

INFINITIF		PRÉSENT	PASSÉ COMPOSÉ	IMPARFAIT	PLUS-QUE-PARFAIT
			INDICATIF		
devenir	je	deviens	suis devenu(e)	devenais	étais devenu(e)
	tu	deviens	es devenu(e)	devenais	étais devenu(e)
	il/elle/on	devient	est devenu(e)	devenait	était devenu(e)
	nous	devenons	sommes devenu(e)s	devenions	étions devenu(e)s
	vous	devenez	êtes devenu(e)(s)	deveniez	étiez devenu(e)(s)
	ils/elles	deviennent	sont devenu(e)s	devenaient	étaient devenu(e)s

		PRÉSENT	PASSÉ	FUTUR SIMPLE	IMPÉRATIF
			CONDITIONNEL		
	je	deviendrais	serais devenu(e)	deviendrai	–
	tu	deviendrais	serais devenu(e)	deviendras	deviens!
	il/elle/on	deviendrait	serait devenu(e)	deviendra	–
	nous	deviendrions	serions devenu(e)s	deviendrons	devenons!
	vous	deviendriez	seriez devenu(e)(s)	deviendrez	devenez!
	ils/elles	deviendraient	seraient devenu(e)s	deviendront	–

		SUBJONCTIF	PARTICIPE PRÉSENT	PARTICIPE PASSÉ
	que je	devienne	devenant	devenu
	que tu	deviennes		
	qu'il/elle/on	devienne		
	que nous	devenions		
	que vous	deveniez		
	qu'ils/elles	deviennent		

VOCABULAIRE français-anglais

The French-English Vocabulary contains all the words and expressions included in the **Vocabulaire** sections at the end of each chapter. Entries are followed by the chapter number (**P** for the **Chapitre préliminaire** and **F** for **Chapitre final**) where they appear. In addition the French-English Vocabulary includes words and expressions used in the **Activités** sections.

Expressions are listed under their key word(s). In subentries, the symbol — indicates the repetition of the key word. Regular adjectives are given in the masculine form, with the feminine ending in parentheses. For irregular adjectives, the irregular ending of the feminine or the whole word is given. Irregular forms of the plural are also indicated. The gender of each noun is indicated after the noun. If the noun has both a masculine and a feminine form, both are listed. If the noun has an irregular form for the plural, this is also indicated in parentheses after the word.

The following abbreviations are used:

m.	masculine	*inv.*	invariable
f.	feminine	*n.*	noun
sing.	singular	*v.*	verb
pl.	plural	*adj.*	adjective
m. pl.	masculine plural	*adv.*	adverb
f. pl.	feminine plural		

A

à *to, in* 3
abord: d'— *first* 4
absolument *absolutely* 2
abstrait(e) *abstract* 9
accro du shopping *(m./f.) shopaholic* 10
acharné(e) *competitive, cutthroat* 7
acheter *to buy* 6
acteur *(m.) actor* 7
actif / active *active, working* 10; **mère** *(f.)* **active** *working mom* 10; **père** *(m.)* **actif** *working dad* 10
activement *actively* 2
actrice *(f.) actress* 7
actualité *(f.) current events*
addition *(f.) check* 6
adolescence *(f.) adolescence* 8
adolescent(e) *adolescent* 8
adorer *to adore* 1
adulte *(adj.) adult* 8; **âge** *(m.)* **— adulthood** 8
adulte *(m./f.) adult* 8
aérobic *(m.) aerobics* 2
aéroport *(m.) airport* 11
affaires *(f. pl.) things, stuff* 4, *business* 7; **homme** *(m.)* **d'— businessman** 7; **femme** *(f.)* **d'— businesswoman** 7
affiche *(f.) poster* P
Afrique *(f.) Africa* 3; **— du Nord** *North Africa* 3; **— de l'Ouest** *West Africa* 3
âge *(m.) age* 8; **— adulte** *adulthood* 8; **Moyen Âge** *Middle Ages;* **troisième — old age, the elderly** 8
agence *(f.) agency;* **— de voyages** *travel agency* 11

agent(e) *(m./f.) officer* 7, *agent* 11; **— de bord** *flight attendant* 11; **— de police** *police officer* 7; **— de la sécurité** *(m./f) security agent* 11; **— de voyages** *travel agent* 11
agneau *(m.) lamb* 5
agrafeuse *(f.) stapler* P
aider *to help* 8
aigle *(m.) eagle* 12
aigre *sour* 5
ail *(m.) garlic* 5
aimer *to like, to love* 1; **— bien** *to like* 1; **— mieux** *to prefer, to like better* 1; **s'— to like / love oneself / each other** 10
ajouter *to add* 5
alcoolisé(e) *alcoholic* 5
aliment *(m.) particular food* 5; **— frit** *fried food* 5; **— industriel** *processed food* 5
Allemagne *(f.) Germany* 3
allemand *(m.) German (language)* P
allemand(e) *German* 3
aller *to go* 2; **— bien** *to look good on someone* 11; **— à la chasse** *to go hunting, to hunt* 4; **— à la pêche** *to go fishing* 4; **— au spa** *to go to the spa* 2; **— en vacances** *to go on vacation* 11; **s'en — to go away** 10
allergie *(f.) allergy* 12
ambitieux / ambitieuse *ambitious* 1
amener *to bring someone* 6
amer / amère *bitter* 5
américain(e) *American* 3
Amérique *(f.) America* 3; **— du Nord** *North America* 3; **— du Sud** *South America* 3
ami(e) *(m./f.) friend* P; **petit(e) — boyfriend / girlfriend** P; **meilleur(e) — best friend** P

amitié *(f.) friendship* 10
amour *(m.) love* 10
amoureux / amoureuse (de) *in love (with)* 8; **tomber — to fall in love (with)** 8
amphithéâtre *(m.) lecture hall* 4
ampoule *(f.) lightbulb* F; **— basse consommation** *energy saving lightbulb* F
amusant(e) *funny* P
amuser *to amuse;* **s'— to have a good time** 10
an *(m.) year* 2
anchois *(m. pl.) anchovies*
ancien / ancienne *former* 11
anglais *(m.) English (language)* P
anglais(e) *British* 3
Angleterre *(f.) England* 3
animal domestique *(m.) pet* 3
animalerie *(f.) pet store* 12
animation *(f.) animation* 9; **film** *(m.)* **d'— (animated) cartoon / animated film** 9
année *(f.) year* 2; **— dernière / passée** *last year* 5; **Bonne —!** *Happy New Year!* 8
anniversaire *(m.) birthday* 2, *anniversary* 8; **— de mariage** *wedding anniversary* 8; **Bon / Joyeux —!** *Happy birthday!* 8; **C'est quand l'— de Samir?** *When is Samir's birthday?* 2; **C'est quand ton / votre —?** *When is your birthday?* 2;
annoncer *to forecast* 2
annulé(e) *canceled*
anorak *(m.) parka* 11
antenne *(f.) antenna, dish* F; **— parabolique** *satellite dish* F

VOCABULAIRE français-anglais

anthropologie (f.) *anthropology* P
antisocial(e) *anti-social* 7
août *August* 2
appareil (m.) *appliance, piece of equipment* 4; — **audiovisuel** *piece of audiovisual equipment* 4; — **ménager** *household appliance* 4; — **photo numérique (APN)** *digital camera* 10
appartement (m.) *apartment* 4
appartenir (à) *to belong (to)*
appeler *to name, to call* 10; **s'** — *to be named / called* 10
appétit (m.) *appetite* 6; **Bon** —! *Enjoy (the meal)!* 6
applaudir *to applaud* 9
apporter *to bring something* 6
apprendre (à) *to learn* 5
après *after* 1
après-midi (m.) *afternoon* 1; **de l'** — *in the afternoon* 1
aquarelle (f.) *watercolor* 9
arbre (m.) *tree* 4
argent (m.) *money* 6
arrêt (m.) *stop;* — **d'autobus** *bus stop* 11
arriver *to arrive* 6
art (m.) *art* P; **galerie** (f.) **d'** — *art gallery* 9; **pop** — *pop art* 9
article (m.) *article* 10
artiste (m./f.) *artist* 9
Asie (f.) *Asia* 3
asperge (f.) *asparagus* 6
aspirateur (m.) *vacuum* 4; **passer l'** — *to vacuum* 4
assez *enough* 1
assiette (f.) *plate* 6
assistance sociale (f.) *social aid* F
assistant(e) social(e) *social worker* 7
assister (à) *to attend*
association (f.) *association, organization* F; — **humanitaire** *humanitarian organization* F
assurance-maladie (f.) *health insurance* 12
astronomie (f.) *astronomy* P
atelier (m.) *art studio* 9
attacher *to tie, to fasten* 11; — **la ceinture de sécurité** *to fasten the seatbelt* 11
attendre *to wait (for)* 6
attentat terroriste (m.) *terrorist attack*
au revoir *goodbye* P
au(x) *at* 1; *to, in* 3
auberge (f.) *hostel* 11; — **de jeunesse** *youth hostel* 11

aubergine (f.) *eggplant* 6
audacieux / audacieuse *daring*
aujourd'hui *today* 1
aussi *too, also* P, *as* 7; —... **que** *as ... as* 7
autant *as many, as much* 7; — **de... que** *as many, as much ... as* 7
auteur (m.) *author* 9; **femme** (f.) — *author (female)* 9
autobus (m.) *bus* 11; **arrêt** (m.) **d'** — *bus stop* 11
automne (m.) *fall* 2
autonome *independent* 7
autre *another, other* 11
autrefois *in the past, long ago* 8
avancement (m.) *promotion* 8; **avoir de l'** — *to get a promotion, to advance (in a job)* 8
avant *before* 1
avant-hier *day before yesterday* 5
avare *stingy, miserly* 10
avec *with* 1
avenir (m.) *future*
averse (f.) *shower* 2
avion (m.) *plane* 11
avis (m.) *opinion;* **À mon (votre) avis...** *In my (your) opinion . . .* 10
avocat (m.) *avocado* 5
avocat(e) *lawyer* 7
avoir *to have* 1; —... **ans** *to be . . . years old* 1; — **besoin de** *to need* 1; — **de la chance** *to be lucky* 1; — **chaud** *to be hot* 5; — **un cours de...** *to have a . . . class* 1; — **envie de** *to feel like* 1; — **faim** *to be hungry* 5; — **froid** *to be cold* 5; — **mal au cœur** *to be nauseated* 12; — **mal à la tête** *to have a headache* 12; — **mal au ventre** *to have a stomach ache* 12; — **peur de** *to be afraid* 1; — **raison** *to be right* 1; — **soif** *to be thirsty* 5; — **sommeil** *to be sleepy* 1; — **tort** *to be wrong* 1
avril *April* 2

B

baba cool (m./f.) *hippy* 10
baccalauréat (m.) *end-of-high-school exam* 7
bague (f.) *ring*
baignoire (f.) *bathtub* 4
bail (m.) *lease* 4
bal (m.) *ball*
baladeur MP3 (m.) *MP3 player* P
balcon (m.) *balcony* 4
ballet (m.) *ballet* 9
banane (f.) *banana* 5

banlieue (f.) *suburbs* 4
banque (f.) *bank* 4
banquet (m.) *banquet* 8
baptême (m.) *baptism* 8
barbe (f.) *beard* 3
barbecue (m.) *BBQ* 2; *barbecue grill* 6; **faire un** — *to have a BBQ* 2
barrer *to cross out*
baseball (m.) *baseball* 2
basket-ball / basket (m.) *basketball* 2
baskets (f. pl.) *sports shoes* 11
bateau (m.) *boat* 4; — **à voile** *sailboat* 4; **faire du** — **(à voile)** *to go (sail) boating* 4
bâtiment (m.) *building* 4
bavard(e) *talkative, gossipy* 10
beau / bel / belle *handsome, beautiful, nice* 2
beaucoup *a lot* 1
beau-fils (m.) *stepson, son-in-law* 3
beau-frère (m.) *brother-in-law, stepbrother* 3
beau-père (m.) *father-in-law, stepfather* 3
beaux-arts (m. pl.) *fine arts* 9
bel (m. before a vowel sound) *handsome, beautiful, nice* 2
belge *Belgian* 3
Belgique (f.) *Belgium* 3
belle (f.) *beautiful, nice* 2
belle-fille (f.) *stepdaughter, daughter-in-law* 3
belle-mère (f.) *mother-in-law, stepmother* 3
belle-sœur (f.) *sister-in-law, stepsister* 3
béquilles (f. pl.) *crutches* 12
bête (adj.) *stupid, idiotic* 10
bête (f.) *beast*
beurre (m.) *butter* 5
bibliothèque (f.) *library* 1
bien *fine* P, *good* 1, *well* 2; — **sûr** *of course* 1
bientôt *soon* P; **À** —. *See you soon.* P
bière (f.) *beer* 5
billet (m.) *bill, banknote* 7, *ticket* 11; — **aller-retour** *round-trip ticket* 11; — **aller-simple** *one-way ticket* 11; — **d'avion** *plane ticket* 11
biodégradable *biodegradable* F; **non** — *nonbiodegradable* F
biologie (f.) *biology* P
biologique (bio) *organic* 6
biscuit (m.) *cookie* 5
bistro (m.) *café-restaurant* 4

bizarre *bizarre* F
blanc / blanche *white* 3
blessure *(f.) wound* 12
bleu(e) *blue* 3, *rare (meat)* 5
bleuet *(m.) blueberry* 5
blog *(m.) blog* 10
blond(e) *(m./f.) blond person* 3; *(adj.) blond* 3
blouson *(m.) heavy jacket* 11; — **en cuir** *leather heavy jacket* 11
blues *(m.) blues, R&B* 9
bœuf *(m.) beef* 6; — **haché** *ground beef* 6
boire *to drink* 5
bois *(m. pl.) woods* 4
boîte (de/d') *(f.) box (of)* 5; — **à lettres** *mailbox* 11; — **(de conserves)** *can (canned goods)* 6; — **de nuit** *nightclub*
bol *(m.) bowl* 6
bon / bonne *good* P, *warm (weather)* 2; **Bonne journée.** *Good day.* P; **Bonne nuit.** *Good night.* P
bonbon *(m.) candy* 5
bonheur *(m.) happiness* 8; **Au — de (qqn)!** *To the happiness of 8 (someone)!* 8
bonjour *hello* P
bonsoir *good evening* P
bottes *(f. pl.) boots* 11
bouche *(m.) mouth* 12
boucherie *(f.) butcher's shop* 6
bouclé(e) *curly* 3
bouger *to move* 11
boulangerie *(f.) bread shop* 6
boule *(f.) ball;* — **de cristal** *crystal ball*
boulot *(m.) job (slang)* 7
bourreau de travail *(m./f.) workaholic* 10
bourse *(f.) scholarship, stock market;* — **(d'études)** *scholarship* 7
bout *(m.) end* 4; **jusqu'au —** *until the end* 4
bouteille (de/d') *(f.) bottle (of)* 5
boutique *(f.) store, boutique* 4
bowling *(m.) bowling* 2
bracelet *(m.) bracelet* 11
bras *(m.) arm* 12
Brésil *(m.) Brazil* 3
brésilien / brésilienne *Brazilian* 3
bricolage *(m.) tinkering, odd jobs* 2; **faire du —** *to tinker, to do odd jobs, to act the handyman/woman* 2
brillant(e) *brilliant* P
brioche *(f.) round egg bread* 6
brocoli *(m.) broccoli* 5

brosse *(f.) brush* 12; — **à cheveux** *hairbrush* 12; — **à dents** *toothbrush* 12; — **(à tableau)** *board eraser* P
brosser *to brush* 12; **se — les cheveux / les dents** *to brush one's hair / teeth* 12
brouillard *(m.) fog* 2
brun(e) *(adj.) brown* 3; *dark-haired person* 3
bureau *(m.) desk* P, *office* 1; — **de poste** *post office* 4
bus *(m.) bus* 11
but *(m.) goal*

C

cachet *(m.) pill, tablet* 12; — **d'aspirine** *aspirin* 12
cadeau *(m.) gift* 8
cadre *(m./f.) executive* 7
café *(m.) café* 1, *coffee* 5
cahier *(m.) notebook* P
calculatrice *(f.) calculator* P
camarade *(m./f.) mate, friend* P; — **de chambre** *roommate* P; — **de classe** *classmate* P
camion *(m.) truck* 11
camionnette *(f.) van, mini van* 11
campagne *(f.) country(side)* 4
camping *(m.) camping* 2; **faire du —** *to go camping* 2
campus *(m.) campus* 4
Canada *(m.) Canada* 3
canadien / canadienne *Canadian* 3
canapé *(m.) couch* 4
canard *(m.) duck* 5
capacité *(f.) skill* 7; **—s de communication** *communication skills* 7
carotte *(f.) carrot* 5
carrière *(f.) career* 7
carte *(f.) card* 2; — **bancaire** *debit card* 7; — **de crédit** *credit card* 7; — **d'embarquement** *boarding pass* 11; **jouer aux —s** *to play cards* 2; — **postale** *(f.) postcard* 11; — **de vœux** *greeting card* 8
casquette *(f.) baseball cap* 11
casser *to break;* **se — (le bras)** *to break one's (arm)* 12
casserole *(f.) saucepan* 5
causerie *(f.) talk show* 9
CD *(m.) compact disc, CD* P
ce *(m. sing.) this* 3
ceinture *(f.) belt;* — **de sécurité** *seatbelt*
célèbre *famous* P

célébrer *to celebrate* 6
célibataire *(adj.) single* 3; **mère** *(f.) — single mother* 10; **père** *(m.) — single father* 10
célibataire *(m./f.) single person* 10
celle *(f.) this one, that one* 9
celles *(f. pl.) these (ones), those (ones)* 9
celui *(m.) this one, that one* 9
cent *one hundred* 1; — **pour cent** *one hundred percent* 1
centième *hundredth* 8
centime *(m.) cent* 6
centre *(m.) center* 4; — **commercial** *shopping center / district* 4; — **sportif** *recreation center* 4; **—-ville** *downtown* 4
céréales *(f. pl.) cereal* 5
cérémonie *(f.) ceremony* 8; — **de remise des diplômes** *graduation ceremony* 8
cerise *(f.) cherry* 6
certain(e) *certain* F; — **(de)** *certain (of)* 11
cerveau *(m.) brain*
ces *these, those* 3
cet *(m. sing. before vowel) this* 3
cette *(f. sing.) this* 3
ceux *(m. pl.) these (ones), those (ones)* 9
chacun / chacune (de) *each (one) (of)* 11
chaise *(f.) chair* P
chambre *(f.) bedroom* 4, *room* 11; — **double** *double room* 11; — **fumeurs / non fumeurs** *smoking / nonsmoking room* 11; — **individuelle** *single room* 11
champ *(m.) field* 4
champignon *(m.) mushroom* 6
chance *(f.) luck* 8; **Bonne —!** *Good luck!* 8
chanceux / chanceuse *lucky*
chanson *(f.) song* 9
chanter *to sing* 1
chanteur *(m.) singer* 7
chanteuse *(f.) singer* 7
chapeau *(m.) hat* 11
chaque (+ noun) *each, every* 8
charcuterie *(f.) deli shop* 6
chariot *(m.) shopping cart* 6
charmant(e) *charming* P
chasse *(f.) hunt, hunting* 4; **aller à la — ** *to go hunting, to hunt* 4
chat *(m.) cat* 3
chaud(e) *hot* 2
chausser *to wear shoe size . . .* 11; **Je chausse du 36.** *I wear a size 36 shoe.* 11

chaussettes *(f. pl.) socks* 11

chaussures *(f. pl.) shoes* 11; — **à talons** *high-heeled shoes* 11

chauve *bald* 3

chef d'entreprise *(m./f.) company president* 7

chef-d'œuvre *(m.) masterpiece* 9

chemise *(f.) shirt* 11

chemisier *(m.) blouse* 11

chèque *(m.) check* 7; **compte-—s** *(m.) checking account* 7; **payer par —** *to pay by check* 7

cher / chère *expensive* 11

chercher *to look for* 1

cheval *(m.) horse* 2; **faire du —** *to go horseback riding* 2

cheveux *(m. pl.) hair* 3; — **blonds** *blond hair* 3; — **bouclés / frisés** *curly hair* 3; — **bruns** *brown hair* 3; — **courts** *short hair* 3; — **longs et raides** *long straight hair* 3; — **noirs** *black hair* 3; — **ondulés** *wavy hair* 3; — **roux** *red hair* 3

cheville *(f.) ankle* 12

chèvre *(f.) goat* 12

chez *at the home / place of* 4

chien *(m.) dog* 3

chiffre *(m.) number* 7; **être bon / bonne avec les —s** *to be good with numbers* 7

chimie *(f.) chemistry* P

Chine *(f.) China* 3

chinois *(m.) Chinese (language)* P

chinois(e) *Chinese* 3

chips *(f. pl.) chips* 5

chœur *(m.) choir* 9

choisir *to choose* 4

chômage *(m.) unemployment* F

chorale *(f.) choir* 9

chose *(f.) thing* 4; **Autre —?** *Anything else?* 6; **—s** *things, stuff* 4

chou à la crème *(m.) cream puff* 6

ciel *(m.) sky* 2; **Le — est couvert.** *It's cloudy / overcast.* 2

cinéma *(m.) movie theater* 4

cinéphile *(m./f.) film enthusiast*

cinq *five* P

cinquante *fifty* P

cinquième *fifth* 8

citron *(m.) lemon* 5; — **pressé** *lemonade* 5; — **vert** *lime* 5

clair(e) *clear* F

classe *(f.) class (of students)* P; — **affaires** *business class* 11; — **économique** *economy class* 11; **première —** *first-class* 11

classer *to classify*

classeur *(m.) folder, binder* P

clavier *(m.) keyboard* F

clé *(f.) key* 11

client(e) *(m./f.) client, guest* 11

clonage *(m.) cloning* F

Coca *(m.) Coca-Cola* 5

cocher *to check*

cochon *(m.) pig* 12

cœur *(m.) heart* 12; — **artificiel** *artificial heart* F

coiffeur *(m.) hairdresser* 7

coiffeuse *(f.) hairdresser* 7

coin: au — **(de)** *on the corner (of)* 4

coincé(e) *uptight* 7

colis *(m.) package* 11

collège *(m.) junior high / middle school* 7

collier *(m.) necklace* 11

colline *(f.) hill* 4

colocataire *(m./f.) roommate, housemate* 4

colonie *(f.) colony* 8

colonisation *(f.) colonization* 8

combien (de) *how much, how many* 4; **Ça fait —?** *How much is it?* 6; **C'est —?** *How much is it?* 6; **— coûte(nt)... ?** *How much is/are . . . ?* 6

comédie *(f.) comedy* 9; — **musicale** *musical (stage, film)* 9

commander *to order* 2; — **une pizza** *to order a pizza* 2

comme *like*

comment *how* P; — **allez-vous?** *(pl./sing., formal) How are you?* P; — **ça va?** *(sing., informal) How is it going?* P; — **s'appelle-t-elle?** *What is her name?* P; — **s'appelle-t-il?** *What is his name?* P; — **t'appelles-tu?** *What's your name?* P; — **vas-tu?** *(sing., informal) How are you?* P;

commerçant(e) *shopkeeper* 7

commerce (international) *(m.) business* P

commode *(f.) chest of drawers* 4

compléter *to fill in*

compositeur *(m.) composer* 9; **femme (f.) — composer (female)** 9

compositrice *(f.) composer (female)* 9

compost: faire du — *to compost* F

comprendre *to understand* 5

comprimé *(m.) tablet* 12

compris(e) *included* 6; **Le service est compris.** *The tip is included.* 6

comptabilité *(f.) accounting* P

comptable *(m./f.) accountant* 7

compte *(m.) account* 7; **—-chèques** *checking account* 7; — **d'épargne** *savings account* 7

concert *(m.) concert* 9

concombre *(m.) cucumber* 6

condoléances *(f. pl.) condolences* 8; **Mes —.** *My condolences.* 8

conduire *to drive* 11

confiture *(f.) jam* 5

confortable *comfortable* 11

conjoint(e) *(m./f.) significant other, (domestic) partner* 3

connaître *to know, to be familiar with* 8; **se —** *to know oneself / each other* 10

connexion *(f.) connection* F; — **Internet à haut débit** *high speed Internet connection* F

conseiller *to advise* 12

conservatoire *(m.) conservatory* 7

conserver *to conserve* F

console *(f.) console* 4; — **de jeux vidéo** *videogame console* 4; — **wii** *wii game box* 6

constamment *constantly* 2

construire *to construct* 11

conte *(m.) tale* 9; — **de fées** *fairy tale* 9

content(e) *happy, content* P

continent *(m.) continent* 3

continuer *to go, to continue* 4

contre *against* 8

contrôle de sécurité *(m.) security check* 11; **passer au —** *to go through security* 11

copain *(m.) friend* P

copine *(f.) friend* P

coq *(m.) rooster* 12

corps *(m.) body* 12

correspondance *(f.) connecting flight* 11

corriger *to correct*

costume *(m.) man's suit* 11

Côte d'Ivoire *(f.) Ivory Coast* 3

côté: à — **(de)** *next (to)* 4

côtelette *(f.) chop* 6; — **d'agneau / de porc** *(f.) lamb / pork chop* 6

cou *(m.) neck* 12

coucher *to put to bed* 12; **se —** *to go to bed* 12

coude *(m.) elbow* 12

couloir *(m.) hallway* 4

coup *(m.) blow, hit* — **de foudre** *love at first sight* 8; **tout d'un —** *all of a sudden* 8

couper *to cut* 5; **se —** *to cut (oneself)* 12

couple (m.) couple 8

courageux / courageuse courageous 1

couramment fluently 2

courriel (m.) email 2

courrier (m.) mail 11

cours (m.) class, course P

course (f.) errand 2; **faire des —s** to run some errands 2

court(e) short (hair) 3

cousin(e) (m./f.) cousin 3

couteau (m.) knife 6

coûter to cost 6

couvert(e) cloudy, overcast 2

couverts (m. pl.) cutlery 6

covoiturage (m.) carpooling 11

craie (f.) chalk (piece of) P

cravate (f.) tie 11

crayon (m.) pencil P

créatif / créative creative 7

créature (f.) creature 12

crème (f.) cream 5, lotion 12; **— à raser** shaving cream 12; **— hydratante** moisturizer 12; **— solaire** sunscreen 12

crevette (f.) shrimp 6

critère (m.) criteria

critique (f.) review, critique 9

critique (m./f.) reviewer, critic 9

croire to believe F

croisière (f.) cruise 11

croissant (m.) croissant 5

cubiste cubist 9

cueillir to pick

cuillère (f.) spoon 5; **— à café (de/d')** teaspoon (of) 5; **— à soupe (de/d')** table / soup spoon (of) 5

cuir (m.) leather 11

cuisine (f.) cooking 2, kitchen 4; **faire la —** to cook 2

cuisiner to cook 1

cuisinier (m.) cook 7

cuisinière (f.) stove 4, cook (female) 7

cuisse (f.) thigh, leg

cuit(e) cooked 5; **bien-—** well-done 5

D

danse (f.) dance, dancing 2; **— classique** classical dance 2; **— moderne** modern dance 2

danser to dance 1

danseur (m.) dancer (male) 9

danseuse (f.) dancer (female) 9

date (f.) date 2; **Quelle est la — (aujourd'hui)?** What's the date (today)? 2

davantage more

de from P; **—... à...** from . . . until . . . 1

débarquer to get off 11; **— de l'avion** to get off the plane 11

débarrasser to clear 6; **— la table** to clear the table 6

début (m.) beginning 9

décédé(e) deceased 3

décembre December 2

décès (m.) death 8

déchet (m.) waste F; **—s domestiques** domestic waste F; **—s industriels** industrial waste F

déclarer to declare 11; **— vos achats** to declare your purchases 11

décolonisation (f.) decolonization 8

découverte (f.) discovery F

décrire to describe

déforestation (f.) deforestation F

déjà already 10

déjeuner (m.) lunch 5; **prendre le —** to have lunch 5

déjeuner (v.) to have lunch

déloyal(e) disloyal 7

deltaplane (m.) hang-gliding 4; **faire du —** to go hang-gliding, to hang-glide 4

demain tomorrow P; **À —.** See you tomorrow. P

demande (f.) request

demander to ask 7; **se —** to wonder 10

démarrer to start up F

déménager to move

demi(e): et — half past 1

démodé(e) old fashioned, out-of-date 11

dent (f.) tooth 12

dentifrice (m.) toothpaste 12

dentiste (m./f.) dentist 7

dépêcher: se — to hurry 10

dépenser (de l'argent) to spend (money) 7

déposer (de l'argent) to deposit (money) 7

déprimé(e) depressed

depuis for, since 2; **— combien de temps** for how long 2; **— quand** how long, since when 6

déranger to bother, to upset 10

derrière behind 4

descendre to go down (to), to get off 6

déshabiller to undress 12; **se —** to get undressed 12

désirer to desire 6; **Vous désirez?** What would you like? 6

désolé(e) sorry 12

dessert (m.) dessert 5

dessin (m.) drawing; **— animé** (animated) cartoon / animated film 9

dessiner to draw, to sketch 2

dessous underneath 6; **au -— (de)** below 6

dessus on top 6; **au -— (de)** above 6

destiné(e) intended

détendre: se — to relax, to take it easy 10

détester to hate 1; **se —** to hate oneself / each other 10

détruire to destroy 11

deux two P; **les —** both

devant in front (of) 4

devenir to become 3

deviner to guess

devoir to have to, must, to owe 7

devoirs (m. pl.) homework P

dieu (m.) god

difficile difficult P

dimanche Sunday 1

dinde (f.) turkey 5

dîner (m.) dinner 5; **prendre le —** to have dinner 5

dîner (v.) to have dinner 1

diplôme (m.) diploma 7; **cérémonie** (f.) **de remise des —s** graduation ceremony 8

dire to say 2

discours (m.) speech

disputer: se — to argue with (each other) 10

disque dur (m.) hard drive F

distrait(e) absent-minded

distributeur automatique (m.) ATM 7

divorce (m.) divorce 8

divorcé(e) divorced 3

dix ten P; **—-huit** eighteen P; **—-neuf** nineteen P; **—-sept** seventeen P

doctorat (m.) doctorate, Ph.D. 7

documentaire (m.) documentary 9

doigt (m.) finger 6

dommage too bad; **C'est —!** That's too bad! 10

donc so, in that case, therefore 1

donner to give 7

dont that, (of) which, (of) whom 11

dormir to sleep 3

dos (m.) back 12

douane (f.) customs 11; **passer à la —** to go through customs 11

douche (f.) shower 4

doucher to shower 12; **se —** to shower 12

doué(e) gifted P

VOCABULAIRE français-anglais

douter *to doubt* F
douze *twelve* P
dramaturge *(m./f.)* *playwright* 9
drame *(m.)* *drama* 9; — **psychologique** *psychological drama* 9
drapeau *(m.)* *flag*
droit *(m.)* *law* 7; **faculté** *(f.)* **de** — *law school* 7
droit *straight* 4; **tout** — *straight ahead* 4
droite *(f)* *right* 4; **à** — **(de)** *to/on the right (of)* 4
drôle *funny, odd* 7
du *from* 3
dynamique *dynamic* P

E

eau *(f.)* *water* 5; — **minérale** *mineral water* 5
écharpe *(f.)* *scarf* 11
échecs *(m. pl.)* *chess* 2; **jouer aux** — *to play chess* 2
éclair *(m.)* *eclair* 6
écœurer *to sicken, to gross out* 10
école *(f.)* *school* P; — **de commerce** *business school* 7; — **professionnelle** *professional / vocational school* 7
écolo(giste) *(m./f.)* *ecologist, environmentalist* 10
écologique *ecological* F
économie *(f.)* *economy* P
économies *(f. pl.)* *savings* 7; **faire des** — *to save money* 7
économiste *(m./f.)* *economist*
écouter *to listen* 1
écran *(m.)* *computer screen* P
écrire *to write* 2; — **des lettres** *to write letters* 2; — **des poèmes** *to write poems* 2; — **des textos** *to write text messages* 2
écrivain / écrivaine *writer* 8
effacer *to delete, to erase* F
effet de serre *(m.)* *greenhouse effect* F
église *(f.)* *church* 4
égoïste *selfish* 10
embarquer *to board* 11; — **dans l'avion** *to board the plane* 11
embêtant(e) *annoying* P
embrasser *to kiss*; **s'**— *to kiss each other* 10
émission *(f.)* *broadcast, TV show* 9; — **sportive** *sports (talk) show* 9; — **de téléachat** *shopping network show* 9; — **de téléréalité** *reality TV show* 9; — **de variétés** *variety show* 9

empereur *(m.)* *emperor* 8
empire *(m.)* *empire* 8
emploi *(m.)* *job* 7
emploi du temps *(m.)* *schedule* 1
employé(e) *employee* 7
emprunter *to borrow* 7
en *to, in* 3; *of them/it, some* 7
enchanté(e) *pleased (to meet you)* P
encore *still* 10
endormir *to put to sleep* 12; **s'**— *to fall asleep* 12
endroit *(m.)* *location, place* 4
énergie *(f.)* *energy* F; — **renouvelable** *renewable energy* F; — **solaire** *(f.)* *solar energy* F
énergique *energetic* P
énerver *to upset*; **s'**— *to get upset* 10
enfance *(f.)* *childhood* 8
enfant *(m./f.)* *child* 3
enfin *finally* 4
ennuyer *to bore*; **s'**— *to be bored* 10
ennuyeux / ennuyeuse *boring* 1
enregistrer *to record, to check*; — **les valises** *(f. pl.)* *to check in luggage* 11
enseignant(e) *instructor, teacher* 7
ensuite *next, then* 4
entendre *to hear* 6; **s'**— **(bien / mal avec quelqu'un)** *to get along (well / badly with someone)* 10
enterrement *(m.)* *burial, funeral* 8
entre *between* 1
entrée *(f.)* *starter, appetizer* 5
entreprise *(f.)* *company* 7
entrer *to enter* 6
entretien *(m.)* *interview*
enveloppe *(f.)* *envelope* 11
environnement *(m.)* *environment* 10
envoyer *to send* 7
épargner *to save up (in a bank account)*
épaule *(f.)* *shoulder* 12
épicé(e) *spicy* 5
épicerie *(f.)* *small grocery store* 6
épinards *(m. pl.)* *spinach* 5
époque *(f.)* *time* 8; **à cette** —-**là** *at that time, in those days* 8; — **contemporaine** *contemporary time* 8
épouse *(f.)* *spouse (female)* 8
époux *(m.)* *spouse (male)* 8
équipe *(f.)* *team* 2
équipé(e) *equipped* 4; **bien** — *well equipped*; **mal** — *poorly equipped*
escalier *(m.)* *staircase* 4
espace *(m.)* *space*

Espagne *(f.)* *Spain* 3
espagnol *(m.)* *Spanish (language)* P
espagnol(e) *Spanish* 3
espèce *(f.)* *species* F; —**s menacées** *endangered species* F
espérer *to hope* 6
essayer (de) *to try (to)* 6
essentiel(le) *essential* 12
est *(m.)* *east* 4
et *and* P
étage *(m.)* *floor* 4; **premier** — *second floor (USA)* 4
étagère *(f.)* *bookshelf* 4
étang *(m.)* *pond* 4
étape *(f.)* *stage* 8; — **de la vie** *stage of life* 8
États-Unis *(m. pl.)* *United States* 3
été *(m.)* *summer* 2
éteindre *to close, to shut off* F
éternuer *to sneeze* 12
étoile *(f.)* *star* 2
étranger: à l'— *abroad, overseas* 11
être *to be* P; — **allergique à** *to be allergic to* 12; — **en avance** *to be early* 1; — **bien dans sa peau** *to have confidence in / to feel good about oneself* 10; — **en forme** *to be in shape* 12; — **à l'heure** *to be on time* 1; — **en ligne (avec)** *to be online (with)* F; — **en retard** *to be late* 1
études *(f. pl.)* *studies* P; — **supérieures** *higher education* 7
étudiant(e) *student* P
étudier *to study* P
Europe *(f.)* *Europe* 3; — **de l'Est** *Eastern Europe* 3; — **de l'Ouest** *Western Europe* 3
évidemment *evidently* 2
évident(e) *obvious* F
éviter *to avoid* 5
examen *(m.)* *exam*; — **médical** *medical exam* 12
excentrique *eccentric* 7
excuser: s'— *to be sorry, to apologize* 10
exigeant(e) *demanding* 7
exiger *to demand* 12
explorateur *(m.)* *explorer (male)* 8
exploratrice *(f.)* *explorer (female)* 8
exposition *(f.)* *exhibition* 9
express: envoyer quelque chose en — *to send something express mail* 11
exprimer *to express* 10
extérieur *(m.)* *outside*
extraverti(e) *(adj.)* *extroverted* 7
extraverti(e) *(n.)* *extrovert* 7

F

face: en — (de) across (from) 4
fâcher: se — to get angry 10
facile easy P
facteur (m.) mail carrier (male) 11
factrice (f.) mail carrier (female) 11
faculté (f.) school, college 7; — **de droit** law school 7; — **de lettres et de sciences humaines** liberal arts college 7; — **de médecine** medical school 7; — **de sciences et de technologie** science and technology college 7
faim (f.) hunger F; **avoir —** to be hungry 5
faire to do, to make 2; **Ça — fait ... euros.** That makes (It costs) . . . euros. 6; — **du...** to be a size . . . 11; — **de l'aérobic** to do aerobics 2; — **attention (à)** to pay attention (to) 5; — **un barbecue** to have a BBQ 2; — **du bateau (à voile)** to go (sail)boating 4; — **du bowling** to go bowling 2; — **du bricolage** to tinker, to do odd jobs, to act the handyman/woman 6; — **du camping** to go camping 2; — **chauffer** to heat 5; — **du cheval** to go horseback riding 2; — **du compost** to compost F; — **des courses** to run some errands 2; — **la cuisine** to cook 2; — **de la danse classique** to do classical dance 2; — **de la danse moderne** to do modern dance 2; — **... degrés** to be . . . degrees 2; — **du deltaplane** to go hang-gliding, to hang-glide 4; — **la fête** to party 2; — **la grasse matinée** to sleep in 2; — **de la gym** to work out, to exercise 2; — **du jardinage** to garden 2; — **du jogging** to go jogging 2; — **du karaoké** to do karaoke 2; — **du lèche-vitrine** to window-shop 2; — **la lessive** to do the laundry 4; — **de la marche** to walk (for exercise) 2; — **le ménage** to do the housework 4; — **de la natation** to swim (for exercise) 2; — **du patinage** to ice skate, to go iceskating 2; — **de la peinture** to paint 2; — **de la photo(graphie)** to practice photography 2; — **un pique-nique** to (have / go on a) picnic 2; — **plaisir à quelqu'un** to please someone 10; — **de la planche à voile** to go wind-surfing 2; — **de la plongée sous-marine** to scuba dive 2; — **la poussière** to dust 4; — **une promenade** to take a walk (in town) 2; — **de la randonnée** to go hiking, to hike 4; — **de la sculpture** to sculpt 9; — **du shopping** to shop, to go shopping 2; — **la sieste** to take a nap 2; — **du ski (alpin)** to go (downhill) skiing 2; — **du ski de fond** to go cross-country skiing 2; — **du ski nautique** to water-ski 2; — **du sport** to work out, to exercise 2; — **du surf** to surf 2; — **la vaisselle** to do the dishes 4; — **les valises** to pack 11; — **du vélo** to go bike riding 2; — **un voyage** to take a trip 2; — **du yoga** to do yoga 2;
fait (m.) fact 10
falloir to be necessary 12
famille (f.) family 3; — **élargie** extended family 3; — **proche** immediate family 3
fana (m./f.) fan, nut 10; — **de la santé** health nut 10
farce (f.) prank
farfelu(e) scatter-brained 7
farine (f.) flour 5
fascinant(e) fascinating P
fast-food (m.) fast food 5
fatigué(e) tired 12
fauteuil (m.) armchair 4
fée (f.) fairy 9; **conte** (m.) **de —s** fairy tale 9
félicitations (f. pl.) congratulations 8
femme (f.) woman P, wife 3; — **d'affaires** businesswoman 7; — **auteur** author 9; — **compositeur** composer 9; — **au foyer** housewife 10; — **ingénieur** engineer 7; — **médecin** doctor 7; — **plombier** plumber 7; — **poète** poet 8; — **politique** politician 8; — **pompier** firefighter 7; — **soldat** soldier 8
fenêtre (f.) window P
férié: jour (m.) — holiday (legal) 8
ferme (f.) farm 4
fermer to close, to shut off F
fête (f.) party 2, holiday, celebration 8; **faire la —** to party 2; — **des Mères** Mother's Day 8; — **nationale** National Holiday 8; — **des Pères** Father's Day 8; — **du Travail** Labor Day 8
fêter to celebrate 8
feu (f.) fire; —**x d'artifices** fireworks
feuille (f.) sheet (paper) P; — **de papier** sheet of paper P
feuilleton (m.) soap opera 9
février February 2
fiançailles (f. pl.) engagement 8
fiancer: se — to get engaged to (each other) 10
fibres (f. pl.) fibers 5
fichier (m.) file F
fidèle loyal 10
fidélité (f.) loyalty 10
fier / fière proud 1
fièvre (f.) fever 12
figure (f.) face 12
fille (f.) girl P, daughter 3
film (m.) film, movie 9; — **d'action** action film 9; — **d'animation** (animated) cartoon / animated film 9; — **d'horreur** horror film 9; — **romantique** romance film 9; — **de science-fiction** sci-fi film 9; — **à suspense** suspense film 9
fils (m.) son 3
fin (f.) end, ending 9
finir to finish 4
fleur (f.) flower 4
fleuve (m.) river 4
flexible flexible 7
fois (f.) time; **d'autres —** other times 10; **une —** once 8
fonder to found 8
football / foot (m.) soccer 2; — **américain** football 2
forêt (f.) forest 4
forme: être en — to be in shape 12
formidable great, awesome 10
foulard (m.) silk scarf 11
four (m.) oven 4; **au —** baked 5; — **(à) micro-ondes** microwave 4
fourchette (f.) fork 6
foyer (m.) household; **femme** (f.) **au —** housewife 10; **homme** (m.) **au —** househusband 10
frais (m. pl.) fees 11; — **de scolarité** tuition 7
frais / fraîche cool (weather) 2, fresh, cool 5
fraise (f.) strawberry 5
framboise (f.) raspberry 5
français (m.) French (language) P
français(e) French 3
France (f.) France 3
franquette: dîner (m.) **à la bonne —** potluck
fréquence (f.) frequency
frère (m.) brother 3
frigo (m.) refrigerator / fridge 4
frisé(e) curly 3

VOCABULAIRE français-anglais

frit(e) *fried* 5
frites *(f. pl.) fries* 5
froid(e) *cold* 2; **avoir froid** *to be cold* 5
fromage *(m.) cheese* 5
fruit *(m.) fruit* 5; **—s de mer** *shellfish* 5
fumer *to smoke* 5
furieux / furieuse *furious* 12

G

gagner *to win, to earn* 7; **— de l'argent** *to earn money* 7; **— sa vie** *to earn a living* 7
galerie *(f.) gallery* 9; **— d'art** *art gallery* 9
gants *(m. pl.) gloves* 11
garage *(m.) garage* 4
garçon *(m.) boy* P
garderie *(f.) daycare center*
gare *(f.) (bus / train) station* 11
gaspiller *to waste* F
gâté(e) *spoiled*
gâteau *(m.) cake* 5
gauche *(f.) left* 4; **à — (de)** *to/on the left (of)* 4
général *(m.) general* 8
génial(e) *great / awesome* 10
génie *(m.) engineering* P; **— civil** *civil engineering* P; **— électrique** *electrical engineering* P; **— mécanique** *mechanical engineering* P
genou *(m.) knee* 12
genre *(m.) genre* 9
gens *(m. pl.) people* 1
gentil / gentille *nice* 1
gentiment *nicely* 2
gérant(e) *manager* 7
gérer *to manage*
gestion *(f.) business administration* P
gilet *(m.) cardigan sweater* 11
gîte du passant *(m.) bed and breakfast* 11
glace *(f.) ice cream* 5
glucides *(m. pl.) carbohydrates* 5
golf *(m.) golf* 2
gomme *(f.) eraser* P
gorge *(f.) throat* 12
goût *(m.) taste* 6; **avoir le — du travail** *to have good work ethic* 7; **C'est à votre —?** *Is it to your liking / taste?* 6
goûter *(m.) snack* 5
goûter *(v.) to snack, to taste* 6
gracieux / gracieuse *graceful, gracious* 10
gramme (de/d') *(m.) gram (of)* 5
grand(e) *big, tall* 3

grand-chose: Pas —. *Not much.* P
grandeur *(f.) greatness* 8
grandir *to grow up* 4
grand-mère *(f.) grandmother* 3
grand-père *(m.) grandfather* 3
grands-parents *(m. pl.) grandparents* 3
gras: en — *boldface*
gratter *to itch, to scratch* 12; **se —** *to scratch (oneself)* 12
grave *serious* 12
grenouille *(f.) frog* 12
grignoter *to snack* 5
grille *(f.) grid*
grillé(e) *grilled* 5
grippe *(f.) flu* 12
gris(e) *gray, dreary (weather)* 2
gros / grosse *fat* 3
grossier / grossière *crude, crass* 10
grossir *to gain weight* 4
guerre *(f.) war* 8; **— mondiale** *world war*

H

habillé(e) *dressed* 10; **bien —** *well-dressed* 10; **mal —** *poorly-dressed* 10
habiller *to dress* 12; **s'—** *to get dressed* 12
habiter *to live (in a place), to reside* 1
habitude *(f.) habit*; **d'—** *usually* 8
hamburger *(m.) hamburger* 5
hamster *(m.) hamster* 12
Hanoukka *(f.) Hanukah* 8
haricot vert *(m.) green bean* 5
hebdomadaire *(m.) weekly (magazine, newspaper) publication* 10
héroïne *(f.) heroine* 8
héros *(m.) hero* 8
heure *(f.) hour, time* 1; **À quelle —...?** *At what time...?* 1; **Il est deux —s.** *It's two o'clock.* 1; **Il est une —.** *It's one o'clock.* 1
heureux / heureuse *happy* 1
hier *yesterday* 1; **— soir** *last night* 5
hip-hop *(m.) hip-hop* 9
hippy *(m./f.) (pl. hippies) hippy* 10
histoire *(f.) history* P, *story* 9
hiver *(m.) winter* 2
hockey *(m.) hockey* 2
homard *(m.) lobster* 6
homme *(m.) man* P; **— d'affaires** *businessman* 7; **— au foyer** *househusband* 10; **— politique** *politician (male)* 8
hôpital *(m.) hospital* 4
horaire *(m.) schedule* 1

horloge *(f.) clock* P
hors-d'œuvre *(m.) starter / appetizer* 5
hôte *(m.) host* 8
hôtel *(m.) hotel* 1; **— de luxe** *luxury hotel, resort* 11; **— trois / quatre / cinq étoiles** *three / four / five star hotel* 11
hôtesse *(f.) hostess* 8
huile *(f.) oil* 5; **— d'olive** *olive oil* 5
huit *eight* P
humains *(m. pl.) humans* 12
humeur *(f.) mood* 7; **être de bonne —** *to be in a good mood* 7; **être de mauvaise —** *to be in a bad mood* 7
hybride *(m.) hybrid animal or plant* F
hygiène *(f.) hygiene* 12
hypermarché *(m.) hypermarket* 6
hypertension *(f.) high blood pressure* 12

I

idée *(f.) idea* 10
identité *(f.) identity* 11; **pièce** *(f.)* **d'—** *form of identification* 11
impatient(e) *impatient* P
impératrice *(f.) empress* 8
imperméable *(m.) raincoat* 11
important(e) *important* P
impressionniste *impressionist* 9
imprimante *(f.) printer* F
imprimer *to print* F
indépendance *(f.) independence* 8
indépendant(e) *independent* P
indiscret / indiscrète *indiscreet* 10
indispensable *indispensable* F
infidèle *disloyal* 10
infidélité *(f.) disloyalty* 10
infirmier *(m.) nurse (male)* 7
infirmière *(f.) nurse (female)* 7
inflexible *inflexible* 7
info(rmation)s *(f. pl.) news broadcast* 9
informaticien(ne) *computer specialist* 7
informatique *(f.) computer science* P
ingénieur *(m.) engineer* 7; **femme** *(f.)* **— engineer (female)** 7
ingrédient *(m.) ingredient* 5
inquiéter *to worry*; **s'— (de)** *to worry (about)* 10
installer: s'— dans / à *to move into, to settle into* 10
instant *(m.) instant*; **à l'—** *a few moments ago*
institut: — (m.) de beauté *spa, beauty parlor* 4
intellectuel / intellectuelle *intellectual* 1
intelligent(e) *intelligent* P

interdire *to forbid* F
intéressant(e) *interesting* P
intéresser: s'— (à) *to be interested (in)* 10
intervention chirurgicale *(f.)* *surgery* 12
introverti(e) *(adj.)* *introverted* 7
introverti(e) *(n.)* *introvert* 7
intrus(e) *one that does not belong*
inutile *not useful, useless* P
invention *(f.)* *invention* F
invité(e) *guest* 8
inviter *to invite* 1
iPod® *(m.)* *iPod®* P
irlandais(e) *Irish* 3
Irlande *(f.)* *Ireland* 3
Italie *(f.)* *Italy* 3
italien / italienne *Italian* 3
ivoirien / ivoirienne *of the Ivory Coast* 3

J

jaloux / jalouse *jealous* 7
jambe *(f.)* *leg* 12
jambon *(m.)* *ham* 5
janvier *January* 2
Japon *(m.)* *Japan* 3
japonais(e) *Japanese* 3
jardin *(m.)* *garden, lawn* 4
jardinage *(m.)* *gardening* 2; **faire du — to garden** 2
jaune *yellow* 3
jazz *(m.)* *jazz* 9
jean *(m.)* *jeans* 11
jeter *to throw (out)* F
jeu *(m.)* *game* 2; **—x de société** *board games* 2; **jouer aux —x de société** *to play board games* 2; **— télévisé** *game show* 9
jeudi *Thursday* 1
jeune *young* 3
jeunesse *(f.)* *youth* 8
jogging *(m.)* *jogging* 2, *sweatpants* 11
joli(e) *pretty* 3
joue *(f.)* *cheek*
jouer *to play* 1; **— de la batterie** *to play the drums* 2; **— aux cartes** *(f. pl.)* *to play cards* 2; **— aux échecs** *(m. pl.)* *to play chess* 2; **— de la guitare** *to play the guitar* 2; **— aux jeux de société** *(m. pl.)* *to play board games* 2; **— de la musique** *to play, to listen to music* 2; **— du piano** *to play the piano* 2; **— au poker** *to play poker* 2; **— du violon** *to play violin* 2; **— du violoncelle** *to play cello* 2

joueur *(m.)* *player (male)* 2
joueuse *(f.)* *player (female)* 2
jour *(m.)* *day* 8; **— de l'Action de Grâce** *Thanksgiving* 8; **— de l'An** *New Year's Day* 8; **— férié** *legal holiday* 8
journal *(m.)* *newspaper* 2; **— intime** *diary* 10
journalisme *(m.)* *journalism* P
journaliste *(m./f.)* *journalist* 7
journée *(f.)* *day;* **— de congé** *day-off* 8
juillet *July* 2
juin *June* 2
jupe *(f.)* *skirt* 11; **mini-—** *(mini) skirt* 11
jus *(m.)* *juice* 5; **— de canneberge** *cranberry juice* 5; **— d'orange** *orange juice* 5
jusque *until* 4
juste / injuste *fair / unfair* F

K

karaoké *(m.)* *karaoke* 2; **faire du — to do karaoke** 2
kilo (de/d') *(m.)* *kilogram (of)* 5
kiosque: — (m.) à journaux *newsstand* 4
kleenex *(m.)* *tissue* 12

L

laboratoire *(m.)* *laboratory* 4
lac *(m.)* *lake* 4
laïc / laïque *secular*
laid(e) *ugly* 3
laisser *to leave* 6; **— un pourboire** *to leave a tip* 6
lait *(m.)* *milk* 5; **— de soja** *soy milk* 5
laitue *(f.)* *lettuce* 6
lampe *(f.)* *lamp* 4
langue *(f.)* *language* P, *tongue* 12
lapin *(m.)* *rabbit* 12
laquelle *which (f. sing.)* 11
lavabo *(m.)* *bathroom sink* 4
laver *to wash* 12; **se — to wash (oneself)** 12
laverie automatique *(f.)* *laundromat* 4
lèche-vitrine *(m.)* *window-shopping* 2; **faire du — to window-shop** 2
lecteur *(m.)* *player (audiovisual equipment)* 4; **— de cédéroms** *CD-ROM drive* F; **— (de) DVD** *DVD player* 4
légume *(m.)* *vegetable* 5
lendemain *(m.)* *next / following day* 1
lentement *slowly* 2
lentilles *(f. pl.)* *lentils* 5
lequel *which (m. sing.)* 11
lesquelles *which (f. pl.)* 11

lesquels *which (m. pl.)* 11
lessive *(f.)* *laundry* 4; **faire la — to do the laundry** 4
lettres *(f. pl.)* *liberal arts* 7; **faculté** *(f.)* **de — et de sciences humaines** *liberal arts college* 7
leur *their* 3, *them* 7
lever *to lift, to raise;* **se — to get up** 12
lèvre *(f.)* *lip* 12
liberté *(f.)* *freedom* 8
librairie *(f.)* *bookstore* 4
licence *(f.)* *bachelor's degree (equivalent of)* 7
lieu *(m.)* *setting*
lion *(m.)* *lion* 12
liquide *(m.)* *cash* 7; **payer en — to pay cash** 7
lire *to read* 2; **— les courriels** *to read e-mail* 2; **— le journal** *to read the newspaper* 2; **— de la poésie** *to read poetry* 2; **— un roman** *to read a novel* 2
lit *(m.)* *bed* 4; **— simple / double** *single / double bed* 11
litre (de/d') *(m.)* *liter (of)* 5
littéraire *literary* 9
littérature *(f.)* *literature* P
livre (de/d') *(f.)* *pound (of)* 5
livre *(m.)* *book* P
livrer *to deliver* 11
location *(f.)* *rental*
logement *(m.)* *lodging*
logiciel *(m.)* *software, program* F
loi *(f.)* *law* 4
loin (de) *far (from)* 4
loisir *(m.)* *leisure activity* 2
long / longue *long* 3
louer *to rent* 4
lourd(e) *heavy, hot (weather), muggy (weather)* 2
loyal(e) *loyal, faithful* 7
loyer *(m.)* *rent* 4
lui *him, her* 7
lundi *Monday* 1
lune *(f.)* *moon* 2
lunettes de soleil *(f. pl.)* *sunglasses* 11
lycée *(m.)* *high school* 4

M

ma *my* 3
madame (Mme) *Ma'am, Mrs.* P
madeleine *(f.)* *madeleine cake* 6
mademoiselle (Mlle) *Miss* P
magasin *(m.)* *store* 6; **— (de produits) bio** *(m.)* *health / organic food store* 6

magazine (m.) *magazine* 4; — **de mode** *fashion magazine* 10
mai *May* 2
maigre *skinny, scrawny* 3
maigrir *to lose weight* 4
maillot (de bain) (m.) *swimsuit* 11
main (f.) *hand* 12
maire (m.) *mayor*
maïs (m.) *corn* 6
mais *but* 1
maison (f.) *house, home* 4; — **de la presse** *newsstand* 4
mal *badly* 2, *bad* 7; **le plus** — *the worst* 7
malade *sick* 12; **tomber** — *to get sick* 12
maladie (f.) *illness* 12
maladroit(e) *clumsy* 10
malheureux / malheureuse *unhappy* 1
mallette (f.) *briefcase* 11
manger *to eat* 1
mangue (f.) *mango* 6
manteau (m.) *overcoat* 11
manuel (m.) *textbook*
maquillage (m.) *makeup* 12
maquiller *to put on make-up (on someone)* 12; **se** — *to put on make-up* 12
marché (en plein air) (m.) *(open air) market* 6
marche (f.) *walking* 2
marché: bon — *inexpensive* 11
marcher *to walk* 1
mardi *Tuesday* 1; — **gras** *Mardi Gras* 8
marelle (f.) *hopscotch*
mari (m.) *husband* 3
mariage (m.) *marriage* 8; **anniversaire** (m.) **de** — *wedding anniversary* 8
marié(e) *married* 3; **nouveaux mariés** (m. pl.) *newly weds* 8
marier: se — *to marry (each other)* 10
Maroc (m.) *Morocco* 3
marocain(e) *Moroccan* 3
marquant(e) *memorable, important* 8
marque (m.) *brand*
marqueur (m.) *marker* P
marron *brown* 3
mars *March* 2
master (m.) *master's degree* 7
match (m.) *game, match* 2; — (m.) **télévisé** *televised game* 9
mathématiques (f. pl.) *mathematics* P
matières grasses (f. pl.) *fats* 5
matin (m.) *morning* 1; **du** — *in the morning* 1; **être du** — *to be a morning person* 7
mauvais(e) *bad* 2; **le/la/les plus** —(s) *the worst* 7

mayonnaise (f.) *mayonnaise* 5
MBA (m.) *MBA* 7
me *me* 7
méchant(e) *mean* P
médecin (m.) *doctor* 7; **femme** (f.) — *doctor (female)* 7
médecine (f.) *medicine*; **faculté** (f.) **de** — *medical school* 7
médicament (m.) *medication* 12
méfier: se — **(de)** *to be suspicious (of)* 10
meilleur(e) *best* P, *better* 7
melon (m.) *cantelope* 6
membre (m./f.) *member* 10; — **de la jet-set** *jet setter* 10
même *same* 11; **le/la/les** —**s** *the same* 11
ménage (m.) *housework* 4; **faire le** — *to do the housework* 4
mensonge (m.) *lie*
mensuel (m.) *monthly publication* 10
menu (m.) *menu* 6
mer (f.) *sea* 4
merci *thank you* P
mercredi *Wednesday* 1
mère (f.) *mother* 3; — **active** *working mom* 10; — **célibataire** *single mother* 10
mériter *to deserve*
merveilleux / merveilleuse *wonderful, marvelous, super* F
mes *my* 3
message (m.) *message*; — **instantané** *instant message* 10
messagerie (m.) *messaging* 10; — **instantanée** *instant messaging* 10
météo (f.) *weather forecast* 2
métier (m.) *trade, vocation* 7
métro (m.) *subway* 11
mettre *to place, to put, to set* 6; — **la table** *to set the table* 6; **se** — **(à)** *to begin (to)* 10
meuble (m.) *piece of furniture* 4
mexicain(e) *Mexican* 3
Mexique (m.) *Mexico* 3
microblogging (m.) *Twitter-like messages* 10
micro-ondes (m.) *microwave* 4
midi (m.) *noon* 1
mieux *better* 7
milieu (m.) *middle* 6; **au** — **(de)** *in the middle (of)* 6
mille *one thousand* 4
milliard (m.) *one billion* 4
million (m.) *one million* 4
mince *slim, lean, slender* 3
ministre (m.) *minister* 8; **premier** — *prime minister* 8

minuit (m.) *midnight* 1
miroir (m.) *mirror* 4
mixeur (m.) *blender* 6
mode (f.) *fashion*; **à la** — *stylish, fashionable* 11
moderne *modern* P
modeste *modest* P
moi *me* P; **Pour** —..., **s'il vous plaît.** *For me . . . please.* 6
moins *less, fewer* 7; — **(de)… que** *less, fewer . . . than* 7; **le/la/les** — *the least* 7
mois (m.) *month* 2; — **dernier / passé** *last month* 5
mon *my* 3
monarchie (f.) *monarchy* 8
moniteur (m.) *monitor* F
monsieur (M.) *Sir, Mr.* P.
montagne (f.) *mountain* 4
monter *to go up, to climb, to get on* 6
montre (f.) *watch* 11
montrer *to show* 7
moralité (f.) *morality* 10
mot (m.) *word*; — **de passe** *password* F
motel (m.) *motel* 11
moto (f.) *motorcycle* 11
mou / molle *soft, no backbone, wimpy* 10
moule (f.) *mussel* 6
mourir *to die* 6
moustaches (f. pl.) *whiskers* 12
moutarde (f.) *mustard* 5
mouvement (m.) *movement* 8
moyen de transport (m.) *means of transportation* 11
musclé(e) *muscular* 3
musée (m.) *museum* 4
musicien(ne) (n. & adj.) *musician* 7
musique (f.) *music* P; — **alternative** *alternative* 9; — **classique** *classical* 9; — **country** *country* 9; — **folk** *folk* 9; —**s du monde** *world music* 9; — **new age** *new age music* 9

N

naïf / naïve *naive* 1
nain(e) *dwarf*
naissance (f.) *birth* 8
naître *to be born* 6
nappe (f.) *table cloth* 6
natation (f.) *swimming* 2
nationalisme (m.) *nationalism* 8
nature (f.) *nature*; — **morte** *still life* 9
navette spatiale (f.) *space shuttle* F
naviguer: — **sur Internet** *to surf the Internet* 1

ne *not* P; —... **aucun(e)** *none, not any* 10; —... **jamais** *never* 1; — … **ni… ni** *neither . . . nor* 10; —... **pas du tout** *not at all* 10; —... **pas encore** *not yet* 10; —... **personne** *nobody, no one* 10; —... **plus** *no longer, no more* 10; —... **que** *only* 10; —... **rien** *nothing, not anything* 10

nécessaire *necessary* P

neige (*f.*) *snow* 2; **bonhomme** (*m.*) **de — ** *snowman*

neiger *to snow* 2

neuf / neuve *new* P; **Quoi de neuf?** *What's new?* P

neuf *nine* P

neuvième *ninth* 8

neveu (*m.*) *nephew* 3

nez (*m.*) *nose* 3

nièce (*f.*) *niece* 3

noblesse (*f.*) *nobility*

Noël (*m.*) *Christmas* 8

noir(e) *black* 3

noix (*f. pl.*) *walnuts* 5

nom (*m.*) *name* P; — **de famille** *last name* P; **Mon — (de famille) est...** *My (last) name is . . .* P; **Quel est ton — (de famille)?** *What is your (last) name?* P

nord (*m.*) *north* 4

normal(e) *normal* F

nos *our* 3

notre *our* 3

nourriture (*f.*) *food* 5

nous *us* 7

nouveau / nouvel / nouvelle *new* 3

nouveaux mariés (*m. pl.*) *newly weds* 8

nouvel (*m. before a vowel sound*) *new* 3

nouvelle (*f.*) *new* 3

nouvelles (*f. pl.*) *news, news items* 9

novembre *November* 2

nuage (*m.*) *cloud* 2

nuit (*f.*) *night* 1

O

obéir (à) *to obey* 4

objet (*m.*) *object* 4

obtenir *to obtain* 7

occuper: s'— (de) *to take care of* 10

octobre *October* 2

œuf (*m.*) *egg* 5

œil (*m.*) (*pl.* **yeux**) *eye* 3

œuvre (*f.*) *work, masterpiece;* — **d'art** *work of art* 9

oignon (*m.*) *onion* 5

oiseau (*m.*) *bird* 12

omelette (*f.*) *omelet* 5

oncle (*m.*) *uncle* 3

ondulé(e) *wavy* 3

onze *eleven* P

opéra (*m.*) *opera* 9

optimiste *optimistic* P

orage (*m.*) *storm* 2

orange (*f.*) *orange* 3; **jus d'— ** (*m.*) *orange juice* 5

orchestre (*m.*) *orchestra* 9

ordinateur (*m.*) *computer* P; — **portable** *laptop computer* P;

ordonnance (*f.*) *prescription* 12

oreille (*f.*) *ear* 12

organisé(e) *organized* 7

organiser *to organize, to throw (party)* 8

organisme (*m.*) *organism;* —**s génétiquement modifiés (OGM)** *genetically modified foods* F

orgueilleux / orgueilleuse (*very*) *proud* 10

orteil (*m.*) *toe* 12

os (*m.*) *bone*

où *where* 4, *when* 11

ouest (*m.*) *west* 4

ouragan (*m.*) *hurricane* 2

ours (*m.*) *bear* 12

ouvrier (*m.*) *worker (factory) (male)* 7

ouvrière (*f.*) *worker (factory) (female)* 7

P

pacifique *peaceful* 8

pain (*m.*) *bread* 5; — **de campagne** *country-style bread* 6; — **au chocolat** *croissant-type pastry filled with chocolate* 6; — **complet** *whole grain bread* 5; — **de mie** *loaf of sliced bread* 6

paix (*f.*) *peace* 8

pamplemousse (*m.*) *grapefruit* 6

panier (*m.*) *basket* 6

pansement (*m.*) *bandage* 12

pantalon (*m.*) *slacks* 11; — **à pattes d'éléphant** *bell bottom pants* 11

papier (*m.*) *paper* P; **feuille** (*f.*) **de — ** *sheet of paper* P

Pâques (*m. pl.*) *Easter* 8

parc (*m.*) *park* 1

parce que *because* 4

parents (*m. pl.*) *parents, relatives* 3

paresseux / paresseuse *lazy* 1

parfois *sometimes, at times* 1

parking (*m.*) *parking lot* 4

parler *to speak, to talk* 1; **se — ** *to talk to oneself / each other* 10

partager *to share* 4

partenaire (*m./f.*) *significant other, (domestic) partner* 3

partir *to leave* 3

pas *not* 1; — **du tout** *not at all* 1

passeport (*m.*) *passport* 11

passer *to pass, to take* 1; *to spend;* — **un examen** *to take an exam* 1; — **par** *to pass by, to go by* 6; **se — ** *to happen* 10

passe-temps (*m.*) *pastime, hobby* 2

pastèque (*f.*) *watermelon* 6

pâtes (*f. pl.*) *pasta* 5

patiemment *patiently* 2

patient(e) (*adj. & n.*) *patient* P, 12

patinage (*m.*) *iceskating* 2

pâtisserie (*f.*) *pastry shop, pastry* 6

patron(ne) *boss* 7

patte (*f.*) *paw* 12

pauvreté (*f.*) *poverty* F

payer *to pay* 6; — **chacun sa part** *to pay, to go Dutch* 6; — **par carte de crédit** *with a credit card* 6; — **par chèque** *to pay by check* 7; — **en liquide** *to pay cash* 6

pays (*m.*) *country* 3

paysage (*m.*) *landscape* 9

peau (*f.*) *skin;* **être bien dans sa — ** *to have confidence in / to feel good about oneself* 10

pêche (*f.*) *fishing* 4, *peach* 6; **aller à la — ** *to go fishing* 4

peigne (*m.*) *comb* 12

peintre (*m./f.*) *painter* 9

peinture (*f.*) *paint* 2, *painting* 9; **faire de la — ** *to paint* 2

peluche: animal (*m.*) **en — ** *stuffed animal*

pendant *during, throughout* 1, *for* 6

pensée (*f.*) *thought* 10

penser *to think* 1

perdre *to lose* 6; **se — ** *to get lost* 10

père (*m.*) *father* 3; — **actif** *working dad* 10; — **célibataire** *single father* 10

périmé(e) *spoiled*

permis (*m.*) *permit, license* 11; — **de conduire** *driver's license* 11

personnage (*m.*) *character* 9

personne (*f.*) *person* 1

pessimiste *pessimistic* P

petit déjeuner (*m.*) *breakfast* 5

petit(e) *small, short* 3

petite-fille (*f.*) *granddaughter* 3

petit-fils (*m.*) *grandson* 3

petits pois (*m. pl.*) *peas* 5

peu *little* 1; **un —** *a little* 1
peut-être *perhaps* 1
pharmacie *(f.) pharmacy* 4
philosophie *(f.) philosophy* P
photo(graphie) *(f.) photo(graph), photography* 2; **faire de la —** *to practice photography* 2
photographe *(m./f.) photographer* 9
photographier *to photograph* 9
physique *(f.) physics* P
pièce *(f.) room* 4, *piece, play* 9; **— de monnaie** *(f.) coin* 7; **— de théâtre** *play (theater)*
pied *(m.) foot* 12; **à —** *on foot* 11
pierre *(f.) stone*
piquant(e) *hot* 5
pique-nique *(m.) picnic* 2; **faire un —** *to (have/go on a) picnic* 2
piqûre *(f.) shot* 12; **faire une —** *to give a shot* 12
pire *worse* 7; **le/la/les —(s)** *the worst* 7
piscine (municipale) *(f.) (public) swimming pool* 4
pizza *(f.) pizza* 5
placard *(m.) closet* 4
plage *(f.) beach* 4
plaisir *(m.) pleasure* 2
plan *(m.) map (of a city)* 4
planche à voile *(f.) windsurfing board* 2
plante *(f.) plant* 4
plat *(m.) course (meals)* 5; **— principal** *main course, dish (kind of food)* 5
plâtre *(m.) cast* 12
pleurer *to cry* 10
pleuvoir *to rain* 2
plombier *(m.) plumber* 7; **femme** *(f.)* **— plumber (female)** 7
plongée sous-marine *(f.) scuba diving* 2
pluie *(f.) rain* 2
plupart *(f.) most*; **la — du temps** *most of the time* 10
plus *plus, more* 7; **— (de)… que** *more . . . than* 7; **le/la/les —** *the most* 7
plusieurs *several* 11
poêle *(f.) fry pan, skillet* 5
poésie *(f.) poetry* 2
poète *(m.) poet (male)* 8; **femme** *(f.)* **— poet (female)** 8
poétique *poetic* 9
poids *(m.) weight*
poignet *(m.) wrist* 12

poils *(m. pl.) animal hair, fur* 12
point *(m.) period, point* 4; **— de suture** *stitch, suture* 12; **à — medium (cooking)** 5
pointure *(f.) shoe size* 11; **Quelle est votre —?** *What is your shoe size?* 11
poire *(f.) pear* 6
poisson *(m.) fish* 5; **— d'avril** *April Fools' Day* 8
poissonnerie *(f.) fish and seafood shop* 6
poitrine *(f.) chest* 12
poivre *(m.) pepper* 5
poivron *(m.) pepper (bell)* 5; **— rouge / vert** *red / green pepper* 5
policier *(m.) crime / detective film* 9
poliment *politely* 2
politique *(f.) politics*; **homme** *(m.)* **— politician (male)** 8; **femme** *(f.)* **— politician (female)** 8
polluer *to pollute* F
pollution *(f.) pollution* F
pomme *(f.) apple* 5; **— de terre** *(f.) potato* 5
pompier *(m.) firefighter* 7; **femme** *(f.)* **— firefighter (female)** 7
pop *(f.) pop* 9
portable *(m.) cell phone, laptop computer* P; **ordinateur —** *(m.) laptop computer* P; **téléphone —** *(m.) cell phone* P
porte *(f.) door* P; **— d'embarquement** *departure gate* 11
porter *to wear* 11
portion *(f.) portion* 5; **— idéale** *ideal portion* 5
portrait *(m.) portrait* 9
poser: — des questions (à) *to ask questions* 4
poste *(f.) post office* 11
poste *(m.) position* 7
potin *(m.) piece of gossip* 10; **—s** *(m. pl.) gossip* 10
potiron *(m.) pumpkin* 6
potluck *(m.) potluck party* 8
poubelle *(f.) waste basket* P, *garbage, trash* 4; **sortir la —** *to take out the garbage, trash* 4
poulet *(m.) chicken* 5
pour *for* 2
pourboire *(m.) tip* 6; **laisser un —** *to leave a tip* 6
pourquoi *why* 4
poussière *(f.) dust* 4; **faire la —** *to dust* 4
pouvoir *to be able, can* 7
prairie *(f.) meadow, grassland, prairie* 4

pratique *practical* P
pratiquer *to practice, to do, to play (a sport)* 1; **— le sport** *to play sports* 1
précis(e) *precise, good with details* 7
préférable *preferable* 12
préférer *to prefer* 6
premier / première *first* 8
prendre *to take, to have* 5; **— le déjeuner / le dîner** *to have lunch / dinner* 5; **— des photo(graphie)s** *(f.) to take photo(graph)s* 9; **— son temps** *to take one's time* 5; **— un verre** *to have a drink* 5
prénom *(m.) first name* P
préoccupation *(f.) concern* F; **— sociale** *social concern* F
préparer *to prepare* 12; **se —** *to get ready* 12
près *near* 4
présenter *to introduce* P
préservation *(f.) preservation, protection* F
préserver *to preserve* F
président *(m.) president* 8
prestige *(m.) prestige* 10
prêt *(m.) loan* 7; **— étudiant** *student loan* 7
prêt(e) *ready*
prétentieux / prétentieuse *pretentious* 10
prêter (à) *to lend* 7
primitif / primitive *primitive, amateur (art)* 9
printemps *(m.) spring* 2
prise de sang *(f.) bloodwork* 12; **faire une —** *to take one's blood* 12
prix *(m.) price* 6
problème *(m.) problem* F
produit *(m.) product* 5; **— laitier** *dairy product* 5; **— de soin personnel** *personal care product* 12
professeur *(m.) professor, teacher* P
profession *(f.) profession* 7
professionnel(le) *professional* 7; **école** *(f.)* **professionnelle** *professional / vocational school* 7
programme *(m.) TV program* 9
projecteur *(m.) projector (overhead)* P
promenade *(f.) walk* 2; **faire une — (en ville)** *to take a walk (in town)* 2
promener *to walk*; **se —** *to take a walk, to stroll* 10
propos: à — de *about / speaking of* 10
propre *clean* 4

propreté (f.) *cleanliness*
protéger *to protect* F
protéines (f. pl.) *proteins* 5
protester *to protest* F
psychologie (f.) *psychology* P
psychologue (m./f.) *psychologist* 7
pub(licité) (f.) *commercial* 9
public / publique *public* 4
publier *to publish* 9
puis *next, then* 4
pull(-over) (m.) *(pullover) sweater* 11;
— **à col roulé** *turtle neck sweater* 11
pyjama (m.) *pyjama* 11

Q

quand *when* 4
quarante *forty* P
quart: et — *a quarter past* 1; **moins le**
— *a quarter to* 1
quartier (m.) *neighborhood* 4
quatorze *fourteen* P
quatre *four* P; **—-vingts** *eighty* 1;
—-vingt-dix *ninety* 1
quatre-quatre (4 × 4) (m.) *SUV* 11
quatrième *fourth* 8
que *what* 1, *that, which* 11; **qu'est-ce**
— *what* 1
Québec (m.) *Quebec* 3
québécois(e) *from Quebec* 3
quel(le) *what, which* 1; **Quelle**
heure est-il? *What time is it?* 1;
Quel jour sommes-nous? *What*
day is it? 1
quelqu'un *someone* 7; **— de/d'**
(+ adjective) *someone (+ adjective)* 7
quelque chose *something;* **— de/d'**
(+ adjective) *something*
(+ adjective) 5
quelquefois *sometimes, at times* 1
quelques *some* 11
quelques-uns / quelques-unes *some,*
a few 11
queue (f.) *tail* 12
qui *who(m)* 4, *that, which* 11
quinze *fifteen* P
quitter *to leave (a place / a person)* 6;
se — *to leave each other* 10
quoi (informal) *what* 4
quotidien (m.) *daily publication* 10

R

R'n'B (m.) *blues, R&B* 9
raconter *to tell (about), to narrate* 10
radiographie (f.) *X-ray* 12
radis (m.) *radish* 6
raide *straight* 3

raisin (m.) *grapes* 5
raisonnable *sensible*
randonnée (f.) *hiking, hike* 4; **faire de**
la — *to go hiking, to hike* 4
ranger *to pick up (the house), to put*
things away 4
rap (m.) *rap* 9
rapidement *fast, quickly, hurry!* 2
rappeler *to call back* 10; **se —** *to*
remember 10
rarement *rarely* 1
raser *to shave* 12; **se —** *to shave (one's*
face, legs, etc.) 12
rasoir (m.) *razor* 12
rat (m.) *rat* 12
rater *to miss, to fail* 1; **— un examen** *to*
fail an exam 1
ravi(e) *pleased* P; **— de faire ta**
connaissance. (sing., informal)
Pleased to meet you. P; **— de faire**
votre connaissance. (pl. / sing.,
formal) *Pleased to meet you.* P
rayon (m.) *aisle, counter* 6; **—**
audiovisuel *audio visual equipment*
aisle 6; **— boucherie** *meat counter*
6; **— boulangerie-pâtisserie**
bakery-pastry aisle 6; **—**
charcuterie *deli aisle* 6; **—**
électroménager *household*
appliances aisle 6; **— maison-**
jardin *home and garden aisle* 6; **—**
poissons et fruits de mer *fish and*
seafood aisle 6; **— surgelés** *frozen*
food aisle 6
réalisateur (m.) *director (TV or movie)*
(male) 9
réalisatrice (f.) *director (TV or movie)*
(female) 9
réalité (f.) *reality;* **— virtuelle** *virtual*
reality F
récent(e) *recent* P
réception (f.) *reception* 8
recette (f.) *recipe* 5
recevoir *to receive* 9
réchauffement climatique (m.) *global*
warming F
recherche (f.) *research*
réconcilier: se — *to make up with each*
other 10
recruter *to recruit*
recyclage (m.) *recycling* F
recycler *to recycle* F
rédacteur (m.) *writer (male)*
rédactrice (f.) *writer (female)*
réfléchir (à) *to reflect (upon), to*
consider 4

réforme (f.) *reform* 8
réfrigérateur (m.) *refrigerator, fridge* 4
refuge (m.) *shelter (animal)* 12
regarder *to look;* **se —** *to look at oneself /*
each other 10
regarder *to watch* 1
régime (m.) *diet* 5; **être au —** *to be on*
a diet 5
registre (m.) *registry*
règle (f.) *rule* 4
règlement (m.) *agreements, rules* 4;
— de location *rental agreements,*
renter rules 4
regretter *to regret, to be sorry about* 10
reine (f.) *queen* 8
rejoindre *to join*
relation (f.) *relationship* 8
rembourser *to pay back* 7
remède (m.) *remedy*
rencontrer *to meet;* **se —** *to meet each*
other 10
rendez-vous (m.) *date, appointment* 8
rendre *to give back, to return* 6;
— quelqu'un (heureux) *to make*
someone (happy) 10; **se — compte**
(de / que) *to realize* 10; **— visite à**
to visit (someone) 6
rentrer *to return, to go home* 6
repas (m.) *meal* 5; **— à emporter** *food*
to go 6
répéter *to repeat* 6
répétition (f.) *rehearsal;* **salle** (f.)
de — *rehearsal room*
réplique (f.) *line (of a dialogue)*
répondre (à) *to answer* 6
reposer: se — *to rest* 10
réputé(e) *known*
requin (m.) *shark* 12
réseau (m.) *network* F; **— sans fil**
wireless network F; **— social**
social network 10
réservation (f.) *reservation* 6
réserver *to reserve* 6
résidence (f.) *residence* 4; **—**
universitaire *university / college*
residence hall 4
residentiel(le) *residential* 4
ressentir *to feel (emotion—sadness)* 10
ressource (f.) *resource* F; **— naturelle**
natural resource F
restaurant (m.) *restaurant* 1; **—**
universitaire (m.) *campus cafeteria* 4
rester *to stay* 6
retirer *to withdraw* 7; **— de l'argent** *to*
withdraw money 7
retourner *to return, to go back* 6

retraite (f.) retirement 8; **Bonne —!** Happy retirement! 8; **prendre sa — to retire** (from a job) 8
retraité(e) (m./f.) retired person 10
réussir (à) to succeed (at, in) 4
réussite (f.) success 8; **À la — de (qqn, qqch)!** To the success of (someone, something)! 8
rêve (m.) dream
réveiller to wake up 12; **se — to wake** oneself up 12
revenir to come back 6
rêver (de) to dream (of, about) 8
revoir to see again 9
révolution (f.) revolution 8
revue (f.) magazine 10
rez-de-chaussée (m.) ground floor, first floor (USA) 4
rhume (m.) cold 12
rideau (m.) curtain 4
rien nothing; **De —.** You're welcome. P; **— de nouveau.** Nothing new. P
rivière (f.) river 4
riz (m.) rice 5
robe (f.) dress 11; **— du soir** evening dress 11
rock (m.) rock 9
roi (m.) king 8
rôle (m.) role 9
roman (m.) novel 2
rosbif (m.) roast beef 6
rose pink 3
rôti (m.) roast 5; **— de porc** pork roast 5
rouge à lèvres (m.) lipstick 12
rouge red 3
roumain(e) Romanian 3
Roumanie (f.) Romania 3
rousse (f.) redhead (female) 3
roux (m.) redhead (male) 3
roux / rousse red (hair) 3
rue (f.) street 4
rugby (m.) rugby 2
russe (m.) Russian (language) P
russe Russian 3
Russie (f.) Russia 3

S

sa his/her/its 3
sac (m.) bag, purse P; **— de** bag (of) 5;
saignant(e) medium rare 5
sain(e) healthy 5
saint (m.) saint; **Saint-Sylvestre** (f.) New Year's Eve 8; **Saint-Valentin** (f.) St. Valentine's Day 8
saison (f.) season 2

salade (f.) salad 5
salaire (m.) salary, pay, wages 7
sale dirty 4
salé(e) salty 5
salir to dirty 4
salle (f.) room 4; **— à manger** (f.) dining room 4; **— de bains** bathroom 4; **— de répétition** rehearsal room; **— de séjour** (f.) living room, family room 4
salon (m.) salon, formal living room 4
salut hello, hi P
samedi Saturday 1
sandales (f. pl.) sandals 11
sandwich (m.) sandwich 5; **— au fromage** cheese sandwich 5
sang (m.) blood 12; **donner son —** to give one's blood 12
sans without
sans-abri (sans domicile fixe) (SDF) (m.) homeless person F
santé (f.) health 5; **À votre —!** To your health! 6
satellite (m.) satellite F
saucisse (f.) sausage 5
saucisson (m.) dry salami type sausage 6
saumon (m.) salmon 6
sauvegarder to save F
sauver to save, to protect F
savoir to know F, to know how to, to know by heart 8
savon (m.) soap 12
science (f.) science P; **faculté** (f.) **de lettres et de —s humaines** liberal arts college 7; **faculté** (f.) **de —s et de technologie** science and technology college 7; **—s politiques** political science P
scientifique (m./f.) scientist
scooter (m.) moped 11
sculpteur (m.) sculptor (male) 9
sculptrice (f.) sculptor (female) 9
sculpture (f.) sculpture 9; **faire de la — to sculpt** 9
sèche-cheveux (m.) hairdryer 12
sécher to dry 12; **se — to dry oneself** 12
secrétaire (m./f.) secretary 7
sécurité (f.) security 11; **agent(e)** (m./f.) **de la — security agent** 11
seize sixteen P
sel (m.) salt 5
selon according to 10
semaine (f.) week 1; **— dernière / passée** (f.) last week 5
semestre (m.) semester, term P

Sénégal (m.) Senegal 3
sénégalais(e) Senegalese 3
sens (m.) sens; **— de l'humour** sense of humor 7
sensible sensitive 7
sentiment (m.) feeling 10
sentir to smell 3; **se — to feel** 10
sept sept P
septembre September 2
série (f.) serial sitcom or TV drama 9
sérieusement seriously 2
sérieux / sérieuse serious 1
serpent (m.) snake 12
serveur (m.) waiter 6
serveuse (f.) waitress 6
servi(e) served 6; **C'est servi avec quoi?** What does this come with? 6
service (m.) service 6; **Le — est compris.** The tip is included. 6; **— de chambre** room service 11; **— à fondue** fondue set 6
serviette (f.) napkin 6, towel 12
ses his/her/its 3
seul(e) alone
shampooing (m.) shampoo 12
shopping (m.) shopping 2; **faire du — to shop, to go shopping** 2
short (m.) shorts 11
siège (m.) seat 11; **— côté couloir** aisle seat 11
sieste (f.) nap 2; **faire la — to take a nap** 2
simple simple 10
sirop (m.) syrup 12; **— contre la toux** cough syrup 12
site (m.) site; **— Web** website 10
six six P
ski (m.) skiing 2; **— alpin** downhill skiing 2; **— de fond** cross-country skiing 2; **— nautique** water-ski 2
Smartphone (m.) Smartphone 10
smoking (m.) tuxedo 11
sociable sociable P
société (f.) society F
sociologie (f.) sociology P
sœur (f.) sister 3
soigné(e) well-groomed, fancy 10
soins médicaux (m. pl.) healthcare
soir (m.) evening 1; **du — in the evening** 1; **être du — to be a night person** 7
soirée (f.) party (evening) 8
soixante sixty P; **—-dix** seventy 1; **— quinzième** seventy-fifth 8
soldat (m.) soldier 8; **femme —** (f.) soldier (female) 8

solde: en — *on sale* 11
soleil *(m.) sun* 2; **Il fait (du)** —. *It's sunny.* 2
solitaire *solitary, loner* 7
solution *(f.) solution* F
sombre *somber, dark* 9
son *his/her/its* 3
sondage *(m.) survey, poll*
sortir *to go out* 3, *to take out* 4; — **la poubelle** *to take out the garbage, trash* 4
soudain *suddenly* 8
souhaiter *to wish* 12
souligner *to underline*
soupe *(f.) soup* 5; — **à la tomate** *tomato soup* 5
sourcil *(m.) eyebrow* 12
souris *(f.) mouse* F
sous-sol *(m.) basement* 4
sous-vêtement *(m.) underwear* 11
souvenir: se — **(de)** *to remember* 10
souvent *often* 1
spécialisation *(f.) major* P; **Quelle est ta** —? *What's your major?* P
spectacle *(m.) show, performance* 9
spiritualité *(f.) spirituality* 10
sport *(m.) sport* 2; **faire du** — *to work out, to exercise* 2
sportif / sportive *athletic* 1
stade *(m.) stadium* 4
stage (de formation) *(m.) internship* 7
steak *(m.) steak* 5
stress *(m.) stress* 12
stressé(e) *stressed*
style *(m.) style* 9
stylo *(m.) pen* P
succès *(m.) success* 8; **Au** — **de (qqn, qqch)!** *To the success of (someone, something)!* 8
sucre *(m.) sugar* 5
sucré(e) *sweet* 5
sud *(m.) south* 4
suffisamment *sufficiently*
Suisse *(f.) Switzerland* 3
suisse *Swiss* 3
suivre *to follow*
sujet *(m.) subject* 9
super *marvelous, wonderful, super* 10
supermarché *(m.) supermarket* 6
supplémentaire *extra, additional* 11
sûr(e) *sure* F
surf *(m.) surfing* 2
surgelés *(m. pl.) frozen foods* 6; **rayon** *(m.)* — *frozen food aisle* 6
surpopulation *(f.) overpopulation* F
surpris(e) *surprised* 12

surréaliste *surrealist* 9
surveiller *to keep watch on*
sweat *(m.) sweatshirt* 11; — **à capuche** *hooded sweatshirt* 11
symptôme *(m.) symptom* 12

T

ta *(fam. & sing.) your* 3
table *(f.) table* P; **À** —! *Let's eat! / The food is ready!* 6
tableau *(m.) chalkboard* P, *painting* 9
tâche *(f.) chore, task* 4; —**s ménagères** *household chores* 4
taches de rousseur *(f. pl.) freckles* 3
taille *(f.) size* 11; **Quelle est votre** —? *What size do you wear?* 11
tailleur *(m.) woman's suit* 11
talentueux / talentueuse *talented* 1
talons: à — *high-heeled* 11
tante *(f.) aunt* 3
taper *to type* F
tapis *(m.) rug* 4
tapisserie *(f.) tapestry* 9
tard *later* P, *late* 4; **À plus** — *See you later.* P; **plus** — *later* 4
tarte *(f.) pie* 5
tasse (de/d') *(f.) cup (of)* 5; **demi-**— *(f.) half-cup* 5
taxi *(m.) taxi* 11
te *you* 7
technologie *(f.) technology* P; —**s de l'information et de la communication (TIC)** *information technology* P
tee-shirt *(m.) t-shirt* 11
téléachat *(m.) TV shopping* 9; **émission** *(f.)* **de** — *shopping network show* 9
télécharger *to download* F
téléfilm *(m.) made-for-TV film* 9
téléphone *(m.) phone* P; — **portable** *cell phone* P
téléphoner *to telephone* 1; **se** — *to telephone each other* 10
télévisé(e) *televised* 9; **jeu** *(m.)* **télévisé** *game show* 9; **match** *(m.)* **télévisé** *televised game* 9
téléviseur *(m.) television set* 4; — **LCD** *flat screen tv* 6
télévision *(f.) television* 1
température *(f.) temperature* 2; **prendre la** — *to take one's temperature* 12; **Quelle** — **fait-il?** *What's the temperature?* 2
temps *(m.) weather* 2, *time*; **de** — **en** — *from time to time* 10; **la plupart**

du — *most of the time* 10; **Quel** — **fait-il?** *What's the weather like?* 2
tennis *(m.) tennis* 2; — **de table** *ping-pong, table tennis* 2
tension (artérielle) *(f.) blood pressure* 12; **prendre la** — *to take one's blood pressure* 12
tente *(f.) tent* 11
tenue *(f.) outfit* 11
tes *(fam. & sing.) your* 3
tête *(f.) head* 12
têtu(e) *stubborn* 7
thé *(m.) tea* 5
théâtre *(m.) theater* 9; **pièce** *(f.)* **de** — *play (theater)* 9; **troupe** *(f.)* **de** — *theater company, troop* 9
tigre *(m.) tiger* 12
timbre *(m.) stamp* 11
timide *shy* P
tissu *(m.) fabric*
tofu *(m.) tofu* 5
toi *you (sing., informal)* P
toile *(f.) canvas*
toilettes *(f. pl.) restrooms* 4
tolérance *(f.) tolerance* 8
tomate *(f.) tomato* 5
tomber *to fall* 6; — **amoureux / amoureuse (de)** *to fall in love (with)* 8; — **malade** *to get sick* 12
ton *(fam. & sing.) your* 3
tornade *(f.) tornado* 2
toucher *to touch, to deeply move* 10
toujours *always* 1
tour *(m.) turn*
tourner *to turn* 4; — **à droite / à gauche** *to turn right / left* 4
tous *every* 1, *all, everyone (m. pl.)* 11; — **les jours** *everyday* 1; — **les soirs** *every evening* 1
tousser *to cough* 12
tout *(m. sing.) all* 6, *everyone* 11; **C'est** —! *That's all.* 6; — **le monde** *everyone* 11
toute *(f. sing.) all, everyone* 11
toutes *(f. pl.) all, everyone* 11
toux *(f.) cough* 12; **sirop** *(m.)* **contre la** — *cough syrup* 12
traduire *to translate* 11
train *(m.) train* 11
traitement *(m.) treatment* 12; — **de texte** *word processing program* F
traiter *to treat*
trajet *(m.) trip, commute* 11; **faire le** — **(entre)** *to travel, to commute (between)* 11

trancher *to slice* 5
transporter *to transport* 11
travail *(m.) work* 7
travailler *to work* 1
travailleur / travailleuse
   hard-working 1
traverser *to cross* 4
treize *thirteen* P
tremblement de terre *(m.)*
   earthquake
trente *thirty* P; **— et un** *thirty-one* P;
   —-et-unième *thirty-first* 8
très *very* P
tricoter *to knit* 2
trimestre *(m.) trimester, term* P
triste *sad* 12
trois *three* P
tromper *to cheat on (someone)* 10;
   se — **(de)** *to be mistaken (about)* 10
trop *too, too much* 1
troupe *(f.) company, troop* 9; **— de**
   théâtre *theater company, troop* 9
trouver *to find* 1; **se —** *to be located* 10
tuer *to kill*
Tunisie *(f.) Tunisia* 3
tunisien / tunisienne *Tunisian* 3

U

un *one* P
universitaire *(adj.) college, university*
   4; **résidence** *(f.) —* *university /*
   college residence hall 4; **restaurant**
   (m.) — *campus cafeteria* 4
université *(f.) university* P
urgences *(f. pl.) emergency room* 12;
   aller aux — *to go to the*
   emergency room 12
utile *useful* F
utiliser *to use* 12

V

vacances *(f. pl.) vacation;* **aller en —** *to*
   go on vacation 11
vaisselle *(f.) dishes* 4; **faire la —** *to do*
   the dishes 4
valise *(f.) suitcase* 11; **faire les —s** *to*
   pack 11; **—s** *luggage* 11
vallée *(f.) valley* 4

valloir mieux *to be better* 12
vapeur: à la — *steamed* 5
veau *(m.) veal* 5
végétalien(ne) *vegan* 5
végétarien(ne) *vegetarian* 5
veille *(f.) day before;* **— de Noël**
   Christmas Eve 8
vélo *(m.) bike, bicycle* 2
vendeur *(m.) salesman* 7
vendeuse *(f.) saleswoman* 7
vendre *to sell* 6
vendredi *Friday* 1
venir *to come* 3; **— à l'esprit** *to come*
   to mind; **— de** *to have just done*
   something 3
vent *(m.) wind* 2; **Il fait du —.**
   It's windy. 2
ventre *(m.) abdomen, belly* 12
verglas *(m.) (black) ice* 2
vérité *(f.) truth*
verre (de/d') *(m.) glass (of)* 5; **—**
   à vin *wine glass* 6
vers *around* 1, *towards* 4
vert(e) *green* 3
vestiaire *(m.) locker, locker room* 12
vêtement *(m.) article of clothing;*
   —s *clothing* 11
vétérinaire *(m.) vet* 12
veuf / veuve *widower / widow* 3
viande *(f.) meat* 5
vie *(f.) life* 2
vieil *(m. before a vowel sound) old* 3
vieille *(f.) old* 3
vieillesse *(f.) old age, the elderly* 8
Viêt Nam *(m.) Vietnam* 3
vietnamien / vietnamienne
   Vietnamese 3
vieux / vieil / vieille *old* 3
vif / vive *bright, lively, colorful* 9
ville *(f.) city, town* 4
vin *(m.) wine* 5; **— d'honneur** *punch,*
   cocktail reception 8
vinaigre *(m.) vinegar* 5
vingt *twenty* P; **— et un** *twenty-one* P;
   —-et-unième *twenty-first* 8;
   —-deux *twenty-two* P
violet(te) *violet, purple* 3
virgule *(f.) comma* 4

visage *(m.) face* 12
visiter *to visit (something)* 6
vite *fast, quickly, hurry!* 2
vivre *to live* 9
vœu *(m.) wish* 8; **Meilleurs —x!**
   Best wishes! 8
voici *here is* P
voilà *there is* P
voir *to see* 9; **se —** *to see oneself /*
   each other 10
voisin(e) *(m./f.) neighbor* 4
voiture *(f.) car* 11
voix *(f.) voice;* **à haute —** *aloud*
vol *(m.) flight* 11; **— direct** *direct*
   flight 11
volaille *(f.) poultry* 5
volley-ball *(m.) volleyball* 2
vos *(formal sing. or pl.) your* 3
votre *(formal sing. or pl.) your* 3
vouloir *to want* 7
vous *you (pl./sing., formal)* P
voyage *(m.) trip* 2; **faire un —** *to take*
   a trip 2; **— de noces**
   honeymoon 8
voyager *to travel* 1
voyageur *(m.) traveler* 11
voyageuse *(f.) traveler* 11
voyant(e) *fortune teller*
vrai(e) *true* F
vraiment *really, truly* 2

W

W.-C. *(m. pl.) toilet (room), restrooms,*
   water closet 4
webcam *(f.) webcam* F
week-end *(m.) weekend* 1
western *(m.) western* 9

Y

y *there, of / about it* 7
yaourt *(m.) yogurt* 5
yeux *(m. pl.) eyes* 3; **— bleus** *blue eyes*
   3; **— yeux marron** *brown eyes* 3;
   — yeux verts *green eyes* 3
yoga *(m.) yoga* 2

Z

zéro *zero* P

to — cold **avoir froid** 5; to — early **être en avance** 1; to — familiar with **connaître** 8; to — hot **avoir chaud** 5; to — hungry **avoir faim** 5; to — late **être en retard** 1; to — lucky **avoir de la chance** 1; to — nauseated **avoir mal au cœur** 12; to — necessary **falloir** 12; to — online (with) **être en ligne (avec)** F; to — on time **être à l'heure** 1; to — right **avoir raison** 1; to — in shape **être en forme** 12; to — a size . . . **faire du...** 11; to — sleepy **avoir sommeil** 1; to — thirsty **avoir soif** 5; to — wrong **avoir tort** 1; to — . . . years old **avoir... ans** 1

beach **plage** *(f.)* 4

bean (green) **haricot vert** *(m.)* 5

bear **ours** *(m.)* 12

beard **barbe** *(f.)* 3

beast **bête** *(f.)*

beautiful **beau / bel / belle** 2

because **parce que** 4

become **devenir** 3

bed and breakfast **gîte du passant** *(m.)* 11

bed **lit** *(m.)* 4; double / single — **lit double / simple** 11

bedroom **chambre** *(f.)* 4

beef **bœuf** *(m.)* 6; ground — **bœuf haché** 6

beer **bière** *(f.)* 5

before **avant** 1

beginning **début** *(m.)* 9

behind **derrière** 4

Belgian **belge** 3

Belgium **Belgique** *(f.)* 3

believe **croire** F

belly **ventre** *(m.)* 12

belong (to) **appartenir (à)**

below **au-dessous (de)** 6

belt **ceinture** *(f.)*; seat— **ceinture de sécurité**

best **meilleur(e)** P

better **meilleur(e)** 7; **mieux** 7

between **entre** 1

bicycle **vélo** *(m.)* 2

big **grand(e)** 3

bike *(v.)* **faire du vélo** 2

bike **vélo** *(m.)* 2; to go — riding **faire du vélo** 2

bill (money) **billet** *(m.)* 7

billion **milliard** *(m.)* 4

binder **classeur** *(m.)* P

biodegradable **biodégradable** F; non— **non biodégradable** F

biology **biologie** *(f.)* P

bird **oiseau** *(m.)* 12

birth **naissance** *(f.)* 8

birthday **anniversaire** *(m.)* 2; Happy —! **Bon / Joyeux anniversaire!** 8

bitter **amer / amère** 5

bizarre **bizarre** F

black **noir(e)** 3

blender **mixeur** *(m.)* 6

blog **blog** *(m.)* 10

blond *(adj.)* **blond(e)** 3

blond *(n.)* **blond(e)** 3

blood pressure **tension** *(f.)* **(artérielle)** 12; to take one's — **prendre la tension (artérielle)** 12

blood **sang** *(m.)* 12; to take one's — **faire une prise de sang** 12

blouse **chemisier** *(m.)* 11

blue **bleu(e)** 3

blueberry **bleuet** *(m.)* 5

blues **blues** *(m.)* 9

board *(v.)* **embarquer** 11; to — the plane **embarquer dans l'avion** 11

board **tableau** *(m.)* P; — eraser **brosse** *(f.)* **(à tableau)** P

boat **bateau** *(m.)* 4; to go (sail)—ing **faire du bateau (à voile)** 4; sail— **bateau à voile** 4

body **corps** *(m.)* 12

boldface **en gras**

bone **os** *(m.)*

book **livre** *(m.)* P

bookshelf **étagère** *(f.)* 4

bookstore **librairie** *(f.)* 4

boots **bottes** *(f. pl.)* 11

bore **ennuyer**; to be —d **s'ennuyer** 10

boring **ennuyeux / ennuyeuse** 1

borrow **emprunter** 7

boss **patron(ne)** 7

both **les deux**

bother *(v.)* **déranger** 10

bottle (of) **bouteille (de/d')** *(f.)* 5

boutique **boutique** *(f.)* 4

bowl **bol** *(m.)* 6

bowling **bowling** *(m.)* 2

box (of) **boîte (de/d')** *(f.)* 5

boy **garçon** *(m.)* P

bracelet **bracelet** *(m.)* 11

brain **cerveau** *(m.)*

brand **marque** *(f.)*

Brazil **Brésil** *(m.)* 3

Brazilian **brésilien / brésilienne** 3

bread **pain** *(m.)* 5; — shop **boulangerie** *(f.)* 6; country-style — **pain de campagne** 6; egg — **brioche** *(f.)* 6;

break *(v.)* **casser**; to — one's (arm) **se casser (le bras)** 12

breakfast **petit déjeuner** *(m.)* 5

briefcase **mallette** *(f.)* 11

bright **vif / vive** 9

brilliant **brillant(e)** P

bring **amener** (someone) 6; **apporter** (something) 6

British **anglais(e)** 3

broadcast **émission** *(f.)* 9

broccoli **brocoli** *(m.)* 5

brother **frère** *(m.)* 3; —-in-law **beau-frère** *(m.)*

brown **brun(e), marron** 3

brush *(v.)* **brosser** 12; to — one's hair / teeth **se brosser les cheveux / les dents** 12

brush **brosse** *(f.)* 12; hair— **brosse à cheveux** 12; tooth— **brosse à dents** 12

building **bâtiment** *(m.)* 4

burial **enterrement** *(m.)* 8

bus **autobus** *(m.)*, **bus** *(m.)* 11; — stop **arrêt** *(m.)* **d'autobus** 11

business **commerce (international)** *(m.)* P, **affaires** *(f. pl.)* 7; — administration **gestion** *(f.)* P; —man **homme** *(m.)* **d'affaires** 7; —woman **femme** *(f.)* **d'affaires** 7

but **mais** 1

butcher's shop **boucherie** *(f.)* 6

butter **beurre** *(m.)* 5

buy *(v.)* **acheter** 6

C

café **café** *(m.)* 1

café-restaurant **bistro** *(m.)* 4

cake **gâteau** *(m.)* 5

calculator **calculatrice** *(f.)* P

call *(v.)* **appeler** 10; to be —d **s'appeler** 10; to — back **rappeler** 10

camera **appareil** *(m.)* **photo**; digital — **appareil photo numérique (APN)** 10

camp *(v.)* **faire du camping** 2

camping **camping** *(m.)* 2; to go — **faire du camping** 2

campus **campus** *(m.)* 4

can (canned goods) **boîte** *(f.)* **(de conserves)** 6

can **pouvoir** 7

Canada **Canada** *(m.)* 3

Canadian **canadien / canadienne** 3

canceled **annulé(e)**

candy **bonbon** *(m.)* 5

cantelope **melon** *(m.)* 6

canvas **toile** *(f.)*
car **voiture** *(f.)* 11
carbohydrates **glucides** *(m. pl.)* 5
card **carte** *(f.)* 2; credit — **carte de crédit** 7; debit — **carte bancaire** 7; greeting — **carte de vœux** 8; to play —s **jouer aux cartes** 2; post— **carte postale** 11
cardigan (sweater) **gilet** *(m.)* 11
career **carrière** *(f.)* 7
carpooling **covoiturage** *(m.)* 11
carrot **carotte** *(f.)* 5
cartoon **dessin** *(m.)* **animé** 9, **film** *(m.)* **d'animation** 9
cash **liquide** *(m.)* 7; to pay — **payer en liquide** 7
cast **plâtre** *(m.)* 12
cat **chat** *(m.)* 3
CD **CD** *(m.)* P
celebrate **célébrer** 6, **fêter** 8
celebration **fête** *(f.)* 2
cell phone **(téléphone) portable** *(m.)* P
cent **centime** *(m.)* 6
center **centre** *(m.)* 4; recreation — **centre sportif** 4; shopping — **centre commercial** 4
cereal **céréales** *(f. pl.)* 5
ceremony **cérémonie** *(f.)* 8; graduation — **cérémonie de remise des diplômes** 8
certain **certain(e)** F; — of **certain(e) de** 11
chair **chaise** *(f.)* P
chalk (piece of) **craie** *(f.)* P
chalkboard **tableau** *(m.)* P
character **personnage** *(m.)* 9
charming **charmant(e)** P
cheat on (someone) **tromper (quelqu'un)** 10
check *(v.)* **cocher; enregistrer** 11; to — in luggage **enregistrer les valises** *(f. pl.)* 11
check **addition** *(f.)* 6; **chèque** *(m.)* 7; —ing account **compte-chèques** *(m.)* 7; to pay by — **payer par chèque** 7
cheek **joue** *(f.)*
cheese **fromage** *(m.)* 5
chemistry **chimie** *(f.)* P
cherry **cerise** *(f.)* 6
chess **échecs** *(m. pl.)* 2; to play — **jouer aux échecs** 2
chest **poitrine** *(f.)* 12; — of drawers **commode** *(f.)* 4
chicken **poulet** *(m.)* 5
child **enfant** *(m./f.)* 3

childhood **enfance** *(f.)* 8
China **Chine** *(f.)* 3
Chinese (language) **chinois** *(m.)* P
Chinese **chinois(e)** 3
chips **chips** *(f. pl.)* 5
choir **chœur** *(m.)* 9
choir **chorale** *(f.)* 9
choose **choisir** 4
chop **côtelette** *(f.)* 6; lamb / pork — **côtelette d'agneau / de porc** 6
chore **tâche** *(f.)* 4; household —s **tâches ménagères** 4
Christmas **Noël** *(m.)* 8
church **église** *(f.)* 4
city **ville** *(f.)* 4
class **classe** *(f.)*, **cours** *(m.)* P; business — **classe affaires** 11; economy — **classe économique** 11; first-— **première classe** 11
classify **classer**
clean **propre** 4
cleanliness **propreté** *(f.)*
clear *(v.)* **débarrasser** 6; to — the table **débarrasser la table** 6
clear **clair(e)** F
client **client(e)** 11
climb **monter** 6
clock **horloge** *(f.)* P
cloning **clonage** *(m.)* F
close *(v.)* **éteindre, fermer** F
closet **placard** *(m.)* 4
clothing **vêtements** *(m. pl.)* 11; (piece of) **vêtement** *(m.)* 11
cloud **nuage** *(m.)* 2
cloudy **couvert(e)** 2
clumsy **maladroit(e)** 10
Coca-Cola **Coca** *(m.)* 5
coffee **café** *(m.)* 5
cold **froid(e)** 2; to be — **avoir froid** 5
cold **rhume** *(m.)* 12
college **faculté** *(f.)* 7; liberal arts — **faculté de lettres et de sciences humaines** 7; science and technology — **faculté de sciences et de technologie** 7
colonization **colonisation** *(f.)* 8
colony **colonie** *(f.)* 8
colorful **vif / vive** 9
comb **peigne** *(m.)* 12
come **venir** 3; to — back **revenir** 6; to — to mind **venir à l'esprit**
comedy **comédie** *(f.)* 9
comfortable **confortable** 11
comma **virgule** *(f.)* 4
commercial **pub(licité)** *(f.)* 9
commute *(v.)* (between) **faire le trajet (entre)** 11

commute **trajet** *(m.)* 11
compact disc **CD** *(m.)* P
company **entreprise** *(f.)* 7; theater — **troupe** *(f.)* **de théâtre** 9
competitive **acharné(e)** 7
composer **compositeur** *(m.)* / **femme compositeur** *(f.)* / **compositrice** *(f.)* 9
compost *(v.)* **faire du compost** F
computer **ordinateur** *(m.)* P; — screen **écran** *(m.)* P; — science **informatique** *(f.)* P; — specialist **informaticien(ne)** 7
concern **préoccupation** *(f.)* F; social — **préoccupation sociale** F
concert **concert** *(m.)* 9
condolences **condoléances** *(f. pl.)* 8; My —. **Mes condoléances.** 8
confidence: to have — **être bien dans sa peau** 10
congratulations **félicitations** *(f. pl.)* 8
connection **connexion** *(f.)* F; high speed Internet — **connection Internet à haut débit** F
conservatory **conservatoire** *(m.)* 7
conserve *(v.)* **conserver** F
consider **réfléchir (à)** 4
console **console** *(f.)* 4; videogame — **console de jeux vidéo** 4
constantly **constamment** 2
construct **construire** 11
content **content(e)** P
continent **continent** *(m.)* 3
continue **continuer** 4
cook *(v.)* **cuisiner** 1, **faire la cuisine** 2
cook **cuisinier / cuisinière** 7
cooked **cuit(e)** 5
cookie **biscuit** *(m.)* 5
cooking **cuisine** *(f.)* 2
cool (weather) **frais / fraîche** 2
corn **maïs** *(m.)* 6
corner **coin** *(m.)*; on the — (of) **au coin (de)** 4
correct *(v.)* **corriger**
cost *(v.)* **coûter** 6
couch **canapé** *(m.)* 4
cough *(v.)* **tousser** 12
cough **toux** *(f.)* 12; — syrup **sirop** *(m.)* **contre la toux** 12
counter **rayon** *(m.)* 6; meat — **rayon boucherie** 6
country **pays** *(m.)* 3
country(side) **campagne** *(f.)* 4
couple **couple** *(m.)* 8
courageous **courageux / courageuse** 1
course **cours** *(m.)* P; **plat** *(m.)* (meals) 5; main — **plat principal** 5

course: of — **bien sûr** 1
cousin **cousin(e)** 3
crass **grossier / grossière** 10
cream **crème** (*f.*) 5; — puff **chou** (*m.*)
  à la crème 6; shaving — **crème à**
  raser 12
creative **créatif / créative** 7
creature **créature** (*f.*) 12
crime film **policier** (*m.*) 9
criteria **critère** (*m.*)
critic **critique** (*f./m.*) 9
critique **critique** (*f.*) 9
croissant **croissant** (*m.*) 5
cross (*v.*) **traverser** 4; to — out **barrer**
crude **grossier / grossière** 10
cruise **croisière** (*f.*) 11
crutches **béquilles** (*f. pl.*) 12
cry (*v.*) **pleurer** 10
cubist **cubiste** 9
cucumber **concombre** (*m.*) 6
cup (of) **tasse (de/d')** (*f.*) 5
curly **bouclé(e), frisé(e)** 3
curtain **rideau** (*m.*) 4
customs **douane** (*f.*) 11; to go
  through — **passer à la douane** 11
cut (*v.*) **couper** 5; to — (oneself) **se**
  couper 12
cutlery **couverts** (*m. pl.*) 6
cutthroat **acharné(e)** 7

D

daily publication **quotidien** (*m.*) 10
dance (*v.*) **danser** 1
dance **danse** (*f.*) 2; classical — **danse**
  classique 2; modern — **danse**
  moderne 2
dancer **danseur / danseuse** 9
dancing **danse** (*f.*) 2
daring **audacieux / audacieuse**
dark **sombre** 9
date **date** (*f.*) 2, **rendez-vous** (*m.*) 8
daughter **fille** (*f.*) 3; —-in-law
  belle-fille (*f.*) 3
day **jour** (*m.*) 8, **journée** (*f.*); Father's —
  fête (*f.*) **des Pères** 8; Labor —
  fête (*f.*) **du Travail** 8; Mother's
  — **fête** (*f.*) **des Mères** 8
daycare center **garderie** (*f.*)
death **décès** (*m.*) 8
deceased **décédé(e)** 3
December **décembre** 2
declare **déclarer** 11; to — your
  purchases **déclarer vos achats**
  (*m. pl.*) 11
decolonization **décolonisation** (*f.*) 8
deforestation F **déforestation** (*f.*)

delete **effacer** F
deli (shop) **charcuterie** (*f.*) 6
deliver **livrer** 11
demand (*v.*) **exiger** 12
demanding **exigeant(e)** 7
dentist **dentiste** (*m./f.*) 7
deposit (*v.*) **déposer (de l'argent)** 7
depressed **déprimé(e)**
describe **décrire**
deserve **mériter**
desire (*v.*) **désirer** 6
desk **bureau** (*m.*) P
dessert **dessert** (*m.*) 5
destroy **détruire** 11
die **mourir** 6
diet **régime** (*m.*) 5
difficult **difficile** P
dinner **dîner** (*m.*) 5; to have — **dîner** 1,
  prendre le dîner 5
diploma **diplôme** (*m.*) 7
director (TV or movie) **réalisateur /**
  réalisatrice 9
dirty (*v.*) **salir** 4
dirty **sale** 4
discovery **découverte** (*f.*) F
dishes **vaisselle** (*f.*) 4; to do the — **faire**
  la vaiselle 4
disloyal **déloyal(e)** 7, **infidèle** 10
disloyalty **infidélité** (*f.*) 10
divorce **divorce** (*m.*) 8
divorced **divorcé(e)** 3
do **faire** 2
doctor **médecin / femme médecin** 7
doctorate **doctorat** (*m.*) 7
documentary **documentaire** (*m.*) 9
dog **chien** (*m.*) 3
door **porte** (*f.*)
doubt (*v.*) **douter** F
download (*v.*) **télécharger** F
downtown **centre-ville** (*m.*) 4
drama **drame** (*m.*) 9, **série** (*f.*)
  (TV) 9; psychological — **drame**
  psychologique 9
draw (*v.*) **dessiner** 2
drawing **dessin** (*m.*) 9
dream (of, about) (*v.*) **rêver (de)** 8
dream **rêve** (*m.*)
dreary (weather) **gris(e)** 2
dress (*v.*) **habiller, s'habiller** 12
dress **robe** (*f.*) 11; evening — **robe du**
  soir 11
dressed **habillé(e)** 10; poorly-— **mal**
  habillé(e) 10; well-— **bien**
  habillé(e) 10
drink (*v.*) **boire** 5
drive (*v.*) **conduire** 11

dry (*v.*) **sécher** 12; to — oneself **se**
  sécher 12
duck **canard** (*m.*) 5
during **pendant** 1
dust (*v.*) **faire la poussière** 4
dust **poussière** (*f.*) 4
dwarf **nain(e)**
dynamic **dynamique** P

E

each (one) (of) **chaque** 8, **chacun /**
  chacune (de) 11
eagle **aigle** (*m.*) 12
ear **oreille** (*f.*) 12
earn **gagner** 7; to — a living **gagner**
  sa vie 7; to — money **gagner de**
  l'argent 7
earthquake **tremblement de**
  terre (*m.*)
east **est** (*m.*) 4
Easter **Pâques** (*m. pl.*) 8
easy **facile** P
eat (*v.*) **manger** 1
eccentric **excentrique** 7
eclair **éclair** (*m.*) 6
ecological **écologique** F
ecologist **écolo(giste)** (*m./f.*) 10
economist **économiste** (*m./f.*)
economy **économie** (*f.*) P
egg **œuf** (*m.*) 5
eggplant **aubergine** (*f.*) 6
eight **huit** P
eighteen **dix-huit** P
eighty **quatre-vingts** 1
elbow **coude** (*m.*) 12
elderly: the — **troisième âge** (*m.*),
  vieillesse (*f.*) 8
eleven **onze** P
email **(e)mail** (*m.*), **courriel** (*m.*) 2
emergency room **urgences** (*f. pl.*) 12
emperor **empereur** (*m.*) 8
empire **empire** (*m.*) 8
employee **employé(e)** 7
empress **impératrice** (*f.*) 8
end **bout** (*m.*) 4, **fin** (*f.*) 9; until the
  — **jusqu'au bout** 4
ending **fin** (*f.*) 9
energetic **énergique** P
energy **énergie** (*f.*) F; renewable —
  énergie renouvelable F; solar
  — **énergie solaire** F
engaged **fiancé(e)**; to get — to (each
  other) **se fiancer** 10
engagement **fiançailles** (*f. pl.*) 8
engineer **ingénieur / femme**
  ingénieur 7

engineering **génie** (m.) P; civil —
génie civil P; electrical — **génie
électrique** P; mechanical
— **mécanique** P
England **Angleterre** (f.) 3
English (language) **anglais** (m.) P
enjoy: Enjoy the meal! **Bon appétit!** 6
enough **assez** 1
enter **entrer** 6
envelope **enveloppe** (f.) 11
environment **environnement** (m.) 10
environmentalist **écolo(giste)** (m./f.) 10
equipment **équipement** (m.) 4;
audiovisual — **équipement
audiovisuel** 4
equipped **équipé(e)** 4; poorly — **mal
équipé(e)** 4; well — **bien équipé(e)** 4
erase **effacer** F
eraser **gomme** (f.) P
errand **course** (f.) 2; to run some —s
faire des courses 2
essential **essentiel(le)** 12
Europe **Europe** (f.) 3; Eastern — **Europe
de l'Est** 3; Western — **Europe de
l'Ouest** 3
eve **veille** (f.) 8; Christmas — **veille de
Noël** 8
evening **soir** (m.) 1
event **événement** (m.); current —s
actualité (f.)
every **tous, toutes** 1, **chaque** 8
everyone **tout, toute, tous, toutes** 11,
tout le monde 11
evidently **évidemment** 2
exam **examen** (m.); medical
— **examen médical** 12;
baccalauréat (m.)
(end-of-high-school) 7
executive **cadre** (m./f.) 7
exercise (v.) **faire de la gym** 2
exhibition **exposition** (f.) 9
expensive **cher / chère** 11
explorer **explorateur / exploratrice** 8
express (v.) **exprimer** 10
extra **supplémentaire** 11
extrovert **extraverti(e)** 7
extroverted **extraverti(e)** 7
eye **œil** (m.) (pl. **yeux**) 3
eyebrow **sourcil** (m.) 12

F

fabric **tissu** (m.)
face **figure** (f.), **visage** (m.) 12
fact **fait** (m.) 10
fail **rater** 1
fair **juste** F

fairy **fée** (f.) 9; — tale **conte** (m.) **de fées** 9
faithful **loyal(e)** 7
fall (v.) **tomber** 6; to — asleep **s'endormir**
12; to — in love (with) **tomber
amoureux / amoureuse (de)** 8
fall **automne** (m.) 2
family **famille** (f.) 3; extended
— **famille élargie** 3; immediate
— **famille proche** 3
famous **célèbre** P
fan **fana** (m./f.) 10
fancy **soigné(e)** 10
far (from) **loin (de)** 4
farm **ferme** (f.) 4
fascinating **fascinant(e)** P
fashion **mode** (f.)
fashionable **à la mode** 11
fast food **fast-food** (m.) 5
fast **rapidement, vite** 2
fasten **attacher** 11; to — the seatbelt
attacher la ceinture de sécurité 11
fat **gros / grosse** 3
father **père** (m.) 3; —-in-law
beau-père (m.); single — **père
célibataire** 10
fats **matières grasses** (f. pl.) 5
February **février** 2
fee 11 **frais** (m.)
feel (emotion—sadness) **ressentir, se
sentir** 10; to — like **avoir envie de** 1
feeling **sentiment** (m.) 10
fever **fièvre** (f.) 12
fewer **moins** 7
fibers **fibres** (f. pl.) 5
field **champ** (m.) 4
fifteen **quinze** P
fifth **cinquième** 8
fifty **cinquante** P
file **fichier** (m.) F
fill (in) (v.) **compléter**
film **film** (m.), **téléfilm** (m.) (made-
for-TV) 9; action — **film d'action**
9; (animated) cartoon / animated
— **film d'animation** 9; — enthusiast
cinéphile (m./f.); horror — **film
d'horreur** 9; romance — **film
romantique** 9; sci-fi — **film de
science-fiction** 9; suspense — **film à
suspense** 9
finally **enfin** 4
find (v.) **trouver** 1
fine **bien** P
finger **doigt** (m.) 6
finish (v.) **finir** 4
fire **feu** (f.); —works **feux** (m. pl.)
d'artifices

firefighter **pompier / femme
pompier** 7
first (adv.) **d'abord** 4
first name **prénom** (m.) P
first **premier / première** 8
fish **poisson** (m.) 5; — and seafood
shop **poissonnerie** (f.) 6
fishing **pêche** (f.) 4
five **cinq** P
flag **drapeau** (m.)
flexible **flexible** 7
flight **vol** (m.) 11; connecting
— **correspondance** (f.) 11
floor **étage** (m.) 4; second — (USA)
premier étage 4
flour **farine** (f.) 5
flower **fleur** (f.) 4
flu **grippe** (f.) 12
fluently **couramment** 2
fog **brouillard** (m.) 2
folder **classeur** (m.) P
follow **suivre**
food **aliment** (m.) 5, **nourriture** (f.) 5;
fried — **aliment frit** 5; processed
— **aliment industriel** 5
foot **pied** (m.) 12; on — **à pied** 11
football **football** (m.) **américain** 2
for **pour** 2, **depuis** 2, **pendant** 6;
— how long **depuis combien de
temps** 2
forbid **interdire** F
forecast (v.) **annoncer** 2
forecast (weather) **météo** (f.) 2
forest **forêt** (f.) 4
fork **fourchette** (f.) 6
former **ancien / ancienne** 11
fortune teller **voyant(e)**
forty **quarante** P
found (v.) **fonder** 8
four **quatre** P
fourteen **quatorze** P
fourth **quatrième** 8
France **France** (f.) 3
freckles **taches** (f. pl.) **de rousseur** 3
freedom **liberté** (f.) 8
French (language) **français** (m.) P
French **français(e)** 3
frequency **fréquence** (f.)
fresh **frais / fraîche** 5
Friday **vendredi** 1
fridge **frigo** (m.), **réfrigérateur** (m.) 4
fried **frit(e)** 5
friend **ami(e)** P, **copain / copine** P;
best — **meilleur(e) ami(e)** P;
boy— / girl— **petit(e) ami(e)** P
friendship **amitié** (f.) 10

fries **frites** (*f. pl.*) 5
frog **grenouille** (*f.*) 12
from **de** P, **du** 3; — . . . until . . .
    de... à... 1
front: in — (of) **devant** 4
frozen foods **surgelés** (*m. pl.*) 6
fruit **fruit** (*m.*) 5
fry pan **poêle** (*f.*) 5
funeral **enterrement** (*m.*) 8
funny **amusant(e)** P
funny **drôle** 7
fur (animal hair) **poils** (*m. pl.*) 12
furious **furieux / furieuse** 12
furniture (piece of) **meuble** (*m.*) 4
future (time period) **avenir** (*m.*)

G

gain (*v.*) (weight) **grossir** 4
gallery **galerie** (*f.*) 9; art — **galerie
    d'art** 9
game **jeu** (*m.*) 2, **match** (*m.*) 2; board
    —s **jeux** (*m. pl.*) **de société** 2;
    — show **jeu** (*m.*) **télévisé** 9; wii
    — box **console** (*f.*) **wii** 6
garage **garage** (*m.*) 4
garbage **poubelle** (*f.*) 4
garden (*v.*) **faire du jardinage** 2
garden **jardin** (*m.*) 4
gardening **jardinage** (*m.*) 2
garlic **ail** (*m.*) 5
gate (departure) **porte** (*f.*)
    d'embarquement 11
general (*n.*) **général** (*m.*) 8
genre **genre** (*m.*) 9
German (*adj.*) **allemand(e)** 3
German (language) **allemand** (*m.*) P
Germany **Allemagne** (*f.*) 3
get: to — along (well / badly with
    someone) **s'entendre (bien / mal
    avec quelqu'un)** 10; to — angry **se
    fâcher** 10; to — off **descendre** 6,
    débarquer 11; to — on **monter** 6;
    to — ready **se préparer** 12;
    to — up **se lever** 12
gift **cadeau** (*m.*) 8
gifted **doué(e)** P
girl **fille** (*f.*) P
give **donner** 7; to — back **rendre**
glass (of) **verre** (*m.*) **(de/d')** 5; wine —
    verre à vin 6
gloves **gants** (*m. pl.*) 11
go (*v.*) **aller** 2, **continuer** 4; to — away
    s'en aller 10; to — to bed **se
    coucher** 12; to — down **descendre**
    6; to — fishing **aller à la pêche**
    4; to — hunting **aller à la chasse**

4; to — to the spa **aller au spa** 2;
to — through security **passer au
    contrôle** (*m.*) **de sécurité** 11;
to — on vacation **aller en vacances**
11; to — out **sortir** 3; to — up
    monter 6
goal **but** (*m.*)
goat **chèvre** (*f.*) 12
god **dieu** (*m.*)
golf **golf** (*m.*) 2
good **bon / bonne** P, **bien** 1; *Good day.*
    Bonne journée. P; *Good evening.*
    Bonsoir. P; *Good night.* **Bonne
    nuit.** P
goodbye **au revoir** P
gossip **potin(s)** (*m.*) 10
gossipy **bavard(e)** 10
graceful **gracieux / gracieuse** 10
gracious **gracieux / gracieuse** 10
gram (of) **gramme (de/d')** (*m.*) 5
granddaughter **petite-fille** (*f.*) 3
grandfather **grand-père** (*m.*) 3
grandmother **grand-mère** (*f.*) 3
grandparents **grands-parents** (*m. pl.*) 3
grandson **petit-fils** (*m.*) 3
grapefruit **pamplemousse** (*m.*) 6
grapes **raisin** (*m.*) 5
grassland **prairie** (*f.*) 4
gray **gris(e)** 2
great **formidable, génial(e)** 10
greatness **grandeur** (*f.*) 8
green **vert(e)** 3
greenhouse effect **effet de serre** (*m.*) F
grid **grille** (*f.*)
grilled **grillé(e)** 5
grocery store (small) **épicerie** (*f.*) 6
gross out **écœurer** 10
ground floor **rez-de-chaussée** (*m.*)
grow up **grandir** 4
guess (*v.*) **deviner**
guest **invité(e)** 8, **client(e)** 11

H

hair **cheveux** (*m. pl.*) 3; black —
    cheveux noirs 3; blond —
    cheveux blonds 3; brown
    — **cheveux bruns** 3; curly
    — **cheveux bouclés / frisés** 3;
    long straight — **cheveux longs et
    raides** 3; red — **cheveux roux** 3;
    short — **cheveux courts** 3; wavy
    — **cheveux ondulés** 3
hairdresser **coiffeur / coiffeuse** 7
hairdryer **sèche-cheveux** (*m.*) 12
half **moitié** (*f.*); —-cup **demi-tasse** (*f.*)
    5; — past **et demi(e)** 1

hallway **couloir** (*m.*) 4
ham **jambon** (*m.*) 5
hamburger **hamburger** (*m.*) 5
hamster **hamster** (*m.*) 12
hand **main** (*f.*) 12
handsome **beau / bel / belle** 2
hang-glide **faire du deltaplane** 4
hang-gliding **deltaplane** (*m.*) 4
Hanukah **Hanoukka** (*f.*) 8
happiness **bonheur** (*m.*) 8; To the
    — of (someone)! **Au bonheur
    de (qqn)!** 8
happy **content(e)** P, **heureux /
    heureuse** 1
hard drive **disque dur** (*m.*) F
hard-working **travailleur /
    travailleuse** 1
hat **chapeau** (*m.*) 11
hate (*v.*) **détester** 1; to — oneself / each
    other **se détester** 10
have **avoir** 1; to — a . . . class **avoir un
    cours de...** 1; to — a good time
    s'amuser 10; to — a headache
    avoir mal à la tête 12; to — a
    stomach ache **avoir mal au ventre**
    12; to — to **devoir** 7
head **tête** (*f.*) 12
health **santé** (*f.*) 5; — insurance
    assurance-maladie (*f.*) 12
healthcare **soins** (*m. pl.*) **médicaux**
healthy **sain(e)** 5
hear (*v.*) **entendre** 6
heart **cœur** (*m.*) 12; artificial — **cœur
    artificiel** F
heat (*v.*) **faire chauffer** 5
heavy **lourd(e)** 2
hello **bonjour, salut** P
help (*v.*) **aider** 8
her **son / sa / ses** 3; **lui** 7
here (is) **voici** P
hero **héros** (*m.*) 8
heroine **héroïne** (*f.*) 8
hi **salut** P
high blood pressure **hypertension** (*f.*) 12
high school **lycée** (*m.*) 4
high-heeled **à talons** 11
hike (*v.*) **faire de la randonnée** 4
hike **randonnée** (*f.*) 4
hiking **randonnée** (*f.*) 4
hill **colline** (*f.*) 4
him **lui** 7
hip-hop **hip-hop** (*m.*) 9
hippy **baba cool** (*m./f.*), **hippy** (*m./f.*)
    (*pl.* **hippies**) 10
his **son / sa / ses** 3
history **histoire** (*f.*) P

hobby **passe-temps** *(m.)* 2
hockey **hockey** *(m.)* 2
holiday **fête** *(f.)* **(nationale)** 2, **jour** *(m.)* **férié** (legal) 8
home **maison** *(f.)*; at the — of **chez** 4
homeless (person) **sans-abri (sans domicile fixe) (SDF)** *(m.)* F
homework **devoirs** *(m. pl.)* P
hope (v.) **espérer** 6
hopscotch **marelle** *(f.)*
horse **cheval** *(m.)* 2; to go —back riding **faire du cheval** 2
hospital **hôpital** *(m.)* 4
host **hôte** *(m.)* 8
hostel **auberge** *(f.)* 11; youth — **auberge de jeunesse** 11
hostess **hôtesse** *(f.)* 8
hot **chaud(e)** 2, **lourd(e)** (weather) 2, **piquant(e)** (spicy) 5
hotel **hôtel** *(m.)* 1; luxury — **hôtel de luxe** 11; three / four / five star — **hôtel trois / quatre / cinq étoiles** 11
hour **heure** *(f.)* 1
house **maison** *(f.)* 4
household **foyer** *(m.)* 10
housemate **colocataire** *(m./f.)* 4
housework **ménage** *(m.)* 4
how **comment**; How are you? **Comment allez-vous?** *(pl./sing., formal)* / **Comment vas-tu?** *(sing., informal)* P; How is it going? **Comment ça va?** *(sing., informal)* P; — many **combien (de)** 4; — much **combien (de)** 4; How much is/are . . . ? **Combien coûte(nt)... ?** 6
humans **humains** *(m. pl.)* 12
hundred **cent** 1
hundredth **centième** 8
hunger **faim** *(f.)* F
hunt **chasse** *(f.)* 4
hunting **chasse** *(f.)* 4; to go — **aller à la chasse** 4
hurricane **ouragan** *(m.)* 2
hurry (v.) **se dépêcher** 10
husband **mari** *(m.)* 3
hybrid (animal or plant) **hybride** *(m.)* F
hygiene **hygiène** *(f.)* 12
hypermarket **hypermarché** *(m.)* 6

I

ice (black) **verglas** *(m.)* 2
ice cream **glace** *(f.)* 5
ice-skate **faire du patinage** 2
iceskating **patinage** *(m.)* 2

idea **idée** *(f.)* 10
ideal **idéal(e)** 5
identity **identité** *(f.)* 11; — papers (form of identification) **pièce** *(f.)* **d'identité** 11
idiotic **bête** 10
illness **maladie** *(f.)* 12
impatient **impatient(e)** P
important **important(e)** P, **marquant(e)** 8
impressionist **impressionniste** 9
in **à, au(x)** 3, **en** 3
included **compris(e)** 6; The tip is —. **Le service est compris.** 6
independence **indépendance** *(f.)* 8
independent **indépendant(e)** P, **autonome** 7
indiscreet **indiscret / indiscrète** 10
indispensable **indispensable** F
inexpensive **bon marché** 11
inflexible **inflexible** 7
ingredient **ingrédient** *(m.)* 5
instructor **enseignant(e)** 7
intellectual **intellectuel / intellectuelle** 1
intelligent **intelligent(e)** P
intended **destiné(e)**
interested **intéressé(e)**; to be — (in) **s'intéresser (à)** 10
interesting **intéressant(e)** P
internship **stage** *(m.)* **(de formation)** 7
interview **entretien** *(m.)*
introduce **présenter** P
introvert **introverti(e)** 7
introverted **introverti(e)** 7
invention **invention** *(f.)* F
invite **inviter** 1
iPod® **iPod®** *(m.)* P
Ireland **Irlande** *(f.)* 3
Irish **irlandais(e)** 3
Italian **italien / italienne** 3
Italy **Italie** *(f.)* 3
its **son / sa / ses** 3
Ivory Coast **Côte d'Ivoire** *(f.)* 3; from the — **ivoirien / ivoirienne** 3

J

jacket (heavy) **blouson** *(m.)* 11; leather — **blouson en cuir** 11
jam **confiture** *(f.)* 5
January **janvier** 2
Japan **Japon** *(m.)* 3
Japanese **japonais(e)** 3
jazz **jazz** *(m.)* 9

jealous **jaloux / jalouse** 7
jeans **jean** *(m.)* 11
jet setter **membre** *(m./f.)* **de la jet-set** 10
job **emploi** *(m.)* 7, **boulot** *(m.)* (slang) 7
jogging **jogging** *(m.)* 2
join **rejoindre**
journalism **journalisme** *(m.)* P
journalist **journaliste** *(m./f.)* 7
juice **jus** *(m.)* 5; cranberry — **jus de canneberge** 5; orange — **jus d'orange** 5
July **juillet** 2
June **juin** 2
junior high **collège** *(m.)* 7

K

karaoke **karaoké** *(m.)* 2
key **clé** *(f.)* 11
keyboard **clavier** *(m.)* F
kill (v.) **tuer**
kilogram (of) **kilo (de/d')** *(m.)* 5
king **roi** *(m.)* 8
kiss (v.) **embrasser**; to — each other **s'embrasser** 10
kitchen **cuisine** *(f.)* 4;
knee **genou** *(m.)* 12
knife **couteau** *(m.)* 6
knit **tricoter** 2
know (v.) **connaître** 8, **savoir** 8; to — oneself / each other **se connaître** 10
known **réputé(e)**

L

laboratory **laboratoire** *(m.)* 4
lake **lac** *(m.)* 4
lamb **agneau** *(m.)* 5
lamp **lampe** *(f.)* 4
landscape **paysage** *(m.)* 9
language **langue** *(f.)* P
laptop (computer) **(ordinateur) portable** *(m.)* P
last **dernier / dernière, passé(e)** 5
late **tard** 4
later **plus tard** 4
laundromat **laverie** *(f.)* **automatique** 4
laundry **lessive** *(f.)* 4; to do the — **faire la lessive** 4
law **droit** *(m.)* 7; — school **faculté** *(f.)* **de droit** 7
law **loi** *(f.)* 4
lawn **jardin** *(m.)* 4
lawyer **avocat(e)** 7
lazy **paresseux / paresseuse** 1
lean **mince** 3

learn **apprendre (à)** 5
lease (apartment or house) **bail** (*m.*) 4
leather **cuir** (*m.*) 11
leave (*v.*) **partir** 3, **laisser** 6, (a place / a person) **quitter** 6; to — each other **se quitter** 10
lecture hall **amphithéâtre** (*m.*) 4
left **gauche** (*f.*) 4; to/on the — (of) **à gauche (de)** 4
leg **jambe** (*f.*) 12
leisure activity **loisir** (*m.*) 2
lemon **citron** (*m.*) 5
lemonade **citron** (*m.*) **pressé** 5
lend **prêter (à)** 7
lentils **lentilles** (*f. pl.*) 5
less **moins** 7
letter **lettre** (*f.*) 2
lettuce **laitue** (*f.*) 6
liberal arts **lettres** (*f. pl.*) 7; — college **faculté** (*f.*) **de lettres et de sciences humaines** 7
library **bibliothèque** (*f.*) 1
license **permis** (*m.*) 11; driver's — **permis de conduire** 11
lie **mensonge** (*m.*)
life **vie** (*f.*) 2
lightbulb **ampoule** (*f.*) F; energy saving — **ampoule basse consommation** F
like (*v.*) **aimer** 1, **aimer bien** 1; to — better **aimer mieux** 1; to — oneself / each other **s'aimer (bien)** 10
like **comme**
lime **citron** (*m.*) **vert** 5
line (of a dialogue) **réplique** (*f.*)
lion **lion** (*m.*)12
lip **lèvre** (*f.*) 12
lipstick **rouge à lèvres** (*m.*) 12
listen (*v.*) **écouter** 1
liter (of) **litre** (*m.*) **(de/d')** 5
literary **littéraire** 9
literature **littérature** (*f.*) P
little **peu** 1
live (*v.*) **habiter** 1, **vivre** 9
lively **vif / vive** 9
living room (formal) **salon** (*m.*) 4
loan **prêt** (*m.*) 7; student — **prêt étudiant** 7
lobster **homard** (*m.*) 6
located: to be — **se trouver** 10
location **endroit** (*m.*) 4
locker (room) **vestiaire** (*m.*) 12
lodging **logement** (*m.*)
loner **solitaire** 7
long **long / longue** 3

look (*v.*) **regarder**; to — at oneself / each other **se regarder** 10; to — for **chercher** 1; to — good on someone **aller bien** 11
lose **perdre** 6; to — weight **maigrir** to 4
lost: to get — **se perdre** 10
lot: a — **beaucoup** 1
lotion **crème** (*f.*) 12
love (*v.*) **aimer** 1; to — oneself / each other **s'aimer** 10
love **amour** (*m.*) 10; to fall in — (with) **tomber amoureux / amoureuse (de)** 8; in — (with) **amoureux / amoureuse (de)** 8; — at first sight **coup** (*m.*) **de foudre** 8
loyal **loyal(e)** 7, **fidèle** 10
loyalty **fidélité** (*f.*) 10
luck **chance** (*f.*) 8; Good —! **Bonne chance!** 8
lucky **chanceux / chanceuse**
luggage **valises** (*f. pl.*) 11
lunch **déjeuner** (*m.*) 5; to have — **prendre le déjeuner, déjeuner** 5

M

Ma'am **madame (Mme)** P
magazine **magazine** (*m.*) 4; fashion — **magazine de mode** 10
magazine **revue** (*f.*) 10
mail **courrier** (*m.*) 11; — carrier **facteur / factrice** 11
mailbox **boîte** (*f.*) **à lettres** 11
major **spécialisation** (*f.*) P
make (*v.*) **faire** 2; to — up (with each other) **se réconcilier** 10
makeup **maquillage** (*m.*) 12
man **homme** (*m.*) P; business— **homme d'affaires** 7
manage **gérer**
manager **gérant(e)** 7
mango **mangue** (*f.*) 6
map (of a city) **plan** (*m.*) 4
March **mars** 2
marker **marqueur** (*m.*) P
market (open air) **marché** (*m.*) **(en plein air)** 6
marriage **mariage** (*m.*) 8
married **marié(e)** 3
marry **se marier** 10
marvelous **super** 10, **merveilleux / merveilleuse** F
master's degree **master** (*m.*) 7
masterpiece **chef-d'œuvre** (*m.*), **œuvre** (*f.*) 9

match **match** (*m.*) 2
mate **camarade** (*m./f.*) P; class— **camarade de classe** P; room— **camarade de chambre** P
mathematics **mathématiques** (*f. pl.*) P
May **mai** 2
mayonnaise **mayonnaise** (*f.*) 5
mayor **maire** (*m.*)
MBA **MBA** (*m.*) 7
me **moi** P, **me** 7
meadow **prairie** (*f.*) 4
meal **repas** (*m.*) 5
mean **méchant(e)** P
means of transportation **moyen** (*m.*) **de transport** 11
meat **viande** (*f.*) 5
medication **médicament** (*m.*) 12
medicine **médecine** (*f.*)
medium rare **saignant(e)** 5
meet (*v.*) **rencontrer**; to — each other **se rencontrer** 10
member **membre** (*m./f.*) 10
memorable **marquant(e)** 8
menu **menu** (*m.*) 6
message **message** (*m.*); instant — **message instantané** 10; text — **texto** (*m.*) 2; (Twitter-like) —s **microblogging** (*m.*) 10
messaging **messagerie** (*m.*) 10; instant — **messagerie instantanée** 10
Mexican **mexicain(e)** 3
Mexico **Mexique** (*m.*) 3
microwave **micro-ondes** (*m.*) 4
middle **milieu** (*m.*) 6
middle school **collège** (*m.*) 7
midnight **minuit** (*m.*) 1
milk **lait** (*m.*) 5; soy — **lait de soja** 5
million **million** (*m.*) 4
mini van **camionnette** (*f.*) 11
minister **ministre** (*m.*) 8; prime — **premier ministre** 8
mirror **miroir** (*m.*) 4
miserly **avare** 10
Miss **mademoiselle (Mlle)** P
miss **rater** 1
mistaken (about): to be — **se tromper (de)** 10
modern **moderne** P
modest **modeste** P
modified **modifié(e)** F; genetically — foods **organismes** (*m. pl.*) **génétiquement modifiés (OGM)** F
moisturizer **crème** (*f.*) **hydratante** 12
monarchy **monarchie** (*f.*) 8
Monday **lundi** 1

money **argent** (m.) 6
monitor **moniteur** (m.) F
month **mois** (m.) 2
monthly publication **mensuel** (m.) 10
mood **humeur** (f.) 7; to be in a bad
   — **être de mauvaise humeur** 7; to be
   in a good — **être de bonne humeur** 7
moon **lune** (f.) 2
moped **scooter** (m.) 11
morality **moralité** (f.) 10
more **davantage, plus** 7; no — **ne...
   plus** 10
morning **matin** (m.) 1; to be a
   — person **être du matin** 7
Moroccan **marocain(e)** 3
Morocco **Maroc** (m.) 3
most **plupart** (f.)
motel **motel** (m.) 11
mother **mère** (f.) 3; —-in-law **belle-
   mère** (f.) 3; single — **mère
   célibataire** 10
motorcycle **moto** (f.) 11
mountain **montagne** (f.) 4
mouse **souris** (f.) F
mouth **bouche** (m.) 12
move (v.) **bouger** 11, **déménager,
   toucher** (feeling) 10; to — into
   s'installer: dans / à 10
movement **mouvement** (m.) 8
movie **film** (m.) 9
movie theater **cinéma** (m.) 4
MP3 player **baladeur** (m.) **MP3** P
Mr. **monsieur (M.)** P
Mrs. **madame (Mme)** P
Mrs. **madame (Mme)** P
much: Not —. **Pas grand-chose.** P
muggy (weather) **lourd(e)** 2
muscular **musclé(e)** 3
museum **musée** (m.) 4
mushroom **champignon** (m.) 6
music **musique** (f.) P
musical (stage, film) **comédie** (f.)
   musicale 9
musician **musicien(ne)** 7
mussel **moule** (f.) 6
must (v.) **devoir** 7
mustard **moutarde** (f.) 5
my **mon / ma / mes** 3

N

naive **naïf / naïve** 1
name (v.) **appeler** 10; to be —d
   s'appeler 10
name **nom** (m.) P; first — **prénom**
   (m.) P; last — **nom de famille** P
nap (v.) **faire la sieste** 2

nap **sieste** (f.) 2
napkin **serviette** (f.) 6
narrate **raconter** 10
nationalism **nationalisme** (m.) 8
nature **nature** (f.) 9
near **près** 4
necessary **nécessaire** P
neck **cou** (m.) 12
necklace **collier** (m.) 11
need (v.) **avoir desoin de** 1;
neighbor **voisin(e)** 4
neighborhood **quartier** (m.) 4
nephew **neveu** (m.) 3
network **réseau** (m.) F; wireless
   — **réseau sans fil** F; social
   — **réseau social** 10
never **ne... jamais** 1
new **neuf / neuve** P, **nouveau / nouvel /
   nouvelle** 3
newly weds **nouveaux mariés**
   (m. pl.) 8
news (broadcast) **info(rmation)s**
   (f. pl.) 9
newspaper **journal** (m.) 2
newsstand **kiosque** (m.) **à journaux** 4
next **ensuite, puis** 4; — (to) **à côté (de)**
nice **gentil / gentille** 1, **beau / bel /
   belle** 2
nicely **gentiment** 2
niece **nièce** (f.) 3
night **nuit** (f.) 1
nightclub **boîte** (f.) **de nuit**
nine **neuf** P
nineteen **dix-neuf** P
ninety **quatre-vingt-dix** 1
ninth **neuvième** 8
nobility **noblesse** (f.)
nobody **ne... personne** 10
none **ne... aucun(e)** 10
noon **midi** (m.) 1
normal **normal(e)** F
north **nord** (m.) 4
nose **nez** (m.) 3
not **ne... pas** P; — at all **ne... pas
   du tout** 10; — yet **ne... pas
   encore** 10
notebook **cahier** (m.) P
nothing **ne... rien** 10
novel **roman** (m.) 2
November **novembre** 2
number **chiffre** (m.) 7; to be good
   with —s **être bon / bonne avec les
   chiffres** 7
nurse **infirmier / infirmière** 7
nut **fana** (m./f.) 10; health — **fana de la
   santé** 10

O

obey **obéir (à)** 4
object **objet** (m.) 4
obtain **obtenir** 7
obvious **évident(e)** F
October **octobre** 2
odd **drôle** 7
of (them/it) **en**
office **bureau** (m.) 1; post — **bureau
   de poste** 4
officer **agent(e)** 7; police — **agent(e)
   de police** 7
often **souvent** 1
oil **huile** (f.) 5; olive — **huile
   d'olive** 5
old fashioned **démodé(e)** 11
old **vieux, vieil, vieille** 3
omelet **omelette** (f.) 5
one **un(e)** P
onion **oignon** (m.) 5
only **seulement, ne... que** 10
opera **opéra** (m.) 9
opinion **avis** (m.); In my (your) — . . .
   À mon (votre) avis... 10
optimistic **optimiste** P
orange (adj.) **orange** 3
orange **orange** (f.) 3
orchestra **orchestre** (m.) 9
order (v.) **commander** 2; to — a pizza
   commander une pizza 2
organic **biologique (bio)** 6
organization **association** (f.) F;
   humanitarian — **association** (f.)
   humanitaire F
organize **organiser** 8
organized **organisé(e)** 7
other **autre** 11
our **nos / notre** 3
outfit **tenue** (f.) 11
out-of-date **démodé(e)** 11
outside **extérieur** (m.)
oven **four** (m.) 4; microwave — **(four)
   (m.) (à) micro-ondes** 4
overcast **couvert(e)** 2
overcoat **manteau** (m.) 11
overpopulation **surpopulation** (f.) F
overseas **à l'étranger** 11
owe **devoir** 7

P

pack (v.) **faire les valises** (f. pl.) 11
package **colis** (m.) 11
paint (v.) **faire de la peinture** 2
paint **peinture** (f.) 2
painter **peintre** (m./f.) 9
painting **tableau** (m.) 9, **peinture** (f.) 9

paper **papier** *(m.)* P; sheet of — **feuille** *(f.)* **de papier** P

parents **parents** *(m. pl.)* 3

park **parc** *(m.)* 1

parka **anorak** *(m.)* 11

parking lot **parking** *(m.)* 4

partner (domestic) **conjoint(e)** *(m./f.)* 3, **partenaire** *(m./f.)* 3

party *(v.)* **faire la fête** 2

party **fête** *(f.)* 2, **soirée** *(f.)* (evening) 8

pass (boarding) **carte** *(f.)* **d'embarquement** 11

pass (by) *(v.)* **passer (par)** 1

passport **passeport** *(m.)* 11

password **mot** *(m.)* **de passe** F

past **passé** *(m.)*; in the — **autrefois** 8

pasta **pâtes** *(f. pl.)* 5

pastime **passe-temps** *(m.)* 2

pastry **pâtisserie** *(f.)* 6; — shop **pâtisserie** *(f.)* 6

patient *(adj.)* **patient(e)** P

patient *(n.)* **patient(e)** 12

patiently **patiemment** 2

paw **patte** *(f.)* 12

pay *(v.)* **payer** 6; to — attention (to) **faire attention (à)** 5; to — back **rembourser** 7; to — by check **payer par chèque** 7; to — cash **payer en liquide** 6; to — with a credit card **payer par carte de crédit** 6

pay **salaire** *(m.)* 7

peace **paix** *(f.)* 8

peaceful **pacifique** 8

pear **poire** *(f.)* 6

peas **petits pois** *(m. pl.)* 5

pen **stylo** *(m.)* P

pencil **crayon** *(m.)* P

people **gens** *(m. pl.)* 1

pepper **poivre** *(m.)* 5, **poivron** *(m.)* 5

percent **pour cent** 1

performance **spectacle** *(m.)* 9

perhaps **peut-être** 1

period **point** *(m.)* 4

permit **permis** *(m.)* 11

person **personne** *(f.)* 1

pessimistic **pessimiste** P

pet **animal** *(m.)* **domestique** 3; — store **animalerie** *(f.)* 12

Ph.D. **doctorat** *(m.)* 7

pharmacy **pharmacie** *(f.)* 4

philosophy **philosophie** *(f.)* P

phone **téléphone** *(m.)* P; cell — **portable** *(m.)* P

photo(graph) **photo(graphie)** *(f.)* 2

photograph *(v.)* **photographier** 9

photographer **photographe** *(m./f.)* 9

photography **photo(graphie)** *(f.)* 2

physics **physique** *(f.)* P

pick *(v.)* **cueillir;** to — up (the house) **ranger** 4

picnic *(v.)* **faire un pique-nique** 2

picnic **pique-nique** *(m.)* 2

pie **tarte** *(f.)* 5

piece **pièce (de monnaie)** *(f.)* 4

pig **cochon** *(m.)* 12

pill **cachet** *(m.)* 12

ping-pong **tennis** *(m.)* **de table** 2

pink **rose** 3

pizza **pizza** *(f.)* 5

place *(v.)* **mettre** 6

place **endroit** *(m.)* 4

plane **avion** *(m.)* 11

plant **plante** *(f.)* 4

plate **assiette** *(f.)* 6

play *(v.)* **jouer** 1, **pratiquer** 1; to — board games **jouer aux jeux** *(m. pl.)* **de société** 2; to — cards **jouer aux cartes** *(f. pl.)* 2; to — the cello **jouer du violoncelle** 2; to — chess **jouer aux échecs** *(m. pl.)* 2; to — the drums **jouer de la batterie** 2; to — the guitar **jouer de la guitare** 2; to — music **jouer de la musique** 2; to — the piano **jouer du piano** 2; to — poker **jouer au poker** 2; to — the violin **jouer du violon** 2

play **pièce** *(f.)* **(de théâtre)** 9

player (audiovisual equipment) **lecteur** *(m.)* 4; DVD — **lecteur (de) DVD** 4

player **joueur / joueuse** 2

playwright **dramaturge** *(m./f.)* 9

please *(v.)* **faire plaisir (à quelqu'un)** 2

pleased **ravi(e)** P; — to meet you **enchanté(e)** P

pleasure **plaisir** *(m.)* 2

plumber **plombier / femme plombier** 7

plus **plus** 7

poem **poème** *(m.)* 2

poet **poète / femme poète** 8

poetic **poétique** 9

poetry **poésie** *(f.)* 2

point **point** *(m.)* 4

politely **poliment** 2

politics **politique** *(f.)*

poll **sondage** *(m.)*

pollute **polluer** F

pollution **pollution** *(f.)* F

pond **étang** *(m.)* 4

pop **pop** *(f.)* 9

portion **portion** *(f.)* 5

portrait **portrait** *(m.)* 9

position (work) **poste** *(m.)* 7

post office **poste** *(f.)* 11

postcard **carte** *(f.)* **postale** 11

poster **affiche** *(f.)* P

potato **pomme** *(f.)* **de terre** 5

potluck (party) **potluck** *(m.)* 8, **dîner** *(m.)* **à la bonne franquette** 8

poultry **volaille** *(f.)* 5

pound (of) **livre** *(f.)* **(de/d')** 5

poverty **pauvreté** *(f.)* F

practical **pratique** P

practice *(v.)* **pratiquer**

prairie **prairie** *(f.)* 4

prank **farce** *(f.)*

precise **précis(e)** 7

prefer **aimer mieux** 1, **préférer** 6

preferable **préférable** 12

prepare **préparer** 12

prescription **ordonnance** *(f.)* 12

preservation **préservation** *(f.)* F

preserve *(v.)* **préserver** F

president (of a company) **chef d'entreprise** *(m./f.)* 7; **président(e)** 8

prestige **prestige** *(m.)* 10

pretentious **prétentieux / prétentieuse** 10

pretty **joli(e)** 3

price **prix** *(m.)* 6

primitive **primitif / primitive** 9

print *(v.)* **imprimer** F

printer **imprimante** *(f.)* F

problem **problème** *(m.)* F

product **produit** *(m.)* 5; dairy — **produit laitier** 5; personal care — **produit de soin personnel** 12

profession **profession** *(f.)* 7

professional **professionnel(le)** 7

professor **professeur** *(f.)*

program (TV) **programme** *(m.)* 9

projector (overhead) **projecteur** *(m.)* P

promotion (work) **avancement** *(m.)* 8; to get a — **avoir de l'avancement** 8

protect **protéger, sauvegarder, sauver** F

protection **préservation** *(f.)* F

proteins **protéines** *(f. pl.)* 5

protest *(v.)* **protester** F

proud **fier / fière** 1, very — **orgueilleux / orgueilleuse** 10

psychologist **psychologue** *(m./f.)* 7

psychology **psychologie** *(f.)* P

public **public / publique** 4

publish **publier** 9
pumpkin **potiron** *(m.)* 6
purple **violet(te)** 3
purse **sac** *(m.)* P
put *(v.)* **mettre** 6; to — on make-up **se maquiller** 12
pyjama **pyjama** *(m.)* 11

Q

quarter **quart** *(m.)* 1
Quebec **Québec** *(m.)* 3
quebecker **québécois(e)** 3
queen **reine** *(f.)* 8
quickly **rapidement** 2
quickly **vite** 2

R

R&B **blues** *(m.)*, **R'n'B** *(m.)* 9
rabbit **lapin** *(m.)* 12
radish **radis** *(m.)* 6
rain *(v.)* **pleuvoir** 2
rain **pluie** *(f.)* 2
raincoat **imperméable** *(m.)* 11
rap **rap** *(m.)* 9
rare (meat) **bleu(e)** 5
rarely **rarement** 1
raspberry **framboise** *(f.)* 5
rat **rat** *(m.)* 12
razor **rasoir** *(m.)* 12
read **lire** 2
ready **prêt(e)**
reality **réalité** *(f.);* virtual — **réalité virtuelle** F
realize **se rendre compte (de / que)** 10
really **vraiment** 2
receive **recevoir** 9
recent **récent(e)** P
reception **réception** *(f.)* 8; **vin** *(m.)* **d'honneur** (cocktail reception) 8
recipe **recette** *(f.)* 5
record *(v.)* **enregistrer** 11
recruit *(v.)* **recruter**
recycle **recycler** F
recycling **recyclage** *(m.)* F
red **rouge** 3, **roux / rousse** (hair) 3
redhead *(n.)* **roux / rousse** 3
reflect (upon) **réfléchir (à)** 4
reform **réforme** *(f.)* 8
refrigerator **réfrigérateur** *(m.)* 4, **frigo** *(m.)* 4
registry **registre** *(m.)*
regret *(v.)* **regretter** 10
rehearsal **répétition** *(f.)*
relationship **relation** *(f.)* 8
relatives **parents** *(m. pl.)* 3
relax *(v.)* **se détendre** 10

remedy **remède** *(m.)*
remember **se rappeler, se souvenir** 10
rent *(v.)* **louer** 4
rent **loyer** *(m.)* 4
rental **location** *(f.)*
repeat *(v.)* **répéter** 6
request **demande** *(f.)*
research **recherche** *(f.)*
reservation **réservation** *(f.)* 6
reserve *(v.)* **réserver** 6
reside **habiter** 1
residence **résidence** *(f.)* 4
residential **résidentiel(le)** 4
resource **ressource** *(f.)* F;
    natural — **ressource naturelle** F
rest *(v.)* **se reposer** 10
restaurant **restaurant** *(m.)* 1
restrooms **toilettes** *(f. pl.)* 4, **W.-C.** *(m. pl.)* 4
retiree **retraité(e)** 10
retirement **retraite** *(f.)* 8
return *(v.)* **rentrer** 6, **retourner** 6, **rendre** (something) 6
review **critique** *(f.)* 9
reviewer **critique** *(m./f.)* 9
revolution **révolution** *(f.)* 8
rice **riz** *(m.)* 5
right **droite** *(f.)* 4; to/on the — (of) **à droite (de)** 4
ring **bague** *(f.)*
river **fleuve** *(m.)* 4, **rivière** *(f.)* 4
roast **rôti** *(m.)* 5; pork — **rôti de porc** 5; — beef **rosbif** *(m.)* 6
rock **rock** *(m.)* 9
role **rôle** *(m.)* 9
Romania **Roumanie** *(f.)* 3
Romanian **roumain(e)** 3
room **pièce** *(f.)* 4, **salle** *(f.)* 4, **chambre** *(f.)* 11; bath— **salle de bains** 4; dining — **salle à manger** 4; double / single — **chambre double / individuelle** 11; family — **salle de séjour** 4; living — **salle de séjour** 4; rehearsal — **salle de répétition**; smoking / nonsmoking — **chambre fumeur / non fumeur** 11
roommate **colocataire** *(m./f.)* 4
rooster **coq** *(m.)* 12
rug **tapis** *(m.)* 4
rugby **rugby** *(m.)* 2
rule **règle** *(f.)* 4, **règlement** *(m.)* 4; rental —s **règlements de location** 4
Russia **Russie** *(f.)* 3
Russian (language) **russe** *(m.)* P
Russian **russe** 3

S

sad **triste** 12
saint **saint** *(m.)*
salad **salade** *(f.)* 5
salami type sausage (dry) **saucisson** *(m.)* 6
salary **salaire** *(m.)* 7
sale: on — **en solde** 11
salesman **vendeur** *(m.)* 7
saleswoman **vendeuse** *(f.)* 7
salmon **saumon** *(m.)* 6
salt **sel** *(m.)* 5
salty **salé(e)** 5
same **même** 11
sandals **sandales** *(f. pl.)* 11
sandwich **sandwich** *(m.)* 5; cheese — **sandwich au fromage** 5
satellite **satellite** *(m.)* F; — dish **antenne** *(f.)* **parabolique**
Saturday **samedi** 1
saucepan **casserole** *(f.)* 5
sausage **saucisse** *(f.)* 5
save **sauvegarder, sauver** F; to — money **faire des économies** *(f. pl.)* 7; to — up (in a bank account) **épargner**
savings **économies** *(f. pl.)* 7
say **dire** 2
scarf **écharpe** *(f.)* 11, **foulard** *(m.)* (silk) 11
scatter-brained **farfelu(e)** 7
schedule **emploi** *(m.)* **du temps** 1, **horaire** *(m.)* 1
scholarship **bourse** *(f.)* **(d'études)** 7
school **école** *(f.)* P, **faculté** *(f.)* 7; business — **école de commerce** 7; law — **faculté de droit** 7; medical — **faculté de médecine** 7; professional / vocational — **école professionnelle** 7
science **science** *(f.)* P; political — **sciences politiques** P; — and technology college **faculté** *(f.)* **de sciences et de technologie** 7
scientist **scientifique** *(m./f.)*
scratch *(v.)* **gratter** 12; to — (oneself) **se gratter** 12
scrawny **maigre** 3
screen **écran** *(m.)* P
scuba diving **plongée sous-marine** *(f.)* 2
scuba-dive **plonger, faire de la plongée sous-marine** 2
sculpt **sculpter, faire de la sculpture** 9
sculptor **sculpteur / sculptrice** 9
sculpture **sculpture** *(f.)* 9

sea **mer** *(f.)* 4
season **saison** *(f.)* 2
seat **siège** *(m.)* 11; aisle — **siège côté couloir** 11
secretary **secrétaire** *(m./f.)* 7
secular **laïc / laïque**
security **sécurité** *(f.)* 11; — agent **agent(e) de la sécurité** 11; — check **contrôle** *(m.)* **de sécurité** 11; to go through — **passer au contrôle de sécurité** 11
see **voir** 9; to — again **revoir** 9; to — oneself / each other **se voir** 10
selfish **égoïste** 10
sell **vendre** 6
semester **semestre** *(m.)* P
send **envoyer** 7; to — something express mail **envoyer quelque chose en express** 11
Senegal **Sénégal** *(m.)* 3
Senegalese **sénégalais(e)** 3
sens **sens** *(m.)*; — of humor **sens de l'humour** 7
sensible **raisonnable**
sensitive **sensible** 7
sept **sept** P
September **septembre** 2
serial sitcom **série** *(f.)* 9
serious **sérieux / sérieuse** 1, **grave** 12
seriously **sérieusement** 2
served **servi(e)** 6
set *(v.)* **mettre** 6; to — the table **mettre la table** 6
setting **lieu** *(m.)*
settle (into) **s'installer dans / à** 10
seventeen **dix-sept** P
seventy **soixante-dix** 1; — fifth **soixante-quinzième** 8
several **plusieurs** 11
shampoo **shampooing** *(m.)* 12
shape **forme** *(f.)* 12; to be in — **être en forme** 12
share **partager** 4
shark **requin** *(m.)* 12
shave *(v.)* **raser, se raser** 12
sheet (paper) **feuille** *(f.)* P
shellfish **fruits** *(m. pl.)* **de mer** 5
shelter (animal) **refuge** *(m.)* 12
shirt **chemise** *(f.)* 11
shoe **chaussure** *(f.)* 11; high-heeled —s **chaussures à talons** 11; — size **pointure** *(f.)* 11; sports —s **baskets** *(f. pl.)* 11
shop *(v.)* **faire du shopping** 2, **faire des courses** *(f. pl.)* 2
shopaholic **accro** *(m./f.)* **du shopping** 10

shopkeeper **commerçant(e)** 7
shopping **shopping** *(m.)* 2; — cart **chariot** *(m.)* 6
short **petit(e)** 3, **court(e)** (hair) 3
shorts **short** *(m.)* 11
shot **piqûre** *(f.)* 12
shoulder **épaule** *(f.)* 12
show (TV) **émission** *(f.)* 9, **spectacle** *(m.)* 9; reality TV — **émission de téléréalité** 9; shopping network — **émission de téléachat** 9; sports (talk) — **émission sportive** 9; variety — **émission de variétés** 9
show *(v.)* **montrer** 7
shower *(v.)* **se doucher** 12
shower **douche** *(f.)* 4, **averse** *(f.)* (weather) 2
shrimp **crevette** *(f.)* 6
shut off *(v.)* **éteindre, fermer** F
shy **timide** P
sick **malade** 12; to get — **tomber malade** 12
sicken **écœurer** 10
simple **simple** 10
since **depuis** 2; — when **depuis quand** 6
sing **chanter** 1
singer **chanteur / chanteuse** 7
single **célibataire** 3; — father **père** *(m.)* **célibataire** 10; — mother **mère** *(f.)* **célibataire** 10
sink (bathroom) **lavabo** *(m.)* 4
Sir **monsieur** (M.) P
sister **sœur** *(f.)* 3; —-in-law **belle-sœur** *(f.)* 3
site **site** *(m.)* 10
six **six** P
sixteen **seize** P
sixty **soixante** P
size **taille** *(f.)* 11
sketch *(v.)* **dessiner** 2
ski *(v.)* **faire du ski** 2
skiing **ski** *(m.)* 2; cross-country — **ski de fond** 2; downhill — **ski alpin** 2; water-— **ski nautique** 2
skill **capacité** *(f.)* 7; communication —s **capacités de communication** 7
skillet **poêle** *(f.)* 5
skinny **maigre** 3
skirt **jupe** *(f.)* 11; mini-— **mini-jupe** 11
sky **ciel** *(m.)* 2
slacks **pantalon** *(m.)* 11; bell bottom — **pantalon à pattes d'éléphant** 11
sleep *(v.)* **dormir** 3; to — in **faire la grasse matinée** 2
slender **mince** 3

slice *(v.)* **trancher** 5
slim **mince** 3
slowly **lentement** 2
small **petit(e)** 3
Smartphone **Smartphone** *(m.)* 10
smell *(v.)* **sentir** 3
smoke *(v.)* **fumer** 5
snack *(v.)* **grignoter** 5, **goûter** 6
snack **goûter** *(m.)* 5
snake **serpent** *(m.)* 12
sneeze *(v.)* **éternuer** 12
snow *(v.)* **neiger** 2
snow **neige** *(f.)* 2; —man **bonhomme** *(m.)* **de neige**
so **donc** 1
soap opera **feuilleton** *(m.)* 9
soap **savon** *(m.)* 12
soccer **football / foot** *(m.)* 2
sociable **sociable** P
social **social(e)**; — aid **assistance** *(f.)* **sociale** F; — worker **assistant(e) social(e)** 7
society **société** *(f.)* F
sociology **sociologie** *(f.)* P
sock **chaussette** *(f.)* 11
soft **mou / molle** 10
software **logiciel** *(m.)* F
soldier **soldat / femme soldat** 8
solitary **solitaire** 7
solution **solution** *(f.)* F
somber **sombre** 9
some **quelques, quelques-uns / quelques-unes** 11
someone **quelqu'un** 7
something **quelque chose** 5
sometimes **quelquefois** 1, **parfois** 1
son **fils** *(m.)* 3; —-in-law **beau-fils** *(m.)* 3
song **chanson** *(f.)* 9
soon **bientôt** P; See you —. **À bientôt.** P
sorry **désolé(e)** 12
soup **soupe** *(f.)* 5; tomato — **soupe à la tomate** 5
sour **aigre** 5
south **sud** *(m.)* 4
spa **institut** *(m.)* **de beauté** 4
space **espace** *(m.)*
space shuttle **navette** *(f.)* **spatiale** F
Spain **Espagne** *(f.)* 3
Spanish (language) **espagnol** *(m.)* P
Spanish **espagnol(e)** 3
speak **parler** 1
speaking of **à propos de** 10
species **espèce** *(f.)* F; endangered — **espèces menacées** F

speech **discours** (m.)
spend (money) **dépenser (de l'argent)** 7
spicy **épicé(e)** 5
spinach **épinards** (m. pl.) 5
spirituality **spiritualité** (f.) 10
spoiled **gâté(e), périmé(e)**
spoon **cuillère** (f.) 5; tea— (of) **cuillère à café (de/d')** 5; table / soup — (of) **cuillère à soupe (de/d')** 5
sport **sport** (m.) 2
spouse **époux / épouse** 8
spring **printemps** (m.) 2
stadium **stade** (m.) 4
stage **étape** (f.) 8; — of life **étape de la vie** 8
staircase **escalier** (m.) 4
stamp **timbre** (m.) 11
stapler **agrafeuse** (f.) P
star **étoile** (f.) 2
start up (v.) **démarrer** F
starter **entrée** (f.) 5, **hors-d'œuvre** (m.) 5
station (bus / train) **gare** (f.) 11
stay (v.) **rester** 6
steak **steak** (m.) 5
steamed **à la vapeur** 5
stepbrother **beau-frère** (m.) 3
stepdaughter **belle-fille** (f.) 3
stepfather **beau-père** (m.) 3
stepmother **belle-mère** (f.) 3
stepsister **belle-sœur** (f.) 3
stepson **beau-fils** (m.) 3
still **encore** 10
still life **nature** (f.) **morte** 9
stingy **avare** 10
stitch **point** (m.) **de suture** 12
stock market **bourse** (f.)
stone **pierre** (f.)
stop **arrêt** (m.); bus — **arrêt d'autobus** 11
store **boutique** (f.) 4; **magasin** (m.) 6; health / organic food — **magasin (de produits) bio** (m.) 6
storm **orage** (m.) 2
story **histoire** (f.) 9
stove **cuisinière** (f.) 4
straight **raide** 3, **droit** 4; — ahead **tout droit** 4
strawberry **fraise** (f.) 5
street **rue** (f.) 4
stress **stress** (m.) 12
stressed **stressé(e)**
stroll (v.) **se promener** 10
stubborn **têtu(e)** 7
student **étudiant(e)** P

studies **études** (f. pl.) P
study (v.) **étudier** P
stupid **bête** 10
style **style** (m.) 9
stylish **à la mode** 11
subject **sujet** (m.) 9
suburbs **banlieue** (f.) 4
subway **métro** (m.) 11
succeed (at, in) **réussir (à)** 4
success **réussite** (f.) 8, **succès** (m.) 8
suddenly **soudain** 8
sufficiently **suffisamment**
sugar **sucre** (m.) 5
suit **costume** (m.) (man's) 11, **tailleur** (m.) (woman's) 11
suitcase **valise** (f.) 11
summer **été** (m.) 2
sun **soleil** (m.) 2
Sunday **dimanche** 1
sunglasses **lunettes** (f. pl.) **de soleil** 11
sunscreen **crème** (f.) **solaire** 12
super **super** 10
supermarket **supermarché** (m.) 6
sure **sûr(e)** F
surf (v.) **naviguer** (Internet) 1; **faire du surf** 2
surfing **surf** (m.) 2
surgery **intervention** (f.) **chirurgicale** 12
surprised **surpris(e)** 12
surrealist **surréaliste** 9
survey **sondage** (m.)
suspicious: to be — (of) **se méfier (de)** 10
suture **point** (m.) **de suture** 12
SUV **quatre-quatre (4 × 4)** (m.) 11
sweater (pullover) **pull(-over)** (m.) 11; turtle neck — **pull à col roulé** 11
sweatpants **jogging** (m.) 11
sweatshirt **sweat** (m.) 11; hooded — **sweat à capuche** 11
sweet **sucré(e)** 5
swim (v.) **faire de la natation** (for exercise) 2
swimming **natation** (f.) 2; (public) — pool **piscine** (f.) **(municipale)** 4
swimsuit **maillot (de bain)** (m.) 11
Swiss **suisse** 3
Switzerland **Suisse** (f.) 3
symptom **symptôme** (m.) 12
syrup **sirop** (m.) 12; cough — **syrop contre la toux** 12

T

table **table** (f.) P; — cloth **nappe** (f.) 6
tablet **cachet** (m.) 12, **comprimé** (m.) 12

tail **queue** (f.)12
take (v.) **passer** 1, **prendre** 5; to — care of **s'occuper (de)** 10; to — an exam **passer un examen** 1; to — one's time **prendre son temps** 5
tale: fairy — **conte** (m.) **de fées** 9
talented **talentueux / talentueuse** 1
talk (v.) **parler** 1; to — to oneself / each other **se parler** 10
talk show **causerie** (f.) 9
talkative **bavard(e)** 10
tall **grand(e)** 3
tapestry **tapisserie** (f.) 9
task **tâche** (f.) 4
taste (v.) **goûter** 6
taste **goût** (m.) 6
taxi **taxi** (m.) 11
tea **thé** (m.) 5
teacher **professeur** (m.) P, **enseignant(e)** 7
team **équipe** (f.) 2
technology P **technologie** (f.); information — **technologies de l'information et de la communication (TIC)** P
telephone (v.) **téléphoner** 1; to — each other **se téléphoner** 10
televised **télévisé(e)** 9; — game **match** (m.) **télévisé** 9
television **télévision** (f.) 1; flat screen — set **téléviseur** (m.) LCD 6; — set **téléviseur** (m.) 4
tell (about) **raconter** 10
temperature **température** (f.) 2; to take one's — **prendre la température** 12
ten **dix** P
tennis **tennis** (m.) 2; table — **tennis** (m.) **de table** 2
tent **tente** (f.) 11
textbook **manuel** (m.)
thank you **merci** P
that (adj.) **ce / cet / cette** 3
theater **théâtre** (m.) 9; — play **pièce** (f.) **de théâtre** 9; — company, troop **troupe** (f.) **de théâtre** 9
their **leur** 3
them **leur** 7
then **ensuite, puis** 4
there (is) **voilà** P
there **y** 7
therefore **donc** 1
these **ces** 3
thigh **cuisse** (f.)
thing **chose** (f.) 4, **affaire** (f.); —s **affaires** (f. pl.) 4
think **penser** 1

thirteen **treize** P
thirty **trente** P; —-one **trente et un** P; —-first **trente-et-unième** 8
this **ce / cet / cette** 3
those **ces** 3
thought **pensée** (f.) 10
thousand **mille** 4
three **trois** P
throat **gorge** (f.) 12
throughout **pendant** 1
throw (out) **jeter** *to* F
Thursday **jeudi** 1
ticket **billet** (m.) 11; one-way — **billet aller-simple** 11; plane — **billet d'avion** 11; round-trip — **billet aller-retour** 11
tie **cravate** (f.) 11
tiger **tigre** (m.)12
time **époque** (f.) 8; at that — **à cette époque-là** 8; contemporary — **époque contemporaine** 8
time **heure** (f.) 1, **fois** (f.), **temps** (m.); from — to — **de temps en temps** 10; most of the — **la plupart du temps** 10
tinker **bricoler, faire du bricolage** 2
tinkering **bricolage** (m.) 2
tip **pourboire** (m.) 6
tired **fatigué(e)** 12
tissue **kleenex** (m.) 12
to **à, au(x), en** 3
today **aujourd'hui** 1
toe **orteil** (m.) 12
tofu **tofu** (m.) 5
toilet (room) **W.-C.** (m. pl.) 4, **toilettes** (f. pl.)
tolerance **tolérance** (f.) 8
tomato **tomate** (f.) 5
tomorrow **demain** P; See you —. **À demain.** P
tongue **langue** (f.) 12
too **aussi** P; — much **trop** 1
tooth **dent** (f.) 12
toothpaste **dentifrice** (m.) 12
top: on — **dessus** 6
tornado **tornade** (f.) 2
touch (v.) **toucher**
towards **vers** 4
towel **serviette** (f.) 12
town **ville** (f.) 4
trade **métier** (m.) 7
train **train** (m.) 11
translate **traduire** 11
transport **transporter** 11
trash **poubelle** (f.) 4
travel (v.) **voyager** 1

traveler **voyageur / voyageuse** 11
treat (v.) **traiter**
treatment **traitement** (m.) 12
tree **arbre** (m.) 4
trimester **trimestre** (m.) P
trip **voyage** (m.) 2, **trajet** (m.) 11; to take a — **faire un voyage** 2
troop (theater) **troupe** (f.) **de théâtre** 9
truck **camion** (m.) 11
true **vrai(e)** F
truly **vraiment** 2
truth **vérité** (f.)
try **essayer** 6
t-shirt **tee-shirt** (m.) 11
Tuesday **mardi** 1
tuition **frais** (m. pl.) **de scolarité** 7
Tunisia **Tunisie** (f.) 3
Tunisian **tunisien / tunisienne** 3
turkey **dinde** (f.) 5
turn (v.) **tourner** 4; to — right / left **tourner à droite / à gauche** 4
turn **tour** (m.)
tuxedo **smoking** (m.) 11
TV shopping **téléachat** (m.) 9; — network show **émission** (f.) **de téléachat** 9
twelve **douze** P
twenty **vingt** P; —-one **vingt et un** P; —-first **vingt-et-unième** 8; —-two **vingt-deux** P
two **deux** P
type (v.) **taper** F

ugly **laid(e)** 3
uncle **oncle** (m.) 3
underline **souligner**
underneath **dessous** 6
understand **comprendre** 5
underwear **sous-vêtement** (m.) 11
undress **déshabiller** 12; to get —ed **se déshabiller** 12
unemployment **chômage** (m.) F
unfair **injuste** F
unhappy **malheureux / malheureuse** 1
United States **États-Unis** (m. pl.) 3
university **université** (f.) P
until **jusque** 4
upset (v.) **énerver, déranger** 10; to get — **s'énerver** 10
uptight **coincé(e)** 7
us **nous** 7
use (v.) **utiliser** 12
useful **utile** F
useless **inutile** F
usually **d'habitude** 8

vacation **vacances** (f. pl.); to go on — **aller en vacances** 1
vacuum (cleaner) **aspirateur** (m.) 4
vacuum (v.) **passer l'aspirateur** (m.) 4
valley **vallée** (f.) 4
van **camionnette** (f.) 11
veal **veau** (m.) 5
vegan **végétalien(ne)** 5
vegetable **légume** (m.) 5
vegetarian **végétarien(ne)** 5
very **très** P
veterinarian **vétérinaire** (m.) 12
Vietnam **Viêt Nam** (m.) 3
Vietnamese **vietnamien / vietnamienne** 3
vinegar **vinaigre** (m.) 5
violet **violet(te)** 3
visit (v.) **rendre visite à** (someone) 6, **visiter** 6 (something)
vocation **métier** (m.) 7
voice **voix** (f.)
volleyball **volley-ball** (m.) 2

wages **salaire** (m.) 7
wait (v.) **attendre** 6
waiter **serveur** (m.) 6
waitress **serveuse** (f.) 6
wake (v.) **réveiller** 12; to — oneself up **se réveiller** 12
walk (v.) **marcher** 1, **faire de la marche** (for exercise) 2, **faire une promenade** 2, **se promener** 10
walk **promenade** (f.) 2
walking **marche** (f.) 2
walnuts **noix** (f. pl.) 5
want **vouloir** 7
war **guerre** (f.) 8; world — **guerre mondiale**
warm **bon / bonne** (weather) 2
warming: global — **réchauffement** (m.) **climatique** F
wash (v.) **laver** 12; to — (oneself) **se laver** 12
waste (v.) **gaspiller** F
waste **déchet** (m.) F; domestic — **déchets domestiques** F; industrial — **déchets industriels** F; — basket **poubelle** (f.) P
watch (v.) **regarder** 1; to keep — on **surveiller**
watch **montre** (f.) 11
water **eau** (f.) 5; mineral — **eau minérale** 5; — closet **W.-C.** (m. pl.) 4, **toilettes** (f. pl.)

watercolor **aquarelle** *(f.)* 9
watermelon **pastèque** *(f.)* 6
wavy **ondulé(e)** 3
wear *(v.)* **mettre, porter, chausser** (shoe size) 11
weather **temps** *(m.)* 2
webcam **webcam** *(f.)* F
website **site** *(m.)* **Web** 10
Wednesday **mercredi** 1
week **semaine** *(f.)* 1; last — **semaine dernière / passée** 5
weekend **week-end** *(m.)* 1
weekly publication **hebdomadaire** *(m.)* 10
weight **poids** *(m.)*
well **bon(ne), bien** 2
well-done (meat) **bien-cuit(e)** 5
well-groomed **soigné(e)** 10
west **ouest** *(m.)* 4
western (movie) **western** *(m.)* 9
what **que, quel(le)** 1, **quoi** *(informal)* 4
when **quand** 4, **où** 11
where **où** 4
which **quel(le)** 1, **lequel / laquelle / lesquels / lesquelles** 11, **que, qui** 11; of — **dont** 11
whiskers **moustaches** *(f. pl.)* 12
white **blanc / blanche** 3
who(m) **qui** 4; of whom **dont** 11
why **pourquoi** 4
widow **veuve** *(f.)* 3
widower **veuf** *(m.)* 3
wife **femme** *(f.)* 3; house— **femme au foyer** 10

wimpy **mou / molle** 10
win *(v.)* **gagner** 7
wind **vent** *(m.)* 2
window **fenêtre** *(f.)* P
window-shop *(v.)* **faire du lèche-vitrine** 2
window-shopping **lèche-vitrine** *(m.)* 2; to go — **faire du lèche-vitrine** 2
windsurfing board **planche** *(f.)* **à voile** 2
wine **vin** *(m.)* 5
winter **hiver** *(m.)* 2
wish *(v.)* **souhaiter** 12
wish **vœu** *(m.)* 8
with **avec** 1
withdraw **retirer** 7
without **sans**
woman **femme** *(f.)* P; business — **femme d'affaires** 7
wonder *(v.)* **se demander** 10
wonderful **super** 10, **merveilleux / merveilleuse** F
woods **bois** *(m. pl.)* 4
word **mot** *(m.)* F; — processing program **traitement** *(m.)* **de texte** F
work *(v.)* **travailler** 1
work **travail** *(m.)* 7; **œuvre** *(f.)* **(d'art)** 9
workaholic **bourreau** *(m./f.)* **de travail** 10
worker **travailleur / travailleuse, ouvrier /ouvrière** (factory) 7, social — **assistant(e) social(e)** 7
working **actif / active** 10; — mom **mère** *(f.)* **active** 10; — dad **père** *(m.)* **actif** 10

worry *(v.)* **s'inquiéter (de)** 10
worse **pire** 7
wound **blessure** *(f.)* 12
wrist **poignet** *(m.)* 12
write **écrire** 2; to — letters **écrire des lettres** *(f.)* 2; to — poems **écrire des poèmes** *(m.)* 2; to — text messages **écrire des textos** *(m.)* 2
writer **écrivain / écrivaine** 8, **rédacteur / rédactrice**

X
X-ray **radiographie** *(f.)* 12

Y
year **an** *(m.)* 2, **année** *(f.)* 2; Happy New —! **Bonne année!** 8; last — **année dernière / passée** 5
yellow **jaune** 3
yesterday **hier;** the day before — **avant-hier** 5
yoga **yoga** *(m.)* 2
yogurt **yaourt** *(m.)* 5
you **toi** *(sing., informal)* P, **te** 7
young **jeune** 3
your **ton / ta / tes** 3, **votre, vos** *(formal)* 3
youth **jeunesse** *(f.)* 8

Z
zero **zéro** P

INDEX